Abbreviations and references

CW01499954

Abbreviations

CIS	Construction Industry S...
DAN	Deferment Approval Number
DGT	Daily Gross Takings
ESL	EC Sales List
HMRC	Her Majesty's Revenue and Customs
MTIC VAT Fraud	Missing Trader Intra-Community VAT Fraud
SAD	Single Administrative Document
SD	Supplementary Declaration
SIVA	Simplified Import VAT Accounting
TURN	Trader's Unique Reference Number
VAT	Value Added Tax
VATA 1994	Value Added Tax Act 1994
VTD	VAT Tribunal Decision
s	Section
SA	Stamp Act 1891
Sch	Schedule

References (*denotes current series)

AC	*Law Reports, Appeal Cases, (Incorporated Council of Law Reporting for England and Wales, 3 Stone Buildings, Lincoln's Inn, London WC2A 3XN)
Ad & E	Adolphus & Ellis's Reports
All ER	*All England Law Reports, LexisNexis Butterworths, 35 Chancery Lane, London WC2A 1EL)
App Cas	Law Reports, Appeal Cases

ATC	Annotated Tax Cases, (Gee & Co (Publishers) Ltd, 7 Swallow Place, London W1R 8AB)
B & Ad	Barnewall & Adolphus's Reports
B & Ald	Barnewall & Alderson's Reports
B & C	Barnewall & Cresswall's Reports
B & S	Best & Smith's Reports
BCLC	*British Company Law Cases
BTC	*British Tax Cases
CB	Common Bench Reports
Ch	*Law Reports, Chancery Division
Ch App	Law Reports, Chancery Appeals
CM & R	Crompton, Meeson & Roscoe's Reports
E & B	Ellis & Blackburn's Reports
East	East's Reports
ECJ	European Court of Justice
Ex D	Law Reports, Exchequer Division
Exch	Exchequer Reports
F(Ct of Sess)	Fraser, Court of Session Cases, 5th Series
FTT	First Tier Tribunal
HL Cas	Clark's House of Lords Cases
IR	*Irish Reports, (Law Reporting Council, Law Library, Four Courts, Dublin)
Ir LR	Irish Law Reports
KB	Law Reports, King's Bench Division
LR	Law Reports (followed by Court abbreviation)
LT	Law Times Reports
M & W	Meeson & Welsby's Reports
P	Law Reports, Probate, Divorce & Admiralty Division
QB/QBD	*Law Reports, Queen's Bench Division
QBR	Queen's Bench Reports
R (Ct of Sess)	Rettie, Court of Session Cases, 4th Series
SC	*Court of Session Cases (Scotland)
Sc LR	Scottish Law Reporter

Tolley's
VAT Planning

Tolley's
VAT Planning

2016–17

by

Graham C Brearley
LLB (Hons)

Members of the LexisNexis Group worldwide

United Kingdom	RELX (UK) Limited trading as LexisNexis, 1-3 Strand, London WC2N 5JR
Australia	LexisNexis Butterworths, Chatswood, New South Wales
Austria	LexisNexis Verlag ARD Orac GmbH & Co KG, Vienna
Benelux	LexisNexis Benelux, Amsterdam
Canada	LexisNexis Canada, Markham, Ontario
China	LexisNexis China, Beijing and Shanghai
France	LexisNexis SA, Paris
Germany	LexisNexis GmbH, Dusseldorf
Hong Kong	LexisNexis Hong Kong, Hong Kong
India	LexisNexis India, New Delhi
Italy	Giuffrè Editore, Milan
Japan	LexisNexis Japan, Tokyo
Malaysia	Malayan Law Journal Sdn Bhd, Kuala Lumpur
New Zealand	LexisNexis NZ Ltd, Wellington
Poland	Wydawnictwo Prawnicze LexisNexis Sp, Warsaw
Singapore	LexisNexis Singapore, Singapore
South Africa	LexisNexis Butterworths, Durban
USA	LexisNexis, Dayton, Ohio

© 2016 RELX (UK) Limited

Published by LexisNexis

ISBN for this volume: 9780754552857

Printed and bound in Great Britain by Hobbs the Printers Ltd, Totton, Hampshire

Visit LexisNexis at www.lexisnexis.co.uk

About this Book

This book addresses the many VAT issues that practitioners encounter on a regular basis. It aims to provide workable solutions to practical VAT problems, rather than to offer a lengthy discourse on VAT legislation. Each chapter analyses the advantages and disadvantages of various VAT positions, includes worked examples of key topics, and is concluded with practical planning points that could help save money for clients. The book has been updated to reflect developments in VAT since the 2015–16 edition was published and includes recent VAT cases to the end of May 2016.

The book includes an introductory section providing an overview of the main VAT changes and a completely updated chapter on recent VAT cases.

Graham C Brearley has worked for the majority of his professional life in VAT. He started out with H M Customs & Excise back in 1974 and worked for 15 or so years in a number of different roles. He joined Grant Thornton in 1989 and has accumulated a further 27 years of experience as a VAT consultant providing VAT advice and solutions across many sectors to many varied clients. Graham is grateful to both Neil Warren (the original author of this work) and to Alex Millar (who updated previous editions).

Graham has written extensively on VAT over the years and is currently consultant editor of *De Voil Indirect Tax Intelligence*.

SLT	Scots Law Times Reports
Sol Jo	Solicitors' Journal, Oyez Publishing Ltd, Norwich House, 11/13 Norwich St, London EC4A 1AB
STC	*Simon's Tax Cases, (LexisNexis Butterworths, as above)
Taunt	Taunton's Reports
TC	*Official Tax Cases, (The Stationery Office, 123 Kingsway, London WC2B 6PQ)
TLR	Times Law Reports
UT	Upper Tribunal
WLR	*Weekly Law Reports, (Incorporated Council of Law Reporting, as above)
WN	Weekly Notes, (Incorporated Council of Law Reporting, as above)

The first number in the citation refers to the volume, and the second to the page, so that [1978] 2 WLR 10 means that the report is to be found on page ten of the second volume of the Weekly Law Reports for 1978. Where no volume number is given, only one volume was produced in that year. Some series, such as the ATC, have continuous volume numbers. Where legal decisions are very recent and in the lower Courts, it must be remembered that they may be reversed on appeal. But references to the official Tax Cases ('TC') may be taken as final.

In English cases, Scottish and N. Irish decisions (unless there is a difference of law between the countries) are generally followed but are not binding, and Republic of Ireland decisions are considered (and vice versa). Privy Council decisions are of persuasive, but not binding, authority.

Acts of Parliament and Statutory Instruments (SI) (formerly Statutory Rules and Orders) (SR & O) are obtainable from:

The Stationery Office

123 Kingsway

London

WC2B 6PQ

Tel: 020 7242 6393/6410;

Fax 020 7242 6394;

Internet: www.the-stationery-office.co.uk.

Email: london.bookshop@theso.co.uk

Contents

Contents

Contents

Contents

Contents

Contents

Contents

Main VAT Changes

This introductory section provides an overview of recent important VAT changes during the 12 months ending 31 May 2016. Most of the changes this year have been brought about by the development of case law rather than through changes in legislation. Some of the changes are still 'on-going' with HMRC yet to finalise its policy in relation to VAT groups and holding companies.

Increased registration and deregistration thresholds

From 1 April 2016, the registration threshold increased from £82,000 to 83,000 (see **1.1**).

From 1 April 2016, the threshold which determines whether a person may apply for deregistration also increased from £80,000 to £81,000 (see **2.1**).

Reduced rate of VAT for the installation of energy-saving materials

In June 2015, HMRC issued Revenue & Customs Brief 13/15 announcing that, as a result of the Court of Justice ruling in *Commission v UK: C-161/14*, it is to consider changing the law to remove reduced rating from supplies of installation of energy-saving materials. The Court found that the UK's application of a reduced rate to such supplies was much wider than allowed by EU law. Changes are not anticipated until *Finance Act 2016* (see **26.14**).

VAT – compulsory charge on single-use carrier bags in England

In August 2015, HMRC announced the introduction of a compulsory charge for the supply of 'single use' carrier bags where such bags are supplied by a business employing 250 or more employees. The minimum value of a carrier bag was set at 5p including VAT. This means that for every carrier bag sold the taxable amount is 4.17p plus VAT of 0.83p.

Deduction of VAT on pension fund management costs

In October 2015, HMRC issued a further Revenue & Customs Brief 17/15 in relation to the recovery of VAT on pension scheme fund management costs. The Brief extended the transitional period for a further year (to 31 December 2016) and also provided an update on HMRC's position on possible arrangements for employers to achieve VAT deduction for the costs of administering occupational pension schemes and managing their assets going forward.

VAT grouping rules and the Skandia judgment

In October 2015, HMRC issued Revenue & Customs Brief 18/15 relating to VAT groups and how the judgment of the Court of Justice in *Skandia America Corp. (USA), filial Sverige v Skatteverket: Case C-7/13* affected UK VAT groups (see Chapter 3).

VAT MOSS – simplifications for businesses trading below the VAT registration threshold

In January 2016, HMRC issued Revenue & Customs Brief 4/16 relating to the VAT MOSS regime (for businesses involved in the supply of electronic/digital services etc to non-business customers in other member states of the EU). The Brief announced some simplifications for smaller businesses. UK micro-businesses, that are below the current UK VAT registration threshold and are registered for the VAT Mini One Stop Shop (VAT MOSS), may use best judgement and base their 'customer location' VAT taxation and accounting decisions on a single piece of information, such as the billing address provided by the customer or information provided to them by their payment service provider (see **14.14, 14.15**).

VAT treatment of conversions of non-residential buildings into dwellings under permitted development rights

In May 2016, HMRC issued Revenue & Customs Brief 9/16 clarifying its policy concerning the VAT treatment of works where an individual planning application is not necessary because statutory planning consent has been granted though Permitted Development Rights (PDRs) (see **26.17**).

Chapter 1

Registration

Key topics in this chapter:

- Turnover limits for compulsory registration.
- Rules for VAT registration when buying a business.
- Applying for a VAT number.
- Registering for VAT on either a voluntary or intending trader basis.
- Input tax recovery on goods or services acquired before the date of registration (and before the date of incorporation for limited companies).
- Situations when a business can apply for exemption from being registered even when it has exceeded the compulsory turnover limits.
- Notifying HM Revenue and Customs (HMRC) of changes to business details.
- Backdating the date of VAT registration and penalties for belated notification.

Introduction

[1.1] A business (defined in the law as a 'taxable person') needs to be registered for VAT in the UK if the value of its taxable supplies in the last 12 months has exceeded the VAT registration threshold – or it expects the value of such supplies to exceed that threshold in the next 30 days.

In addition, since 1 December 2012 overseas businesses making taxable supplies in the UK have not benefited from the UK VAT registration threshold. In most cases they are required to register for VAT in the UK unless their customers account for the VAT due via the reverse charge. An exception is that VAT registration will not be required if HMRC are satisfied that all of the taxable supplies qualify for zero-rating. This change is included in *Finance Act 2012*, which added *Sch 1A* to *VATA 1994*.

The VAT registration threshold was increased to £83,000 on 1 April 2016.

Recent VAT registration thresholds are as follows:

1 April 2015 to 31 March 2016	£82,000
1 April 2014 to 31 March 2015	£81,000
1 April 2013 to 31 March 2014	£79,000

1 April 2012 to 31 March 2013	£77,000

A 'taxable person' is defined in UK legislation as being someone who is either registered for VAT or is required to be registered for VAT. This is an important point and means that anyone who is not yet registered but should be (on the basis that the value of their taxable sales has exceeded the registration threshold at some point in the past) is still classed as a taxable person.

There are occasions when a business can be registered for VAT even if the limits above have not been exceeded (voluntary registration) and there are also instances when a business can register without ever having made any taxable supplies in the past (intending trader).

If a business fails to notify its liability to be registered for VAT, then it will face penalties based on the length of time it was late with its notification, and in cases where the VAT registration date should have been after 1 April 2010, based on the behaviour of the taxpayer that led to the late registration.

The key point to remember is that it is only the value of taxable supplies that counts towards the registration threshold quoted above. If a business has exempt, non-business (or outside the scope) income, these amounts are excluded from the calculation. This is a technical issue that can cause confusion with many clients and advisers – see Example 1.

Example 1

John trades as an estate agent and in the 12-month period ending 30 June 2015, his total income is as follows:

- commission earned from selling houses (taxable) £60,000
- commission earned from selling mortgages (exempt) £30,000

Does John need to register for VAT?

Solution – although John's total income of £90,000 is above the VAT registration threshold, the key figure is the value of his taxable income ie £60,000. As this is less than the VAT registration threshold, he has no legal obligation to register for VAT.

Note – 'taxable' income is any income where the goods or services supplied by the business would be charged at a VAT rate (ie either 0% (zero-rate), 5% (reduced rate) or 20% (standard rate)). Don't forget that a zero-rated supply is still classed as taxable – but the rate chargeable is 0%.

Example 2

Jane is a consultant with income from UK clients of £60,000, and income from French business clients of £30,000.

Solution – the income from French business clients is outside the scope of UK VAT because the place of supply is France (where the customer is based). Jane does not need to register for VAT in the UK because her taxable sales are less than the VAT registration threshold.

Note – see Chapter 13 for a detailed analysis of the place of supply rules.

Compulsory registration

Turnover limits, EU acquisitions, services received from abroad

[1.2] As explained above, there are two main situations when a business needs to be VAT registered on a compulsory basis – ie if the annual turnover threshold has been exceeded or if it is expected that the annual limit will be exceeded in the next 30 days. In effect, the latter rule means that any large business that has significant trading income will, more than likely, need to be VAT registered from its first day of trading.

However, there are four other situations when a business will also have to register:

(a)   if the value of its 'acquisitions' (ie the value of goods bought from other EU countries) exceeds certain limits. The rules state that if the value of acquisitions made by a business at the end of any month, in the period beginning with 1 January in that year, have exceeded the annual UK VAT registration threshold or are expected to exceed that threshold in the next 30 days, then the business must register for VAT. See **11.11** for an example of how this rule works in practice;

(b)   if an unregistered business receives certain services from abroad, then it may need to register if the value of these supplies (and any other taxable supplies it makes) exceeds the UK registration threshold. See **14.6** for practical examples of how this rule works in practice;

(c)   from 1 December 2012 an overseas business that does not have a place of establishment in the UK will not benefit from the UK VAT registration threshold and will have to register for VAT in the UK if it has any customers that do not account for the VAT due via the reverse charge. However, HMRC may grant exemption from the requirement to be registered if they are satisfied that the only taxable supplies to be made by the business will be zero-rated;

(d)   if it is supplying consumers in other EU countries with broadcasting, telecommunications or electronically supplied services and it wants to register to use the Mini One Stop Shop as an alternative to registering for VAT in each EU country where the customers are located. See **14.9** for details of the 1 January 2015 change to the place of supply rules.

In the case of the annual turnover threshold being exceeded, then notification of the liability to be registered must be made within 30 days of the end of the month in which the threshold was exceeded. The registration date will then be the first date of the following month.

The effect of the annual registration test is that an unregistered business needs to review, on a rolling 12-month basis, the value of its taxable supplies at the end of each calendar month. See Example 3.

Example 3

> Steve is a self-employed plumber (making wholly taxable supplies), and the value of work carried out in recent months has been as follows:
>
> | | |
> |---|---|
> | 12 months to 31 March 2016 | £79,500 |
> | 12 months to 30 April 2016 | £80,500 |
> | 12 months to 31 May 2016 | £81,500 |
> | 12 months to 30 June 2016 | £84,500 |
>
> When should he become VAT registered?
>
> **Solution** – until 31 March 2016, the annual VAT registration limit was £82,000 – this figure was increased to £83,000 from 1 April 2016. The point at which Steve has exceeded the limit is 30 June 2016 – which means he must notify HMRC of his liability to be VAT registered within 30 days of this date, and his registration will be effective from 1 August 2016.

As illustrated by Examples 1 and 2, it is important to remember that only the value of taxable supplies is taken into account for the registration threshold – any exempt or non-business supplies are ignored. As a separate point, a new business will need to monitor its turnover from its first day of trading because it is possible that it might exceed the VAT registration threshold after, for example, the fifth month of trading. It is not advisable to wait until after the first year of trading has been completed to identify whether registration was needed earlier in the year.

If a business trades as a second-hand car dealer or any other trader dealing in second-hand goods that uses a margin scheme, the taxable turnover is the full value of the sale, not the margin being achieved.

However, in the case of a tour operator using the tour operators' margin scheme, the taxable supplies represent the full margin (ie difference between buying prices and selling prices).

Transfer of a going concern

[1.3] If a person takes over a business as a going concern, then it is necessary to take into account the taxable sales of the previous owner to determine if VAT registration is required. If the previous owner's taxable supplies exceeded the threshold, then the new owner must also register for VAT from the first day he takes ownership of the business. See Example 4.

(HMRC Notice 700/1, para 3.8).

Example 4

> Jean took over a florist shop as a going concern. The supplies of the previous owner (all taxable) were £125,000 per year. Jean has decided not to register for VAT until her own sales have exceeded the VAT registration threshold.

Solution – Jean's decision is incorrect – as the new owner, she needs to take into account the turnover of the previous owner and because this was in excess of the registration limit, she needs to register from her first day of trading.

Note – it is also a condition of the transfer of going concern rules (under which the transfer of a business is disregarded for VAT purposes, so that no VAT is chargeable on the transaction) that the new owner must either be VAT registered at the time of the sale or liable to be registered.

Applying for VAT registration

[1.4] When a business applies for VAT registration, the majority of applications will be made to register a business as a sole trader, partnership or limited company and most will now be completed online.

Standard paper applications need to be sent to the national registration unit (based at 62–70 Tettenhall Road, Deansgate, Wolverhampton, WV1 4TZ) and the business must be registered from its principal place of business (it is not acceptable to register the address from an accountant's office or postal address).

As a useful tip, it is usually of benefit if a taxpayer's VAT quarters coincide with its financial year. In many cases, a new business will have a year end of 31 March to coincide with the tax year, so a request for this date (or any other date for different year ends) can be made at the time of application for VAT registration.

Providing full and complete information at the time an application is submitted should help HMRC process the application within a reasonable time. It may be useful to provide supporting evidence to prove that an application is genuine – HMRC look very closely at applications where it suspects a possible link to what is known as 'carousel (or MTIC) fraud' (see Chapter 19). In cases where it needs further information, HMRC will write to the business requesting more details to verify the application.

If HMRC are satisfied with the application, a certificate of registration, confirming the effective date of registration, the registration number, the date on which the first accounting period ends and the length of future VAT accounting periods (ie quarterly, monthly, annual) will be issued. From the effective date of registration, a business must start keeping appropriate records and begin charging VAT to its customers.

Since April 2012 virtually all VAT registered businesses have been required to submit their VAT returns online and pay any VAT due electronically, regardless of when the business registered for VAT.

Sales made before a VAT number has been allocated

[1.5] What happens if a business needs to start charging VAT from, say, 1 June, but that date arrives and it has still not received details of its VAT registration number from HMRC?

The rules state that a business must start charging VAT from the date it knows it has to be registered. This means that it can charge VAT before it is actually registered but, until it has received a VAT registration number, it must not show VAT as a separate item on any invoice raised. This can be achieved by changing its prices to include VAT and explaining to any VAT registered customers (who will want to be able to reclaim input tax) that it will send them VAT invoices at a later date. When the business has received confirmation of its VAT number, it must then send the necessary invoices showing VAT within 30 days.

The positive point about these procedures is that the business will still be collecting VAT from its customers at the time an invoice is raised.

Input tax on goods and services obtained before VAT registration

[1.6] When a business first registers for VAT, it is possible that it may have incurred input VAT on expenditure before its date of registration. The positive point is that there is some scope to reclaim this VAT on the first return submitted by the business. The rules for making such a claim depend on whether the expenditure in question is related to goods or services.

(1)   Goods – the following conditions must be satisfied:
  (a)   the goods are still held at the time when the business became VAT registered;
  (b)   they must have been supplied to the registered business within the four-year period before the date of VAT registration (assuming the date of registration is 1 April 2009 or later – but without bringing back into time a period that was out of date on 31 March 2009 when a three-year limit was in place);
      Example – if the date of registration is 1 October 2009, the goods must have been purchased after 1 April 2006. If the date of registration is 1 May 2010, the goods must have been purchased after 1 May 2006. The four-year limit is fully effective in this situation because the date of registration is after 1 April 2010.
  (c)   the goods are to be used by the business that is now registered for VAT, and in connection with its taxable supplies (ie, no partial exemption or non-business issues);
  (d)   all the normal rules allow the input tax to be reclaimed, ie holding proper tax invoice etc.
  In effect, the goods in question will either relate to capital items being used by the business, eg computers, fixtures and fittings etc, or stock bought before the date of registration that will be sold after the business becomes VAT registered.
(2)   Services – the following conditions must be satisfied:
  (a)   the services are for the purpose of the business that is now VAT registered;
  (b)   the services were acquired within the six-month period before the date of registration;

(c)   the services have not been supplied by the taxable person before he became registered, ie they have not been recharged to a customer.

With the exception of capital items acquired after 1 January 2011 and within the capital goods scheme (see Chapter 9) there is no scope to extend either the four-year time period in relation to goods or the six-month period in relation to services. HMRC can, however, allow a VAT registration to be voluntarily backdated by up to four years at the time the application to register is submitted. A registration which has been backdated by four years could, for example, allow VAT to be recovered on goods purchased eight years before the application to register is submitted, subject to the conditions referred to above being met. Backdating a VAT registration will, however, also have implications in relation to the output tax that is due from the effective date of VAT registration. The choice of effective date of VAT registration should be carefully considered because once it has been agreed HMRC will not normally allow it to be changed.

An interesting tribunal case was *Sassoon Bury Ltd v Revenue and Customs Comrs* (TC01633) [2011] UKFTT 797 (TC). Sassoon Bury Ltd was incorporated on 27 May 2009 and incurred significant costs fitting out a hairdressing salon before starting to trade on 5 September 2009. The VAT registration threshold was reached during April 2010 and the company was registered for VAT with effect from 1 June 2010. The first VAT return included a claim for input tax on the fitting out costs incurred between 27 May 2009 and 5 September 2009.

HMRC argued that the input tax related to a supply of services to the appellant and was not allowable as the costs were incurred more than six months before the date of VAT registration. However, the tribunal found that some of the input tax related to goods and the taxpayer's appeal was allowed in part. The case demonstrates the importance of distinguishing between goods and services and selecting the most appropriate VAT registration date.

HMRC policy, as reflected in VAT Manual VIT32000, is that use of assets before the effective date of registration affects the amount of VAT that can be recovered. An example is provided in VAT Manual VIT32000 of a business trading below the VAT registration threshold acquiring a van that is still used by the business when it registers for VAT three years later.

(HMRC Notice 700/1, para 5.2). (VAT Manual VIT32000.)

Input tax on goods or services before incorporation

[1.7] It is very common for a private individual to purchase an asset before he starts his business, and then to trade as a limited company when trading actually starts.

Again, there are rules that allow input tax to be reclaimed on pre-incorporation expenditure:

(1)   the person to whom the supply was made must become a member, officer or employee of the company and is to be reimbursed (or receives an undertaking to be reimbursed) by the company for the whole amount of the price paid for the goods or services;

(2)   the person to whom the supply was made was not a taxable person at the time the expenditure was incurred, ie no input tax has been reclaimed already through another business;

(3)   the other rules mentioned above concerning input tax on goods and services have been fully met, eg four-year time limit in relation to purchase of goods and six-month period for services.

Voluntary registration

[1.8] The analysis at **1.2** explains the various procedures that apply when a business has to be VAT registered on a compulsory basis. In these situations, the business has no choice but to be registered and join the 'VAT club'.

However, there are various situations when it is in the interests of the business to be VAT registered, even when its turnover has not exceeded the annual limits. There are three main situations when a business would want to register for VAT on a voluntary basis as follows.

•   *Most or all business income is zero-rated* – this means that the business would be able to avoid charging VAT on all or most of its income, but would benefit from input tax recovery on its costs and overheads. The net result would be that the business would be a repayment trader as far as VAT is concerned.

•   *The majority of sales are to other VAT registered businesses* – if a business makes sales wholly or mainly to other VAT registered businesses, then the VAT it charges to its customers is not a problem because they can usually claim it back as input tax. This assumes that the customer in question does not suffer an input tax restriction through being exempt or partly exempt. By being VAT registered in this situation, a business can then benefit from input tax recovery on its costs without suffering any competitive disadvantage on the output tax charged to its customers.

•   *A business is incurring major amounts of VAT on capital expenditure* – a new business that is investing major sums of money on capital expenditure may decide that it wants to register for VAT as soon as possible in order to reclaim input tax at the earliest opportunity. The thinking may be that if the business develops as intended with future growth, then it will need to be VAT registered anyway. It would therefore be sensible to register from day one, and boost cash flow when it is needed most, ie by recovering input tax on relevant costs.

See Example 5 to identify when a business could benefit from being VAT registered on a voluntary basis.

(HMRC Notice 700/1, para 3.9).

Example 5

Geoff is a self-employed carpenter, who makes wooden tables for a wide range of businesses that are registered for VAT. He spends a lot of money on raw materials and tools, and has also bought a new van for £20,000 plus VAT. His annual sales are £75,000.

Gordon is a self-employed tax adviser, who does a lot of work advising insurance companies on tax issues. His annual income is £75,000.

What is the best VAT route for these two businesses?

Solution – it is definitely in Geoff's interest to become VAT registered as soon as possible. He will be able to reclaim input tax on all of his raw materials and tools, and on the purchase of his van. The VAT he charges to his customers will not be a problem because they are registered for VAT themselves, and can therefore reclaim input tax.

However, it is best for Gordon to remain as an unregistered business. The nature of his business means he is unlikely to have any significant input tax to reclaim, and the additional VAT charged on his fees will be a problem for his clients because insurance companies are mainly exempt from VAT and are, thus, unable to reclaim any VAT charged.

In practice, HMRC are generally very accommodating when it comes to approving registrations on a voluntary basis. As long as it is satisfied that the business has a genuine need for registration and is carrying on a legitimate taxable activity, it tends to approve applications without any problem.

An intention to trade in the future

[1.9] It is common practice for certain types of business to incur large amounts of expenditure before they actually make a taxable supply. Examples could include a business that builds new houses, or a new business that needs to carry out major property alterations before it can start trading.

In such cases, a business can register for VAT as an intending trader – however, it is important to remember the following points:

* HMRC will look very closely at intending trader applications. It will need to be convinced that the business has a genuine intention to make taxable supplies and that the application is not just an attempt to obtain large amounts of VAT repayments on a non-business project;
* it is important that traders provide HMRC with as much evidence of their intention to trade as possible. This evidence could be in the form of planning permission from a local authority to trade as a certain business and correspondence with potential customers or suppliers;
* HMRC will want to know the likely date when taxable supplies will commence – this could be evidenced by, for example, a cash flow forecast or a business plan.

Exemptions and exceptions from being registered

[1.10] In most cases, a business that exceeds the VAT registration limits must register for VAT in accordance with the rules mentioned earlier in this chapter.

However, there is scope for a business to request exemption from registration if it can satisfy HMRC that:

- the business is wholly making zero-rated supplies and would, therefore, always be a repayment trader if it registered for VAT; or
- the business mainly makes zero-rated supplies and even though some supplies are standard or reduced rated, the business would still be in a net repayment position, ie input tax exceeds output tax on a regular basis; or
- although the business has exceeded the compulsory registration limits, this situation was caused by a one-off sale (or unusual trading circumstances). A letter should be sent to HMRC advising of this situation but with a request for the registration to not be processed on the basis that future trading by the business will again be below the deregistration limit.

Note – in the first two situations above, a business is requesting 'exemption' from being VAT registered on the basis that it would be a repayment trader. It must therefore still complete an application to register but request exemption. In the third situation, ie where the registration limit has been exceeded due to a 'one-off' good sale, this relates to an 'exception' arrangement. The letter to request an exception from being registered should be sent to HMRC within 30 days of the limit being exceeded. There have been many cases over the years where a business that has failed to register for VAT at the correct time (after exceeding the registration threshold) could probably have applied for exemption from registration on the basis that it only made zero-rated supplies. In most cases it is not possible to backdate an application for exemption from registration.

The main disadvantage of not being VAT registered is that a business is sacrificing the opportunity to reclaim input tax on goods or services purchased for the business. In reality, the key point will be for a business to carry out an analysis of the costs and benefits of being registered. See Example 6.

(HMRC Notice 700/1, paras 3.7 and 3.11).

Example 6

Jean rents a small unit in a shopping centre selling fruit (zero-rated). Her sales for the previous 12 months were £90,000, exceeding the VAT limit for the first time. Her main costs in the business are rent (exempt from VAT), the wages of two employees (outside the scope) and the fruit she buys for resale (zero-rated).

Solution – the main overheads and costs of the business do not attract any VAT, so Jean will have negligible input tax to reclaim if she became VAT registered. Her best option is to notify her liability to be registered for VAT but, at the same time, to apply to HMRC to receive exemption from registration on the basis that she makes only zero-rated sales and would, therefore, always be a repayment trader.

An important point to remember as far as exemption from VAT registration is concerned is that the taxpayer still has a responsibility to notify HMRC of any material change in the business that could affect the decision of HMRC to grant exemption from VAT registration. Any such change needs to be notified to HMRC within 30 days of the day on which the material change took place – see Example 7.

Example 7

ABC Ltd trades from a small shop in the High Street, selling take-away sandwiches that are zero-rated for VAT purposes. The company received exemption from VAT registration because it managed to convince HMRC that it would always be in a net repayment situation.

On 3 May, the business diversified its activities by opening a café on its premises to sell sandwiches and light meals to customers – it will also continue to do take-away sales.

Solution – the new café represents a material change to the business of ABC Ltd. The company has 30 days from 3 May to notify HMRC of the change, and will probably need to be VAT registered due to the fact that the catering sales made on the premises will be standard rated.

Changes of business details

[1.11] It is important that a business ensures that its VAT registration details with HMRC are accurate. This means that changes in any of the following details must be notified when they take place:

- names of the proprietors or partners in the business;
- trading name, trading activity or address of principal place of business;
- any additional partners taken on by the business and the relevant date when this happened;
- any change in legal entity (the same VAT number can be retained in most cases by completing Form VAT 68), eg transfer from a sole trader to a limited company.

Note – it is now possible to apply for VAT registration and notify changes by using HMRC's eVAT service. The business must first be authorised to use the eVAT service, which can be done via VAT Online Services on the GOV.UK website (at www.gov.uk/government/organisations/hm-revenue-customs).

The 'VAT trap'

[1.12] Many businesses that have traded below the VAT registration limit will be faced with a dilemma when they increase their sales to the point when they may need to be VAT registered. In basic terms, the question that all businesses will need to consider is: should I expand my business and register for VAT, even though my profits could reduce by being VAT registered? Or should I restrict my level of activity by trading just below the VAT registration limits?

See Example 8 for an example of how being VAT registered can adversely affect the trading of a business. This particular business has been caught by what is sometimes known as the 'VAT trap'.

Example 8

Alan is a mobile caterer selling hot food from a small unit to customers who cannot recover VAT. His prices are determined by the prices charged by similar outlets in the same area. His sales have always been just below the VAT registration limit, but he has now been approached by a potential new customer who wants to buy £6,000 of beef burgers from him each year. This extra business will take him above the VAT registration limit. Should Alan accept the business offered by the new client?

Solution – most of Alan's purchases are zero-rated so he would have very little input tax to reclaim if he became VAT registered. It would also be difficult for him to increase prices charged to his customers because this could make him less competitive in the market place – he would probably have to absorb the VAT chargeable within his existing prices.

If Alan's sales increased from £78,000 to £84,000 as a result of the extra order, the likely impact on his business could be as follows:

- the new order will create additional profit of perhaps £3,000 (assuming 50% gross profit);
- by being VAT registered and not able to increase selling prices, the business will be worse off by having to pay £14,000 in output tax (£84,000 × 1/6 with a VAT rate of 20%) with very little, if any, input tax to reclaim on its expenses;
- the business has been caught by the 'VAT trap' and is worse off financially than if it had continued to trade below the VAT registration limit.

Consequences of late registration

Identifying the correct date of registration

[1.13] An unregistered business has a duty to monitor its activity levels on a monthly basis, and then register for VAT when it has exceeded certain limits as specified at **1.2**.

If a business fails to register for VAT at the correct time, there are two main consequences:

- the correct date of registration will be established by HMRC and the business will become VAT registered and liable to VAT on its taxable supplies from that date;
- the business could also be faced with a penalty for belated notification of its liability to be VAT registered.

If an adviser is acting for a client where HMRC has attempted to backdate the registration, there are a number of measures to take to ensure the revised date is correct:

- the calculation of supplies should only take taxable supplies into account. If a business makes some sales that are exempt or outside the scope of UK VAT, then the value of these sales should not be included in the calculation, as illustrated in Examples 1 and 2;
- the calculations should also exclude the sale of any capital assets made by the business;
- if a business exceeded the registration limit because of a one-off large sale, then it can potentially escape the need to be VAT registered if it notifies HMRC within 30 days of the time it exceeded the limit and is able to convince HMRC that it expected its future taxable sales would be less than the deregistration limit at the time it exceeded the limit, ie an 'exception' situation would be relevant as considered in **1.10** above;
- remember that the registration limit changes each year. It is important to ensure that the officer has used the limits in force at the correct period of time, eg if checking the level of sales for the calendar year 2014, then the relevant limit in that year was £79,000 up to 31 March and £81,000 from 1 April;
- if an officer has used annual accounts to arrive at an effective date of registration, then check that the accounts do not include adjustments that would not have created a tax point for VAT purposes, eg if the accounts to 31 December include closing work in progress of £10,000 within the sales figure, then the relevant date for VAT registration purposes is when this work was completed or invoiced (obviously at a later date);
- ensure that the officer's arithmetic is correct and that he has extracted his figures from the correct accounting records relevant to sales.

Note – be aware that HMRC share information between different sections of the department. For example, a review of figures submitted by taxpayers on their self-assessment tax returns could identify situations when a business should be VAT registered on the basis that sales have exceeded the relevant limits. This situation was highlighted in the case of *Reza Rastegar T/A Mo's Restaurant v Revenue and Customs Comrs* (TC00733) [2010] UKFTT 471 (TC), a restaurant owner who had never registered for VAT despite exceeding the turnover limit since 1999. HMRC discovered his lateness through his self-assessment tax returns and calculated arrears of tax for the late period of £268,000.

Arrears of tax through late registration

[**1.14**] If a business was registered for VAT from an incorrect date, then it will be required to complete a single VAT return to cover the period from when it should have been registered to the date when it actually became registered. In some cases, this period can be for many years.

The ideal situation for a business will be to recharge its customers for any unpaid VAT – this situation is most likely to be practical if the customer is VAT registered and able to recover input tax. The VAT charge should be 20% of the original value of the services performed or goods supplied (assuming the sale was made on or after 4 January 2011 when the standard rate increased from 17.5% to 20%) and should be made by issuing a VAT-only invoice. However, no output tax needs to be declared on zero-rated or exempt sales made by the business. It is also important to remember that some sales could be subject to the reduced rate of VAT (5%) – see Chapter 22 for further details.

If a business is unable to recharge VAT to its customers, then the standard rated sales made in the period under review will be deemed by HMRC to have been made on a VAT inclusive basis.

The positive point is that the business will be able to reclaim input tax (subject to normal rules) on its expenses for the period covered by the return.

An important point to remember is that the backdating of VAT registration will affect the profits made by a business – so income tax, corporation tax or Class 4 National Insurance savings could be made to help alleviate the impact of any VAT bill.

Penalty calculation and possible mitigation

[1.15] The calculation of a belated notification penalty is based on the net amount of tax payable for the period from when the business should have registered for VAT to the time when it actually became registered. The amount of the penalty then varies according to the total length of this period.

If the date of registration should have been before 1 April 2010:

*   where the period is less than 9 months a maximum penalty of 5% (or £50 if greater) will be applied;
*   for a period of between 9 and 18 months, a maximum penalty of 10% (or £50 if greater) will be applied;
*   for a period exceeding 18 months, a maximum penalty of 15% (or £50 if greater) will be applied.

If the date of registration should have been any date on or after 1 April 2010:

*   a penalty of between 10% and 30% of the tax outstanding can be charged, ie based on the rates that apply for showing a lack of reasonable care. However, HMRC have confirmed that most penalties will be in the lower range, taking into account the quality of disclosure made by the taxpayer in informing HMRC about the amount of VAT owed;
*   there is no penalty if the late registration has not produced a tax loss – this is good news for any business that wholly or mainly sells zero-rated items and would be in a VAT repayment position;
*   if a person makes a full and unprompted disclosure less than 12 months after the time when the tax first becomes unpaid the penalty can be reduced to zero.

In a First Tier Tribunal case the Tribunal decided that the time when the tax first becomes unpaid is the date on which the taxpayer would have been obliged to make its first VAT payment to HMRC if it had been registered for VAT on time.

In *Taste of Thai Limited v Revenue and Customs Comrs* (TC02721) [2013] UKFTT 318 (TC), [2013] SWTI 2187 the company was late notifying HMRC of its liability to register for VAT. HMRC accepted that the failure to notify was not deliberate and the company had made an unprompted disclosure. In such circumstances, if the notification was made less than 12 months late the penalty should be 0%, but if the notification was made later the penalty should be 10% of the potential lost revenue. The Tribunal considered the legislation at *FA 2008, Sch 41 para 13*, which refers to 'less than 12 months after the time when the tax first becomes unpaid'.

HMRC argued that the time when the tax first becomes unpaid was the date from which the company was obliged to be registered for VAT, which was more than 12 months before the company made its unprompted disclosure.

The company argued that the time when the tax first becomes unpaid was the date on which it would have been obliged to make its first VAT payment to HMRC if it had been registered on time, which was less than 12 months before it made its unprompted disclosure.

The Tribunal decided that no penalty was due as the company had made an unprompted disclosure to HMRC of its non-deliberate failure to notify within 12 months of the date when it would have been obliged to make its first VAT payment to HMRC if it had been registered on time.

There are two main ways of reducing the penalty or seeking its total withdrawal:

(a)   reasonable excuse provisions – if it can be shown that the business had a reasonable excuse for belated notification, then a penalty will not be charged by HMRC;

(b)   HMRC has the power to mitigate the penalty.

In terms of the reasonable excuse situation, HMRC has indicated that the following reasons for late registration may be acceptable as possible explanations.

- *Compassionate circumstances* – where an individual is totally responsible for running a small business and he, or a member of his immediate family, was seriously ill or recovering from such an illness at the time notification was required.
- *Doubt about liabilities of supplies* – where there is written evidence of an enquiry to HMRC about the liability of supplies and the liability has remained in doubt.
- *Uncertainty about employment status* – where there are genuine doubts as to whether a person is employed or self-employed or where correspondence with HMRC can be produced about these doubts.

If a taxpayer cannot convince HMRC (or an independent VAT tribunal) that he had a reasonable excuse for registering late, his priority should then be to ensure the penalty is as low as possible through mitigation.

The officer will take a number of factors into account when reviewing a penalty charge – including the following general headings:

(i)   how the infringement occurred;

(ii)   the degree of co-operation received from the taxpayer in quantifying the arrears;

(iii)   any other relevant factors that may be put forward by the taxpayer or an adviser acting on his behalf.

Registering for VAT with no UK income (service business)

[1.16] The place of supply for most services is based on the location of the customer, assuming the customer is in business. So a UK accountant doing accountancy work for business clients in France (EU) or Australia (non-EU) will not charge UK VAT.

In such cases, the business can still register for VAT in the UK and benefit from input tax recovery on its costs and overheads. This facility is allowed as long as the services in question would be taxable if supplied to a UK customer (ie not exempt).

(HMRC Notice 700/1, para 2.9).

Planning points to consider

[1.17] The following planning points should be given consideration.

*   A new or existing business will need to monitor the level of its taxable sales at the end of each calendar month to identify if it has exceeded the VAT registration limit. It is not advisable to wait until the end of the first 12 months of trading and then apply the relevant test.
*   Remember, that it is only taxable sales that count in deciding whether the registration limit has been exceeded, not exempt or non-business sales. Many sales of services to overseas customers will also be excluded from the calculations because these sales are outside the scope of UK VAT under the place of supply rules.
*   A transferee taking over a business as a going concern must take the turnover of the previous owners into account when deciding if it needs to be VAT registered from its first day of trading.
*   A business trading in second-hand goods must base the value of its taxable turnover on the full value of the sale, not just the margin that would be used under a second-hand VAT scheme.
*   To make accounting simpler, it is worthwhile for a business to seek VAT periods at the time of registration that coincide with its financial year, eg a business with 31 March year end should request calendar quarter VAT periods.
*   Ensure that a newly registered business has identified opportunities to reclaim input tax on any relevant expenditure incurred before its date of registration. However, expenditure on goods must have been in-curred within the four-year period before the registration date; a six-month time limit is imposed for services.

- It may be in the best interest of many businesses to register for VAT on a voluntary basis – particularly if they are making mainly zero-rated supplies or mainly working for other VAT registered businesses. Advisers should regularly review the activities of all non-registered clients to see if they could benefit from voluntary registration.
- If HMRC backdates a registration, make sure the officer's calculations and procedures for calculating the actual date are correct. Remember that if any arrears of VAT are established through the backdating of the registration, there is likely to be scope to reduce self-assessment tax liabilities because of reduced profits.
- A new penalty system took effect for all late registrations where the correct date of registration falls on or after 1 April 2010. There is an incentive with the new system to notify HMRC of the late registration within 12 months of when the business should have been registered because a zero penalty will usually apply.
- A potential planning opportunity could make it worthwhile for a business to register for VAT on a voluntary basis in order that it can make tax savings by using the flat rate scheme. The scheme is analysed in Chapter 8. A business using the flat rate scheme gets an extra 1% discount on its relevant flat rate category in its first year of VAT registration.
- Be aware that since 1 December 2012 only entities with an establishment in the UK can benefit from the UK VAT registration threshold.

Chapter 2

Deregistration

Key topics in this chapter:

- Opportunities for a business to deregister from VAT and occasions when this would be beneficial.
- Situations when deregistration is compulsory – eg sale of a business, ceasing to trade.
- Procedures for reclaiming input tax on post deregistration expenses using Form VAT 427.
- Sale of a business – either cancelling an existing VAT registration or new owners retaining the same VAT number.
- Dealing with a change in legal entity – VAT 68 procedures.
- Output tax liability on stock and assets owned by a business at the time it deregisters from VAT.
- Output tax issues on land and property owned at time of deregistration.
- Administration procedures for deregistration.

Introduction

[2.1] It is often assumed that once a business becomes VAT registered and joins the 'VAT club', it will remain registered until it is either sold or ceases to trade. In reality, this is not necessarily true. There are a number of situations where a tax adviser can be proactive as far as VAT deregistration is concerned, often to the clear benefit of the client.

Going back to basics, the main rule as far as VAT registration is concerned is that a business must register for VAT when it has made taxable supplies in the previous 12 months exceeding the VAT registration threshold (£83,000 from 1 April 2016) or expects to make taxable supplies exceeding the VAT registration threshold in the next 30 days. The latter rule effectively means that all large businesses have to register for VAT as soon as they start to trade.

Once registered, a business will charge VAT on its taxable supplies, and as long as it is not making exempt or non-business supplies, will recover input tax on relevant expenditure.

Deregistration must be requested if a business has ceased to make taxable supplies, ie the business has closed down or has been sold – but there are two other main situations where a business can request deregistration:

- if HMRC are satisfied that the value of taxable supplies in the next 12 months will not exceed the deregistration threshold (£81,000 from 1 April 2016. This figure usually increases in the Budget each year in the same way as the registration limit;
- most or all sales are zero-rated and the business submits repayment VAT returns (needless to say, not many businesses seek to deregister under this clause).

(HMRC Notice 700/11, para 3.2).

Reasons for voluntary deregistration

[2.2] The main reasons why some businesses would be keen to deregister at the earliest opportunity are as follows:

(a)   the majority of sales are standard rated and made to members of the public or to other businesses who are not VAT registered – in other words, VAT is an extra cost to these customers because they do not have the opportunity to reclaim input tax. In the case of sales to non-registered businesses, VAT would become an extra cost that they would treat as a business overhead. Remember, it is not just small businesses that may not be VAT registered but also large companies who cannot register because they only make exempt supplies – most insurance companies and some financial institutions;

(b)   the nature of the business means there is very little input tax to reclaim – this is particularly the case for many service-based businesses. This situation could mean that even though output tax charged to customers is not an issue (if supplies are made to other businesses able to reclaim input tax), the negligible input tax to reclaim could mean it is not productive to spend unnecessary time on the administration of VAT, ie completing returns, keeping certain records etc.

Note – in the case of (b), it is possible that the business is using the flat rate scheme, and saving tax by using the scheme compared to normal VAT accounting. It may be unwise to deregister if this was the case. The scheme is fully analysed in Chapter 8.

The above situations therefore mean that it is important for advisers to review the trading levels of certain clients – to see if a request for deregistration could be worthwhile. This is particularly relevant in the current economic climate where many businesses have suffered reduced sales.

See Example 1 which illustrates the impact of VAT on different types of business.

Example 1

John provides accountancy services and tax advice to funeral directors. He is VAT registered and his normal charge out rate is £100 per hour plus VAT.

Jill provides accountancy services and tax advice to funeral directors. She only works on a part-time basis so has always traded below the VAT registration limits. Her charge out rate is £100 per hour – no VAT.

Jack provides accountancy services and tax advice to butchers' shops. All of his customers are VAT registered and he charges £100 per hour plus VAT.

Which of the three businesses above is suffering a loss of competitiveness because of VAT?

Solution – in this example, only one business is suffering a commercial disadvantage by being VAT registered, namely John. This is because funeral directors are partially exempt, and are unable to reclaim all of their input tax. In effect, VAT becomes part of their overhead cost – in contrast to a butcher's shop, which is able to reclaim all of the VAT charged by Jack as input tax. In reality, the funeral directors would save money by using the services of Jill – who does not have to charge VAT.

Reductions in future turnover

[2.3] At **2.1** above, it was explained that one of the reasons why a business could request deregistration from VAT is if it can satisfy HMRC that its taxable turnover in the next 12 months will be less than the deregistration threshold. Be aware that deregistration can only be requested from a current or future date, ie not on a retrospective basis (HMRC Notice 700/11, para 3.4).

The main reasons why this situation could emerge are as follows:

• the business has lost a key customer(s) that has not been replaced by new customers. In such cases, the value of future sales will obviously decrease;

• the business owner may decide to simplify his operation, the result of which could be a decrease in income and expenditure – for example, a carpet fitter employing ten people and renting premises may decide to make all staff redundant, close the premises and just trade on his own fitting carpets;

• the business owner may decide to reduce his working hours – to a level where he expects to trade below the VAT deregistration limits – for example, an architect working five days a week making a lifestyle decision to only work four days a week will (all things being equal) encounter a 20% reduction in his turnover.

In the case of a business seeking deregistration on the basis of future reduced turnover, it is important that the owner considers the impact of the VAT charge on his selling prices. For example, a surveyor currently charging £70,000 plus VAT of £14,000 has total sales of £70,000 but if he deregisters and does not reduce his total VAT inclusive fees (ie continues to collect £84,000 from his customers), then his expected sales in the next 12 months are £84,000, ie above the deregistration limit. He cannot seek to deregister (HMRC Notice 700/11, para 3.2).

Example 2 illustrates a typical situation (extending Example 1) where a business could encounter a trading problem that produces a VAT benefit.

Example 2

> John, from Example 1 above (who provides accountancy and tax services to funeral directors), has relied on one particular funeral director for nearly 25% of his £100,000 per annum turnover. The funeral director in question has now closed his business, and will no longer require the services of an accountant. John has therefore decided that this is a good opportunity for him to work less hours – he therefore does not intend to replace the lost business with any new clients.
>
> *Solution* – in this example, it is clear that John's taxable turnover in the future will be about £75,000 per year (ie £100,000 × 75%) – well below the deregistration threshold. He is entitled to deregister.
>
> The dilemma now faced by John is whether he can increase his charge-out rate to remaining customers, who will be financially better off anyway because of the VAT saving on his fees. An increase from £100 per hour to £105 per hour would probably compensate John for the loss of input tax he will suffer as a result of not being VAT registered – but his clients (all partly exempt businesses) are still better off by the new arrangement.

Anti-avoidance measure

[2.4] As with many aspects of VAT, HMRC has anti-avoidance measures in relation to deregistration, namely that the expected reduction in sales must not be because a business intends to suspend trading for 30 days or more. See Example 3.

Example 3

> Bill trades as a fish and chip shop, and his taxable sales are £7,000 per month (£84,000 per annum). He is VAT registered. Next year, he is planning to close his shop for 8 weeks to go on a long holiday to Australia – he sees an opportunity to deregister for VAT as his taxable turnover will be less than the deregistration threshold in the next 12 months.
>
> *Solution* – it is clear that the reason for the decrease in turnover is because of the suspension of trading for more than 30 days. In reality, the business is still trading above the VAT threshold in normal circumstances. Any request for deregistration would be refused.

Exclusion of capital assets

[2.5] One point to remember is that the sale of capital assets is excluded when considering if taxable turnover in the next year will be less than the deregistration threshold.

For example, if a business expects sales to be £100,000 in the next 12 months but this includes the sale of a machine that is a capital asset of the business for £30,000, then the relevant figure to consider is £70,000. An application to deregister could therefore be made.

Administrative savings by not being VAT registered

[2.6] A business can also deregister if it can convince HMRC that all, or most, of its sales are, or will be, zero-rated, and therefore any VAT return submitted would always be a repayment claim.

In most cases, a business making zero-rated supplies will be reluctant to deregister because of the loss of input tax recovery. However, certain businesses have negligible input tax to claim, and therefore gain little advantage in being registered. See Example 4.

Example 4

Mrs E runs a business that buys eggs (zero-rated) from a local farm and sells them to surrounding shops. Her turnover from this activity is £100,000 per annum. She makes all of the collections and deliveries on her bicycle and therefore incurs no motoring expenses. She works from home and therefore suffers no premises costs. The accountant she uses is not registered for VAT, but charges her £500 per year to complete four VAT returns, which have no output tax and only about £10 per quarter input tax on a small amount of telephone and stationery expenditure.

Solution – it is clearly a 'win:win' situation for Mrs E to deregister for VAT – she will save £460 per year (£500 accountancy fees less the £40 loss of input tax) and HMRC will not have to administer a registration that does not produce any tax revenue.

As an extra point, the circumstances in the case of Mrs E above are very clear because she is only making zero-rated supplies. However, HMRC will also allow a business to deregister or not register in the first place if there are some standard rated supplies being made as well. The key test it will consider is whether input tax is likely to exceed output tax on a regular basis. Once it has established this is the case, the taxpayer's request for deregistration is likely to be granted.

Compulsory deregistration

Ceasing to trade

[2.7] The examples illustrated at 2.2–2.6 above considered situations where a taxable person 'may' request deregistration – in other words, he or his adviser has identified that he is entitled to exit the VAT system, and it is in his best interests to do so.

There are other circumstances where deregistration is compulsory, ie the business 'must' cancel its VAT registration.

The obvious situation is where a business has ceased to trade. Another situation where deregistration is compulsory is where a business continues to trade but now only makes exempt supplies and has ceased to make any taxable supplies. The effective date of deregistration is the date when the final taxable supply was made, and deregistration is applied for online or by completing and submitting Form VAT 7. The legislation requires that the application must be submitted within 30 days of cessation. HMRC have the power to charge a penalty if this deadline is not met.

In reality, it is unlikely that HMRC will charge a penalty if the 30-day notification is not made. This is because many businesses delay cancelling their registration as a matter of course because they want to recover input tax on all outstanding expenses – and think this can only be done by retaining their VAT registration number. The correct approach is to notify HMRC immediately (within 30 days) that cessation has taken place – and then make post deregistration claims of input tax on Form VAT 427. See Example 5.

Example 5

Mrs Smith ceased to trade as a computer consultant on 31 March. Her accountant will not be doing her final self-employment accounts until September – and will raise his invoice for this work (£800 + VAT) in October. Mrs Smith is VAT registered and submits VAT returns on a calendar quarter basis.

Solution – the incorrect approach (but adopted by many people in practice) would be for Mrs Smith to retain her VAT number until the end of December – so that she can recover input tax on her accountancy fees on the VAT return for the quarter to 31 December.

The correct approach would be for her to notify HMRC of the cessation of trading within 30 days and then submit Form VAT 427 at a later date to recover the input tax on her accountancy fees.

Claiming VAT after deregistration

[2.8] With regard to Form VAT 427 to reclaim VAT on post deregistration expenses:

- a claim cannot be made for any goods purchased after the registration has been cancelled – this is a reasonable rule because HMRC will not be receiving any output tax on these goods, so they are unlikely to allow any input tax claim;
- a claim for services can only be made if the services were received for the purposes of taxable business activities;
- any claim must be submitted with original invoices (copies are not accepted);
- claims must be submitted within four years of when the expenditure was incurred (this limit took effect on 1 April 2009). This is a later date than the date of deregistration;
- no claim can be made on expenses relevant to exempt or non-business activities. The partial exemption *de minimis* limits do not apply to expenses incurred after the date of deregistration.

See **2.15** below for the HMRC address where claims should be sent.

(HMRC Notice 700/11, section 9).

Sale of a business

[2.9] A business owner must also deregister if he sells his business, although it is possible that the new owner may want to retain the same VAT registration number. Is this wise?

- The main disadvantage with new owners taking over an existing VAT registration is that they are also agreeing to take over any potential VAT debts of the previous business.
- This could cause problems if, for example, a VAT inspection going back four years found a number of underpayments that were relevant to the period when the previous owner was running the business. The new owner would then be liable to pay this debt to HMRC.

HMRC should not, however, apply any penalty against the new owner of the business for any period before he took ownership.

The procedure for retaining a VAT number is that the new and former owners of the business must complete and sign Form VAT 68 – which must be approved by HMRC who will carry out various checks.

(HMRC Notice 700/11, para 2.4).

In the majority of circumstances it would be regarded as unwise for the new business owner to agree to take over the existing VAT registration number. There is no compulsion to do so, so why take the risk that an unknown VAT liability may be discovered? Much better to obtain a 'clean' VAT registration number where there can be no surprises.

Change of legal entity

[2.10] The other main situation where a registration must be cancelled is if a business changes its legal entity. For example, a common situation in recent years (due to favourable rates of corporation tax) has been for a sole trader or partnership to incorporate its business.

In such situations, there are again two options:

- the parties involved can sign Form VAT 68 so that the new entity retains the same VAT registration number. This arrangement would be sensible in the case of incorporation mentioned above – as the same persons are involved in both businesses;
- to apply for a new VAT registration number – this might be the best approach when, for example, a sole trader takes on a partner, ie there are different people involved in the old and new business.

(HMRC Notice 700/11, para 2.4).

Note – the situation when an existing partnership takes on an extra partner is not a change in legal entity. In such cases, the only information needed by HMRC is a new VAT 2 (list of partners) to reflect the addition of the new partner.

Note – where a new entity retains the VAT registration number of the previous business, the requirement from 1 September 2007 is that the new owner (or buyer) must retain the business records of the previous owner. This will enable the buyer to comply with his obligations to HMRC, eg being able to produce records in the event of a VAT visit.

Consequences of deregistration

Output tax on stock and assets held at time of deregistration

[2.11] When a business deregisters from VAT, it must account for output tax on any stocks and assets held at the time of deregistration. There is legislation at *VATA 1994, Sch 4, para 8* which outlines that this output tax can be ignored if the total VAT declared on all stock and assets would be less than £1,000 (ie gross value of less than £6,000 with a VAT rate of 20%).

With regard to these rules, there are a number of important points to take into account, all of which help to reduce the output tax liability, in many cases to zero.

- Output tax is not due on any stocks or assets where input tax has not been claimed on the original purchase. In effect, HMRC are acknowledging that because no input tax credit has been given on the goods in question, it will not seek an output tax payment. However, this does not apply if the goods in question were not subject to a VAT charge because they were acquired as part of a transfer of a going concern.
- No output tax is due on goods that are zero-rated or exempt, eg a newsagent selling newspapers.
- No output tax is due on intangible assets such as copyrights and goodwill – these assets are ignored and the rules only apply to tangible assets.
- In many situations, assets or stock held will be taken into the private ownership of the business owners or will be used to carry on trading in the future (if the business is deregistering due to the turnover rules rather than because it is closing down). In such cases, output tax will be due at cost price on the stock items, ie there is no requirement to include a profit element on the goods. To quote from paragraph 7.8 of HMRC Notice 700/11 'You should normally value your land or goods at the price you would expect to pay for them, or for similar land or goods, in their present condition.' This enables the calculation to take into account the impact of any out-of-date or damaged goods.
- In all cases of estimates, HMRC would expect calculations to be based on a fair and sensible approach – for example, it would not be reasonable to declare that a van was worth £3,000, if the van in question was bought for £10,000 only three months before the business deregistered.
  (HMRC Notice 700/11, section 7).

The rules become more complicated if land and property assets are involved – for further details, see **2.13** below.

For an illustration of the above issues, see Example 6.

Example 6

Mike runs a shop that sells confectionery, tobacco and newspapers. His taxable turnover for the 12 months to 31 March was £53,000 and his expected taxable sales for the next 12 months are expected to be £55,000. He has decided to deregister from VAT.

The cost value of Mike's stock at 31 March was £20,000 (cost price excluding VAT) – of which newspapers were £4,000. He also has a car that he bought 12 months ago for £10,000 plus VAT and a computer that he bought from a friend (not VAT registered) for £1,000.

Solution – it is clear that the value of stock and assets on hand exceeds £5,000 excluding VAT – so Mike has an output tax liability to declare on his final VAT return. However, he can ignore the computer because it was bought from an unregistered person. In the case of the car, Mike would not have reclaimed input tax on the initial purchase (non-deductible input tax) so the onward supply is exempt under *VATA 1994, Sch 9, Group 14*. The newspapers are zero-rated so they can also be excluded. Output tax is therefore due on the remaining stock (£16,000 × 20% = £3,200).

It is important that the impact of any output tax liability is discussed at the planning stage of any discussions about deregistering for VAT. It can be a shock to many business owners if they suddenly have a large output tax liability on stock and assets – in many cases, the impact of this bill could make the option of deregistration much less attractive.

Transfer of a going concern

[2.12] Another important consideration is to assess whether deregistration is taking place because a business is being sold or transferred as a going concern. In such cases, the transfer of stock and assets is outside the scope of VAT, with no output tax payment needed by the seller.

One requirement for a transfer of a going concern situation is for the new owner to be VAT registered, or liable to be VAT registered, at the time of the transfer but there are other important rules to follow as well. See Chapter 4 for a detailed analysis of the issues involving the transfer of a going concern.

Land and property issues

[2.13] As explained at **2.11** above, output tax is due on the value of any stock and assets owned by the business at the time of deregistration on which input tax has been claimed.

In the case of land and property, a number of different situations apply as far as output tax is concerned at the time of deregistration.

Note – in the examples that follow, it is being assumed that a business is deregistering on the basis of reduced turnover but is retaining land or buildings within the business.

- **The land or buildings were bought as an exempt supply but the option to tax has been exercised since that date.**
  In this situation, the business would have charged output tax on any supplies connected with the property since it made the option to tax election on the property, eg rent charged to a tenant. It would have also reclaimed input tax on any related costs, eg refurbishment. The positive point, however, is that there is no output tax liability to declare on the final VAT return at the time of deregistration on the value of the opted land or buildings. This is because no input tax claim was made when the land or buildings were first purchased.
  However, it needs to be recognised that an option to tax election is effective for 20 years once it has been made. So, if the business sells the property at a future date, then it will need to reregister for VAT and account for tax on the sale proceeds, assuming the sale takes place within the 20-year life of the option.

- **The land or buildings were purchased with VAT and input tax reclaimed – but the supply would now be classed as exempt from VAT if sold to a third party.**
  The above situation could apply if a business purchased a brand new commercial property but never opted to tax the property (it would still be able to recover input tax on the initial purchase as long as the building was used for its own trading purposes, making taxable supplies). Once the property was then three years old, the onward sale of the property would be exempt. The output tax liability at the time of deregistration would not apply because it excludes all zero-rated or exempt goods – so as long as a sale of the property would be an exempt supply if sold at the date of deregistration, there is no output tax liability.
  However, there may be a problem for the business in this situation with the capital goods scheme – if the property in question cost more than £250,000 plus VAT when it was first purchased and deregistration is taking place within ten years of this date. The end result could be an extra disallowance of input tax on the final VAT return submitted by the business. See Chapter 9 for details about the capital goods scheme.

- **The land or buildings were purchased with VAT and input tax reclaimed – the buyer made the election to opt to tax the property.**
  In this situation, an output tax liability exists at the time of deregistration because input tax was claimed on the initial purchase of the land or buildings and the option to tax election makes this a taxable supply. Note – the reality of this situation is that the business would be unlikely to deregister because of the high output tax payment that would be due on the market value of the land or buildings on its final VAT return. The sensible and possibly only option would be for the business to defer the cancellation of its VAT registration until the property is sold.

(HMRC Notice 700/11, para 7.4).

Note – as an example of a land and property/deregistration arrangement that went wrong, the case of *Mollan and Co Ltd v Revenue and Customs Comrs* (TC00828) [2010] UKFTT 578 (TC), [2011] SWTI 283 gives an important warning. In this case, the taxpayer's final VAT return omitted output tax on the market value of a property it owned and on which it had claimed input tax and made an option to tax election. The market value of the property at the date of deregistration was deemed to be £200,000, and as the deregistration date was when the standard rate was 15% (June 2009), this created an output tax liability of £30,000 on the final VAT return. To make matters worse, HMRC not only assessed the tax but also a careless error penalty of £4,500, ie the minimum 15% penalty for a prompted disclosure (it was HMRC that queried the issue of output tax on stock and assets by issuing a post-deregistration questionnaire to the directors). The penalty was upheld in this case, ie a total bill of £34,500 for the company.

Administration issues

[2.14] When the date of cancellation of registration has been arranged, either a formal notice of cancellation will be sent (Form VAT 35) or a formal notice of exemption from registration is sent (Form VAT 8). Assuming that the VAT registration number has not been reallocated to a new owner, the final VAT return (VAT 193) must be completed in the normal way and sent to HMRC with full payment due.

Once the VAT registration is cancelled, it is important that the business does not issue any more VAT invoices (showing its VAT registration number) or charge VAT to any customers. HMRC should be consulted about the situation where a business uses an existing stock of business stationery, but crosses out the VAT registration number (HMRC Notice 700/11, para 8.3).

* *Deregistration date* – in the case of *Vass (Peter) v Revenue and Customs Comrs* (TC00510) [2010] UKFTT 208 (TC), the taxpayer's accountants claimed to have submitted Form VAT 7 to HMRC in order to deregister their client on 30 June 2008. HMRC claimed never to have received the form on the date specified, and allowed deregistration from when they subsequently received another form on 27 October 2008. The deregistration date was slightly backdated to 30 September 2008. The tribunal supported HMRC on this issue, ie producing an output tax bill for Mr Vass that he was not expecting from 1 July to 30 September 2008. As a principle of VAT, a request to deregister on a voluntary basis (ie due to reduced turnover levels) cannot be backdated and it is important to follow up paperwork sent by post to ensure it has been received.

Bad debt relief

[2.15] A business can claim relief for VAT paid on bad debts after it has deregistered as long as it paid output tax on the sales in question while it was VAT registered, and also meets the conditions for claiming bad debt relief, ie invoice is more than six months overdue for payment and has been written off in the business accounts. No claim can be made more than four years after the relief became reclaimable.

A claim for bad debt relief is made on Form VAT 427, ie the same form that is used for claiming VAT on expenditure incurred after a business has deregistered. Claims should be sent to the address shown on the claim form.

Form VAT 427 can be accessed from this link:

www.gov.uk/government/publications/vat-reclaim-or-claim-vat-relief-on-canc elling-vat-registration-vat427

Planning points to consider

[2.16] The following points should be given consideration.

- Review the VAT registration position of all businesses on an annual basis to see if a client could be eligible for deregistration and, if he is, whether it would be commercially beneficial for him to do so.
- Any request for deregistration based on future turnover cannot be made because of a decision to suspend trading for 30 days or more.
- A business that is in a repayment situation but has taxable supplies exceeding the VAT limits can still apply for deregistration. This could be worthwhile if the business does not claim much input tax, and wants to save the administrative burden of being registered.
- Remember that a deregistered business can claim input tax on certain relevant expenses after it has been deregistered by using Form VAT 427. Any claim must be supported by original tax invoices.
- The same VAT number can be retained by the new owners when a business has been transferred as a going concern. However, there are potential risks for the new owner, who is taking over the possible VAT debts of the seller.
- There is no output tax liability on the value of stocks and assets held at the time of deregistration if the total amount of VAT involved is less than £1,000. Don't forget that no output tax is due on zero-rated or exempt goods or other items where input tax was blocked from being claimed when the goods were bought; output tax calculations are based on the present condition of the goods, ie taking damage and depreciation into account.
- If a business owns land and property at the time of deregistration, then it is important to be clear about the output tax rules that apply in relation to the option to tax and potential problems with the capital goods scheme.

- A deregistered business can claim bad debt relief in some cases after it has deregistered, subject to the usual bad debt relief rules being met. Claims are made on Form VAT 427.

Chapter 3

Group Registration and Divisional Registration

***

Key topics in this chapter:

- Main rules for group registration – the 'control' test.
- Forms to complete and procedures to follow if applying for a group registration.
- Benefits and consequences of a group registration.
- Being aware of anti-avoidance powers available to HMRC if it considers that group registration structures are being abused.
- The need for holding companies to make genuine taxable supplies if they are to be registered for VAT in their own right.
- Group registrations where the only taxable supplies are between group members.
- Key rules and procedures for divisional registration.

***

Introduction

[3.1] This chapter reflects the current treatment of VAT groups in the UK as at May 2016. The composition of a VAT group and the criteria necessary to form a VAT group are topics that have come under scrutiny at the Court of Justice of the European Union during 2015 (see the joined cases *Beteiligungsgesellschaft Larentia + Minerva mbH & Co KG v Finanzamt Nordenham: Case C-108/14* [2015] STC 2101 and *Finanzamt Hamburg-Mitte v Marenave Schiffahrts AG: Case C-109/14*. See also *Skandia America Corp (USA), filial Sverige v Skatteverket: Case C-7/13* [2015] STC 1163). In light of the above judgments it seems inevitable that UK law on VAT groups will need to change. Indeed, in January 2016, HMRC issued Revenue & Customs Brief 3/16 which announced that a consultation exercise is to be undertaken to consider the impact of the Court of Justice judgments in the above cases. What follows is therefore a reflection of the existing rules but it is highly likely that, within the next 12 months or so, the VAT grouping provisions of UK law will change substantially.

Under the UK's existing rules, the basic principle of a group registration is that a number of different legal entities (usually limited companies under common control) can be registered for VAT as a single taxable person, ie instead of each entity submitting its own VAT return, there is only one return submitted for the entire 'group'.

There are a number of important rules to be met before a group registration can be established, the main rule being that the companies within the group must all be under the control of one individual or one entity. This entity may be in the VAT group itself but it is not compulsory.

In the *Larentia & Minerva/Marenave* cases, the Court of Justice confirmed that *article 11* of the *VAT Directive* does not restrict membership of VAT groups only to corporate entities nor is it necessary for those entities to be under common control. Consequently, in principle, any entity may be a member of a VAT group. The only conditions laid down in *article 11* is that the entities must be established in the territory of a member state and while legally independent, the entities must be closely bound to one another by financial, economic and organisational links. Even then, *article 11* is a permissive Article (ie, member states are not obliged to allow VAT groups at all). If a member state does permit VAT groups it is entitled to adopt any measure needed to prevent tax evasion or avoidance through the use of the VAT group rules. Following the consultation, it remains to be seen how VAT groups will develop in the UK.

The two main advantages of being registered for VAT on a group basis are as follows:

(a)   there is no VAT charged on supplies made between group members (as the VAT group is regarded as a single taxable person which cannot supply itself with goods or services);

(b)   from an administrative point of view, there is only one quarterly (or monthly) VAT return to submit for the entire group.

The key challenge for HMRC in recent years has been to ensure that group registrations cannot be used (or, in HMRC's view, abused) to give an unfair recovery rate on input tax attributable to exempt supplies. See **3.5** below.

Divisional registration exists when one corporate body is split into a number of self-accounting units (divisions) and the company wishes to register each unit separately for VAT. Each unit will submit its own VAT return. However, the corporate body still remains liable for all of the debts and VAT responsibilities of each division.

Rules for group registration

[3.2] The key rule for group registration is that the group of companies seeking to be registered must meet the 'control test'. If the control rule is not met, then the application for group registration will be refused.

The control test can be met if any of the following situations apply:

•   the controlling company or individual has a majority of the voting rights in the other companies – this is usually achieved by owning at least 51% of the ordinary share capital of the subsidiary company;

•   the controlling company is a member of the subsidiary company and has the right to appoint or remove a majority of its board of directors;

•   the subsidiary company is a subsidiary company of another company which is also owned by the controlling company.

In the case of *European Commission v United Kingdom: Case C-86/11* [2013] All ER (D) 42 (May), [2013] SWTI 1775, ECJ, it was considered whether a VAT group can include non-taxable persons. The European Commission applied to the Court of Justice of the European Union (the Court), seeking a declaration that by permitting non-taxable persons to be members of a group of persons regarded as a single taxable person for purposes of VAT (a VAT group), the UK had failed to fulfill its obligations under *Directive 2006/112/EC, arts* 9 and 11. The Court dismissed the application and decided that *article 11* did not distinguish between taxable persons and non-taxable persons, using the word 'persons' rather than 'taxable persons' and noted that there was no case law to support the European Commission's argument. A VAT group can include non-taxable persons.

See Example 1 for an illustration of a practical example of how the control test would be applied.

Example 1

ABC Holding Co Ltd owns 75% of the shares in DEF Ltd. The latter company owns 100% of the shares in GHI Ltd. ABC Holding Co Ltd also has a joint venture arrangement whereby it owns 50% of the shares in JKL Ltd.

To date, each of the companies has been registered for VAT in its own right – but the group Finance Director now wishes to apply for a group registration to bring all four companies under one VAT group.

Solution – there is no problem with DEF Ltd being part of the group registration as it is controlled by ABC Holding Co Ltd because of share capital ownership. Equally, GHI Ltd is effectively owned by ABC Holding Co Ltd as well through its relationship with DEF Ltd. However, JKL Ltd cannot be part of the group because it is not controlled by ABC Holding Co Ltd. A separate company has the same level of control over the company (the joint owner) so the control test is not met.

It is possible that, following the consultation, JKL will be entitled to join the VAT group if it is deemed to be closely bound to the other companies by financial, economic and organisational links.

Note – it is possible that the control objective can be met by one private individual owning the majority of shares in a number of different companies. Equally, two or more individuals as a partnership can control all of the other entities. However, the most common arrangement is where a holding company owns shares in a series of trading companies.

Other rules that need to be met in order to satisfy the group registration requirements are as follows:

*   each of the bodies within the group must be established in the UK or have a fixed establishment in the UK;

- where applicable, the group structure must satisfy the anti-avoidance rules specified by HMRC to avoid the rules being exploited for an unfair tax advantage (these rules are mainly designed to counter specific planning measures carried out by larger organisations so are outside the scope of this book – see **3.5** below for a brief summary of the key points).

A company is established in the UK if its principal place of business is in the UK, and the management and control of the company is UK based. A company is classed as having a fixed establishment in the UK if it has a real and permanent trading presence in the UK.

For VAT purposes, a company is not classed as being established in the UK or having a fixed establishment in the UK just by being incorporated in the UK and having its registered office in the UK.

(HMRC Notice 700/2, para 2.8).

Applying for a group registration

[3.3] The basic outcome of applying for a new group registration is that the existing VAT registration numbers of the separate entities will be cancelled, and a new registration formed for the group. The business will need to select one of the proposed group members to act as a 'representative' member. This does not necessarily have to be the holding company. The new group registration will be in the name of the representative member.

Once a group registration has been created, it is fairly simple to add new entities to the group or, where appropriate, remove individual members from the group.

There are three main forms to complete when applying for a group registration:

- VAT 1 – main registration form signed by the representative member;
- VAT 50 – signed by either the applicant company or the person controlling the group;
- VAT 51 – relevant to each company applying to join the group (signed by the same person as the Form VAT 50).

Note – there is also Form VAT 56 that is used if there is a change in the representative member of the group.

Once a group registration has been established, Forms VAT 50 and VAT 51 will also need to be completed for each company that joins or leaves the group.

(HMRC Notice 700/2, paras 2.11, 2.12 and 6.3).

HMRC aim to respond within ten working days of receipt of an application for a group registration to confirm the application was received and either confirm that the application has been approved or advise that further enquiries need to be made. HMRC have 90 days from the date of receiving a completed application to make enquiries about the application and confirm its validity. The main aims of its checking procedures are as follows:

- to confirm that the control test for the group is properly achieved;
- to ensure that there are no revenue risks as far as the application is concerned.

In reality, the main reasons why an application would be refused to protect the revenue are as follows:

- the group's members have a poor history of complying with VAT requirements, which might pose a threat to HMRC's ability to collect VAT;
- HMRC suspect that the applicants intend to manipulate the group registration process through the use of tax avoidance schemes;
- group registration would create a distortion in the VAT liability of the group's supplies eg through partial exemption calculations.

(HMRC Notice 700/2, para 2.17).

Note – HMRC have confirmed that it will not refuse an application where the revenue loss follows from the normal operations of the group, eg because of the elimination of the VAT charge on supplies between group members. See Example 2.

Example 2

Jones Ltd is the holding company of two companies: Jones Estate Agency Services Ltd and Jones Surveyors Ltd. Jones Ltd employs ten staff carrying out head office functions such as central finance, purchasing and marketing. It makes a quarterly management charge of £50,000 plus VAT to each of the two trading companies. Each of the three companies (the holding company and two trading companies) is registered for VAT on an individual basis – Jones Surveyors Ltd is fully taxable but Jones Estate Agency Services Ltd has some exempt income relevant to fees for arranging mortgages. What are the benefits in forming a group registration?

Solution – one of the main benefits of group registration is that supplies between group members are ignored for VAT purposes. Jones Ltd can continue to charge its subsidiary companies £50,000 per quarter for its management services but the group registration arrangement means it must not add VAT to this fee. This does not produce any tax saving to Jones Surveyors Ltd because this company is fully taxable and is able to recover any VAT it is charged as input tax. However, Jones Estate Agency Services Ltd has some exempt income, so would, ordinarily, suffer a restriction on the input tax charged by its parent company. With a VAT group, the supply of management services by the holding company to Jones Estate Agency Services Ltd would be ignored meaning that no VAT would be charged and, as a result, there would be no input tax to consider in the first place.

In the situation above, there is a tax saving as a result of group registration but this is a normal benefit of the group structure, so would not be blocked by HMRC on avoidance grounds.

If HMRC are not satisfied with the validity or fairness of an application, it will seek further information to establish the motives for requesting group registration. In reality, the motives should be mainly linked to the administrative benefits of the arrangement, namely the need to avoid charging VAT on intra-group supplies and the benefits of only completing one VAT return each period.

Ultimately, whether a VAT group is permitted is down to HMRC's discretion and it will make that judgment based on the information it has received. Any refusal of the taxpayer to co-operate in providing the requested information will be taken into account when it makes its decision.

Benefits and implications of group registration

[3.4] Once a group registration has been established, the following key advantages and implications will follow.

- *Only one return needs to be completed for each VAT period* – however, there could still be considerable work involved in collating the figures submitted by each individual member of the group so it is important that the person completing the VAT return has good communication within the VAT group to ensure that all relevant figures are included in the consolidated return.
- *No VAT needs to be accounted for on supplies between group members* – there is also no need for VAT invoices to be issued for supplies between group members – inter-company charges could therefore be dealt with by raising journals through inter-company accounts in the nominal ledger.
- *All members of the group are jointly and severally liable for any VAT due from the representative member* – this means that if the VAT group (through its representative member company) cannot pay the debt owing to HMRC on the group VAT return, then each individual member of the VAT group is held jointly and severally liable for the amount of the debt until it is discharged (HMRC Notice 700/2, para 2.1).
- *The cash accounting limits, partial exemption de minimis limits, payment on account limits – all apply on a group basis* – this situation means, for example, that if company A has taxable turnover of £700,000 per year and company B has taxable turnover of £800,000 per year, then both companies would each be able to use cash accounting if they were registered for VAT on a separate basis. However, if the two companies were registered as part of a VAT group, then the combined taxable turnover of £1,500,000 becomes relevant – and this exceeds the cash accounting limit of £1,350,000 per year.

  HMRC Notice 700/60 provides details of how payments on account works and what a business must do if it is liable to make payments on account. Payments on account must be made by any business that accounts for VAT by submitting quarterly returns and has a VAT liability of more than £2.3 million in any period of 12 months or less. If a company is a member of a VAT group the VAT liability of the whole group determines whether payments on account are required and all members of the group are jointly and severally responsible for each payment on account (HMRC Notice 700/60, paras 1.1 and 2.3.5).

- *Input tax recovery is based on how the VAT group as a whole uses the goods and services received by each individual member* – this is a very important point and is illustrated in Example 3 below (HMRC Notice 700/2, para 5.5).

- *Error correction limits are based on the group as a whole* – if company A identifies an underpayment of £100,000, this would normally need to be corrected by making a disclosure to HMRC on Form VAT 652 because the amount of tax clearly exceeds the error correction limits (a disclosure must be made if the net error is more than £10,000 or 1% of the Box 6 outputs figure on the return where the error is being corrected, up to a maximum figure of £50,000). However, if company B is in the same VAT group and has identified an error of £95,000 overpaid VAT, then the net group error of £5,000 is now less than the disclosure limits. The net underpayment of £5,000 can be corrected on the next VAT return submitted by the group.

(HMRC Notice 700/2, paras 2.2 and 2.3).

Example 3

Following on from Example 2, Jones Ltd purchases new computer equipment that it leases to Jones Estate Agency Services Ltd for £2,000 per quarter. Jones Estate Agency Services Ltd uses the equipment to store all details of its mortgage customers and mortgage lenders with whom it deals.

Solution – although the supply from Jones Ltd to Jones Estate Agency Services Ltd is taxable (lease of computer equipment), the key point is that the VAT group is using the equipment in connection with its exempt supplies, ie arranging mortgages. The VAT group treatment is what counts and, therefore, Jones Ltd (as representative member of the VAT group) cannot reclaim the input tax on the initial purchase of the equipment.

Anti-avoidance measures

[3.5] As explained at **3.1** above, HMRC have attempted to close loopholes in the legislation that have allowed certain group structures to produce unfair results in terms of input tax recovery. For example, certain groups have benefited from an unfair recovery by introducing or taking a partly exempt company out of the group at a critical stage.

HMRC have extensive powers to deal with the manipulation of VAT groups – but these powers will mainly be applied to larger company structures where the amount of tax at stake is considerable.

The best advice to any adviser is to be very wary about implementing any scheme or structure for a client that appears too good to be true. One of the key principles of VAT is that input tax can be recovered to the extent that it relates to taxable supplies. If an arrangement appears to give high input tax recovery on an expense or asset that appears mainly attributable to exempt supplies, then there will almost certainly be a problem with the validity of the scheme.

(HMRC Notice 700/2, para 6.5).

Holding companies

[3.6] The main function of many holding companies is to own shares and receive dividends in subsidiary companies – but they will sometimes make management charges to these subsidiary companies, and employ staff in support functions such as finance and administration.

As long as the management services are genuine supplies, then the holding company will be able to register for VAT in its own right, as these supplies are taxable. However, it is more common for the company to be a member of a VAT group.

When reviewing the validity of management services, HMRC take the following points into account.

•   Does the holding company employ any staff – ie who are capable of producing work or providing services that could be recharged to a subsidiary company as a genuine management charge?

•   Are the directors the only people employed by the holding company – and are they also directors of the subsidiary companies as well? In such cases, there is unlikely to be a management charge arrangement.

•   What supplies are covered by the charge? Is there evidence of purchase invoices being processed through the accounts of the holding company (for example, a group purchasing arrangement may be in place for certain overheads)? This type of arrangement would then add credibility to a recharge arrangement for services provided to subsidiary companies.

•   Does the management charge have a proper basis of calculation – for example, cost basis plus percentage mark-up or recharge based on number of labour hours provided by the holding company to its subsidiaries?

Note – in the case of *Stirling Investments v Revenue and Customs Comrs (VAT)* (TC00374) [2010] UKFTT 61 (TC), the taxpayer managed to convince the tribunal that a payment from its associated business Stirling Investments Ltd related to a dividend payment rather than a fee for management services. This issue was important because the activity of Stirling Investments Ltd was exempt from VAT, so any VAT it paid on management services would create an input tax cost under the partial exemption rules. A dividend payment is outside the scope of VAT because it relates to an extraction of profit for the shareholders, rather than payment for a supply of services.

Note – in the case of *Norseman Gold plc v Revenue and Customs Comrs* [2016] UKUT 69 (TCC), the Upper Tribunal dismissed the taxpayer's appeal in a case relating to the supply of management services by a holding company.

In this case, the company provided services to an Australian subsidiary but did not stipulate a payment date in respect of the charges made. The tribunal found, therefore, that there was no consideration for the supplies of management services and, in the absence of consideration, there can be no supply for VAT purposes.

Management services to a group member – being the only taxable supplies

[3.7] There is no problem forming a group registration if the only taxable supplies relate to management services supplied by one group member to another. The initial thinking might be that this measure would be blocked because it will, in reality, generate nil VAT returns in most cases.

If one of the entities is making taxable supplies that would make it liable or eligible to register for VAT in its own right a VAT group can be formed, subject to the other conditions for VAT group registration being met. The group will, however, not be able to recover any input tax unless it makes taxable supplies outside the group, or makes supplies outside the UK that would be taxable supplies if made in the UK, or makes exempt supplies of financial or insurance services to customers outside of the EC. VAT returns must be submitted even if they are nil returns.

See Example 4 to illustrate this point.

(HMRC Notice 700/2, para 2.4).

Example 4

Good Causes Ltd is a registered charity that owns a trading subsidiary called Good Causes Trading Ltd. Neither company is registered for VAT because their supplies are either outside the scope of VAT or exempt from VAT. However, Good Causes Ltd incurs costs on behalf of Good Causes Trading Ltd, and wants to make a management charge of £100,000 per annum for these services.

Solution – The problem with the above situation is that as a separate entity not in a VAT group, Good Causes Ltd would need to charge output tax on the management services once it has exceeded the VAT registration limit but Good Causes Trading Ltd would be unable to reclaim this VAT as input tax because it is not making any taxable supplies.

However, the two companies could register for VAT as a group registration (the control conditions are met without any problem), which means that supplies of goods and services between group members are made without charging VAT.

The end result is that the VAT returns will always be nil because there is no taxable income being generated by either company outside of the VAT group. This is not a problem. The reality is that Good Causes Ltd is making supplies that would require it to register for VAT in its own right – but these supplies escape a VAT charge because they are being made to another entity in the same VAT group.

Note – the case of *Skandia America Corp (USA), filial Sverige v Skatteverket: Case C-7/13* [2015] STC 1163 has the potential to dramatically change the landscape in relation to VAT groups in the UK in the future. The case related to supplies of services between Skandia America Corp and a branch of that entity established in Sweden. Following an earlier judgment of the Court of Justice (*Ministerio dell'Economica e delle Finanze v FCE Bank plc: Case C-210/04* [2007] STC 165), supplies between a parent company and its branch were ignored for VAT purposes as the parent and the branch were considered to be the same entity (and thus it could not, by definition, supply services to itself). However, In *Skandia*, the Swedish branch was, along with other Swedish companies, a member of a Swedish VAT group. The Court of Justice considered that a VAT group is a separate person for VAT purposes. In essence, for VAT purposes, each constituent member of the VAT group (including the branch of the American company) lost its own individual identity. Any supply of services by the parent company was, thus, not regarded as made to its branch in Sweden, but to the separate taxable person that was the VAT group itself. Accordingly, the charges for services rendered by the American parent were charges to the VAT group as a whole and subject to Swedish VAT under the reverse charge rules. This is a seminal judgment of the court which is likely to have far reaching consequences for VAT groups. The consultation exercise announced by HMRC in January 2016 is to consider the implications of this judgment for the future.

Property transactions

[3.8] An option to tax election made on land or buildings by a member of a VAT group will apply to all other members of the same VAT group (see Chapter 28 for a detailed analysis of the option to tax regulations). The election will also apply to future group members, ie those that join the group after the election has been made. The election will also remain valid for those companies that may leave the VAT group in the future.

The capital goods scheme is a complex part of the VAT legislation (see Chapter 9) and a scheme adjustment may be needed when a company leaves or joins a VAT group.

Divisional registration

[3.9] As explained at **3.1** above, divisional registration allows a company that is divided into self-accounting units to submit divisional VAT returns – rather than one overall return for the company. Each division will have its own VAT registration number – however, the corporate body is still treated as a single taxable person and is responsible for the VAT debts and responsibilities of all the divisions.

The main reason why a company could request divisional registration is because it would anticipate genuine difficulties in getting all of its VAT figures together within the 30-day deadline to submit one corporate return.

HMRC rules for divisional registration to be granted are as follows:

- all divisions must be independent accounting units with their own accounting system – and must either be operating from different geographical locations, supplying different commodities or carrying out different functions, eg manufacture, wholesale, retail, export etc;

- all the divisions must be registered, even those whose turnover is below the compulsory registration limits;
- the corporate body as a whole must be, or be treated as being, fully taxable, ie if there are any partial exemption implications, then the corporate body as a whole must be *de minimis*;
- all divisions must complete VAT returns for the same periods – ie it is not allowed for some divisions to complete their returns under calendar quarters and others to complete their returns in months ending April, July, October and January.

(HMRC Notice 700/2, para 8.5).

An important point to remember is that charges between different divisions of the same company do not qualify as supplies for VAT purposes – and no VAT should be charged (or VAT invoices issued) for these transactions (HMRC Notice 700/2, para 8.13).

A company applying for divisional registration must make its application by letter and send it to the National Registration Service, along with Form VAT 1 for each division of the company. The letter must state why the company has a need for divisional registration. The application can only be from a current date, unless there are exceptional circumstances that require an earlier date. (HMRC Notice 700/2, paras 8.6 and 8.7).

Note – a corporate body constituted outside the UK may apply for divisional registration as long as it has at least two self-accounting units in the UK and it can also comply with the above conditions.

Avoiding an overlap between group and divisional registration

[3.10] If a company that belongs to a VAT group wishes to benefit from divisional registration, it will firstly have to leave the VAT group and then make an application for divisional registration. This is because group registration is only available to corporate bodies under common control, not divisions of those corporate bodies. Equally, an existing divisional registration must be cancelled if the corporate body wishes to join a VAT group.

Overall, therefore, group registration and divisional registration operate totally independently – currently, there is no scope for any overlap of the two arrangements.

(HMRC Notice 700/2, para 1.4).

Planning points to consider

[3.11] The following points should be given consideration.

- For a group registration to be accepted by HMRC, the control test needs to be fully met.

- A holding company making management charges to its trading subsidiaries will have to charge VAT on these supplies if it is registered for VAT. This could lead to a source of non-claimable VAT if the recipient company makes some exempt supplies. A group registration avoids this problem because no VAT is charged on supplies between entities within the same group.

- However, be aware of the need to consider input tax for the group as a whole and its relationship to supplies made to external customers. If input tax incurred by one group company relates to exempt supplies made by another group company, then the input tax will be classed as relevant to an exempt supply, ie partial exemption implications.

- Ensure that a holding company registered for VAT is making genuine taxable supplies for consideration to its trading subsidiaries, eg for management services, consultancy fees, etc.

- There is scope for a group registration to be formed even if the only taxable supplies relate to management services between group members. This strategy will avoid output tax being charged on such supplies.

- A request for divisional registration must clearly explain why the business feels it needs this facility – usually this is because of difficulties collating all figures together within one VAT return for a company based on different regions, products, etc.

Chapter 4

Transfer of a Going Concern

Key topics in this chapter:

- What constitutes the transfer of a going concern (transfer of a business).
- Key rules that need to be in place for an arrangement to qualify as the transfer of a going concern.
- Important points to consider for a property rental business or for a sale that involves a property where the option to tax has been exercised.
- Input tax deduction on the costs of selling a business.
- Approach adopted by HMRC when reviewing transfers of a going concern.
- VAT liability of goodwill payments.
- Record-keeping rules following the transfer of a business.
- The option to retain the seller's VAT number.

Identifying a transfer of a going concern

Introduction

[4.1] There is a widely used phrase in accounting circles: 'If in doubt, charge VAT'.

However, there is one situation where this phrase should not be used – that is, concerning the transfer of a business (for a consideration) as a going concern. Basically, this is because HMRC have the power in certain circumstances to disallow any input tax claimed by the buyer, even if he holds a proper tax invoice and the seller has accounted for output tax on the amount charged.

The transfer of a going concern rules basically state that, if certain important conditions are met, then the sale proceeds of the transfer (including all assets sold) will not constitute a supply – in other words, the transaction will be outside the scope of VAT.

In reality, charging or not charging VAT on the transfer of a business as a going concern is a very important topic – simply because the amounts of money involved can be so large.

What is the transfer of a going concern?

[4.2] For a transfer of a going concern to exist, there must be the sale of the whole business, or a part of a business. A mere transfer of assets will not be regarded as a transfer of a going concern. If the business is not being transferred as a going concern, then normal VAT rules will apply, ie output tax must be charged on the supply, unless it is specifically zero-rated, exempt or outside the scope of VAT. See Examples 1 and 2 below.

Example 1

Mr Jones owns a jeweller's shop in a local town centre, and has decided he wants to retire and live in Spain. He holds a big closing down sale to sell his stock; he then sells the fixtures and fittings to another jeweller's shop in the next street; a property developer buys the freehold of the shop because he wants to convert the property into luxury flats.

Solution – in this particular case, there is no transfer of a going concern, and the VAT liability of each separate sale must be considered. The sale of stock, and any fixtures and fittings will, generally, be standard rated, and the sale of the freehold property will be exempt unless the seller has opted to tax the property at any time or if it is less than three years old.

However, if Mr Jones had sold the business as a whole and the buyer was continuing to trade as a jeweller's shop, then this would have been a transfer of a going concern, and no VAT would have been charged if all of the relevant rules were met.

Example 2

Mrs Smith runs a bakery shop in the local town centre. She does not own the property from which she trades – this is rented on a five-year negotiable lease. However, she owns the fixtures and fittings and other plant and equipment, and the business name of 'Smiths Bakeries' has established a good reputation during the last 20 years.

Mrs Smith has decided to retire and sells the business to one of her staff, Miss Baker, who will continue trading as a baker, but changes the name of the business to 'Eat Well'.

Solution – although Mrs Smith does not own the property from where the business trades, she is still selling a business to Miss Baker, and therefore the transfer of a going concern rules will apply. Miss Baker will benefit from the use of all assets bought from her employer, as well as the business location, good trading name, supplier accounts and experience of the staff in the business.

The key point here is that Miss Baker is continuing the same type of business as Mrs Smith (we develop the theme of what constitutes the same business in the next section). It is irrelevant that Miss Baker intends to change the trading name of the business – it is what the business is doing that counts (ie continuing to trade as a baker), not what it is called.

Key rules for transfer of a going concern situations

[4.3] The two examples illustrated at **4.2** were both very clear-cut. In the first example, there was no business sale, and the assets of the business were being sold off on a piecemeal basis. In the second example, an actual business was being sold – in effect, all that was changing was the ownership of the business from one person to another.

There are other situations where the rules may not be so simple, for example, in the following scenarios.

- What would happen if the person buying the business wanted to change the activity slightly – for example, buying an Indian restaurant but changing it into a Chinese restaurant?
- What if the new owner wanted to close the business down for six months and go on a world cruise before he started trading? Does the break in trading jeopardise the transfer of a going concern rules?
- What if the new owner had no intention of running the business himself – but wanted to sell it straight away for a profit to a third party?

There are five main conditions (discussed below) that need to be met to satisfy the transfer of a going concern rules – as long as these are all satisfied, then the supply from the vendor to the buyer can be made without charging VAT.

(HMRC Notice 700/9, paras 1.2 and 2.3).

(A) Same type of business must be operated by new owner

[4.4] The person buying the business must intend to use the assets to carry on the same kind of business as the seller. If this is not the case, then the transfer is not as a going concern, and VAT must be charged.

HMRC are quite flexible on this rule – partly because it accepts that there can be grey areas as to whether exactly the same kind of business is being operated.

Note – a key word above is 'intend'. This means that if a buyer intends to use the assets, eg to trade as a builder like the seller, then the situation regarding the going concern rules will not change if he discovers after two months of ownership that the building business is not profitable and he totally changes the activity. It is the buyer's intentions at the time of the transfer that are important.

To quote two tribunal cases:

- The going concern rules applied in the case of *Tahmassebi t/a Sale Pepe v Customs and Excise Comrs* (2 March 1995, unreported) (MAN/94/197 13177). In this case, an Indian restaurant became an Italian restaurant, and the decision confirmed that the same kind of business was being operated, ie a restaurant, even though the menu was different.
- In the case of *G Draper (Marlow) Ltd v Comrs of Customs and Excise* (28 April 1986, unreported) (LON/85/439 2079), the ownership of a public house was transferred, but the new owners altered the business to appeal to a totally different client base (eg a local beer drinking pub

was turned into a trendy wine bar). The tribunal agreed that the new business was carrying on the same business as its predecessor, ie the sale of alcohol to the general public, even though its customer base was different.

However, the rules do need to be carefully considered to avoid potential pitfalls – see Example 3.

Example 3

> ABC Ltd owns a pub which it rents out to a tenant – the tenant is effectively in business on its own account, selling beers, wines and spirits to the general public. ABC Ltd exercised the option to tax on the pub when it first acquired the freehold interest.
>
> The pub performs so well that another company, DEF Ltd, agrees to buy the pub from ABC Ltd – which it will operate as a pub on its own account.
>
> *Solution* – the initial conclusion might be to say that the business has been sold as a going concern and therefore no VAT is due on the consideration paid by DEF Ltd.
>
> However, ABC Ltd is in the business of property rental, and the new owner is in the business of running a pub. So there is a change in activity – which means the going concern rules have not been met. As ABC Ltd has opted to tax the property, it must charge VAT on the proceeds. DEF Ltd should be able to recover the VAT charged as input tax but will suffer the initial cash flow outlay. In addition, because Stamp Duty Land Tax (SDLT) is chargeable on the VAT-inclusive cost of property, DEF Ltd will incur a higher SDLT charge than if the going concern rules had been met.
>
> Note – the Scottish Land and Buildings Transaction Tax (LBTT) is chargeable on the VAT-inclusive cost of property in Scotland.

In Example 3 above the vendor was the landlord (ABC Ltd) and the purchaser (DEF Ltd) intended to operate the pub on its own account. If a different transaction had taken place so that the tenant sold the pub business of selling beers, wines and spirits to the landlord and surrendered the lease of the pub to the landlord, the transfer of going concern provisions should apply. (Revenue & Customs Brief 27/14).

(B)   Any part transfer must be capable of separate operation

[4.5] It is possible that a vendor may decide to sell a specific part of his business and retain ownership of another part. For example, a publican operating a catering function within his pub may decide to sell the catering arm of his business, but retain the wet sales.

However, the key point is that the person selling the business must be able to continue running the remaining part of the business without the part that has been sold. In most cases, this should not prove a problem.

(C) The new owner must be VAT registered if the seller was registered

[4.6] This is an important point for all tax advisers acting for a vendor. If the vendor is VAT registered, or liable to be VAT registered, then the buyer must also be VAT registered, or liable to be registered, in order for the sale to be outside the scope of VAT.

In effect, the new owners are likely to be VAT registered as a matter of course, but there are some situations that could avoid a need for registering:

- If, at the date the transfer takes place, the buyer does not anticipate that his sales in the next 12 months will exceed the VAT deregistration threshold, then he has no obligation to register for VAT. This could apply, for example, if he decides to work shorter hours.
- If the seller was registered for VAT on a voluntary basis, then the buyer will not have an obligation to register because the turnover in the previous 12 months was below the compulsory registration threshold (which is relevant for the new owner – if the compulsory VAT registration limit was exceeded by the previous owner in his last 12 months, then he has an obligation to register himself as well from the first day he takes ownership of the business).

In theory, it is possible for a buyer to not have a VAT number at the time of the transfer. This is because the strict wording of the law (*SI 1995/1268, reg 5*) states the condition as being that the buyer 'immediately becomes as a result of the transfer a taxable person'. A 'taxable person' is defined as someone who is registered or should be registered for VAT. However, it is recommended that any element of doubt be avoided by ensuring that the buyer is VAT registered at the time of the transfer.

Note – the wording of the legislation means that if an exempt business is being sold or a business has traded below the VAT limits (eg an insurance broker) then a transfer of a going concern situation will apply, ie there is no need for the buyer to be registered at the time of the transfer (HMRC Notice 700/9, para 2.3.5).

Consider the circumstances illustrated at Example 4.

Example 4

Mr Giles trades as a surveyor and is selling his practice as a going concern to Mr Hardwick on 1 July. The taxable turnover of the business in the 12 months to 30 June was £90,000 – ie above the compulsory VAT registration limit. However, Mr Hardwick enjoys fishing and has decided to reduce the activity of the practice and only work four days a week instead of the five worked by Mr Giles.

Solution – in effect, Mr Hardwick's expected turnover in the next 12 months will be £72,000 (all other things being equal) which is below the VAT deregistration threshold. He does not need to register for VAT.

If Mr Hardwick does not register for VAT, then the transfer of a going concern conditions are not met and Mr Giles must charge VAT on the sale proceeds.

Note – remember, however, that the option of voluntary VAT registration is always open to a business, even if it trades below the compulsory VAT registration threshold.

(D)   The transfer must put the new owner in possession of a business which can be operated as such and the business must be a going concern at the time of the transfer

[4.7] In this situation there should be no break in trading immediately before or after the transfer.

There will inevitably be situations where a business has ceased to trade because of lack of profits and commercial viability. In such cases, employees will be laid off, stock will have been sold, and advertising to generate new business will have been cancelled.

If the business is then sold, possibly to a company that thinks it can recreate a profitable operation, then it has to be carefully considered whether the business is now a 'going concern' at the time of transfer. If not, then the transfer conditions have not been met, and VAT must be charged on the supply.

HMRC state that the business, or part business, must be a 'going concern' at the time of the transfer. It can still be a 'going concern' even though it is unprofitable, or is trading under the control of a liquidator or administrative receiver, or a trustee in bankruptcy, or an administrator appointed under the *Insolvency Act 1986*.

(HMRC Notice 700/9, para 2.3.1).

In effect, the key question to consider is whether the new owner is placed in a position after the transfer where he is in possession of a business, or whether he has effectively bought an empty shell that he needs to build up from scratch.

As a separate point, a break in trading does not necessarily mean that a business is not a going concern. For example, if a seaside guest house only trades from May to September when the weather is good, then it will still be a going concern if it is sold the following March, even though it would not have traded for six months. This is because the break in trading is due to the seasonal nature of its trade, not the fact that it has been permanently closed down.

Again, the new owner should not have a long break in trading after he has bought the business. For example, a three-month closure for redecoration works would not be a problem – but closure for 12 months while the new owner went on a round the world cruise is not likely to be acceptable.

(E)   There should not be consecutive transfers of the same business

[4.8] There are some situations where company A will sell its assets to company B, which immediately sells them to company C. This arrangement can sometimes apply to property rental businesses, where lease issues are quite complex.

In such cases, company B is not eligible to benefit from the special transfer provisions – because it is not carrying on the same business as company A.

Option to tax

[4.9] With most complex subjects on VAT, issues concerning property and the option to tax are never too far away.

The key point as far as land and buildings are concerned is to remember that there is an extra stage to the rules.

Basically, if the seller has opted to tax the property that is now being sold, then the buyer must also make an election to tax the property in question before the supply is made and it must confirm in writing to the seller that this option to tax will not be disapplied. If this condition is not met, then the seller must charge VAT on the property part of the deal, even if the transfer of going concern rules are otherwise fully met in relation to the other assets being transferred. See Example 5.

(HMRC Notice 700/9, para 2.4).

Example 5

Mr Smith is selling his restaurant business as a going concern to Mr Jones, and the sale proceeds of £2m can be split as follows: £400,000 fixtures and fittings; £600,000 goodwill; freehold property on which an option to tax election has been made is £1m. What is the position as far as the transfer of the freehold is concerned?

Solution – before the deal is completed, Mr Jones must opt to tax the property with HMRC (complete Form VAT 1614A) and provide evidence of this action to Mr Smith. Assuming that all other conditions are met, the whole deal will then qualify as a transfer of a going concern and be outside the scope of VAT.

However, if Mr Jones fails to make the election, or decides it is not in his best interests to make the election (eg he expects to make a big profit on selling the property in a few years' time to a buyer that may not be able to recover VAT), then the seller will have to charge £200,000 VAT on the property only, ie £1m x 20%. The fixtures, fittings and goodwill will still be outside the scope of the tax.

Property rental business

[4.10] A situation that has become quite common in recent years has been where a property has been sold to a third party – but with an existing lease in place with a tenant. In these situations, the sale can qualify as a transfer of a going concern (sale of a property rental business).

(HMRC Notice 700/9, para 2.5 and section 6).

However, if the seller has opted to tax the property in question, then the buyer must also elect to tax the property himself before a tax point arises (complete Form VAT 1614A). If an election is made, a VAT charge can be avoided. A tax point in relation to a property transaction can arise upon the payment of a deposit (see the case of the *Higher Education Statistics Agency Ltd v Comrs of Customs & Excise* [2000] STC 332).

Note – the rules concerning transfers of a going concern and property can be quite complex. For example, a challenge can occur when a seller is transferring a block of properties, some with tenants in place and others that might be empty. In such cases, there could still be the opportunity for the block sale to be outside the scope of VAT as a transfer of a property rental business. To directly quote from HMRC Notice 700/9, para 6.4.1:

> '6.4.1 Transfers of a number of sites or buildings
>
> The transfer of a number of sites or buildings where some of the sites or buildings are let, or partially let and some are unlet, needs to be considered on a case by case basis. The nature of the sites or building and their use are all factors for consideration. It is important to look at whether the assets can be identified as a single business or an identifiable part of a business. In addition all the conditions as set out at sections 1.2 and 2.3 of this notice would need to be met. For example the sale of a chain of shops or pubs could be a TOGC whereas the sale of a grouping of disparate properties might not.'

Following the 2012 case of *Robinson Family Limited* [2012] UKFTT 360 (TC), [2012] SWTI 2519, HMRC now accept that transfer of going concern treatment can apply to the transfer of a property letting business where the vendor retains a small reversionary interest in the property transferred, providing all the other conditions for transfer of going concern treatment are met.

HMRC previously took the view that, if the transferor retained any interest in the property transferred it prevented the transaction being treated as a transfer of a going concern. This incorrect approach, which was reflected in HMRC guidance, could have resulted in VAT being charged when none was due and an excessive amount of SDLT being paid. For those affected, Revenue & Customs Brief 30/12 (issued on 16 November 2012) and Revenue & Customs Brief 8/13 (issued on 15 April 2013) are worth reading in full.

Revenue & Customs Brief 30/12, referred to above, announced a change in HMRC policy in relation to grants of leases. In July 2014 Revenue & Customs Brief 27/14 announced a change in HMRC policy in relation to surrenders of leases.

HMRC policy regarding the surrender of a lease was previously that the surrender of a lease is not covered by the transfer of going concern provisions. This was stated in the following terms in the HMRC VAT Manual VTOGC6450, prior to being amended following the change of policy—

> 'In a surrender, the tenant surrenders his lease to the landlord and the lease is brought to an end. Thus the asset used by the seller no longer exists and will not [be] used by the purchaser (i.e. the landlord) in carrying on the business. The property rental business carried on by the lessee has ceased and cannot be transferred as a going concern, even if the sub-tenants remain in occupation. The right to receive rental income derives not from the transfer of the lease but from the landlord's rights as freeholder. The surrender of a lease is therefore not covered by the TOGC provisions.
>
> In certain circumstances, particularly in relation to Scottish land law, the original lease will not be extinguished on surrender. It is our policy however, to see the

continuation as merely an enabling document which returns the property to the landlord but, as it does not affect the landlord's right to collect rent, it is not used to carry on the same kind of business.'

HMRC now considers that there is in principle no obstacle to the surrender of a lease being covered by the transfer of going concern provisions, subject to all the normal conditions. This will apply, for example, where a tenant subletting premises by way of business subsequently surrenders its interest in the property together with the benefit of the sub-tenants, or where a retailer sells its retailing business to its landlord. In substance the landlord has acquired the tenant's business. HMRC have confirmed that this applies equally where the landlord's interest is held via one or more nominees, so that the transaction involves a transfer to the nominee(s) for the landlord's benefit. (Revenue & Customs Brief 27/14).

New developments of dwellings, relevant residential or relevant charitable purpose buildings

[4.11] Revenue & Customs Brief 27/14, referred to above, also announced a change in HMRC policy in relation to the transfer as a going concern of new developments of dwellings, relevant residential or relevant charitable purpose buildings.

The first grant by a person constructing dwellings, relevant residential or relevant charitable purpose buildings or a person converting non-residential buildings into dwellings, relevant residential or relevant charitable purpose buildings is zero-rated – see **27.12**. Having 'person constructing' or 'person converting' status is therefore important in terms of input tax recovery. Prior to the Revenue & Customs Brief being issued in July 2014, HMRC's policy was that 'person constructing' and 'person converting' status does not move to the person acquiring completed buildings transferred as a going concern.

Revenue & Customs Brief 27/14 confirms that HMRC now accept that a person acquiring a completed residential or charitable development as part of a transfer of a going concern inherits 'person constructing' status and is capable of making a zero-rated first major interest grant in that building or part of it as long as—

(a) a zero-rated grant (see **27.15**) has not already been made of the completed building or relevant part by a previous owner – HMRC consider that the grant that gives rise to the transfer of going concern should be disregarded for this purpose;

(b) the person acquiring the building as a transfer of a going concern (the transferee) would suffer an unfair VAT disadvantage if the transferee's first major interest grant was treated as exempt – see Example 6 below; and

(c) the transferee would not obtain an unfair VAT advantage by being in a position to make zero-rated supplies, for example, by recovering input tax on a refurbishment of an existing building.

The above also applies in relation to 'person converting' status (for buildings converted from non-residential to residential use) and 'person substantially reconstructing' status (for substantially reconstructed listed buildings).

Example 6

A property development company (the transferor) restructures its business in a way that involves the transfer as a going concern of its entire property portfolio of newly constructed residential/charitable buildings to an associated company (the transferee). The transferee sells the buildings to third parties. If the sale of the buildings by the transferee was treated as exempt, the transferee could become liable to repay input tax recovered by the transferor on development costs under the capital goods scheme or partial exemption claw back provisions and would incur input tax restrictions on costs it incurs selling the buildings.

It is understood that HMRC would regard the potential repayment of input tax and the input tax restrictions on selling costs as an unfair VAT disadvantage for the purpose of (b) above.

Input tax

[4.12] Although the sale of a business as a going concern is not regarded as a supply (taxable or otherwise), input tax can still be recovered on the related costs of the sale (eg solicitors' fees) as long as the business in question was only making taxable supplies, ie able to fully recover its input tax. If the business was partly exempt, then the costs would be classed as a general overhead item and input tax would need to be apportioned according to its partial exemption method.

Note – if part of a business is being sold, then input tax claimed on disposal costs will depend on whether the part being sold made wholly taxable or exempt supplies, or possibly both. So an estate agent earning commission on selling houses (taxable) and mortgages (exempt) would not be able to claim input tax on disposal costs if it just sold its mortgage brokerage, ie the input tax relates to the sale of an exempt business.

(HMRC Notice 700/9, para 2.6).

See Example 7.

Example 7

Mike owns an estate agency business, which has two main sources of income: the sale of houses on a commission-only basis (taxable activity); and fees earned on arranging insurance products and mortgages for customers (exempt activity).

The business has always adopted the standard method of calculation as far as partial exemption is concerned (non-attributable input tax apportioned according to income percentages) and the taxable sales have always been 60% of total sales.

Mike is now selling the business to John for £1.3m and the sale qualifies as a going concern because all of the relevant conditions have been met – no output tax is therefore charged on the proceeds. Mike's legal and other costs related to the sale are £65,000 plus VAT.

Solution as part of Mike's activities are exempt, he cannot recover all of the input tax incurred on the costs of selling his business to John. The VAT charge on the selling costs is classed as non-attributable (also known as residual) input tax within his partial exemption calculation, so he can only recover 60% of this amount on his return, ie £65,000 x 60% x 20%. If Mike's activities were wholly taxable (ie commission from house sales only) then he would have been able to recover all of the VAT on his disposal costs.

HMRC approach to a transfer

[4.13] Imagine the following situation: Mr Jones has traded as a limited company and now sells his jewellery business for £430,000 as a going concern, and charges output tax of £86,000 to the new owner (assuming VAT rate of 20%). He then disappears to Spain, and liquidates the company without ever paying the final output tax liability to HMRC. This is bad news for HMRC because it has no way of recovering the VAT debt because the company no longer has any assets – and the chances are that Mr Jones will be out of sight, out of mind.

In this situation, HMRC will probably use its powers to confirm that the business was the transfer of a going concern, meeting the various rules, and that the supply was therefore outside the scope of VAT. The input tax then claimed by the buyer would be non-reclaimable on the basis that it does not relate to a taxable supply.

In effect, therefore, sound VAT advice on transfer of a going concern issues is probably quite unique in that it is probably more important for the buyer to get it right than the seller. The other relevant point is that even if the buyer is able to recover input tax on any charge, there is a significant cash flow disadvantage if he has to pay 20% of the buying price as VAT, and then wait three months to recover the money on his first VAT return.

As far as identifying a transfer of a going concern situation is concerned, HMRC will obviously analyse the key issues described at **4.3–4.8**.

However, it is also advised to take the following points into account when determining whether there has been the transfer of a going concern.

- *Goodwill* – a charge for goodwill (see **4.14**) normally indicates a transfer of a going concern because the buyer is making payment for an intangible asset. However, the absence of goodwill does not necessarily mean that there is no transfer of a going concern.
- *Customer lists, knowledge of customers* – the sale or transfer of a list of potential or previous customers is normally a good indication of a transfer of a going concern. Equally, if a purchaser takes over existing contracts with suppliers or customers (and related obligations) then this also suggests that the buyer is carrying on the business of the seller.
- *Stock* – the transfer of stock to a single purchaser can indicate a transfer of a going concern. In contrast, the sale of stock to a number of different parties could indicate that assets are being divided rather than a business being transferred.
- *Premises, plant and equipment* – many businesses are closely linked to their premises, and the transfer/sale of the premises clearly suggests a transfer of a going concern, as long as the buyer is not intending to

totally change the nature of trading in the building. The sale of plant and equipment is also a good indicator, however, it is possible that the buyer may already have his own equipment, so there could still be a perfectly valid transfer of a going concern arrangement without plant and equipment being a part of the sale.

- *Staff* – if the new business takes over the contracts of existing staff, this will again suggest a transfer of a going concern
- *Advertisements* – the way in which a sale is publicised is also relevant. For example, a newspaper advertisement using the phrase: 'under new management' clearly indicates an existing business is being continued but by a new owner.

It is important to look at the bigger picture when making conclusions about whether an arrangement qualifies as the transfer of a going concern. It is not appropriate to make a conclusion based on one piece of information in isolation. For example, it would be wrong to conclude that a transfer of a going concern situation could not apply just because the new owners did not buy the fixtures and fittings from the previous owner (in this situation, the decision not to buy the fixtures and fittings is likely to be for commercial motives).

The VAT and Duties Tribunal (and now the First Tier Tax Tribunal) is littered with many failed cases on this issue. There are a number of leading decisions most of which give great weight to a judgment from the High Court (Queen's Bench) in a case called *Kenmir v Frizzel* [1968] 1 All ER 414, [1968] 1 WLR 329. Although not a VAT case, it laid down the appropriate rules to determine whether or not a business had been transferred. The court adopted a substance over form approach. In simple terms, one needs to consider all of the factors indicating that a business has been transferred and weigh those factors against factors which indicate the opposite. In most cases whichever factors have more weight will inform the answer to the puzzle.

Readers should also be aware of the judgment of the Upper Tribunal in *Royal College of Pediatricians and Child Health v Revenue and Customs Comrs* [2015] UKUT 38 (TCC). In that case, the college wished to move to a new building where the vendor had opted to tax. The college was partially exempt and was, therefore, unable to reclaim all of the VAT that would be chargeable by the vendor. The college attempted to get round that problem by granting to a prospective tenant an agreement to lease. The prospective tenant was already a tenant in the college's existing building. By inserting the tenant, the college assumed that the transfer of the property by the vendor would qualify as a transfer of a going concern and that, as a result, no VAT would be charged. The Upper Tribunal allowed HMRC's appeal. In the circumstances there was not a transfer of a property letting business as a going concern and VAT was due on the purchase price.

On a similar note, advisers need to be aware that 'timing is everything'. For a transfer of an opted property to qualify as an asset being transferred as part of a transfer of a going concern, the purchaser must notify its option to tax in advance of any tax point (see *Higher Education Statistics Agency Ltd* [2000] STC 332).

Finally, advisors need also to be aware of an Upper Tribunal judgment from 2015 relating to the transfer of a business to a company within a UK VAT Group. In *Intelligent Managed Services Ltd* [2015] UKUT 341 (TCC), a business was transferred to a company that was a member of a UK VAT group. The business it acquired was then 'carried on' solely within the VAT group and HMRC took the view that as there were no external supplies (ie to customers outside of the VAT group) made by the company, it was not 'carrying on' the business. The Upper Tribunal dismissed that view. The business of the vendor was continued after the disposal albeit wholly within a VAT group.

Goodwill

[4.14] The key advantage for a person selling his business as a going concern (in the general sense of the phrase, not the VAT-specific sense), rather than the separate sale of assets, is that he should also be able to receive some payment for goodwill.

Goodwill is an intangible asset, and reflects the difference between the value of the assets a person is buying, and the payment made. For example, if a business comprises stock, fixtures and fittings and a freehold property with a combined value of £380,000, but the business is sold for £430,000, then the additional £50,000 relates to goodwill (the buyer is effectively paying for the benefit he will gain from the trading name, customer database, location of the shop and possibly staff that will continue to be employed by the new owners).

In normal circumstances, for VAT purposes, the money received for the sale of goodwill is standard rated – unless the transfer of a going concern rules are met.

Change in legal entity and sales of shares

Change in legal entity

[4.15] A common situation that occurs in business is where a sole trader decides to expand his activities by taking on a partner. Equally, an existing partnership may be expanded to include an extra partner and, very common in recent times, a sole trader or partnership business may incorporate and become a limited company.

As far as VAT is concerned, a change in legal entity (ie sole trader business becoming a partnership) represents the transfer of a going concern. However, the addition of a new partner to an existing partnership does not produce a transfer of a going concern situation as a partnership remains a partnership.

The VAT registration issues of a change in legal entity are considered at **2.10**.

Sale of shares

[4.16] When there is a transfer of shares in a limited company from one person to another the assets still belong to the limited company. There is no change in the ownership of the assets and therefore no supply to which the transfer of going concern provisions could apply.

(HMRC Notice 700/9, para 1.3.)

Record-keeping requirements

[4.17] The seller of a business will retain the records of his business that are relevant to the period before the date of the sale. However, since 1 September 2007:

- The seller must give the buyer any information the latter needs to comply with his duties under the *VATA 1994*.
- If the buyer of the business decides to retain the VAT number of the seller (see **4.18**), then the seller is still required to transfer his records to the buyer. However, the seller has the right to approach HMRC for permission to retain his records if this is appropriate to his circumstances.
- HMRC can also disclose to the buyer any information it holds on the business that is needed for him to comply with his VAT obligations.

Note – the three main situations where the above conditions become relevant relate to partial exemption issues (agreed special methods in the past etc), option to tax elections (in relation to commercial property) and the capital goods scheme. The capital goods scheme requires input tax adjustments for up to ten years in the case of land and property transactions, and is often still relevant when a business is transferred.

(HMRC Notice 700/9, para 3.6).

Retaining the seller's VAT number

[4.18] It is possible for the buyer of a business to retain the seller's VAT registration number by completing Form VAT 68. However, this is an unwise move in most cases because the new owner is also taking over the potential VAT liabilities of the previous business. It is suggested that a new VAT registration number be obtained to avoid this potential risk.

(HMRC Notice 700/9, para 3.4).

Planning points to consider

[4.19] The following points should be given consideration.

- When acting for the buyer of a business, ensure that VAT is not incorrectly charged by the vendor – if a transfer of a going concern arrangement is evident, then HMRC has the power to disallow any input tax claimed by the buyer, even if he holds a proper tax invoice and has paid the VAT to the seller in good faith. Remember – the transfer of a going concern rules are compulsory – it is not possible to choose to 'opt out' by, for example, playing safe and charging VAT.

- It is also important for buyers to avoid paying VAT if possible because of the cash flow problems of paying the VAT to the seller and then waiting up to three months to reclaim it on a VAT return. In addition, avoiding VAT if possible should reduce the Stamp Duty Land Tax (SDLT) or Scottish Land and Buildings Transaction Tax (LBTT) charge when property is purchased.

- If acting for the seller, remember that the buyer must be VAT registered or be liable to be VAT registered as a result of the sale – otherwise the transfer of a going concern rules are not met.

- In most cases, it will be clear if a business is being sold as a going concern, or whether individual assets are being sold. Advisers need to be aware of the key rules to consider in cases that are not as clear-cut – as explained at **4.3**.

- Be aware that even though the proceeds from a transfer of a going concern sale are outside the scope of VAT, the related input tax on selling costs can still be reclaimed as long as the business has activities that are wholly taxable. If part of the business income is exempt, then a restriction on the input tax claimed will be evident using the normal partial exemption method adopted by the business.

- There are important issues to consider if the sale of a going concern includes a property where the option to tax election has been made by the seller – as explained at **4.9**. The decision to opt to tax a property is very important for any business, because once made, it cannot be revoked for 20 years.

Chapter 5

Separation of Business Activities

Key topics in this chapter:

- What constitutes an artificial separation of business activities.
- Legislation and rules to determine whether two or more businesses will be classed as one business.
- Financial, organisational and economic links between businesses.
- The importance of normal commercial arrangements between two separated businesses.
- The motive to avoid paying VAT.
- Arrangements for businesses involving members of the same family.
- Effect of an HMRC direction that only one business exists in practice.
- Case examples on artificial separation of business activities.
- Approach to be adopted when dealing with clients.

Separating business activities

Introduction

[5.1] Many clients have an interest in more than one business – and from a VAT perspective, a challenge can occur when one of these businesses is VAT registered, and the other trades below the VAT registration threshold. If the business trading below the VAT threshold is mainly dealing with members of the public (ie who are unable to reclaim any of the VAT they pay as input tax) then it is in the interests of the owners to avoid VAT registration if possible.

However, HMRC have extensive powers to direct that two or more businesses should be treated as a single business, effectively bringing all entities into the VAT system. It will take this course of action if it considers that the separation of business activities has been carried out in an 'artificial' manner, with the primary intention being to avoid registering for and paying VAT.

For tax advisers, there are many opportunities available to advise clients about the correct manner of properly setting up separate business activities – but it is important that clients follow through any advice given with proper action. A review of tribunal cases on this subject highlights that most arrangements that fail are due to the fact that the owner(s) did not create a clear division between their different business activities.

Definition of an 'artificial' scheme

[5.2] The dictionary definition of artificial is 'something that is not real'. In effect, therefore, the key question an adviser should ask when discussing the separation of business activities with a client is:

'Is this a genuine business arrangement made for commercial reasons and with commercial motives – or is it an artificial measure designed to avoid paying VAT?'

Consider Example 1 below.

Example 1

Mr A owns 12 laundrettes, each with taxable turnover of about £60,000 per year. Each laundrette operates in a different town, under the trading name of 'Keep Clean'.

Mr A decides to set up a separate limited company for each different outlet thinking that, as each limited company will be trading below the VAT registration limit each limited company can avoid the need to register for VAT. This is important for him on a commercial basis, because all of the customers are members of the public, unable to recover any VAT charged as input tax.

Solution – this situation illustrates both the motives and benefits of separating business activities. It is clear that there is, in reality, only one business, but Mr A has devised a specific scheme to try and create 12 different businesses. In this situation, HMRC could issue a direction that there is only one actual business, with a combined turnover exceeding the VAT registration threshold.

Note – it is important that HMRC have the power to take action in these situations, otherwise there would be a massive competitive disadvantage for other laundrettes who accept the requirement to be VAT registered.

Legislation and key rules

[5.3] The power of HMRC to deal with artificial business separations is contained in *VATA 1994, Sch 1, para 1A(1) and (2)* which say:

'1A

(1) *Paragraph 2* below is for the purpose of preventing the maintenance or creation of any artificial separation of business activities carried on by two or more persons from resulting in an avoidance of VAT.

(2) In determining for the purposes of *sub-paragraph (1)* above whether any separation of business activities is artificial, regard shall be had to the extent to which the different persons carrying on those activities are closely bound to one another by financial, economic and organisational links'.

We will consider each of the points mentioned in the last sentence of *sub-para (2)* above – and the key questions HMRC consider when looking at a particular arrangement.

(a) Financial links:
- Is financial support given by one of the businesses to another?
- Would one of the businesses not be financially viable without support from another of the businesses?

- Is there a common financial interest in the proceeds of the businesses as a whole?
(b) Economic links:
- Are both businesses trying to realise the same economic objective?
- Do the activities of one part of the business benefit the other part?
- Are both businesses supplying the same circle of customers?
(c) Organisational links:
- Do both businesses have common management?
- Are there common employees?
- Are premises shared?
- Is there common use of the same equipment?

Normal commercial arrangements

[5.4] One of the main changes in VAT thinking in recent years has been for tribunals and higher courts to consider an issue based on what the customer perceives to be happening – or what he perceives he is buying with his money.

Consider the circumstances in Example 2.

Example 2

Mr B provides accountancy services from his office in the High Street. Mr C trades from the same premises, offering a service to complete tax returns. Neither of the two businesses is VAT registered, as they each have taxable income of only £45,000 per annum. The following facts apply to their respective organisations:

- Mr B and Mr C use the same computers to carry out their work – they sit together in an open plan office in the same room;
- they have many common clients, with Mr B doing the accounts work and Mr C the tax returns for these clients;
- Mr B employs a receptionist who also spends a lot of her time working for Mr C;
- Mr C employs a secretary who also spends a lot of her time doing work for Mr B;
- they have a joint advert in the local newspaper – promoting a combined service of 'preparing accounts and completing tax returns for small businesses and individuals'.

They receive a visit from HMRC, who decide that there is only one business trading above the VAT registration threshold.

Solution – this particular arrangement has made it very easy for HMRC to direct that there is only one business. As mentioned at 5.3, there are clearly financial, economic and organisational links between the two businesses. Of equal importance, any customer dealing with the business would perceive that there was, in reality, only one business.

At this stage, it is useful to consider three key words on this topic – 'normal commercial arrangements'.

The key question to consider when looking at an arrangement is to ask the question: Are the links between the two businesses based on normal commercial arrangements?

For example, in the case of Mr B and Mr C at Example 2, there is a situation of staff being employed by one of the businesses but partly used by another business. In such situations, it would be expected that any time spent doing the work of the other party would be charged at an agreed rate on a time basis, with an invoice raised explaining the services carried out.

Equally, if one business benefits from using the assets of another business (and it should be noted that from an accounting aspect, an asset can only be owned by one business) then it would be expected that a charging arrangement would be evident for these supplies.

In reality, if a formal charging structure is not in place for two closely linked businesses, then it will be a clear indication to HMRC that it is dealing with a case of artificial separation.

Motive to avoid paying VAT

[5.5] As discussed at **5.3**, a key phrase in the legislation at *para 1A(1)* is 'resulting in an avoidance of VAT' (*VATA 1994, Sch 1 para 1A(1)*).

Consider the following examples.

Example 3

Mary and June share the premises of a unit in a local village, running a health food shop. They both trade as separate legal entities, and neither is VAT registered. Their combined turnover is £100,000 per year. Mary sells organic fruit and June sells organic vegetables (all take-away sales). They maintain that the reason for keeping their businesses separate is because Mary has a high level of expertise in issues concerning fruit, and June specialises in vegetables.

Solution – the key point with this situation is that the supplies made by Mary and June would all be zero-rated if they became VAT registered – so the arrangement between them regarding the structure of the business does not result 'in an avoidance of VAT'. It could be argued that there would be benefits in both of them registering for VAT on a voluntary basis, because they could then recover input tax on overheads they incur – producing a direct improvement to overall profits.

Example 4

Bill and Ben are sole traders, working from a small unit offering carpentry services to the general public. Bill makes and repairs tables – Ben makes and repairs chairs. Their turnover is £35,000 each – and they have very close organisational, financial and economic links, sharing the same equipment, premises and customer base.

Solution – the structure would be prone to challenge by HMRC – but the key point is that the combined turnover of Bill and Ben (£35,000 × 2 = £70,000) is still below the VAT registration threshold. The motive to avoid VAT cannot therefore be proved by HMRC.

However, if the businesses grow so that combined trading exceeds the VAT registration limit, then the operation will need to be reviewed to ensure that there will be no problems with HMRC in the future.

In effect, therefore, the approach adopted by HMRC is to clearly identify situations where tax is being lost through the creation of artificial arrangements.

Family business arrangements

[5.6] It is more difficult for HMRC to combine businesses where the individuals are not members of the same family. This is because one of the key arguments that could be put forward for individuals who are not related to each other is as follows:

'The main reason for having two separate businesses is not the avoidance of VAT but because we want to ensure that we are each rewarded with profits according to our own efforts'.

In other words, there are clear commercial reasons for separate trading, even though the arrangement may appear artificial.

However, the reasons why many family business arrangements fail to convince HMRC is due to the following reasons.

- Normal commercial arrangements do not tend to be followed in such a strict manner. For example, if the husband is running one business, and the wife running another business that is closely linked to the husband's business, then there should be market rate charges made for any shared overheads, equipment, staff etc.
  In reality, this principle of recharging for shared overheads tends to be forgotten where family members are involved.
- In many cases, the activities of one part of the business benefit the other part. For example, a common situation where many taxpayers have encountered problems is where the husband operates as a publican for the wet sales (and is VAT registered) and the wife operates as a sole trader running the catering part of the business (trading below the VAT limits).
- Problems in such cases tend to be that cash takings for the two parts of the business can be confused; staff on duty carry out work for both parts of the business (even though they are only on the payroll of the publican); there is no formal charging arrangement to cover the cost of equipment and overheads used by the wife in her catering activity. Again, the family issue in this arrangement makes it less important to ensure arm's length transactions are the norm.
- Common management – in reality, the husband and wife are likely to make joint decisions regarding the overall direction of the combined business – rather than each separate part. This makes it more difficult to convince HMRC that there are two distinct businesses in operation.

However, despite the list of potential problems above, it is by no means impossible for family members to have separate businesses which are acceptable to HMRC.

Effect of an HMRC direction

[5.7] A positive point is that HMRC cannot issue a direction on a retrospective basis. This is confirmed in *VATA 1994, Sch 1 para 2*:

> '... the persons named in the direction shall be treated as a single taxable person carrying on the activities of a business named in the direction and *that taxable person shall be liable to be registered under this Schedule with effect from the date of the direction or, if the direction so provides, such later date as may be specified therein.*' (emphasis added)

The above regulation means that separation could prove effective until it is discovered by HMRC, which could be many years. However, there is still a risk that HMRC could take a stronger view and rule that there never was a separation of activities. For example, a chaotic arrangement between a husband and wife (no written agreements, separate structures, etc) could be deemed to have been one business from the first day of trading. Furthermore, a backdated registration is not limited to a three or four-year adjustment period as with VAT errors – in the worst case scenario, a registration could be backdated 20 years.

As explained above, HMRC will carry out a very detailed review of a commercial arrangement where it considers there has been an artificial separation of business activities. The officer will fully consider the motives of the separation – the avoidance of VAT obviously being the prime consideration.

If he is satisfied that an arrangement is artificial, then a direction will be issued which effectively treats the combined business entities as a single taxable person from the date of the direction. The taxable person is then liable to be registered from the date of the direction. The direction must be served on each person named in it.

The effects of a direction are as follows:

(a)   in reality, if two or more persons are trading individually, then the combined business will be treated as a partnership;

(b)   as far as VAT is concerned, each constituent member is jointly and severally liable for any VAT due from the taxable person;

(c)   in effect, any failure to comply with VAT requirements is treated as a failure by each of the constituent members severally.

Note – in the case of *PC & VL Leonidas* (VTD 16588), a married couple tried to separate ice cream sales from a café on the same premises, but the structure was so disorganised that HMRC ruled that there had only ever been one business in existence and collected output tax on a retrospective basis. This is a key point – if there never were two businesses in place, then the normal VAT registration rules apply to the combined income of the two entities. This could produce a significant historic VAT bill for the owners.

Tribunal cases and case law

[5.8] There have been many significant VAT tribunal cases on this subject over the years.

Cases won by HMRC

[5.9] HMRC was successful in the three cases summarised below.

(a) *Smith t/a Ty Gwyn Hotel v Customs and Excise Comrs* (3 September 2001, unreported) (MAN/01/0065 17406) – in this particular case, Mrs Smith ran the catering part of the business, but the only payment she made to her husband towards the facilities she enjoyed was to provide free sandwiches to pub customers on a Thursday night. It was argued by the Smiths that this was her way of paying for the kitchen and equipment facilities she enjoyed within the premises.

However, the reality of the situation is that no person in business would sublet such a large part of his premises and allow gas and electric supplies to be freely used in return for a weekly plate of sandwiches.

Comment – this case illustrates the importance of ensuring 'normal commercial arrangements' are in place for two businesses that are closely linked.

(b) *Williams v Customs and Excise Comrs* (7 July 1987, unreported) (LON/87/132 2445) – in this case, a married couple were carrying on business as a café and bread shop from the same premises. Customs ruled that there was only one business.

Comment – it would be very difficult in this particular case to prove there were separate businesses because it would be quite complicated to keep the purchases separate. For example, if the two businesses were using the same kitchen, then they would be presumably using the same bread, rolls and cakes served in each part. Again, overhead issues would need to be very clearly analysed and recharged at an appropriate market rate in order to highlight that normal commercial arrangements were in place.

(c) *Osman v Customs & Excise Comrs* [1989] STC 596 – this is a High Court judgment. HMRC issued a 'single taxable person' direction against Mr Osman, his wife, a partnership (consisting of Mr Osman and his wife) and a limited company where Mr Osman and his wife were Directors and shareholders. Each of the entities purported to carry on separate trading activities below the VAT registration threshold.

Comment – it was shown that all the persons named in the direction had conducted their activities from the same office, that they had provided similar services, that they had used the same employees and that almost all the fees received had been paid into a joint account of the taxpayer and his wife. The VAT and Duties Tribunal (as it then was) and the High Court agreed that HMRC's decision to treat all of the entities as a single taxable person was reasonable.

Cases won by the taxpayer

[5.10] In each of the cases below, there are a number of key themes that recur, explaining why the taxpayers were successful in their appeal:

- motives for separation of the businesses other than the avoidance of paying VAT;
- normal commercial arrangements between the parties when it comes to issues such as dealing with shared overheads;
- separate accounting arrangements in place, separate purchasing, invoicing procedures, bank account, completion of tax returns, etc.

The following three cases were won by the taxpayer.

(a) *Skelton Waste Disposal v Customs and Excise Comrs* (6 July 2001, unreported) (MAN/00/866 17351) – in this case, Dean Langton (son of Maurice) was very ambitious and keen to branch off with a separate business of his own. He formed Skelton Mini Skips, which was not VAT registered, and claimed successfully that this was a different business from Skelton Waste Disposal (in which he was a partner with his father).

Comment – the key point in this situation was that the motivation for the arrangement was not considered to be the avoidance of VAT – but the opportunity for Dean Langton to trade independently of his father and develop profits in his own right. All of the arrangements were based on normal commercial terms, and the fact that both businesses had 'Skelton' within the trading name was not considered the key issue overall. The case also highlights that members of the same family can operate separate business activities, as long as they are properly formulated.

(b) *Townsend v Customs and Excise Comrs* (9 October 2000, unreported) (LON/00/349, LON/00/350 17081) – the Townsends ran separate pottery businesses – Mrs Townsend painted and decorated pottery blanks, and Mr Townsend made studio pieces. The tribunal considered that the arrangements for the two businesses were made on normal commercial terms, and that they were operated at arm's length to each other. These factors were considered more important than the fact that the couple were married and involved in a similar trade.

Comment – this case emphasises the point that it is up to HMRC to prove artificial separation of business activities, not the taxpayer to prove his innocence. In this situation, HMRC failed to convince the tribunal that there was only one business in existence.

Approach for advisers acting for clients

[5.11] A key tip for tax advisers is to stand back and ask the question: 'How would this arrangement look in the eyes of an HMRC officer?' Would the arrangement come across as being two or more distinct businesses, each aiming to make profits in their own right, or would it appear that an artificial situation has been created, with the aim of ensuring at least one of the businesses (possibly all of them) does not have to register and pay VAT.

To help with this assessment, there are five key questions to ask.

(a)   *What is the key motive for separating the business?* Just because two parties are married or living together does not mean they cannot run separate businesses. The human rights legislation has been well publicised in recent years, and one of these rights is the opportunity to trade in business for a profit.

The key point is to be satisfied that VAT avoidance is not the main motive for separating a business.

(b)   *Do normal commercial relationships exist for all issues affecting the businesses?* As a matter of course, most businesses use assets and incur overheads. It is therefore important that if each of the two businesses are to be considered genuine trading entities, they must pay for any assets used or overheads incurred. Equally importantly, these overheads must be paid for at reasonable levels, ie open market rates.

(c)   *What do the customers perceive to be happening?* An example is where two ladies trade from the same premises, one selling dietary supplements and vitamin pills, the other selling health foods. Would customers recognise the independence of the two entities? They may if they could only purchase one category of goods from one lady and the other category of goods from the other lady.

(d)   *Does one of the parties have a controlling influence over the other party?* Going back to the laundrette example at **5.2**, one of the main features of this situation was that one director and one shareholder had control of all twelve of the different limited companies. In effect, this is displaying common financial, organisational and economic links.

(e)   *How will the arrangement look in the eyes of an HMRC officer?* Although effective tax planning is the right of any taxpayer, there is sometimes a thin line between avoidance and evasion. It is important to assess whether there is any blatant limitation in the arrangement being reviewed, that would make it look like a VAT evasion scheme rather than a genuine business arrangement.

It is important to remember that just because the arrangement may pass the test on a number of issues (for example, separate invoicing and banking arrangements), it is the overall picture that is important.

Planning points to consider

[5.12] The following points should be given consideration.

•   If advising clients on the separation of business activities, it is important to ensure that avoidance of VAT is not the main motive for the arrangement.

•   Remember, there will only be a potential problem with HMRC if the arrangement results in a loss of VAT – two businesses with a combined turnover of less than the registration limits, or businesses selling wholly or mainly zero-rated items (where a registration would produce VAT repayments) is not a problem.

- The emphasis on normal commercial arrangements between different entities is vital to the success of a separation. Any overheads, shared assets, staff costs etc must be properly charged at a fair market rate.
- History tends to show that there are more problems with the separation of business activities when members of the same family are involved. If possible, consider whether a third party could become involved with the ownership of one of the businesses, which gives increased independence.
- Don't forget that there are only VAT advantages to be gained if the non-registered business is trading with members of the public (or VAT-exempt businesses) who cannot reclaim any VAT charged as input tax. If the business which is not VAT registered is mainly working for other registered entities, then it is probably in its best interests to register for VAT on a voluntary basis, to benefit from the opportunity to recover input tax.

Chapter 6

Cash Accounting Scheme

Key topics in this chapter:

- Conditions for joining the cash accounting scheme, including turnover limits and record-keeping requirements.
- How the scheme operates in practice.
- Limitations of the scheme for certain businesses, eg businesses selling mainly zero-rated items.
- Potential problems with the scheme for advisers to be aware of, for example, dealing with part-payments, part exchange transactions, discounts etc.
- Completing VAT returns.
- Rules for leaving the cash accounting scheme.

Introduction

[6.1] An intention of government policy has always been to try and simplify VAT procedures for small businesses. The cash accounting scheme is one such measure, allowing certain businesses to pay output tax when they receive payment from customers, rather than, under the ordinary VAT rules the earlier date when a sales invoice is raised. In the current economic climate, when customers are taking longer to pay their bills, this is a very worthwhile benefit.

The scheme can be adopted by any business that expects its taxable sales in the next 12 months to be £1,350,000 or less (excluding VAT).

The two main advantages of the scheme are automatic bad debt relief (output tax is never included on a VAT return until payment has been received from a customer, so there is no need to worry about trying to recover VAT on unpaid sales invoices) and the deferral of the time for payment of VAT where extended credit is given. Retailers would never use the scheme because they already account for VAT at the time they receive payment from a customer.

The main disadvantage of the scheme is that input tax can only be reclaimed when payment is made to suppliers – not on the date of the purchase invoice. However, this negative point tends to be outweighed for most taxpayers by the advantages gained by the output tax benefits.

Conditions for joining the scheme

[6.2] Unlike many special schemes, there is no requirement to notify HMRC in advance that a business intends to adopt cash accounting. If a business is eligible to use the scheme, then it can join at the beginning of any VAT accounting period.

However, there are a number of important conditions that must be met before the decision to adopt the scheme can be made, as follows.

- *Turnover limit* – as mentioned at **6.1**, the cash accounting scheme can only be used by a small business with an expected annual taxable turnover (VAT exclusive) of £1,350,000 or less in the next 12 months. This amount includes zero-rated, reduced-rated and standard rated supplies, but excludes any exempt sales or sales of capital assets (eg sale of plant, equipment or a van).
  Note – HMRC Notice 731, para 2.4 confirms that a business will not be penalised if its actual turnover in the next 12 months exceeds the scheme's joining limit, providing the business can show that there were reasonable grounds for its estimated turnover. The key issue is that it expected its sales to be under the limit at the time it joined.
- *Returns and payments are up to date* – a business should have submitted all of its returns for previous periods. With regard to payments, a business must also be up to date with its VAT payments to HMRC. However, it is also acceptable if a 'time to pay arrangement' is in place for past arrears.
- No *major VAT problems in the last 12 months* – the business must not have been convicted of any VAT offences during the previous 12 months. Also, it must not have incurred any penalty for VAT evasion involving dishonest conduct in the same period.
- No *retrospective use of the scheme* – any use of the cash accounting scheme can only be from a current date. It is not permissible to backdate the scheme and gain advantages in earlier VAT periods.

How the scheme works

Output tax is declared when payment is received from a customer

[6.3] As explained at **6.1**, the main advantage of the scheme is that a business has no output tax liability until the date when payment is received from a customer – in other words, no money received means no VAT bill due to HMRC. This is in contrast to the normal VAT accounting rules, where VAT is payable on the date of an invoice or receipt of payment, whichever happens sooner. See Example 1.

Example 1

Anita is a self-employed computer consultant and requires all of her customers to pay sales invoices within 60 days of the date of the invoice. She raises the following sales invoices during her VAT quarter to 30 September (based on VAT rate of 20%):

31 July	£10,000 plus VAT	– invoice paid 2 October
31 August	£5,000 plus VAT	– invoice paid 23 October
30 September	£7,000 plus VAT	– invoice paid 30 November

Solution – under normal VAT accounting rules, the date of the sales invoice would create a tax point and a VAT liability for each of the above sales invoices. Anita would therefore account for output tax of £4,400 on her VAT return for the quarter (ie £22,000 × 20%).

However, if she had made a decision to adopt the cash accounting scheme from the beginning of the quarter (and remember, there is no requirement to advise HMRC of this decision), then her cash flow position would be improved because she would not need to account for the output tax of £4,400 until she completed her VAT return for the following quarter, ie to coincide with payment dates.

Note – the position above with normal VAT accounting does not produce a disastrous result for the business because two out of the three invoices raised will have been paid by customers before the VAT bill becomes due. However, imagine the potential problems a business could face if it was paying VAT to HMRC on sales invoices that were still unpaid at the time when the VAT bill is due for payment.

A frequently asked question concerns the treatment of bounced cheques. In reality, a bounced cheque means that a customer has not made payment, and therefore no output tax liability exists under the cash accounting scheme. However, if the cheque is automatically represented by the bank and then is successfully cleared, VAT will then become payable.

Input tax can only be reclaimed when payment is made to suppliers

[6.4] The main principle of the scheme is to base VAT payments on 'cash-book' accounting rather than a 'day-book' basis. This principle applies to input tax as well as output tax, meaning that input tax can only be reclaimed when a purchase invoice has been paid to a supplier.

In effect, the input tax rule means that the scheme will be unsuitable for some businesses – or it may be suitable for some businesses in the future, but not at the current time. See Examples 2 and 3.

Example 2

John trades as an exporter of handbags to the USA. He buys the handbags from wholesalers in the UK – who give him 90 days credit. He also incurs input tax on a wide range of other expenses from UK suppliers for various services – who also give him good payment terms because they realise that it takes a long time for him to be paid by his American customers.

Solution – the cash accounting scheme is totally unsuitable for John. This is because he is gaining no output tax advantage because all of his sales are zero-rated as export of goods to a non-EU country.

In effect, his cash flow will be adversely affected by the scheme because it will delay the point when he can reclaim input tax on his purchase invoices by at least one VAT quarter.

Example 3

Jack has just started in business as a wholesaler of stationery, selling goods to retail stationers throughout the country. He is registered for VAT and trades from a small industrial unit. He has purchased goods costing £20,000 plus VAT as the initial stock in his unit, and has also paid an additional £20,000 plus VAT for various items of equipment, fixtures and fittings.

He has managed to negotiate generous payment terms with both the stock and asset suppliers. He wants to know if the cash accounting scheme will be worthwhile for him.

Solution – in the longer term, the cash accounting scheme should benefit Jack because the output tax gains will exceed the negative point about input tax claims being delayed until supplier invoices are paid.

However, in the first few months, the initial outlay of expenditure on stock and capital equipment means that his input tax will almost certainly exceed his output tax, ie repayment position as far as VAT is concerned. It is therefore probably sensible to delay using the cash accounting scheme until the time when the business will be in a net VAT payment situation.

Adjustments when a business first uses the scheme

[6.5] If an existing business decides to use the scheme, a key issue will be to ensure that output tax is not paid twice on the same supplies, and that input tax claims are, likewise, not duplicated.

For example, if a sales invoice is raised on 31 March, and paid in April, then a business on calendar VAT quarters and normal VAT accounting will account for output tax on the return to 31 March. If a decision is then made to adopt cash accounting with effect from 1 April, this particular invoice must be excluded from the cash accounting calculations for the quarter to 30 June – otherwise the output tax liability will be duplicated. The same principle must be applied with purchase invoices.

The other situation that could arise for a new business that adopts the scheme from the day it first becomes VAT registered is where it wants to reclaim input tax on the first return relevant to assets/stock purchased before it became registered for VAT. These expenses were obviously paid before the business became registered (ie payment date outside of the VAT period) but HMRC still allows the VAT on such purchases to be reclaimed on the first return.

Allocation of part payments on invoices with supplies at different rates of VAT

[6.6] Where a part-payment is received from a customer, which is not directly linked to specific invoices, then the payment must be allocated to invoices in date order (earliest first). This situation is then likely to mean that one sales invoice is part paid – and if this invoice includes a standard rated and zero-rated element, then the VAT payment should be apportioned according to the percentage of standard rated sales on the invoice. See Example 4. (HMRC Notice 731, para 5.7 and section 8).

Example 4

Doreen uses the cash accounting scheme and has two sales invoices unpaid from her customer ABC Ltd:

- invoice no 234 (dated 1 August) – £2,000 plus VAT (at 20%) of £400 – total £2,400; and
- invoice no 238 (dated 15 August) – £5,000 plus VAT of £200 – because £4,000 of goods on this invoice were zero-rated – total £5,200.

She receives a lump-sum payment on account from ABC Ltd for £4,000.

Solution – the first £2,400 of the payment will be allocated to the earliest sales invoice no 234, creating an output tax liability of £400.

The balance of the payment (£1,600) will be allocated to sales invoice no 238. The output tax to declare on this part of the payment is: £1,600 divided by £5,200 × £200 = £61.53. The remaining output tax on this invoice (£138.47) will be declared on future receipts of money from the customer.

Payments in kind: part exchange transactions

[6.7] It is possible that a business could receive part or full payment for its supplies as non-monetary consideration, for example, a part exchange transaction. In such cases, output tax is due on the full value of the supply. For a business using the cash accounting scheme, this principle still applies, and the 'payment' date is deemed to be when the non-monetary consideration is received. See Example 5.
(HMRC Notice 731, para 5.9).

Example 5

DEF Ltd sells tractors and is VAT registered using the cash accounting scheme. It sells a tractor to Mr Smith for £10,000 plus VAT and receives £6,000 cash plus Mr Smith's old tractor to settle the account. Mr Smith is not VAT registered.

> *Solution* – the cash book entry for this transaction will be £6,000 for the payment by Mr Smith – but the output tax liability is £2,000 with a VAT rate of 20%, ie on the full value of the supply. Assuming that the business took ownership of Mr Smith's old tractor on the same date as Mr Smith made payment for the balance due, then this will be the date when output tax is payable under the cash accounting scheme.

Prompt payment discount

[6.8] With a prompt payment discount a customer receives a discount if they pay within a certain time, for example, 5% within 14 days of the invoice date. Prior to the changes noted at the following two bullet points, the consideration for VAT purposes was reduced by a prompt payment discount even when the customer did not take advantage of the prompt payment discount. This meant that businesses (including businesses using the cash accounting scheme), accounted for output tax according to the amount of VAT shown on the invoice, which was previously calculated on the assumption that the customer took advantage of the prompt payment discount.

- From 1 May 2014 output tax must be accounted for on the actual consideration received for supplies of broadcasting and telecommunication services made in circumstances where a VAT invoice is not required and on terms which allow a discount for prompt payment.
- From 1 April 2015 output tax must be accounted for on the actual consideration received for all other supplies made on terms which allow a discount for prompt payment.

The above changes are intended to prevent the loss of output tax that can arise when a supplier accounts for output tax based on consideration reduced by a prompt payment discount rather than the actual consideration received.

(*VATA 1994, Sch 6 para 4; Finance Act 2014, s 108*).

Partial exemption

[6.9] A business that makes both taxable and exempt supplies is classed as partially exempt as far as VAT is concerned (see Chapters 24 and 25). In most cases, this means there is a restriction on input tax recovery based on the standard method of calculation for partial exemption – whereby taxable outputs are calculated as a proportion of total outputs, ie including exempt supplies to give an input tax recovery rate on general overheads.

For a business on the cash accounting scheme, the same principle of input tax restriction applies, but the outputs calculation under the standard method is based on payments received for taxable and exempt supplies in a VAT period, not on invoices raised.

Input tax recovery for a partly exempt business using the cash accounting scheme will still be based on payments made.

(HMRC Notice 731, para 4.6).

Completing VAT returns

[6.10] One of the main aims of the cash accounting scheme is to simplify the administrative burden of VAT for a small business – as well as the other two main benefits of automatic bad debt relief and a delay in paying output tax until payment is received from a customer.

For a small business, the record keeping process is simplified because a cash book system can be used as the main record, avoiding the need for a sales day book and purchase day book to be maintained as well.

In terms of completing the VAT return, the points below are relevant.

Box 1 – output tax will be based on payments received from customers during the period covered by the VAT return. This will include payments by cash, cheque and other means, as well as the value of any non-monetary payments such as part-exchange transactions (see **6.7**).

Box 4 – input tax will be based on payments made to suppliers during the period covered by the VAT return. This will include payments by cash, cheque, standing orders, direct debit and credit card – for credit card transactions, the key date is when the supplier makes out the sales voucher, not the date when payment is made to the card company.

Box 6 – the value of outputs (VAT exclusive) will also be based on payments received from customers.

Box 7 – the value of inputs (VAT exclusive) should also be based on payments made to suppliers.

Box 8 – this box is the exception to the rule. In the case of the sale of goods to VAT registered customers based in other EU countries, the Box 8 entry should be based on the value of goods supplied to customers, not on the total value of payments received.

Note – in effect, the consistency between Boxes 1, 4, 6 and 7 as far as the method of calculation is concerned (that is, based on payments rather than invoices) should enable the usual ratio checks to apply between the boxes:

- Box 6 figure multiplied by 20% should be equal to Box 1 output tax figure if the business only makes standard rated supplies;
- Box 7 figure multiplied by 20% should be equal to or greater than Box 4 input tax figure.

Leaving the scheme

[6.11] There are three situations which would result in a business withdrawing from the scheme:

(a)   voluntary withdrawal – a business may withdraw from the scheme at the end of any VAT period (see **6.12**);

(b)   turnover above the limits of the scheme – if a business expands so that its taxable turnover exceeds £1.6m per annum (excluding VAT), then it may need to withdraw from the scheme, however, HMRC allow continued use of the scheme in certain circumstances (see **6.13**);

(c)   compulsory withdrawal – due to non-compliance with HMRC regulations (see **6.14**).

If a business leaves the scheme, there are various transitional rules in place regarding the payment of tax that need to be carefully considered (see **6.15**).

Voluntary withdrawal

[6.12] A business is entitled to withdraw from using the scheme at the end of any VAT period; there are a number of commercial reasons why it might make this decision, for example:

- *change in mixture of goods being sold* – if a business that previously sold all standard rated items suddenly changes its activity so that the majority of sales are zero-rated, then the benefits of using the scheme could be eroded. This is because the benefits in delaying payment of output tax will not be relevant if sales are mainly zero-rated – the delay in reclaiming input tax until payment is made to suppliers may then be more of a problem;
- *customers make payment quicker than suppliers are paid* – this would be an enviable position for any business as far as cash flow is concerned, ie where customers make instant payment (or even payment in advance) but the business is able to enjoy extended payment terms with its suppliers. In such cases, the output tax benefits of the cash accounting scheme will be eroded but the delay in reclaiming input tax may be a problem.

Key point – as with entry to the scheme, there is no requirement to notify HMRC of the decision to leave. A business can rejoin again at the beginning of any VAT period if it is eligible (HMRC Notice 731, para 6.3).

Withdrawal due to turnover limit being exceeded (and opportunity to remain in scheme if limit was exceeded temporarily)

[6.13] Although the entry limit for a business is an annual taxable turnover of £1,350,000, a business does not have to withdraw from the scheme until the value of its taxable supplies in the previous 12 months has exceeded £1,600,000 (both figures exclude VAT). The only disadvantage is that the exit calculation must include the disposals of any stock or capital assets.

A business using the cash accounting scheme should monitor the level of its taxable supplies regularly as the test applies on a rolling 12 monthly basis. If taxable turnover in the immediately preceding 12 months exceeds £1,600,000 the business will normally be required to leave the scheme at the end of the VAT period in which the limit was exceeded.

However, HMRC will exceptionally allow a business to remain in the scheme as long as it can prove the following:

- the limit was exceeded because of a large 'one-off' increase in sales which has not occurred before and is not expected to occur again (eg the sale of a capital asset or an exceptional sale outside of the normal activities of the business); and

- the sale arose from a genuine commercial activity; and
- there are reasonable grounds for believing that turnover in the next 12 months will be below £1,350,000.

For an extension to be granted, all three of the above conditions must be met – and applications must be made to (and granted by) HMRC for a business to remain in the scheme. See Example 6.

(HMRC Notice 731, para 2.6).

Example 6

JKL Ltd is a company that offers computer consultancy services. It does not usually sell computer equipment but as a one-off transaction imported a special shipment of computers and sold them to a client for a good profit.

The sales value of these computers was £900,000 and the transaction resulted in the company having taxable turnover for a 12-month period in excess of £1,600,000 for the first time. This is the first time the company has been involved in the sale of goods, and the situation is not expected to repeat itself.

The company has been using the cash accounting scheme for many years and has enjoyed the benefits because many customers take a long time to settle their invoices.

Solution – if the above facts are as stated, then HMRC will almost certainly allow the business to continue using the scheme, even though its taxable turnover exceeded the £1,600,000 limit. The reason the limit was exceeded was due to a one-off sale that is unlikely to be repeated, and expected turnover for the following 12 months is expected to be within the scheme limits.

Compulsory withdrawal

[6.14] The legal basis of the cash accounting scheme is in *VAT Regulations 1995 (SI 1995/2518), regs 56–65*.

A business will be expelled from using the scheme in the following circumstances:

- if it fails to meet the record-keeping requirements to enable calculations to be properly made for VAT purposes;
- if it has been convicted of an offence in connection with VAT since using the scheme or accepted an offer to compound proceedings in connection with a VAT offence;
- if it has been assessed for a VAT penalty involving dishonest conduct.

In the above cases, HMRC will write to the taxpayer to withdraw the use of the scheme.

As a separate point, HMRC also has the power to withdraw the use of the scheme for any other reason where it feels it is necessary to safeguard the tax yield.

Rules to apply when a business withdraws from the scheme

[6.15] Unless special transitional rules can be applied (see **6.16**), a business must account for VAT as follows on the final return it submits when it is within the cash accounting scheme:

*   all VAT that it would have been required to pay to HMRC during the time the scheme was operated if it had not been operating the scheme, *minus*
*   all VAT accounted for and paid to HMRC in accordance with the scheme, subject to any adjustments for input tax credit.

In effect, the above conditions mean that at the point of leaving the scheme, the business will have accounted for, and declared, a total output tax figure (and reclaimed total input tax) the same as if it had never been in the scheme in the first place. In other words, output tax will be declared on unpaid sales invoices on this return (unless bad debt relief can be claimed) and input tax will be claimed on any unpaid purchase invoices.

(HMRC Notice 731, para 6.4).

Transitional rules when a business leaves the scheme

[6.16] The rules discussed at **6.15** could create a large and unexpected VAT bill for a business on the final return it submits when it is within the cash accounting scheme.

In order to alleviate the effect of this large payment, special transitional rules are available for businesses that leave the scheme either because of the turnover limits or because they choose to withdraw on a voluntary basis. The transitional rules are not available to any business where use of the scheme has been withdrawn by HMRC because of non-compliance issues. There is also an exclusion from using the transitional rules for any business whose taxable turnover exceeded £1,350,000 in the three-month period in which it ceases to operate the scheme.

The transitional rules can be summarised as follows:

*   the business can continue to operate the scheme in respect of its 'scheme supplies' for six months after the end of the VAT period in which it ceased to operate the scheme;
*   'scheme supplies' means supplies made and received while the business operated the scheme;
*   on the VAT return for the first period that ends six months or more after the end of the VAT period in which it ceased to operate the scheme, the business must then pay VAT under the rules at **6.15**, ie to bring its VAT accounting up to date again.

In effect, the transitional rules are extending the benefits of the scheme for six months after its official use has been withdrawn. There is no need to apply to HMRC to use the transitional arrangements.

Key point – if sales invoices are still unpaid at the end of the transitional six-month period, there may be scope to claim bad debt relief if they are more than six months overdue for payment and are written off in the business accounts.

Cash accounting scheme – other matters

Transfer of a going concern

[6.17] When a business is transferred as a going concern, then one of two situations will apply: either the new business retains the VAT registration number of the old business or the new business applies for its own VAT number. In the latter case, the transferor must, within two months or longer period as HMRC allows, account for and pay VAT due on all supplies made and received which have not otherwise been accounted for on any return (less input tax credit).

If the same VAT number is retained, the transferor must advise the new owner of the use of the scheme, and the new owner then takes over the accounting responsibilities in the normal way, ie as if there had been no change in ownership.

Cessation of business

[6.18] The two-month rule described above must also be applied if a business ceases to trade. However, HMRC will normally allow the business to continue to use the cash accounting scheme while stocks and assets are being sold – it is only when the final return is then submitted that all output tax on unpaid sales invoices needs to be accounted for (subject to bad debt relief being claimed and input tax credits also being adjusted).

Anti-avoidance measures

[6.19] A risk to HMRC is the situation when an advance tax invoice could be raised by a supplier, giving his customer the chance to reclaim input tax on the invoice, even though payment will not be made for many months. The delay in payment will then avoid an output tax declaration by the supplier if he is on the cash accounting scheme.

However, HMRC has rules in place to avoid this abuse – the scheme specifically excludes any supplies where a VAT invoice is issued and full payment of the amount shown on the invoice is not due within six months from the invoice date. Also, the scheme excludes any supplies where a VAT invoice is raised in advance of goods being delivered or services performed.

In reality, HMRC wants to avoid the situation where it is allowing a business to reclaim input tax on supplies where the output tax payment on the same supply is being delayed on either a temporary or permanent basis.

(HMRC Notice 731, para 2.7).

Factored debts

[6.20] Where debts are sold or transferred to become the debts of a factor company, output tax must be accounted for on their full value in the period in which they are sold or assigned. Obviously, this date will usually occur before payment is made by the final customer. Again, if the transfer occurs as soon as a sales invoice is raised, then the benefits of the cash accounting scheme may be negligible for the business in question.

An alternative scheme used in factoring arrangements is where the business retains ownership of the customer's debt, but receives advances of money from the factor company, usually based on a percentage of its turnover. The customer will then remit payment direct to the factor company to settle his account. In this situation, the business must declare output tax in the VAT period in which the customer pays the factor. The actual date of payment will be shown on statements issued by the factor company, and it is important to remember that output tax is due on the full value of the payment made by the customer – not net of any commission charged by the factor company.

(HMRC Notice 731, paras 5.3 and 5.4).

Flat rate scheme and annual accounting scheme

[6.21] A business cannot use the cash accounting scheme and flat rate scheme at the same time. However, a flat rate scheme user can, instead, account for VAT by adopting what is known as the 'cash-based turnover' method. This method gives the same outcome as the cash accounting scheme, ie no tax is declared on a VAT return until payment has been made by a customer. Full details of the flat rate scheme are considered in Chapter 8.

However, there is no problem with a business using the cash accounting scheme and annual accounting scheme at the same time. The main benefit of the annual accounting scheme is that a business completes one VAT return each year instead of 4 or 12, making regular payments on account throughout the year. See Chapter 7.

(HMRC Notice 731, para 2.8).

Planning points to consider

[6.22] The following points should be given consideration.

- Review client lists to identify those that could benefit from adopting the scheme, ie those within the annual turnover limit of £1,350,000 per year (taxable sales excluding VAT) and whose trading circumstances could produce worthwhile benefits.
- The cash flow benefits and automatic bad debt relief given by the scheme could be particularly useful for many clients.
- The scheme is probably not suitable for taxpayers selling mainly zero-rated items, or for a business where customers pay in advance or as soon as sales invoices are raised.

- The greatest benefits of the scheme will be enjoyed by a business that mainly sells standard-rated items, and also gives generous payment terms to its customers.
- Always review whether the scheme continues to benefit clients – a change in the mixture of standard/zero-rated goods could mean it is more beneficial for a business to account for VAT under normal accounting rules.
- A business that exceeds the exit level of £1.6m per annum in taxable supplies can still remain in the scheme if it can prove to HMRC that the increase in sales for the year in question was due to a one-off sale and that it expects taxable supplies in the next 12 months to be less than £1,350,000.
- Be aware of HMRC anti-avoidance rules that exclude transactions from the scheme that are invoiced in advance of goods being supplied to customers or services performed (or where payment is not due for six months or more). It is not acceptable to HMRC for a business to claim input tax when another business is able to delay paying output tax on the same supply.

Chapter 7

Annual Accounting Scheme

Key topics in this chapter:

- The rules that apply for a business to join the annual accounting scheme.
- How the scheme works in practice – one VAT return each year, regular payments on account and balancing payment due at the end of the accounting period.
- Withdrawal from the scheme – turnover limits, compulsory withdrawal, voluntary withdrawal.
- Disadvantages and potential problems of using the scheme.
- Types of business that could benefit from using the scheme.

Introduction

[7.1] The aim of the annual accounting scheme is to reduce the administrative burden of VAT for a small business by only requiring the submission of one annual VAT return instead of four quarterly (or 12 monthly) returns.

A business can join the scheme if it expects that its annual taxable turnover (excluding VAT) will be £1,350,000 or less in the next 12 months.

The basic rules of the scheme are as follows:

- a business submits one VAT return per year, usually coinciding with its financial year;
- the business gets an extra month to submit the annual return, ie it is due two months after the end of the period rather than one;
- VAT is usually paid on a monthly basis throughout the year – any remaining balance is then paid or repaid at the end of the year after the annual return has been submitted.

Eligibility to use the scheme

[7.2] A business is able to apply for and adopt annual accounting if the following condition is met:

* *Taxable turnover in the next 12 months is expected to be £1,350,000 or less* – the turnover level excludes the sale of capital assets and also the value of any exempt supplies made by the business. Once a business has joined the scheme, it can remain in the scheme until the value of its annual taxable sales (VAT exclusive) exceeds £1,600,000.

(HMRC Notice 732, section 2).

A business can apply to join the annual accounting scheme as soon as it becomes VAT registered, as long as it expects its taxable sales in the 12-month period to be £1,350,000 or less.

The scheme is generally open to all businesses that meet the above criteria, however, there are a few exceptions when HMRC will refuse an application:

(a)   a business cannot join the scheme if it is part of a group or divisional registration;

(b)   once a business has left the scheme, it cannot rejoin for at least 12 months;

(c)   a business can be refused admission if it has a rising VAT debt. There should not be a problem if this rising debt is still a small amount, and if settlement has been negotiated through a time to pay agreement;

(d)   an insolvent business cannot join the scheme.

How the scheme works

Application process

[7.3] An application to use the scheme must be made on form VAT 600(AA). There is another form that can be used if a business wishes to join the annual accounting and flat rate schemes at the same time (VAT 600(AA) and FRS). The forms can be downloaded from the GOV.UK website (www.gov.uk/gove rnment/organisations/hm-revenue-customs).

If a business chooses to make its regular payments on account by direct debit (a scheme condition is that payments on account must be made electronically) then it must also complete Form VAT 623 at the time of making its application.

All correspondence with HMRC concerning the scheme (including joining, leaving and changing payment on account arrangements) is dealt with by the Annual Accounting Registration Unit at the following address:

Annual Accounting Registration Unit
National Registration Service
Imperial House
77 Victoria Street
Grimsby DN31 1DB

Note – tips on how to complete the application form for the scheme are given in HMRC Notice 732, section 8.

Once HMRC approves a business to use the scheme, it will confirm the amount and timing of the interim payments made by electronic means and the due date for the annual return and balancing payment.

At this stage, it is important that a business reviews the level of payments being proposed to ensure they are reasonable:

- if the payments are too low, then the business will face a large balancing payment at the end of its accounting year;
- if the payments are too high, then working capital could be stretched for the business until the overpayment is corrected at the end of the year.

First year of using the scheme

[7.4] One of the rules of the scheme is that no annual accounting period can exceed 12 months (apart from a new business that is applying to use the scheme from the date it registered for VAT, in which case 12 months and 30 days is possible). In effect, a business applying to join the scheme midway through its chosen accounting year will have one return to complete of less than 12 months, followed by annual returns thereafter. See Example 1.

Example 1

John trades as a plumber and decided to join the annual accounting scheme. He applied to join on 10 July 2014 and chose an accounting year of 31 March. He was previously on calendar VAT quarters.

Solution – the first period that John needs to submit a return for under the scheme is the period from 1 July 2014 to 31 March 2015. He will then submit an annual return each year up to 31 March. It would not be possible for John's first period to cover 1 July 2014 to 31 March 2016 because the period would then exceed 12 months, contrary to the scheme rules.

Payments on account

[7.5] A key condition of the scheme is the requirement to make regular payments on account throughout the year. The rules for these payments are as follows.

(a)   For the first accounting period of less than 12 months (as per Example 1 above), there are special transitional rules regarding payments on account. These rules depend on the number of months in the period, however, if the period is less than four months, no interim payments are required. There will also need to be agreed payments on account for a newly registered business that is joining the scheme from its date of registration – based on expected VAT payments in its first 12 months of trading.

Note – a business completing a first VAT return of less than four months when it first joins the scheme must complete the return and pay tax due within one month of the period end, ie rather than two months (HMRC Notice 732, para 3.6).

(b)   Normal accounting year – the procedures for payments on account in a full accounting year (ie a 12-month period) are as follows:

- the total VAT paid in the previous 12 months is calculated; 10% of this amount is then due for each payment in months 4 to 12 of the accounting year. However, a business can alternatively apply to make quarterly payments on account at the end of months 4, 7 and 10. In such cases, the payments made will be each based on 25% of the previous year's VAT liability;
- the monthly or quarterly payments in each of the above months will be made by electronic means on the last working day of the month;
- a business can make additional voluntary payments at any time, as long as the payments are in multiples of £5 and made by electronic means;
- the balance of tax is payable two months after the end of the accounting period when the annual return is submitted;
- if a business expects its actual liability of VAT to increase or decrease compared to the previous year (eg because of a significant change in trading levels), then it should contact the Annual Accounting Registration Unit (address at **7.3** above) with information on how it has calculated the revised interim payments.

For an illustration of the workings of the payment arrangement, see Example 2.

Example 2

ABC Ltd paid VAT of £22,000 in the year to 31 March 2014. It was approved to use the annual accounting scheme with effect from 1 April 2014. For the year ended 31 March 2015, it paid nine monthly instalments of £2,200 each from July 2014 to March 2015, ie based on 10% of the previous year's liability for each period. When the company submitted its annual VAT return for year ended 31 March 2015, the actual amount due was £25,000.

Solution – a balancing payment of £5,200 was due by 31 May 2015, ie within two months of the end of the annual accounting period. This figure is the difference between the VAT liability for the year (£25,000) and the interim payments made from months 4 to 12 (£2,200 × 9 = £19,800). The payments on account for the following year will each be £2,500, ie £25,000 × 10%.

Repayment traders

[7.6] There is no problem with a repayment trader applying to join the annual accounting scheme. A repayment trader is defined as a trader whose VAT returns regularly show that input tax exceeds output tax. This situation would mainly apply to a business where most or all sales are zero-rated, eg newsagents, farmers, milkmen, builders working on new residential properties, export traders.

However, the problem for a repayment trader adopting the scheme is that any repayment due from HMRC would not be paid until the annual return has been submitted. This is likely to create a negative result as far as cash flow is concerned – particularly if the business had a large amount of input tax to reclaim early in the accounting year, for example on capital equipment.

(HMRC Notice 732, para 7.1).

Leaving the scheme

[7.7] A business ceases to be eligible to use the scheme in the following circumstances.

- *Turnover exceeds £1.6m* – the key figure is the taxable sales for the 12-month period shown on the annual return (excluding VAT).
- *Expulsion by HMRC* – HMRC have the power to withdraw the use of the scheme for any business that does not comply with the rules. In reality, this means that if a business has a poor compliance record as far as making payments are concerned, or has failed to submit two annual returns on time, then it can be removed from the scheme. HMRC also have the power to withdraw a business from the scheme if it considers it to be necessary 'for the protection of the revenue', ie to safeguard the tax yield.
- *Cessation of trading* – if a business ceases to trade or ceases to be VAT registered, then it will obviously withdraw from using the scheme.

Note – a business may elect to use the scheme but then decide it would prefer to revert to submitting quarterly returns and to adopt normal VAT accounting. It can leave the scheme at any time by writing to HMRC – this means that a final return must be completed under the scheme, with the balance of any tax being paid within two months of the termination date. If a business has chosen to withdraw from the scheme, it cannot apply to rejoin again for at least 12 months.

(HMRC Notice 732, para 7.5).

Incorrect estimates of future taxable sales

[7.8] One of the rules of admission is that a business can only join if it expects the value of its VAT-exclusive taxable turnover to be less than £1,350,000 in the next 12 months. However, even if it gets its estimate wrong and exceeds this limit, there is no problem as long as the actual taxable sales do not exceed £1.6m. See Example 3.

(HMRC Notice 732, para 2.5).

Example 3

ABC Ltd joined the annual accounting scheme on 1 April and expected its sales in the next 12 months to be £1,125,000. However, the trading year proved exceptionally strong and actual taxable sales during the period were £1,500,000.

Solution – although ABC Ltd should not have joined the annual accounting scheme, it will not be penalised for getting its turnover estimate wrong, and can remain in the scheme as long as actual sales are always less than the exit level of £1.6m per year.

Note – the key challenge for a business is to be able to show to HMRC that there were 'reasonable grounds' for thinking that taxable sales in the next 12 months would be less than £1,350,000 at the time it applied to join the scheme, eg as supported on cash flow projections, business plans etc.

Annual accounting scheme – potential problems

[7.9] The scheme has not been as popular as originally anticipated by HMRC when it was first introduced. The following are potential problems of which advisers need to be aware.

- *Payments on account could be too high* – if a business identifies at any time that its payments on account are too high, it can make an application to HMRC to reduce them. This request should be made to the Annual Accounting Registration Unit (address at **7.3** above). In reality, however, this effectively means that a business needs to calculate its VAT liability anyway (in order to confirm the payments on account are reasonable) and so it may want to complete quarterly returns in the normal way.

- *Payments on account could be too low* – the risk that payments on account could be too low and a business does not anticipate the high balancing payment is another limitation of the scheme.
  This situation could be particularly relevant for an expanding business that has increased its activity levels, eg turnover doubled in the last 12 months. Imagine if a busy company was trading very heavily, and accepting low payments on account under the annual accounting scheme. The annual return is then submitted, producing an unexpected balancing payment that could cause immediate cash flow problems.

- *Discipline of quarterly VAT returns is lost* – the discipline of completing a quarterly VAT return is a good way of ensuring that business accounting records are kept reasonably up to date. If this discipline is removed by the annual accounting scheme, there is a risk that accounts will be completed at the end of the year on a last-minute basis. This increases the risk of errors in the records.

It is well known that a large number of self-assessment tax returns are filed close to the deadline each year due to the natural tendency of many people to leave things to the last minute. The annual accounting scheme, by effectively extending deadlines, could contribute further to this approach.

Types of business to benefit from use of the scheme

[**7.10**] Although the scheme has definite limitations (see **7.9**), there are many instances where it could be worthwhile. The following examples make it worthy of consideration.

- If a client has a persistent record of putting VAT returns in late, and incurring default surcharges, then the reduced number of returns and discipline of monthly electronic payments may be beneficial. In reality, the client could save time on completing returns – and spend more time running his business.
- The scheme is quite attractive to businesses that are partly exempt because they only have to do one partial exemption calculation per year. The annual accounting period would coincide with the partial exemption year, and there would effectively be no need for an annual adjustment in the scheme because this would be automatic with the 12-month return (HMRC Notice 732, para 7.3). Many small partly exempt businesses could be voluntary/non-profit making organisations (eg a members' golf club) so volunteer officers would welcome the reduced administration time.
- There could also be financial savings for any business that does not feel confident about completing its own VAT return and has to pay for external expertise. Although it would be fair to argue that there is more work involved in completing an annual return rather than quarterly returns, there should still be a welcome saving of fees for the client.
- HMRC does not penalise a business that has low payments on account and a high balance of tax due after the year end, so there is scope for a growing (but well-managed) business to gain a cash flow advantage from the scheme. However, the directors will need to ensure that money is put aside for the balancing payment due after the end of the year. See Example 4.

Example 4

John used the annual accounting scheme and paid VAT of £30,000 (including the balancing payment) for a particular year. During the following year he paid nine instalments of £3,000 – each instalment being 10% of the previous year's liability. However, John's business has enjoyed significant trading growth, and his actual VAT liability for the year is £60,000.

Solution – John will have a large balancing payment of £33,000 (£60,000 less £27,000) to make when he submits his annual VAT return. However, the payment delay has given him a positive cash flow benefit compared to normal quarterly returns. The priority though, is to ensure he has funds available to pay the amount due and that it has not already been spent.

Planning points to consider

[**7.11**] The following points should be given consideration.

- Payments on account that are either too high or too low can be adjusted during the year by writing to the Annual Accounting Registration Unit (address at **7.3** above) and requesting revised payment terms. The payments on account are based on the previous year's VAT liabilities and some businesses may owe less tax in the current year.

- It is unlikely that the scheme will benefit repayment traders because they have to wait until the end of the accounting year to receive any repayment due. Any scheme users that have recently become repayment traders (eg change in activity so that most sales are zero-rated rather than standard rated) would almost certainly benefit from applying to leave the scheme on a voluntary basis.

- Be aware of the potential advantages of the scheme that may appeal to certain traders – particularly the time-saving benefits of completing only one return each year. The scheme may also appeal to partly-exempt taxpayers who will only need to make one partial exemption calculation per year.

- There is no problem using both the annual accounting and flat rate schemes at the same time. The flat rate scheme also produces worthwhile time (and sometimes tax) savings for a small business and is considered in Chapter 8.

Chapter 8

Flat Rate Scheme

Key topics in this chapter:

- Turnover limits for using the FRS.
- How the scheme works.
- Applying to use the scheme and potential problems for users.
- Input tax issues – opportunity to claim input tax on some items of capital expenditure.
- Choosing the relevant flat rate percentage to apply for a particular business and the importance of choosing the right percentage when a business first joins.
- Sources of business income that need to be included in the scheme in some cases, eg buy-to-let income, sale of capital assets.
- Bank interest received – clarification of treatment by courts.
- Situations where the scheme could produce tax savings.
- Completing VAT returns.
- The three alternative methods of calculating sales – basic turnover method, cash-based method and retail method.
- Dealing with EU acquisitions and other international transactions.
- Rules for leaving – voluntary and compulsory withdrawal.
- Potential problems if a business is associated with another business.

Introduction

[8.1] The FRS was introduced in April 2002, with the aim of simplifying the record-keeping requirements of a small business in relation to VAT.

The basic principles of the scheme are as follows:

- It is only available to a small business where VAT exclusive annual taxable turnover in the next 12 months is expected to be less than £150,000 (HMRC Notice 733, section 3).
- A business still charges VAT on its sales invoices in the normal way, ie adding 20% VAT for standard rated sales, 5% for reduced rate sales and 0% for zero-rated sales.

- Instead of paying VAT based on output tax less input tax, a business will apply a given flat rate percentage to its gross (VAT inclusive) income – the percentage is based on the category of business to which it belongs.

A business using the scheme does not reclaim input tax, unless it relates to capital expenditure goods costing at least £2,000 including VAT. The definition of capital expenditure goods follows that of normal accounting principles, eg it includes money spent on vans, plant and machinery, fixtures and fittings for use in the business but with an exception if the asset is used for hiring or letting.

(HMRC Notice 733, para 2.4 and section 15).

HMRC publicises the scheme to promote the potential time saving and administrative benefits for a small business. VAT specialists and accountants generally publicise the tax savings for certain users whose specific circumstances produce a good result. HMRC's approach is understandable – the aim of the scheme is to be tax neutral rather than to create savings for certain types of business. However, the reality of the situation is that most clients are more interested in the tax savings rather than the time savings.

The limited scope to claim input tax results in the following potential time saving benefits:

- Purchase invoices do not need to be analysed in detail for VAT return purposes.
- No scale charge arises for private use of car fuel.
- For a partly exempt business, no complicated partial exemption calculations are required.

How the scheme works

[8.2] The scheme is simple to operate and works on the following basis:

- under normal accounting, a business separately records the VAT on its sales (usually invoices) as output tax and the VAT on its purchase and expense invoices as input tax. Its VAT liability for a period equates to output tax less input tax. With the FRS, there is no need to record sales or purchase invoices in this manner;
- the FRS only requires a business to record the value of its VAT inclusive sales or takings for a period – this sales figure also includes any zero-rated or exempt supplies made during the period – see **8.10–8.16**. However, any sales that are outside the scope of VAT are excluded from the calculation. This exclusion would apply to any services provided to overseas customers where the place of supply is established as being outside the UK;
- a specific percentage is applied to the VAT inclusive sales figure, and this becomes the VAT payable by the business in the relevant period. The percentage to apply depends on the trade sector of the business in question – see **8.8**;

- if a business buys capital expenditure goods exceeding £2,000 including VAT, it is entitled to reclaim input tax on these items subject to the normal rules. The items must be used in relation to the business – not purchased for resale and not purchased to lease, let or hire (see **8.32** and **8.33**);
- there are special rules in place to deal with stock and assets held at the time of VAT registration – so that a claim for input tax can be made where appropriate on the first VAT return submitted by the business.

See Example 1 to illustrate the workings of the scheme in a practical situation.

Example 1

ABC Management Consultants Ltd is VAT registered, completes VAT returns on a calendar quarter basis and uses the FRS. The value of sales invoices raised in the VAT quarter to 31 March was £20,000 plus VAT, ie £24,000 including VAT. However, the company purchased a highly sophisticated piece of capital equipment for use in its business on 28 February, at a cost of £1,900 plus VAT. How much VAT is due under the flat rate scheme (based on a VAT rate of 20%)?

Solution – because the equipment purchased is a capital item costing more than £2,000 including VAT (£1,900 plus VAT at 20% = £2,280) the input tax on this purchase can be claimed separately, ie outside the scheme.

A management consultant has a flat rate of 14% under the scheme and must apply this percentage to its VAT inclusive sales figure of £24,000.

The amount of tax due under the scheme is, therefore £2,980, ie £3,360 output VAT less £380 input VAT.

Note – if the business sells the capital asset in the future, it must account for output tax on the proceeds of the sale in Box 1 of its return, that is on the basis that it has obtained input tax recovery on the purchase of the asset. It is not acceptable to include the sale of the asset within the scheme calculation, ie output tax must be accounted for on the full selling price using the relevant VAT fraction at the time (20/120 for a 20% VAT rate).

Applying to use the scheme

[8.3] As explained above, any business can apply to use the scheme if it meets the relevant turnover limit given at **8.1**. The business must also ensure it does not have a problem with the 'associated business' rules – see **8.30**. The application can be made at any time (usually from the beginning of a VAT period) – either by post (Form VAT 600 (FRS)), e-mail or telephone (the VAT Helpline can take application details over the phone on 0300 200 3700).

HMRC has the power to refuse use of the scheme if it considers it necessary to safeguard the tax yield. It will notify the business that its application has been accepted (or declined) and the date from which it can operate the scheme. If the application is denied, then the reasons for the refusal will be given.

An important benefit of adopting the scheme for a newly registered business is that it will benefit from an extra 1% discount from its usual flat rate percentage in its first year of VAT registration. For a business with turnover at the maximum level allowed by the scheme (£150,000 plus VAT), this 1% discount could be worth up to £1,800.

Note – be clear that the 1% discount is available to a business in its first year of VAT registration, not the first year that it uses the scheme. So a business that has already been VAT registered for at least a year when it joins the scheme will not obtain the discount.

(HMRC Notice 733, section 5).

Potential problems of using the scheme

[8.4] As with many aspects of tax, a situation that may be suitable for one business may prove totally unsuitable for another. Example 2 illustrates one situation where the scheme produces a disastrous result for a taxpayer. Advisers should be aware of the important points in relation to the scheme that are mentioned in this section.

Example 2

John trades as an accountant and tax adviser, subcontracting a lot of work to three local practitioners, all of whom are VAT registered.

John's annual sales figure is £100,000 (excluding VAT) and his sole expense is the subcontractor fees of £40,000 (excluding VAT). Should he use the flat rate scheme?

Solution – John should avoid the flat rate scheme. Under normal accounting, with a VAT rate of 20%, his annual VAT bill would be £12,000 (output tax of £20,000 less input tax of £8,000). However, the flat rate scheme (14.5% flat rate for accountants) gives him a tax bill of £17,400 (£100,000 x 1.2 x 14.5%). He is worse off by £5,400. This is because the nature of his trading produces exceptionally high input tax – far greater than is recognised by the 14.5% flat rate for accountants.

Appropriate scheme percentage needs to be applied to all sales

[8.5] The appropriate scheme percentage needs to be applied to zero-rate, lower-rate and exempt sales (see **8.10**) – not just standard-rated sales.

This is possibly the point that causes most confusion among many clients, and some advisers. Basically, the flat rate percentage is applied to the gross receipts of a business, so effectively it means that some VAT is being paid on zero-rated or exempt supplies that are made. The flat rate percentages are lower for trade sectors with a high prevalence of zero-rated or exempt sales (eg the flat rate percentage for a business retailing food, confectionery, tobacco, newspapers or children's clothing is 4%) but the scheme may not be favourable for a business where the extent of zero-rated sales is unknown on a period-by-period basis. For an illustration of this point, see Example 3.

Example 3

DEF Builders Ltd is registered for VAT and uses the FRS. It has just completed a large job erecting a new roof for a builder on a new residential property (zero-rated supply). The value of the work carried out was £30,000 and it was the only job the company performed during the VAT quarter ended 31 March. A sales invoice was raised for the completed work on 31 March.

GHI Builders Ltd is registered for VAT and uses the FRS. It has just completed a large job erecting a new roof for a builder on an existing residential property (standard-rated supply). The value of the work carried out was £30,000 plus VAT and it was the only job GHI performed during the VAT quarter ended 31 March. A sales invoice was raised for the completed work on 31 March.

What is the VAT position of the two companies?

Solution – assuming that both companies supply labour and materials, the flat rate for general building or construction services is 9.5%. This will produce a VAT bill of £2,850 for DEF Builders Ltd (ie £30,000 × 9.5%), and leave them with net income on the job carried out of £27,150 (ie £30,000 less £2,850).

GHI Builders Ltd will have a VAT bill of £3,420 (ie £30,000 × 1.2 × 9.5%), leaving them with net income on the job carried out of £32,580 (ie £36,000 less £3,420).

As can be seen, the FRS has produced a very bad result for DEF Builders Ltd because it has produced an output tax liability on a job where the company charged no VAT. However, for GHI Builders Ltd (and for any building company carrying out wholly or mainly standard-rated work), the 9.5% flat rate may prove very attractive.

FRS is not suitable for repayment traders

[8.6] The lowest flat rate percentage for any trade sector is 4%. Therefore, it is impractical for any repayment trader (eg a business with wholly or mainly zero-rated sales) to use the scheme because it is impossible to obtain repayments from HMRC. In reality, the scheme is only suitable for businesses that, over a period of time, are in a net payment position to HMRC.

FRS may produce a high tax bill for a business with two different activities

[8.7] A scheme rule is that if a business has two or more different activities, the flat rate to be chosen will be based on the activity that represents the greater or greatest proportion of its turnover. In some cases, this situation may produce a very favourable result for a taxpayer – for example, where the VAT bill on his secondary activity would be higher than on his main activity – but the opposite result can also occur.

If the mix of sales between the two different activities changes (ie creating the situation when the secondary activity becomes the primary activity) then the flat rate percentage will need to reflect this change – but from the date that coincides with the anniversary of the business joining the scheme in the first place.

An interesting tribunal case involving a publican was *Morgan (t/a The Harrow Inn) v Revenue and Customs Comrs* (30 June 2006, unreported) (MAN/05/0726 19671). The case produced a bad result for the taxpayer, due to the fact that the catering part of the business became more significant in terms of turnover than the wet sales.

At the time of applying to join the FRS, the Morgans described their business as a pub and used the appropriate flat rate of 5.5% from 1 January 2004. However, the catering activity soon became the greater part of total sales, meaning that the flat rate percentage should have been increased to 12% (percentage for catering) on the anniversary date of when the scheme was first adopted, namely 1 January 2005. The Morgans failed to adjust the percentage, and the tribunal supported HMRC's assessment to the higher rate.

The essential learning point from the *Morgan* case is that the mix of sales for any business using the FRS should be reviewed on, at least, an annual basis. If a higher rate becomes appropriate, then the taxpayer must either pay an increased amount of tax or withdraw from the scheme and adopt normal VAT accounting methods.

Choosing a business category

[8.8] The choice of the trade sector and the relevant flat rate percentage to adopt is down to the individual business to choose from the table in the *VAT Regulations 1995 (SI 1995/2518), reg 55K*. In making a choice, the everyday meaning of the words should be used. HMRC has published guidance in VAT Manual FRS7200 on its website.

Once HMRC has approved a business to join the scheme, it will not change the category of business on a retrospective basis as long as the choice made by the business was reasonable and records have been kept as to why it was chosen. For example, there may be certain businesses that could overlap into two different categories, and the final choice will require a careful analysis of the business activity to decide the most appropriate category.

Many advisers and clients are concerned about the prospect of an HMRC officer making a routine visit and telling the taxpayer he has chosen the wrong flat rate percentage (too low), and that a retrospective assessment for the last four years will be issued.

However, reassurance is given by HMRC's VAT Notice 733, para 4.2, which states:

> 'If you have made a mistake choosing an incorrect sector you may pay too much tax or too little. Paying too little could mean that you are faced with an unexpected VAT bill at a later date.
>
> HMRC will not change your choice of sector retrospectively as long as your choice was reasonable. It will be sensible to keep a record of why you chose your sector in case you need to show HMRC that your choice was reasonable.'

A list of categories and the appropriate percentage rates can be found at Appendix 8A.

Paragraph 4.2 of HMRC Notice 733 acknowledges that some business activities can reasonably fit into more than one sector, but indicates that HMRC will not change a choice of sector retrospectively as long as the choice was reasonable. Paragraph 4.4 of HMRC Notice 733 provides HMRC's guidance regarding what trade sector each of the business activities in question fall into. The table below is based on the information in paragraph 4.4 of HMRC Notice 733:

Business activity	Trade sector
Engineering consultants and designers	Architects, civil and structural engineers
Agents	Business services that are not listed elsewhere
Barristers	Lawyers or legal services
Florists	Retailing that is not listed elsewhere
Agronomists	Management consultancy
Television cameramen	Film, radio, television or video production

The First-tier Tribunal considered HMRC's guidance in paragraph 4.4 of VAT Notice 733 in the separate cases of *Idess Ltd* (TC03638) and *SLL Subsea Engineering Ltd* (TC04256). In particular, the Tribunal considered the guidance that engineering consultants and designers fall into the category for architects, civil and structural engineers or surveyors. This category currently has a flat rate percentage of 14.5%.

In both cases the companies, which provide mechanical engineering services, chose the 'any other activity not listed elsewhere' category, which currently has a flat rate percentage of 12%. In both cases HMRC decided that the companies should have used the higher percentage for the 'architect, civil and structural engineer or surveyor' category.

HMRC decided that the original choice of category by both companies was unreasonable and decided to change the choice of category retrospectively by issuing assessments. HMRC also decided to impose a penalty on Idess Limited. The penalty was initially 35% but was reduced to 15% following an internal review by HMRC which decided that the 'error' was careless rather than deliberate but not concealed.

The Tribunal was not convinced by HMRC's argument, which was essentially the same in both cases and was that the choice of category was unreasonable because it was not made in accordance with the guidance in paragraph 4.4 of VAT Notice 733.

Paragraph 4.4 of VAT Notice 733 has no legal effect so the Tribunal focused on the statutory wording of the *VAT Regulations 1995 (SI 1995/2518), reg 55K*, which has a category with the description 'architect, civil and structural engineer or surveyor'.

In *Idess Ltd* the Tribunal considered that the term 'civil and structural engineer' in *reg 55K*, whether read alone or in the context of architects and surveyors, was relevant to operations relating to land, buildings and other structures. To quote an extract from the Tribunal report – 'The adjectives, civil and structural, were, we must assume, chosen consciously and deliberately by the draftsman'. The Tribunal noted that the services provided by Idess Ltd did not involve land, buildings and other structures, but rather plant and machinery.

In *SLL Subsea Engineering Ltd* the company also provided mechanical engineering services. The Tribunal considered that if Parliament had intended that all engineering fell into the 'architect, civil and structural engineer or surveyor' category in *reg 55K* there would have been no reason whatsoever to introduce the words 'civil' and 'structural'.

In both cases the Tribunal considered that choice of category made by each company was reasonable and allowed the appeals against HMRC's decisions.

Retrospectively changing your choice of flat rate category

[8.9] As explained above, HMRC should not challenge a taxpayer's choice of category on a retrospective basis as long as the initial choice was sensible. This is important because not every business will exactly fit into one of the 55 different categories, so an element of judgement is needed by taxpayers in many cases.

However, what happens if a new scheme user plays safe and adopts a category with a high flat rate percentage and then subsequently discovers that this choice was incorrect?

The case of *Archibald & Co Ltd v Revenue and Customs Comrs (VAT)* (TC00336) [2010] UKFTT 21 (TC) related to a chartered accountant whose main activity was to provide tax advice to investment funds and management companies, supplemented by some exam marking. She joined the scheme in March 2007, and chose the flat rate category of 'Accountancy or bookkeeping'.

However, in 2009 she requested a retrospective change in her chosen category to 'Business services that are not listed elsewhere' (with a lower flat rate percentage) on the basis that she was not doing traditional accountancy work. Her revised choice was sensible but HMRC refused to backdate her new category on the basis that her first choice was reasonable. The tribunal supported HMRC.

The message of the *Archibald* case is that an assertive approach is needed when users first join the scheme and choose their category. As long as a decision can be supported by a sensible analysis, then no retrospective challenge should be made by HMRC.

Consider all forms of business income

[8.10] It is crucial that all advisers are aware of the issues raised in this section because the income sources are very common for many individuals.

The starting point is to remember that a VAT registration includes all supplies made by a 'taxable person'. Hence, a sole trader who runs a restaurant and also repairs cars will need to account for VAT on both activities if he is registered. However, there would be no problem if the two activities were under different legal entities, eg if the sole trader was in a partnership in the car repair business with his friend.

(HMRC Notice 733, para 6.2).

Buy-to-let income – excluded or included?

[8.11]

Example 4

Steve is an accountant who is registered for VAT as a sole trader. He uses the flat rate scheme (14.5% rate for accountants) and also owns a flat in Leicester that he rents out for £1,000 per month. Does he also apply the FRS percentage to his rental income?

Solution – as explained in a previous section, a disadvantage of the scheme is that the relevant percentage is applied to exempt and zero-rated business income, and rental income is definitely exempt. However, is the income from a buy-to-let arrangement classed as business or private income? Unfortunately, any income derived from the exploitation of land is always classed as business income.

The view of HMRC (with which the author agrees) is that rental income must be included because of the EU definition of 'economic activity' (*Directive 2006/112/EC, art 9(1)*). To quote from the Directive:

'The exploitation of tangible or intangible property for the purposes of obtaining income therefrom on a continuing basis shall in particular be regarded as an economic activity.'

Unfortunately, the above definition also captures any rental income earned by a person who rents out his own private residence.

The VAT registration of a sole trader includes all of his activities – it is the person rather than the business that is registered. However, the good news is that many clients will avoid this problem if they have different legal entities for their business and property income.

So if this example does apply to your client, should you go back four years (the time limit for adjusting errors on past VAT returns) and calculate any underpaid VAT on the rental income and adjust your next VAT return (if it is below the error notification limit of £10,000 or 1% of Box 6 outputs to a ceiling of £50,000)? And moving forward, should you withdraw from the scheme if the inclusion of rental income means you are worse off with the scheme? Or should you consider a change in the legal entity of the business or property?

The answer is 'yes' with the first question and 'possibly' with the others.

Note – see **8.27** with regard to withdrawing from the scheme.

The principle of buy-to-let income being included in the FRS calculations was confirmed in the case of *ICAN Finance v Revenue and Customs Comrs* (TC00958) [2011] UKFTT 81 (TC):

- A sole trader had two sources of income – trading as a finance broker and also renting out a series of buy-to-let investment properties.
- The taxpayer used the FRS but had excluded rental income from buy-to-let properties from his scheme calculations – HMRC assessed tax of £8,269 + £750 on this income. The taxpayer classed the rental activity as separate to his business as a finance broker.
- The taxpayer also put forward the view that he should not be charged a penalty on the errors – however, he was actually being charged interest (commercial restitution) and not a penalty.
- Appeal dismissed – based on principles explained in this section.

Sale of capital assets – included or excluded?

[8.12]

Example 5

> Steve from the previous example has enjoyed a very profitable month. He has sold his buy-to-let flat in Leicester for £200,000 and his Mercedes business car for £20,000. What are the FRS issues?
>
> **Solution** – going back to the basic scheme rules, the relevant percentage is applied to exempt and zero-rated business income. This creates a VAT liability for a taxpayer on income where no VAT has been charged to a customer.
>
> The two asset sales in this example are both sources of exempt income, and we have already confirmed that the property activity is classed as 'business' within EU law. In technical terms, the car sale is exempt under *VATA 1994, Sch 9, Group 14* ('Supplies of goods where input tax cannot be recovered', ie including motor cars available for private use).
>
> The logical solution is for Steve to withdraw from the scheme before these two assets are sold – and revert to normal VAT accounting. The VAT bill of £31,900 (£200,000 + £20,000 x scheme percentage of 14.5% for accountants) would definitely outweigh any other gains!

However, what are the issues if the horse has already bolted and you have a client who had a similar situation to Steve, perhaps sold a property last year and did not account for VAT through the flat rate scheme?

The good news is that HMRC accepts that the issue of 'proportionality' would be relevant, and they would almost certainly allow the business to withdraw from the scheme on a retrospective basis. Proportionality is a rule of EU law that embodies a basic principle of fairness, ie it is relevant when the application of the law goes beyond its intended objectives.

However, placing reliance on proportionality for the car sale can be risky, as HMRC could potentially argue that the flat rate percentages already take into account the fact that many businesses have some exempt income.

Bank interest excluded from flat rate scheme turnover

[8.13] HMRC has previously taken the view that bank interest earned on a business account is within the FRS because it is both exempt income and business related. However, this view was successfully challenged in the joined VAT tribunal case of *Fanfield Ltd and Thexton Training Ltd v Revenue and Customs Comrs* (TC00919) [2011] UKFTT 42 (TC).

Following the VAT tribunal case referred to in the previous paragraph, HMRC included the following statement in VAT Notes 3/2011:

'In the Tribunal cases of *Thexton Training Limited* and *Fanfield Limited* the ruling was that where the receipt of bank interest is derived from the taxable activity of a business:

- such interest is a relevant supply for the purposes of the FRS.

Conversely, where the receipt of bank interest is not a direct result of the taxable activity of a business:

- such interest falls outside the scope of VAT and is not a relevant supply.

This gives rise to the potentially confusing situation where FRS users will need to determine whether or not to include bank interest in their flat rate turnover. Therefore, HMRC has decided that, for simplification purposes, all FRS users can exclude interest from their flat rate turnover.'

Note – if your clients have declared FRS tax on bank interest received, you can go back four years and adjust as an overpayment on your next VAT return (assuming the tax involved is less than £10,000). HMRC has confirmed it is not appealing the outcome of the case.

International trade – included or excluded?

Selling goods and services outside the UK

[8.14]

Example 6

Steve has now produced accounts for a French business customer and charged a fee of £5,000. He has also sold the same customer a computer for £1,000. He has not charged VAT on either sale – what about the FRS?

Solution – Steve is correct to not charge VAT to his customer. The completion of the accounts represents a B2B (business to business) service covered by the general rule that applies since 1 January 2010, ie the place of supply is where the customer is based in France. So the French business customer will deal with VAT under the reverse charge procedures. The sale is outside the scope of UK VAT.

The sale of the computer is a sale of goods to another EU business, which is zero-rated as long as Steve shows the VAT number of the customer on his sales invoice and holds proof that the computer has left the UK. The French customer will again deal with the VAT on his own return by accounting for acquisition tax in Box 2.

With regard to the FRS, there is good and bad news. The good news is that the accountancy fee is excluded from the scheme calculation because the income is outside the scope of UK VAT. However, the sale of the goods is included because it is zero-rated.

Buying services from abroad

[8.15] If a UK business buys services from abroad, then no overseas VAT will be charged by the supplier in most cases – a UK customer (not using the FRS) then treats the expense as his own income and declares the reverse charge in Box 1 (output tax) and Box 4 (input tax) on his relevant VAT return. This approach assumes the business is not partly exempt and does not have an input tax restriction.

However, a positive outcome is that a business using the FRS does not have to increase its tax bill by accounting for output tax on the value of the services bought from abroad. These supplies should be dealt with outside of the FRS, ie they are excluded from flat rate turnover but recorded in boxes 1 and 4 of the VAT return, as under normal accounting. This produces a trading advantage compared to buying the same service from a UK supplier, where VAT would be paid to the supplier in most cases but without being able to claim input tax under the FRS.

(HMRC Notice 733, para 6.4).

Buying goods from another EU country

[8.16] The same outcome is not achieved if a business buys goods from a supplier based in another EU country. In such cases, the EU supplier does not charge VAT on the sale to the UK business because it has acquired the VAT registration number of the UK customer, ie the sale is zero-rated. However, the UK customer must account for acquisition tax at the standard rate of VAT in Box 2 of its relevant VAT return, even though it uses the FRS, but without being able to reclaim input tax in Box 4 of the same return. This produces an increase in the amount of VAT payable for the period by the scheme user but is a fair outcome because VAT would have been paid to a UK supplier if the same goods had been purchased in the UK.

(HMRC Notice 733, para 6.4).

FRS – potential savings

[8.17] As explained at **8.1**, HMRC is very keen to promote the time saving and administrative benefits of the FRS, rather than any potential tax savings for certain categories of business. However, the fact remains that the nature of the scheme and its calculations produce some winners and some losers. It is important to identify those clients who will benefit from using the scheme, and those clients who should avoid it at all costs because of the higher VAT bill they could encounter, ie as illustrated in Example 2.

In some cases (and this is the point that would be stressed by HMRC) it may be beneficial for a business to still use the scheme, even if it produces a slightly higher tax bill. For example, if a business finds the record-keeping requirements of normal VAT accounting very onerous, it may be prepared to enjoy the simplicity of the FRS even if there is a financial cost in terms of extra VAT to pay. If a business has been submitting late returns and incurring default surcharge penalties due to record-keeping problems, then the FRS will prove a winner if it avoids future penalties.

However, an adviser should be aware of the situations discussed at **8.18–8.22** when reviewing the VAT affairs of a client (and it is worthwhile to review the possible benefits of the scheme on an annual basis).

Making use of the flat rate percentage for activities not listed elsewhere

[8.18] One of the aims of the FRS is to ease administrative burdens for a small business. As a result of this aim, HMRC sensibly limited the total number of different categories within the scheme to 55. After all, it would be a minefield of bureaucracy if a small business owner had to go through a list of 500 different categories of business, all with different flat rate percentages, to see where he belonged.

As a result of the limit in the number of categories, there are two categories that can benefit certain businesses, and both enjoy a flat rate percentage of 12%:

- any other activity that is not listed elsewhere; and
- business services that are not listed elsewhere.

The above percentage is very favourable for any qualifying small business that has negligible input tax – see Example 7.

Example 7

James is VAT registered and considering the use of the FRS. The nature of his business means that all of his outputs are standard rated and he has negligible input tax to reclaim on his costs (total of £500 per year). His taxable sales are expected to be £149,000 per year excluding VAT.

An examination of the various categories under the FRS shows there is no specific category for the type of business being carried out by James, so he would qualify for the 12% rate as an activity that is not listed elsewhere. Is it worthwhile for James to adopt the FRS?

Solution – by adopting the scheme, James' annual VAT bill will be calculated as follows:

Gross turnover (£149,000 × 1.2) × 12% flat rate = £21,456

Under normal VAT accounting, his VAT bill would be:

Output tax (£149,000 × 20%) = £29,800

Input tax = £500

Payable = £29,300.

The net VAT saving to James is £7,844 per year, ie £29,300 less £21,456.

Note – the two reasons why the scheme produces such a good deal in this particular example is because the nature of the business means that James has very little input tax and also the activity he carries out does not have its own flat rate category and therefore can benefit from the generous flat rate of 12%. If James was newly VAT registered, he could save even more money in his first year of registration because of the extra 1% discount explained at **8.20**.

In reality, the nature of the global economy and the emphasis of the UK economy on service trades means that many business activities could fall into one of these two categories. Unless these businesses have a high amount of input tax, then the scheme should prove a winner.

Note – in reality, a taxpayer (or adviser) does not need to worry about the difference between the two 'sweep up' categories, ie whether it is providing a 'business service' or 'other activity' because both have the same flat rate percentage of 12%.

Businesses with more than one activity

[8.19] The rules of the FRS state that where a business has turnover generated from two or more activities, then the flat rate percentage applied should be the percentage appropriate to the main business activity as measured by turnover. This situation can also produce tax savings for certain categories of business – see Example 8.

Example 8

A business repairs cars (flat rate percentage 8.5%) and operates a mini cab taxi service (flat rate percentage 10%). The expected turnover for the business in the next 12 months is expected to be £110,000 net of VAT, £80,000 of which relates to repairing cars and £30,000 of which relates to providing taxi services. The business should apply the lower flat rate percentage of 8.5% to the VAT-inclusive turnover from both activities because repairing cars is the main activity as measured by turnover.

The situation in Example 8 could apply to many other businesses that have a core activity with a lower flat rate percentage, and a secondary activity that would be liable to a higher flat rate.

The flat rate scheme may be less appropriate if the core activity has the higher flat rate percentage, or if the balance between the parts of the business changes so that the activity with the higher flat rate percentage becomes the primary activity.

(HMRC Notice 733, paras 4.6 and 4.7).

1% extra saving in first year of VAT registration

[8.20] As explained in an earlier section, a 1% reduction in the relevant flat rate percentage is also given to a newly VAT registered business in its first year of VAT registration.

(HMRC Notice 733, para 4.5).

Example 9

JKL Accounting Services Ltd is a new business that achieved turnover of £125,000 in its first year (VAT exclusive) – it became VAT registered from day one, and applied the flat rate percentage for accountants of 14.5%. The company estimated that the flat rate scheme would not save any money compared to normal VAT accounting but would save administration time in preparing the quarterly returns (as explained above, saving of time is the key benefit publicised by HMRC).

At the end of the year, the company discovers that it should only have accounted for VAT at 13.5% of its gross income, due to the 1% discount in its first year of registration. This results in a VAT rebate of £1,500 (£125,000 plus VAT × 1%) – the FRS has now proved a financial winner for the company.

As an interesting aside, there may be cases where a business uses the FRS in its first year of trading but then decides that the loss of the 1% first year discount will not make it worthwhile to continue with the scheme thereafter. A plus point is that there is no minimum period where a business must stay in the scheme – it can leave voluntarily at the end of any VAT period, as long as written notification is made to HMRC. However, once it has withdrawn from the scheme it cannot rejoin for at least 12 months.

Flexible use of flat rate percentages

[8.21] As explained at **8.8,** one of the conditions of the FRS is that it is up to the taxpayer to identify which category he belongs to – and HMRC should not challenge this decision as long as the choice made was reasonable and records are kept as to why it was chosen. HMRC have published guidance in VAT Manual FRS7200 on the website.

In reality, any situation where decisions are based upon words and the interpretation of words means there may be different conclusions reached on the same situation by different people. In situations where the most appropriate category is not obvious it is important that tax advisers look very carefully at the flat rate percentages and record their reasons for choosing a particular category.

Construction industry

[8.22] As a final example on the benefits of the FRS, be aware that a construction business must choose between one of two FRS categories, depending on whether it is classed as a labour only builder or one that also supplies materials as part of its service. The labour only FRS percentage is 14.5%, compared to a FRS percentage of 9.5% for general building or construction services.

The decision as to which category to apply is helpfully clarified by the following sentence, which is included in the category of business at *reg 55K* of the *VAT Regulations 1995*:

'Labour-only building or construction services' means building or construction services where the value of materials supplied is less than 10 per cent of relevant turnover from such services; any other building or construction services are 'general building or construction services'.

If a business in the construction industry can show that its material costs are more than 10% of turnover, there is, potentially, a big saving of tax to be claimed by utilising the lower FRS percentage.

Completing VAT returns

[8.23] The following boxes need particular care when completing VAT returns for businesses that are using the flat rate scheme:

- Box 1
- Box 4
- Box 6
- Box 7

Each of the nine VAT return boxes should be treated as follows:

Box 1 – the figure to include in Box 1 will often just be the VAT due after applying the appropriate flat rate scheme percentage. However, box 1 should also include any VAT calculated in the normal way if any capital items have been sold on which input tax has been claimed (see **8.32**) and any VAT due on services subject to the reverse charge (see **8.15**).

Box 2 – Box 2 should include any VAT due on goods acquired from other EU countries (see **8.16**). Participation in the flat rate scheme does not affect how the Box 2 figure is calculated.

Box 3 – The Box 1 figure plus the Box 2 figure.

Box 4 – The figure to include in Box 4 will often be zero but input tax can be claimed on capital expenditure goods with a VAT-inclusive cost exceeding £2,000. Input tax can also be claimed in relation to stocks and assets on hand at the date of VAT registration and services subject to the reverse charge (see **8.1** and **8.15**). Claims for bad debt relief should also be included in Box 4 (see **8.35**).

Box 5 – The Box 3 figure minus the Box 4 figure.

Box 6 – Box 6 should include the VAT-inclusive turnover figure to which the appropriate flat rate scheme percentage is applied and the VAT-exclusive value of supplies accounted for outside of the flat rate scheme, for example supplies of capital items on which input tax has been claimed (see **8.32**).

Box 7 – As with Box 4, the figure to include in Box 7 will often be zero. However, Box 7 should include the VAT-exclusive cost of capital items on which input tax is being claimed and goods acquired from other EU countries.

Box 8 – The total value of goods supplied to other EU countries.

Participation in the flat rate scheme does not affect how the Box 8 figure is calculated.

Box 9 – The total value of goods acquired from other EU countries. Participation in the flat rate scheme does not affect how the Box 9 figure is calculated.

(HMRC Notice 733, para 7.5).

Example 10

Peter has been a VAT-registered self-employed photographer for many years. During the quarter ended 30 June he issued invoices for £10,000 plus VAT. In addition, he had rental income of £2,000 from a residential property that he lets out. He did not buy or sell any capital items and did not have any transactions with other EU countries. How should Peter complete Box 1 and Box 6 of his VAT return for the quarter?

Solution – Box 1 will show a figure of £1,540, being the flat rate percentage of 11% for photography applied to the Box 6 figure of £14,000. The Box 6 figure being the VAT-inclusive amount invoiced for photography services (£12,000) plus the exempt rental income (£2,000).

Incidentally, in the above example the following boxes should all show zero:

*   Box 2
*   Box 4
*   Box 7
*   Box 8
*   Box 9

(HMRC Notice 733, para 7.5).

Other matters

[8.24] The points below should also be taken into account when dealing with the scheme.

Basis of calculating turnover

[8.25] There are three methods that can be used to calculate turnover in a relevant period – the basic turnover method, the cash-based turnover method and the retailer's method. Once adopted, a method should normally be used for at least 12 months.

The *basic turnover* method will be based on sales made with a tax point in the relevant VAT period (ie date of invoice or receipt of payment, whichever happens sooner) and will usually be based on invoices raised. See Example 10.

The *cash-based turnover* method is based on supplies for which a business has been paid during a period and can benefit a business that gives extended credit terms to its customers. The basic rules of the cash-based turnover method are the same as for cash accounting.

The *retailer's turnover* method uses daily gross takings as the basis for calculating its sales value.

(HMRC Notice 733, para 6.1).

Disbursements

[8.26] A business that makes genuine disbursements on behalf of a client can exclude the value of these disbursements from the turnover calculation it makes under the scheme. An example of a genuine disbursement relates to MoT test fees recharged by a car repair business to his customer or a solicitor who invoices his customer for, eg stamp duty or land registry fees paid on his behalf in relation to a property deal.

However, a recharge of expenses for providing a service is not classed as a disbursement. See Example 11.

Example 11

Jane is a tax lecturer and charges £1,000 for giving a lecture in Edinburgh. She also charges her client £100 for her return rail fare and £100 for her overnight accommodation. How does she deal with the VAT?

Solution – Jane will charge 20% VAT on her total fee of £1,200. The total amount charged (£1,440 including VAT) is then the relevant figure for her FRS calculations. The rail fare and hotel expenses are not classed as disbursements.

Leaving the scheme

[8.27] Be aware that the limits for when a business must leave the scheme are higher than for the joining levels. This is a useful planning point for a growing business (*VAT Regulations 1995 (SI 1995/2518), reg 55(M)*). A flat rate trader ceases to be eligible to use the scheme when:

• at the anniversary date of when he joined the scheme, the total value of his income in the period of the year just ended was more than £230,000; or

- there are reasonable grounds to believe that the total value of his income in the next 30 days will exceed £230,000.

However, a trader does not need to leave the scheme if he can persuade HMRC that the total value of his income in the next 12 months will not exceed £191,500.

In considering the above limits, the sale of capital assets is ignored but VAT is included.

The following is an extract from HMRC Notice 733, para 11.2:

'What if the increase in my turnover is a one-off?'

If, when you do your annual check you find that your turnover has gone above the £230,000 limit but you expect that your turnover in the next year will fall below £191,500 in the next year, you may be able to remain on the scheme with our agreement. If you wish to remain on the scheme in those circumstances, apply in writing to:

National Registration Service

HM Revenue & Customs

Imperial House

77 Victoria Street

Grimsby

Lincolnshire

DN31 1DB.'

Backdated request to join the scheme

[8.28] A common question that is often asked is whether it is acceptable to backdate an application to join the FRS, ie to recalculate previous VAT liabilities using the scheme rather than normal VAT accounting. This question is obviously raised in relation to circumstances where the scheme produces an exceptionally good result for a taxpayer and he would like to extend these benefits on a historic basis.

The answer to this question is essentially 'no', even though the regulations (*VAT Regulations 1995, reg 55B(1)(b)*) authorise HMRC to allow traders to join the scheme on any date it approves, ie past, present or future. However, its policy is to only allow backdated entry 'in exceptional circumstances'.

Note – the argument of HMRC in this situation is that the aim of the scheme is to save time and administration for a small business, and this cannot be achieved if a VAT return has already been submitted for a period based on normal VAT accounting principles. According to the letter of the law, a business can join the FRS from the beginning of the next VAT period after its application to join has been received by HMRC but in practice HMRC allows a business to join from the beginning of the current VAT period, as long as the return in question has not already been submitted.

(HMRC Notice 733, para 5.5).

HMRC approach to the scheme

[8.29] A major concern for any taxpayer using the scheme would be if an HMRC officer made a routine VAT visit and told the taxpayer he had chosen the wrong flat rate percentage (too low) and he wanted to issue a retrospective assessment for the last four years. As explained above, the policy of HMRC is to not challenge a taxpayer's chosen flat rate category as long as the choice was made on a sensible and reasonable basis. This is the correct approach because the aim should be to encourage more users – not less.

As a separate comment, do not assume that HMRC's decision regarding a taxpayer's flat rate category is always final and correct. A tribunal case to support this statement is *Calibre TAS Ltd* (27 September 2007, unreported) (LON/07/594 20508).

The taxpayer's activity was to produce reports in personal injury cases, assessing the injured party's earnings potential before and after the injury.

The appellant joined the flat rate scheme on 1 April 2004 under the category of 'Business services that are not listed elsewhere' at 11%. However, HMRC strangely challenged this conclusion, and initially deemed the taxpayer to be a 'Lawyer' at 13%. HMRC subsequently changed its thinking so that he was classed as a 'Management consultant' at 12.5%.

The tribunal considered the definition of 'management consultancy' to broadly mean 'advice as to how a business should be run or restructured' – and concluded that the appellant did not provide such services. It agreed with the taxpayer's view that the 11% rate was correct for 'Business services that are not listed elsewhere' – and allowed the taxpayer's appeal with costs.

Associated business rules

[8.30] Be aware that the legislation prevents a business from joining the scheme if it is 'associated' with another business (or has been in the last 24 months). If a business already in the scheme becomes 'associated' with another business at any time in the future, then it must withdraw from the scheme at the time the association is formed.

However, not all connected business situations will produce a problem with the scheme. The relevant extract from HMRC's Notice 733, para 3.8 is as follows in relation to the definition of association:

- '• one business is under the dominant influence of another
- • two businesses are closely bound by financial, economic and organisational links
- • another company has the right to give directions to you
- • in practice your company habitually complies with the directions of another. The test here is a test of the commercial reality rather than of the legal form.'

The key phrase is 'closely bound by financial, economic and organisation links' – the key word being 'and' rather than 'or'. So a problem is only evident if all three links are established. See **5.3** for what HMRC consider to be relevant to each link.

However, to give some good news on this topic, para 3.9 of HMRC Notice 733 helpfully confirms that if a husband and wife are separately VAT registered in different types of business, they will not be 'associated'. This applies even if they share premises, as long as the costs are charged at a market rate between the two entities.

Note – the above restriction on associated businesses was confirmed in the tribunal case involving *R D F Management Services Ltd v Revenue and Customs Comrs* (TC00387) [2010] UKFTT 74 (TC). RDF was the only source of income for another company BBE Ltd (financial link), which was under common ownership of the same shareholder (organisational link) and each company benefited from the activities of the other (economic link). HMRC used their powers to terminate RDF's use of the scheme back to 5 October 2007 (when it first joined), producing a tax bill of £17,546 for the company. (HMRC Notice 733, para 3.8).

Insurance pitfall

[8.31] Imagine the following situation: your client who uses the FRS has suffered a fire at his office, and the cost of repairing all the damage is £10,000 plus £2,000 VAT. A claim is submitted to the insurance company to recover an amount of £12,000 – but is this correct?

The insurance company will only refund the net amount of a claim if an insured person is VAT registered and can reclaim input tax. So is it correct for a scheme user to reclaim £12,000 from the insurance company rather than £10,000 on the basis that input tax cannot be claimed?

The key point to recognise is that the various flat rate percentages take into account the input tax not being claimed by a business. So if a scheme user can benefit from both a reduced flat rate percentage and a VAT refund from his insurer in the event of a claim, this is technically producing a double VAT windfall.

It might be necessary to withdraw from the scheme to enable a full input tax reclaim on the repair damage (£2,000) as the insurance company is only likely to refund the net cost of £10,000. This option assumes a better result is obtained by claiming input tax than by sacrificing input tax on the repair costs and continuing to use the FRS.

Input tax on capital goods (£2,000 limit)

[8.32] A scheme user does not generally claim input tax, the main exception being in relation to capital goods costing at least £2,000 including VAT.

There is good news in relation to the £2,000 limit. HMRC has confirmed that the limit is met if two different assets are purchased at the same time from the same supplier on the same purchase invoice as long as the total invoice value in relation to capital goods exceeds £2,000.

Example 12

Three laptops are purchased by John at the same time from the same supplier on the same invoice, each costing £900 plus VAT. One of the laptops will be immediately sold for a profit and the other two will be used in his business as assets. He is VAT registered and uses the FRS. Can input tax be claimed on the computers?

Solution – the first laptop is not an asset. However, the other two computers will qualify for input tax deduction because the total amount on the invoice (£2,160 including VAT) exceeds £2,000.

Don't forget that input tax cannot be claimed on capital expenditure if it relates to services, eg building work. This was confirmed in the tribunal case (*March (Sally) v Revenue and Customs Comrs* (TC00062) [2009] UKFTT 94 (TC)) where VAT paid by a business that was building a new riding arena for a riding school did not qualify for an input tax claim within the scheme. This is because the supplies in question were of 'building services' rather than 'capital goods'. The bricks and materials bought in relation to the project were also excluded from any input tax claim.

(HMRC Notice 733, paras 15.4 and 15.5).

What if assets are bought to 'lease, let or hire'?

[8.33] Where capital goods are bought with the intention of generating income from them either directly (eg boats for hire on a boating lake) or indirectly (eg a company van used for deliveries during the week and hired out at weekends), then they are not capital expenditure goods no matter how much they cost.

(HMRC Notice 733, para 15.7).

Selling an asset when input tax has been claimed

[8.34] If input tax has been claimed on an asset, either because it was bought before the business joined the scheme, or because it qualified with the £2,000 limit, then the sale proceeds are excluded from the scheme calculations and the full amount of output tax charged on their sale is included in Box 1 of the VAT return in the normal way. This is reasonable because it ensures a business cannot gain a tax advantage by buying and selling an asset with different VAT rules.

(HMRC Notice 733, para 15.9).

Bad debt relief

[8.35] An interesting point about the flat rate scheme is that bad debt relief can be claimed on more VAT than has been paid to HMRC in the first place. This point is illustrated by Example 13 and Example 14.

Example 13

Sue provides secretarial services and calculates her flat rate scheme turnover using the basic turnover method (see 8.25). Sue paid VAT of £156 to HMRC in relation to an invoice for £1,000 plus VAT, having applied the appropriate percentage for secretarial services (13%) to the VAT inclusive amount invoiced (£1,200). The conditions for claiming bad debt relief have been met. How much bad debt relief can Sue claim?

Solution – the answer is that Sue can claim bad debt relief of £200 in Box 4 of her VAT return. It may seem odd that the claim for bad debt relief is £44 greater than the £156 Sue originally paid to HMRC. However, £44 is the difference between the VAT element of the payment she should have received from her client and the amount Sue originally paid to HMRC. In effect, Sue is being compensated for the input tax that she may have incurred providing the secretarial services but is unable to claim because she uses the flat rate scheme.

Example 14

Sid also provides secretarial services but calculates his flat rate scheme turnover using the cash-based turnover method (see 8.25). Sid has not paid any VAT to HMRC in relation to an invoice for £1,000 plus VAT because the invoice has not been paid. The conditions for claiming bad debt relief have been met. Can Sid claim bad debt relief when he has not paid HMRC any VAT in relation to the invoice?

Solution – the answer is that Sid can claim bad debt relief of £44 in Box 4 of his VAT return. It may seem odd that a claim for bad debt relief can be made when Sid has not paid any VAT to HMRC in relation to the invoice. However, like Sue, Sid is being compensated for the input tax that he may have incurred providing the secretarial services but is unable to claim because he uses the flat rate scheme.

(HMRC Notice 733, section 14).

Impact on the profit and loss account

[8.36] Using the flat rate scheme has an impact on the annual accounts and the direct tax position of the business. Direct tax is beyond the scope of this book but the following is an extract from HMRC Notice 733, para 7.8:

'It is expected that accounts for businesses who are using the scheme will be prepared using gross receipts, less the flat rate VAT percentage, for turnover and that expenses will include the irrecoverable input VAT.'

Planning points to consider

[8.37] The following planning points should be given consideration.

- Note that the FRS allows a business buying capital goods costing at least £2,000 including VAT to reclaim input tax on the purchase of the assets. There may be opportunities for a business to buy a slightly more expensive asset (eg upgraded computer) to exceed the £2,000 limit to benefit from the VAT saving.

- However, be aware that an input tax claim does not apply in relation to building projects, eg an office extension, because the supplies in such cases are of 'building services' rather than 'capital goods'. Input tax can only be claimed on capital expenditure goods costing at least £2,000.

- Be aware of the main disadvantage of the FRS – namely that the flat rate percentage needs to be applied to zero-rated and exempt sales. This could make the scheme very unattractive to taxpayers who have an unpredictable level of zero-rated sales, such as builders.

- Exempt income is included in the scheme calculations if it relates to the business, and this includes buy-to-let rental income and the sale of certain property assets as well (assuming the income is from the same legal entity as the VAT registered business). Withdrawal from the scheme might be the best option in certain situations when exempt income is a large amount of money.

- The FRS offers potential savings of tax to certain users. As with any scheme based on averages, there will always be winners and losers – and the examples given at **8.18–8.22** illustrate where a lot of money can be saved by using the scheme.

- Review a client's turnover on each anniversary date of joining the scheme. Even if a business has exceeded the VAT-inclusive turnover limit of £230,000 for leaving the scheme, there may be scope to remain within the scheme if HMRC is satisfied that the total business income in the next 12 months will be less than £191,500 including VAT.

- Review a client's chosen flat rate category on an annual basis to ensure it is still valid. This is particularly important for a business with two or more activities because the flat rate is based on the activity with the greater (greatest) percentage of turnover. If the secondary activity overtakes the main activity in terms of turnover, then this will become the relevant activity as far as the scheme is concerned.

- Remember that a business can benefit from an extra 1% discount on the relevant flat rate % in its first year of VAT registration. This could produce a considerable saving of tax in a 12-month period.

Appendix 8A — Trade Sectors and Flat Rate Percentages

The table below shows the trade sectors and flat rate percentages in alphabetical order that have applied since 4 January 2011 when the standard rate of VAT increased to 20%.

Trade sector	Flat rate percentage
Accountancy or book-keeping	14.5%
Advertising	11%
Agricultural services	11%
Any other activity not listed elsewhere	12%
Architect, civil and structural engineer or surveyor	14.5%
Boarding or care of animals	12%
Business services that are not listed elsewhere	12%
Catering services, including restaurants and takeaways	12.5%
Computer and IT consultancy or data processing	14.5%
Computer repair services	10.5%
Dealing in waste or scrap	10.5%
Entertainment or journalism	12.5%
Estate agency or property management services	12%
Farming or agriculture that is not listed elsewhere	6.5%
Film, radio, television or video production	13%
Financial services	13.5%
Forestry or fishing	10.5%
General building or construction services	
Note – Use 'General building' if the value of materials supplied is more than 10% of your turnover. If the value of the materials is less than this, use the 'Labour only' flat rate.	9.5%
Hairdressing or other beauty treatment services	13%
Hiring or renting goods	9.5%
Hotel or accommodation	10.5%
Investigation or security	12%
Labour-only building or construction services	
Note – Use 'Labour-only' if the value of materials supplied is less than 10% of your turnover. If the value of the materials is more than this, use the 'General building' flat rate.	14.5%
Laundry or dry-cleaning services	12%
Lawyer or legal services	14.5%
Library, archive, museum or other cultural activity	9.5%
Management consultancy	14%
Manufacturing food	9%
Manufacturing that is not listed elsewhere	9.5%
Manufacturing yarn, textiles or clothing	9%
Manufacturing fabricated metal products	10.5%
Membership organisation	8%
Mining or quarrying	10%
Packaging	9%

Trade sector	Flat rate percentage
Photography	11%
Post Offices	5%
Printing	8.5%
Pubs	6.5%
Publishing	11%
Real estate activity not listed elsewhere	14%
Repairing personal or household goods	10%
Repairing vehicles	8.5%
Retailing food, confectionery, tobacco, newspapers or children's clothing	4%
Retailing pharmaceuticals, medical goods, cosmetics or toiletries	8%
Retailing vehicles or fuel	6.5%
Retailing that is not listed elsewhere	7.5%
Secretarial services	13%
Social work	11%
Sport or recreation	8.5%
Transport or storage, including couriers, freight, removals and taxis	10%
Travel agency	10.5%
Veterinary medicine	11%
Wholesaling agricultural products	8%
Wholesaling food	7.5%
Wholesaling that is not listed elsewhere	8.5%

Chapter 9

Capital Goods Scheme

Key topics in this chapter:

- Situations when the capital goods scheme will apply.
- Capital expenditure that is included (and excluded) within the scheme.
- How to calculate the annual adjustments required by the capital goods scheme.
- New rules concerning non-business use of a capital asset since 1 January 2011.
- Ships and aircraft costing more than £50,000 have been included within the scheme since 1 January 2011.
- Rules effective from 1 January 2011 in relation to claiming input tax on a capital item that was owned before the business became VAT registered.
- Part disposals of a capital item must be adjusted after 1 January 2011, ie so that the remaining scheme intervals only apply to the part of the asset that remains in the business.
- Dealing with the sale of capital items before the end of the final adjustment period.
- The disposal test and rules for final adjustment periods after an asset has been sold.
- The requirement for the buyer of a business to take over the remaining intervals for capital items included within the scheme.
- Five or ten-year scheme intervals could be reduced after 1 January 2011 if owner's interest in the capital item is less than this period of time.

Introduction

[9.1] The capital goods scheme is intended to prevent a business from gaining an unfair rate of input tax recovery on its capital expenditure. The scheme applies to land and building capital expenditure exceeding £250,000 and computer assets exceeding £50,000 (both figures exclude VAT). Since 1 January 2011, the scheme has also been extended to include ships, boats and aircraft costing more than £50,000.

Basically, the scheme means that when considering input tax recovery on major capital expenditure, it is necessary to consider the use of the item over a five or ten-year period, not just at the time when a relevant asset is purchased.

In effect, input tax claimed on the initial purchase is, depending on the type of asset, adjusted over a five or ten-year period. The capital goods scheme is mainly relevant to businesses making some exempt or non-business supplies. If an asset is purchased and used wholly for taxable purposes in the five or ten-year adjustment period relevant to it, then the input tax deduction made when the asset was first purchased will not require any future adjustment.

Note – the five-year period applies to computer, aircraft or boat-related expenditure and ten years is relevant for land and building expenditure.

Capital goods scheme – relevant situations

[9.2] If a business only makes exempt supplies, then it will not be VAT registered because it is not making taxable supplies. In such cases, any VAT charged on the purchase of capital equipment becomes part of the cost of the equipment, ie the gross amount of the invoice is capitalised to the fixed asset account. A business only making exempt supplies has no opportunity to reclaim any input tax on its purchases.

If a business wholly makes taxable supplies, and no exempt or non-business supplies, then input tax can be fully reclaimed on the purchase of any capital equipment used for the business (with the exception of motor cars in most cases). If the business continues to make wholly taxable supplies over a five or ten-year period, then there will be no adjustment to make to the initial claim of input tax.

The scheme recognises that the use of an asset (for both taxable and exempt/non-business purposes) may fluctuate over time. The capital goods scheme is relevant where a business makes some exempt supplies and some taxable supplies (or non-business supplies) over the relevant adjustment period – see Example 1.

Example 1

ABC Ltd bought a freehold unit for £400,000 plus VAT to use for its taxable activity of providing accountancy and taxation services. At the time, it reclaimed all of the VAT as input tax on its VAT return.

Five years later, the company decided to move its accountancy and tax practice to a new location, and use the freehold unit to develop a new activity acting as insurance brokers (an exempt activity).

Solution – the initial purchase of the freehold unit is within the capital goods scheme (to confirm which items are included and which are excluded, see 9.3) so input tax needs to be reviewed and adjusted over a ten-year period as the expenditure relates to property.

In effect, the end result is that the company will recover only half of the input tax. This is because the building was used to make taxable supplies for five years and exempt supplies for five years. However, in terms of cash flow, the initial input tax would have been fully recovered, and then half of the input tax would have been paid back to HMRC in years six to ten (see **9.6** on how calculations are made under the scheme).

Items within the capital goods scheme

[9.3] The situation at Example 1 above illustrates why the capital goods scheme plays an important part in ensuring a 'fair' rate of input tax recovery on a major item of expenditure. Consider what would happen if, for example, there was no adjustment period, and that the change of use to the insurance brokers office took place after one year instead of five years.

In such a situation, the initial input tax would be reclaimed in full (as attributable to taxable supplies at the time of purchase) and no clawback of tax would be required after the change in activity. This would be commercially unfair to other insurance brokers not able to gain any input tax recovery.

This chapter deals specifically with the capital goods scheme. For the general clawback and payback provisions that apply when there is a change of intended use of goods or services, see **24.23**.

So what items are included within the capital goods scheme?

Basically, the following main categories of expenditure need to be taken into consideration (all quoted figures exclude VAT):

- a computer, or an item of computer equipment, costing £50,000 or more;
- ships, boats or other vessels costing £50,000 or more (since 1 January 2011);
- aircraft costing £50,000 or more (since 1 January 2011);
- land, a building or part of a building or civil engineering work or part of a civil engineering work where the value of the interest supplied to the owner is £250,000 or more (excluding any zero-rated or exempt elements);
- a building or civil engineering work (the latter since 1 January 2011) which the owner alters, or an extension to an annexe which he constructs, where the value of the work in connection with the alteration or extension is £250,000 or more (note – a condition concerning an extra 10% floor area being created in connection with an extension was withdrawn on 1 January 2011);
- a building or civil engineering work (the latter since 1 January 2011) which the owner refurbishes or fits out where the value of the expenditure on the taxable supplies of services and of 'goods affixed' to the building (excluding any zero-rated expenditure) is £250,000 or more. However, only capitalised expenditure is included – not repairs and maintenance costs charged to the profit and loss account. Note – the provision about 'goods affixed' to the building was also withdrawn on 1 January 2011. The key issue now is whether the expenditure is treated as capital for balance sheet purposes if it relates to the building project. This change is intended to simplify the scheme.

Since 1 January 2011, the relevant value of a capital project to identify if the £50,000 or £250,000 limit has been exceeded will also include the non-business element of a project as well. So a building project costing £300,000 will be in the scheme, even if there is 25% non-business use of the building, ie the business element is less than £250,000 (£300,000 x 75% = £225,000). It is the total cost that is relevant, ie £300,000 in this example. Until 31 December 2010, the relevant figure would have been £225,000 (business use) so the project would have been excluded from the capital goods scheme until this date.

There was an opportunity for owners of buildings costing less than £250,000 that used them to provide self-storage facilities to choose, by 31 March 2013, to treat their building as a capital item for the purpose of the capital goods scheme. An example would be a self-storage business (ie a business that provides customers with discrete areas of storage) that bought a building for £200,000 plus VAT in October 2011. At the time of purchase the business may have decided not to recover input tax on the basis that it intended to use the building to make exempt supplies. However, *Finance Act 2012* introduced a change to the VAT legislation so that, with effect from 1 October 2012, the business is treated as making a taxable supply of the grant of facilities for self-storage of goods. If the business was not able to choose to treat the building as a capital item for the purpose of the capital goods scheme it would be stuck with not having claimed any input tax and could be disadvantaged compared to a self-storage business that bought a more expensive building costing at least £250,000 plus VAT. This illustrates how the capital goods scheme can work to the taxpayer's advantage.

The opportunity referred to in the previous paragraph was helpful for self-storage businesses who had bought buildings costing less than £250,000 prior to the 1 October 2012 change to the VAT legislation.

Self-storage businesses buying buildings costing less than £250,000 after the 1 October 2012 change to the VAT legislation should be able to recover the input tax to the extent that the building is intended to be used in making a taxable supply of the grant of facilities for the self-storage of goods. Buildings costing more than £250,000 will be subject to the capital goods scheme rules explained in this chapter.

Capital expenditure for property

[9.4] In many cases, a property transaction will include the initial purchase of land, plus the construction of a building on the land in question. In such cases, the combination of the land and property costs form one capital project as far as the £250,000 limit is concerned. However, if the purchase price of the land was zero-rated or exempt (eg no option to tax election in place for the seller of the land), this cost would be excluded.

As far as the items classed as capital expenditure are concerned, this will include the following:

* taxable goods and services supplied in connection with the construction (but excluding zero-rated items);

- the interest in the land if the supply was taxable (other than zero-rated land);
- the costs of making the building ready for occupation including: professional and management services (eg architects, surveyors, site managers); demolition and site clearance costs; materials used in the course of construction; equipment hire; haulage; landscaping; services relevant to building and civil engineering work.

(HMRC Notice 706/2, para 4.7).

Tips to consider

[9.5] The above categories usually make it reasonably easy to identify if a project falls within the capital goods scheme. However, a few points need to be remembered.

- The scheme requires expenditure on computer equipment, aircraft and boats to be considered over a five-year period – all other expenditure over a ten-year period. This is known as the 'adjustment period'.
- With regard to computer equipment, the scheme only applies to individual computers, and items of computer equipment. It would not therefore include a computerised telephone exchange or any item of computer software.
- The purchase of 50 separate computers at £1,000 each would not be included within the scheme – even though the total value of the expenditure reaches the £50,000 limit. However, a new computer server costing £50,000 or more would be within the scheme.
- All values relevant to the capital goods scheme are VAT exclusive. So a new computer costing £52,000 including VAT would not be included.
- The capital goods scheme only applies to capital items purchased by the business – and not items that are purchased for resale. A business involved in selling computers would therefore exclude all goods bought for resale to customers.
- Work that is classed as 'civil engineering' relates to the everyday meaning of the term – including work on roads, bridges, golf courses, running tracks and installation of pipes for connection to main services.
- Be aware of the impact of a phased refurbishment. If it is clear that there is only one overall refurbishment contract, then this would be included within the capital goods scheme if the value of the expenditure exceeded £250,000. But if the refurbishments were carried out in very distinct parts and with distinct contracts (eg first floor refurbished in 2010; ground floor in 2011; second floor in 2012) then the value of each project would be taken in isolation. (HMRC Notice 706/2, para 4.12).
- There may be occasions during the life of an asset when it is not used by the business eg a computer that has broken down and needs major repair works. In such situations, calculations for the capital goods scheme are made as if the asset is still being used by the business.

Note – it is important to be clear about what actually constitutes capital expenditure. In basic terms, the VAT definition follows normal accounting principles. If the expenditure is capitalised to the balance sheet as a fixed asset addition, then it needs to be taken into account. In the case of computer equipment, the amount capitalised includes any delivery or installation costs.

To highlight the principles explained above, see Example 2.

Example 2

Alan is a VAT consultant for Kelly and Co accountants, and has four queries from clients as to whether their proposed projects fall within the capital goods scheme.

- Client A runs a large restaurant in a 10,000 square metre complex which he owns. He is planning to build a 1,500 square metre extension at a cost of £200,000 excluding VAT.
- Client B is to undertake a massive office refurbishment project costing £300,000 excluding VAT – analysed as follows: new windows and air conditioning system £170,000; new office furniture £130,000.
- Client C runs a carpet warehouse and intends to build a new car park on some land at the back of the building. The cost of the building works on the car park will be £260,000 including VAT.
- Client D has decided to install Sage Line 50 to all of its computers across the country – at a total cost of £60,000 excluding VAT.

The answer to the above queries is that none of them fall within the capital goods scheme!

- Although Client A is building an extension that adds more than 10% floor space to his existing premises (which was a relevant factor until 31 December 2010), the value of the project is less than £250,000. The project is not covered by the scheme.
- For Client B, the office furniture is not classed as building work – so this expenditure of £130,000 is not taken into account for the capital goods scheme – the balance of the expenditure on the windows and air conditioning is then under the £250,000 limit and is not within the scheme.
- Client C escapes the capital goods scheme because the VAT exclusive value of the project is less than £250,000.
- Client D has no worries because the expenditure is on computer software.

Calculation method for the scheme

[9.6] Having fully analysed the scope of the capital goods scheme, the next stage is to look at the calculations, and how these are carried out in practice. This paragraph assumes that the asset in question only has taxable and exempt use – **9.7** below considers changes introduced on 1 January 2011 if an item has non-business use as well. Since this date, the five or ten interval adjustments under the scheme take into account any change in non-business use of the asset as well as the change in taxable and exempt use. This is an important change, and particularly relevant for aircraft and boats where non-business use is likely to be an important aspect.

There are three key principles to consider:

* if an item of qualifying expenditure is wholly used by a business in making taxable supplies throughout the five or ten-year adjustment period relevant to the asset then there will be no adjustments to make. This is because the 100% taxable use would have produced a full input tax recovery on the initial expenditure – and as the asset continues to be used wholly for the taxable activities of the business, this 100% recovery continues to be correct;
* if an item of qualifying expenditure is wholly used by the business in making exempt supplies throughout the five or ten-year adjustment period relevant to the asset then there will again be no adjustments to make. This is because the initial purchase would not have recovered any input tax – and as the asset continues to be wholly used for the exempt part of the business, the 0% recovery rate continues to be correct;
* in effect, therefore, the only adjustment that needs to be made is if the item in question is used by the business for both taxable and exempt activities (or for private/non-business purposes in certain cases) where the extent of taxable, exempt or private/non-business use of the asset changes each year under the partial exemption method, or if there is a clear change of use at some time during the ten-year period – as in Example 1 at **9.2**.

The formula that should be used each year to make the necessary scheme calculations is as follows:

$$\frac{\text{Total input tax on the capital item}}{A} \times \text{the adjustment \%}$$

Where 'A' = number of adjustment years relevant to the asset, ie five for computer, aircraft or boat expenditure and ten for all land and buildings.

The adjustment % is the difference (if any) between the extent to which the item was used in making taxable supplies (taxable use) at the time of the initial purchase and the extent of such use in the period being adjusted.

A number of other key points need to be taken into account:

* the first interval under the five or ten-year interval period relates to the period from the date the item is bought up to the end of the partial exemption year of the business. In effect, this means up to 31 March, 30 April or 31 May – depending on when the VAT periods end;
* any adjustment of VAT payable or repayable under the scheme needs to be corrected on the second VAT return of the following tax year, ie the VAT return which incorporates 30 September for a business making quarterly returns (May for a business on monthly returns). So a business on calendar VAT quarters would make the capital goods scheme adjustment for the year ended 31 March 2015 on its September 2015 return. Any adjustment should be added to or deducted from Box 4.

(HMRC Notice 706/2, para 8.1).

Example 3

ABC Ltd (from Example 1) purchased a new computer server for its head office at a cost of £100,000 plus VAT on 1 October 2008 (when the standard rate of VAT was 17.5%).

The equipment will be used for the overall company business, ie relevant to both taxable supplies (accountancy and taxation services) and exempt supplies (insurance brokers). There is no non-business or private use of the asset.

The company is on the standard method for partial exemption purposes (input tax on residual expenditure apportioned according to the ratio of taxable income to total income, ie taxable plus exempt income) and has the following recovery rates for each of the tax years ending 31 March 2009 to 31 March 2013: 32%, 40%, 26%, 38%, 39%.

Solution – the first interval covers the period October 2008 to 31 March 2009 – producing an initial input tax recovery of £5,600 (ie £17,500 × 32%).

The taxable use has increased in the second interval from 32% to 40% – an additional 8%. Using the standard formula for the capital goods scheme, the additional input tax recovery for year ended 31 March 2010 will be: £17,500 × 8% divided by 5 = £280. This amount will be reclaimed in box 4 of the September 2010 return.

The taxable use in the third interval has decreased to 26% – and this will now produce a repayment to Customs of £210 on the September 2011 return, ie £17,500 × 6% divided by 5. In the final two intervals, additional amounts reclaimed will be £210 and £245.

Looking at the overall picture, the total input tax recovery on this item is as follows:

Year ended 31 March 2009	£5,600
Year ended 31 March 2010	£280
Year ended 31 March 2011	(£210)
Year ended 31 March 2012	£210
Year ended 31 March 2013	£245
Total recovery of tax	£6,125

Taking the average (mean) recovery rate for the five-year period, for example:

(32 + 40 + 26 + 38 + 39 divided by 5 = 35)

confirms the accuracy of our overall figure: £17,500 × 35% = £6,125.

This brings us back to the key overall principle of the capital goods scheme – which is fairness to both the taxpayer and HMRC. The capital goods scheme recognises that a business uses capital assets for the purpose of its business over a much longer period of time. For a business making both taxable and exempt supplies, the extent to which an asset will be used for making taxable supplies may fluctuate over time. The way that the scheme works is to iron out those fluctuations so that the extent of taxable use over the whole of the adjustment period is more accurately reflected. Without the scheme, a business could plan to purchase an affected asset at a time when the value of its taxable activities was very high. In accordance with the normal rules, the initial recovery of input tax would, correspondingly, also be high. If no further adjustments were required, the business could be at an unfair advantage over its competitors.

Non-business use – included since 1 January 2011

[9.7] Since 1 January 2011, recovery of input tax for certain assets has been limited to the extent to which the asset is used for business purposes. In effect, this means that the *Lennartz* mechanism (full input tax recovery at the time when an asset is purchased, with output tax declared over the life of the asset to reflect non-business or private use) was withdrawn for the following assets where there was some non-business or private use:

• land and property;
• ships, boats or other vessels;
• aircraft.

The change applies irrespective of the asset cost.

Since this date, ships, boats, other vessels and aircraft have been included in the capital goods scheme where they cost £50,000 or more – land and buildings costing more than £250,000 continue to be in the scheme as before, along with computer equipment costing more than £50,000.

As an important change to the scheme, the interval adjustments for all capital items purchased after 1 January 2011 must now reflect any change in the percentage of non-business use, as well as changes in taxable and exempt use. This works as follows:

Establishing taxable use

• *Step 1* – carry out a business/non-business use calculation at the time an asset is purchased, eg an aircraft will be used for 60% hirings and 40% private use of the directors – only 60% of the VAT is classed as input tax. The non-business calculation can be made using any method that is fair and reasonable.
• *Step 2* – how much of the input tax from Step 1 is to be used for taxable supplies rather than exempt purposes? If there is no exempt use, the answer will be 100% and this amount will be claimed on the VAT return relevant to the period when the asset is bought. If there is both exempt and taxable use, then the amount of input tax claimed will be based on the partial exemption method used by the business (usually the standard

---

> method where input tax recovery is based on the proportion of taxable income compared to taxable plus exempt income).

Interval adjustments over five or ten years

For assets purchased on or after 1 January 2011, the capital goods scheme adjustments will now include private/non-business use changes of the asset, as well as an adjustment for partial exemption purposes (the latter reflecting the change each year between taxable/exempt use of the asset). See Example 4.

Example 4

A business purchased a building for £1m plus £200,000 VAT on 1 February 2013. The building is to be used for 60% business purposes and 40% non-business purposes. The business use is for both exempt and taxable purposes, and for partial exemption year ending 31 March 2013, the standard method recovery percentage is 50% for residual input tax (ie costs relevant to both taxable and exempt activities). How much input tax will be initially reclaimed on the asset?

Solution – the input tax figure is £120,000, ie relevant to business use (£200,000 x 60% = £120,000). The property is used for both taxable and exempt purposes so the £120,000 input tax figure is classed as residual input tax for partial exemption purposes, ie £60,000 will be claimed on the March 2013 VAT return based on the standard method.

Note – in effect, 30% of the total VAT has been claimed by the business in its first interval within the capital goods scheme, ie £60,000 claimed out of total VAT charge of £200,000. The remaining nine intervals of the capital goods scheme will adjust this 30% figure (upwards or downwards) whereas until 31 December 2010, the adjustment would only have been based on the input tax relevant to business use.

Capital items purchased before VAT registration

[9.8] An unregistered business is able to claim input tax on goods (including stock) bought within the four-year period before its date of VAT registration, as long as the item is still held on the first day of VAT registration and is used for the purpose of the business (ie for taxable purposes). The claim is made on the first VAT return submitted by the business. In the case of services obtained before the date of VAT registration (including building services), the four-year period is reduced to six months.

In the case of a business making an option to tax election on a property, and then registering for VAT once the option had been made, there had, until 1 January 2011, been no legal opportunity to reclaim input tax on the property outside the four-year period (or six months in the case of building services).

However, a facility existed to allow some recovery of input tax in such cases, linked to a capital goods scheme type calculation. This facility was withdrawn for registrations effective from 1 January 2011.

However, new rules with legislative force took effect instead on 1 January 2011, with the intention of giving a fair and reasonable input tax recovery in relation to a taxpayer holding a capital goods scheme asset when they first register.

• Expenditure incurred on assets falling within the capital goods scheme will be brought into the scheme on the first day of registration if the total expenditure exceeds the relevant £50,000/£250,000 limit.
• When the business registers for VAT, one interval period will be taken away for each complete year that the asset was used by the business before its date of VAT registration. So if a qualifying property asset was purchased and first used by a business on 1 January 2011, and it registered for VAT on 1 March 2013, then the usual ten intervals will be reduced to eight, ie to reflect the passing of two complete years in the period before VAT registration.
  Note – in most cases, the first use of an asset will coincide with the time when it was first purchased. The exception would usually be if a property was purchased and then kept empty (unused) until a future date. First use cannot apply before input tax has been incurred on the asset, eg when buying a property
• The business will not have claimed any input tax on the capital asset while it was not VAT registered, so the baseline starting point for the capital goods scheme will be nil as far as input tax is concerned.
• The first interval will run from the date of first use to the day before the start of the tax year for the newly registered business, ie until 31 March, 30 April or 31 May depending on when VAT periods end. The legislation treats this as a subsequent interval and so any taxable use of the asset in this period will enable the business to make an adjustment in its favour. Because pre-registration use is accounted for by a (potential) decrease in the number of intervals, only use in the registration period needs to be taken into account in considering the first interval adjustment.
• The business then needs to monitor taxable use over remaining subsequent intervals, making adjustments in the normal way.

Note – the legislation above means that VAT on capital assets can no longer be claimed through the normal rules for claiming pre-registration input tax on the first VAT return submitted by a business.

See Example 5 (which is directly taken from section 13 of HMRC's Notice 706/2).

Example 5

A business purchased a building while it was unregistered for £250,000 and incurred VAT of £50,000 (assuming a 20% rate of VAT for simplicity). It first used the building on 1 October 2009. On 1 January 2011, it registers for VAT and its first tax year starts on 1 April 2011. It uses the building entirely for making taxable supplies after it registers for VAT.

The CGS period of adjustment for the building is ten intervals and the baseline recovery percentage is nil. However, as one complete year has elapsed between first use of the building and the date the business registered for VAT, the CGS period of adjustment is reduced by one to nine intervals. The first interval runs from 1 October 2009 to the day before the business's first VAT tax year which, in this example, is 31 March 2011. As the legislation treats this interval as a subsequent interval, the business needs to establish the recovery percentage for its first interval.

As the business only makes taxable supplies in the first interval, it is entitled to recover 100% of 50,000/10 = £5,000 in relation to the first interval. The definition of the first interval covers all the way back from first use but this simply sets the CGS running. As exempt pre-registration use is reflected by the number of intervals being reduced (in this case from ten to nine) that use does not need to be taken into account again in the first interval adjustment. So it is only the use while registered that is taken into account.

Assuming the building is used entirely for taxable purposes in subsequent intervals, the business will also be entitled to recover 100% of 50,000/10 = £5,000 in respect of the remaining eight intervals (as the period of adjustment has been reduced to 9 to reflect use of the asset when the business was unregistered).

Sale of capital items during the adjustment period

[9.9] The circumstances at Example 3 above assume that the asset in question is owned for the full five-year period relevant to the capital goods scheme for computer equipment costing more than £50,000. However, it is possible that the item could be sold before the five-year period has expired (ten years for buildings).

HMRC is often suspicious that complex VAT avoidance schemes could result in an unfair recovery of input tax. Anti-avoidance legislation is therefore in place through what is known as a 'disposal test'.

The basic rules for dealing with the sale of an asset during the adjustment period are as follows:

- for the interval period when the asset is sold, a normal calculation under the scheme is carried out, ie as if the asset was owned for the full period
- for the remaining complete intervals in the adjustment period, the input tax recovery will by 100% if the sale of the asset was a taxable supply (subject to the disposal test) and 0% if the sale of the asset was an exempt supply (ie as in certain property transactions). However, as well as the 'disposal test' (see **9.10**) another condition is that the value of the input tax recovered in the remaining complete intervals cannot exceed the output tax chargeable on the supply of the capital item.

(HMRC Notice 706/2, para 9.1).

The disposal test

[9.10] The disposal test is not applied to bona fide commercial transactions – and is only in place to prevent a partly exempt business such as a bank or an insurance company obtaining an unfair rate of input tax recovery through the disposal of a capital asset. This could occur if, for example, they made a significant exempt supply of a long lease of a property, followed immediately by the taxable disposal of the freehold for low consideration.

The basic rule of the disposal test (if it applies) is that the total amount of input tax reclaimed on the item (including the initial deduction in the first interval, and subsequent adjustments under the scheme) cannot exceed the output tax charged on the ultimate supply of the capital item.

(HMRC Notice 706/2, para 11.1).

However, the key point is that the disposal test only applies when HMRC considers a business is trying to gain an unjustified tax advantage. It will not be applied in the following circumstances:

- sales of computer equipment;
- where the owner sells an item at a loss due to the market conditions, eg a downturn in property prices;
- where the value of the capital item has depreciated (as would normally be the case with computers);
- where the value of the capital item is reduced for other legitimate reasons (eg discounted price for a quick sale);
- where the amount of output on disposal is less than the total input tax claimed only due to a reduction in the VAT rate; and
- where the item is used only for taxable (including zero-rated) purposes throughout the adjustment period (which includes the final disposal).

(HMRC Notice 706/2, para 11.2).

Dealing with part disposals of a capital item

[9.11] Until 1 January 2011, the capital goods scheme period of adjustment was only brought to an end when the owner sold his complete interest in the item. So if, for example, part of a refurbishment was destroyed in a fire, or part of a building was sold, then a business would in theory continue to apply scheme adjustments on all of the VAT incurred on the asset, including that element sold or destroyed.

The new law since 1 January 2011 means that a business must carry out a final adjustment in respect of the value of the part disposal, and only carry out future scheme adjustments on that part of the capital goods scheme asset that is still in existence or which it still owns. This change in law is intended to assist the process whereby a business gets a fair and reasonable recovery of input tax over the life of the asset, ie the main aim of the capital goods scheme.

If part of an asset is disposed by a transfer of a going concern (TOGC) arrangement, there has been no supply for VAT purposes (outside the scope of VAT if TOGC conditions are met – see Chapter 4) and no final adjustment is made for any remaining complete intervals in relation to the VAT on that part of the scheme asset that has been transferred. However, adjustments are still required in relation to that part of the scheme asset that is retained in accordance with the normal rules (even if related expenditure of the asset falls below the scheme threshold). If the part disposed is by TOGC, the scheme item is split into two parts and adjustments in relation to the element transferred will be continued by the transferee.

The application of the above principle is likely to be limited in practice so is not developed further.

Note – the disposal test has also been updated to deal with part disposals but will only apply in cases of avoidance or abuse.

(HMRC Information Sheet 06/11, section 7 which includes a worked practical example).

Sale of a capital item when a business is sold

[9.12] The proceeds from the sale of a business are usually outside the scope of VAT as long as certain important conditions are met (see Chapter 4 – Transfer of a Going Concern). However, the new owner must take over the responsibility for dealing with any remaining adjustment periods for assets subject to the capital goods scheme. In effect, the capital goods scheme does not cease to be relevant just because an asset has been transferred to a new owner.

To give an example, if Bill bought a property on 1 June 2008 which was subject to the capital goods scheme, and sold it to Ben as part of a business sale on 1 August 2013, the following outcome would apply.

*   Bill would have accounted for six annual adjustments within the capital goods scheme, ie the first interval period to 31 March 2009 (assuming he is on calendar VAT returns), followed by 4 annual adjustments to 31 March 2013, and a final adjustment from 1 April 2013 to 31 July 2013.
*   Ben takes over the remaining four interval periods (to complete the ten that are required for property transactions within the capital goods scheme), which must be made on the anniversary of when he bought the business, ie 1 August 2014 to 2017. He will still include any under or overpayment of tax on the second tax return after the end of his partial exemption year, ie the VAT return that includes 30 September (assuming he is on calendar VAT returns).

The outcome of the above arrangement is that Ben might need to pay additional tax to HMRC, or, if the calculations are favourable, claim some tax in the final four adjustment periods. He needs to be aware of this situation when he buys the business from Bill. The other priority is for Ben to ensure he acquires adequate records from Bill about the original transaction (date when asset was purchased, initial deduction of input tax, copy of purchase invoice etc) to support his calculations in the event of a VAT visit.

(HMRC Notice 706/2, section 9).

Period of adjustment linked to owner's interest

[9.13] The following change affects capital goods scheme assets for which the period of adjustment (under the old rules) had not started before 1 January 2011:

- in some cases, an owner's interest in a scheme asset lasts for less than ten years (land and buildings) or five years (computers, aircraft, boats etc). Until 31 December 2010, five or ten interval adjustments were still required through the capital goods scheme;
- from 1 January 2011, the number of scheme intervals will be capped at the length of the owner's interest in the asset plus one year if this figure is less than five or ten. This change only applies if the difference between the length of the owner's interest and the five or ten-year period is greater than one. The minimum number of intervals must still be three. See Example 6.

Note – the aim of this change is to ensure that a business gets a fair and reasonable recovery of input tax over the period it uses the asset rather than the standard five or ten-year limit that normally applies with the capital goods scheme.

Example 6

A business acquires a seven-year interest in a building that falls within the capital goods scheme (ie purchase price exceeding £250,000 excluding VAT). The number of capital goods scheme intervals for a building is ten years but the number will reduce to eight in this situation, ie seven years plus one year = eight years. This situation applies because ten exceeds seven by more than one.

Note – the denominator part of the fraction used for the scheme adjustments will change from ten to eight in this example.

Planning points to consider

[9.14] The following planning points should be given consideration.

- It is important that tax advisers do not see the capital goods scheme as a threat – by recommending to clients that they deliberately try to keep projected capital expenditure below the £50,000 and £250,000 limits. In the case of a partly exempt business that expects to increase its level of taxable activities in the future, any expenditure on assets relevant to taxable and exempt supplies will actually produce a tax advantage by being within the scheme.

- Remember, the key aim of the scheme is 'fairness' – so if the final calculations indicate that a business with 90% exempt income has somehow managed to reclaim 50% of the input tax on a capital item, then there is likely to be an error in the computations.

- Although a business is only obliged to keep records for six years, it is important to ensure that records relating to a capital goods scheme item are kept for the full ten-year period (if the item relates to property).

- Be aware of the 'disposal test' to ensure that there is no unfair input tax recovery on assets that are sold by a partly exempt business before the end of the adjustment period.

- Remember, a business that wholly makes taxable supplies over a five or ten-year period (ie no exempt or non-business supplies) will not be affected by the scheme calculations. This is because it will reclaim 100% of the input tax on the initial purchase of the asset (subject to normal rules) and will not have any need to amend this percentage because the exclusive taxable use continues over the relevant five or ten-year period.

- Annual adjustments are always declared on the second VAT return following the end of the tax year (ie the return which includes 30 September for a business on calendar quarterly returns). This is different to the annual adjustment for partial exemption, which is either declared on the return at the end of the tax year (31 March, 30 April or 31 May) or the first return of the new tax year.

- Individual computers purchased with a total value exceeding £50,000 are excluded from the capital goods scheme. It is only relevant if one item of equipment is being bought worth more than £50,000. Expenditure on computer software is also excluded from the scheme.

- Do not forget that the new owner must take over the responsibility for any remaining scheme calculations of the seller in the event of a business sale (transfer of a going concern). It is important that the buyer is given adequate records from the seller to ensure accurate calculations can be carried out.

- Be aware of rules that took effect on 1 January 2011 that apply to capital assets owned by a business before it became VAT registered (these rules are mainly relevant in the case of property assets). The method of claiming input tax is intended to reflect taxable use of the asset after the period when the business became VAT registered.

- Since 1 January 2011, scheme calculations also take into account changes in the percentage of non-business use of a capital item, as well as changes in exempt or taxable use. This change will mainly affect some charitable and educational establishments.

- Private use factors are also included in the scheme adjustments as 'non-business' (eg a director using a company aircraft at weekends for his social purposes). This situation recognises the fact that the *Lennartz* accounting method was withdrawn in the UK on 1 January 2011 for aircraft and boats so input tax apportionment (rather than full input tax recovery and output tax on private use accounted for over the life of the asset) is the only available option from this date.

Chapter 10

Retail Schemes and Second-hand Margin Schemes

Key topics in this chapter:

- The five different retail schemes approved by HMRC that can be used by a retail business that is registered for VAT.
- The rules and potential problems of each of the five different retail schemes.
- A practical example of each of the five different schemes – looking at situations when a scheme can produce a higher/ lower tax bill for certain types of business.
- Calculation of daily gross takings for a retail business.
- The rules for issuing less detailed tax invoices (value less than £250).
- Procedures concerning second-hand margin schemes – available to traders dealing in second-hand goods.

Introduction

[10.1] There are certain businesses that are allowed to calculate their output tax using a special method approved by HMRC – the main example being retailers. It would be very difficult for a retailer dealing mainly in small cash transactions to issue a tax invoice for every sale – a retailer is therefore allowed to use one of five different retail schemes.

Equally, many businesses that deal in second-hand goods (eg car traders, antique dealers) would be at a disadvantage under normal VAT accounting rules (ie output tax due on full value of supply) because most of the goods they purchase are bought from the general public, that is, there is no source of input tax to reclaim. In such cases, VAT would cease to be a margin tax and become a sales tax – but this situation is assisted by second-hand schemes for these types of traders.

Retail schemes

Introduction

[10.2] The aim of a retail scheme is to enable a retailer to calculate his output tax liability in a simple, cost effective manner. If the retailer only sells goods at one rate of tax, then his output tax position is very simple but it becomes more complicated if he sells goods at different rates of tax. See Example 1.

Example 1

Jones is a clothes retailer and has two shops in the local High Street. The first shop sells women's clothes; the second shop sells a mixture of women's and girls' clothing.

On 15 July, the gross takings from the first shop were £2,400; the sales of the second shop were £3,250.

What is the position of the two shops as far as output tax is concerned?

Solution – there is no problem with the output tax position of the first shop because all goods are being sold at one rate of tax, ie standard rated for adult clothing. The output tax liability with a 20% rate of VAT will be: £2,400 × 1/6 = £400.

Note – 1/6 is the fraction relevant to a VAT rate of 20%.

However, there is a problem for the second shop because some of the sales are standard rated (adult clothing) and some sales will be zero-rated as children's clothing. A special method of calculation will be needed to establish how much of the £3,250 is zero-rated and how much is standard rated – this objective will be achieved by the business adopting one of the five retail schemes published by HMRC – see 10.3.

As far as HMRC is concerned, it is content for a retailer to choose his own preferred scheme (as long as he is eligible) – the choice will often depend on the extent of computer technology available to him and how comfortable he is using this technology. Equally, however, the retailer may prefer a particular scheme due to a potential tax saving with its operation.

As with many VAT issues, HMRC has the power to refuse the use of a particular retail scheme in the following circumstances:

- if the use of a particular scheme does not produce a fair and reasonable result;
- it is necessary to do so for the protection of the revenue, ie to safeguard the tax yield;
- the retailer could reasonably be expected to account for VAT in the normal way.

Note – the condition about a scheme producing a fair and reasonable result does not mean that HMRC will direct the trader to adopt the scheme that produces the largest output tax liability. It means the method chosen must, objectively, give a sensible overall calculation as far as output tax is concerned.

Five approved retail schemes

[10.3] A business with annual VAT exclusive turnover exceeding £130m (£100m until 31 March 2009) is only eligible to use a retail scheme if it agrees a bespoke scheme with HMRC.

There are five different schemes that are available to a business with turnover less than £130m as follows:

* Point of Sale Scheme – see **10.4**;
* Apportionment Scheme 1 – see **10.6**;
* Apportionment Scheme 2 – see **10.9**;
* Direct Calculation Scheme 1 – see **10.12**;
* Direct Calculation Scheme 2 – see **10.15**;

To assist with the understanding of each scheme, we will consider three points in each case:

(a)   the rules that apply;
(b)   types of business that may wish to use the scheme and potential problems; and
(c)   a worked example of each scheme.

Point of Sale Scheme

Rules

[10.4] The rules of the scheme are as follows:

* this is the only scheme that can be adopted if all sales are standard rated or all sales are only taxable at the reduced rate;
* the turnover limit is £130m (£100m until 31 March 2009) excluding VAT;
* it can be used for services as well as goods, eg catering activities;
* there is no need to work out stock values at the end of a period or expected selling prices;
* no annual adjustment is required;
* the VAT liability of supplies needs to be correctly identifiable at the point of sale – usually with a multi-button till, electronic till or bar-coding system. These supplies could be zero-rated, standard rated, exempt or subject to VAT at the reduced rate – the correct VAT liability needs to be identified when the sale is made. See Example 2 below.

(HMRC Notice 727/3; HMRC Notice 727, paras 3.4 and 3.5).

Types of business

[10.5] The types of business that could use the scheme and potential problems are as follows:

* the scheme is simple to use and would therefore benefit users who want to simplify their VAT affairs as much as possible;

- the scheme largely relies on electronic tills that could be expensive to purchase. It is also important that staff are able to correctly operate these tills;
- as long as the tills and staff operating them are effective, the scheme gives a very accurate declaration of output tax due on goods or services supplied by a business;
- for a multi-button till system, lack of experience or knowledge by a member(s) of staff could prove costly for the business if staff members incorrectly classify zero-rated items as standard rated;
- to counter the above problem, a simple system of having, for instance, a different coloured price sticker for zero-rated goods, could help reduce errors made at the checkout.

Example 2

Smith Chemists sell a range of goods that are subject to VAT at standard rate, zero-rate and the reduced rate of VAT. A multi-button till is used to identify the VAT liability at the point of sale. All staff using the till are well trained on the VAT treatment of specific products.

The daily gross takings for the business in the VAT quarter ended 31 May are as follows:

Standard-rated sales	£32,385
Zero-rated sales	£14,265
Reduced rate sales	£2,485

What is the output tax liability for the business?

Solution – output tax for the period is:

$(£32,385 \times 1/6) + (£2,485 \times 1/21) = £5,397.50 + £118.33 = £5,515.83$.

Note – the main products sold by a chemist that are subject to the reduced rate of VAT are contraceptive products and smoking cessation products.

Apportionment Scheme 1

Rules

[10.6] The rules of the scheme are as follows:

- an annual turnover limit (VAT exclusive) of £1m;
- the scheme requires a business to calculate the proportion of purchases in each VAT period that are bought at different rates of VAT – these different proportions are then applied to the sales made by the business in the same period to calculate output tax;
- an annual adjustment is required with the scheme – up to the end of March, April or May each year depending on the date that coincides with the end of the VAT period;

- the scheme cannot be used for supplies of services;
- the scheme does not require stock valuations or calculations of expected selling prices.

Types of business

[10.7] The type of business that could use Apportionment Scheme 1 and potential problems are as follows:

- the scheme is suitable for a small business that does not have electronic equipment or suitable methods of identifying the correct VAT liability at the point of sale;
- all sales made by a business can be entered at the point of sale without being concerned about the rate of VAT that applies to the goods in question;
- the scheme cannot be used for a business selling services – these sales will need to be recorded separately outside of the retail scheme;
- the main disadvantage of the scheme is that because it is based on purchases, it will produce a higher tax bill (compared to a point of sale scheme) for a business that achieves a higher mark-up on zero-rated goods. This is an important point for a business such as a confectioner, tobacconist and newsagent where a higher mark-up is achieved on newspapers (zero-rated) compared to cigarettes (standard rated).

See Example 3 below.

Calculating output tax

[10.8] The following is an illustration of how to calculate output tax with the scheme.

For each VAT period (quarterly or monthly):

Step 1	Add up daily gross takings =	A
Step 2	Add up the cost, including VAT, of all goods received for resale at the standard rate =	B
Step 3	Add up the cost, including VAT, of all goods received for resale at the reduced rate =	C
Step 4	Add up the cost, including VAT, of all goods received for resale at standard, reduced and zero-rates =	D
Step 5	Calculate the proportion of daily gross takings from sales at the standard rate by dividing the total at Step 2 by the total at Step 4 and multiplying by the total in Step 1	
Step 6	Calculate the proportion of daily gross takings from sales at the reduced rate by dividing the total at Step 3 by the total at Step 4 and multiplying by the total in Step 1	

Step 7   To calculate output tax, add the total at Step 5 multiplied by the VAT fraction for standard-rated goods to the total at Step 6 multiplied by the VAT fraction for reduced rate goods

In algebraic form (based on standard rate of 20% and reduced rate of 5%):

Output tax = ((B divided by D) x A x 1/6) + ((C divided by D) x A x 1/21).

Example 3

Janet sells newspapers and cigarettes and has decided to use Apportionment Scheme 1 as far as calculating her output tax liability is concerned. For quarter ended 30 June, the total purchases of newspapers were £8,000 and cigarettes £12,000 plus VAT.

The daily gross takings of the business for the period were £28,000 including VAT. What is Janet's output tax liability?

As a separate point, Janet estimates that her newspaper sales for the period were £12,000. Is Apportionment Scheme 1 the most appropriate retail scheme for her to use? Would she be better advised to invest in a multi-button till and adopt the Point of Sale Scheme?

Solution – the proportion of standard-rated purchases is (£12,000 + VAT) divided by (£12,000 + VAT + £8,000). It is important to note that the standard-rated proportions include VAT because the calculations are being applied to a daily gross takings figure that also includes VAT.

The proportion of standard-rated goods (64.29%, ie £14,400 divided by £22,400) gives an output tax liability as follows:

£28,000 × 64.29% × 1/6 = £3,000.20.

The next question is to consider whether the Point of Sale Scheme would give a better result. In principle, the answer is likely to be yes, because the mark-up achieved on newspapers is always higher than that achieved on cigarettes – and Apportionment Scheme 1 rarely (if ever) produces a favourable outcome where a higher mark-up is achieved on zero-rated goods.

If Janet estimates that her newspaper sales in the period are £12,000, this means her cigarette sales would be £16,000 (£28,000 gross takings less £12,000 for newspaper sales), giving an output tax liability of £2,666.67 (£16,000 × 1/6). This is a saving of £333.53 compared to Apportionment Scheme 1.

Note – remember that Janet will also need to do an annual adjustment with Apportionment Scheme 1.

Apportionment Scheme 2

Rules

[10.9] The rules of the scheme are as follows:

- the taxable turnover is less than £130m excluding VAT (£100m until 31 March 2009);
- supplies must be made at two different rates of VAT;
- the scheme is based on calculating expected selling prices of goods either used from stock or purchased during a period;
- supplies of services (eg catering) must be dealt with outside the scheme;
- no annual adjustment is required but a rolling calculation method is used;
- a stocktake is required at the beginning of the scheme being used, but not thereafter.

Types of business

[10.10] The types of business that could use Apportionment Scheme 2 and the potential problems are as follows:

- the scheme will provide a more accurate calculation of output tax compared to Apportionment Scheme 1 because it is based on selling rather than purchase prices – and output tax is a tax on sales;
- the scheme can be complex to operate – especially in the early stages when opening stock valuations need to be included;
- an example of a business that could benefit from using the scheme is the newspaper/cigarette sales business highlighted in Example 3, ie with a higher mark-up on zero rated goods. A business with a higher mark-up on zero-rated goods will enjoy the benefits of the scheme because the expected selling prices form the basis of the output tax calculation.

See Example 4 below.

Calculating output tax

[10.11] The following are illustrations of how to calculate output tax with the scheme.

(a) **For the first three quarterly VAT periods or the first 11 monthly VAT periods:**

Step 1	Calculate the expected selling price, including VAT, of standard-rated goods for retail sale in stock at the commencement of using the scheme =	A
Step 2	Calculate the expected selling price, including VAT, of reduced rated goods in stock for retail sale at the commencement of using the scheme =	B
Step 3	Calculate the expected selling price, including VAT, of all goods in stock for retail sale at the commencement of using the scheme (ie including zero-rated goods) =	C
Step 4	Add up daily gross takings for the VAT period =	D
Step 5	Add up expected selling prices, including VAT, of standard-rated goods:	
	(i) received, made or grown for retail sale since starting to use the scheme; and	

(ii)   acquired from other EC countries since starting to use the
       scheme =   E

Step 6   Add the total in Step 5 to the total in Step 1

Step 7   Add up expected selling prices, including VAT, of reduced rated
            goods:

            (i)   received, made or grown for retail sale since starting to use
                   the scheme; and

            (ii)   acquired from other EC countries since starting to use the
                   scheme =   F

Step 8   Add the total in Step 7 to the total in Step 2

Step 9   Add up expected selling prices, including VAT, of all goods (stan-
            dard rated, reduced rated and zero-rated):

            (i)   received, made or grown for retail sale since starting to use
                   the scheme; and

            (ii)   acquired from other EC countries since starting to use the
                   scheme =   G

Step 10   Add the total in Step 9 to the total in Step 3

Step 11   Calculate the proportion of gross takings from sales at the standard
            rate by dividing the total at Step 6 by the total at Step 10 and mul-
            tiplying by the total at Step 4

Step 12   Calculate the proportion of gross takings from sales at the reduced
            rate by dividing the total at Step 8 by the total at Step 10 and mul-
            tiplying by the total at Step 4

Step 13   To calculate output tax, add the total at Step 11 multiplied by the
            VAT fraction for standard-rated goods to the total at Step 12 multi-
            plied by the VAT fraction for reduced rated goods

In algebraic form, output tax (based on standard-rate of 20% and reduced rate
of 5%) is:

$((A + E)$ divided by $(C + G) \times D \times 1/6) + ((B + F)$ divided by $(C + G) \times D \times 1/21)$.

**(b) For the fourth and all later quarterly VAT periods or the twelfth and all later monthly
VAT periods:**

Step A   Add up daily gross takings for the VAT period =   H

Step B   Add up expected selling prices, including VAT, of standard-rated
            goods:
            (i)   received, made or grown for retail sale; and

            (ii)   acquired from other EC countries in the current VAT period
                   and the previous three quarterly (or 11 monthly) VAT peri-
                   ods =   J

Step C   Add up expected selling prices, including VAT, of reduced rated
            goods
            (i)   received, made or grown for retail sale; and

(ii) acquired from other EC countries in the current VAT period and the previous three quarterly (or eleven monthly) VAT periods =   K

Step D Add up expected selling prices, including VAT, of all goods standard rated, reduced rated and zero-rated)

(i) received, made or grown for retail sale; and

(ii) acquired from other EC countries in the current VAT period and the previous three quarterly (or 11 monthly) VAT periods =   L

Step E Calculate the proportion of gross takings from sales at the standard rate by dividing the total at Step B by the total at Step D and multiplying by the total in Step A

Step F Calculate the proportion of gross takings from sales at the reduced rated by dividing the total at Step C by the total at Step D and multiplying by the total at Step A

Step G To calculate output tax, add the total at Step E multiplied by the VAT fraction for standard-rated goods to the total at Step F multiplied by the VAT fraction for reduced rated goods

In algebraic form, output tax (based on standard-rate of 20% and reduced rate of 5%) is:

(J divided by L x H x 1/6) + (K divided by L x H x 1/21).

Example 4

John is a clothes retailer and has been using Apportionment Scheme 2 for many years.

He is about to complete his VAT return for period ended 30 June, and has extracted the following key figures from his records:

*   expected sales of standard-rated goods purchased during the last four quarters up to 30 June – £360,000 including VAT;
*   expected sales of all goods purchased during last four quarters up to 30 June – £450,000;
*   daily gross takings for period – £300,000.

What is John's output tax liability using Apportionment Scheme 2?

Solution – the proportion of expected standard-rated sales (based on goods purchased for the last four quarters) is £360,000 divided by £450,000 (ie 80% to two decimal places).

If this proportion is applied to daily gross takings for the period, the output tax liability is as follows:

£350,000/£450,000 x £300,000 × 1/6 = £40,000.

Direct Calculation Scheme 1

Rules

[10.12] The rules of the scheme are as follows:

- the annual VAT exclusive turnover must not exceed £1m;
- identify the rate of VAT which is in the minority for the business, eg if 70% of sales made by the business are standard-rated and 30% of sales are zero-rated, the minority rate of tax is zero-rated;
- calculate the expected selling price of minority rate goods bought during the VAT period in question;
- supplies of services with the same VAT liability as the minority goods must be dealt with outside the scheme;
- any supplies of catering must be dealt with outside the scheme;
- no annual adjustment or stocktaking is required.

Types of business

[10.13] The types of business that could use the Direct Calculation Scheme 1 and the potential problems are as follows:

- the scheme is fairly simple to operate and could benefit a business that has, for example, a very small volume of sales at one particular rate of VAT (eg 99% of sales are standard-rated and 1% of sales are zero-rated). In such cases, it would not be worthwhile for the business to invest in electronic equipment to identify the VAT liability at the point of sale or to carry out some of the detailed computations involved with the other schemes;
- there is scope for the scheme to be based on the mark-up of the 'majority' goods rather than the minority goods if this is easier to calculate. For example, a business mainly selling newspapers may find it easier to mark-up these goods (because the paperwork may be easier to handle) than for tobacco/confectionery items which could have been bought through multiple small transactions;
- the main problem with the use of the scheme would be if the expected selling prices are not calculated correctly. If, for example, the mark-up on zero-rated goods is overstated, then the output tax paid by the business will be too low.

Calculating output tax

[10.14] If the minority goods are zero-rated, then output tax will be calculated by deducting the expected selling prices of zero-rated items from the daily gross takings figure for the period. Output tax will then be due at 1/6 of the remaining figure if the rate of VAT is 20% (this assumes the business does not have any reduced rate or exempt supplies).

If the minority goods are standard rated, then the daily gross takings figure becomes irrelevant. This is because output tax will be due on 1/6 of the expected selling price of standard-rated goods (this again assumes the business does not have any reduced rate supplies). See Example 5 below.

It is important to note that the scheme will also allow the majority item to be marked up where this is easier to calculate.

Example 5

Jill is VAT registered and trades as a sports retail shop. All sales are standard rated with the exception of books on fitness, which are zero-rated as printed matter.

Her gross takings for the VAT period ending 30 June were £23,000 including VAT. She bought 50 fitness books during the quarter for £5 each – she applies a 50% mark up to each book that is purchased.

What is Jill's output tax for this period using Direct Calculation Scheme 1 (based on a VAT rate of 20%)?

Solution – the expected selling price of the books (minority goods) is £375, ie cost price of £250 plus mark up of 50%.

This gives an output tax liability of: £23,000 less £375 × 1/6 = £3,770.83.

Note – in effect, the tax saving for Jill is only £62.50 (£375 × 1/6) compared to the situation where she treated all sales as standard rated. In effect, there is little incentive for her to spend resources on electronic tills or point of sale training just for the VAT benefits.

Direct Calculation Scheme 2

Rules

[**10.15**] Exactly the same rules as for Direct Calculation Scheme 1 (see **10.12**), apart from the fact that it can be used by a business with annual sales of between £1m and £130m. There is also a requirement to carry out an annual stock-take adjustment.

(HMRC Notice 727/5, para 3.5).

Types of business

[**10.16**] The scheme could produce benefits compared to Direct Calculation Scheme 1 where the minority goods are standard rated, and these goods are slow moving as far as stock turnover is concerned. In these cases, the scheme delays paying output tax on these goods until they are sold – instead of the period when they were purchased.

Calculating output tax

[**10.17**] How to calculate output tax with the Direct Calculation Scheme 2:

* for each VAT period, the same rules apply as for Direct Calculation Scheme 1;

- an annual adjustment is required after the fourth quarter in which the scheme is used (and annually thereafter) which takes into account the opening and closing stock values of the minority rate goods. The calculation made applies a mark-up to the cost of goods sold by the business (ie opening stock *plus* purchases *minus* closing stock) rather than the goods purchased by the business during the year;
- the difference in output tax identified in the fourth quarter (compared to the four quarterly calculations) will produce either an under or overpayment of tax. This difference should be adjusted on this return.

See Example 6.

Example 6

Jean sells children's clothes as a retailer (zero-rated). Her only standard-rated supplies relate to the sale of wardrobes. Each wardrobe is purchased for £1,000 plus VAT and sells for £2,000 plus VAT. Jean has been using the Direct Calculation Scheme 2 for many years.

For year ended 30 June 2015 the quantity of wardrobes she purchased was as follows:

Opening stock 1 July 2014	15
Quarter ended 30 September 2014	12
Quarter ended 31 December 2014	30
Quarter ended 31 March 2015	10
Quarter ended 30 June 2015	18
Closing stock 30 June 2015	35

What is the output tax position for Jean using Direct Calculation Scheme 2 compared to Direct Calculation Scheme 1?

Solution – under Direct Calculation Scheme 1, Jean would account for output tax on the expected selling prices of goods purchased during the four periods in question: £2,000 × 70 wardrobes × 20% = £28,000

Under Direct Calculation Scheme 2, the output tax liability will be based on the actual quantity of wardrobes sold, ie adjusting for opening and closing stock. The annual adjustment calculation will be made on the June 2015 return.

The total output tax declared in the four quarters (including the annual adjustment) will be as follows:

£2,000 × 50 wardrobes sold x 20% = £20,000.

Note – 50 wardrobes sold equates to opening stock of 15 wardrobes plus 70 wardrobes bought during the year less 35 wardrobes held in stock at 30 June 2015. In reality, the output tax saving for Jean with Direct Calculation Scheme 2 is due to the fact that she has not yet accounted for tax on the stock increase of wardrobes that was evident during the year (ie 20 additional wardrobes in stock x £2,000 x 20% = £8,000).

Other issues for retailers

Tax invoices

[10.18] A retailer makes most or all of his sales to the general public, and does not therefore have an obligation to issue a tax invoice for every sale that is made. However, he should issue an invoice if requested by a customer – it could be that the customer is buying, for example, stationery items from a retail outlet and wants to reclaim input tax on his own VAT return.

When a retailer is asked for an invoice, there are two options available to him.

Less detailed tax invoice

[10.19] If the value of the sale is £250 or less, and provided the supply is not to a person in another EU country, a VAT invoice only needs to record the following details:

- the name, address and VAT registration number of the retailer;
- the date of the sale;
- a description to identify the goods or services sold;
- the gross amount of the sale (ie including VAT);
- for each rate of VAT chargeable, the gross amount payable including VAT, and the rate of VAT that applies.

Modified tax invoice

[10.20] This invoice is very similar to a full tax invoice, but the main difference is that it only shows the VAT inclusive price of each standard rated or reduced rated supply rather than the VAT exclusive price, ie £120 including VAT rather than £100 + £20 VAT.

Note – there is no £250 limit for a modified tax invoice – but it can only be issued with the agreement of the customer.

Daily gross takings

[10.21] The key challenge for any retailer is to be able to accurately record his daily gross takings. It is not acceptable for him to just record a weekly or monthly takings total – takings must be recorded on a daily basis.

HMRC considers retailers to be high risk in terms of a potential tax loss because of the emphasis on cash transactions. But there are other issues to consider as far as recording takings are concerned – see Example 7.

(HMRC Notice 727, paras 4.4 and 4.6).

Example 7

Janet is the owner of the White Horse pub in Bournemouth. The cash in her till (adjusting for float) at the end of the day's trading is £350. However, she is unsure about how to deal with the following issues as far as VAT is concerned:

- A member of staff stole £50 of cash from the till – she has now been sacked.
- The window cleaner was paid £20 cash from the till for cleaning the pub windows.
- Janet enjoys a drink herself and consumed four glasses of wine without paying for them – the retail selling price of a glass of wine is £3 and the cost price is £1.50.

Solution – remember the basic definition of VAT, ie a tax on the 'supply of goods or services'. This means the £70 cash removed from the till (illegally in the case of the staff member) relates to sales that have already taken place. The amount of £70 should therefore be included in the takings figure.

Sales to the business owner also need to be included because a supply of goods has again taken place (even though no money has been exchanged). However, the good news for Janet is that she only needs to account for output tax on the cost price of the goods, ie £1.50 x 4 glasses = £6.

The total daily gross takings figure for VAT purposes is therefore £426 (£350+£50+£20+£6).

Flat rate scheme

[10.22] The flat rate scheme (FRS) is available to a business with annual taxable sales of less than £150,000 (excluding VAT) and essentially means that VAT payable on a return is calculated by applying a specific flat rate percentage to the gross sales made by a business. This is in contrast to the usual method of VAT accounting, ie VAT payable = output tax *minus* input tax. A full analysis of the scheme is given in Chapter 8.

Although the aim of the FRS is to simplify VAT accounting, it can save a lot of tax for certain types of business. There is no problem with a retailer adopting the FRS and here is an example of a significant tax saving for a retailer.

Example 8

Steve sells ice-creams, chocolates and cans of drink from a small kiosk on Blackpool beach – all of his sales are standard rated. His only overheads are the rent of the kiosk and staff costs, ie no input tax to reclaim.

His figures for the VAT quarter ended 31 March (all relevant to 20% VAT) are as follows:

- Sales including VAT – £36,000 (ie £30,000 plus VAT of £6,000);
- Cost of goods for resale – £15,000 plus VAT of £3,000 = £18,000 (ie 50% gross profit being achieved).

Should Steve use the FRS to calculate his VAT rather than a retail scheme?

Solution – Steve's business qualifies for a very generous flat rate percentage of 4% – 'Retailing food, confectionery, tobacco, newspapers or children's clothing'.

Under normal VAT accounting, his annual VAT bill will be £3,000 (£6,000 output tax less £3,000 input tax). With the flat rate scheme his bill will be £1,440 (£36,000 x 4%) – a big saving of £1,560 for the period.

Final points

[10.23] In concluding this section, a few other points should be noted as far as VAT and retail sales are concerned:

- VAT Notice 727 is the main source of information published by HMRC as far as retail schemes are concerned. The notice has the force of law and considers each of the five different retail schemes in detail;
- where a business has both retail and non-retail sales, a retail scheme can only be used for the retail sales. VAT on the non-retail sales must be accounted for outside the scheme in the normal way;
- there is no problem with a retailer using the annual accounting scheme if his yearly sales are less than £1.35m excluding VAT (see Chapter 7);
- the Court of Justice recently confirmed (in the case of *Dixons Retail plc v Revenue and Customs Comrs: Case C-494/12* [2014] STC 375, ECJ that a retailer must account for VAT on the income it receives in a case where the customer has used a stolen credit card for the purchase. The Court considered that there has still been a supply of goods for consideration and that VAT is payable.

Margin schemes for second-hand goods

Introduction

[10.24] The basic rule of VAT is that output tax is due on the full value of goods sold by a business (unless the goods are specifically zero-rated, exempt or subject to the reduced rate of VAT).

However, there are special schemes in place that reduce the output tax liability on goods sold by certain businesses – through what is known as a second-hand margin scheme.

The following traders can apply a margin scheme:

- motor vehicle dealers;
- businesses trading in works of art, antiques or collectors' items;
- second-hand goods dealers;
- traders who obtain goods in their own name, but are acting as an agent, in relation to a supply.

Note – the following HMRC notices have useful information regarding schemes:

- Notice 718 – The VAT Margin Scheme and global accounting;
- Notice 718/1 – The VAT Margin Scheme on second-hand cars and other vehicles;

- Notice 718/2 – VAT Auctioneers' scheme (a variation on the VAT Margin Scheme).

How a margin scheme works

[10.25] Under a margin scheme, VAT is accounted for on the difference between the purchase price and the selling price of eligible goods in each VAT period. In effect, output tax is being declared on the 'profit margin' – if no profit is made, then no VAT is payable. The seller's margin is not revealed to the buyer.

The VAT registration test for a trader dealing in margin goods is still based on the gross value of his sales, and the record keeping requirements for a business using a margin scheme are very strict. If these requirements cannot be met, then a business could be ineligible to use a second-hand scheme and would then have to account for output tax on the full value of a sale in the normal way.

As a separate point, the scheme cannot be used for any goods that have been purchased on a VAT invoice on which input tax is recoverable. However, input tax incurred on expenditure to improve the item can be reclaimed in the normal way, eg an antique dealer paying a fee to a restorer to renovate an item can reclaim input tax on the charges made by the restorer. However, the cost of the restoration cannot be added to the purchase price of the item under the margin scheme.

For an illustration of a typical margin scheme transaction for a car dealer, see Example 9 below.

Example 9

Local Motors purchases a second-hand car from a member of the public for £2,000. An amount of £500 plus VAT is paid to a local repair firm to re-spray the car, and then £100 plus VAT is paid to a valet company to clean the interior. The car is then sold to another member of the public for £3,000.

What is the VAT position based on a VAT rate of 20%?

Solution – Local Motors must ensure they keep proper records concerning the buying and selling of this vehicle, and record the car in a proper stock book giving full details of, eg registration number, date of purchase/sale etc.

The input tax on the repair/valeting charges can be reclaimed in Box 4 of the relevant return in the normal way.

The margin made by the business on the sale is £1,000 (ie £3,000 less £2,000) and this margin is treated as VAT inclusive. An output tax liability of £166.67 must be included in Box 1 of the relevant return, ie £1,000 × 1/6 (assuming a VAT rate of 20%).

Conditions of the scheme

[10.26] HMRC has very strict rules in place to ensure that the benefits of the scheme are not misused:

- When buying goods from a private person or unregistered dealer, the buyer must make out a purchase invoice showing the seller's name and address, the date of the transaction, the total price paid for the goods, the invoice and stock book number and a description of the goods (including any unique identification, eg vehicle registration number).
- A stock book with the full details of each item bought and sold by the business must be kept.
- When selling goods, a sales invoice should be raised for the customer. The invoice should record details of the stock book number, date of sale, description of the goods (including any unique identification number, eg vehicle registration number) and total price including VAT.
- The sales invoice should be noted along the lines of:

    'This is a second-hand margin scheme supply'.

    In effect, this is confirmation to the customer that the goods have been accounted for under the margin scheme.
- The customer must be given the invoice for his retention – the seller must retain a copy and also update his stock book so that the margin on the deal can be properly calculated.

The conditions of the margin scheme have the force of law. Therefore, if HMRC is not satisfied with the standard of record-keeping, it has the power to assess output tax on the full selling price of the goods. The exercise of this power would be disastrous for any business using the scheme, so the importance of accurate accounting should be stressed to all clients.

As a general point, the quality of accounting under the margin scheme is often dependent on the standard of the stock book maintained by each particular business. For example, in the case of an antique shop, it is important that items are fully described – the phrase 'antique table' is not particularly useful if the shop has 50 different tables in stock!

(HMRC Notice 718, para 2.3 and section 5).

Information in a stock book

Purchase details

[10.27]

- stock number in numerical sequence;
- date of purchase;
- purchase invoice number;
- name of seller (ie the person from whom the item is purchased);
- any unique identification number (eg car registration);
- description of the goods (eg type, make or model).

Sales details

- date of sale;
- sales invoice number;
- name of buyer (ie the person to whom the item is sold).

Accounting details

- purchase price;
- selling price or other method of disposal;
- margin on sale;
- VAT due.

The purchase price must be the price shown on the invoice that has been agreed between the buyer and seller. It must not be altered. Separate entries must be made where a bulk purchase of a number of items is made and where the items are to be sold separately.

(HMRC Notice 718, para 5.2).

Goods sold at a loss or nil profit

[10.28] A common mistake made by many businesses using the margin scheme is to add up all of the selling prices of goods sold in a VAT period to give a total selling price; they then enter the purchase prices against each item and add this list of figures up to give a total purchase price; they then account for output tax on the difference between the two figures.

The above approach sounds logical but the mistake being made is that the margin is effectively being reduced by any loss that is made on an item. The rule as far as the scheme is concerned is that no output tax is due on a loss – but the loss cannot be offset against profits made on other items. This principle is illustrated by Example 10.

Example 10

Daphne is registered for VAT selling antique furniture and accounts for output tax using the margin scheme. She has made only two sales for the VAT period ending 31 May – one at a loss of £2,000 and the other at a profit of £1,500.

Solution – although Daphne has made an overall loss of £500 (£2,000 less £1,500), she still has an output tax liability of £250 on the item sold at a profit (£1,500 x 1/6). There is no scope to reduce this liability against the second item. In effect, Daphne's trading loss for the period is now £750 (ie the loss of £500 plus the output tax of £250 she must now pay).

As a final point, if an item is sold at a nil profit (ie selling price equals purchase price) then no output tax liability exists on the sale if the margin scheme is being used.

Completing a VAT return

[10.29] The completion of the VAT return for a business using the margin scheme follows similar principles as for any other trader:

Box 1 (output tax) – records the output tax payable on the margin.

Box 4 (input tax) – this figure will be nil as far as goods purchased under the scheme are concerned – but would include input tax incurred by the business on expenses and overheads.

Box 6 (outputs) – records the total selling price, less output tax accounted for on the margin.

Box 7 (inputs) – records the purchase price paid for the goods.

(HMRC Notice 718, para 5.4).

Sales to other EU businesses

[10.30] VAT often becomes interesting when two different aspects of the system overlap into one transaction. Consider the following example.

Example 11

Jeff is registered for VAT in the UK and has bought an antique table for £2,000 from a private individual in Birmingham. The table is now being sold to an antique dealer who is registered for VAT in Holland. The selling price is £5,000. What is the best option as far as VAT is concerned?

Solution – the margin scheme is available throughout the EU, so the antique dealer in Holland will probably be keen to acquire the goods under the margin scheme himself. This means that he can resell the goods in Holland and only account for output tax on his own profit margin.

The alternative situation would be for the goods to be excluded from the margin scheme and be treated as a normal sale of goods. This means that Jeff will zero-rate the supply of goods to the Dutch customer (as long as he shows the customer's VAT number on his invoice and obtains proof that the goods left the UK) – the latter must then account for acquisition tax in Box 2 of his own VAT return in Holland, based on the standard rate of VAT in Holland). He will then reclaim input tax in Box 4 of his return (same amount) but he will then have to account for output tax on the full selling price of the item when it is eventually sold.

The conclusion is that the margin scheme is a good result for the Dutch customer – but normal accounting outside of the margin scheme is a good result for Jeff because he has no output tax liability on his supply (through zero-rating the goods as a sale to a VAT registered business in another EU country).

(HMRC Notice 718, para 7.3).

Global Accounting

[10.31] At this point, a few readers may be thinking of the administrative nightmare of the margin scheme for clients who sell a high volume of goods at very low selling prices. For example, think of a business that trades in second-hand thimbles, buying thimbles from car boot sales and then selling them on to members of the public. The paperwork involved in each transaction would be very cumbersome, for example, having to fill in a purchase and sales invoice every time a £1.50 thimble is sold!

In this situation, a business can adopt what is known as Global Accounting which allows accounting for output tax on the total margin made during a VAT period, ie not on an item by item basis.

Again, HMRC imposes very strict rules about which businesses are eligible to use Global Accounting – not least because any business adopting the scheme is gaining automatic VAT relief on items sold at a loss.

The principal rules for the scheme are as follows:

- every individual item for which the scheme is used must have been obtained for a price of £500 or less;
- the goods were not purchased on an invoice on which VAT was shown separately;
- the goods are not sold on a VAT invoice or similar document showing an amount as being VAT or as being attributable to VAT;
- records and accounts are kept as specified by HMRC;
- the scheme cannot be used for sales of motor vehicles; motor cycles; aircraft; boats and outboard motors; caravans and motor caravans; horses and ponies.

In the case of motor vehicles, there is scope to use Global Accounting if the vehicle is broken up and individual components are sold as scrap (as long as no individual component is valued at more than £500).

Note – when a business first starts to use Global Accounting, it must calculate an opening stock figure that will be counted as purchases in its first VAT period. The basis of the stock valuation should be as accurate as possible. A closing stock adjustment will be needed on the final VAT return if a business ceases to use the scheme.

(HMRC Notice 718, sections 14 and 15).

Horses and ponies

[10.32] As a final point, it is very common for the margin scheme to be used for trading in horses and ponies. The scheme will not apply to the sale of a horse that the trader has bred himself – simply because it is not classed as second-hand at this point in time.

The values of deals for horses and ponies can be significant – so the British Equestrian Trade Association is a good point of contact for any assistance. The Association has even produced forms that can be used for individual transactions covered by the scheme – very useful to ensure HMRC's conditions are properly met.

(HMRC Notice 718, section 16).

Planning points to consider

[**10.33**] The following planning points should be given consideration in relation to retail or margin schemes:

- A business may need to justify to HMRC why it cannot adopt a Point of Sale retail scheme by, for example, using a multi-buttoned till. The Point of Sale scheme should give the most reliable output tax calculation because the VAT liability is based on actual sales made by the business.

- Each retail scheme has potential benefits as well as potential problems for users. For example, a Point of Sale method using a multi-button till will only be accurate if the staff operating the till know how to determine the VAT position for each sale. Proper staff training is an important issue.

- Apportionment Scheme 1 avoids the need to identify the VAT liability at the point of sale. However, it is only available to businesses with annual VAT exclusive sales of less than £1m, and can produce a higher than usual tax bill for a business that has a higher mark-up on zero-rated goods.

- It is important to remember that most retail schemes need to exclude the value of services provided by a business – or non-retail sales. These supplies should be accounted for outside of the scheme.

- Apportionment Scheme 2 calculates output tax using expected selling prices – so will deal with the problem mentioned above with Apportionment Scheme 1, ie where there is a higher mark-up made by the business on its zero-rated goods.

- Direct Calculation Scheme 2 could benefit a business that has slow moving stock of minority standard-rated items. This is because the scheme makes an annual adjustment for stock so that output tax is not actually paid until the goods are sold. Direct Calculation Scheme 1 produces an output tax liability in the period that the goods are purchased.

- Remember that some smaller retailers could benefit from using the flat rate scheme if their annual taxable sales are less than £150,000 excluding VAT. The scheme produces winners and losers in terms of VAT payments – see Example 8 in this chapter which highlights a winning outcome.

- Second-hand margin schemes are very worthwhile for businesses dealing in second-hand goods. However, it is important to ensure the record keeping requirements of HMRC are fully met, otherwise it could base output tax on the full selling price of an item rather than the profit margin.

- To avoid common mistakes when operating margin scheme calculations, consider the following precautions:
  - ensure that any losses made on items are not netted off for VAT purposes against items on which a profit has been made.
  - Remember that the value of the margin cannot be reduced by any expenditure incurred to improve the condition of the item (eg restoration fees for an antique trader) but input tax can be reclaimed on such expenditure subject to the normal rules.

- A business selling high quantities of small value items could benefit from using Global Accounting – the main benefits of which relate to the reduced record-keeping requirements (compared to the main margin scheme) and the automatic loss relief available on items sold at a loss.

Chapter 11

Imports (and Acquisitions)

Key topics in this chapter:

- The difference between imports (goods brought into the UK from non-EU countries) and acquisitions (goods brought into the UK from other EU countries) and practical examples to show the VAT treatment in each case.
- Administration issues relevant to VAT on imported goods.
- The benefits of having a duty deferment account and the forms to complete to obtain an account.
- The benefits of using Simplified Import VAT Accounting (SIVA) to reduce the level of bank guarantees required for a business with a deferment account.
- Evidence needed by importers to reclaim input tax on their VAT returns (C79 certificates).
- Procedures for dealing with postal imports.
- Goods imported into the UK that are not subject to VAT, eg zero-rated goods, consignments with a value of less than £15.
- Removal of Low Value Consignment Relief (LCVR) from all goods imported into the UK from the Channel Islands from 1 April 2012.
- The requirement for certain businesses to complete additional declarations regarding EU transactions through the system known as Intrastat.
- The possibility of an unregistered business having to register for VAT if the value of its acquisitions exceeds the registration limits during the course of a calendar year.
- Deciding whether the importation of computer software represents an import of goods or services for VAT purposes.

Introduction

[11.1] For VAT purposes, the rules are different according to whether the goods are arriving from an EU or non-EU country:

- *imports* – only goods arriving from non-EU countries are classed as imports;
- *acquisitions* – goods arriving from EU countries are known as 'acquisitions' and it is important to be clear about which countries are in the EU (the Channel Islands are not part of the EU for VAT purposes).

(HMRC Notice 702, para 1.1).

Imports

[11.2] VAT is charged and payable at the point when the goods enter the UK – either at the port, airport, or other boundary point. The VAT payable on the goods is charged at the same rate as if the goods were supplied in the UK. This means, for example, that zero-rated goods, eg children's clothes will be imported without VAT – although there could be customs duty chargeable on the goods. As long as the goods are used by the importer for the purpose of making taxable supplies (which will usually be the case because most imported goods will be sold in the UK as an onward supply), then the VAT paid at the time of importation can be reclaimed as input tax. The usual evidence for claiming input tax is import VAT certificate C79.

Note – input tax deduction on imports is subject to the usual rules that apply for domestic purchases, eg input tax cannot be claimed on a motor car available for private use.

(HMRC Notice 702, para 2.3).

Acquisitions

[11.3] Goods bought from a VAT registered trader in another EU country will be 'acquired' without VAT being charged by either the supplier or HMRC at the point when the goods enter the UK. The EU supplier is allowed to zero-rate his supply as long as he obtains the VAT registration number of his UK customer and records this on his sales invoice. However, the UK customer is then required to account for the output tax of the supplier by making a declaration in Box 2 of his VAT return. This declaration is based on the value of the goods being imported, multiplied by the rate of UK VAT applicable to those goods. However, the UK customer now has a source of input tax that he can reclaim in Box 4 of the same VAT return, assuming the goods are used for taxable supplies. There is a neutral VAT effect with the above entries in most cases.

(HMRC Notice 725, section 7).

VAT on imports and acquisitions

[11.4] The rules in many situations regarding VAT and imports can be quite complicated, for example, for issues such as temporary imports and goods to be repaired in the UK etc. The aim of this chapter is to consider only the main practical points concerning VAT on the importation of goods, which will be relevant to the vast majority of import transactions.

To clarify the principles explained above, see Examples 1 and 2 to illustrate the different VAT treatment of goods entering the UK from an EU and non-EU country.

Example 1

John is registered for VAT in the UK – his main activity is to import plant pots and sell them to garden centres throughout the north of England. He has bought 500 plant pots for £10 each from a Belgian supplier (EU) and has given the supplier his UK VAT number.

What is the VAT position?

Solution – as the Belgian supplier now holds John's UK VAT registration number, he can invoice John for the plant pots without charging Belgian VAT. This is because the deal is between traders in two different countries within the EU. However, the Belgian supplier must retain evidence that the goods have left Belgium in case a VAT officer in Belgium queries the invoice.

John must account for VAT in Box 2 of his VAT return relevant to the supply (£5,000 × 20% = £1,000) but he can reclaim the same amount of VAT as input tax in Box 4 of his return because he is using the goods to make a taxable supply. John must also include the net value of the purchase in Box 7 of his VAT return (ie the inputs value) and also in Box 9 of the return (for acquisitions from the EU). When he sells the goods in the UK, output tax will be declared in Box 1 of his return in the normal way, with the net value of the sale recorded in Box 6.

Example 2

John, from Example 1, has imported 500 special plant pots at a cost of £20 each from a supplier in Hong Kong (outside the EU). The pots will attract Customs duty of £10 each when they arrive in the UK.

What is the VAT position?

Solution – VAT is charged and payable on the importation of goods into the UK – and the VAT is charged on the value of the goods, including customs duty. The total amount of VAT charged on the importation is £3,000 (500 × £30 (£20 cost plus £10 duty) × 20%) and John can reclaim this amount in Box 4 of his next VAT return, supported by a C79 certificate as evidence of VAT payment. No entry is needed in Box 9 of the return because the purchase is not an acquisition of goods from another EU country.

(HMRC Notice 702, para 3.1).

Overall, therefore, the purchase of goods from another EU country is fairly simple, however, more procedures are relevant to goods purchased from outside the EU. The following points are relevant to import transactions:

(a)   goods imported from abroad are declared to Customs using the Single Administrative Document (SAD) (Form C88). Import VAT is dealt with in the same way as customs duty;

(b)   the import declaration must normally be accompanied by a declaration of value on Form C105, C105A, C105B or C109 as appropriate;

(c)   unless the goods are placed under excise warehousing or a specified customs arrangement, then VAT must normally either be paid at the time of importation or be deferred if the importer or his agent have been approved for deferment – see **11.5**;

(d)   any VAT-registered business that imports goods or exports goods outside the EU will need to acquire an EORI (Economic Operator Registration and Identification) number. The starting point is to complete application form C220.

Deferment of VAT

[11.5] Ordinarily, import VAT is payable at the point when the goods arrive at the UK border. However, HMRC allows an importer to delay paying import VAT at the time the goods arrive in the UK providing he holds a Deferment Approval Number (DAN). An agent who enters goods for an importer or owner may also use the deferment scheme.

The two main benefits for a business having a deferment account are:

(a)   cash flow is improved by the delay in payment; and
(b)   the process of importation is not delayed whilst payment of VAT and duty are arranged.

The key procedures for a deferment arrangement are as follows:

*   charges deferred (including VAT, customs and excise duties) during a calendar month must be paid by the importer on the 15th day of the following month – payment to be made by BACS rather than cheque or cash. Form C1202 needs to be completed by the applicant to set up an appropriate direct debit arrangement with the applicant's bank;
*   in order to set up a deferment arrangement, an importer must obtain a guarantee from his bank (or other approved lender) that the amounts deferred will be covered by the bank, up to a certain limit;
*   the form to complete to apply for a deferment arrangement is Form C1200 – the form to be completed in order to guarantee payment of sums to HMRC is Form C1201;
*   an agent making an entry can request deferment against his principal's approval number provided he is authorised to do so. This can either be executed through completion of Form C1207N or, if relevant to a 'one-off' consignment of goods, by completing Form C1207S;
*   HMRC sends out 'periodic deferment statements' on a weekly basis, summarising the deferments made for the relevant period. The statement will also show the total amount of tax deferred in the month to date.

Note – deferment statements cannot be used as evidence for input tax deduction – see **11.7**.

If the tax due on imported goods during a particular period exceeds the deferment limit of the importer, then he must pay the additional tax due at the point of import.

A business wishing to apply for a deferment number – or raise any other query on this subject should contact:

HM Revenue & Customs
Central Deferment Office
6th Floor NW
Alexander House
21 Victoria Avenue
Southend-on-Sea
Essex
SS99 1AA

(HMRC Notice 702, para 2.2).

Simplified import VAT accounting (SIVA)

[11.6] The deferment system explained at **11.5** can cause problems for certain businesses trying to get a sufficient level of guarantee from their bank to cover the VAT and duty payable to HMRC in a typical month.

An arrangement is available for importers who hold a deferment account (or who are applying for one), to allow them to reduce the level of financial guarantee required to operate it for VAT purposes only. Customs and excise duties must still be fully secured.

The arrangement, known as SIVA, could apply if applicants can satisfy the following criteria:

* they must have been VAT registered for at least three years;
* they must have a good VAT compliance history;
* they must have a good payment record with HMRC;
* they must have sufficient financial means to meet any amount deferred under SIVA;
* they must have a good HMRC record (serious offences will result in automatic expulsion);
* they must have at least a 12-month record of international trade operations;
* they must have a good compliance record for international trade.

The SIVA application form (SIVA1) can be downloaded from the GOV.UK website (www.gov.uk/government/organisations/hm-revenue-customs). The completed form needs to be sent to:

HM Revenue and Customs
SIVA Approvals Team
Ruby House
8 Ruby Place
Aberdeen AB10 1ZP

The result of a successful application will be as follows:

* the business will have a deferment account limit which must be sufficient to cover all deferred charges for VAT, customs duty and excise duty;

- the business will have a deferment guarantee level which must be supported by a deferment guarantee able to cover all deferred customs and excise duties.

(HMRC Notice 101, paras 5.8–5.10).

Evidence for input tax deduction (Form C79)

[11.7] Import VAT can only be reclaimed by a business that is registered for VAT in the UK. If a business is not registered for VAT (for instance, because it trades below the VAT registration limits or because it is involved in making exempt supplies), then there is no scope to reclaim input tax.

Equally, input tax can only be reclaimed by a VAT-registered business if the goods are to be used to make taxable supplies and if adequate evidence is held to support the claim.

As explained at **11.5**, weekly deferment statements issued by HMRC are not acceptable as evidence to support an input tax claim. The main document for this purpose is the Import VAT Certificate (Form C79). C79 certificates are issued by HMRC on a monthly basis, usually on the 12th day of the following month. They are issued to the VAT registered person whose registration number, plus a three-digit suffix, is shown on the import entry SAD/C88.

(HMRC Notice 702, para 8.2).

As far as input tax is concerned, the key date is the accounting date alongside each item, not the date when the certificate is issued. This applies even where the business uses the cash accounting scheme, as imports are excluded from cash accounting treatment.

(HMRC Notice 702, para 8.4).

If a monthly certificate is mislaid, replacements can be obtained (for up to six years) by writing to:

HM Revenue and Customs
Microfilm Section
8th Floor Alexander House
Victoria Avenue
Southend SS99 1AU

Note – the request should be made on business headed paper, quoting the VAT registration number of the business and the date(s) of the missing certificate(s).

(HMRC Notice 702, para 8.10).

An importer will often use an agent to complete the import formalities at the port of entry. If this is the case, and the agent has to pay VAT on behalf of the importer, then the agent will invoice the importer to recover this VAT. However, the VAT shown on this invoice cannot be used by the importer as evidence to reclaim input tax – only the C79 documentation is acceptable. From a client perspective, there is clearly a risk here that the agent's invoice will be processed through the purchase system and input VAT claimed while, at the same time, the C79 will also be used. This could result in a double claim.

Note – the reason that input tax cannot be reclaimed by a shipping or forwarding agent acting for an importer and paying VAT on his behalf is because the goods in question are not being used by the agent for the purpose of his business. The only exception is that there are certain times when HMRC will repay import VAT paid by an agent but not repaid to him by his client, eg if the client became insolvent.

(HMRC Notice 702, paras 2.4 and 2.5).

Postal imports

[11.8] The procedures considered in this chapter so far assume that goods enter the UK by port or airport. There are special rules that apply if goods are imported by a postal arrangement.

- *Consignments (other than International Datapost/EMS packets) not exceeding £2,000* – a VAT-registered person importing goods for business purposes does not have to pay VAT immediately on importation. Instead, he may account for the VAT due in Box 1 of the VAT return covered by the period of importation. Subject to the normal rules, the same amount of input tax can then be reclaimed in Box 4 of the return. The charge label, postal wrapper and any customs declaration attached to the package must be kept to support the claim to input tax (Form CN22 and CN23).
- *International Datapost/EMS packets not exceeding £2,000 in value* – for such imports, the Royal Mail or Parcelforce require payment of the VAT when the package is delivered. The charge label attached must be kept to support any claim to input tax. It is not possible to defer payment of import charges.
- *Consignments over £2,000 in value* – for these imports, a declaration on Form C88 (which will be sent to the consignee) must be made and returned to HMRC together with an invoice or other acceptable evidence of value. VAT and other charges due at importation are payable immediately unless the consignee is approved to use the deferment scheme. After payment, HMRC sends the consignee a copy of the entry to support any claim to input tax.

(HMRC Notice 702, para 4.3).

Goods not subject to an import VAT charge

[11.9] There are a range of goods that can be imported into the country without VAT being charged – the obvious example being any goods that would be zero-rated if supplied in the UK. Another common example of goods that can be imported without a VAT charge are miscellaneous items where the value of the consignment does not exceed £15.

The £15 consignment limit is often referred to as Low Value Consignment Relief (LVCR). LVCR does not apply to imports of alcoholic beverages, tobacco products, perfumes or toilet waters, and, from 1 April 2012, does not apply to any goods imported from the Channel Islands.

The other main categories of reliefs that are potentially available apply to the following general headings – further information is available on the GOV.UK website:

- aircraft ground and security equipment;
- capital goods and equipment on transfer of activities from abroad;
- certain imports by, and for, charities;
- decorations and awards;
- electricity and natural gas;
- fuel, animal fodder and feed, and packaging necessary during transportation;
- funerals, war graves etc;
- goods for examination, analysis or test purposes;
- goods imported for sale to another EU country;
- health, including animals and biological or chemical substances for research, blood and human organs;
- inherited goods;
- personal belongings;
- printed matter;
- promotion of trade;
- re-imported goods;
- rejected goods;
- small non-commercial consignments;
- temporary importations;
- travellers' allowances;
- United Nations visual and auditory materials;
- visiting forces;
- works of art and collectors' pieces.

(HMRC Notice 702, para 5.1).

Intrastat

[11.10] All VAT-registered businesses trading in goods with VAT-registered businesses in other EU countries outside the UK must complete Boxes 8 and 9 of their VAT returns.

- Box 8 records the total value of sales of goods (dispatches) to other EU countries. This entry not only includes sales of goods to other VAT registered businesses in EU countries but also the value of goods despatched from the UK to a destination in another EU country, even if no actual sale is involved or the sale is being invoiced to a person located outside the EU. The figure in Box 8 will exclude sales to non-VAT registered customers in other EU countries, assuming the business is trading below the distance selling thresholds in that country.

- Box 9 records the total value of acquisitions of goods from other EU countries. The value to be included is the invoice (or contract) price, including directly related services such as freight and insurance. The receipt of other services should not be included.

The figures included in Boxes 8 and 9 will determine if a business needs to involve itself in the completion of Supplementary Declarations (SDs) which form part of what is known as the Intrastat system. Intrastat is the name given to the system for collecting statistics on the trade in goods between EU countries. The Intrastat system is only relevant to VAT registered businesses (ie not unregistered businesses or private individuals).

A business does not need to complete Intrastat declarations if it trades below the thresholds:

- the exemption threshold for arrivals is £1,500,000;
- the exemption threshold for dispatches is £250,000.

(HMRC Notice 60, para 3.1).

The thresholds apply on a calendar year basis, that is, January to December. From 1 January 2014 to 31 December 2014 the exemption threshold for arrivals was £1,200,000.

If a business has acquisitions or dispatches that do not exceed these limits, then information recorded in Boxes 8 and 9 is sufficient to give details of its EU trade. If a SD form needs to be completed, then a full explanation of the key issues can be found in Customs Notice 60.

From 1 April 2012 Intrastat declarations must be submitted electronically and the submission date has been brought forward from the last day to the 21st day of the month following the month to which the declarations relate.

Example 3

Month (2015)	Dispatches	Arrivals
January	£20,000	£5,000
February	£30,000	£30,000
March	£80,000	£40,000
April	£50,000	£40,000
May	£100,000	£40,000
June	£50,000	£50,000
July	£20,000	£80,000

Solution – the £250,000 threshold for dispatches is exceeded in May and the HMRC Intrastat Enquiries team must be notified at that point.

The £1,500,000 threshold for arrivals is not exceeded at all, so SDs are not required for arrivals.

Additional information relating to delivery terms needs to be included on the SDs if the delivery terms threshold for the previous calendar year was exceeded and the delivery terms threshold for the current calendar year will be exceeded. The delivery terms threshold for arrivals and dispatches is currently £24 million.

The delivery terms threshold applies separately to arrivals and dispatches so that if the delivery terms threshold is exceeded for arrivals but not for dispatches the additional information need only be included in relation to arrivals. Likewise, if the delivery terms threshold is exceeded for dispatches but not for arrivals, the additional information need only be included in relation to dispatches.

(HMRC Notice 60, para 3.3).

Registration for VAT and EU acquisitions

[11.11] The need to be registered for VAT is usually based on the level of taxable supplies made by a business. If the value of these taxable supplies in the immediately preceding 12 months has exceeded the VAT registration threshold or is expected to exceed the VAT registration threshold in the next 30 days, there is a requirement for the business to be VAT registered.

However, there is another situation when a business or person may need to be registered for VAT, based on the value of its 'acquisitions' (ie value of goods bought from other EU countries) rather than its taxable supplies. In this situation the same VAT registration threshold is relevant but instead of looking back at the value of taxable supplies in the immediately preceding 12 months the business monitors the level of taxable supplies made from the beginning of each calendar year.

The rules on this subject state that if the value of acquisitions made by a business at the end of any month, in the period beginning with 1 January in that year, have exceeded the VAT registration threshold or are expected to exceed the threshold in the next 30 days, then the business must be VAT registered.

In the case of the threshold being exceeded on an historic basis, the notification of the need to be registered must be made within 30 days of the end of the month in which the threshold has been exceeded. The registration date will then be the first date of the following month.

Example – threshold exceeded in May – notification to HMRC must be made by 30 June, and effective date of registration will be 1 July.

When it is expected that the VAT registration threshold will be exceeded in the next 30 days, VAT registration is effective from the beginning of the 30-day period. See Example 4.

Example 4

On 12 June, a company that is not registered for VAT expects the value of its relevant acquisitions in the next 30 days to exceed the registration threshold. This is because a major purchase order has been raised to buy goods from Italy on 28 June.

Solution – the business will be liable to register for VAT on 12 June and must notify HMRC of its liability to register by 11 July. HMRC will register the company with effect from 12 June.

Import of computer software – goods or services?

[**11.12**] Think of an importer's predicament as he buys the latest technology product from the USA – does he have to declare his product as an import of goods (pay VAT at the time of import into the UK and reclaim this amount as input tax on his VAT return)? Or is he making an import of services, in which case he can import the product VAT free, and deal with the VAT on his next return using the reverse charge system? (Output tax is declared in Box 1; input tax reclaimed in Box 4 – subject to normal rules). See **14.6** for further detail on this process.

The positive point is that the rules in the above situation are helpfully clarified by HMRC in Notice 702, section 7.

- If a mass-produced item is imported, this is treated as an import of both goods (the medium carrying the data, eg discs) and services (the data itself). If the value of the goods and services are not itemised separately (almost certainly they will be imported with an inclusive value), the supply is wholly treated as goods.
- If a customer designed product is imported (ie a bespoke package), this is again treated as an import of both goods and services – but in this case, an inclusive price means the whole supply is treated as a supply of services.

Planning points to consider

[**11.13**] The following planning points should be given consideration.

- Different VAT rules apply depending on whether goods being acquired from overseas are imports (ie from a non-EU country) or acquisitions (ie from another EU country). Advisers should ensure that relevant clients have procedures in place to deal with the two different situations.
- No VAT is due on imported goods if the item in question would be zero-rated if supplied in the UK.
- Be aware of the main benefits of holding a deferment account with HMRC to delay paying VAT on imports until the 15th day of the following month. However, remember that periodic deferment statements are not acceptable as evidence for input tax purposes – the C79 certificate is needed to support any input tax claim.
- It is worthwhile for importers with (or applying for) a deferment account to utilise the SIVA arrangements. This scheme reduces the level of a bank guarantee required for VAT on imports via a deferment account.
- If a business is not registered for VAT, it is important to regularly review the value of its EU acquisitions to ensure they do not exceed the VAT registration limits during a calendar year on a cumulative basis. If the limits are exceeded, then the business will need to register for VAT.
- Be aware that Low Value Consignment Relief no longer applies to goods imported to the UK from the Channel Islands.

Note – the Union Customs Code (UCC) finally took effect on 1 May 2016, replacing the outdated 1992 Community Customs Code. This is European legislation governing customs declarations and import duty payments throughout all 28 EU member states. Any business with a SIVA authorisation in force when UCC became effective will have its authorisation reviewed by HMRC in due course. Only businesses with Authorised Economic Operator (AEO) approval will continue to benefit from being relieved from the requirement to provide financial guarantees to HMRC for the import VAT.

Chapter 12

Exports (and Dispatches)

Key topics in this chapter:

- The different VAT rules that apply depending on whether goods are sold to an EU or non-EU customer.
- The different VAT rules that apply depending on whether an EU customer is registered for VAT or not.
- The importance of obtaining proper evidence to confirm that goods have left the UK.
- Procedures for sales to non-registered customers in another EU country – under distance selling arrangements.
- Triangulation arrangements – supplies of goods from a UK supplier to a customer's customer – where both customers are based in different EU countries.
- Procedures for completing an EU sales list – recording sales made to VAT registered businesses in other EU countries outside of the UK.
- Dealing with the situation where goods are collected from a UK supplier and exported by the customer. Cases are reviewed where customers have falsified export evidence.
- Practical examples of common export transactions and the VAT treatment in each case.
- The benefits of the retail export scheme.

Introduction

[12.1] The VAT treatment of goods supplied to a destination outside the UK depends on two key facts:

- whether the goods are supplied to a country that is inside or outside the EU;
- if the goods are supplied to a person that is based in another EU country, then it is relevant to consider whether the customer is VAT registered or non-registered.

In VAT terms, an export situation only applies if the goods are sold to a non-EU customer. In such cases, all sales of goods are zero-rated, irrespective of the status of the customer, as long as the exporter holds proper evidence that the goods have left the EU. This evidence must be available for inspection by an HMRC officer carrying out a VAT visit.

If the goods are sold to a customer in another EU country outside the UK, then UK VAT must be charged where appropriate if the customer is not registered for VAT in his own country. If the customer is registered for VAT, then he must give details of his VAT number to the UK supplier – the latter must then include the number on his sales invoice in order to zero-rate the supply of goods.

As with the supply of goods outside EU boundaries, a supplier of goods within the EU must obtain evidence that the goods have left the UK if no VAT is being charged.

If the value of sales to non-registered customers exceeds certain limits in specific EU countries, then a UK supplier will be obliged to register for VAT in that country through what is known as distance selling.

The other main situation where a UK supplier will become involved with an export arrangement is as a retailer selling goods to a customer who belongs overseas but who intends to take the goods outside of the EU. In such cases, the customer could be entitled to a refund of VAT on the goods in question through the retail export scheme.

The VAT rules regarding certain export transactions can become very complicated but the aim of this chapter is to consider the basic principles and arrangements that will apply in the majority of cases.

Export of goods and sale of goods within the EU

[12.2] To illustrate the different VAT treatment of EU and non-EU sales, consider the following example.

Example 1

Jill buys plant pots in the UK and sells them to a variety of customers throughout the world. In the next VAT quarter, her sales will include the following transactions and she is keen to understand the VAT implications:

(a)   500 pots will be sold to a business in Russia (outside the EU);
(b)   5 pots will be sold to a private individual in Russia;
(c)   500 pots will be sold to a VAT registered company in Belgium (inside EU);
(d)   5 pots will be sold to a private individual in Belgium.

Solution – a 20% VAT charge is made in the case of (d) above – the other sales are zero-rated. In situations (a)–(c), it is important that Jill obtains export/shipping documentation to confirm that the goods have left the UK. The standard of proof is considered at **12.3**.

For the goods supplied to Russia, it does not make any difference whether the customers are private individuals or business customers. All exports of goods to a country outside of the EU are zero-rated.

In the case of the 500 pots supplied to the Belgian company, the company should provide Jill with its Belgian VAT number, and Jill should show this number on the sales invoice she raises at the time the goods are sold. She can then zero-rate the supply of goods to the Belgian company. In the absence of a VAT number, Jill would be required to charge UK VAT at the appropriate rate.

However, in the case of the five pots sold to the private individual in Belgium, UK VAT (standard rate) must be charged on these goods. Jill should also record the total value of sales made to non-registered customers in Belgium to ensure she does not exceed the distance selling levels – see **12.5**.

Note – a UK business should take reasonable steps to confirm the validity of the VAT numbers given to it by overseas customers. Each EU country has a specific format for its VAT numbers, so it should be initially confirmed that the number provided by the customer follows this format. See **19.11** and Box 1 for further details.

Evidence of exportation

[12.3] HMRC is very specific about the type of evidence it requires to support export sales, a position that is confirmed by the legislation on this subject.

Evidence may consist either of official evidence such as a Single Administrative Document (SAD) (eg Form C88 stamped by Customs) or commercial evidence concerning the transaction – the latter is more usual.

All documents retained as evidence of export must give the following details:

*   the identity of both the exporter and the customer;
*   the destination of the goods must be clearly given and the method of transportation;
*   identification of the goods themselves.

Commercial evidence of export will either be primary evidence, eg authentication documents issued by shipping lines, air lines, railway companies etc or secondary evidence, eg documentation issued by freight forwarders exporting on behalf of a number of exporters and who will themselves obtain and retain the primary evidence.

For exports by sea, exporters should obtain a copy of the bill of lading or sea waybill. If the export process is by air, then an air waybill is required. In export methods falling outside the norm, section 6 of HMRC Notice 703 should be consulted regarding the appropriate evidence in most cases.

Evidence concerning proof of export to support zero-rating should be retained by a business for six years as part of its business records.

(HMRC Notice 703, para 6.7).

The time of supply of exported goods is usually the earlier of the date when the supplier sends the goods to the customer or when the customer collects the goods or the customer pays for the goods in full. In most cases, if the supplier has not obtained valid evidence that the goods have been exported within three months of the time of supply it should amend its VAT records and account for the appropriate amount of VAT. For goods that are sent to another business for processing or to be incorporated into other goods prior to export, the time limit for obtaining valid evidence of export is six months from the time of supply. Subject to conditions, a six-month limit, and in some cases a 12-month limit, for obtaining valid evidence of export applies to the export of thoroughbred racehorses.

If the transaction has become standard rated because evidence of export has not been received within the required time limit the business should amend its VAT records and account for the VAT accordingly. For a VAT rate of 20% the amount of VAT would be equivalent to one-sixth of the consideration. The VAT records are amended by making an entry equivalent to the VAT that has become due on the 'VAT payable' side of the VAT account. This amount should be included in box 1 of the VAT return for the period in which the time limit for obtaining evidence has expired. If evidence of export is subsequently received the business can adjust its VAT position and VAT records for the period in which the evidence was received.

(HMRC Notice 703, paras 2.13, 3.5, 11.2, 11.3).

An interesting situation can arise where a VAT officer raises an assessment for insufficient export evidence – where the exporter subsequently obtains the evidence – see Example 2.

Example 2

ABC completes VAT returns on a calendar quarterly basis. In March a customer from the USA arranged for goods worth £30,000 to be collected from ABC's premises and told ABC that the goods were being shipped to the USA and that valid evidence of export would be provided in due course. ABC treated the sale as a zero-rated export when completing its VAT return for the quarter to 31 March.

When ABC was completing its VAT return for the quarter to 30 June it had not received valid evidence of export but did not amend its VAT records or account for output tax of £5,000 (£30,000 x 1/6) in box 1 of its VAT return for that period.

A VAT officer making a routine visit in September assessed VAT on the goods as if they had been supplied in the UK. He raised an assessment for £5,000 and HMRC calculated an interest charge of £300.

ABC subsequently provided the officer with evidence that the goods were exported – but the officer refused to reduce the assessment, instead instructed the company to adjust the VAT on its next return.

Solution – The approach of HMRC in this situation is that the assessment is correct because at the time of the visit, the export evidence was inadequate. It is only at a later date that the evidence is produced – hence the instruction to adjust a current VAT return.

The negative outcome of this situation is that the interest charge of £300 will stand because the assessment has not been withdrawn.

Inadequate evidence – case law

[12.4] The exportation of goods to a non-EU country can either be a 'direct' export (where the UK supplier arranges for the goods to be delivered to the overseas customer, or through an agent he appoints) or an 'indirect export' (where the customer arranges for the collection of the goods from the UK supplier, and then takes them outside of the EU).

Under EU VAT law (*Directive 2006/112/EC, art 146(1)(b)*) no VAT is due on indirect exports, provided the overseas customer does not have a business establishment in the supplier's country. The UK has implemented this condition into national law but prior to 1 October 2013 the UK had included an additional requirement that the customer must not be registered for VAT in the UK. This additional requirement that the customer must not be registered for VAT in the UK no longer applies. Zero-rating can therefore apply to indirect exports where the customer is registered for VAT in the UK as a non-established taxable person (see **15.2**) (*SI 1995/2518, reg 129(1)(a); SI 2013/2241*).

(HMRC Notice 703, paras 3.3 and 3.4).

In the case of indirect exports, the UK supplier is relying on the customer to forward adequate evidence that the goods have left the EU (proof of export), otherwise HMRC could assess tax as if the goods had been supplied in the UK.

A problem may occur if the evidence provided by the customer is subsequently found to be false – but the supplier is unaware of this fact. This situation occurred in the following cases and, encouragingly, the courts supported the taxpayer:

- *R (on the application of Teleos plc) v Customs and Excise Comrs: C-409/04* [2008] QB, 600, [2007] ECR I-7797, [2008] STC 706, ECJ. The taxpayer relied on commercial road transport documents as proof that goods had left the UK (in this particular case, the destination was another EU country – but the principles are the same). The documents were subsequently found to be false, so HMRC assessed tax as if the goods had been supplied in the UK. The ECJ ruled that as long as a supplier acts in good faith and has no involvement in tax evasion (and takes every reasonable step to ensure the transaction does not involve tax evasion), then he should not be required to account for VAT on those goods if the evidence subsequently proves to be false. See Revenue & Customs Brief 61/07 for further detail on this case and the implications for taxpayers affected by the issues.

- *Netto Supermarket GmbH & Co OHG v Finanzamt Malchin: C-271/06* [2008] ECR I-771, [2008] STC 3280, ECJ. The same circumstances applied as in the *Teleos* case, but concerning export evidence in relation to goods supplied to Polish customers (before Poland joined the EU). The outcome was the same:

  'It would clearly be disproportionate to hold a taxable person liable for the shortfall in tax caused by fraudulent acts of third parties over which he had no influence whatsoever.'

The First Tier Tribunal case involving *Jane Louise Eydmann* (TC01569) [2011] UKFTT 732 (TC) illustrates the approach of the courts on evidence of dispatch of goods to another EU country.

Miss Eydmann was VAT registered in the UK as a sole trader selling kitchen carcasses to a customer in Spain (Robert Bradbury) who provided a Spanish VAT number to support the zero-rating of the sales in question. It transpired that the VAT number was not genuine and that Mr Bradbury was not VAT registered in Spain.

A supplier of goods has some responsibility to confirm that a VAT number provided by an overseas customer is genuine – it should at least be in the format of a VAT number relevant to the country in question.

HMRC assessed tax against Miss Eydmann on the basis that one of the conditions for zero-rating the sale of goods to an EU business customer had not been met and the tribunal accepted that she had not applied adequate checks to confirm the number was genuine.

Comment – the three conditions for zero-rating the sale of goods to an EU customer are clearly explained in HMRC's VAT Notice 725, para 4.3:

'A supply from the UK to a customer in another EC Member State is liable to the zero rate where:

• You obtain and show on your VAT sales invoice your customer's EC VAT registration number, including the 2-letter country prefix code, and
• The goods are sent or transported out of the UK to a destination in another EC Member State, and
• You obtain and keep valid commercial evidence that the goods have been removed from the UK within the time limits set out at paragraph 4.4.'

(The conditions have the force of law and are clearly marked to that effect in the Notice).

As a warning point, it is important that a customer provides the VAT number that has been allocated to his business for the purposes of intra-EU trade, rather than an internal tax or fiscal number that is only relevant in his own country.

Be aware of the opportunity to check the validity of a customer's VAT registration number using the 'Europa' website facility (google 'Europa VAT number checker'). The guidance of HMRC in relation to checking overseas VAT numbers as noted at paragraphs 4.10 to 4.12 of Notice 725 is quoted below:

'**4.10 Will I have to account for VAT if my customer's VAT number turns out to be invalid?**

No. But only if you have genuinely done everything you can to check the validity of the VAT number; can demonstrate you have done so; have taken heed of any indications that something might be wrong and have no other reason to suspect the VAT number is invalid.

4.11 What is meant by 'reasonable steps'?

HMRC does not expect you to go beyond what is reasonable but will be seeking to identify what actions you took to check the validity of your customer's EU VAT registration number. This will focus on the due diligence checks you undertook and, most importantly, the actions taken by you in response to the results of those checks. We would consider 'reasonable steps' to be, you genuinely doing everything you can to check the integrity of the VAT registration number, being able to demonstrate you have done so and taking heed of any indications that the number may be invalid. Some examples of not having taken 'reasonable steps' would be:

• using a VAT number that does not conform to the published format for your customer's Member State as shown in paragraph 16.19, or

- using a VAT number that you have not regularly checked using the Europa website or with HMRC
- using a VAT number which you have already been informed is invalid, or
- using a VAT number which you know does not belong to your customer.

4.12 Will VAT be chargeable if reasonable steps are not considered to have been taken?

Yes. You will have to account for VAT at the appropriate UK rate.'

In the *Eydmann* case, the taxpayer should have been more cautious because the customer in question (Robert Bradbury) owed £10,000 to a separate business owned by Miss Eydmann's father, a debt that had been written off by her father. So there were past trading problems that the Tribunal felt should have persuaded Miss Eydmann to adopt a more cautious approach in her dealings with him.

Note – even if a customer provides a genuine overseas VAT number, it is recommended by HMRC that the validity of the number is checked on a regular basis. What would happen, for example, if the business deregistered, but continued, due to using the number, to receive zero-rated supplies?

Distance selling limits

[12.5] 'Distance selling' is the term used for the sale of goods to customers in other EU countries outside the UK that are not VAT registered and where the supplier is responsible for their delivery. The same principles apply if a supplier in an EU country sells goods to non-registered customers in the UK. The sales in question often relate to mail order or Internet sales.

As explained at **12.1**, the sale of goods by a UK business to a non-registered customer in another EU country (outside of the UK) will be subject to VAT at the same rate as if the goods were sold in the UK. In most cases, the goods will be standard rated and subject to VAT although some goods will be zero-rated, eg children's clothing or books.

The main problem with the above arrangement is that a company could gain a competitive advantage by fixing its main place of business in a country with a relatively low rate of VAT. If a business is a large international mail order company, making sales worth many millions of pounds, then the VAT saving could be considerable – hence the need for the distance selling rules.

The distance selling rules are as follows:

- each EU country has the option to choose one of two distance selling thresholds – if this annual threshold is exceeded by a business making sales to unregistered persons in that country on a calendar year basis, it must register for VAT in that country;
- the relevant distance selling thresholds are €35,000 and €100,000;
- examples of countries that have adopted the lower thresholds (as at April 2016) are Belgium, Finland, Greece, Ireland, Italy, Portugal and Spain;

- examples of countries that have adopted the higher threshold (as at April 2016) are France, Germany, Luxembourg, Netherlands and the UK (the UK limit is £70,000 as it is not in the Euro);
- the distance selling thresholds do not apply to excise goods, for example, cigarettes and wine – if a business makes distance sales of any excise goods to customers in another EU country it must register for VAT and account for VAT in that country;
- once registered for VAT in that country, a business will charge VAT according to the rate that applies to the sale of the goods in that country, and complete regular VAT returns and pay VAT to the tax authorities.

In effect, the distance selling rules mean that certain large companies trading across the EU could be registered for VAT in all EU member states.

Note – the calculations to check if the distance selling limits have been exceeded are based on sales to unregistered persons in a particular country for a calendar year. This is in contrast to the usual VAT registration test, which is based on taxable sales made on a rolling 12-month basis. See Example 3.

Example 3

Susan's only income is from selling handbags to individuals via the internet. She is currently registered for VAT in the UK where she lives and is not currently registered for VAT in any other EU country. Some of Susan's sales are distance sales to individuals in other EU countries.

Susan needs to monitor the level of her distance sales to customers in each EU country from the beginning of each calendar year to see if the level of sales to customers in any EU country exceeds the relevant distance selling threshold for that country. If Susan's sales to customers in, for example, Italy, exceed the distance selling threshold for Italy at any point during a calendar year Susan must immediately register for VAT in Italy and start accounting for Italian VAT rather than UK VAT on sales to customers in Italy.

If Susan's distance sales to customers in another EU country do not exceed the relevant distance selling threshold for that country during a calendar year she can ignore those sales for distance selling threshold purposes but must continue to monitor the level of sales made to customers in that country during the following year.

Susan does not have to wait until the level of her sales to customers in an EU country exceeds the distance selling threshold for the country before she registers for VAT in that country. She could register for VAT in any EU country on a voluntary basis in relation to sales she makes to customers in that country. This may be an attractive option for Susan if the amount of VAT she has to account for in the other country is less than the VAT she would otherwise have to account for in the UK in relation to sales she makes to customers in that country.

(HMRC Notice 725, para 6.4).

Triangulation

[12.6] Triangulation applies where goods are delivered directly by a supplier (UK based) to his customer's customer – where the customer and his customer are both located in different EU countries outside of the UK.

In such circumstances, both the UK supplier and his customer may zero-rate their supplies (assuming all parties are registered for VAT). See Example 4 for an illustration of this situation.

Example 4

Jeff is VAT registered in the UK and has received an order to supply goods to a Spanish customer. However, the Spanish customer is reselling the goods to a French customer, and has asked for the goods to be shipped directly to France rather than via Spain. The Spanish and French customers are both registered for VAT in their own countries.

Solution – as long as Jeff obtains proof that the goods have left the UK, and obtains the VAT number of his Spanish customer, he can zero-rate the supply of goods on his invoice to the Spanish customer.

Through a simplified procedure agreed by EU countries to avoid unnecessary VAT registrations being created the Spanish customer can then zero-rate his supply to the French customer as long as he obtains his French VAT registration number. The French customer will effectively account for the output tax by declaring acquisition tax in Box 2 on his own VAT return in France.

Note – as a final requirement, the Spanish customer should endorse his invoice to the French customer with the words: 'VAT: EC Article 28 simplification invoice'.

The simplified procedure explained in the above example aims to avoid the need for unnecessary VAT registrations – the Spanish supplier avoids the need to become VAT registered in France. However, the triangulation arrangements cannot work where there are more than three parties to a chain transaction. In such cases, additional VAT registrations are almost always required. In Example 4 the Spanish business is regarded as the intermediary in the triangular transaction.

(HMRC Notice 725, section 13).

EU sales lists and completing VAT returns

[12.7] A business must complete and submit an EU sales list (ESL) if it:

* makes supplies of goods to a customer that is registered for VAT in another EU country;
* is the intermediary in a triangular transaction (see **12.6**);
* makes supplies of services that are subject to the reverse charge in the EU country where the customer belongs.

An ESL can be submitted electronically or on paper format (Form VAT 101).

Most businesses that are required to submit ESLs are required to submit them on a monthly or a calendar quarterly basis. Businesses that sell goods where the value of the sales that need to be included on the ESL has exceeded £35,000 in the current or previous four quarters must complete monthly returns. Certain businesses with annual sales to other EU countries of not more than £11,000 can apply to HMRC for approval to submit an ESL once a year. The due date for submitting a paper ESL is within 14 days of the end of the period to which it relates and for an electronic ESL within 21 days of the end of the period to which it relates.

A business that submits ESLs on a calendar quarter basis but submits its VAT returns on a different quarterly basis can apply to HMRC to change its VAT return periods so that they coincide with its calendar quarter ESL periods.

The details to be disclosed in the ESL are as follows:

- the date of submission of the ESL and the last day of the period to which the ESL refers;
- a two-letter prefix code identifying each customer's country and the VAT registration number of each person acquiring, or deemed to have acquired, goods in the period (eg the prefix for a French customer is FR, Denmark is DK);
- the total value of the goods (or services) supplied in the period to each person above;
- a code '1' entry is made if a sale relates to goods; code '2' if the sale involves a triangulation arrangement (see **12.6**); code '3' if relevant to services.

Note – the ESL does not include sales of goods to any customers registered for VAT in other EU countries but where the VAT number is not known. Sales of goods to these customers would be taxable because the supply could not have been zero-rated without the customer's registration number. Supplies to non-registered customers in other EU countries are also excluded from the ESL (distance sales).

In terms of time intervals, a business selling services will have to complete an ESL on a calender quarter basis. A business selling goods where the value of the sales that need to be included on the ESL has exceeded £35,000 in the current or previous four quarters must complete monthly returns.

Other information about the ESL

[12.8]

- In the case of a business selling EU services only, there will have been no Box 8 entry on a VAT return, so it is up to the business to notify HMRC of the need to complete an ESL, not the other way round.
- An incomplete line cannot be accepted on the form, so no entry will be made if either zero sales have been made to a customer in a period, or if the customer does not have a VAT registration number.

Goods collected in the UK by a customer

[12.9] A situation may arise where an EU customer (VAT registered) or non-EU customer collects goods himself from the UK supplier, and personally arranges for the goods to be taken out of the country.

In such cases, the onus is still on the UK supplier to obtain proof that the goods have left the UK. As this type of situation is high risk (in the sense that HMRC will be keen to ensure the goods have not been diverted to the UK market), the standard of export evidence required is very high. See **12.4** to illustrate potential problems in this area that have led to court cases being necessary.

In reality, a sensible approach would probably be for the seller of the goods to take a deposit from the customer equal to the amount of VAT on the supply – this deposit to be refunded once satisfactory evidence is received to confirm the goods have left the UK. See **19.13** and Example 5 below.

(HMRC Notice 703, paras 6.6 and 6.9).

Example 5

Julie sells photocopiers and is based in the UK. She has received an order from a French customer (registered for VAT in France) for 10 photocopiers costing £2,000 each. However, the customer will collect the goods and ship them to France.

Solution – Julie can zero-rate the sale of the photocopiers as the supply is to a business registered for VAT in an EU country outside the UK. However, this zero-rating is subject to the two key rules that she obtains the French VAT number of the customer, and proof that the goods have left the UK. It would be sensible for her to take a deposit for the VAT from the customer on the basis that this will be refunded when satisfactory evidence has been received to confirm the goods have left the UK.

If this deposit is not taken, the French customer has no incentive to ensure the relevant evidence is acquired and forwarded to Julie. HMRC would then almost certainly treat the sales as standard rated on the basis that the goods could have been diverted to the UK market.

Single movement of goods but multiple transactions

[12.10] As global trade becomes more sophisticated, there will inevitably be various situations arising with the movement of goods that will need to be addressed as far as VAT is concerned.

One common situation is where a single movement of goods occurs but more than two parties are involved in the sale (as with triangulation – see **12.6**).

With regard to overseas sales of goods (excluding the triangular arrangement), if a single movement of goods is supported by two or more transactions, the legislation states that only the final transaction can be zero-rated – see Example 6.

(HMRC Notice 703, para 4.1).

Example 6

Smith Inc is based in America and orders goods from ABC Ltd in the UK. ABC Ltd purchases the goods from DEF Ltd, also based in the UK. However, to avoid double handling of the goods, it is agreed that DEF Ltd will send the goods directly to the customer in America.

Solution – the supply of goods from DEF Ltd to ABC Ltd has taken place in the UK and DEF Ltd must therefore charge output tax on its sales invoice to ABC Ltd (assuming the goods are subject to VAT). However, ABC Ltd can zero-rate its supply to Smith Inc, as long as it obtains evidence of export to confirm that the goods have left the UK.

Other common export/dispatch problems

[12.11] Highlighted below are four common export/dispatch problems that have been raised on many occasions over the years. They are all relevant to practical situations that could be encountered by advisers in the course of their work:

- Example 7 – customer based outside the EU but goods never leave the EU;
- Example 8 – customer based in the EU but goods are shipped outside the EU;
- Example 9 – customer based in the UK but goods are shipped to another EU country;
- Example 10 – customer is VAT registered in another EU country but goods do not leave the UK.

Example 7

A business registered for VAT in the UK receives an order from a private individual based in America, who wants the goods to be shipped to her niece in Italy as a birthday present.

Solution – in this situation, the goods do not leave the EU so cannot be classed as an export. It is a requirement for zero-rating as an export that proof of export is held that the goods have left the EU. If the goods have been shipped to Italy, they have never left the EU so this condition is not met. The customer in America is not VAT registered in the EU so there is no scope to zero-rate the sale as a supply between two VAT registered businesses in different EU countries.

The American customer must therefore be charged UK VAT on her order – assuming the goods in question are not zero-rated.

Example 8

A business registered for VAT in the UK receives an order from a private individual based in Italy, who wants the goods to be shipped to her niece in America as a birthday present.

Solution – the goods have left the EU so can be classed as an export. It is a requirement for zero-rating as an export that proof of export is held that the goods have left the EU – this should not be a problem as the business is arranging the export.

The Italian customer does not therefore need to be charged UK VAT on her order – the sale is zero-rated.

Example 9

A UK company based in London receives an order for goods from a business customer in Wales. To save costs, the customer asks for the goods to be delivered directly to its customer based in France.

Solution – the London company is making a sale to another customer based in the UK. There is no scope to zero-rate the sale even if the Welsh customer is VAT registered because Wales is part of the UK. However, the London company will forward documentation to the Welsh customer to prove that the goods have left the UK and this would enable the Welsh customer to not charge VAT to the French customer if he was VAT registered in France and supplied his French VAT number (the Welsh customer must record this number on his VAT invoice).

Example 10

A UK company receives an order for goods from a German business customer, VAT registered in Germany. However, the German customer asks for the goods to be delivered to his customer based in Wales, ie within UK.

In this situation, the goods have never left the UK, so all supplies are taking place within the UK. It is irrelevant that the first customer is based in Germany.

In effect, the first outcome is that the German customer will be charged UK VAT – but can he reclaim this VAT as either input tax or by an overseas repayment claim?

The answer is 'no' in relation to the overseas repayment claim because the supply relates to the sale of goods in the UK. The German company cannot reclaim UK VAT on its own German VAT return.

If the German business does not have a physical presence in the UK (ie if it is a non-established taxable person) then it will not benefit from the UK VAT registration threshold and will have to register for VAT in the UK on a compulsory basis. It could then claim the VAT charged by the UK supplier as input tax on its UK VAT return.

Retail exports

[**12.12**] The retail export scheme gives the opportunity for overseas visitors coming to the UK to receive a refund of VAT paid on goods they buy in shops, as long as the goods are exported to a destination outside the EU. The onus is on the retailer to ensure that export evidence is held to support zero-rating of the goods – if this evidence is missing or unacceptable, then HMRC will treat the goods as having been supplied in the UK.

There is a time limit as far as a VAT refund is concerned – the overseas customer must leave the UK for a final destination outside the EU (with the goods in question) by the last day of the third month following that in which the goods were purchased.

The retail export scheme is optional for a retailer – it gives two main advantages:

* reduced prices for eligible customers who can effectively buy goods on a VAT free basis;
* customer satisfaction – the business may attract more overseas customers if it adopts the retail export scheme.

Details about the retail export scheme, including forms to complete and procedures to adopt, are given in HMRC Notice 704.

Note – there is no problem with a retailer making an administration charge to customers for the time spent dealing with the paperwork created by the scheme.

Planning points to consider

[**12.13**] The following planning points should be given consideration.

* Remember that an export of goods outside the EU is always zero-rated, irrespective of the status of the customer. However, the priority is to ensure that proper export evidence is held to confirm that the goods have left the EU.
* Goods supplied to an EU customer can be zero-rated as long as the customer is registered for VAT in his own country and provides his VAT registration number to the UK supplier. Again, proof of shipment is a priority issue.
* The importance of obtaining proper export evidence to support zero-rating cannot be emphasised enough. If HMRC is not satisfied with the evidence provided, it can treat the goods as being supplied in the UK. This could create an output tax charge if the goods in question are standard rated.
* Be aware of the distance selling rules that may require a UK supplier to register for VAT in another EU country if the value of its sales to non-registered customers exceed certain limits. Remember that countries have the choice of adopting one of two annual turnover thresholds, ie €35,000 or €100,000.

- If goods are collected and taken out of the country by an overseas customer eligible for zero-rating, it is worthwhile to collect a deposit from the customer equal to the amount of VAT due on the supply. The deposit can then be refunded to the customer when he provides export evidence to confirm the goods have left the UK.
- The retail export scheme can offer commercial benefits to some retailers by giving certain overseas customers the chance to buy goods on a VAT-free basis.
- A UK trader whose sales are wholly or mainly exports will probably be in a repayment situation on his VAT returns. The cash flow benefits of submitting monthly rather than quarterly returns should therefore be considered.
- Be aware of the need for a business selling goods to VAT registered customers in other EU countries to complete a monthly EU sales list (ESL) rather than quarterly if the value of such sales within the EU has exceeded £35,000 in the current or previous four quarters.

Chapter 13

International Services: Place of Supply

Key topics in this chapter:

- The importance of establishing the 'place of supply' of services as far as VAT liabilities are concerned.
- How the reverse charge works and its importance in the VAT system.
- The current position with the place of supply rules after major changes introduced in 2010 and 2011.
- The difference between B2B (business to business) and B2C (business to consumer) sales and why this is important.
- The EC Sales List which needs to be completed for services supplied to a business customer in another EU country if the service is covered by the reverse charge.
- Land-related services – an exception to the general B2B rule.
- Other services when VAT must still be charged to an overseas customer.
- Sales of services to customers outside the EU where no VAT is charged (including B2C sales).
- Practical examples of situations where a UK supplier provides services to an overseas customer.
- Identifying the country in which a business is based – very important with place of supply rules.
- Common questions (with answers) in relation to the place of supply rules post 2010 and 2011 changes.

Introduction

[13.1] The rules concerning supplies of goods and services to an overseas customer are very different as far as VAT is concerned. The VAT rules concerning the supply of goods basically involve looking at where the goods are shipped, and the status of the customer. The rules concerning the supply of services can vary according to the type of service being performed, where the work is being performed, as well as the status and location of the customer.

Important changes were introduced to the place of supply rules on 1 January 2010 and 2011. The main impact of these changes is that in the case of most B2B (business to business) supplies, the VAT charge (or otherwise) depends on where the customer is based rather than the supplier. These changes mean that a lot more transactions avoid a domestic VAT charge on B2B sales. The position is unchanged for B2C (business to consumer) supplies, ie the location of the supplier remains the default position but there are again exceptions to this rule, one of which relates to supplies of broadcasting, telecommunications and electronic services after 31 December 2014 (see **14.9**).

The main exception when the VAT charge to an overseas business customer does not depend on where the customer is based relates to a land-related service. The location of the land is then the key issue, ie a building service (or professional service) linked to UK land will mean VAT is charged to an overseas customer in exactly the same way as to a UK customer, ie the location of the customer is irrelevant.

The first challenge on this subject is to be clear about the difference between a supply of goods and a supply of services.

- *Goods* – in general terms, a supply of goods involves a change of ownership of goods from a supplier to a customer. In most cases, the supply will be for a physical product that can be touched, and the transfer of ownership will normally take place by the supplier raising an invoice and the customer providing payment to settle his account.
  Examples of goods – computers, washing machines, cars, furniture.
- *Services* – as a useful guideline, any supply that is not a supply of goods will be a supply of services. There is usually an indication of work being performed, eg a tax consultant providing advice or a decorator painting a wall. The value of the service is usually confirmed by the payment provided by the customer, which will form the basis of the VAT charge. No VAT is payable on a free supply of services.
  Examples of services – writing an article for a magazine (copyright service), building services, hotel accommodation, an entertainer performing at a show.

Place of supply – basic principles/reverse charge

[13.2] The intention of the new rules introduced on 1 January 2010 and 2011 was to simplify procedures. The aim of this chapter is to look at the basic rules on the subject that can be applied in the majority of cases to arrive at a sensible conclusion regarding the VAT liability of the service being performed.

The phrase 'place of supply' is crucial because this rule establishes the country within which the particular supply takes place and the jurisdiction where any VAT will be due. If the 'place of supply' is deemed to be in another EU country outside of the UK, then the VAT due on that supply will be payable in that country – not the UK. If the place of supply is outside the EU, then no VAT is payable, although the country in question may have its own indirect tax system similar to VAT with issues to consider. In most cases, the VAT due in other EU countries will be paid by the customer by applying the reverse charge, on other occasions, by the UK supplier registering for VAT in that particular country. From 1 January 2015 it will be possible for UK suppliers of broadcasting, telecommunications and electronic services to consumers in other EU countries to account for the VAT due in the other EU countries using the Mini One Stop Shop facility as an alternative to registering for VAT in the other EU countries (see **14.9**).

Example – A UK business receives accountancy services worth £10,000 from a Danish supplier. The Danish accountant will not charge Danish VAT (the place of supply for such services is the location of the customer under the default rule for B2B sales) but the UK business will instead account for output tax of £2,000 in Box 1 of its own VAT return through the reverse charge mechanism (the rate of VAT that applies for the reverse charge entry depends on the rate of VAT in the customer's country rather than that of the supplier, ie 20% in the UK).

If the UK business is making taxable supplies and therefore able to reclaim input tax (no partial exemption problems etc) then the same amount of £2,000 will be included in Box 4 of the same VAT return. This produces a nil VAT payment overall. Entries of £10,000 (the net value of the service) will also be included in Boxes 6 and 7 of the return (sales and purchases).

Note – the Box 6 entry in this type of transaction often causes confusion for advisers, ie why is the payment to a supplier being treated as income (outputs) of the customer when he completes his UK VAT return. The logical way of justifying this approach is to recognise that the customer is avoiding the need for the overseas supplier to register for VAT in the UK. So the VAT return entries that would have been made by the supplier if he had a UK VAT registration (ie output tax in Box 1 and net sales recorded in Box 6) are instead being made by the customer. The customer is treating the transaction as both his own income and his own expenditure.

The two key rules for a UK business are as follows:

* *If a UK business supplies services and the place of supply is the UK,* then UK VAT must be charged on the supply (assuming the services in question are subject to VAT). This applies regardless of where the customer belongs. In other words, a customer in, eg Sweden, is dealt with in exactly the same way as a customer in Scotland.

* *If a UK business supplies services and the place of supply is in another EU country,* subject to the registration limits in that country either the UK supplier or the customer is liable to account for any VAT due in that country (where the customer is liable to account for the supplier's output tax, this will be done through the reverse charge mechanism).

See Examples 1 and 2 for an illustration of the different VAT treatment of the above situations.

Example 1

ABC Ltd is VAT registered in the UK and does some work for a business customer that is based in Belgium (EU country). The work relates to a UK building.

What is the VAT position for both the UK supplier and the Belgian customer?

Solution – ABC Ltd must charge UK VAT on the work performed (assuming the rate of VAT that applies on this particular service is standard rated) because the place of supply for land-related services depends on where the land is situated. This UK VAT charge is made even though the customer is based in Belgium.

However, all is not lost for the Belgian customer. Although he will not be able to reclaim the UK VAT on his Belgian VAT return, he may be able to make a claim to the UK to recover this VAT through the overseas VAT repayment system. Alternatively, if he is using the UK premises to make taxable sales (eg a retail shop), then he can register for VAT in the UK and get input tax recovery on UK costs in the usual way.

The overseas VAT refund system gives scope for a business registered for VAT in an EU country to reclaim VAT incurred in another EU country other than its own. A full analysis of the system is considered in Chapter 15 at **15.3**.

Example 2

ABC Ltd provides a different service to the same Belgian customer. The rules for this particular service state that the place of supply is based on the general rule of the customer's location (eg accountancy services).

What is the VAT position for both the UK supplier and the Belgian customer?

Solution – ABC Ltd will raise a sales invoice to the Belgian business customer without charging VAT. It should be satisfied that the customer has a bona fide VAT registration in Belgium (or can provide some other evidence of being in business). The invoice will be noted along the lines of: 'this supply is subject to the reverse charge'.

However, the services are still subject to VAT and the Belgian customer will account for the output tax on his VAT return. He will apply the Belgian rate of VAT to the value of the invoice raised by the UK supplier, and will include this amount of tax in Box 1 of his VAT return. As long as the service carried out by the UK supplier relates to a taxable supply (ie not relevant to an exempt or non-business activity), then the same amount of VAT can be reclaimed in Box 4 of the return as input tax. The net value of the transaction will be recorded in Box 6 and Box 7 as well.

The transaction has a nil overall effect on the Belgian's VAT return but is still declaring output tax on the transaction in question.

An important point to remember about this subject is that the performance of standard rated services by an EU supplier for any EU customer will include VAT at some point. VAT will either be charged in the supplier's own country (and declared on his own return), or declared in the customer's country, as in Example 2 above.

Here are a couple of other key points with the reverse charge:

- *Ignore Box 8 and Box 9 of VAT return* – if a transaction involves the sale or purchase of services, then entries are never made in Box 8 or 9 of the UK VAT return by either the supplier or the customer. These two boxes only relate to trading in goods between businesses in different EU countries (with VAT registration in their own country). For a business that only sells services, eg a firm of accountants, these boxes will always be zero.

- *Sale of services included in Box 6* – the sales of services to overseas customers are always included in Box 6 (outputs) of the VAT return completed by the seller even though they are outside the scope of UK

VAT in most cases (eg because the place of supply is in the customer's country). The exception is if the supplier uses the flat rate scheme (FRS) because the Box 6 entry is only made if a sale is included in the scheme calculations – and no FRS tax is due on income that is outside the scope of VAT.

(HMRC Notice 741A, paras 5.2 and 5.3 and section 18).

Summary of the changes to the place of supply rules

Introduction

[13.3] As a brief summary, four boxes are shown below that highlight the changes made to the place of supply rules on 1 January 2010, 1 January 2011, 1 January 2013 and 1 January 2015. Take time to read through them and note the range of services where the rules changed.

As a separate summary, a key question now being asked by advisers is: when must VAT still be charged by a UK business on a service carried out for an overseas customer? The following summary highlights the main situations.

VAT must still be charged on services to an overseas customer in the following situations:

* *land-related services where the land is situated in the UK* – unless the services are specifically zero-rated work (eg building services on a new residential dwelling) or certain other services (see **13.5**);
* *admission to a UK event (B2B or B2C)* – eg an accountancy CPD seminar organised by a commercial training provider;
* *car hire – B2B – hire period less than 30 days* – where the car is made available to the customer in the UK;
* *B2C sales to EU customers* – general default position for place of supply is the location of the supplier;
* *many B2C sales to non-EU customers* – but see **13.8** below for exceptions.

Box 1 – changes introduced on 1 January 2010

* The place of supply for most B2B (business to business) services is now dependent on where the customer is based rather than the supplier. So if the customer is based outside the UK and is in business (EU or non-EU), then UK VAT is not charged in most cases.
* A UK business making sales to EU business customers where no VAT is charged should declare these sales each calendar quarter by completing an EU Sales List (ESL).
* The basic rule above did not apply in 2010 to those services listed in Box 2 until further changes were introduced on 1 January 2011. In 2010, the place of supply for those services in Box 2 depended on where they were actually performed.

- The place of supply for land-related services is not where the customer is based but where the land is located.
- The place of supply for most B2C (business to non-business) sales is where the supplier is based, although there are exceptions if the customer is based outside the EU.

Box 2 – changes introduced on 1 January 2011

- For business and non-business customers, the place of supply in respect of the following services is where the events actually take place: services in respect of admission to cultural, artistic, sporting, scientific, educational, entertainment or similar events (including fairs and exhibitions), and ancillary services relating to admission to such events.
- For non-business customers, the place of supply of the following services is where the activities concerned actually take place: services relating to cultural, artistic, sporting, scientific, educational, entertainment or similar activities (including fairs and exhibitions) and ancillary services relating to such activities, including services of organisers of such activities.
- For other services linked to these categories, the place of supply will resort to the default position, ie location of the customer for B2B sales. It is only the *admission* to cultural, artistic events etc that will have a place of supply based on where the event takes place in the case of B2B sales.

Box 3 – changes introduced on 1 January 2013

- The changes introduced on 1 January 2013 affect B2C supplies of long-term hiring of means of transport.
- Details of the changes are included at **13.11**.

Box 4 – changes introduced on 1 January 2015

- The changes introduced on 1 January 2015 affect B2C supplies of broadcasting, telecommunications and electronic services.
- Details of the change are included in Chapter 14.

Services relating to land

[13.4] The VAT liability of services relating to land is dependent on where the land in question is situated. If the land is situated in the UK, then UK VAT will be charged (assuming the work in question is not zero-rated). If the land is located in another EU country, then the supply is regarded as taking place in that country.

The services covered by these rules include:

*   any works of construction, demolition, conversion, reconstruction, alteration, enlargement, repair or maintenance of a building or civil engineering work;
*   services such as those provided by estate agents, auctioneers, architects, surveyors, engineers and others involved in matters relating to land;
*   services provided by hotels and similar establishments.

Note – an accountant producing accounts for an overseas landlord in relation to his UK property portfolio is not supplying a land-related service. He is still providing the services of an accountant.

If the land in question is located outside the EU, then the supply is outside the scope of UK and EU VAT.

The main problem with the rules on services relating to land is that it could create a liability for a UK supplier to register for VAT in another EU country. Think of a UK builder doing some work for private customers (non-business) in France. However, if the customer is VAT registered in the country where the land is located, then it may be possible to avoid registering for VAT through the customer applying the reverse charge mechanism. We allow this process in the UK to avoid having a lot of overseas VAT registrations being created, possibly for only one transaction.

Note – the place of supply rules in relation to land were not affected by the changes introduced on either 1 January 2010 or 2011.

See Examples 3 and 4 for practical examples of how VAT is dealt with on typical land transactions.

Example 3

ABC Construction Services Ltd is based in the UK, and has been asked to build an extension to a property in Dublin that is owned by an Italian company. All work will obviously be carried out where the property is located, ie Ireland. The value of the building works is £500,000.

What is the VAT position?

Solution – ABC Construction Services Ltd is making supplies in Ireland that exceed the Irish VAT registration threshold. The company must therefore register for VAT in Ireland, and charge Irish VAT to the Italian customer. There is no scope for any reverse charge to be carried out by the customer because he is not VAT registered in the country where the land is based. The option of ABC registering for VAT in Ireland is the only available option to deal with the Irish VAT issue.

Example 4

A very wealthy individual resident in Dubai has purchased a big residential property in London and arranged for a UK builder to carry out a lot of improvement work on the property. What is the VAT position?

Solution – in this situation, the place of supply is where the building is based, ie the UK. All other issues are irrelevant, including the fact that the sales invoice is being raised to a resident outside the EU. The work carried out by the builder is subject to UK VAT in the normal way.

Note – the same rule also applies to land-related services provided to a business client. So if a UK architect provides building plans for a German or Australian-based business customer, and the building in question is in the UK, a 20% UK VAT charge will apply in both cases.

Example 5

A UK-based architect is providing services to a wealthy private individual who lives in Spain, in relation to a property that is being built for the customer in Denmark. What is the VAT position?

Solution – the place of supply for land-related services is the location of the land in the case of professional as well as construction services, so the architect is making supplies in Denmark. If the value of his services exceeds the VAT registration threshold in Denmark, then he must register for VAT in Denmark and charge Danish VAT to his customer in Spain. This process might seem laborious but it is ensuring that the Spanish customer cannot gain an unfair tax advantage if he uses an architect based in a country with a lower rate of VAT (the UK rate of 20% is much lower than the Danish rate of 25%).

(HMRC Notice 741A, section 6).

HMRC policy on certain land-related services

[13.5] On 2 August 2012 HMRC issued Revenue & Customs Brief 22/12 which included details of changes to their policy in relation to the place of supply of certain land-related services, in particular, stand space at conferences and exhibitions, storage and warehousing, and access to airport lounges. A summary of the revised HMRC policy is as follows:

Stand space at conferences and exhibitions

HMRC will continue to regard the supply of specific stand space at a conference or exhibition as a supply of land where no accompanying services are provided. However, where stand space is provided with accompanying services as a package, the package (stand space and services) will be subject to the general place of supply rule for B2B supplies when supplied to business customers ie the place of supply will be where the business customer is located. Accompanying services include the design and erection of a temporary stand, security, power, telecommunications, hire of machinery and publicity material.

Storage and warehousing

Where a supplier grants the right to use a specific area of a UK warehouse or storage area for the exclusive use of the customer to store goods (ie a self-storage facility), the service will be treated as relating to land and subject to VAT in the UK. However, where the supplier agrees to store goods but does not grant a right to a specific area for the exclusive use of the customer, this will not be seen as a land related supply but will be subject to the general place of supply rule for B2B supplies when supplied to business customers ie the place of supply will be where the business customer is located.

Access to airport lounges

HMRC now regard the supply of access to airport lounges as a land-related supply and VAT, if applicable, will be due in the country where the airport lounge is located.

Receiving land services from abroad

[**13.6**] The main problem with the rules on services relating to land is that it could create a liability for a UK supplier to register for VAT in another EU country or vice versa. However, this is not a problem in the UK in some cases because an overseas builder/land-related professional working on UK land does not need to become VAT registered if his customer is in the UK and is VAT registered. The UK customer is able to account for the reverse charge on such supplies.

This opportunity is confirmed in HMRC Notice 741A through the extension of the 'reverse charge' procedures. It relates to builders/land-related professionals based in both EU and non-EU countries.

'18.11 Extension to other services supplied in the UK

The reverse charge also applies to the following services when they are made in the UK:

• services relating to land and property (see section 6)

18.11.1 When does the extension to the reverse charge apply?

The extension to the reverse charge applies if you are UK VAT registered and receive B2B supplies of the services listed in paragraph 18.11 which are supplied in the UK where your supplier belongs outside the UK.'

(HMRC Notice 741A, section 18).

Example 6

Athens Builders, is an overseas trader based in Greece, and staff of the company travel to the UK (after 1 December 2012) to do some bricklaying work at a new extension for a retailer based in London. The place of supply is the UK (where the building is based) and the value of the work is £50,000. As the supply takes place after 1 December 2012, the Greek company cannot benefit from the UK VAT registration threshold. However, the Greek company can avoid the need to become VAT registered in the UK because the retailer can account for the VAT instead by doing a reverse charge calculation on its own VAT return. If the customer was not VAT registered, then the Greek builder would need to register for VAT in the UK as an overseas trader.

Note – the Greek company can still register for VAT in the UK if it wishes to do so, rather than have its VAT registered customer account for the VAT via the reverse charge. This would create an easier route for reclaiming VAT paid on UK expenses – input tax can be claimed on a VAT return compared to an overseas refund claim.

Services which are supplied where physically carried out

[13.7] A supply of the following services is treated as being made where the services are physically carried out, as long as the customer is not in business, ie it is a B2C sale:

- cultural, artistic, sporting, scientific, educational or entertainment services and any services ancillary to any such services;
- services relating to exhibitions, conferences or meetings and any services ancillary to (including organising) any such services;
- ancillary transport services.

Regarding the VAT treatment of services in the above categories:

- with the exception of the supply of electronic services – an overseas supplier providing services to a person in the UK that is not in business (ie B2C sales) must register for UK VAT immediately he begins to make taxable supplies.

Note – the place of supply in relation to admission charges to such events are taxable according to the country where the event takes place. So admission to a UK accountancy conference (regarded as educational services in the list above) would be subject to UK VAT if carried out by a commercial training provider in the UK.

No VAT charge on some supplies to non-business customers (outside EU)

[13.8] So far in this chapter, we have established that the basic rule since 1 January 2010 is that the place of supply for B2C sales is based on the location of the supplier. An exception to this rule relates to supplies of broadcasting, telecommunications and electronic services to EU consumers after 31 December 2014 which is covered in Chapter 14. This section deals with the important exceptions to this rule in cases where the customer is outside the EU.

Many readers will recall the list of services known as 'Schedule 5' services that used to determine situations when the VAT charge was determined by the location of the customer before 1 January 2010. 'Schedule 5' is no longer needed because of the basic rule for B2B sales – but a new *Schedule 4A (para 16)* of *Value Added Tax Act 1994 (VATA 1994)* has been introduced instead. This produces the outcome that the place of supply for the old 'Schedule 5' services is protected for any customer not in the EU, ie including B2C sales to a non-EU customer.

The relevant rule is as follows:

- if the service is listed in *Schedule 4A, para 16*, then the supply is treated as taking place where the recipient belongs if the recipient belongs outside the EU and the Isle of Man. In such cases, the supply is outside the scope of UK VAT.

See Example 7 for an illustration of the above points in a practical situation.

Example 7

Accountancy (and tax) work is included in the list of *Schedule 4A, para 16* services (see below). Smith and Smith accountants are VAT registered in the UK and are currently working on three important jobs for overseas customers (all work being physically carried out in the UK):

- completing an audited set of accounts for a VAT-registered business based in Spain (EU customer);
- completing a UK tax return for a private individual who lives in Spain;
- completing a UK tax return for a private individual who lives in Australia (non-EU).

What is the VAT liability of the three jobs?

Solution – the supply to the Spanish business will be made without charging UK VAT. This is because the customer is in business in another EU country (B2B sale). The output tax on the supply will be accounted for by the Spanish customer who will apply the reverse charge on his own VAT return in Spain, ie output tax in Box 1 of the return and input tax reclaimed in Box 4 as long as the work in question relates to a taxable supply.

The private individual in Spain is not in business, so the supply reverts to the usual 'place of supply' rule for B2C sales, which is that it takes place where the supplier is based (ie in the UK). The individual will therefore be charged UK VAT at the standard rate.

The Australian individual will not be charged VAT because 'accountancy' services are included in *Schedule 4A, para 16*, so the place of supply is Australia even though he or she is not a business customer. However, Smith and Smith will need to ensure they do not incur any liability to register for any sales/turnover based tax in Australia.

Schedule 4A para 16 services	*Example of services included*	*Comments*
Transfers and assignments of copyright, patents, licences, trademarks and similar rights.	The granting of a right by a photographer for one of his photographs to be published in a magazine article.	
Advertising services.		
Services of consultants, engineers, consultancy bureaux, lawyers, accountants and similar services; data processing and provision of information, other than any services related to land.	An accountant completing a private tax return for a customer.	Note – this is an interesting category and needs to be approached with care. For example, a consultant's services are only covered if he is working in his own field of expertise.

Schedule 4A para 16 services	Example of services included	Comments
		In reality, the section requires a degree of expertise within the work being performed. For example, accountancy services do not include clerical or secretarial services.
Acceptance of any obligation to refrain from pursuing or exercising, in whole or part, any business activity or any such rights.		
Banking, financial and insurance services (including reinsurance) other than the provision of safe deposit facilities.	Debt collection services.	
The provision of access to, and of transport or transmission through, natural gas and electricity distribution systems and the provision of other directly linked services.		
The supply of staff.		
The letting on hire of goods other than means of transport.	The hire of computer and office equipment.	Note – this paragraph contains an interesting clause that goods include all forms of movable property or equipment but not land and property or equipment and machinery installed as a fixture. It is also important to look at where the enjoyment of the goods takes place. See Example 8.
Telecommunication services, radio and television broadcasting services, electronically supplied services.	Transmission or delivery of another person's material by electronic means.	Note – this section considers supplies made over the Internet or other electronic networks. The provisions are quite complicated and specialist advice may be appropriate to establish the correct VAT position.

Example 8

ABC VAT Consultants have been asked to advise on the VAT liability of the following supplies of services.

(a)   An American tourist in the UK hires a video camera from a UK provider for use during her visit.

(b)   A UK golf club hires out a set of golf clubs to a UK customer for use on his holiday in the USA. The clubs will be used exclusively in the USA – at no times will they be used to play golf in the UK or any other EU country.

(c)   A satellite TV company based in India supplies broadcasting services to UK subscribers. The services are used and enjoyed in the UK.

Solution –

(a)   VAT needs to be charged at the standard rate. This is because the use of the goods is taking place in the UK.
(b)   The place of supply is outside the EU as long as the customer can demonstrate that the goods are only being used in the USA. If not, then the supply will be deemed to be taking place in the UK and subject to VAT at the standard rate.
(c)   The services are used and enjoyed in the UK and are subject to UK VAT. The place of supply is the UK even though the supplier is based in India.

Transport services

[13.9] As a general rule, the VAT liability of B2C transport services depends on where the transportation is carried out. For supplies of intra-Community haulage transport (B2B), the place of supply follows the general rule that it is the location of the customer that counts.

Example – the place of supply for transporting goods from London to Rome for an Italian business customer is Italy and the supply would be subject to the reverse charge there.

VAT treatment of B2B supplies of services relating to the transportation of goods when performed wholly outside of the EU

[13.10] Think of a UK supplier working for a UK business customer supplying freight transport services that are performed wholly outside of the EU. From 1 January 2010 VAT is due on most services based on where the business customer is located. In the absence of special rules UK VAT would be due on such freight transport services and the services may also be subject to local indirect taxes in the countries where the transportation actually takes place. *VATA 1994, Sch 4A, paras 9B* and *9C* are special rules which have the effect of treating B2B services relating to the transportation of goods as made wholly outside of the EU, providing the transportation takes place wholly outside of the EU.

In essence a supply of services to a relevant business person consisting of the transportation of goods that would otherwise be treated as made in the UK is to be treated as made wholly outside of the EU providing the transportation takes place wholly outside of the EU. This VAT treatment also applies to ancillary transport services supplied to a relevant business person, such as loading, unloading and handling goods, providing the services are physically performed wholly outside of the EU.

The hiring of a means of transport

[13.11] The place of supply rules relating to the hire of a means of transport changed on 1 January 2010 and on 1 January 2013.

From 1 January 2010 the rules are dependent on whether the customer is a business customer (B2B) or a consumer (B2C) and whether the period of hire is long term or short term. Long-term hire means hire for a period exceeding 30 days, or exceeding 90 days in the case of a vessel. Other periods of hire are regarded as short-term hire.

The change on 1 January 2013 affects B2C supplies of long-term hiring of means of transport.

A summary of the rules is included below:

Rules before 1 January 2010

*   The place of supply was where the supplier belonged.

Rules from 1 January 2010 to 31 December 2012

*   B2B and B2C short-term hiring of means of transport are supplied where the means of transport is put at the disposal of the customer, that is, where the customer takes control of the means of transport.
*   B2B supplies of long-term hiring of means of transport are supplied where the customer belongs.
*   B2C supplies of long-term hiring of means of transport are supplied where the supplier belongs.

Rules from 1 January 2013

*   B2B and B2C short-term hiring of means of transport are supplied where the means of transport is put at the disposal of the customer, that is, where the customer takes control of the means of transport.
*   B2B and B2C supplies of long-term hiring of means of transport are supplied where the customer belongs, except for B2C supplies of long-term hiring of a pleasure boat.
*   B2C supplies of long-term hiring of a pleasure boat are supplied where the pleasure boat is put at the disposal of the customer where the service is provided from the supplier's place of business or fixed establishment in that place.

(HMRC Notice 741A, section 7).

Example 9

A UK car hire company rented a car to a French business customer for 31 days in October 2010. The car was made available to the customer in the UK. What is the VAT position?

Solution – the place of supply before 1 January 2010 was the location of the supplier, so UK VAT would have been charged on the hiring before this date. However, the October 2010 hiring was for more than 30 days to a business customer outside the UK and the place of supply is now France, ie where the customer is based. The French hirer will account for the reverse charge on his own return.

Evidence of business status

[13.12] In the earlier sections, we have considered the phrase B2B – but how do we know if a customer is 'in business'?

*   In the case of EU businesses, the best proof is evidence of the customer's VAT registration number. The VAT number should be recorded on the sales invoice.

- If the EU customer is 'in business' but does not have a VAT registration number (think of a small bookkeeping business in the UK trading below the VAT registration threshold), then the regulations allow alternative evidence of business status to be acquired, eg website details, letter-headings, business stationery, Chamber of Commerce membership.
- Alternative evidence (other than a VAT number) will also be needed for business customers outside the EU.
- If the supplier cannot determine where his customer belongs, or obtain evidence of his business status, he should normally charge his customer VAT.

EC Sales List

[13.13] An important change introduced on 1 January 2010 means that a UK business selling services to an EU business customer where the customer must account for the reverse charge must record details of all such transaction on an EC Sales List (ESL). The ESL is relevant to all services where the EU customer declares the reverse charge, not just the new situations that apply after 1 January 2010.

The ESL (VAT101) has been in place for many years and has been completed by UK businesses that sell goods to VAT registered businesses in other EU countries. The only difference for a supply of services is that a code 3 entry will need to be made in the end column of the form.

The aim of the ESL is to enable the tax authorities to ensure that reverse charge entries are correctly being made by those businesses that are receiving services without being charged VAT. This is particularly relevant if the business in question is partly exempt and cannot fully reclaim input tax.

The key rules for ESL forms are as follows:

- The forms must be completed on a calendar quarter basis, either in paper format or online. An extra seven days (21 instead of 14) are given if the form is completed online.
- It is possible that some supplies will be made to business customers in other EU countries who are not VAT registered. These sales will not be recorded on the ESL because each entry requires a VAT registration number otherwise the form will be rejected.
- The entries on the ESL only relate to the supply of taxable services not to those that are exempt from VAT.
- The ESL forms are not covered by the new penalty regime. However, a penalty of £5, £10 or £15 per day can be charged if the ESL is submitted late and a potential penalty of £100 could be charged for a material inaccuracy on the form, unless there is a reasonable excuse for such an inaccuracy.

As a final point, HMRC recognises that the completion of ESL forms is an extra challenge for UK businesses and has confirmed it will 'keep administrative burdens and VAT costs to a minimum.'

Supplies to be used by the customer for non-business purposes

[13.14] Here is another major difference between the old and new rules, again explained by a practical example. The basic principle is that the reverse charge concept will apply to services supplied to a VAT registered customer in another EU country (where the default position applies), even if the customer uses a particular service for non-business purposes.

Example 10

Jones is an accountant based in London and he has done some work for a VAT registered charity based in Denmark (EU country) in relation to its non-business activities. What is the VAT position?

Solution – the place of supply is based on the location of the customer for B2B sales. This situation also applies in relation to non-business activities after 1 January 2010 as long as the business (charity in this case) has some business supplies. This is a further simplification measure that makes life easier for a UK business. If it receives a VAT registration number from its customer, it does not need to worry about whether it is working for the business or non-business part of the organisation. *Article 43* of the *VAT Directive* confirms that a taxable person (as defined) who also carries out transactions that are not considered to be taxable supplies of goods or services shall be regarded as a taxable person in respect of all services rendered to him.

Time of supply

[13.15] The tax authorities are keen to ensure that there is a cross-reference facility between an entry on an ESL (EC Sales List as explained in **13.13**) and on the customer's VAT return (reverse charge entry). This is an important control to counter the risk of either VAT fraud or major errors taking place. To facilitate this process, new time of supply rules took effect on 1 January 2010.

- *Single supplies* – the key date is when the service has been completed or paid for, whichever happens first. A single supply relates to the situation when a service has a clear start and finish date, eg repairing a vehicle. The completion date will usually coincide with an invoice being raised, so this will hopefully be the key date in most cases.
- *Continuous supplies with regular billing periods* – for example, the hire of a photocopier machine. In such cases, a reverse charge entry must be made when either an invoice is raised or payment received, whichever happens first.
- *Continuous supplies that are not subject to regular billing or payment periods* – in such cases, the regulations create an annual tax point of 31 December each year.

It may be complicated in some cases to determine the time of supply, and as such, the HMRC guidance states:

'we are aware of the difficulties, for example, in determining when a service has been completed. Events such as entry of a transaction into the accounts, receipt of an invoice or date of payment might be appropriate indicators of when that point is reached.'

(HMRC Notice 741A, para 18.6).

Where is a business actually based?

[13.16] In most cases, for the purposes of determining the place of supply of services, it will be fairly easy to decide in which country a customer or supplier is based. For example, if a supply of services is made to a private individual and used for his private or non-business purposes, then he is treated as belonging in the country where he has his 'usual place of residence.'

In the case of services provided to a business customer, the approach to adopt is as follows:

- the services are supplied in the country where he has a 'business establishment' or some other 'fixed establishment' and no such establishment elsewhere;
- if he does not have a 'business establishment' or other 'fixed establishment', then the place of supply is based on his 'usual place of residence.'

The phrase 'business establishment' is not defined in the legislation but is taken by HMRC to mean the principal place of business. This means the head office, headquarters or 'seat' from which the business is run. There can only be one such place and it may be an office, showroom or factory.

Example – a business has its headquarters in the UK and branches in Spain, Italy and France. Its business establishment is in the UK.

An important point to remember is that just because a company might be incorporated in the UK, this does not necessarily mean that its business establishment is in the UK.

Example – a UK incorporated company trades entirely from its head office in Switzerland. Its business establishment is in Switzerland.

The phrase 'fixed establishment' is an establishment other than a 'business establishment' and the guidance from HMRC is that it 'has both the technical and human resources necessary for providing and receiving services on a permanent basis.'

Note – the word permanent is important, meaning that a temporary presence in a country is usually not enough to create a fixed establishment.

Example – an overseas business sets up a branch comprising staff and offices in the UK to provide services. The UK branch is a 'fixed establishment'.

The challenging question is: what happens if a business has establishments in more than one country? Which establishment is relevant as far as the place of supply rules are concerned?

In this situation, the place of supply is based on the country which is most relevant for the services in question, ie in which country are the services most directly used or to be used. The answer to this question could be linked to the address that appears on contracts, correspondence and invoices or where the directors dealing with a contract are permanently based. Another indicator could be to consider where decisions are made and controls exercised over the performance of the contract. See Examples 11 and 12.

Example 11

John trades in the UK and supplies staff to retail establishments throughout the world. He has been asked by a UK customer with its head office in the UK (business establishment) to supply staff for its retail branch in the USA (fixed establishment). John will raise his sales invoice to the UK head office, which will pay him for the services he has provided.

John's service in this situation (a supply of staff) is being provided to a customer outside the UK because the American fixed establishment is effectively receiving the direct benefit of the staff he has provided. He does not charge VAT to the UK company because the place of supply for the staff is based on the location of the customer, which is outside the UK in this example. John will need to be careful that he does not need to register for any indirect tax system in America.

Note – this example is quite an unusual situation because you would normally expect the branch in America to recruit its own staff rather than through its head office in another country. But from a VAT position, the end result is the same because it is the establishment that is receiving the benefit of the services that matters rather than the establishment that is organising the service.

Example 12

Jane is VAT registered in the UK and provides advertising services to clients throughout the world. She has been asked to provide services to a customer with its head office in Germany (business establishment) regarding an advertising promotion campaign for a branch of the German company based in London (fixed establishment). Although Jane mainly liaises with staff from the UK branch on a day-to-day basis, to assess their advertising needs and target market, all of the artistic and other decisions concerning the adverts are made by the German head office.

Jane's services are being provided to the head office in Germany to which she is contracted. This is because the German base is the source of control and decision-making. The place of supply for advertising services is based on the location of the customer for B2B supplies, therefore Germany in this case. No UK VAT is charged, which is dealt with by the German customer using the reverse charge mechanism.

Example 13

A UK bank receives some VAT consultancy advice from a UK VAT consultant. It asks the consultant to raise an invoice for his services to its Swiss subsidiary company. The place of supply is still the UK because the UK-based customer has enjoyed the benefit of the supply. The invoice address in this situation is irrelevant.

Note – the significance of these rules is that they prevent the situation where, for example, a UK business unable to reclaim input tax (for example, if it only makes exempt supplies) can avoid a VAT charge on its expenses by asking suppliers to raise an invoice to eg a small head office in Switzerland. The logic of such a measure would be to try and avoid a VAT charge on the basis that the place of supply is where the customer is based in Switzerland but this is incorrect.

The legislation effective from 1 January 2010 (*Finance Act 2009, Sch 36*) introduced two new concepts of a 'relevant business person' and a 'relevant country' as far as the rules on belonging to a country are concerned. A 'relevant country' means:

- the country in which the person has a business establishment, or some other fixed establishment (if it has none in any other country);
- if the person has a business establishment, or some other fixed establishment or establishments, in more than one country, the country of the relevant establishment (ie the establishment most directly connected with the supply); and
- otherwise, the country of the person's usual place of residence (in the case of a body corporate, where it is legally constituted).

In basic terms, a relevant business person means someone receiving services otherwise than in a private capacity. As explained above, a supply to someone who is not a relevant business person depends on his usual place of residence (HMRC Notice 741A, section 3).

Input tax issues for a business making all supplies outside the UK? (EU and non-EU)

[13.17] The main general principle as far as input tax is concerned is that a business based in the UK is able to reclaim input tax on UK costs relevant to an activity where the place of supply is outside the UK, as long as the activity in question would be taxable if it were supplied in the UK. This important point is highlighted by Example 14.

(HMRC Notice 741A, para 2.12).

Example 14

John is the sole trader of his own accountancy practice in the UK earning £50,000 per annum. His only cost is that he uses the services of a VAT registered subcontractor in the UK to carry out a lot of the accountancy work. John's clients are all business customers based in France. What can John do to improve his VAT position?

The situation is as follows:

- The place of supply for accountancy services to EU business customers is where the customer is located, ie France. So John does not charge UK VAT on the value of his services. The French customers will deal with the VAT on their own returns using the reverse charge.

- John is allowed to register for VAT in the UK (even though the place of supply of his services is France and he has no UK sales) and reclaim input tax on all of his UK expenses (subject to normal rules), including the fees of the subcontractor he uses to prepare accounts. His VAT registration in the UK will be made on a voluntary basis.

The end result is that the above situation is fair. If John had some UK income and some French income, he would be able to register for VAT in the UK and fully reclaim input tax – it is only reasonable that he is not denied the same privilege just because all of his customers are based in France.

Common questions on place of supply rules

[13.18] The changes introduced in 2010 and 2011 produced a number of challenging issues for a business to consider. This section considers some of the practical questions that have been asked by advisers.

- *Does the default position apply to services provided to a VAT registered person based in another EU country for his private purposes (as opposed to non-business services)?*
  No. To give an example, if a UK accountant is completing the private tax return of an individual who lives in Portugal, this is not classed as a B2B sale, even if the Portuguese person gives you proof that he is in business. The service is classed as a B2C supply and UK VAT must be charged. This is a reasonable outcome because a private customer has no way in most cases of paying over the VAT through, eg a reverse charge calculation if he is not registered for VAT.
- *Can the same EC Sales List (ESL) be used for a business that sells goods and services to VAT registered businesses in the EU?*
  Yes. The only difference is that entries on the ESL relevant to services will be given a 'code 3' entry on the form.
- *How does a business register to complete an ESL?*
  A service business that needs to complete an ESL can register in one of three ways:
  - register (via the GOV.UK website) to use the ESL service and submit the return online; or
  - download a blank form from the GOV.UK website and submit a paper return; or
  - contact HMRC's VAT Helpline on telephone number 0300 200 3700 and ask them to post out a blank form.
  As explained in an earlier section, the return can be submitted in either paper format or online, an extra seven days will be given to those businesses that choose the online option.
  If a business has no relevant sales to include on an ESL in a period, it does not need to complete a nil return.
- *What happens if an EU customer is in business but not registered for VAT?*

In such cases, the customer will not be able to provide a VAT registration number as evidence of his business status. This could apply if the customer is trading below the VAT registration limits that apply in his country.

However, alternative evidence can be acquired from the customer such as business stationery, certificates from fiscal authorities, letters from the Chamber of Commerce etc. No ESL entry is made for a business customer that is not VAT registered.

- *What happens about the services of intermediaries?*
  The place of supply for the services of an intermediary used to be based on where the underlying supply was arranged. Since 1 January 2010, such services are covered by the new general rule for B2B supplies, ie based on the location of the customer.

- *What about restaurant and catering supplies?*
  The position is unchanged – it is where the meal is consumed that counts.

- *What about work carried out on repairing or valuing goods?*
  These services are covered by the general rule, ie the place of supply depends on the location of the customer for B2B supplies after 1 January 2010. See Example 15.

Example 15

Warranty work is carried out by a UK plumber on boilers manufactured by a Canadian company. All work is carried out on UK boilers. An invoice is raised to the manufacturer in Vancouver. Until 31 December 2009, the place of supply was based on where the work was physically performed, ie the UK. Since 1 January 2010, the location of the customer is the key issue, ie no UK VAT is charged by the plumber because he is working for a Canadian business.

- *The ESL form does not apply to any exempt supplies made to a business customer. How will a UK business know if a service is taxable or exempt in, say, Germany?*
  This is a question that could be quite relevant in relation to supplies of some financial services and it is worthwhile contacting the VAT Helpline (tel. 0300 200 3700) in areas of doubt. But the VAT liability of most services in other countries tends to be the same as in the UK.

- *Will reverse charge entries also apply to services bought by a UK business from business suppliers outside of the EU – say in India?*
  Yes. This has always applied in relation to many services bought from non-EU suppliers but was extended after 1 January 2010. This could produce an extra source of non-recoverable VAT for exempt businesses in the UK in some cases, ie output tax is declared in Box 1 through the reverse charge but the corresponding entry in Box 4 is blocked as attributable to exempt activities.

- *What happens if a UK business incorrectly pays VAT to a supplier based in another EU country?*

Example 16

Think of the situation where a UK business pays VAT to an Italian business on advertising services. This is incorrect because the place of supply for advertising services is the location of the customer in the case of B2B supplies. So the Italian business should not have charged VAT on its invoice, the VAT being dealt with in the UK under the reverse charge procedures.

In the above situation, an attempt to reclaim this VAT under the overseas refund system should be rejected by the Italian tax authority. They should instruct the UK business to seek a VAT credit note from the Italian supplier to correct the situation.

But what happens if time has passed (claims can in some cases be submitted up to 21 months after an expense was incurred) and the supplier cannot be traced?

In such cases, a possible solution is to quote the ECJ case of *Reemtsma Cigartettenfabriken GmbH v Ministero delle Finanze: Case C-35/05* [2007] ECR I-2425, [2008] STC 3448, ECJ. This case concerned a German company that had incorrectly paid VAT to an Italian supplier but which the Italians had paid to their tax authorities on their own VAT return. The Italian authorities denied the German claim, producing a tax windfall for the Italian authorities. However, the EU principles of 'fiscal neutrality, effectiveness and non-discrimination' allowed national legislation to reimburse VAT unduly paid to the tax authorities.

- *If a client makes a sale to a business customer in another EU country which is not VAT registered, what entry is made on the EC Sales List (ESL)?*
  The ESL requires a VAT registration number for each line that is recorded. So if a business customer does not have a VAT registration number, for whatever reason, the sales to that customer are excluded from the ESL.

- *If I supply a service to a business customer who is not VAT registered in the EU country in which he is based, must I charge him VAT?*
  The key point is that the place of supply for most B2B sales will depend on where the customer is based if the customer is 'in business'.
  The best evidence of being 'in business' is a VAT registration number but there are certain businesses that might not have a VAT number for very valid reasons, eg trading below the VAT threshold in that country. In such cases, alternative evidence of business status should be obtained.

- *I have a UK business client who buys legal services from a Dutch firm of lawyers. At what point must my client do the reverse charge entry on his VAT return in relation to these services?*
  Another less publicised change introduced on 1 January 2010 related to the time of supply rules, more commonly known as the tax point rules. Under the previous regime, the reverse charge entry would have been made according to the date when your client paid the lawyer – however, the new rules require the entry to be made when the service is performed. The latter definition can cause a few problems but usually means the date of a sales invoice.
  (HMRC Notice 741A, para 18.6).

Planning points to consider

[13.19] The following planning points should be given consideration.

- Be aware that the place of supply rules were subject to major changes on both 1 January 2010, 2011 and 2013. The aim of the new rules is to take away domestic charges of VAT on most B2B sales, so it is important that a UK business does not incorrectly pay overseas VAT to an EU supplier.

- Even if an EU business outside the UK is charged UK VAT on services it receives, eg land-related services, this is not necessarily a problem. There may be scope for the overseas customer to recover UK VAT. The process is explained in Chapter 15 at **15.4**.

- The VAT on services relating to land, eg building work carried out by a tradesman depends on where the land is located. This is likely to mean, for example, that a UK company providing construction services on, eg property in France, will need to register for VAT in France. However, this need to register may be avoided if the French customer applies the reverse charge to account for the output tax on his own return.

- Don't forget there is a separate list of services (see **13.8**) where no UK VAT will be charged, even if the customer is a non-business customer.

Chapter 14

International Services – Other Issues

Key topics in this chapter:

- Territorial boundaries of the UK and EU as far as VAT is concerned.
- The need for an unregistered business or person in the UK to take into account the value of certain services it receives from abroad in determining whether it should be registered for VAT.
- International services that are zero-rated.
- Supplies of broadcasting, telecommunication and electronic services to EU consumers.

Introduction

[14.1] In Chapter 13 we considered the 'place of supply' rules as far as international services are concerned – which is important to determine the place of the relevant supply.

In effect, if the place of supply is considered to be outside the UK, the services are outside the scope of UK VAT. Where the place of supply is deemed to be within the UK, the services are subject to normal UK VAT rules, ie the supply will be standard rated, zero-rated or exempt (or subject to the reduced rate of VAT) as if the services were being supplied between two UK parties.

This chapter considers three main issues:

- the territorial boundaries of the UK;
- the need for an unregistered business in the UK to take into account the value of some services it receives from abroad in deciding whether it must register for VAT;
- examples of international services that qualify for zero-rating within the zero-rated schedule, ie which are charged without VAT irrespective of the place of supply outcome; and
- supplies of broadcasting, telecommunication and electronic services to EU consumers.

Note – the reverse charge is given this title because it reverses the usual position of output tax being accounted for by the supplier to the situation where output tax is accounted for by the customer.

Territorial boundaries of the UK

[14.2] The UK comprises Great Britain, Northern Ireland and the territorial sea of the UK (ie waters within 12 nautical miles of the coastline).

The Isle of Man is deemed to be part of the UK as far as VAT is concerned – but the Channel Islands and Gibraltar are excluded.

Territorial boundaries of the EU

[14.3] Since 1 July 2013, the EU has been made up of 28 member states. It is important that a business is aware of the countries that are inside or outside the EU because this can have an impact on the VAT liability of a supply. To give an example, a UK accountant completing a private tax return for an EU individual will charge standard rate VAT but not if the customer is outside the EU.

The VAT territory of the EU consists of

- Austria
- Belgium
- Bulgaria
- Croatia (with effect from 1 July 2013)
- Cyprus (including the British Sovereign Base Areas of Akrotiri and Dhekelia but excluding the UN buffer zone and the part of Cyprus to the north of the buffer zone where the Republic of Cyprus does not exercise effective control)
- Czech Republic
- Denmark (excluding the Faroe Islands and Greenland)
- Estonia
- Finland (excluding the Aland Islands)
- France (including Monaco but excluding Martinique, French Guiana, Guadeloupe, Reunion and Saint-Martin and Mayotte)
- Germany (excluding the island of Heligoland, and Busingen)
- Greece (excluding Mount Athos (also known as Agion Oros))
- Hungary
- Ireland
- Italy (excluding Campione D'Italia, the Italian waters of Lake Lugano and Livigno)
- Latvia
- Lithuania
- Luxembourg
- Malta
- Netherlands (excluding the Antilles)
- Poland
- Portugal (including the Azores and Madeira)
- Romania
- Slovakia
- Slovenia
- Spain (including the Balearic Islands but excluding the Canary Islands, Ceuta or Melilla)

- Sweden
- United Kingdom (including the Isle of Man but excluding the Channel Islands and Gibraltar)

Other areas not within the VAT territory include Leichtenstein, the Vatican City, Andorra and San Marino. (HMRC Notice 725, paras 2.4–2.6).

The special territories

[14.4] The special territories are part of the EU for customs purposes, but not for fiscal purposes. Goods imported from these countries are free of customs duty but subject to excise duty and import VAT. The special territories are:

- The Aland Islands
- Channel Islands
- The Canary Islands
- The overseas departments of the French Republic (Guadeloupe, Martinique, Reunion and French Guiana)
- Mount Athos (Agion Poros)

(HMRC Notice 143, para 4.3).

Turkey

[14.5] Many goods can be imported from Turkey free of customs duty but excise duty and import VAT still apply.

UK customer receives a service from a person who belongs outside the UK where the place of supply is the UK and no VAT has been charged by the supplier

[14.6] A key objective of the VAT system is to create a level playing field as far as competition in business is concerned. For example, it would be totally unfair if a UK person or business could avoid paying VAT on a service it receives by simply obtaining this service VAT free from a supplier in another country. The rules applied throughout the EU are designed to avoid this situation happening – even if they are somewhat complicated in the process.

Example 1

John has a very successful business as an accountant in the UK and is not VAT registered. The process adopted by his business is that all accounts preparation work is carried out in India by a firm that charges John for its work. John then reviews the work and agrees the accounts with his clients.

Most of John's clients are small businesses in the UK that are not VAT registered.

The annual value of John's turnover is £70,000 and he pays £20,000 per year to the Indian company for its services.

Are there any VAT consequences with this arrangement?

Solution – the initial thinking might be that John has created an excellent business structure where there is no need to worry about VAT – good news for his customers because they are not VAT registered, so VAT would be an extra cost to their business.

However, the reverse charge rules apply to a 'person' rather than a 'taxable person' who receives a service from outside the UK where the place of supply is the UK and no VAT has been charged by the supplier.

John therefore has an obligation to treat the charge from the Indian business as a taxable supply for his own purposes. This means that the total value of John's taxable supplies are £90,000 per year (£70,000 from clients fees plus £20,000 through the reverse charge mechanism) meaning he must be registered for VAT as this exceeds the VAT registration threshold.

The other main situation where a UK business may be tempted (incorrectly) to use the services of an overseas entity is if the business is not registered for VAT in the UK because it only makes exempt supplies. See Example 2 for an illustration of this point.

Example 2

DEF Insurance Brokers Ltd is based in the UK but is not registered for VAT because it only makes exempt supplies linked to insurance services.

The managing director of the company has devised a strategy that he thinks will save £24,000 VAT per annum (based on 20% rate of VAT):

- the company auditors in the UK charge £50,000 plus VAT for their services – he intends to use an American company to do this work for the same fee but without VAT being charged;
- the company pays £70,000 plus VAT each year for computer consultancy services. He intends to use a firm in India to carry out this work – again for the same fee but without VAT being charged.

The result of the above measures (he thinks) is that the company will save irrecoverable VAT of £24,000 (ie £120,000 × 20%) – is he correct?

Solution – again, the company is affected by the fact that the reverse charge rules apply to a 'person' in business not just a 'taxable person' that is already registered for VAT. If the company proceeds with the strategy being proposed by the managing director, it will be liable to be VAT registered because the value of its reverse charge services will exceed the VAT registration limit on an annual basis.

Once registered, the company will account for output tax on the overseas services in Box 1 of quarterly VAT returns (£120,000 × 20% = £24,000) – but will not be able to reclaim input tax in Box 4 because the services are attributable to exempt supplies. The end result is that the company is in the same VAT position if it uses an overseas company to carry out various works as if it used a UK supplier, ie the VAT rules have ensured that a level playing field exists for all EU businesses.

Note – the relevant legislation on the reverse charge rules is *VATA 1994, s 8*, as amended by *Finance Act 2009, Sch 36, para 5*.

Services covered by the reverse charge

[14.7] The reverse charge procedure explained in **14.6** applies to all services where:

(a)   the place of supply is the UK; and
(b)   the supplier belongs outside the UK; and
(c)   the recipient is a VAT registered person who uses the services for business purposes.

The above situation covers services relating to land.

The reverse charge cannot apply to these services if the recipient is not already registered for VAT in the UK. In such cases, the supplier must account for the VAT due.

Note – the existence of the reverse charge procedure for the services listed above does not prevent overseas suppliers from registering for VAT in the UK under normal rules. If they do register, they must invoice UK VAT in the normal way and the recipient is not then required to account for VAT under the reverse charge procedure.

See Example 3 for an illustration of this point.

Example 3

Athens Builders, is an overseas trader based in Greece, and staff of the company travel to the UK (after 1 December 2012) to do some bricklaying work at a new extension for a retailer based in London. The place of supply is the UK (where the building is located) and the value of the work is £50,000. As the supply takes place after 1 December 2012, the Greek company cannot benefit from the UK VAT registration threshold and would, ordinarily, be required to register for VAT in the UK. However, the Greek company can avoid the need to become VAT registered in the UK because the customer (the retailer) can account for the UK VAT instead by doing a reverse charge calculation on its own VAT return. If the customer was not VAT registered, then the Greek builder would need to register for VAT in the UK as an overseas trader.

International services that are zero-rated

[14.8] The examples considered in this chapter and in Chapter 13 have illustrated situations when VAT is not charged by suppliers in many cases because the customer has taken responsibility for paying output tax through the reverse charge procedure. The end result is still the same – an output tax declaration has been made on the services supplied (but by the customer rather than the supplier).

In other cases, VAT has not been charged on a supply because the recipient of a service has been based outside the EU.

In basic terms, the key approach is to identify the place of supply – and if this is outside the UK, then the services are outside the scope of UK VAT. If the place of supply is deemed to be inside the UK, the services are subject to normal UK rules concerning VAT.

The other occasion when a UK supplier can avoid a VAT charge to an overseas customer is if the service he is performing is specifically zero-rated or exempt under UK legislation (*VATA 1994, Schs 8* and 9). See Chapter 21 for details of supplies that are exempt and Chapter 22 for an analysis of zero-rated supplies.

Specific services that will be zero-rated if supplied in the UK to an overseas customer are as follows (under *Group 7* of *Sch 8*):

• **Training supplied in the UK to overseas governments for the purpose of their sovereign activities (not their business activities).**
  The supplier must retain a statement in writing from the government concerned certifying that the trainees are employed in the furtherance of its sovereign activities, eg armed forces, public servants, police etc. The zero-rating does not extend to the business activities of a government, eg training for staff employed by a nationalised company. (HMRC Notice 741A, para 8.2).

• **Work on goods obtained, acquired or temporarily imported for that purpose and subsequent export.**
  The supply of services of work carried out on goods which, for that purpose, have been obtained or acquired in, or imported into, any EU country is zero-rated provided that the goods are intended to be (and are) subsequently exported to a place outside the EU. Normal rules apply concerning proof of export.
  Any goods used in connection with the work performed (eg spare parts) should also be treated as part of the supply of services.
  An example of work eligible for zero-rating is a classic car imported from America, repaired by a UK company and re-exported to America. The charge by the UK repair company to its American customer will be zero-rated even though the work is physically performed in the UK. (HMRC Notice 741A, para 8.6).

• **Services of intermediaries.**
  If the place of supply is deemed to be in the UK, then the supply will be zero-rated if consisting of the making of arrangements for the export of any goods to a place outside the EU.
  The intermediary's services can be supplied to the supplier (in finding a customer) or the customer (in finding a supplier) or both.
  For example, Intermediary A arranges for a supply of goods to take place between UK supplier X and Russian customer Y where the goods will move from the UK to Russia. The fee earned by Intermediary A for brokering the deal will be zero-rated irrespective of whether he is acting for UK supplier X or Russian customer Y.
  (HMRC Notice 741A, section 13).

Supplies of broadcasting, telecommunication and electronic services to consumers from 1 January 2015

[14.9] From 1 January 2015 all supplies of broadcasting, telecommunication and electronic services (collectively known as digital services) to EU customers are subject to VAT where the customer belongs, regardless of the status of the customer (business or consumer) or the location of the supplier (EU or non-EU). The only exception relates to when the services are effectively used and enjoyed outside of the EU.

The 1 January 2015 change to the place of supply rules affects businesses supplying digital services directly to consumers. Supplies to VAT registered business customers in other EU countries were, and continue to be, subject to VAT where the customers belong via the reverse charge procedure described at **13.2**.

If a customer in another EU country does not have a VAT registration number, or at least does not provide their VAT registration number to the supplier, the supplier should usually treat the customer as a consumer. Suppliers can accept alternative evidence that the customer is a business customer but the tax authorities in the country where the customer belongs may not necessarily accept the alternative evidence. There is therefore a risk that the supplier, rather than the customer, will remain liable for accounting for the VAT due in the country where the customer belongs.

If the customer does not have a VAT registration number the reverse charge procedure cannot be applied. The supplier should account for the VAT that is due either by registering for VAT where the customer is located or by using the Mini One Stop Shop (MOSS). The MOSS provides UK VAT registered businesses that supply digital services to consumers in other EU countries with an alternative to registering for VAT in each of those other EU countries (see **14.15**).

Example 4 provides an illustration of the above points.

Example 4

> Ann's business is registered for VAT in the UK. She sells downloaded applications (apps), over the internet to private individuals located in the UK, France and Germany. Before 1 January 2015 Ann accounted for UK VAT on all of her sales. The 1 January 2015 change to the place of supply rules mean that Ann should now be accounting for UK VAT in relation to sales to UK customers, French VAT in relation to sales to French customers, and German VAT in relation to sales to German customers. Ann can account for the French and German VAT either by registering for VAT in France and Germany or by using the MOSS.

Unlike the distance selling rules that apply to goods, there are currently no thresholds below which a supplier of digital services to consumers in other EU countries can continue to charge VAT based on where the supplier belongs. If Ann in Example 4 made a single one euro sale to a consumer in Italy she would need to account for Italian VAT in relation to that sale, either by registering for VAT in Italy or by using the MOSS.

Supplying an app is an example of a digital service affected by the 1 January 2015 change to the place of supply rules. The phrase 'digital services' is used as a collective term for the broadcasting, telecommunication and electronic services that are affected by the 1 January 2015 change to the place of supply rules. The EU legislation implementing the change does not provide an exhaustive or definitive list of all digital services and the nature of digital services is that they are subject to technological developments. It may be almost impossible to list all the digital services that are currently available and it is certainly impossible to list all of the digital services that may be available in the future. Examples of broadcasting, telecommunication and electronic services are included below.

Broadcasting services

[14.10] Broadcasting services relate to the provision of audio/audio-visual content for simultaneous listening/viewing on the basis of programme schedule, to the general public, via communications networks by, and under the editorial responsibility of, media service providers.

See Example 5 for an illustration of the above.

Example 5

Bob's business provides the right of access to premium sports channels and has editorial responsibility over the content. Bob's business is providing broadcasting services.

Catherine's business buys the right of access to premium sports channels and forwards the signals on but has no editorial responsibility over the content. Catherine's business is not providing broadcasting services but is providing electronic services.

Examples of broadcasting services are:

(a)   radio or television programmes transmitted or retransmitted over a radio or television network;

(b)   radio or television programmes distributed via the internet or similar electronic network (IP streaming) if they are broadcast simultaneously to their being transmitted or retransmitted over a radio or television network.

Broadcasting services include the provision of radio or television programmes that can be recorded by the listener or viewer, or that can be listened to or viewed via the internet within a particular time frame. However, radio or television programmes that can be accessed at any time by the listener or viewer from a catalogue of programmes selected by the media service provider are an example of electronic services.

Telecommunication services

[**14.11**] Telecommunication services relate to the transmission, emission or reception of signals, words, images and sounds or information of any nature by wire, radio, optical or other electromagnetic systems, including the related transfer or assignment of the right to use capacity for such transmission, emission or reception, with the inclusion of the provision of access to global information networks. Examples of telecommunication services are:

(a)   fixed and mobile telephone services for the transmission and switching of voice, data and video, including telephone services with an imaging component (videophone services);
(b)   telephone services provided through the internet, including voice over Internet Protocol (VoIP);
(c)   voice mail, call waiting, call forwarding, caller identification, three-way calling and other call management services;
(d)   paging services;
(e)   audiotext services;
(f)   facsimile, telegraph and telex;
(g)   access to the internet, including the World Wide Web;
(h)   private network connections providing telecommunications links for the exclusive use of the client.

Electronic services

[**14.12**] Electronic services relate to the provision, via the internet or an electronic network, of services which are essentially automated and involve minimal human intervention. Examples of electronic services are:

(a)   the supply of digitised products generally, including software and changes to or upgrades of software;
(b)   services providing or supporting a business or personal presence on an electronic network such as a website or a webpage;
(c)   services automatically generated from a computer via the internet or an electronic network in response to specific data input by the recipient;
(d)   online auction services which involve the transfer for consideration of the right to put goods or services up for sale on an internet site operating as an online market on which potential buyers make their bids by an automated procedure and on which the parties are notified of a sale by electronic mail automatically generated from a computer;
(e)   Internet Service Packages (ISP) of information in which the telecommunications component forms an ancillary and subordinate part and which go beyond mere internet access and include other elements, for example, content pages giving access to news, weather or travel reports or access to online debates;
(f)   downloaded applications (apps);
(g)   movie downloads, music downloads, e-books, online games, online newspapers and journals;
(h)   the provision of online advertising space including banner advertisements on a website or web page;
(i)   website hosting and webpage hosting;

(j)   automated online distance maintenance of programmes;
(k)   automated online distance learning services;
(l)   radio or television programmes that can be accessed at any time by the listener or viewer from a catalogue of programmes selected by the media service provider.

A question to ask when considering if a service is an electronic service is – does delivery of the service require more than minimal human involvement by the service provider? If the answer is 'Yes', the service is unlikely to be an electronic service. See Example 6 for an illustration of this point.

Example 6

Derek's business supplies tax advisory services to private individuals in other EU countries and he communicates the advice via email. The emails are not automatically generated. The emails are written by Derek and are specific and unique to each individual client.

The delivery of the service requires more than minimal human involvement. Derek's business is not supplying electronic services.

When considering if a service is an electronic service it is important to consider the nature of what is being supplied to the customer. If what is being supplied to the customer is a supply of goods the supply will not be a supply of electronic services. See Example 7 for an illustration of this point.

Example 7

Edith's business specialises in selling CDs and DVDs via a website to private individuals in other EU countries. Edith's business is supplying goods, the CDs and DVDs are tangible items. Edith's business is not supplying electronic services.

Note – If sales exceed the relevant distance selling thresholds Edith's business will be required to register for VAT in the other EU countries in accordance with the distance selling rules that apply to goods and which are explained at **12.5**. There are no thresholds below which a supplier of digital services to consumers in other EU countries can continue to charge VAT based on where the supplier belongs.

Identifying who is making the supply to the final consumer

[14.13] From 1 January 2015 all supplies of digital services to EU customers are subject to VAT where the customer belongs. However, in situations where the customer and supplier belong in different countries, the status of the customer affects who is responsible for accounting for the VAT that is due. If the customer is a business customer (registered for VAT) in another EU country the customer is responsible for accounting for VAT via the reverse charge procedure. If the customer is a consumer, the supplier is responsible for accounting for VAT either by registering for VAT where the customer belongs or using the MOSS scheme. If the customer and supplier belong in the same country the supplier is always responsible for accounting for the VAT that is due on digital services.

In a supply chain involving several businesses it is necessary to identify which business is making the supply of digital services to the final consumer. It is that business that will be liable for accounting for the VAT that is due where the consumer belongs. It will often, but not always be clear which business is making the supply to the final consumer. If a business does any one of the following:

- authorises the charge to the consumer; or
- authorises the delivery (for example, authorises the download) of the service to the consumer; or
- sets the general terms and conditions,

the business will be treated as making the supply to the final consumer and will be responsible for accounting for VAT based on where the consumer belongs.

Other businesses may be involved in the process without necessarily making the supply to the final consumer. Examples include companies providing business to business supplies of website hosting services or payment processing services. A question to ask is who is supplying what to whom?

Examples 8 and 9 illustrate the above points.

Example 8

Pearl is a popular singer who has her own website selling her music downloads to consumers. Pearl pays a website hosting company to host her website and a payment processing company to process, but not to authorise, the online debit and credit card transactions.

Pearl's website is highly automated and

(1)   authorises the charges to consumers;
(2)   authorises the music downloads;
(3)   sets the general terms and conditions.

Pearl is supplying electronic services to consumers and is responsible for accounting for VAT based on where the consumers belong.

The website hosting company and the payment processing company are making business to business supplies to Pearl.

Example 9

Robert creates apps and contracts with an online app store where a consumer purchases an app. Who has supplied the app to the consumer?

If the app store actions any of the following the app store must be treated as supplying the consumer.

(1)   Authorises the charges to consumers.
(2)   Authorises the download of the app to the consumer.
(3)   Sets the general terms and conditions.

If Robert rather than the app store actions the above, and if Robert is referred to as the supplier, for example, on the invoice or receipt issued to the consumer, Robert will be treated as supplying the consumer.

Supply chains for digital services can vary in length and involve lots of different businesses. However, at some point at least one business in the supply chain must authorise the charge to the consumer, or authorise delivery of the service to the consumer, or set the general terms and conditions. That business will be responsible for accounting for VAT where the consumer belongs.

There is a distinction between authorising the charge to the consumer and processing the payment, although it is possible that the same business could do both. Businesses that simply provide payment processing services are not treated as authorising the charge to the consumer. Businesses that provide payment processing services sometimes get involved in other activities related to payment processing services, for example, accepting bad debt risk. Another example of an activity related to payment processing services is providing first line customer care, which in essence means re-directing the customer to the supplier except where the customer care relates to the payment processing itself. Businesses that only provide payment processing services and related activities such as accepting bad debt risk or providing first line customer care are not treated as the supplier to the consumer.

Identifying where the final consumer belongs

[14.14] From 1 January 2015 suppliers of digital services to consumers must account for the VAT that is due either by registering for VAT where the customer is located or by using the Mini One Stop Shop (MOSS). It is necessary to identify where customers are located, either for the purpose of registering for VAT in the relevant countries, or for the purpose of completing the relevant entries in the MOSS returns.

A consumer is normally treated as belonging where they are established, have their permanent address, or usually reside. For example, a UK expatriate that spends most of their time living in Spain should be regarded as belonging in Spain. That is where they will be consuming digital services and therefore Spanish VAT should be accounted for on those services.

It may not always be clear where a consumer is established, has their permanent address, or usually resides. In some situations a supplier may have a choice as to which EU country they treat a consumer as belonging in for the purpose of accounting for the VAT that is due on the services. The following are examples of questions clients may ask and the possible solutions:

Questions	Solutions
Digital services are supplied through a telephone box, telephone kiosk, a wi-fi hot spot, an internet café, a restaurant or a hotel lobby – where is the consumer located?	The supplier can treat the consumer as located where the services are provided, for example, in the EU country where the internet café is located. If the supplier adopts this treatment they need only retain one item of evidence confirming the location.

If the supplier does not adopt this treatment and decides to treat the consumer as located in a different EU country they need to retain three items of non-contradictory evidence which support that decision. |
| Digital services are supplied on transport, for example a train, travelling within the EU – where is the consumer located? | The supplier can treat the consumer as located in the EU country where the consumer's journey began (the country of departure). If the supplier adopts this treatment they need only retain one item of evidence confirming the location.

If the supplier does not adopt this treatment and decides to treat the consumer as located in a different EU country they need to retain three items of non-contradictory evidence which support that decision. |
| Digital services are supplied through an individual consumer's telephone landline – where is the consumer located? | The supplier can treat the consumer as located where the landline is located. If the supplier adopts this treatment they need only retain one item of evidence confirming the location.

If the supplier does not adopt this treatment and decides to treat the consumer as located in a different EU country they need to retain three items of non-contradictory evidence which support that decision. |
| Digital services are supplied through a mobile phone – where is the consumer located? | The supplier can treat the consumer as located in the country relevant to the code of the SIM card. If the supplier adopts this treatment they need only retain one item of evidence confirming the location.

If the supplier does not adopt this treatment and decides to treat the consumer as located in a different EU country they need to retain three items of non-contradictory evidence which support that decision. |
| Digital services are supplied through a decoder – where is the consumer located | The supplier can treat the consumer as located in the country where the decoder was sent or installed. If the supplier adopts this treatment they need only retain one item of evidence confirming the location.

If the supplier does not adopt this treatment and decides to treat the consumer as located in a different EU country they need to retain three items of non-contradictory evidence which support that decision. |

Other situations may arise that are not covered by the above examples and a supplier will need to decide where a consumer is located based on such information as is available or that can be obtained. In these situations two items of non-contradictory evidence from the following list should be retained to support the decision regarding where the consumer is located:

- the consumer's billing address;

- the Internet Protocol (IP) address of the device used by the consumer;
- the location of the consumer's bank;
- the country code of the consumer's SIM card;
- the location of the consumer's fixed land line via which the service is supplied;
- other commercially relevant information, for example, product coding information which electronically links the sale to a particular country.

For many micro and small businesses the above requirements may be challenging. In their published guidance for business supplying digital services to private consumers HMRC have suggested a different method of identifying the location of the customer that micro and small businesses that use payment service providers can use. The suggested method involves such businesses having a website sales process whereby customers are asked to provide either their billing address, including the country, or their telephone number, including the country dialling code, at the point of sale. Providing this information is consistent with the two-digit country code that can be requested from the payment service provider, the information can be relied on to identify the location of the customer. If the information provided by the customer and the payment service provider does not tally the supplier will need to contact the customer and ask them to reconcile the discrepancy between the two pieces of information.

The method referred to above involves micro and small businesses having a website sales process whereby customers are asked to provide either their billing address, including the country, or their telephone number, including the country dialling code, at the point of sale. In its published guidance for business supplying digital services to private consumers HMRC have indicated that UK micro-businesses that operate below the UK VAT registration threshold, that register for the Mini One Stop Shop (MOSS), and that use payment service providers, may base their decisions regarding customer location entirely on the information provided to them by their payment service provider.

As noted at **14.13** it is the business that makes the supply to the final consumer that is responsible for accounting for the VAT due based on where the consumer belongs. Some businesses may prefer to sell digital services to other VAT registered businesses, rather than to consumers, in order to avoid having to identify where the consumers belong.

Update – responding to feedback from small businesses, HMRC announced in early 2016 that it was to simplify the rules concerning evidence of customer's belonging for those businesses trading below the VAT registration threshold. Revenue & Customs Brief 4/16 sets out HMRC relaxation of the rules on obtaining evidence of a customer's belonging. Business trading below the VAT registration threshold can now use a single piece of information (as opposed to two pieces previously required). Accordingly, UK micro-businesses, that are below the current UK VAT registration threshold and are registered for the VAT Mini One Stop Shop (VAT MOSS), may use best judgment and base their 'customer location' VAT taxation and accounting decisions on a single piece of information, such as the billing address provided by the customer or information provided to them by their payment service provider.

HMRC have also stated in Revenue & Customs Brief 4/16 that, having analysed the MOSS returns submitted during 2015, it appears that many small businesses may not actually be in business at all but simply conducting a hobby. If this is the case, then such activities are outside the scope of VAT.

The Mini One Stop Shop (MOSS)

[14.15] The MOSS provides UK businesses that supply digital services to consumers in other EU countries with an alternative to registering for VAT in each of those other EU countries. Instead, one return is submitted to HMRC covering supplies of digital services to consumers in other EU countries for each calendar quarter. The VAT due on those supplies is paid to HMRC rather than directly to each of the EU countries to which the VAT relates.

UK businesses who want to use the MOSS must be registered for VAT in the UK and make, or intend to make, supplies of digital services to at least one consumer in at least one other EU country.

In their published guidance for business supplying digital services to private consumers HMRC have explained that UK businesses that have taxable turnover below the VAT registration threshold can register for VAT in the UK in order to use the MOSS to account for VAT on sales of digital services to consumers in other EU countries, without having to account for VAT on UK sales. Businesses in this position that do not account for VAT on UK sales should not recover as input tax VAT charged on business expenses relating to UK sales but can recover as input tax VAT charged on business expenses directly related to sales of digital services to customers in other EU countries.

MOSS returns are submitted electronically, with each return covering a calendar quarter. The deadline for submission of MOSS returns and payment of the VAT due is the 20th day of the month following the end of each calendar quarter. The total value of supplies of digital services to consumers in each member state during the period covered by a MOSS return should be entered separately in sterling, using the exchange rates published by the European Central Bank on the last day of the period covered by the MOSS return. If exchange rates are not published on the last day of the period covered by the MOSS return, the exchange rates for the next day of publication should be used.

MOSS returns deal with the output tax due on digital services supplied to consumers in other EU countries. UK input tax incurred is claimed on the normal VAT returns, even if the input tax relates to costs incurred when supplying digital services to consumers in other EU countries.

Businesses that are registered to use the MOSS must submit nil returns for any quarters during which they make no supplies of digital services to consumers in other EU countries.

Amendments to MOSS returns should be made in relation to the return for the period to which the amendment relates rather than by making an adjustment on a later MOSS return. The general rule is that amendments can be made up to three years after the end of the period to which the amendment relates. However, the time period for amending each entry on a MOSS return will depend on the nature of the amendment and the rules of the country to which the amendment relates. For example, if the entry relates to supplies to consumers in a country which allows 15 days for making an amendment after issuing a credit note that rule will apply to that amendment.

In some cases it may be possible for amendments to be made after three years have elapsed from the end of the period to which the amendment relates, but only by contacting the tax authorities in the country to which the amendment relates. Such amendments are not part of the MOSS scheme.

Records relating to MOSS returns should be retained for a period of ten years from the end of the calendar year during which the transaction was carried out. The tax authorities in each EU country have the right to check the VAT records of businesses making supplies to their country. However, HMRC are likely to be the main tax authority that most UK businesses using the MOSS get involved with, unless there are disputes, penalties or fines, in which case it may be necessary to deal directly with the tax authorities concerned.

(*VATA 1994, Sch 3BA; Finance Act 2014, Sch 22*).

The MOSS provides UK businesses that supply digital services to consumers in other EU countries with an alternative to registering for VAT in each of those other EU countries. Some businesses may prefer to sell digital services to other VAT registered businesses, rather than to consumers, in order to avoid having to either use the MOSS or register for VAT in other EU countries.

Note – in Revenue & Customs Brief 4/16 HMRC confirmed that registration under MOSS is only applicable where suppliers of digital services are in business for VAT purposes. Suppliers should give consideration to whether their activities constitute a business activity or are more akin to a hobby undertaken on a minimal and occasional basis. Those suppliers that are not 'in business' are not required to account for VAT on their supplies.

Overseas suppliers of broadcasting, telecommunication and electronic services to consumers

[14.16] Just as HMRC are responsible for providing a MOSS scheme for businesses registered for VAT in the UK (see **14.15**), the tax authorities in each of the other EU countries are responsible for providing a MOSS scheme for businesses registered for VAT in their country. This provides those businesses with an alternative to registering for VAT in each of the EU countries where they make supplies of broadcasting, telecommunication, or electronic services to consumers.

The MOSS scheme which the UK and the other EU countries are responsible for providing to businesses registered for VAT in the EU is known as the Union VAT MOSS scheme. Another scheme, known as the non-Union VAT MOSS scheme is relevant to non-EU businesses making supplies of broadcasting, telecommunication, or electronic services to EU consumers. A non-EU business can use the non-Union VAT MOSS scheme in one EU country to account for the VAT that is due in each EU country in which they make supplies to consumers. Alternatively, the non-EU business would need to register for VAT in each of those countries.

The non-Union VAT MOSS scheme is a modified version of the VAT on E-Services (VoES) scheme that non-EU suppliers of electronic services to EU consumers could use in relation to electronic services supplied prior to 1 January 2015.

(*VATA 1994, Sch 3B; Finance Act 2014, Sch 22*).

Planning points to consider

[**14.17**] The following planning points should be given consideration.

- It should be noted that the Isle of Man is deemed to be part of the UK as far as VAT is concerned but that the Channel Islands are excluded.
- It is important to remember that the reverse charge legislation applies to 'persons' in the UK not just 'taxable persons'. This means that a business not registered for VAT will need to take into account the value of services it receives from abroad in calculating whether it needs to be VAT registered according to the relevant turnover limits.
- Be aware of opportunities when a UK business can avoid being charged VAT by an overseas company, ie when the reverse charge mechanism can be applied. The reverse charge mechanism can also avert the need for an overseas supplier to register for VAT in the UK.
- Certain services provided by a UK supplier to an overseas customer are zero-rated under *VATA 1994, Sch 8*. In such cases, there is no VAT charge on these services, even if the place of supply is in the UK. See **14.8** for examples of zero-rated services that fall into this category.
- Since 1 January 2015 businesses supplying broadcasting, telecommunication or electronic services to consumers in other EU countries have been required to account for VAT based on where the consumers belong. For many businesses the Mini One Stop Shop scheme may be a more attractive alternative than registering for VAT in the EU countries where the consumers belong.
- Consider whether the supplier of digital services is actually 'in-business' or is he providing services on a minimal and occasional basis such that the activity could be regarded as a hobby.
- The reverse charge procedure continues to apply to supplies of broadcasting, telecommunication and electronic services to VAT registered business customers in other EU countries. In some situations it may be appropriate to consider making intra-EU supplies to another business rather than directly to consumers.

Chapter 15

Overseas Traders and UK VAT (plus Overseas Refunds for a UK Business)

Key topics in this chapter:

- Circumstances when an overseas trader will need to register for VAT in the UK, including the *Finance Act 2012* change effective from 1 December 2012.
- Appointing a UK agent to deal with the VAT affairs of an overseas trader.
- Opportunities for businesses based in other EU and non-EU countries to reclaim VAT paid in the UK.
- Opportunities for UK businesses to reclaim VAT or indirect taxes paid in other EU and non-EU countries.
- Electronic procedures to claim VAT paid in other EU countries.
- Submitting a claim to recover incorrectly charged VAT – ECJ case law example.

Introduction

[15.1] An overseas trader is any person who:

- is not normally resident in the UK;
- does not have a 'business establishment' in the UK;
- if a company, is not incorporated in the UK.

As far as the phrase 'business establishment' is concerned, this normally indicates that the business actually trades from a location in the UK. In such cases, the business is not an overseas trader and must be registered for VAT in the UK at the address of its principal UK place of business (assuming the value of its taxable supplies exceeds the VAT registration threshold).

If a business has a business establishment in the UK, then it must retain its books and records from this address, which must be made available to HMRC if it wants to conduct a VAT inspection. An authorised person must be responsible for handling the VAT affairs of the business from the UK address.

Important improvements were made to the system for reclaiming VAT paid in other EU countries with effect from 1 January 2010. The procedures for making a claim have historically been very inefficient so the revised procedures based on electronic submissions are very welcome.

Registering an overseas trader for UK VAT

[15.2] Before 1 December 2012 an overseas trader could benefit from the UK VAT registration threshold. In general terms this meant that an overseas trader could make taxable supplies in the UK up to the level of the VAT registration threshold without being required to register for VAT in the UK. It was possible for the overseas trader to register for VAT voluntarily, for example to claim input tax on imported goods, but there was no obligation to do so, providing they did not breach the VAT registration threshold with reference to the level of their UK supplies and/or the level of their acquisition of goods in the UK from other EU countries.

The general rule is that from 1 December 2012 an overseas trader will be required to register for VAT in the UK if they make any taxable supplies in the UK. The exceptions to the general rule are:

• when the customer accounts for VAT via the reverse charge mechanism;
• when the overseas trader uses the Mini One Stop Shop (MOSS) scheme (see **14.16**);
• when HMRC agrees to exempt an overseas trader from the requirement to register for VAT in the UK on the basis that it is satisfied that the only taxable supplies that the trader makes would be zero-rated. However, most traders who only make zero-rated supplies prefer to register for VAT in order to recover input tax.

There are three options as to how the VAT registration of an overseas trader is co-ordinated:

(a) he can appoint a VAT representative who will be jointly and severally liable for any VAT debts incurred by the business. However, the application of this option is limited in practice because very few representatives would be prepared to be liable for the VAT debts of an overseas trader;

(b) he may personally deal with all the VAT obligations of the business – including registration, record-keeping and completion of returns. In such cases, he should register for VAT with HMRC as a non-established taxable person; and

(c) he can appoint an agent to deal with his UK VAT affairs. The agent is not responsible for any debts owed to HMRC although could be held responsible for his part in any VAT fraud committed by the business.

The overseas trader must complete a VAT registration form in the normal manner – but must also submit a letter of authority to confirm the involvement of the agent. For an illustration of an authority letter, see Example 1.

(HMRC Notice 700/1, sections 9–11, 15).

Example 1

ABC Inc is based in America but makes taxable supplies in the UK and has therefore been required to register for VAT in the UK. The company wishes to appoint London based accountants Smith and Smith to deal with its UK VAT affairs.

HMRC requires an authorisation letter confirming that Smith and Smith are the appointed UK agents to deal with the VAT issues pertaining to ABC Inc.

Solution –

To: HMRC

We the directors of ABC Inc, based in Las Vegas, USA, hereby appoint Smith and Smith of London to act as agent for dealing with all the legal obligations of the company in respect of UK VAT. This letter authorises Smith and Smith to sign VAT Return Forms 100 and any other documents needed for the purpose of enabling the agent or employee of the agent to comply with the VAT obligations of ABC Inc.

Signed: Director authorised to sign on behalf of company

. . . .

Date:

. . . .

The VAT registration forms to complete are as follows:

- VAT 1 if in respect of taxable supplies being made in the UK;
- VAT 1A if in respect of distance sales;
- VAT 1B if in respect of acquisitions.

Refunds of VAT for persons established in other EU countries

Basic principles of a refund claim

[15.3] A business can only reclaim input tax on its VAT return if the tax in question was incurred in the country in which it is registered for VAT. Therefore, if a UK business makes a trip to France in the course of business, and incurs French VAT, then it is not permitted to reclaim this VAT in Box 4 of its UK VAT return.

Equally, a business registered for VAT in another EU country cannot reclaim UK VAT on its return – only input tax it incurs in its own country.

However, there is a refund system in place to enable a business to reclaim VAT paid in EU countries other than its own. This scheme would apply to a UK business paying VAT in any other EU country and vice versa for an EU business registered outside the UK paying VAT in this country.

An important point is that the VAT paid in the other EU country must be deductible under the normal VAT rules of the country where the expenditure was incurred. See Examples 2 and 3.

(HMRC Notice 723A, section 2).

Example 2

ABC Ltd is registered for VAT in the UK. The managing director of the company has been on a business trip to Paris to visit a major French customer. He stayed in a hotel in the middle of Paris for three nights and incurred French VAT of €200.

What is the position regarding the French VAT that has been paid by the company?

Solution – although the trip is business related, and there is scope to recover VAT paid under the overseas refund system, one of the rules of French VAT is that input tax cannot be recovered on hotel bills. The €200 cannot therefore be reclaimed.

Note – other expenditure that is non-reclaimable in France includes entertainment, restaurant expenses, passenger transport and motor fuel (apart from diesel).

Example 3

The managing director of ABC Ltd's French customer (registered for VAT in France) now comes to the UK and stays at a luxury hotel in London for three nights. He pays UK VAT of £250.

As input tax is recoverable on hotel bills in the UK (ie for UK businesses registered for VAT), then the £250 VAT on the hotel bill can be reclaimed by the French company through the refund procedures.

Procedures to reclaim VAT paid in EU countries

[15.4] This section is based on the procedures for making refund claims that were introduced on 1 January 2010.

- Claims must be submitted to the tax authority in the country where the claimant is VAT registered, ie to HMRC in the case of a UK business. The previous system was based on submitting the claim to the overseas authority where the VAT was paid. The first thing a UK business will need to do is register for the scheme through the Government Gateway. (HMRC Notice 723A, para 4.1).

- Claims must be submitted in an electronic rather than paper format. Most details on the form are completed by filling in boxes with numbers, rather than requiring any significant amount of text. In relation to text, most countries have also confirmed they will accept English as a common language.

- The deadline for submitting claims is nine months after the end of a calendar year, ie by 30 September. A business will be able to make a maximum of five claims in a year to each relevant country where it has paid VAT. This allows four quarterly claims to be made, plus a final claim to sweep up any expenses that might have been overlooked during the year. (HMRC Notice 723A, paras 4.2 and 4.3).

- The member state of refund must notify the applicant of the decision to approve or refuse the application within four months of the date they first received the application. If the member state of refund requires additional information in order to process the application, it can request this from the applicant, the applicant's tax authority, or a third party before the expiry of the four-month period. The additional information must be provided by the person to whom the request is made within one month of receiving the request. Once the member state of refund has received the additional information it has two further months in which to notify its decision. If further additional information is requested by the member state of refund the final deadline for making a decision can be extended up to a maximum of eight months from the date they received the application. Payment must be made within ten working days following expiry of the appropriate decision deadline. (HMRC Notice 723A, para 2.18).

Practical implications of the refund system

[**15.5**] The refund system based on electronic procedures should simplify the administrative process of making a claim. The following are a number of practical issues that should now be evident.

- By submitting a claim to its own tax authority, claimants no longer need to provide a VAT certificate of status with each claim. This is an administrative saving for claimants.
- As a general principle, the claim forms are easier to complete. There is an increased emphasis on using codes and numbers rather than text.
- The claim form requires a business to record a 'Business Activity Code' – this confirms the nature of its business.
- The form also introduces ten different 'Expenditure Codes' – which categorise the VAT being claimed under different headings. For example, fuel has been allocated as code '1'. The full codes are as follows:
  (1) Fuel.
  (2) Hiring of means of transport.
  (3) Expenditure relating to means of transport.
  (4) Road tolls and road user charge.
  (5) Travel expenses, such as taxi fares, public transport fares.
  (6) Accommodation.
  (7) Food, drink and restaurant services.
  (8) Admissions to fairs and exhibitions.
  (9) Expenditure on luxuries, amusements and entertainment.
  (10) Other.
Many member states will require sub-codes in addition to the main codes set out above, to the extent that such information is necessary due to restrictions on the right to deduct in those member states. Where applicable, these sub-codes will appear as completion options on the electronic portal. Where code 10 is used, without an accompanying sub-code, a narrative description of the goods or services must be

entered in a free text box, using the language(s) required by the member state of refund. If an invoice includes items covering more than one code the code relating to the highest proportion of expenditure is the one that should be used.
(HMRC Notice 723A, para 3.10).

- The positive point about the ten codes is that they give an opportunity for input tax blocks to be identified in relation to claims made for each EU country at the time the claim is being submitted.
  For example, an overseas business making a claim to recover UK VAT needs to be aware of the input tax blocks that apply to car leasing (codes 2/3), business entertainment (which could be relevant to codes 6, 7 and 9). Example 2 highlighted how input tax cannot be claimed on hotel expenses in France – so a potential block would occur on code 6 claims.

- The previous system required original purchase invoices to be submitted with the claim, and photocopies were not acceptable. The new regime requires invoices to be scanned and submitted electronically, unless the invoice value is below a certain limit. This limit is 1,000 Euros in most cases, or 250 Euros in the case of fuel. However, a business should retain all invoices as a matter of course, in case they are requested by the tax authority receiving the claim.
  (HMRC Notice 723A, para 2.14).

- The tax authorities will only repay VAT that has been correctly charged by a supplier in the first place. To give an example, a claim to recover VAT on advertising expenses will be rejected because the place of supply for advertising services is based on the location of the customer, ie no VAT should be charged by the supplier if he is raising an invoice to a business based in an EU country other than his own. In such cases, the correct approach is to seek a VAT credit note and refund from the supplier who has incorrectly charged VAT.
  (HMRC Notice 723A, para 2.9).

Note – it is important that advisers take into account the place of supply rules which are considered in detail in Chapter 13.

Does the electronic claims system work?

[15.6] HMRC has always been very efficient in processing refund claims submitted by overseas businesses based in both EU and non-EU countries. The tax authorities in many other countries have also earned a good reputation for dealing with claims in an efficient manner, eg Denmark, Sweden, Holland and Belgium.

The new system appears to be a significant improvement on the previous regime but only time will tell if the system will provide greater certainty to UK businesses that the claims they make to certain countries will be paid promptly.

Overall, it is suggested that advisers acting for UK clients should still adopt a cautious approach when informing clients about the efficiency of the EU refund system and the length of time it will take for a repayment claim to be made in various countries. However, a successful claim now has to overcome a lot less obstacles because of the electronic procedures (eg language issues, problems with the postal system, finding out where to send the claim in another country), so the signs are encouraging.

Rules in particular countries

[15.7] As explained earlier, each country in the EU has different rules as far as input tax recovery is concerned – as mentioned with the French rules in Example 2 above. A few other interesting points regarding specific countries are as follows (but the list is obviously not exhaustive):

- claims in Denmark must exclude hotel expenses, car rental charges and entertainment costs – these categories tend to be disallowed in most countries;
- claims in Italy must, among other things, exclude luxury items such as furs, sparkling wines and oriental carpets;
- claims in Greece must exclude, among other things, food, drink and tobacco products.

The key point is to research the rules for the country in question, and ensure that all claims for VAT comply with these rules.

There is a link providing contact details for the tax authorities in other EU member states in Notice 723A, section 8 (http://ec.europa.eu/taxation_custo ms/resources/documents/taxation/vat/traders/vat_refunds/refund_contact_det ails_table_en.pdf).

Refunds of UK VAT for persons established in non-EU countries

[15.8] EU VAT law requires each EU country to adopt a scheme that allows non-EU businesses to also recover VAT.

However, an obligation to adopt the refund scheme only exists with countries that have a reciprocal arrangement in their country. Obviously, this reciprocal arrangement may not necessarily involve VAT – but the similar turnover tax adopted by the country in question, for example, GST (Goods and Services Tax) in Australia. However, in the case of claims to the UK, we acknowledge that many countries do not have an indirect tax system that is the equivalent of VAT, so we allow claims to be submitted from these countries in most cases. It is only if a country has an indirect tax system in place and precludes a claim by UK businesses to recover that tax that the UK will deny a claim by a business in that country.

The provisions apply to any registered trader carrying on a business established in a country outside the EU – provided that the trader meets the following rules:

- he was not registered or liable to be registered in the UK;
- he was not established in any EU country;
- he made no supplies of goods or services in the UK.

An important point to note is that there is a different time period for submitting non-EU refund claims – the 'prescribed period' is the 12-month period ending 30 June, and claims have to be made within six months of the 'prescribed period'.

The basic rules are the same as for EU refund claims, apart from the fact that claims are submitted by paper format (VAT 65A) rather than by electronic methods. To give an example, an overseas business (EU or non-EU scheme) cannot reclaim UK VAT on an item of expenditure that is not reclaimable under normal UK rules.

The Form VAT 65A is available on the GOV.UK website. The legislation permits use of a similar form if it is produced by an official authority and contains the same information and declaration set out in Form 65A. The form must be completed in English and submitted with original invoices to:

HM Revenue & Customs
VAT Overseas Repayment Unit
PO Box 34
Foyle House
Duncreggan Road
Londonderry
BT48 7AE

Sections 5 and 6 of Notice 723A, are particularly relevant in relation to refunds of UK VAT for persons established in non-EU countries.

Submitting a claim to recover incorrectly paid VAT

[15.9] The rules concerning VAT and international services are complex. In the commercial world, there will inevitably be situations when a supplier wrongly charges VAT to an overseas customer (and the customer pays this VAT in good faith) – and the overseas customer then submits a VAT refund claim to the supplier's country to reclaim this VAT. What happens if the tax authority receiving the claim reject it on the basis that the VAT should not have been charged in the first place?

In such cases, the claimant should go back to his supplier and acquire a VAT refund – and then account for the VAT on his own return using the reverse charge procedures. However, what if the supplier in question has disappeared and there is no scope to contact him about the overcharged VAT?

In such instances, it is useful for advisers to note the outcome of the ECJ case *Reemtsma Cigarettenfabriken GmbH v Finance Minister: C-35/05* [2007] ECR I-2425, [2008] STC 3448, ECJ, which was based on the following situation:

- A German based customer received advertising services from an Italian based company – under the place of supply rules, no VAT should have been charged by the Italian company, with tax being accounted for by the German customer using the reverse charge rules (the place of supply for advertising services is based on the location of the customer, ie Germany). However, Italian VAT was incorrectly charged on the service – and paid in good faith by the German customer.

- The Italian supplier paid the incorrectly charged VAT to the Italian authorities – the German customer then tried to recover this VAT by making an overseas refund claim to the Italian authorities.

- The Italian authorities rejected the claim on the basis that VAT should not have been charged in the first place. However, the German customer was unable to trace the Italian company to acquire a VAT credit, leaving it out of pocket having paid the VAT in good faith. But, the ECJ ruled in favour of the taxpayer, on the basis that the principles of neutrality, effectiveness and non-discrimination allowed national legislation to reimburse VAT unduly paid to the tax authorities.

Planning points to consider

[15.10] The following planning points should be given consideration.

- An overseas trader having business dealings with the UK must clearly establish whether it is making taxable supplies in the UK and has a liability to register for VAT in the UK.

- Remember that a UK agent dealing with the VAT obligations of an overseas trader must be properly authorised by the trader through a written letter to HMRC.

- Be aware of the electronic procedures that apply to overseas VAT refund claims made on or after 1 January 2010. Claims are made via the taxpayer's own tax authority, rather than to the country where the VAT was paid.

- It is important to note that various EU and non-EU countries have specific rules about categories of expenditure on which VAT cannot be reclaimed.

Chapter 16

Dealing with Errors and Interest Charged on Errors

Key topics in this chapter:

- Options for dealing with VAT errors – increased error notification limits from 1 July 2008.
- The difference between an error and an adjustment.
- Error correction procedures – forms to complete and information required.
- Four-year time limits for correcting errors.
- The importance of 'unjust enrichment' on any errors that have resulted in an overpayment of tax.
- The effect of charging the wrong amount of VAT on an invoice.
- Dealing with input tax claims on late purchase invoices.
- The HMRC approach to dealing with errors.
- Default interest charged on errors made by a taxpayer and occasions when HMRC may pay interest in the case of an official error.

Introduction

[16.1] It is inevitable that mistakes will be made by many businesses in calculating their VAT liabilities. These mistakes will sometimes be identified before the return has been submitted, this is helped by having strong internal controls and an effective system of checking the figures. In such cases, the procedure for dealing with errors is not an issue – the figures on the return can be amended before it is submitted to HMRC.

However, there will be occasions when mistakes are identified after the return has been submitted, resulting in an underpayment or overpayment of tax. In basic terms, the following key rules apply with regard to the correction of errors:

- The error can be adjusted on the next VAT return submitted by the business if the net value of all errors is less than £10,000 or less than 1% of the Box 6 outputs figure for the return when the error is discovered, up to a ceiling of £50,000.

- If the net value of errors exceeds £10,000 and also exceeds 1% of the Box 6 outputs figure for the return when the error is discovered or £50,000, then an error notification must be made to HMRC (Form VAT 652), giving full details of the errors and the VAT periods to which they relate.

- HMRC will usually charge interest on underpayments of tax made by an error notification, reflecting 'commercial restitution', ie the fact that tax has been paid after the due date.

  Note – an 'error' is relevant to a situation where there has been no deliberate attempt to underpay VAT. If an underpayment has been caused by deliberate actions, then it is excluded from the error adjustment regulations and disclosure to HMRC must be made in all cases, ie rather than tax being included on the next VAT return.

(HMRC Notice 700/45, section 4).

Difference between an error and an adjustment

[16.2] There is a big difference between an error and an adjustment – it is only errors that need to be corrected by making a notification to HMRC. See Example 1.

Example 1

ABC Ltd is a partly exempt company, with taxable supplies from selling houses on a commission basis and exempt sales from arranging financial services products.

The company has come to the end of the tax year 31 March 2015, and calculated its annual adjustment for partial exemption purposes. An amount of £2,400 is payable to HMRC. The company has also identified that a sales invoice it raised in July 2014 has never been paid – the VAT involved is £800 and the company wants to claim bad debt relief.

Finally, the company reclaimed £2,750 of input tax on the purchase of a new car in December 2014, a vehicle not exclusively for business use, and also available for private use (ie input tax should not have been claimed).

What is the VAT position?

Solution – the partial exemption annual adjustment and claim for bad debt relief are not VAT errors – they are standard accounting adjustments. The partial exemption annual adjustment needs to be declared on either the March 2015 or June 2015 return in accordance with partial exemption rules. The bad debt relief adjustment can be made at any time by the taxpayer, as long as the debt is more than six months (but not more than four years and six months) overdue for payment and has been written off in the business accounts.

As the amount of VAT reclaimed on the car is less than the error notification limits, the VAT can be adjusted on the next VAT return, rather than as a separate notification to HMRC. However, the taxpayer should be aware that a separate notification of this error to HMRC is still advisable to avoid a potential penalty for making a 'careless' error. The inclusion of an error on a VAT return is not classed as a full disclosure for penalty purposes ie to mitigate a potential penalty of 30% down to zero. So the tax overclaimed on the car will still be included on the VAT return (less than £10,000 limit etc), with a separate letter or Form VAT 652 being sent to HMRC giving full details of the error (Chapter 17).

However, some errors in accounting can occur (for instance due to invoicing errors) that result in an under or overpayment of VAT but which cannot be corrected by an error notification. See Example 2 for a typical illustration.

Example 2

X Ltd raises a sales invoice for £30,000 plus £6,000 VAT on 31 March, and accounts for output tax on its quarterly VAT return for the quarter to 31 March, submitted on 14 April.

However, the day after the return has been submitted, it is discovered that the invoice should have been for £3,000 plus £600 VAT – meaning that output tax has been overcharged by £5,400.

Solution – if the invoice clerk at X Ltd had not made the error when raising this invoice, then the VAT payment to HMRC for the quarter to 31 March would have been reduced by £5,400 (ie £6,000 – £600). However, the issuing of the invoice to the customer has created a tax point for VAT purposes, and the customer could reclaim input tax on this invoice. The correct procedure is for X Ltd to raise a credit note during the quarter to 30 June to correct the invoicing error in the previous quarter. Output tax for the quarter to 30 June will then be reduced by £5,400.

Error correction procedures

[16.3] The new penalty system introduced by HMRC in relation to VAT returns due on or after 1 April 2009 means that some errors could be subject to a penalty, even where the business makes a disclosure of the error to HMRC or corrects the error on its next VAT return. See Chapter 17 for further details.

The following is a summary of the key phrases that are relevant when dealing with VAT errors.

* All errors discovered by a taxpayer must be corrected as soon as they are discovered (or noted in the VAT file to be corrected on the next VAT return submitted by the business if the net value of the errors is below certain limits). This means that all errors are within the 'error correction' procedures.
* Certain errors can be corrected by a taxpayer on his next VAT return – if the net value of the errors is:
  — less than £10,000; or
  — less than £50,000 and also less than 1% of the Box 6 outputs figure on the VAT return on which the errors are being corrected.

- If the net value of errors discovered by a taxpayer is above these limits, they cannot be adjusted on a VAT return. An 'error notification' must be made to HMRC to advise them of the error(s) – this can either be done by completing Form VAT 652 or by writing a separate letter giving full details of the various errors and the periods to which they relate.

(HMRC Notice 700/45, section 4).

Method of disclosure

[16.4] As explained at **16.1**, it is the net value of errors that needs to be considered when deciding whether errors can be adjusted on the next VAT return submitted by a business. See Example 3 which illustrates the method of calculating the net error.

Example 3

John's accountants have just carried out their annual review of his books, and identified the following VAT errors:

- John omitted two sales invoices from his sales day book, underpaying output tax by £13,250;
- John forgot to reclaim input tax of £3,500 on the purchase of his business computer system, incorrectly thinking the expense was zero-rated.

The net effect of the errors is that John has underpaid VAT by £9,750. As this amount is less than £10,000, John can adjust it on his next VAT return. However, he may still want to notify HMRC about the error to avoid or reduce a potential penalty for making a 'careless' error. See Chapter 17.

When a business has to notify HMRC of an error for any reason, there are two methods it can adopt, either to:

- complete Form VAT 652 (obtainable from the VAT Helpline on 0300 200 3700 or can be downloaded from the GOV.UK website) – this form ensures that all relevant details are given about the error; or
- write to HMRC at

  HM Revenue and Customs
  VAT Error Correction Team
  13th Floor North
  Euston Tower
  286 Euston Road
  London
  NW1 3UH
  Telephone: 0300 200 3700

In either of the above cases, information must be given about the errors as follows:

- how each error arose;
- the VAT period in which it occurred;
- if it was an input tax or output tax error;

- the VAT underdeclared or overdeclared in each VAT period;
- how the VAT underdeclared or overdeclared has been calculated;
- the total amount to be adjusted.

(HMRC Notice 700/45, para 4.4).

If an amount of tax has been underpaid, it is important to give as much detail as possible about the error.

Once the notification has been processed by HMRC, it will issue a 'statement of account', confirming the amount of tax and interest payable.

The amount payable should be remitted by the taxpayer within 30 days of the calculation date, otherwise further interest could be charged. Where a repayment is due by HMRC, it will first net the repayment off against any tax payable, and then repay the remainder by BACs or payable order.

Time limit for corrections

[16.5] In general terms, errors cannot be corrected more than four years after the VAT period in which they arose. The previous time-cap until April 2009 was three years. The extra year is good news in the case of overpayments, but not such good news if big underpayments of VAT have taken place.

Example 4

The accountant at DEF Ltd has just discovered that, for the last ten years, the company has failed to reclaim input tax on the petrol element of mileage allowances paid to employees for their business travel. However, it is also discovered that input tax has been fully reclaimed on the costs of the office Christmas party for the last ten years, even though 50% of the guests were non-employees, ie where input tax should have been disallowed on 50% of the costs as relevant to business entertainment.

Solution – the company has made two VAT errors, one resulting in an underpayment of tax and one in an overpayment of tax. A correction can only be made for the last four years in both cases, which is good news for the company if the underpayments exceed the overpayments – but not such good news if it is the other way around. The correct approach is for the accountant to calculate the net tax due (or repayable) over the last four years. If the amount exceeds the error notification limits, HMRC must be notified of the error (by Form VAT 652 or by letter) – if it is less than these limits, an adjustment on the next VAT return can be made.

Unjust enrichment

[16.6] In certain cases, a business could identify that it has made a major error of principle that has produced a significant overpayment of tax – for example, where a zero-rated product has been charged at the standard rate of VAT. This error could have been ongoing for many years.

In many cases, the taxpayer will be prevented from claiming a windfall from HMRC through the rules of 'unjust enrichment'. These rules basically state that no taxpayer can be unjustly enriched through making VAT errors – and it needs to be identified who has borne the cost of any incorrectly charged VAT. For example, in most cases where VAT has been charged to a customer on an item, the correct procedure will be for this VAT to be refunded to the customer, not to treat it as a cash windfall for the taxpayer who should not have charged tax in the first place.

A detailed analysis of the issues concerning unjust enrichment is included in Chapter 20.

(HMRC Notice 700/45, section 9).

Input tax claims on late purchase invoices

[16.7] In an ideal world, all suppliers would submit their purchase invoices on time – not least because it will be in their own interests to get paid quicker.

However, in reality there is often a situation where a supplier submits a late purchase invoice, after the relevant VAT return has already been submitted. So the question then is: can input tax on the late purchase invoice be treated as an error notification to HMRC and be submitted as an overpayment on Form VAT 652? Or is the late purchase invoice a normal accounting adjustment to include on the next VAT return submitted?

The decision will be made by the taxpayer and will usually depend on the amount of tax involved. HMRC Notice 700/45,para 6.1 states:

> 'In practice, most traders will deduct any input tax they are entitled to on the next VAT return after they have received the invoice from their supplier.'

Adjustments required when incorrect VAT is shown on a VAT invoice

[16.8] It is possible that in some situations an invoice will be issued where the VAT charge has been calculated incorrectly. For example, £100 + £10 VAT instead of £100 + £20 VAT. It is also possible that VAT could have been charged on a zero-rated supply.

In such situations, the best option is for both the supplier and the customer to agree to a VAT adjustment being made. As long as the error occurred within the last four years, this can be achieved by one of the following methods:

- the original invoice can be cancelled and the supplier issues a replacement showing the correct charge of VAT;
- the supplier can issue a credit note or supplementary VAT invoice to his customer;
- the customer can issue a debit note to the supplier (in reality, this option is less likely – very few taxpayers become involved with debit notes).

If the above situation is not applied, then the priority is for HMRC to ensure it is not out of pocket by the error. There are two possible courses of action:

(a)   if the VAT shown on the invoice is too high – the supplier must account for the higher amount in his records and the customer must only include the amount which should have been charged in his records; or

(b)   if the VAT shown on the invoice is too low – the supplier must account
        for the amount which should have been charged and the customer must
        only include the lower amount actually shown on the invoice.

The essential point with errors in these situations is that there is no error
notification procedure required – HMRC sets the rules to ensure that the
output tax accounted for by the supplier is either equal to or greater than the
input tax reclaimed by the customer.

(HMRC Notice 700/45, paras 3.2–3.3).

HMRC approach to dealing with error notifications

[16.9] There is often a fear among clients and advisers that if they notify an
underpayment to HMRC, it will immediately result in an army of VAT
inspectors arriving at the door to carry a full audit going back four years.

In reality, this is rarely the case, because HMRC recognises that errors will be
made, even with the increasing use of computers to deal with standard VAT
calculations. However, it is always useful to ensure that a 'one off' error is
clearly explained as such in a letter. It would be considered a more serious
problem if the errors were caused by a fundamental defect in the accounting
system of a business.

Another important point is to ensure that if the notification results in money
being repaid by HMRC, then as much supporting evidence about the claim as
possible should be given. For example, if the notification is due to input tax not
being reclaimed on a new piece of equipment, then it is worthwhile to provide
a copy of the purchase invoice with the claim letter. If the error has been
identified and corrected by various spreadsheet or nominal ledger reconcilia-
tions, then copies of these calculations and supporting printouts would again
be useful.

In effect, the approach to adopt is to ensure that HMRC can obtain a full
picture of how and why the error occurred, and also to give it confidence that
the error has been corrected in an accurate manner.

Although HMRC has a responsibility to process voluntary disclosure claims
promptly, it also has the right to seek further information where it is not
satisfied with the figures. This can either be done through a written request for
further information, or by asking to attend the premises and examine the
business records.

Errors discovered on a VAT visit

[16.10] The routine VAT visit where HMRC attends a taxpayer's premises
and looks at all records for the previous four years is becoming less common.
Many visits are now conducted on a risk-based assessment, and may only look
at one aspect of the accounting system.

If an officer finds errors during an inspection, usually resulting in an underpayment of tax, he or she will often send a letter to the taxpayer showing the calculations made to arrive at an assessment. This gives the taxpayer the chance to review the figures (possibly with an accountant or adviser) and raise any points in dispute.

In cases where the amount of VAT cannot be agreed, then the taxpayer has the right of appeal, firstly by asking for an internal review by an HMRC officer not connected with the original case. If necessary, it can then be considered by an independent VAT tribunal.

Charging of interest

[16.11] In general terms, HMRC only charges interest where it considers it represents 'commercial restitution', ie compensation for the loss of use of any underpaid tax. It normally only charges interest if it has been deprived of this money for a period of time. It would not, for example, normally charge interest on an output tax underpayment that would have been reclaimed as input tax by a third party.

HMRC uses the following guidelines to decide if an interest charge for commercial restitution is appropriate, usually when either an officer assessment is raised or an error notification is processed.

(a)   Overclaimed input tax:
- Is the input tax properly reclaimable by another registered person (who is not partly exempt)? If so, then no interest will be charged as the input tax would still be recovered from HMRC.
- Is there any other reason why interest should not be charged? This gives the officer the chance to review whether there are other reasons why an interest charge should not be made.

(b)   Underpaid output tax:
- Is the underdeclaration an additional assessment, ie where HMRC has assessed for a period in the absence of a return and the true liability is later found to exceed the assessment? In such cases, interest will be charged.
- For VAT errors – is the error wholly within an accounting system, eg arithmetical and accounting errors, retail scheme errors, calculation errors? If so, interest will be charged.

HMRC will seek to charge interest on all errors notified to it, irrespective of whether the tax could have been adjusted on a VAT return, ie errors below £10,000 or 1% of Box 6 turnover up to £50,000 etc. So the key message is to adjust an error on a VAT return if it is eligible for such treatment in order to avoid any potential interest charge. Interest is not charged by HMRC in the following situations:

- where VAT has been declared on returns but not paid;
- central assessments initially raised in the absence of a VAT return for a period;
- interest is not charged on penalties and interest;

- amendments made to VAT returns before they are fully processed.

(HMRC Notice 700/43, para 2.4).

Note – interest is charged from the date when the tax should have been paid to the date when it was actually charged on the notice issued by HMRC. If the amount charged is not paid within 30 days from the date of the notice, then a further charge of interest is made.

(HMRC Notice 700/43, paras 2.6 and 2.8).

Interest repaid by HMRC

[**16.12**] A business is entitled to repayment supplement where HMRC does not make any repayment due within a specified time. However, as a general principle, HMRC does not pay interest to a taxpayer on any amounts of overpaid tax, unless it (HMRC) caused the error – see Example 5.

Example 5

ABC Ltd received a ruling from HMRC in 2010 that it could not reclaim input tax on the costs of the staff Christmas party. The director of ABC Ltd has now discovered that this ruling was incorrect, and that the company could have claimed £700 input tax on each of its December returns in years 2010 to 2012.

Solution – as well as being able to reclaim £2,100 input tax on the staff party for the three years, the director can also apply for HMRC to pay interest on the input tax claimed late as the delay in the claim was due to an official error by HMRC.

Planning points to consider

[**16.13**] The following planning points should be given consideration.

- It is important to ensure that all adjustments or error corrections made on VAT returns are fully supported by working papers and schedules to prove the figures in the event of a future VAT visit. If a separate notification is made to HMRC, ensure supporting evidence is given where appropriate, particularly in the case of a tax overpayment.
- There is no need to be concerned about errors on VAT returns (underpayments or overpayments) that go back beyond four years – they are out of date and cannot be adjusted. The only exception is if fraud is involved, in which case HMRC can collect tax for the last 20 years.
- Always thoroughly review any assessment raised by HMRC following a VAT visit – there may be scope to request a reconsideration of the assessment if the officer has not taken important information into account within his calculations.
- It is important that a taxpayer pays error notifications or officer assessments within 30 days otherwise interest will continue to accrue on the non-payment.

- If a client is due a big tax rebate due to an error of principle, make sure that the issue of 'unjust enrichment' is fully considered before the client spends the rebate. In most cases, any overcharged VAT must be refunded to customers, not treated as a cash windfall by the business in question.

- Be aware of the impact of penalty rules that came into effect on 1 April 2009 (see Chapter 17). The regulations mean that a taxpayer's error could still be subject to a penalty, even when he has corrected the error on a VAT return.

Chapter 17

Penalties

Key topics in this chapter:

- Penalties for errors on VAT returns.
- The default surcharge regime (current at the time of writing).
- The replacement for the default surcharge regime.
- Other VAT penalties.

Introduction

[17.1] The penalty regime for failure to notify HMRC on time of the requirement to be registered for VAT was considered in detail in Chapter 1. Chapter 16 considered how errors on VAT returns could be corrected and disclosed and the interest charges that can arise. This chapter will look at the penalty regime for errors on VAT returns, the default surcharge regime and its replacement, and finally, other VAT penalties.

Please note that a replacement for the default surcharge regime was introduced by *Finance (No 3) Act 2010, ss 26* and *27* and *Schs 10* and *11* but at the time of writing has not yet been implemented.

How penalties are calculated

[17.2] *Finance Act 2007, Sch 24* introduced a penalty regime that applies to VAT returns filed after 31 March 2009. The aim of the regime is to encourage compliance and not to penalise innocent errors.

The three categories of behaviour that give rise to penalties are listed in *Finance Act 2007, Sch 24 para 3* and can be summarised as:

- *Careless* – where the inaccuracy is due to a failure to take reasonable care.
- *Deliberate but not concealed* – where the inaccuracy is deliberate but arrangements are not made to conceal it.
- *Deliberate and concealed* – where the inaccuracy is deliberate and arrangements are made to conceal it (eg by preparing false documents in an attempt to support the inaccuracy).

It is important to note that the legislation treats an innocent error as careless if the taxpayer, on becoming aware of the error, does not take reasonable steps to inform HMRC. The thinking behind this may be that an innocent error ceases to be innocent if the taxpayer becomes aware of it and fails to notify HMRC.

The penalty is calculated by applying a percentage (see Table 1), based on the category of behaviour giving rise to the penalty, to what is referred to as 'potential lost revenue'. In the context of VAT, the term 'potential lost revenue' broadly means the additional VAT which would have been due had the VAT return not contained the inaccuracy. However, the term 'potential lost revenue' can also apply when HMRC have under-assessed a taxpayer, for example, because VAT returns have not been submitted. The message here is that a taxpayer cannot avoid penalties for inaccuracies by not submitting VAT returns.

The percentage that is applied to the potential lost revenue can be reduced if the taxpayer makes a disclosure to HMRC. The amount of the reduction will depend on whether the disclosure is prompted or unprompted (see Table 1) and the quality of the disclosure (see **17.3**).

TABLE 1: SUMMARY OF HOW PENALTIES ARE CALCULATED

Reason for penalty	Standard penalty	Minimum reduced penalty for un-prompted disclosure	Minimum reduced penalty for prompted disclosure
Careless error	30%	0%	15%
Deliberate but not concealed error	70%	20%	35%
Deliberate and con-cealed error	100%	30%	50%
Incorrect assessment	30%	0%	15%

Disclosure

[17.3] The aim of the penalty regime is to encourage compliance, which includes encouraging taxpayers to notify HMRC of inaccuracies in their VAT returns or in HMRC assessments, ie by making a disclosure. Penalties can be reduced by the quality of the disclosure and whether it is unprompted or prompted. A paraphrased summary of *Finance Act 2007, Sch 24 para 9*, which provides details of what is meant by the quality of a disclosure and whether a disclosure is unprompted or prompted is as follows:

A person discloses an inaccuracy or an under-assessment by—

- telling HMRC about it,
- giving HMRC reasonable help in quantifying the inaccuracy or the under-assessment, and
- allowing HMRC access to records for the purpose of ensuring that the inaccuracy or the under-assessment is fully corrected.

Disclosure is 'unprompted' if made at a time when the person making it has no reason to believe that HMRC have discovered or are about to discover the inaccuracy or the under assessment, and otherwise, is 'prompted'.

In relation to disclosure, 'quality' includes timing, nature and extent.

Penalty suspension

[17.4] HMRC can suspend all or part of a penalty for careless inaccuracy for a period of up to two years. Providing the taxpayer is compliant throughout the suspension period (by meeting any conditions HMRC set), the amount of the penalty that is suspended is cancelled.

Penalty appeals

[17.5] If a taxpayer or their adviser does not accept a penalty, or believe that it should be suspended, they can ask HMRC to reconsider their decision, by requesting an internal review, or they can appeal directly to the tribunal. The important point to note is that action must be taken to either request an internal review or lodge an appeal within 30 days of the penalty being issued. If an internal review is requested and the outcome is not acceptable a further 30 days is then available to appeal to the tribunal.

The rules and procedures concerning the penalty for belated notification of VAT registration are analysed in detail in Chapter 1.

Tribunal cases involving penalties for inaccurate VAT returns

[17.6] There have been a number of tribunal cases involving penalties for inaccurate VAT returns that have clarified how the penalty regime should operate. The following paragraphs provide examples.

Athenaeum Club (TC00833) [2010] UKFTT 583 (TC), [2011] SWTI 284 – input tax dilemma

[17.7] Have you ever looked at a purchase invoice or bill and not been totally sure whether it includes VAT or not? This was the problem for the treasurer of the Athenaeum Club in relation to a £216,871 water bill for its commercial premises, and she couldn't establish whether it included VAT or otherwise. She liaised with two officers of HMRC, one of whom had carried out a recent VAT visit, and she was also reassured by correspondence she saw from Anglia Water indicating that VAT was due on water charges for commercial properties. She therefore claimed input tax of £28,287 based on a VAT rate of 15% that applied at the time of the bill (VAT fraction 3/23).

It was subsequently found that the water bill did not include VAT so HMRC, on reviewing the return submitted by the taxpayer, reduced the input tax. They also assessed a 15% careless error penalty, the minimum penalty that can be applied if an error is 'prompted', ie discovered by HMRC rather than notified by the taxpayer.

However, fair play and common sense prevailed and the tribunal reversed the penalty. To quote directly from the case report:

> 'Mrs Jones had been misled by the letters from Anglia Water and the bill from Essex & Suffolk Water. The advice supplied by Graham Back from HMRC further confused the issue.
>
> We find that Mrs Jones did take reasonable care and was not careless. We found it somewhat illogical that HMRC refused to suspend a penalty on the grounds that the Appellant was unlikely to do it again.'

GD and Mrs D Lewis (t/a Russell Francis Interiors) (TC00983) [2011] UKFTT 107 (TC) – timing error

[17.8] The most important VAT issues to get right often involve property transactions. Here are the circumstances of the *Lewis* case:

- Partnership bought a property in 2009 – exchange of contracts was on 23 May 2009 (£25,000 plus VAT of £3,750) and completion date was 14 July 2009 (an additional £225,000 plus VAT of £33,750).
- Input tax of £37,500 was claimed on June 2009 VAT return – instead of £3,750 – and queried by HMRC – this was an error as input tax of £33,750 should have been claimed the following quarter ie based on completion date.
- HMRC reduced the input tax claim by £33,750 and assessed a 15% careless error penalty of £5,063 for June 2009 – on the basis that the adjustment was a 'prompted disclosure' and this is the minimum penalty within the legislation.
- Taxpayer appealed – on the basis that the penalty was exceptionally high for a timing error – judge agreed and felt HMRC should have treated the situation as a 'special circumstance' (*Finance Act 2007, Sch 24, para 11*). He reduced the penalty to 7.5% of the tax error, ie £2,531.

Comment – there is no doubt that the above error was 'careless' and also that HMRC 'prompted' the disclosure by querying the input tax on the June 2009 return submitted by the taxpayer. But is a 15% penalty fair when there was no error involved that would have created a permanent loss of tax to the Exchequer?

HMRC had three escape routes within the legislation to reduce or cancel the penalty against the Lewis family – they opted for none of them:

- *Finance Act 2007, Sch 24, para 11* – gives HMRC the power to reduce the minimum penalties in 'special circumstances'.
- *Finance Act 2007, Sch 24, para 14* – gives HMRC the power to suspend a penalty (see **17.4**) for up to two years, ie a bit like the yellow card in football, you can stay on the field but one more slip-up and you're off! However, a suspended penalty was not appropriate in this case because the deal was a one-off transaction and unlikely to be repeated in the future.

- They could have treated the error as a timing error – they didn't in this case but see **17.11** regarding an important change of policy on this issue, almost certainly as a result of this case.

Express Food Supplies (TC00728) [2010] UKFTT 466 (TC), [2010] SWTI 3048 – errors by third parties

[17.9] If a taxpayer appoints an agent to handle his tax affairs, and complete his VAT returns, then he has immediately shown a degree of 'reasonable care'. But the fact that an agent has completed a VAT return does not mean that the taxpayer will avoid a reasonable care penalty at all costs. If the taxpayer should have queried the accuracy of a return because the figures looked incorrect, then he can still be held liable to a penalty. Here are the circumstances of the *Express Food Supplies* case:

- VAT period April 2009 – repayment return for £21,660.82 – totally out of trend with normal returns of the business.
- HMRC wrote to the taxpayer asking if the return was correct and asking for copies of major purchase invoices to support input tax claimed.
- The return had been completed by a temporary bookkeeper who had posted zero-rated purchase invoices in the VAT column – the correct repayment was £1,082.23 and the taxpayer's accountant notified HMRC of this figure.
- HMRC assessed a careless error penalty equal to 15% of the potential lost revenue (ic £21,661 – £1,082 x 15%).
- 15% penalty is the minimum penalty for a 'prompted disclosure' when an error(s) is careless – it could be as high as 30%. Prompted means that it was action by HMRC that led to the error being discovered and corrected.
- The taxpayer admitted he had been careless – the repayment was four times more than his biggest ever VAT repayment so he should have been aware of the potential for error, even though his bookkeeper completed the records and the VAT return.

Comment – this was a clear-cut case. Even though a temporary bookkeeper completed the records for the period in question, the taxpayer should have known that the end result of her work was a totally inaccurate return. He should have asked more questions to establish why the return showed such a big repayment. As the old saying goes, if something appears too good to be true, it probably is!

The taxpayer Mr Nassan Ali Al-Faham claimed that he was 'not a bookkeeper' and should not therefore be penalised for the bookkeeper's shortcomings but the fact was that the highest ever VAT repayment for his business in its trading history had been £5,500, so he should have challenged why the work of an inexperienced person had suddenly resulted in a rebate that was equal to four times this amount. He lost the case.

Mollan and Co Ltd (TC00828) [2010] UKFTT 578 (TC), [2011] STI 283 – deregistration 'disaster'

[17.10] Any business that deregisters from VAT must ensure that output tax is declared on any standard-rated stock or assets owned by the business on the final day when a business is registered, and on which input tax has been claimed. In some cases, the potential output tax liability means a business should withdraw its application to deregister.

In the case of *Mollan and Co Ltd*, the taxpayer's final VAT return committed the cardinal sin . . . it omitted output tax on the market value of a property it owned and on which it had claimed input tax and made an option to tax election. The market value of the property at the date of deregistration was deemed to be £200,000, and as the deregistration date was when we had 15% VAT (June 2009), this created an output tax liability of £30,000. HMRC also imposed a 15% careless error penalty of £4,500. The tribunal upheld the penalty.

Revised HMRC policy on timing errors

[17.11] The legislation imposes a penalty of 5% per annum, adjusted on a time basis (eg 1.25% for three months) where an error corrects itself on the following VAT return, eg a sales invoice entered late or purchase invoice entered early (the latter problem applied in the case of *GD and Mrs D Lewis* – see **17.8**). The previous HMRC policy was that both VAT returns must have been submitted by the taxpayer before the timing penalty applied – so that HMRC could see the automatic correction of the error in the following period.

HMRC has sensibly revised its policy by issuing Revenue & Customs Brief 15/11 on 6 April 2011, confirming that if it is satisfied the error would have been corrected on the subsequent return, ie in cases where the business has submitted the first return which has been checked by HMRC before the second one is legally due, then it will apply the timing penalty rather than the higher level of penalties based on 'careless error' situations. This is very sensible and welcome and would be relevant to the *Lewis* case considered above.

VAT compliance activity by HMRC

[17.12] HMRC now identify a lot of errors by reviewing VAT returns in the comfort of their offices. Contrast that to the policy that applied in the past when officers usually made a visit to the premises of the taxpayer to carry out checks and reviews. The message is clear – although there are less HMRC visits taking place, they are still making enquiries into VAT returns and figures by telephone calls or by writing to the taxpayer.

The office-based reviews referred to in the previous paragraph focused on VAT compliance activity in relation to VAT-registered businesses. HMRC have also recently been looking at individuals and businesses operating above the VAT threshold who have not registered for VAT. For example, HMRC wrote to over

40,000 businesses during 2011 to highlight an opportunity they referred to as 'the VAT Initiative'. By 31 December 2011, when the opportunity to come forward under the terms of the initiative closed, 844 businesses notified HMRC that they should previously have registered for VAT and wished to take part in the campaign. At 31 March 2012, 851 businesses had registered for VAT through the initiative, which resulted in revenue of over £9m when 467 of those newly registered businesses had submitted their first VAT return.

HMRC have made increasing use of technology, together with information and intelligence gathered from many different sources, to find businesses that are not, but should be, registered for VAT. As well as specialist technology, the information widely available on the internet can assist HMRC to identify businesses that may be attempting to operate 'under the radar'.

There have been a number of HMRC direct tax campaigns focusing on specific sectors such as e-traders, plumbers, electricians and tutors and there are often VAT implications for those affected.

Default surcharge

[17.13] A replacement for the default surcharge regime was introduced into the legislation at *Finance (No 3) Act 2010, ss 26* and *27* and *Schs 10* and *11*. However, at the time of writing it has not yet been implemented. Before looking at the replacement regime in detail we will look at the existing default surcharge regime.

The legislation covering the existing default surcharge regime is at *VATA 1994, ss 59, 59A* and *59B*.

Late returns and payments

What happens when returns and payments are made late?

[17.14] Many clients will sometimes face a cash flow problem – which means either paying suppliers on time (to keep the flow of goods coming into the business) or paying the quarterly VAT return on time (and keeping HMRC happy).

Note – the starting point for any business that is unable to pay its tax bill is to contact HMRC's Business Payment Support Service (BPSS) and negotiate a time to pay arrangement. See **30.5** for further details.

The question that clients often ask is: 'What will happen if I pay my VAT late?' The approach taken by HMRC in relation to late VAT returns and payments is as follows.

- *Surcharge liability notice* – on the first occasion that a return or payment is submitted late, a taxpayer will be issued with a surcharge liability notice. This notice confirms that he is in default in respect of a VAT period, and that if another default occurs within the next 12 months, he will be liable to a default surcharge penalty.

Note – in the case of a small business with turnover of £150,000 per year or less, the first default does not produce a surcharge liability notice, but a letter from HMRC offering help and support. It is only if another default occurs within the next 12 months that the surcharge liability notice is issued. (HMRC Notice 700/50, para 4.2).

- *Default surcharge* – if the taxpayer defaults within the next 12 months (the surcharge period), then he will be liable to pay a default surcharge. The surcharge is calculated as a percentage of the VAT that is unpaid at the due date. The first late payment in a surcharge period attracts a 2% surcharge and an extension to the surcharge period – see comments below regarding the surcharge liability extension notice.
  The rate of surcharge then increases progressively to 5%, then 10%, and then 15% for subsequent late payments in the surcharge period, with the surcharge period being extended each time.
  (HMRC Notice 700/50, para 4.3):
- *Surcharge liability extension notice* – a business only comes out of the default surcharge system when it has submitted and paid four successive VAT returns on time (assuming a business on quarterly returns). The initial surcharge liability notice covers a 12-month default period from when the first late payment or return occurs – but each additional default within this 12-month period sees a surcharge liability extension notice issued to extend the period up to the 12-month anniversary of the relevant default. Basically, to come out of the default surcharge system, a taxpayer needs to submit all returns and pay all tax on time for a full 12-month period.

There are some important points to note regarding the default surcharge penalties imposed following an offence:

- Where a liability to surcharge is established, HMRC will not issue a surcharge assessment at the 2% or 5% rates for an amount of less than £400. However, a default will still be recorded, and a surcharge liability extension notice will also be issued (HMRC Notice 700/50, para 4.5);
- If the taxpayer can convince HMRC (or a VAT tribunal if he takes the case to appeal) that he had a 'reasonable excuse' for the VAT not being paid (or return despatched) then the default will be withdrawn.

See Example 1 for an illustration of the workings of the default surcharge system.

Example 1

Jones Wholesalers submitted its October 2010 return late and received a default surcharge liability notice. It then submitted its January 2011 and April 2011 returns on time, but made a late payment in July 2011. The payment due for the July 2011 period was £20,500. It was also late in October 2011 (VAT due was £7,500) and again in January 2012 (VAT due was £3,500). What penalties are due?

Solution – having submitted its October 2010 return late, the company needed to be on time and fully compliant with the next four VAT returns up to and including the period ending 31 October 2011 – it did not achieve this goal.

The next default in July 2011 attracts the initial 2% penalty of £410 (£20,500 × 2%), and the next period attracts a 5% penalty of £375 (£7,500 × 5%). However, good news on this one – because the total penalty is less than £400, and it is relevant to the 5% penalty period, then no penalty is issued. The penalty for January 2012 is also less than £400 (£3,500 × 10% = £350) but this penalty is applied because we are no longer in either the 2% or 5% period – hence the £400 *de minimis* situation does not apply.

An interesting point to note: just because the 5% penalty was wavered in October 2011, it does not mean that the next default attracts only a 5% penalty – the next period still suffers a 10% rate.

When does a default occur?

[17.15] The relevant date as far as the VAT return or payment is concerned, is not the date it was posted by the trader – but the date it was received by HMRC. And for cheque payments made after 1 April 2010, the cheque needs to have cleared HMRC's bank account by the date when the VAT return is due for payment.

Over the years, the posting issue has caused great controversy – with some interesting tribunal cases. Since 1 April 2012 virtually all VAT-registered businesses have been required to submit their VAT returns and pay any VAT due electronically so postal delays should now be less of an issue.

Payments on account

[17.16] As explained above, a surcharge penalty is based on the 'outstanding VAT' due for the period. This means that the penalty is reduced if some payment on account has been made on time to meet the liability – see Example 2.

Example 2

DEF Ltd is in the default surcharge system, and the next default will attract a 10% penalty. The VAT return for December 2011 shows a payment due of £30,000 but the company accountant can only pay £13,000 by the due date of 7 February 2012 (an extra seven days are given to file and pay online return) because a key customer has not settled his account on time.

Solution – the 10% penalty will be based on the unpaid VAT of £17,000, ie £1,700. In effect, the company has a strong incentive to at least pay some of the VAT liability in order to reduce the extent of the penalty.

As a useful planning point, it is possible to make a part-payment to avoid a default surcharge if the penalty based on the outstanding tax is under the *de minimis* penalty of £400 for the 2% and 5% rates. See Example 3.

Example 3

JKL Ltd is in the default surcharge system and liable to a 2% penalty if it defaults in the October 2011 period. It submits the October 2011 return on time, but instead of paying the full tax due amount of £25,000 can only make a part-payment of £5,000. The company's VAT adviser suggests the part-payment be increased to £5,001.

Solution – the surcharge penalty is based on the amount of outstanding VAT for the period not paid by the due date. In this particular case, the amount is £19,999 – a 2% penalty therefore equates to £399.98 – but this will be waived because it is less than the £400 *de minimis* limit that applies for the 2% and 5% periods. The extra pound makes all the difference!

Impact of 15% penalty charge

[17.17] Once a business is paying the maximum 15% surcharge, then all future defaults within the default surcharge period will automatically be charged at 15%. This will become very costly for most businesses – and the hope by this point is that either a business has restructured its accounting system (if slow bookkeeping is the reason for defaults) or refinanced the business or its cash management procedures (if lack of cash was the problem).

For smaller businesses (taxable turnover excluding VAT is less than £1,350,000 per annum), it may be worth considering the possible benefits of using the annual accounting scheme if bookkeeping issues are the cause of defaults being incurred. The annual accounting scheme means an eligible business will only complete one VAT return each year instead of four. See Chapter 7 for a detailed analysis of the scheme.

If a business has very high output tax (ie all standard-rated sales) and negligible input tax (eg a service-based business where the biggest overhead of labour does not produce any input tax) then the impact of the 15% penalty will be enormous. It will be a priority for the business to take measures to ensure returns and payments are submitted on time or seek a time to pay agreement with HMRC's Business Payment Support Service (see **30.5**).

Avoiding a penalty

[17.18] When a business has submitted one return or payment late, then it is issued with a default surcharge notice. It then needs to submit the next four returns and payments on time (assuming quarterly returns are submitted) so that it has a clean record for the next 12 months. At this point, the business will be taken out of the default surcharge system, meaning that it can make one more return or payment late without incurring a penalty.

Some useful points to remember are as follows:

- if a repayment return (or nil return) is submitted late, then a default surcharge liability extension notice will be issued but there will be no penalty applied. This is because penalty calculations are always based on the amount of tax unpaid by the due date;

- a penalty can be avoided if a taxpayer can prove that the return and payment were despatched on time (and hence should have been received on time); or
- a penalty should not be applied because there was a reasonable excuse for not paying the tax on time – see **17.19**;
- if a business does not submit its return on time, but pays the full amount of tax due on time, then the late return will be recorded as a default but there will be no surcharge because the tax has been paid by the due date.

Note – the recent case of *Enersys Holdings UK Ltd v Revenue and Customs Comrs* [2010] UKFTT 20 (TC), [2010] SFTD 387, [2010] SWTI 1765 concerned a default surcharge penalty of £131,000, caused by the fact that the taxpayer submitted and paid a VAT return one day late. The business was subject to a 5% default surcharge. The judge withdrew the surcharge and allowed the taxpayer's appeal on the basis that it was 'wholly disproportionate' to the offence committed. Although this case does not set a precedent to similar situations, it is a useful case to quote if you have default surcharge situations where the amount charged appears to be excessive.

Note 2 – however, be aware of the Upper Tribunal judgment in the case of *Trinity Mirror plc*.

Trinity Mirror appealed to the First Tier Tribunal arguing that a penalty of £70,000 for being a day late with its balancing payment was wholly disproportionate. The First Tier Tribunal agreed and allowed the appeal. When compared to the *Enersys Holdings* case where the courts had found a default surcharge to be disproportionate, it was clear to the First Tier Tribunal that the surcharge in this case was also disproportionate and allowed the taxpayer's appeal. HMRC appealed.

The Upper Tribunal overturned the First Tier's decision and allowed HMRC's appeal. The Upper Tribunal considered that the First Tier erred in law. By comparing the level of the surcharge in *Trinity Mirror* to the level of surcharges in other cases, it made the wrong comparison. It should have focused on the amount of VAT that had been paid late (ie £3.5m) and, if it had done so, it would have seen that a penalty of 2% (a 'modest' percentage of the tax paid late) was not disproportionate and did not go beyond the objective of ensuring compliance and the timely payment of tax due.

In the circumstances, there was no reasonable excuse for the delay in paying the balancing payment and the imposition of the 2% surcharge was not disproportionate. HMRC's appeal was allowed. Given that the Upper Tribunal's judgment is binding, it seems clear now that the decision in *Enersys Holdings* does not stand up.

Reasonable excuse

[17.19] As with most decisions made by HMRC, the taxpayer has the right of appeal if he disagrees with either the issuing of a default surcharge liability notice or a subsequent default penalty.

The main reason for appeal is where the taxpayer considers that he has a 'reasonable excuse' for failing to submit his return or pay his tax on time. As a general point, the law stipulates that a lack of funds constitutes a reasonable excuse for non-payment of VAT, unless the circumstances are exceptional. Equally, it is not acceptable to blame a third party for failing to carry out a task (eg 'my accountant forgot to ask me for a cheque for my VAT payment') unless exceptional events again apply, such as death, serious illness, etc.

The phrase 'reasonable excuse' is not actually defined in the legislation and therefore individual situations depend on the interpretation of the facts by HMRC or, if that fails, by the view of an independent VAT tribunal.

The following circumstances could be accepted as a reasonable excuse by HMRC or a tribunal.

- *Computer breakdown* – if essential records are maintained on a computer, which suffers a major breakdown, then a reasonable excuse argument could be made. However, HMRC will expect to see evidence of an engineer being called to try and solve the problem – and probably a copy of his report.
- *Illness or compassionate reasons* – if it can be shown that the person normally responsible for preparing the return was either seriously ill or recovering from such an illness, then a reasonable excuse situation could apply. However, this argument would not work for a larger organisation for example, where it would be expected that more than one person would be capable of completing the return.
- *Unexpected cash crisis* – as explained above, insufficient funds is not a reasonable excuse for a default. However, if a cash crisis was caused by the sudden non-payment of money by a normally reliable customer, then a reasonable excuse could apply. Again, however, it would have to be proved that this customer's business represented a major part of the company's trading – it would be unacceptable to say that a late VAT return by a company with £5m turnover per year was caused by a customer not paying his £1,000 invoice.
- *Loss of records* – a genuine fire, flood or burglary would certainly create a 'reasonable excuse' situation if the records for the current VAT period were lost. In such circumstances, however, there would again need to be evidence of the problem (eg insurance claim for a fire; photographic evidence of fire damage etc). The other point to bear in mind is that if records are unavailable, a business has the facility to estimate its VAT figures in the absence of records – so there is still an opportunity to submit the return and pay the tax on time.

For an illustration of when a reasonable excuse situation could apply, see Example 4.

(HMRC Notice 700/50, section 6).

Example 4

Smith Ltd has submitted three successive VAT returns late for different reasons. The managing director wants to know which of the following issues would be classed as a reasonable excuse:

- the return for the quarter to 30 June was late because the bookkeeper had a week's holiday in Italy and was therefore out of the country in the week when the return was due;
- the return for the quarter to 30 September was late because the company's computer crashed and an engineer had to collect the computer and take it away for repair;
- the business encountered cash flow problems the following January – an important customer, accounting for 4% of the company's total turnover, did not pay his account on time. The amount unpaid equalled 50% of the VAT bill for the quarter to 31 December.

How many of the defaults would qualify as a reasonable excuse?

Solution – in reality, the bookkeeper's holiday is a non-starter. It would be expected that she would be able to complete the return before she went on holiday or, alternatively, arrange for the company accountants to come in and do the return.

The computer crash would probably be acceptable as long as there was clear evidence of the crash – and HMRC were satisfied that the circumstances were genuine.

The non-payment of money by the customer in January would not qualify as a reasonable excuse – the unpaid debt is only a small percentage of company sales.

Overall, a worthwhile approach for advisers dealing with reasonable excuse situations is to stand back and ask: 'Was my client late because of a genuine excuse, or is he trying to use this excuse to disguise the real reason for default, such as forgetting to do the return or, more likely, because he cannot afford to pay the tax due?'

The replacement of the default surcharge regime

[**17.20**] As noted at **17.13**, a replacement for the default surcharge regime was introduced into the legislation at *Finance (No 3) Act 2010, ss 26* and *27* and *Schs 10* and *11* but has not yet been implemented. A key difference between the new regime and the default surcharge regime is that late filing and late payments each attract separate penalties. It will be possible to incur a late filing penalty even if a VAT repayment is due.

The new late filing penalties

[**17.21**] Details of the late filing penalties are at *Finance (No 3) Act 2010, Sch 10* and are summarised in Table 2 below:

TABLE 2: SUMMARY OF NEW LATE FILING PENALTIES

	Quarterly VAT returns	Monthly VAT returns
First late return	£100	£100
	Start of 1-year penalty period	Start of 1-year penalty period
Second late return	£200	£100
(first in penalty period)	Penalty period extended	Penalty period extended

	Quarterly VAT returns	Monthly VAT returns
Third late return (second in penalty period)	£300 Penalty period extended	£100 Penalty period extended
Fourth late return (third in penalty period)	£400 Penalty period extended	£100 Penalty period extended
Fifth late return (fourth in penalty period)	£400 Penalty period extended	£100 Penalty period extended
Sixth late return (fifth in penalty period)	£400 Penalty period extended	£100 Penalty period extended
Subsequent late returns (in penalty period)	£400 Penalty period extended	£200 Penalty period extended

Notes:

(1) Each late return extends the penalty period to the anniversary of the filing date of the most recent late return.

(2) For returns which are over six months late there is a penalty of the greater of £300 and 5% of the VAT due.

(3) A further penalty of the greater of £300 and 5% of the VAT due applies to returns which are over 12 months late.

(4) For returns which are over 12 month late for which the taxpayer deliberately withholds information which would enable or assist HMRC to assess the VAT due the penalty can potentially be up to 100% of the VAT due.

Under the default surcharge regime late filing was seldom a concern for businesses making mainly zero-rated supplies and they often submitted VAT returns monthly in order to obtain the VAT repayment sooner. Under the *Finance (No 3) Act 2010, Sch 10* regime a late filing penalty can apply even when a VAT repayment is due. This is illustrated at Example 5.

Example 5

Fred is a farmer who receives VAT repayments every month but is always a few days late filing his VAT returns.

Solution – Table 3 below illustrates why it may be appropriate for Fred to consider moving to filing VAT returns quarterly if he finds it difficult to file his VAT returns on time.

TABLE 3: ILLUSTRATION OF HOW THE NEW LATE FILING PENALTIES COULD AFFECT FRED THE FARMER IN EXAMPLE 5

	Quarterly VAT returns (Calendar quarters)	Monthly VAT returns
January	n/a n/a	£100 Start of 1-year penalty period
February	n/a n/a	£100 Penalty period extended
March	£100 Start of 1-year penalty period	£100 Penalty period extended

	Quarterly VAT returns (Calendar quarters)	Monthly VAT returns
April	n/a	£100
	n/a	Penalty period extended

The new late payment penalties

[**17.22**] Fred the Farmer in Example 5 may not be too concerned about the new late payment penalties but many other businesses will be. Details of the late payment penalties are at *Finance (No 3) Act 2010, Sch 11* and are summarised in Table 4 below:

TABLE 4: SUMMARY OF NEW LATE PAYMENT PENALTIES

	Quarterly VAT returns	Monthly VAT returns
First late payment	No penalty	No penalty
	Start of 1-year penalty period	Start of 1-year penalty period
Second late payment	2% of the late payment	1% of the late payment
(first in penalty period)	Penalty period extended	Penalty period extended
Third late payment	3% of the late payment	1% of the late payment
(second in penalty period)	Penalty period extended	Penalty period extended
Fourth late payment	4% of the late payment	1% of the late payment
(third in penalty period)	Penalty period extended	Penalty period extended
Fifth late payment	4% of the late payment	2% of the late payment
(fourth in penalty period)	Penalty period extended	Penalty period extended
Sixth late payment	4% of the late payment	2% of the late payment
(fifth in penalty period)	Penalty period extended	Penalty period extended
Seventh late payment	4% of the late payment	2% of the late payment
(sixth in late payment)	Penalty period extended	Penalty period extended
Eighth late payment	4% of the late payment	3% of the late payment
(seventh in penalty period)	Penalty period extended	Penalty period extended
Ninth late payment	4% of the late payment	3% of the late payment
(eighth in penalty period)	Penalty period extended	Penalty period extended
Tenth late payment	4% of the late payment	3% of the late payment
(ninth in penalty period)	Penalty period extended	Penalty period extended
Subsequent late payments	4% of the late payment	4% of the late payment
(in penalty period)	Penalty period extended	Penalty period extended

Notes:

(1)   Each late payment extends the penalty period to the anniversary of the most recent default.

(2)   The penalty percentage applies to the amount of VAT paid late – paying at least some VAT on time should reduce the amount of the late payment penalty.

Other VAT penalties

[17.23] The penalty regime for failure to notify HMRC on time of the requirement to be registered for VAT was considered in detail in Chapter 1. Earlier in this chapter the penalty regime for errors on VAT returns, the default surcharge regime and its replacement were considered. The following paragraphs provide a brief overview of other VAT penalties which advisers may come across from time to time.

Missing trader inter-community fraud (MTIC VAT fraud)

[17.24] Chapter 19 describes how MTIC VAT fraud works and the importance for traders of knowing their suppliers and customers. This section focuses on penalties that can be imposed on traders who get involved in MTIC VAT fraud.

As a general point any criminal fraud in relation to VAT can potentially result in a prison sentence of up to seven years and an unlimited fine. Criminal fraud in relation to VAT is where a person deliberately makes arrangements to evade VAT or to enable another person to evade VAT.

The level of penalty for a criminal prosecution in relation to VAT fraud depends on whether the conviction is a summary conviction in a Magistrate's Court or a conviction on indictment (a conviction before a jury) in a Crown Court. A conviction in a Magistrate's Court can result in a prison sentence of up to six months and a fine of up to £5,000, or three times the VAT evaded, whichever is greater. A conviction in a Crown Court can result in a prison sentence of up to seven years and an unlimited fine. For a criminal prosecution to succeed there must be proof 'beyond reasonable doubt'.

Civil fraud is the civil equivalent of criminal fraud but it is easier for HMRC to prove – the standard of proof required is 'on the balance of probabilities'. The penalty for civil fraud is 100% of the VAT evaded, although this can be reduced in certain circumstances. The penalty is in addition to the VAT evaded, which must be paid in full.

A 'penalty' for traders involved in supplies of the types of goods and services commonly involved in MTIC VAT fraud (eg mobile telephones and computer chips) is that of joint and several liability for any VAT that goes unpaid anywhere in the supply chain. In essence, if a trader is involved in a chain of transactions involving certain specified supplies, and at the time the supply was made to the trader, the trader knew or had reasonable grounds to suspect that some or all of the VAT payable in respect of that supply, or any previous or subsequent transaction in the chain, would go unpaid, HMRC can serve a notice on the trader which has the effect of making the trader and other traders jointly and severally liable for the unpaid VAT.

It is important to note that the joint and several liability provisions referred to above are intended to be applied in cases of MTIC VAT fraud as described in Chapter 19, rather than to ordinary manufacturers, retailers and businesses buying goods or services for their own use. The provisions are also not intended to apply in cases of genuine bad debts or genuine business failures.

A joint and several liability notice can be appealed, for example, where the business can demonstrate that it has done all that it reasonably can to check the integrity of the supply chain and to check that the 'favourable' price of the goods or services was unconnected with MTIC VAT fraud. For example, a supply of apparently 'cheap' mobile phones may be OK if the model had been replaced and was being sold at a reduced price because if was considered to be out of date.

Another 'penalty' that can be applied for MTIC VAT fraud is for HMRC to refuse an input tax claim where they can ascertain that the claim is being made by a person who knew, or should have known, that the input tax claim relates to goods connected with the fraudulent evasion of VAT. This penalty is often applied in situations where a trader purchases goods for a zero-rated dispatch or export from the UK and seeks to recover the input tax he has been charged when he knew, or should have known, that VAT has fraudulently been evaded on the goods earlier in the supply chain.

Unauthorised issue of VAT invoices

[17.25] Unauthorised issue of VAT invoices can include:

* A VAT invoice being issued when a person has applied for, but not yet received, a VAT registration number – see 1.5 for the correct procedure in these circumstances.
* A VAT invoice being issued for an exempt supply – adding VAT does not make an exempt supply taxable.
* A VAT invoice showing a false VAT number being issued by a person who is not registered for VAT and who has no intention of registering for VAT or accounting to HMRC for the VAT charged.

A civil penalty can be applied ranging from between 10% and 100% of the VAT incorrectly shown on the invoices. A penalty will not be due if there is a reasonable excuse.

Incorrect certificates

[17.26] An example is a person incorrectly issuing a certificate so that construction services can be zero-rated – see Chapter 26.

The standard penalty is 100% of the VAT undercharged as a result of the incorrect certificate but can be appealed against if there is a reasonable excuse.

EC Sales List

[17.27] When goods or services are sold to VAT-registered customers in other member states an EC Sales List must be submitted detailing the sales by customer – see 12.7.

Financial penalties can be imposed for late and/or inaccurate EC Sales Lists but can be appealed against if there is a reasonable excuse.

Civil penalties for import/export non-compliance

[17.28] A civil penalty regime applies to importers and exporters of goods to and from the EU. In addition to penalties for non-compliance, which can be appealed if there is a reasonable excuse, HMRC can seize goods.

Failure to notify the use of VAT avoidance schemes

[17.29] *Finance Act 2004* introduced various disclosure requirements in relation to the use of VAT avoidance schemes. HMRC Notice 700/8 is a useful source of information in relation to the disclosure requirements and the penalties that can be applied.

Breaches of walking possession agreements

[17.30] A walking possession agreement may be entered into when HMRC arrange for bailiffs to call on a person who has refused or neglected to pay VAT. In essence a walking possession agreement is an agreement that certain property, whilst remaining in the possession of the person in default, cannot be moved without the consent of HMRC. In effect, it prevents the person in possession of the goods from moving them to another location.

The standard penalty for breach of a walking possession agreement is 50% of the unpaid VAT. The penalty can be appealed if there is a reasonable excuse. The legislation is at *VATA 1994, s 68*.

Breaches of regulations and other breaches

[17.31] *VATA 1994, s 69, s 69A* and *s 69B* detail the penalties that can apply for various breaches of VAT regulations. *Section 69* deals with breaches of any kind, *s 69A* deals with breaches in relation to transactions in gold and *s 69B* deals with breaches in relation to record-keeping requirements imposed by directions.

Penalties relating to Mini One Stop Shop (MOSS) schemes

[17.32] *VATA 1994, Sch 3B* and *Sch 3BA* provide details of the penalties that can apply in relation to the non-Union VAT MOSS scheme and the Union VAT MOSS schemes respectively (see **14.15** and **14.16**). *VATA 1994, Sch 3B* was amended by *Finance Act 2014, Sch 22* and *VATA 1994, Sch 3BA* was introduced by *Finance Act 2014, Sch 22*.

Planning points to consider

[17.33] The following planning points should be given consideration.

- It is always worth considering appealing against a default surcharge penalty if a reasonable excuse can be made – some taxpayers have won tribunal cases against the odds by putting forward their case.

- Be aware of the *de minimis* limit of £400 for a default surcharge relevant to the 2% and 5% periods. A part payment of tax could be made to reduce the chargeable penalty to less than £400, in which case no penalty will be applied.

- Consider requesting a time to pay arrangement with the Business Payment Support Service (BPSS) if a VAT bill cannot be paid. An agreed payment arrangement before the tax is due will avoid a potential default surcharge.

- Remember that in the case of some penalties, HMRC has the power to mitigate the amount of the penalty to reflect co-operation levels and the amount of work done by a taxpayer to correct errors.

- The aim of the penalty system is to encourage taxpayers to take their VAT affairs seriously (and in relation to other taxes as well) and avoid making careless or deliberate errors. The best strategy at all times is to fully disclose errors as they are discovered and co-operate with HMRC to calculate the amount of any tax underpaid. This should reduce potential penalties in most cases.

Chapter 18

Relationships with HMRC

Key topics in this chapter:

- The emphasis of HMRC on a risk-based approach to VAT visits.
- The importance of a taxpayer meeting his VAT obligations – suggested checklists to improve VAT accounting issues.
- The opportunity to use HMRC's Business Payment Support Service if tax cannot be paid by the due date.
- How to keep up to date with changes in VAT.
- The problems of getting a written ruling (or telephone answer) from HMRC on a VAT issue – alternatives ways of finding a solution.
- Shared information between different sections of HMRC.
- Procedures for a VAT visit: before, during and after the visit.
- Complaints about HMRC or an officer in HMRC.
- How to appeal to a VAT tribunal or request an internal review by HMRC.
- Action plan (**18.25**) to ensure that a business gets the most out of its dealings with HMRC.

Introduction

[**18.1**] The relationship between HMRC and a business as far as VAT is concerned has changed over the years. It is vital that a business develops a relationship with HMRC to ensure that it gets its VAT right (or as right as it can) or, in some cases, to seek help and guidance from the authorities on a relevant issue. The other key point is that HMRC has placed great emphasis on the use of the word 'customer' rather than 'taxpayer' in its dealings with those who pay tax. It is therefore logical to conclude that if you are a business that gets its VAT affairs in order and pays the right amount of tax at the right time that you will be given 'special status' from HMRC, ie a relaxed existence should be evident because you are classed as one of their best customers.

Many small businesses with low tax risks (eg a baker selling zero-rated goods) will probably never receive a VAT visit, although they will still receive correspondence and other communications from HMRC. There is also scope for these businesses to develop a positive working relationship with HMRC – and these issues are considered in this chapter.

Submit VAT returns and pay tax on time

[18.2] This is a priority for any business.

From 1 April 2012 almost all businesses are required to submit VAT returns online and make VAT payments electronically.

The following are a few important tips in relation to submitting VAT returns and paying tax:

- A business normally submits VAT returns on a quarterly basis. However, if the business regularly receives VAT repayments (eg the majority of its income is zero-rated) then there is scope to submit monthly VAT returns. This will improve the cash flow of the business by producing more regular repayments, although obviously means that 12 rather than four VAT returns will need to be submitted each year.
- A return submitted on time with full payment of tax will avoid any default surcharge being incurred by the business. The default surcharge system is analysed in Chapter 17 and can result in penalties of up to 15% of any unpaid tax being levied against a business.
- If it is not possible to pay the full amount of tax that is due, and attempts to raise finance have failed, then the business should approach HMRC's Business Payment Support Service (BPSS) – see **18.3**.
- A business that struggles to submit quarterly returns and pay tax on time should consider the annual accounting scheme if it is eligible (ie where only one VAT return each year needs to be submitted). See Chapter 7.

Business Payment Support Service (BPSS)

[18.3] The BPSS was set up by HMRC in 2008 to assist businesses of all sizes that were encountering cash flow problems due to the economic downturn. It covers a wide range of taxes – including VAT, National Insurance and self-assessment tax.

The priority is to contact the BPSS before a VAT liability becomes due – if a time-to-pay agreement is then confirmed, this will avoid any default surcharge being incurred for the period in question.

Contact telephone number: 0300 200 3835

Opening hours: Monday–Friday 8am to 8pm; Saturday and Sunday 8 am to 4pm.

Ensuring VAT returns are accurate

[18.4]–[18.8] The penalty system that came into effect on 1 April 2009 for VAT considers a taxpayer's behaviour in relation to underpayments of tax. The essential question is, did the taxpayer take reasonable care in ensuring his VAT return was accurate?

It is accepted by HMRC (and a fact of human nature) that errors will be made – but it is a responsibility of the taxpayer to minimise the risk of errors taking place by applying sensible checks on the returns before they are submitted. The four checklists that follow give practical tips and advice to help a business not only get its VAT affairs right but also to identify some tax saving opportunities and measures that could help to simplify VAT accounting procedures:

VAT returns

- Are all VAT returns and payments up to date?
- If payments are not up to date, has a payment schedule been agreed with HMRC's Business Payment Support Service?
- Does the VAT creditor balance in the nominal ledger reconcile to the Box 5 payment figure on the relevant VAT return?
- Have any VAT errors been adjusted by the client on recent VAT returns? If they were underpayments, should a separate disclosure be made to HMRC to avoid a potential 'careless error' penalty in the future? (See Chapter 17).
- Does the total 'outputs' figure in Box 6 reconcile to the 'sales' figure on the profit and loss account for the same period – particularly important for cash traders?
- Has VAT on goods bought from EU suppliers outside the UK been correctly declared in Box 2, and claimed in Box 4 (assuming no input tax restriction). And has the reverse charge been accounted for on any services bought from abroad without VAT being charged (Box 1/Box 4 entries)?

Output tax issues

- Does the client have any other forms of income within the same legal entity that should be declared as far as VAT is concerned – it is the legal entity that is registered for VAT (eg sole trader, partnership), not the business?
- Has the VAT liability of all income sources been correctly established? If income is zero-rated, exempt or subject to the 5% rate of VAT, is the legal basis for this correct?
- Does the business supply any services to overseas customers? If so, have the place of supply rules been considered, particularly important after major changes were introduced on 1 January 2010?
- Have any fixed assets been sold – has output tax been accounted for where appropriate?

- Inter-company charges for, eg management services or goods supplied, will be subject to VAT unless a group registration is in place. Has output tax been charged on such transactions and input tax claimed by the recipient (subject to normal rules)?
- Does the business sell goods to overseas customers – if so, has proof of shipment been retained as evidence of export? This is very important in the event of a future VAT review by HMRC.
- Are the tax point rules being correctly applied – is output tax being accounted for on advance payments, is a sales invoice being raised within 14 days of a supply taking place?
- If the client has a connected business that is not VAT registered, ensure there is not a potential problem with the business splitting rules (ie disaggregation), ie proper recharging, separate bank accounts, invoicing, buying etc.

Input tax issues

- Has input tax been apportioned on private expenses or output tax accounted for on private use, eg fuel scale charges for road fuel?
- Confirm that no input tax has been claimed on business entertaining expenses (other than staff or overseas customers) or other non-deductible items such as motor cars available for private use or private expenses of the director (does he enjoy a game of golf?).
- Confirm that input tax has been adjusted on any invoices that are more than six months overdue for payment (but input tax can be claimed again at a later date when the invoices are eventually paid).
- Have C79 certificates been acquired and retained to support any input tax claimed on imports?
- Is the business partly exempt? If so, are partial exemption calculations being carried out correctly, including an annual adjustment at the end of the tax year?
- Has input tax been properly claimed (or not claimed in the case of most cars) on fixed assets acquired during the year?

VAT planning checklist

- Is the client using the flat rate scheme (annual taxable sales less than £150,000) and is it worthwhile? If the scheme is not being used, would there be potential VAT and time savings by adopting it in the future?

- Is VAT being accounted for on a cash received basis through the cash accounting scheme (annual taxable sales must be less than £1.35m)? If not, would it be worthwhile, taking into account the fact that input tax cannot then be claimed until a supplier has been paid?
- If the client is not VAT registered, are there potential savings with voluntary registration? This could be worthwhile if a client's income is either mainly zero-rated or he works for VAT registered customers able to reclaim input tax.
- Is there scope for some income to be zero-rated or exempt rather than standard rated? This would be very useful for a business trading with the general public.
- Has bad debt relief been claimed on any sales invoice more than six months overdue for payment and which has been written off in the accounts (assuming business is not using the cash accounting scheme where relief is automatic).
- Is there scope for a business supplying services on an ongoing basis, eg accountants/builders to issue 'applications for payment' rather than tax invoices to delay the tax point until payment has been received from a customer.
- If a business is partly exempt, is there scope to use a special method to produce a fairer recovery of input tax than the standard method based on income?
- For smaller businesses that are partly exempt, have you checked if they are *de minimis* for a period or year and therefore able to reclaim all of their input tax on exempt supplies? (See **24.10–24.16**)
- If the business has suffered reduced sales is it appropriate to deregister if expected taxable sales in the next 12 months are less than the deregistration threshold? But don't forget about output tax issues concerning assets owned at the time of deregistration.

Keeping a VAT account

[18.9] The record-keeping requirements of HMRC tend to be quite limited as far as VAT is concerned, as long as they are sufficient to enable accurate calculations to be made.

(HMRC Notice 700/21, section 2).

One legal requirement is for the taxpayer to keep a VAT account, which shows how the various figures on the VAT return have been compiled. It is sensible to keep a VAT file, which would not only show details extracted from the VAT account but also details of any correspondence received from HMRC or professional advisers on VAT rulings etc.

(HMRC Notice 700/21, section 3).

A typical VAT account is shown in Example 1.

Example 1

John is completing his VAT return for the quarter ended 30 June. He is calculating his output figure for the period and recording this in his VAT account.

Solution – an example of how the output tax section of John's VAT account would look is shown as follows.

Output tax

Sales day book totals		
April	£1,500	
May	£1,200	
June	£1,100	Total
		£3,800

Error on previous VAT return – VAT on sales invoice 345 omitted	£80

Total output tax due = £3,880

(HMRC Notice 700/21, para 3.3 gives a full example of a VAT account).

Other record-keeping requirements

[18.10] As explained above, HMRC's main requirement is that the records maintained by a business must enable accurate VAT returns to be completed. In reality, most computer accounting packages automatically ensure this objective is achieved, being able to produce a series of VAT reports that show a clear audit trail.

However, there are other aspects of VAT accounting that require separate records to be kept to ensure figures are accurate and can be supported with appropriate evidence:

- Paperwork in relation to the export of goods – proof that the goods have left the EU;
- Paperwork in relation to sales of goods to VAT registered businesses in other EU countries – proof of a customer's VAT number and proof the goods have left the UK;
- Imports of goods – ensure C79 documents are properly retained;
- Bad debt relief claims – see **31.19** to confirm conditions for claiming bad debt relief are met;

- International services – a proper record of all work carried out for overseas customers needs to be kept, eg in some cases, the place of supply rules require that supplies are received by the customer for the purpose of his business so proof of this business status (usually a VAT registration number) needs to be kept.

Note – a business must retain all records for six years – however, there could be an opportunity to request a reduced retention period. To quote from HMRC Notice 700/21, para 2.4:

'If the six-year rule causes you serious storage problems or undue expense, or you need advice on records for other types of tax, then you should consult our advice service. We may be able to allow you to keep some records for a shorter period.'

An exception to the general rule regarding retention of records relates to businesses using the VAT MOSS scheme (see **14.15**). VAT MOSS records must be kept for a period of ten years from 31 December of the year during which the transactions to which the records relate were carried out.

Keeping up to date with VAT changes

[**18.11**] VAT can be a fast moving tax and for practitioners with a client base in a range of different businesses, it can be a challenge keeping up to date with the many changes that take place.

As a starting point, a very useful tip is to regularly check the 'VAT Latest documents' section on the GOV.UK website (www.gov.uk/business-tax/vat/latest). This section highlights new information that has been published by HMRC.

HMRC only tends to announce either a change in the way it interprets legislation (eg following a court case verdict) or new legislation that is being introduced or has been introduced. For obvious reasons, it does not tend to publicise VAT planning measures or potential opportunities to reclaim tax with a wider interpretation of a court case verdict.

There are a number of ways that a practitioner can keep up-to-date on the thinking of the profession on VAT matters – reading commentary and articles in leading tax publications, attending VAT Update courses, branch meetings, online updates etc.

As a separate tip, where information is used from the GOV.UK website to determine the VAT treatment of a transaction, it is important to be aware that some of the information could be out-of-date or even incorrect. In cases where errors are alerted to it, HMRC will remove the information from the website or amend the details – so it is important to print out any information you use, keep it in the VAT file discussed at **18.9** and highlight the section that has been adopted.

Written advice from HMRC

[18.12] This has proved a controversial subject. The basic approach of HMRC is to encourage taxpayers to reach a decision about a VAT issue by making use of published HMRC Notices and guidance on the GOV.UK website. When HMRC are asked for advice on a VAT issue, often the reply will refer to the relevant paragraph or section of a published Notice. This can be particularly frustrating if the adviser is aware of the Notice but does not understand what it means. If the published guidance is inadequate HMRC can be asked to provide a non-statutory clearance in relation to a particular transaction.

The importance of providing all of the facts

[18.13] When HMRC are asked to provide a non-statutory clearance it is important that they are supplied with all of the facts. Let me highlight a case that illustrates the importance of giving full facts in writing concerning a transaction.

In the case of *R (on the application of the Medical Protection Society Ltd) v Revenue and Customs Comrs* [2009] EWHC 2780 (Admin), [2010] STC 555, the taxpayer acquired a ruling from HMRC about dealing with the reverse charge on its VAT returns, but a subsequent VAT visit challenged the accounting being carried out by the company and raised an assessment of tax.

Without going into detail, the tribunal did not give the taxpayer protection on the basis of 'misdirection' by HMRC because the directors had not disclosed the full facts of the transaction in their initial written enquiry.

Telephoning HMRC

[18.14] It can also be a frustrating experience when attempting to speak to HMRC by telephone on its VAT Helpline (0300 200 3700). A query about any technical matter of detail will again either refer the enquirer to public notices or published guidance, or ask for the issues to be put in writing.

In reality, it would be very dangerous for a taxpayer to rely on a verbal conversation in relation to any important VAT matter, especially as the meaning of words can become distorted by regional accents or badly used phrases. A written ruling or professional advice is always the best option.

One suggestion may be to try the search facility on the HMRC section of the GOV.UK website (www.gov.uk/government/organisations/hm-revenue-customs). However, as explained in **18.11**, be mindful to always print off this information (and date it and retain it) just in case there is any problem with the accuracy of the guidance.

The helpline service is very effective for:

- Giving contact addresses and telephone numbers of different offices and sections of HMRC, eg where do I send a VAT 1 application to register for VAT?

- Posting public notices and giving details about where to find information on the website.
- Providing details of VAT forms that need to be completed in certain circumstances.

Telephone horror stories

[**18.15**] The case of *Acrylux Ltd v Revenue and Customs Comrs* (TC00173) [2009] UKFTT 223 (TC), [2009] SFTD 763, [2010] SWTI 1453 considered whether the renting out of a country home for weekend functions and weddings related to an exempt supply of rental income, or a standard rated supply on the basis that the country home was a 'similar establishment' to a hotel.

The tribunal decided that the income was standard rated but the key point in the case appears to be that the taxpayer received incorrect or misleading advice from the HMRC telephone helpline service. Did the taxpayer ask the wrong question, for example, the question: 'I am renting out a house – should I charge VAT?' would probably lead to a 'no' answer from the HMRC staff, and there is no reason why further questions should be asked. However, the interesting issue is that the tribunal reversed a serious misdeclaration penalty charge made by HMRC in this case so the quality of the advice must definitely have been questionable. The tribunal accepted that the taxpayer had acted responsibly at all times in trying to get his VAT right – but the penalty 'added salt to the wounds' and was inappropriate.

The case of *Abdul Noor* (TC01209) [2011] UKFTT 349 (TC); revsd [2013] UKUT 071 (TCC) considered whether the First Tier Tribunal had jurisdiction to consider legitimate expectation in relation to a claim to recover pre-registration input tax on costs incurred on services more than six months prior to the date of VAT registration.

Mr Noor incurred legal costs in 2007 and 2008 in relation to problems he had with a builder he had engaged to construct a small commercial property. Wanting to recover VAT on the costs, he went to an HMRC office and was directed to a telephone in the office so that he could contact HMRC's National Advice Service (NAS).

The advice the NAS provided to Mr Noor over the telephone appears to have been based on the pre-registration input tax rules relating to goods rather than services. The rules at the time were that, subject to certain other conditions being met, pre-registration input tax can be recovered on goods purchased in the three years (currently four years) prior to the date of VAT registration. The relevant time for services was, and continues to be, six months prior to the date of VAT registration. Mr Noor chose a VAT registration date based on the advice the HMRC NAS had provided.

When Mr Noor submitted his first VAT return HMRC refused the claim for VAT on the legal costs on the basis that they were services incurred more than six months prior to the date he was registered for VAT. Mr Noor appealed to the First Tier Tribunal who allowed his appeal on the basis that the telephone advice he had received from the HMRC NAS meant that he had a legitimate expectation of recovering the input tax on the legal costs.

The concept of legitimate expectation is referred to in the HMRC Manual ADML 1200, an extract from which is quoted below:

> 'In some cases, HMRC might act in such a way that it leads a person to believe he is acting correctly when in law he is not. In this situation, the person might be entitled to rely on the advice he received from HMRC. The person has a "legitimate expectation" that HMRC will treat him in a certain way and is protected by the courts on the basis that the principles of fairness, proportionality, predictability and certainty should not be disregarded.'

HMRC appealed to the Upper Tribunal against the decision of the First Tier Tribunal. The Upper Tribunal considered whether the First Tier Tribunal had jurisdiction to consider legitimate expectation in relation to the recovery of pre-registration input tax on supplies of services and decided that it did not.

The Upper Tribunal decision means that Mr Noor was not entitled to his claim for input tax on the cost of services incurred more than six months prior to his date of VAT registration.

The Upper Tribunal decision confirms that even when HMRC has provided the wrong advice it will not always be bound by that advice.

While the EU principle of legal certainty – in a VAT sense the principle of legitimate expectation – is not to be confused with the UK equitable principle of estoppel, it is a similar concept. The tribunal has no jurisdiction to consider matters of legitimate expectation and so the Upper Tribunal overturned the First Tier's decision. Short of taking the case to the Ombudsman (on maladministration grounds) or an MP, or seeking judicial review, a taxpayer has little recourse. One would only hope that in cases where it is clear that HMRC has given wrong or misleading advice that it does the 'right thing'! Notice 700, para 2.5 states:

> 'HMRC aims to provide information and advice that will give certainty to customers concerning the tax consequences of their transactions, their obligations, liabilities and entitlements. The general principle, therefore, is that you should be able to rely on any information or advice HMRC provides, because it is correct.
>
> There may be a small number of cases where HMRC provides information or advice that is incorrect in law. Where this happens, HMRC will be bound by such advice provided that it is clear, unequivocal and explicit, and that you can demonstrate that—
>
> - you reasonably relied on the advice
> - where appropriate, you made a full disclosure of all the relevant facts
> - the application of the law would result in your financial detriment.
>
> Where HMRC has given incorrect information or advice, our primary duty is to collect the correct amount of tax as required by the law, and therefore there will be some circumstances where HMRC will not be bound by the advice given.
>
> Where HMRC provides you with erroneous advice that is binding on us, and subsequently notify you that it is incorrect, you will only be required to start accounting for tax on the correct basis from the date of that notification.'

VAT inspections

Background

[18.16] As explained at the beginning of this chapter, routine VAT visits for many businesses are now very unusual. The focus of HMRC is to adopt a risk-based approach to deciding which businesses should be targeted. The following businesses tend to be considered higher risk and could receive more regular visits:

- cash traders – where there is a risk that sales (and therefore output tax) could be understated;
- traders dealing in 'relevant goods and services' – eg mobile phones and computer chips that have been the subject of widespread VAT fraud (see Chapter 19);
- land and property traders – either businesses dealing in property or providing building services that have complex liability issues;
- partly exempt businesses – this is always one of the most complicated areas of VAT and subject to detailed calculations that could produce significant VAT errors;
- businesses with a poor compliance record – ie a history of assessments on previous VAT visits, non-payment of tax/late submission of returns.

An important point to recognise is that a VAT visit concluded without any errors being found does not mean a business has submitted totally correct VAT returns in the past or that the periods checked by the officer cannot be reviewed again in the future.

Before the visit

[18.17] Before a visit, HMRC should confirm the following details:

- the person the VAT officer wants to see;
- a mutually convenient appointment date and time;
- the name and contact number of the officer carrying out the visit;
- which records the officer will need to see, and for which tax periods; and
- how long the visit is likely to take.

HMRC should confirm all the above information in writing unless the time before the visit is too short to allow it. HMRC should generally provide at least seven days' notice of any visit unless an earlier visit is required.

In some cases, VAT officers will visit without making an appointment. If they do they should explain why.

During a visit

[18.18] For the purpose of the visit itself, HMRC officers should:

- identify themselves by name on arrival and, if requested, produce an identity card;

- explain the main purpose of the visit;
- discuss various aspects of the business at the outset so as to keep claims on staff time to a minimum (although new points may arise as they review the records);
- examine the records of the business and, where appropriate, inspect the premises;
- deal with VAT affairs confidentially in a polite and considerate manner;
- advise of overpayments as well as underpayments; and
- where possible, try to resolve matters during the visit.

It is possible that the officers may also want to record details of suppliers and customers of the business, to check correct VAT figures are declared in their records as well.

End of the visit

[18.19] At the end of the visit, HMRC should:

- review the main work done;
- explain any areas of concern in relation to that work, discuss them and agree any future action that needs to be taken; and
- explain as fully as possible the size and reason for any adjustment to the VAT payable, and describe how the adjustment will be made.
- advise of any under or overpayments of tax that need to be assessed; the officer should also advise on the appeals procedure if the taxpayer disagrees with the assessment.

After the visit, HMRC will:

- where requested, or where it feels it necessary, put in writing a summary of the visit, any rulings, agreements or recommendations; and
- where matters are unresolved, give the business a reasonable time within which to provide further information or comment.

Complaints about officers

[18.20] If a taxpayer or adviser has a complaint against HMRC, and is unable to resolve it with the officer concerned, he has a number of options available to take the matter further:

- contact one of the Regional Complaints Units within the Department, giving full details of the complaint and the reasons why it could not be resolved at a local level. The local manager at the Unit will then make enquiries into the problem and aim to give a full reply within ten days of the original complaint. Where appropriate, the Unit will consider reimbursing reasonable costs incurred by the complainant, such as telephone or postage costs. However, the compensation is unlikely to include time spent on the complaint unless loss of earnings can be clearly shown. There is also scope to make a payment to the complainant to cover distress that may have been caused – this payment tends to range from £25 to £500;

- complain to the independent Adjudicator. The Adjudicator is uncon-nected with the Department and will consider many different types of complaint, including complaints about delays, improper behaviour and rudeness. The Adjudicator cannot examine cases that are applicable to a VAT tribunal nor intervene once a matter is before the criminal courts. The address of the Adjudicator is:

  The Adjudicator's Office
  PO Box 10280
  Nottingham
  NG2 9PF
  Tel: 0300 057 1111
- complain to a Member of Parliament.

Appeals system

[18.21] If an officer raises a VAT assessment that is challenged by the taxpayer or his adviser, then there has always been a very clear appeals process that can, in limited cases, end up with a case being considered by the European Court of Justice.

However, in most cases, appeals will be dealt with on a local basis, and the importance of local reviews was strengthened on 1 April 2009 with the introduction of the tribunal appeals system for all taxes.

- The tribunal appeals system consists of a two-tier tribunal system with routine appeals being heard by the First Tier Tax Tribunal and complex appeals being heard by the Upper Tribunal.
- Before reaching the tribunal stage, a taxpayer has the new legal right for the decision to be reviewed at a local office level by a trained review officer who has not previously been involved with that decision. In the majority of cases, the review officer will be outside the immediate line management chain of the decision maker.
- Local reviews must be completed within 45 days (unless another period is agreed between HMRC and the taxpayer).
- The main point is that HMRC prefers to resolve disputes on a local basis without going to a tribunal if this can be avoided. Although previous regimes have always had the facility for a local reconsidera-tion, the indications are that review officers will be better trained and more independent than their predecessors.

Early experiences with the internal review system

[18.22] The internal review system sounds a sensible procedure with a lot of potential advantages. However, the early indications as far as VAT is con-cerned are that most disputed decisions are unchanged on review, ie the internal review officer reaches the same conclusion as his colleague who gave the initial decision. Is this unexpected? After all, the internal review officer probably makes contact with his colleague to discuss the reasons behind the initial decision but how often does he contact the taxpayer to discuss the reasons behind the appeal and clarify any issues that are not clear from the taxpayer's appeal letter (or the letter sent by his adviser)?

As a general observation, an appeal against a penalty or default surcharge on the basis of a 'reasonable excuse' situation appears to have more chance of success at the internal review stage than a challenge against a technical point, eg whether a supply is exempt rather than standard rated.

HMRC's increased powers – April 2009

[18.23] The way that HMRC carries out compliance checks (VAT inspections) was changed on 1 April 2009. The new system is designed to make the tax system simpler and more consistent.

From this date, HMRC will have one set of powers covering all taxes:

- a set of powers to examine business records without a right of appeal;
- the ability to inspect business records, assets and premises;
- the ability to correct errors going back four years – in the case of VAT, this used to be a three-year limit. The 20-year limit for correcting fraudulent errors remains unchanged;
- a new statutory ban on inspecting purely private dwellings without consent;
- a statutory requirement for HMRC to give at least seven days' notice prior to making a visit, unless either an unannounced visit is necessary, or a shorter period is agreed;
- a statutory requirement on HMRC to act reasonably;
- a new requirement that unannounced visits must be approved beforehand by a specially trained HMRC officer.

There has been a lot of concern within the profession about the increased HMRC powers. However, going back to the observation I made at the beginning of this chapter, they should not be relevant to a compliant taxpayer that is fully meeting its VAT responsibilities.

Sharing of information

[18.24] In a multi-tax system, it is inevitable that different sections within HMRC will utilise information about taxpayers that are held by other parts of the department.

In the case of *Baljit Singh t/a BS Construction v Revenue and Customs Comrs* (TC00194) [2009] UKFTT 245 (TC), the taxpayer's date of VAT registration was backdated to 2003. The source of information for HMRC was that it had used data from the client's self-assessment tax returns to identify a level of sales considerably in excess of the VAT registration limits by a trader who was not registered for VAT!

Alternative dispute resolution process

[18.25] The Alternative Dispute Resolution (ADR) process is an alternative way of dealing with disputes with HMRC. A taxpayer can apply to HMRC for the ADR process before or after an HMRC officer has made a decision. It does not affect the taxpayer's right to appeal or right to ask for a decision to be reviewed by another HMRC officer not previously involved in the dispute.

The ADR process is led by a person who has not been involved with the dispute and who works with the taxpayer and the HMRC officer with a view to resolving the dispute, or at least getting agreement on the outstanding issues, which may need to be taken for a legal ruling. The process will typically involve meetings and/or telephone conversations and in some cases may involve agreeing with HMRC to jointly pay for a professional independent mediator.

Examples of situations where the ADR process may be helpful include the following.

- The taxpayer and HMRC do not agree about the facts.
- Communication between the taxpayer and HMRC has broken down.
- It is not clear why HMRC have not agreed evidence.
- It is not clear what evidence or information HMRC are using.
- It is clear what evidence or information HMRC are using but it is not clear why HMRC are using that evidence or information.
- It is not clear why HMRC have made certain assumptions or come to certain conclusions.

There are situations when HMRC will not agree to the ADR process, for example, disputes about default surcharges. In some situations it may not be clear whether HMRC will agree to the ADR process but if the taxpayer or adviser feel it is appropriate they can ask HMRC to at least consider an application for the ADR process.

Planning points to consider

[18.26] The following action plan should help a business or adviser to get the most out of its relationship with HMRC and avoid any major problems:

- Always aim to pay tax and submit VAT returns on time.
- Ensure that a senior employee in a client's business spends time carrying out a thorough review of a VAT return before it is submitted to HMRC (see **18.4–18.8** for suggested checks). This will hopefully avoid a penalty being incurred for failing to take reasonable care.
- In the event that VAT cannot be paid, contact HMRC's Business Payment Support Service before a debt becomes due to negotiate a time to pay agreement.
- Use the 'VAT Latest documents' section on the GOV.UK website (www.gov.uk/business-tax/vat/latest) to keep up to date on VAT developments – supported by information from other publications within the tax profession.

- Always try to solve a VAT problem by using HMRC's public notices or other written guidance. The HMRC search engine is also a useful tool to direct a user to the appropriate section. The occasions when HMRC will give a written ruling on a subject are now very limited.

- The HMRC telephone helpline service is very useful for basic enquiries – but not for detailed technical questions that should be resolved by other methods. Do not base an important VAT decision (eg concerning the VAT liability of sales) on a telephone call.

- VAT visits tend to be determined by risk factors. Be aware that many businesses will not receive a VAT visit for many years so it is important that procedures and systems are in place to ensure a visit does not produce any major problems. Errors can now be adjusted going back four rather than three years.

- VAT assessments raised by HMRC can be reviewed by an independent officer within the department if they are disputed by a taxpayer. The officer is trained to make a thorough review of the facts, although early indications suggest that a large number of review decisions are being upheld in favour of HMRC, with the main successful review outcomes for the taxpayer being linked to penalty-related issues, eg the 'reasonable excuse' provisions.

- The alternative dispute resolution process may help resolve certain disputes with HMRC, or at least help to obtain agreement on the outstanding issues.

Chapter 19

Knowing your Suppliers and Customers

Key topics in this chapter:

- How Missing Trader Intra-Community (MTIC) fraud works.
- HMRC efforts to combat MTIC fraud – and their current approach to the problem.
- The need for a business to take 'reasonable steps to ensure the integrity of its supply chain' – practical examples of how this can be achieved.
- The reverse charge rules for supplies of mobile phones, computer chips, emissions allowances and wholesale supplies of gas and electricity.
- Checks to apply when taking on a new overseas customer.
- Avoiding problems with HMRC if export documents provided by an overseas customer prove to be false.

Introduction

[19.1] The impact of the global economy means that many more businesses are involved in international transactions which, in turn, means that VAT decisions and issues have international factors to consider. For example, a UK business providing consultancy services to a Swedish business customer knows it will not charge UK VAT if it acquires evidence that the customer is 'in business' – this evidence usually means obtaining details of the customer's VAT number in his own country. But how do we know if it is a genuine VAT number? What happens if it is subsequently found to be false?

In terms of buying goods, the impact of Missing Trader Intra-Community VAT fraud, commonly known as MTIC VAT fraud, has been enormous in terms of a loss of tax to the treasury.

The extent of the fraud has caused great concern at all levels of government. Measures have been taken to strengthen the powers of HMRC to deal with the fraudsters, the aim being to prevent fraud in the first place.

The issue of MTIC fraud is particularly relevant for advisers who have clients dealing in high-risk goods such as computer chips, telephone chargers, memory cards and mobile telephones. However, it is becoming clear that the fraudsters are extending the scope of their trade, moving to other high value, small volume goods such as razor blades and fizzy drinks.

The key point is that if a business buys goods from a supplier and either knows, or had reason to suspect that they were part of an illegal supply chain (and that output tax might not be paid to HMRC in the normal manner further up or down the chain), then HMRC have the power to disallow input tax claimed by the buyer, even if he met the usual rules for claiming input tax, ie holding a proper tax invoice with a VAT registration number, relevant to goods sold to him as a taxable supply. The phrase to explain this legislation is 'joint and several liability'.

How missing trader and carousel fraud works

[19.2] It is important that advisers know the basis of MTIC fraud (also referred to as 'carousel fraud' because the same goods go round in a trading circle, often many times) in order to advise clients how to avoid becoming innocently involved in an illegal trading chain.

MTIC VAT fraud basically works by the creation of a supply chain – where at some stage, a key player in the chain disappears. The chain normally involves goods being purchased from a supplier in another EU country – who does not charge VAT to his UK customer because he is given the customer's UK VAT number. See Example 1.

Example 1

ABC Ltd is VAT registered in the UK and buys 100,000 mobile phones from DEF, based in Holland for £400,000. DEF does not charge VAT on the supply of goods because it receives and quotes the VAT number of the UK customer (ABC Ltd) on its invoice.

ABC Ltd is a fraudulent company and sells 10,000 mobile phones to ten different companies for £36,000 plus VAT (ie 10% below bulk cost). The ten companies all pay ABC Ltd £43,200 each – and reclaim input tax of £7,200 on the tax invoices issued by ABC Ltd (based on VAT rate of 20%). However, ABC Ltd disappears as a 'missing' trader without ever paying HMRC the output tax due of £72,000. The company has effectively made a profit of £32,000 (£432,000 – £400,000) – wholly at the expense of HMRC.

Solution – the input tax claimed by the ten UK companies on invoices raised by ABC Ltd will be examined very closely by HMRC under the legislation (*VATA 1994*, s 77A). If HMRC have strong reason to suspect that the companies knew or should have known that ABC Ltd was a fraudulent company and that the transactions were connected with VAT fraud, then the input tax could be disallowed.

The above example illustrates how illegal companies can effectively sell goods at a loss and still make a reasonable profit – at the expense of HMRC. And the customers of ABC Ltd are delighted – because they have bought goods very cheaply (below cost) – which they can sell at a higher price.

The development of the above scheme creates an even bigger problem for HMRC, when the same goods go round in a circular trading cycle. This means that the fraudsters have the opportunity to steal money from the Exchequer on many occasions. In one fraud case, HMRC apparently proved that the same goods went round in a circle of business deals no less than 35 times.

HMRC approach to the problem

[19.3] The basic argument put forward by HMRC is that a person in business can only trade successfully if he is aware of the market price of goods he buys and sells. So if an unknown supplier suddenly offers him an excellent deal, he should seriously challenge the reasons for the low price on offer. To quote the phrase used by HMRC, it is expected that the buyer will 'take reasonable steps to verify the integrity of the supply chain'. In simple terms, if something sounds too good to be true, it probably is!

HMRC need to look at each transaction in a supply chain on an individual basis and decide whether the buyer of the goods had reason to doubt the legitimacy of the trader from whom he was buying. If so, then the input tax claimed by the buyer can be disallowed. The latter measure then compensates HMRC for the undeclared output tax lost on the sale of the goods.

(HMRC Notice 726, section 2).

Taking 'reasonable steps' to ensure the 'integrity of the supply chain'

[19.4] Think of situations where you could purchase goods at genuinely low prices. For example, if an item has been superseded by more up-to-date technology, then it is likely to be sold cheaply because its place in the market has been eroded. Items that are damaged or have suddenly become unfashionable may also be sold cheaply.

In the cases above, the supplier will have a good reason for charging low prices – but equally, the onward supply by his customer will also be at a lower price to reflect the problems with the goods. Contrast this with MTIC frauds, where the goods are bought cheaply and sold at top price.

Points to consider when reviewing the integrity of a supply chain are noted at section 6 of VAT Notice 726, and the main ones are as follows:

- review the supplier's history in the trade – the fraudulent companies often surface and disappear very quickly;
- ensure normal commercial practices have been adopted in negotiating prices;
- confirm the goods actually exist and the price being charged is sensible within the market place;
- verify VAT registration details with HMRC (call the National Helpline);

- seek a trade reference;
- carry out credit checks and company searches;
- ensure supplementary paperwork is completed – eg purchase orders, delivery notes, inspection reports;
- be suspicious of any payments to third parties – why is this the case?

The above measures are not an exhaustive list. HMRC takes the view that if it produced a standard checklist for all businesses to follow, then this would encourage the fraudsters to beat the system. See Examples 2 and 3.

Example 2

The Managing Director of Mobiles Phones Ltd has been approached by the director of a newly formed company, Very Dodgy Ltd, who offers to sell him a mobile phone component that he normally pays £1.50 for on the open market. The price being proposed is £1.35 per component. The credit search on Very Dodgy Ltd shows it is a new company, and the directors are all based overseas. The company does not have any UK trading premises, and is unable to give any trade references or UK bank account details. The company has asked for payment for the goods to be made direct to an overseas bank account.

Solution – there are strong indications that this company is not a bona fide organisation – it would be sensible to avoid trading with it to avoid potential problems with HMRC in the future.

Example 3

The Managing Director of Mobile Phones Ltd has been approached by an alternative supplier, Not Dodgy Ltd, and the director offers to sell him a mobile phone component that he normally pays £1.50 for on the open market. The price being proposed by Not Dodgy Ltd is £1.35 per component. A credit search carried out on Not Dodgy Ltd confirms it has been trading for 23 years, and has trading premises in Southampton. A reputable firm of accountants has prepared the audited accounts, and the company has net assets exceeding £1m.

The director of Not Dodgy Ltd explains why he can sell the components so cheaply – it is because the company is manufacturing the components at a new specialised factory in Southampton – pictures and manufacturing specs are seen to confirm this information. A telephone call to HMRC confirms the validity of the VAT registration number.

Solution – Mobile Phones Ltd has taken 'reasonable steps' to 'establish the legitimacy of the supplier' (Notice 726, para 4.5). It would be unlikely to be involved in a loss of input tax through an MTIC VAT fraud.

Safety of innocent businesses from 'joint and several liability' legislation

[**19.5**] In reality, any business that trades in either computer or mobile phone goods must now have very clear procedures in place to check out the validity of all suppliers. Although this sounds common sense, there are always temptations to ignore procedures when a good deal appears to be on the table.

HMRC has indicated that:

- it will only issue a notice of liability if the goods in question were sold as an onward sale – there would be no problem if, for example, the equipment was adopted for the company's own use. This is because it is recognised that a company buying assets will not have the same knowledge of pricing issues as a company involved in the distribution of the goods;
  (HMRC Notice 726, para 4.9).
- each case is independently reviewed and authorised by a central team within HMRC before further action is taken;
- HMRC recognises that the onus of proof is on itself to prove a trader had grounds to suspect there could be a problem. The actual wording in para 4.1 of Notice 726 refers to a situation where 'there is sufficient evidence on a balance of probabilities to show the requisite knowledge';
- with regard to price, HMRC will only issue a notice if it is sure that the price paid by the company was less than the lowest price that might reasonably be expected to be payable on the open market. This would also be less than the price previously paid on the supply of the same goods.

It is important that advisers do not find themselves acting for fraudulent companies that are going to cause problems – the following questions should therefore be considered before a letter of engagement is agreed.

- Is the business being managed by young men with no indication of past business experience or a past track record in the goods with which they are trading? Do these men have any detailed knowledge about the range of goods they are selling?
- Has the company any previous history in terms of length of trading, past accounts, bank references? It is very unusual for a new business to suddenly start trading in goods worth millions of pounds – how is such trade being financed?
- Does the business have buying links with Netherlands, Spain and France and selling links with Dubai or Hong Kong? These countries are very often the start and finish points of the chains.
- The level of business (turnover) carried out by fraudulent companies is very high. So an important question is to consider cash flow and credit arrangements, ie how is a business funding the purchase of goods in advance of receiving payment from a customer.

The list is not exhaustive and there is no substitute for having a general feel that the issues surrounding the arrangement do not look genuine.

Approach of courts

[19.6] The starting point for a tribunal is to consider whether a taxpayer:

'knew or had reasonable grounds to suspect that some or all of the VAT payable in respect of that supply, or on any previous or subsequent supply of those goods, would go unpaid' (*VATA 1994, s 77A(2)*).

It is clear that many companies are unaware that the goods they are buying might be relevant to fraudulent activities. However, this is not the end of the story. As the extract above explains, the consideration is to then consider whether the taxpayer ought to have known the goods were fraudulent, ie had 'grounds to suspect' etc.

The following is a summary of important cases along with comments on the key issues.

- *Red 12 Trading Ltd* (16 December 2008, unreported) (LON/07/1345 20900) – the company exported mobile phones and claimed to have no knowledge that there was any connection with fraud. However, the tribunal referred in its report to 'the sheer improbability of these trades being genuine'. Red 12 should have known that its claim for input tax could not succeed – HMRC was correct in its action.

  Comment – HMRC was able to illustrate that the phones being traded in this case had no commercial basis or logic. The phones could not be used in the UK, were being bought in from countries where they were quite expensive to buy, and ended up in countries where they were already relatively cheap in the domestic market.

- *Blue Sphere Global Ltd* (17 December 2008, unreported) (LON/07/0934 20901) – BSG was a relatively small company with no previous trading history in mobile phones that suddenly became involved with large scale deals. For each sale, there was a customer already identified for BSG by the supplier of the phones – so if the deals were genuine, why would the supplier sacrifice some of his margin by involving another company that had little value to offer? The tribunal's conclusion was that 'BSG ought to have known that, by its purchases, it was participating in transactions connected with the fraudulent evasion of VAT'.

  Comment – as explained above, the fraudsters seem to have taken advantage of BSG's vulnerability. Why did BSG not consider the reasons it was being presented with easy deals and profit, ie because of the link with tax fraud?

- *Megtian Ltd (in admin)* (11 December 2008, unreported) (LON/07/0980 20894) – the owner of Megtian made a big mistake in his evidence by referring to 'everyone' in the supply chain, which challenged his claim that he dealt with no-one but his supplier and customer. The tribunal again concluded that Megtian knew that its transactions were connected with fraud.

  Comment – HMRC was fortunate to win this case as one of its main arguments was that an alleged 95% of trading in mobile phones was fraudulent at the time and as such, Megtian should have been aware of this and avoided getting involved with the deal. The tribunal rejected this argument. However, it was the behaviour of the taxpayer and the knowledge he should have possessed that was relevant to the case.

Reverse charge accounting – sales of certain goods

[19.7] HMRC introduced reverse charge rules with effect from 1 June 2007 in relation to the sale of mobile telephones and computer chips between VAT registered traders in the UK. The rules were subsequently extended to include emissions allowances from 1 November 2010 and wholesale supplies of gas and electricity from 1 July 2014. The reverse charge rules basically transfer the output tax liability in the sale of high-risk items from the supplier to the customer.

The reverse charge only applies to the sale of mobile telephones and computer chips if the invoice value of the items in question exceeds £5,000 (excluding VAT). See Example 4 for an illustration of this point.

Note – full details about the reverse charge procedures in relation to the sale of mobile phones and computer chips are given in HMRC Notice 735.

With effect from 1 February 2016, reverse charge accounting was extended to supplies of wholesale telecommunications services between counterparties established in the UK. The reverse charge will cover telecommunications services which enable:

- speech communication instantly or with only a negligible delay between the transmission and the receipt of signal;
- the transmission of writing, images and sounds or information of any nature when provided in connection with services described above.

In this context, the term 'wholesale supplies' is defined as normal business to business transactions that are purchased for the purpose of resale (ie they are not services that are 'consumed' by the purchaser but are supplied onwards).

(Revenue & Customs Brief 1/16: VAT– domestic reverse charge for businesses wholesaling telecommunications services).

Example 4

ABC Ltd is VAT registered in the UK and buys 100,000 mobile phones from DEF, based in Holland for £400,000. DEF does not charge VAT on the supply of goods because it quotes the VAT number of the UK customer (ABC Ltd) on its invoice.

ABC Ltd then sells the goods to GHI Ltd in the UK but does not charge any output tax on the supply. It quotes the VAT registration number of GHI Ltd on its sales invoice. However, GHI Ltd must account for the output tax of ABC Ltd by making an entry in Box 1 of its own VAT return (based on the price paid for the goods × standard rate of VAT), claiming the same amount back as input tax in Box 4 of the same return. It has applied the reverse charge mechanism by making these entries.

Solution – if ABC Ltd disappears before it has submitted and paid its VAT return, then a large VAT debt to HMRC has hopefully been avoided. This is because the output tax liability has been transferred to GHI Ltd.

Reverse Charge Sales List (RCSL)

[19.8] Any business making sales of mobile telephones, computer chips, emissions allowances and supplies of gas and electricity that are subject to the reverse charge rules must complete another return each VAT quarter, namely the Reverse Charge Sales List (RCSL). Businesses supplying wholesale telecommunications do not need to complete this return (see Revenue & Customs Brief 1/16, para 5.2).

The form is not complicated, and can be accessed through the GOV.UK website. The form is submitted for the same period as the taxpayer's VAT return and basically requires a declaration of sales made to VAT registered businesses which are covered by the reverse charge scheme. The declaration gives a monthly breakdown of sales to each VAT registered trader, obviously quoting their VAT registration number.

(HMRC Notice 735, section 11).

£5,000 de minimis limit for mobile telephones and computer chips

[19.9] As noted at **19.7** the reverse charge only applies to the sale of mobile telephones and computer chips if the invoice value of the items in question exceeds £5,000 (excluding VAT). The reverse charge applies to supplies of emissions allowances and wholesale supplies of gas and electricity and from 1 February 2016, the wholesale supply of telecommunications services regardless of the value.

The £5,000 *de minimis* figure for mobile telephones and computer chips is calculated on an invoice basis, ie the reverse charge applies if the total VAT-exclusive value of all the specified reverse charge items shown on an invoice is £5,000 or more. In that event, the reverse charge applies to the total value of the specified reverse charge items on that invoice.

If supplies of any other goods or services are shown on the same invoice as the reverse charge items, the reverse charge does not apply to the other supplies.

If an itemised invoice relates to a single supply, for example a computer, which is not subject to the reverse charge, VAT should be charged as normal on the supply, even if certain of the itemised components are reverse charge goods.

Many businesses issue several separate invoices in relation to a single order, eg a separate invoice for each delivery. Where the order value is larger than the invoice value, it will be acceptable to apply the reverse charge to all invoices relating to the order so long as the order value exceeds the £5,000 threshold, if both parties agree.

Where VAT is due on a value reduced by an unconditional discount then the discounted value is to be used to establish the value for the purpose of applying the *de minimis* rules. However, where there are contingent discounts or a delayed reduction in price, the full value shown on the invoice is to be used.

(HMRC Notice 735, section 6).

Are your overseas customers genuine?

[19.10] Keeping records for VAT purposes is not just about retaining copies of sales and purchase invoices. In the age of the global economy, there is a burden on taxpayers to keep a wide range of records and seek information from both customers and suppliers, often before a deal is completed.

Selling a service to an overseas customer

[19.11] Imagine the following situation: I am doing some VAT consultancy work for a French accountant based in Paris. I know that my fee will be outside the scope of UK VAT as long as I acquire and retain proof that my customer is 'in business', ie a 'business to business' (B2B) sale. The best evidence of business status is the customer's VAT number in France, which he duly gives me as 12365478901. How do I know it is a genuine number?

Each EU country has a different format for its VAT numbers – they don't all have nine numbers like we have in the UK. You can check the format of each country's VAT numbers by reviewing the list in HMRC Notice 725, para 16.19, which confirms that French VAT numbers contain 11 digits, and can include a letter rather than number in the first or second digit (or both).

A way of checking the actual validity of a specific VAT number is to use the Europa website. See Box 1.

Box 1 – validating a customer's VAT number

- http://ec.europa.eu/taxation_customs/vies (or do a 'google' search on 'VAT number check')
- enter member state of customer using drop down menu (this identifies prefix of country eg FR = France), and then VAT number provided by customer

---

How much protection is given to a taxpayer?

[19.12] HMRC is very aware that a fraudulent business could obtain a VAT number in order to receive VAT-free goods from an overseas supplier in another EU country (the sale of goods to a VAT-registered customer in another EU country is zero-rated) and then deregister at some future date, and continue to receive VAT-free goods for a period.

A one-off check of a customer's VAT registration number when you first do business with him is not the end of the road as far as verification is concerned. To illustrate this point, I have quoted below an extract from para 4.9 of HMRC's Notice 725.

'When making an enquiry on the Europa website you must identify yourself by entering your own VAT registration number and print out a record of the date and time that the enquiry was made and the result of the enquiry. If it later turns out that the customer's number was invalid, eg the tax authorities database was not up to date, you will be able to rely on the validation record as one element to demonstrate your good faith as a compliant business and, in the UK, to justify why you should not be held jointly and severally liable for any VAT fraud and revenue losses which occur.

You must also regularly check your EC customer's VAT registration number to make sure that the details are still valid and that the number has not been recently deregistered.

Alternatively you can contact the VAT Helpline on 0300 200 3700 to validate your customer's VAT registration number and verify that the name and address is correct.

Evidence relating to export of goods

[19.13] The export of goods outside the EU (or sale of goods to a VAT registered customer in another EU country when the goods leave the UK) is zero-rated; a condition of zero-rating being that the customer retains proof of shipment to prove to HMRC (if necessary) that the goods have left the UK.

Note – export proof must be retained for six years (HMRC Notice 725, para 5.6).

In the case of an indirect export (where the customer collects the goods from a UK supplier and is responsible for shipping them himself – see **12.4**), it is up to the exporter to forward proof of export to the supplier. He must normally do this within three months of collecting the goods from the supplier, ie within three months of the date of the supply. The following is an extract from HMRC Notice 725, para 5.5, including the useful tip that suppliers should consider taking a 'VAT deposit' from the customer, to be refunded when he provides acceptable proof of shipment:

'If your VAT registered EC customer is arranging removal of the goods from the UK it can be difficult for you as the supplier to obtain adequate proof of removal as the carrier is contracted to your EC customer. For this type of transaction the standard of evidence required to substantiate VAT zero-rating is high.

Before zero-rating the supply you must ascertain what evidence of removal of the goods from the UK will be provided. You should consider taking a deposit equivalent to the amount of VAT you would have to account for if you do not hold satisfactory evidence of the removal of the goods from the UK. The deposit can be refunded when you obtain evidence that proves the goods were removed within the appropriate time limits.

Evidence must show that the goods you supplied have left the UK. Copies of transport documents alone will not be sufficient. Information held must identify the date and route of the movement of goods and the mode of transport involved.'

False evidence – case law

[19.14] What would happen if a UK business sold ten computers to a French trader (VAT registered) who collected them from the UK office and forwarded shipping documents two weeks later, which proved to be false? The goods were actually deflected to private UK customers, and sold as 'cash' deals. Even worse, HMRC have picked up on the problem and now want to assess the UK supplier for 1/6 of its sales (1/6 is the VAT fraction for a 20% rate of VAT) because of the false documents.

The good news is that two ECJ cases (*Teleos plc and Others v C & E Commrs: C-409/4* [2008] QB 600, [2008] STC 706, ECJ, and *Netto Supermarket GmbH and Co OHG v Finanzamt Malchin: C-271/06* [2008] ECR I-771, [2008] STC 3280, ECJ) cleared the waters on this issue a number of years ago, and basically confirmed that as long as a supplier has acted in good faith and had no involvement in tax evasion (and had taken every reasonable step to ensure tax evasion was not an issue) then he should not be held responsible for the VAT loss on these goods if the evidence he has relied upon subsequently proves to be false.

See also Revenue & Customs Brief 61/07 (issued 10 October 2007) and VAT Information Sheet 13/07 (issued 28 September 2007) for further information – both issued after the *Teleos* case.

Reverse charge for wholesale supplies of gas and electricity

[19.15] A reverse charge applies to wholesale supplies of gas and electricity after 30 June 2014 (that is, if the tax point is after 30 June 2014). The reverse charge only applies to supplies to customers who are registered for VAT (or liable to be registered for VAT) and who resell or trade the gas or electricity (wholesale supplies). Supplies to customers for their own consumption are not affected.

Businesses are not required to complete a reverse charge sales list (see **19.8**) in relation to wholesale supplies of gas and electricity but there is no *de minimis* limit (see **19.9**) excluding wholesale supplies of gas and electricity with a value below £5,000 from the reverse charge.

When issuing an invoice for a supply to which the reverse charge applies, suppliers should show all the information normally required on a VAT invoice. The amount of VAT due under the reverse charge should be stated on the invoice but not included in the amount shown as total VAT charged. The invoice should be annotated to make it clear that the reverse charge applies and that the customer is required to account for the VAT.

The VAT should be shown in box 1 of the customer's, rather than the supplier's, VAT return. The customer can claim the VAT as input tax in box 4 of their VAT return, subject to the normal rules for claiming input tax.

The value of the supply excluding VAT should be included in box 6 of the suppliers VAT return and box 7 of the customers VAT return as normal.

Completion of a Reverse Charge Sales List is not required in relation to supplies of gas and electricity.

(Revenue & Customs Brief 23/14 issued on 29 May 2014) (*SI 2014/1458*; *SI 2014/1497*).

Reverse charge for wholesale supplies of telecommunications services

[19.16] With effect from 1 February 2016, reverse charge accounting was extended to supplies of wholesale telecommunications services between counterparties established in the UK. The reverse charge will cover telecommunications services which enable:

- speech communication instantly or with only a negligible delay between the transmission and the receipt of signal;
- the transmission of writing, images and sounds or information of any nature when provided in connection with services described above.

In this context, the term 'wholesale supplies' is defined as normal business to business transactions that are purchased for the purpose of resale (ie they are not services that are 'consumed' by the purchaser but are supplied onwards).

Planning points to consider

[19.17] The following planning points should be given consideration.

- It is important that advisers know how MTIC fraud works and the main goods used by the fraudsters. This is not only to ensure they do not act for fraudulent companies – but also to advise innocent traders of the potential risks of receiving goods in a fraudulent supply chain.
- Recent court cases have supported HMRC's strategy of disallowing input tax on the purchase of any fraudulent goods if it can prove that the trader had reason to suspect that the goods were part of an illegal supply chain where output tax was unlikely to be declared by the supplier. In other words, the onus is on HMRC to prove that the trader knew or ought to have known that he was dealing in goods where the intention was to fraudulently evade VAT.
- It is important that all traders take adequate measures to 'ensure the integrity of their supply chain'. HMRC does not produce an exhaustive list of the measures that need to be taken – but it gives very clear guidelines as to the issues that should be considered.
- Be aware of the reverse charge rules whereby the output tax liability for certain goods and services between VAT registered traders in the UK is transferred in some cases from the seller to the buyer. This is an attempt by HMRC to eliminate MTIC fraud by preventing the seller of the goods from disappearing without declaring output tax he has received from his customer.
- Any UK business selling goods or services to overseas customers should take steps to verify the bona fides of the customer. This process might involve checking the accuracy of the customer's VAT registration number in his own country or obtaining other information to confirm he is bona fide.

Chapter 20

Best Judgement and Unjust Enrichment

Key topics in this chapter:

- The powers of HMRC officers to issue best judgement assessments when records and VAT returns are incomplete or inaccurate.
- The approach adopted by HMRC when raising best judgement assessments.
- Suggested approach for tax advisers reviewing best judgement assessments.
- The key concepts of unjust enrichment and when they apply.
- Procedures for reimbursing customers in cases where unjust enrichment applies for VAT errors made.
- The difference between an error and an adjustment.

Introduction

[20.1] This chapter considers two important topics that could arise for a business in its dealings with HMRC.

- *Best judgement assessments* – in the case of a business with incomplete records, or where HMRC feel that returns submitted are not correct, the officer(s) has powers under the *VATA 1994, s 73* to assess the amount of tax due using his 'best judgement'. Unfortunately for the taxpayer, if he has no records to challenge the best judgement assessment, he will find it very difficult to claim the officer's figures are incorrect. The law stipulates that an officer must employ 'best' judgement not just any old judgement. The tribunals and courts have battled with this concept over the decades culminating in a 'standard' which the courts will employ.
- *Unjust enrichment* – the concept of unjust enrichment states that no taxpayer can be financially enriched because of VAT errors that have been made in the past. For example, if output tax has been incorrectly charged to customers (eg on supplies subsequently found to be zero-rated), and this VAT has been added to the cost of the goods or services provided by the business (rather than VAT being absorbed as part of an inclusive price) then the correct procedure is for this VAT to be refunded to customers, not treated as a windfall for the business.

The main point about the topics above is that in many cases the principles are far from clear-cut – for example, one officer may forget a key point in his calculations; in the case of unjust enrichment, an officer rejecting a claim may not fully understand the way that a business fixes its selling prices.

The power to make 'best judgement' assessments

The legislation

[20.2] Before looking at some practical situations of best judgement, it may be useful to directly review the key legislation on this topic:

- *Failure to make returns*:

  'Where a person has failed to make any returns required under this Act or to keep any documents . . . or where it appears to the Commissioners that such returns are incomplete or incorrect, they may assess the amount of VAT due from him to the best of their judgement and to notify it to him'. [*VATA 1994, s 73(1)*].

- *Evidence of supplying goods*:

  ' . . . if he fails to prove that goods that he has acquired (either by supply, acquisition or importation) have been or are available to be supplied by him . . . they may assess to the best of their judgement and notify to him the amount of VAT that would have been chargeable in respect of the supply of the goods if they had been supplied by him'. [*VATA 1994, s 73(7)*].

In reality, there are two main situations when an officer will use his powers to assess tax under best judgement:

- when records are incomplete or inadequate; or
- when records are fully complete, but the officer has reason to doubt the credibility of the figures.

See Examples 1 and 2.

Example 1

Bill has been trading for one year as a fish and chip shop and has never kept any record of his takings figures – he has also destroyed all purchase invoices and receipts. He has never submitted a VAT return, and only paid central assessments issued by HMRC, which he considers to be an accurate assessment of his VAT liability.

Bill receives a VAT visit, and the officer considers that the central assessments issued by HMRC are too low.

Solution – in this case, the officer will try to establish the correct amount of VAT he considers to be due by using his best judgement. His initial approach may be to look at the outgoings of the business to try and estimate the level of takings needed for the business to cover its costs. He will also look at profit margins and the money taken out of the business by Bill for his own needs. It is also likely that he will ask

Bill to keep a record of his takings for a period of time to estimate total income since the business became VAT registered.

Overall, the officer will be interested in assessing the output tax due from the business – he is unlikely to give any significant credit for input tax because the main supplies will be zero-rated (food purchases) and also because Bill does not hold proper tax invoices to support an input tax claim.

Example 2

An officer of HMRC enters the premises of a fish and chip shop in the local High Street at 11.00 pm on a Friday night, just before the shop is due to close. He asks the manager on duty to cash up in front of him, which confirms takings of £1,200 for the night.

However, a routine VAT inspection carried out six months earlier noted that the best ever declared Friday night takings for the business was £800.

The officer is satisfied that he has evidence of underpaid output tax and, more importantly, incomplete VAT returns. He calculates average declared Friday night sales over a 12-month period (£650) and calculates a suppression of sales rate equal to 85% of declared sales (£1200 – £650 divided by £650 × 100). He applies this percentage to all declared sales made by the business during the last four years (error adjustment period allowed by the legislation), and issues a very large assessment.

Solution – the officer is in a very strong position because he has what appears to be clear evidence of incorrect accounting – the credibility of the taxpayer's takings records is clearly in doubt. Has he exercised his powers honestly? The key point is that the officer has calculated the average Friday night takings figure for the last 12 months – it would not have been acceptable if he had calculated a suppression of sales rate by comparing the £1,200 figure to the lowest Friday night sales figure in the last 12 months! This would certainly have been rejected by a tribunal.

However, has he considered whether there are any reasons why the Friday night on which he entered the premises produced such a high takings figure? For example, is it a Bank Holiday weekend? Is there a local festival that would have generated extra business?

In reality, HMRC should have already researched such issues – its aim on entering the premises is to choose an average night that will not be distorted by events such as those mentioned above.

Approach adopted by HMRC

[20.3] As explained above, officers of HMRC have extensive powers to raise best judgement assessments – and are not obliged to spend excessive amounts of time reconstructing records for every single VAT period over the last four years to arrive at an amount of tax due.

However, as with all aspects of VAT, the taxpayer has the right to ask for an independent review by another HMRC officer or appeal to an independent tribunal if he or she is not happy with the action taken by HMRC.

The key rules on best judgement assessments are as follows:

- HMRC must exercise its powers honestly and must have material before it on which to make its judgment;
- decisions reached must be based on factual information but the officer is under no obligation to carry out exhaustive investigations to calculate the tax he considers due;
- the officer must take into account all information presented to him – although he can obviously make a decision to ignore such information if he considers it is not relevant to his calculations;
- the role of the VAT tribunal is to act as supervisor – confirming that the 'best judgement' criterion has been fairly applied by the officer – in other words, he has not acted in a dishonest or vindictive manner, or made unreasonable estimates when carrying out his calculations.

Decisions based on factual information

[20.4] The assessment issued by the officer at Example 2 at **20.2** is based on two pieces of information – the physical cash takings after he entered the premises, and the record of daily takings declared by the business in the previous 12 months.

However, imagine if the officer had decided to add an extra 10% to the suppression rate on the basis that he felt that some of the business takings had found its way into the back pocket of the sole proprietor, ie never being entered into the till. A conclusion of this nature may be reasonable – but there is no factual evidence to support it, other than the gut instinct of the officer.

It is important that advisers reviewing a best judgement assessment ensure that HMRC have clearly acted on known facts and information, not on gut feelings or assumptions.

Taking account of all relevant information

[20.5] The officer is obliged to take account of all information given to him although he can obviously ignore information that he considers to be irrelevant to his calculations – or where he considers the information given is inaccurate.

For example, let us assume that our fish and chip shop owner in Example 2 above suddenly reveals to the officer that for the last four Fridays, he has opened the shop for an extra two hours a night, eg opening hours are now 4.00 pm–11.00 pm instead of 6.00 pm–11.00 pm. At the time of the last VAT visit, the trading hours for the period in question had only been 6.00 pm–11.00 pm.

In reality, the approach of the officer will be to assess whether he is being told the truth with the statement being made. If he is satisfied on this point, he must take the information into account and readjust his figures.

Innocent until proven guilty

[20.6] The key point with best judgement situations is that the onus is on HMRC to prove that an assessment is appropriate because the taxpayer has declared an incomplete return – not on the taxpayer to prove his innocence where the evidence against him is vague or incomplete – see Example 3. However, once it has been established that an assessment is appropriate, it is up to the taxpayer to demonstrate that the assessment has not been made to the officer's best judgement.

Example 3

ABC Ltd trades as a confectioner, tobacconist and newsagent (CTN) in a busy High Street. The company has a routine VAT inspection and the inspector challenges the 20% gross profit margin being declared by the business. He says that he has carried out three other inspections on CTNs in the town, where the average declared gross profit margin was 28%. He tells the director of ABC Ltd that he intends to raise an assessment for the difference of 8%, going back three years.

Solution – in this situation, the officer has no evidence of incomplete returns being submitted by ABC Ltd – the fact that similar businesses have a higher gross profit margin is irrelevant (it could be that they are better managed, charge higher prices or have a better location in the town).

In effect, the officer of HMRC will always need to have some tangible evidence to support his best judgment calculations – the key thinking he should adopt is: 'I have firm evidence that this trader has not declared all of his output tax – I must therefore use my best judgement powers under *s 73* of the *VATA 1994* to realistically and objectively assess the extent of the underdeclared tax'.

Approach of tax advisers

[20.7] What should be the approach of advisers when dealing with a best judgement assessment raised against a client?

- The adviser will need to obtain as much information about the client business as possible, enabling him to then reach conclusions as to why the HMRC figures could be inaccurate. These factors will then need to be explained in an appeal letter to the officer (local reconsideration always comes before an appeal to an independent tribunal), and the impact on the assessment needs to be established.
- Many best judgement assessments raised by VAT officers will subsequently find their way to colleagues in the direct tax part of the department. An assessment based on underdeclared takings for VAT purposes could therefore be further assessed for underdeclared profits for self-assessment or corporation tax purposes. So there are large sums of money at stake.
- One of the questions often asked by accountants is whether VAT officers deliberately make an initial best judgement assessment as high as possible, meaning that if the figures are challenged and subsequently reduced, they still end up with a good result. The answer to this

question should be in the negative – officers have a duty to take all relevant information into account when raising their assessment and, in effect, should give the taxpayer the benefit of the doubt in cases where there are two sides to the argument. See Example 4.

Example 4

Jennifer and Magnus Smith are partners in business, running the White Horse pub in a local village in Somerset. A VAT officer was concerned about the low gross-profit margin of the business, and carried out a mark-up exercise to calculate projected sales, based on brewery and cash and carry purchases. Projected sales are £60,000 more than declared sales over a four-year period, so the officer raises an assessment for underdeclared output tax.

Solution – for a public house business, there are many situations where purchases made do not achieve the full selling price. For example, beer is lost through pipe cleaning, spillage and drawing off – bottled products may be broken, stolen or thrown away if they are past their sell-by date.

There are other occasions where discount could be given for, eg 'happy hour' promotions, staff discounts or own consumption for the partners. It is possible that the business may also sell bottled beer at a reduced price for take-away purposes.

John and Mary's advisers will need to review the above allowances to make sure the officer has taken them fully into account. Also, officer's projections are often based on purchases for a limited period, so unusual buying trends in this period should also be considered. Overall, there should be plenty of scope to review the content of the officer's assessment.

Unjust enrichment

Basic principle of unjust enrichment

[20.8] The basic principle of unjust enrichment is that no taxable person should make a financial gain from making VAT errors. In effect, if any VAT rebate is paid by HMRC, the key question to ask is whether the rebate belongs to the taxpayer or to his customer that he has incorrectly charged VAT to in the first place. See Example 5.

Example 5

Smith Builders has just carried out some building work for a customer, and charged £5,000 plus £1,000 VAT. The customer pays £6,000 to settle his account. Smith subsequently discovered that the work in question qualified for the 5% VAT rate so only £250 VAT should have been charged.

Smith reduces the Box 1 figure (output tax) by £750 on his next VAT return – and uses the £750 windfall to pay for a week's holiday in Spain.

Solution – the correct procedure is for Smith to issue a VAT credit to his customer for £750 – as it is the customer not the business who has paid the incorrect VAT. Smith should then send the customer a cheque (or cash) for £750. He is then entitled to reduce his Box 1 figure by £750.

When unjust enrichment applies and factors to consider

[20.9] The legislation for unjust enrichment is contained in the *VATA 1994, s 80(3)* and, as with most aspects of VAT, there can be grey areas as far as the application of the law is concerned.

The point to emphasise is that the onus is on HMRC to prove a case of unjust enrichment – not the other way round. In reality, this means it must prove that someone other than the business bore the cost of the incorrectly charged VAT.

Here are two direct extracts from manuals within HMRC's Internal Guidance:

VR3400

'The first thing that we must prove is whether the business is claiming an amount that they have passed on to their customers. If the evidence is that the tax improperly accounted for has been passed on to the claimant's customers, it will be reasonable, on the face of it, to conclude that payment of the claim would lead to the claimant receiving that amount twice – once from the customer and once from HMRC.

We should not invoke the defence of unjust enrichment before we have adequate proof to discharge the evidential burden so far as both pass-on and economic loss or damage is concerned.'

VR3700

'In simple terms, we use the phrase "unjust enrichment" to describe the situation where the crediting or payment of a claimant's claim would put him in a better economic position than he would have been if he had not mistakenly accounted for the tax, in other words, where he would get a "windfall" profit.

However, principles of Community law tell us that unjust enrichment can only be successfully invoked where it can be proven on a balance of probabilities that someone other than the claimant effectively bore the economic burden of the wrongly charged tax and that the claimant did not suffer economic loss or damage as a consequence of their mistaken assumptions about the VAT wrongly charged.

The defence is for HMRC to invoke and therefore for HMRC to prove. It is not for the claimant to prove that he would not be unjustly enriched if we were to settle his claim. It is for us to prove that he would. Thus, to successfully invoke the unjust enrichment defence HMRC must prove two things; that the whole or part of the erroneously charged VAT charge was passed on to the customer (consumer) and that the claimant did not suffer economic loss or damage as a consequence.'

In the case of Smith at Example 5, it is very easy to illustrate that it would be incorrect for him to pocket the £750 windfall – it is quite clearly his customer who has paid the initial VAT charge, so it is the customer who should financially gain from the zero-rating now established.

However, there are other cases where a taxpayer can benefit from the windfall – as long as he can prove that it was his business that bore the impact of the VAT rather than the customer – see Example 6.

Example 6

Mr Jones is a clothing retailer on the High Street, and has to price his goods extremely carefully because of competition from two similar shops in the next street.

His accountant has discovered that he has standard-rated one item of clothing for the last three years that should have been zero-rated as children's clothing. Gross sales of the item are £30,000 per annum. What is the VAT position?

Solution – in this situation, Mr Jones can put forward a very strong case that he has priced the item in question to achieve sales in the market place – rather than on a cost plus basis where he has collated his costs, added a profit margin and then added VAT.

It would be very difficult for HMRC to prove a case of unjust enrichment.

Note – It is important to consider how a business dealt with pricing issues when the standard rate of VAT increased on 1 January 2010 and 4 January 2011, ie were the VAT rate increases passed on to customers or absorbed within existing prices.

The two examples considered so far have been very clear-cut as far as unjust enrichment is concerned, but in reality, there will be borderline cases where a full analysis of the facts will be needed. The following points are highlighted by HMRC.

- *Basis of pricing* – if the structure of a business is such that prices are mainly based on calculating costs and then adding a profit margin and then VAT, then it would be very difficult to convince an officer that an item is being costed on a VAT inclusive basis. For example, if a product was sold for £100 plus VAT in the UK, and then exported for £100 with no VAT added, then it would be virtually impossible to pocket the VAT if the item was found to be zero-rated.

- *Are customers generally VAT registered* – if a business sells mainly to other VAT registered businesses, able to recover input tax, then it will be virtually impossible to avoid an unjust enrichment situation. In reality, HMRC would be out of pocket if any overcharged output tax was kept by the taxpayer.

- *Decline in profits* – if a business that has recently become VAT registered can show that its profits have declined since it registered, then this adds to the argument that it has absorbed the VAT element, rather than added to its prices. An example of such a situation could be a mobile caterer, who needs to price his hot dogs at a certain price to achieve a sale irrespective of whether the price is VAT inclusive or exclusive.

- *Necessity of goods/addictiveness* – this is a tricky one. The basic argument is that if an item is needed by a customer for addictive reasons, eg cigarettes, then the demand for the goods is less sensitive to price. It is more likely that VAT has been added to the price rather than absorbed by the retailer.

Note – the concept of unjust enrichment is exceptionally complex. The First Tier Tax Tribunal has recently issued a judgment in the case of *The Berkshire Golf Club and Ors* (TC04774) [2015] UKFTT 627 (TC). This was a test case which followed on the heels of the *Bridport and West Dorset* judgment of the Court of Justice (Case C-495/12). Here, the golf club claimed that green fee income (charges to non-members for the right to play golf) should have been exempt from VAT. The Court of Justice confirmed that to be the case and, as such, a VAT refund was due to Bridport. HMRC took the point that the refund would unjustly enrich the golf club as, in essence, it was the visitors paying the green fees that had borne the burden of the tax. *The Berkshire Golf Club and Ors* tested this assertion at the First Tier Tribunal which concluded that, on the evidence (very extensive evidence given by expert economists), only 10% of the VAT charged on the green fees had been borne by the customer. 90% of the VAT had been borne by the golf club. HMRC have accepted the tribunal's decision and is not to appeal it further.

The extent of unjust enrichment (or otherwise) is a science in itself. In summary, a business will need to be able to demonstrate through objective evidence that it, and not its customer, has borne the burden of the tax.

Part refunds

[20.10] It is possible to have a situation where HMRC accept that part of a VAT charge has been 'passed on' to a customer and part of the VAT charge has been 'absorbed' within the taxpayer's pricing structure. In this situation, only the 'absorbed' VAT can be retained by the taxpayer.

Procedures for reimbursing customers

[20.11] The worst case situation for a busy taxpayer is where he has missed out on his expected VAT windfall because of an unjust enrichment ruling, and then has to pay VAT back to his customers, giving him a lot of extra paperwork in the process.

HMRC have very tight procedures for ensuring that any VAT rebate it pays back is passed on to the correct person. In reality, HMRC will only repay any overpaid VAT if, on or before the time of making the claim, the claimant signs a written undertaking to confirm the following points:

- he is able to give the names and addresses of the customers he has reimbursed or intends to reimburse;
- the reimbursements will be paid to customers no later than 90 days after the repayment by HMRC;
- no deduction in the amount of VAT paid to customers will be made for either management or administration time;
- reimbursement will only be made by cash or cheque;
- any part of the relevant amount that is not reimbursed within the 90-day period will be paid back to HMRC;
- full records of the reimbursement will be kept, ie names, amounts etc; and
- details must be produced to a VAT officer if requested.

The aim of HMRC is very clear – to ensure a business is unable to prosper financially as a result of making VAT errors, hence the strict rules above.

HMRC Internal Manual – VR4800 – Unjust enrichment: Reimbursement: Pre-undertaking procedures.

Note – Manual VR4820 gives officers the power to extend the 90-day reimbursement period if genuine efforts are being made to repay customers. However, the wording of the note is that only 'a slightly longer period' should be allowed.

Difference between an error and an adjustment

[20.12] An important point to remember is that unjust enrichment situations are only relevant to dealing with errors rather than dealing with normal accounting adjustments. For example, an adjustment of VAT for bad debt relief is not the correction of an error. Equally, the annual adjustment made each year for a business that is partly exempt is also an accounting adjustment rather than an error.

However, incorrectly charging output tax on a zero-rated supply is an error, as is charging output tax on a supply that should have been exempt from VAT.

Finally, note that unjust enrichment situations only apply where the taxpayer is making a financial gain from VAT errors he has made.

Planning points to consider

[20.13] The following planning points should be given consideration.

- Always consider the credibility of a client's explanations regarding any best judgement assessment – how would the explanations appear in the eyes of an HMRC officer? And, more importantly, would they appear sensible reasons to an independent tribunal?
- For best judgement assessments based on outputs calculations, there are many reasons for discrepancies – advisers needs to explore issues such as stock losses, wastage, discounted sales, own consumption, theft, breakages, seasonal variations. In reality, any challenge to an assessment needs to show proper evidence and realistic calculations.
- Always ensure that an officer's best judgement assessment is based on factual information and logical conclusions, not on assumptions, personal views or gut instinct.
- In cases where HMRC is claiming unjust enrichment exists, look very closely at the client's pricing structure, to see if he has actually absorbed the VAT within his price, rather than added VAT to his net costs and profit margin. It is easier to challenge an unjust enrichment ruling where sales are to the general public, rather than another VAT registered business.

- When a client has to repay overcharged VAT to customers, always ensure the correct procedures are followed. It is important that clients do not make an administration charge to customers for reimbursing VAT – this will be assessed as tax due by officers reviewing the calculations.

Chapter 21

Exempt Outputs

Key topics in this chapter:

- VAT implications for a business making exempt supplies.
- Example of how VAT exemption can improve the profits of a business.
- List of exempt supplies within the *VATA 1994, Sch 9*.
- Basic situations when supplies involving land are exempt or taxable.
- VAT exemptions available to non-profit making sports clubs, for example, on competition fees, membership subscriptions, fundraising events.
- Situations when a supply of goods is exempt from VAT.
- Postal services provided by Royal Mail are no longer exempt (since 31 January 2011) – other than public postal services.

Introduction

[21.1] In general terms, a supply or source of income can be allocated to one of five different categories as far as VAT is concerned:

- standard-rated supply – currently 20%;
- reduced-rated supply – currently 5%;
- zero-rated supply – 0%. The zero-rate means that a business can still reclaim input tax on its expenses (subject to normal rules) but does not have to pay output tax on its sales;
- exempt supply – a business does not charge VAT on an exempt supply, but a business that only makes exempt supplies cannot register for VAT and recover input tax, and a business that makes some exempt supplies and some taxable supplies will be subject to the partial exemption rules which affect input tax recovery;
- outside the scope or non-business – eg for many grant payments and donations and many services where the place of supply is outside the UK.

In effect, a business that only makes exempt supplies does not need to register for VAT, irrespective of its level of turnover. The only exception to this statement is if it acquires goods from other EU countries and needs to register for VAT through the acquisition rules (or it purchases certain services from abroad where the place of supply is the UK) – see **11.11**.

Basic principles of exempt supplies

[21.2] The goods or services that qualify as being exempt from VAT are listed under various group headings within the *VATA 1994, Sch 9*. See **21.3**.

As explained above, a business that only makes exempt supplies is not a taxable person under UK law and cannot register for VAT. However, many large businesses that make exempt supplies also have some taxable supplies, and therefore have an obligation to register for VAT if the value of these taxable supplies exceeds the current VAT registration limits. The business will then be partly exempt as far as VAT is concerned with an input tax restriction on its expenditure (see Chapters 24 and 25). See Example 1.

Note – under UK law (*VATA 1994, s 3(1)*) the term 'Taxable Person' means a person who is, or is required to be registered for VAT under the Act. Compare this with the definition of a taxable person in the VAT Directive. *Article 9(1)* of *Directive 2006/112/EC* defines a taxable person as being any person who independently carries out an economic activity, whatever the purpose or result of that activity. The Directive makes no distinction between a person who is registered for VAT and one who is not so registered. What matters is whether the person is engaged in an economic activity not whether he is registered for VAT. Technically therefore, under EU law, a person that makes only exempt supplies is a taxable person (albeit that he has no entitlement to register for VAT).

Example 1

ABC Ltd is a major insurance company with 100 offices across the UK. Its turnover from its insurance activity is £350m per year. In each office it has a vending machine for staff tea and coffee, and each vending machine has sales of £1,200 per year. What is its VAT position?

Solution – insurance income is exempt from VAT, so this activity does not create a need for the company to be VAT registered. However, the supply of catering is taxable (standard rated) and the total income from this activity is £120,000 (100 offices × £1,200 each), which exceeds the VAT registration threshold. The company therefore needs to be registered for VAT. In this example £20,000 of the total income of £120,000 would represent output tax (ie £120,000 × 1/6).

If a business only makes exempt supplies, this creates two outcomes as far as VAT is concerned:

- no output tax is due on any income received or supplies made. This can produce a competitive advantage to a business that deals with the general public or other exempt businesses because it is not making a tax charge that adds to the cost of the goods or services it provides;
- the business does not have any opportunity to recover input tax because it is not making any taxable supplies – any costs it incurs within its business will therefore be based on the gross charge including VAT. See Example 2.

Example 2

DEF Ltd is a registered charity and is organising a fundraising dinner where the costs for meals, cabaret, venue hire etc are £20,000 plus VAT at 20% and income from ticket sales is £40,000.

JKL Ltd is a profit making company and is organising a similar event the following week, with the same income and expenditure amounts. JKL Ltd is not a registered charity or eligible body.

Solution – the income from the fundraising dinner organised by DEF Ltd is exempt from VAT under *Group 12* of *Sch 9*. The overall profit from the dinner will therefore be as follows:

Income	£40,000	(no output tax due on ticket sales – exempt supply)
Costs	£24,000	(ie gross amount because no input tax recoverable)
Profit	£16,000	

The event organised by JKL Ltd is taxable and will have a profit as follows:

Income	£33,333	(ie £40,000 less VAT of £6,667 based on a VAT rate of 20%)
Costs	£20,000	(ie net amount because input tax is reclaimed)
Profit	£13,333	

In effect, DEF Ltd has made extra profit of £2,667 – which is the difference between the output tax it has saved by making an exempt supply (£6,667) less £4,000 it has lost by not being able to recover input tax on its costs.

An important point to emphasise is that a business cannot charge VAT on exempt supplies to try and improve its input tax recovery position. It would not be acceptable to put forward the argument that because HMRC is gaining output tax on the supply, it should not worry about whether it should actually have been exempt.

Exempt supplies within VATA 1994, Sch 9

[21.3] There are 16 different group headings within *Sch 9*, as follows. The relevant HMRC public notice giving further analysis about each heading is shown in brackets, and the easiest way to view the notices is on the GOV.UK website at www.gov.uk/government/collections/vat-notices-numerical-order.

- *Group 1*: Land – see **21.4** (Notice 742);
- *Group 2*: Insurance (701/36);
- *Group 3*: Postal services – see **21.10** (701/8);
- *Group 4*: Betting, gaming and lotteries (701/29);
- *Group 5*: Finance (701/49);
- *Group 6*: Education (701/30);
- *Group 7*: Health and welfare (701/2, 701/31, 701/57);
- *Group 8*: Burial and cremation (701/32);

- *Group 9*: Subscriptions to trade unions, professional bodies and other public interest bodies (701/5);
- *Group 10*: Sport, sports competitions and physical education – see **21.5** (701/45);
- *Group 11*: Works of art (701/12);
- *Group 12*: Fundraising events by charities and other qualifying bodies – see **21.8**;
- *Group 13*: Cultural services etc – admissions to museums, exhibitions, zoos and performances of a cultural nature supplied by public bodies and eligible bodies (701/47);
- *Group 14*: Supplies of goods where input tax cannot be recovered – see **21.9**;
- *Group 15*: Investment gold (701/21);
- *Group 16*: Supplies of services by groups involving cost sharing (VAT Information Sheet 7/12).

The key VAT issues and some planning points on some of the more commonly used groups are now considered in more detail.

Land

[21.4] A basic starting point with land and buildings is that many sources of property income tend to be exempt from VAT. However, the VAT issues concerning land and property transactions need to be treated with great care (not least because of the generally high value of land transactions) and this book considers the key issues at Chapters 26 to 28.

Sport, sports competitions and physical education – fundraising events

[21.5] Many accountants and tax advisers are involved with sports clubs, either on a client basis or through a voluntary arrangement by being treasurer of, for example, the local golf club. This section will therefore focus on some important planning points to consider which may benefit such clubs as far as exempt supplies are concerned.

Entry fees for competitions

[21.6] An entry fee for the right to enter a competition is normally standard rated. However, there are circumstances where the income can be classed as exempt if the following conditions are met:

- they are to a competition in sport or physical education and the total amount of the entry fees charged is returned to the entrants of that competition as prizes; or
- they are to a competition promoted by an eligible body, which is established for the purposes of sport or physical recreation.

(HMRC Notice 701/45, para 6.1).

Note – a members' golf club run by a volunteer committee would normally qualify as an eligible body for this purpose.

HMRC gives a very clear definition as to what it considers to be a competition: 'a structured and organised contest, tournament or race where prizes or titles are awarded'.

As far as the definition of sport or physical recreation is concerned, HMRC accepts any activity recognised as a sporting activity by Sport England. The obvious sports include football, cricket, golf and tennis, but less obvious ones include angling and dancing (chess, card games and dominoes are excluded as is (possibly) the playing of bridge (see Upper Tribunal judgment in *English Bridge Union v Revenue and Customs Comrs* [2015] UKUT 401 (TCC), [2016] STC 25 which referred the question to the CJEU).

(HMRC Notice 701/45, para 3.2).

Finally, an eligible body means a non-profit making body which cannot distribute any profit it makes otherwise than to another non-profit making body or its own members on winding up or dissolution. A members' golf club managed by a volunteer committee is an example of an eligible body.

(HMRC Notice 701/45, para 4.1).

Example 3 demonstrates how a competition organised by a golf club can qualify for VAT exemption on its entry fees.

Example 3

Big Town Golf Club is a commercial body organising its annual handicap competition for 150 players at an entry fee of £30 each. The gross receipts of £4,500 are used to purchase trophies at £35 each for the top ten players, and then a large cup for the winner worth £500. The winner also receives a cheque for £2,500 and the runner-up receives a cheque for £1,150.

Solution – the income from this event is exempt (even though organised by a commercial business) because all of the entry fees have been allocated to prizes and trophies.

Services closely linked with and essential to sport or physical education

[**21.7**] The supply, by an eligible body to an individual, of services closely linked with and essential to sport or physical education in which the individual is taking part, is exempt from VAT. Before 1 January 2015 UK VAT law excluded from this exemption supplies to non-members of eligible bodies operating a membership scheme, but HMRC now accepts that this exclusion was invalid under EU VAT law.

An organisation is an eligible body for the purpose of the VAT exemption for sport, sports competitions and physical education if it meets all of the following conditions:

• It is non-profit making.
• Its constitution includes a non-distribution clause or limits any distribution of profits or surpluses to another non-profit making organisation or to the organisation's members on a winding up or dissolution.

- It uses any profits or surpluses derived from the provision of its playing facilities to maintain or improve those facilities or for the purposes of a non-profit making organisation.
- It is not subject to commercial influence or part of a wider commercial undertaking.

Whether an organisation is non-profit making is decided by looking at the organisation's constitution, its activities, and its use of funds, in order to determine whether it was established with a purpose which excludes the distribution of profits to those with a financial interest in it. Although a non-distribution clause in the constitution of an organisation does not in itself mean that it is non-profit making, a non-distribution clause, or a clause which limits the distribution of any profits or surpluses to another non-profit making organisation, or to the organisation's members on a winding up, is essential for eligible body status.

HMRC has produced a list of activities that qualify for exemption in Notice 701/45 – the key condition is that the activity must comprise some element of physical activity intended to improve physical fitness. A few unusual examples that are included are: octopush, tang soo do, kabaddi and unihoc. Interestingly, snooker, billiards and motor sports are also included as designed to improve physical activity.

The following are considered to be supplies closely linked with and essential to sport or physical education:

- playing, competing, refereeing, umpiring, judging, coaching or training (but not attending as a spectator or involvement in administration);
- use of changing rooms, showers and playing equipment together with storage of equipment essential to the sporting activity;
- match fees charged by an 'eligible body' for use of the playing facilities; and
- mooring, hangarage and use of workshop facilities (but not the use of parts, or the services of an engineer).

See Example 4 to consider the VAT liability of some of the main sources of income for a members' club.

(HMRC Notice 701/45, para 3.3.1).

Example 4

Big Town Golf Club is an eligible body for the purpose of the VAT exemption for sport. It has 300 playing members paying an annual subscription of £2,000 and social members who enjoy the bar and catering facilities paying £50 a year. In addition, the club has three other sources of income:

- it allows non-members to play a round of golf for £35;
- it charges playing members £5 a week for the use of a locker in the club changing rooms;
- it produces a quarterly magazine charging £5 a copy (paper rather than electronic format).

Solution – the VAT liability needs to be considered in each case. The playing subscription paid by members is exempt from VAT, however, the social membership is standard rated because the use of the bar and catering facilities is not closely linked to sport. The fee charged to non-members for playing a round of golf is exempt from VAT and the locker facility for members qualifies for exemption because it is linked to the participation in sport. Finally, the magazine is zero-rated as reading matter (*VATA 1994, Sch 8, Group 3*).

Fundraising events

[21.8] The exemption for fundraising events applies to the supply of goods or services in connection with an event where the primary purpose is to raise money and which is promoted as such. The event must be organised by an eligible body. The key point is that HMRC needs to be convinced that the aim of the function is to raise money. This can be proved by minutes of meetings, costings and publicity material. An eligible body for this section of the law also includes charities and their trading subsidiaries.

The scope for exemption is very wide, and includes income received from admission charges, the sale of advertising space in brochures and items sold at the event, eg auctioned goods. Examples of events that could qualify for exemption include dinner dances, discotheques, concerts, fêtes, dinners and lunches.

The exemption in relation to fundraising events applies to:

- charities and their trading subsidiaries;
- non-profit making bodies such as a members' golf club.

A few rules exist that limit the scope of exemption, for example, there is a maximum number of events of the same kind that can be held at the same location (ie 15 maximum in a financial year).

Similar kinds of events held in different locations qualify for exemption provided all the other conditions are met, for example, 30 dinners held by a national charity in different towns in the same financial year would all qualify for exemption. See **35.12** for an example of how the exemption for fundraising activities applies in practice.

(HMRC Notice 701/1, para 5.9).

Supplies of goods where input tax cannot be recovered

[21.9] A supply of goods is an exempt supply where the following conditions are all met:

- the person making the supply incurred input tax on the item in question; and
- all of the input tax incurred on the item was not reclaimed because it was classed as 'non-deductible input tax'.

Non-deductible input tax comprises three main categories:

(a)   input tax used on goods to make exempt supplies;
(b)   input tax which is wholly excluded from credit under the provisions relating to non-deductible items such as business entertainment, motor cars and non-building materials incorporated in a building or its site;

(c)   VAT incurred by the person concerned when he was not a taxable person (ie when he was not registered or liable to be registered).

See Example 5 for an illustration of how this principle works in a practical situation.

Example 5

> ABC Ltd supplies computer software and is registered for VAT. The company bought a brand new car for the sales director and did not reclaim input tax of £3,500 on the purchase because the car is not wholly used for business purposes and is also available for private use. The car was used by the director for only 12 months and then sold by the company for £10,000.
>
> DEF Ltd is an insurance broker making exempt supplies, and purchased two computers for £80,000 each. As the computers were used wholly within the insurance business, no input tax could be reclaimed by DEF Ltd. The computers were used by the company for 18 months, but now need to be upgraded. The company has been offered £50,000 for each of the computers. The directors are concerned that these sales may be taxable and will take the company above the VAT registration threshold and the company may need to register for VAT.
>
> **Solution** – the money received from the sale of the car in the first situation is exempt from VAT because no input tax was claimed on the original purchase of the car (non-deductible item). The sale of the computers in the second situation is also exempt from VAT because there was no input tax claim on the original purchase because the expenditure was wholly attributable to the company's exempt insurance supplies.

Postal services exemption

[21.10] Since 31 January 2011, the exemption for postal services has been restricted to supplies of public postal services (and incidental goods) by the universal service provider (USP – currently Royal Mail). Postal services supplied on terms that are individually negotiated, and services not subject to price or regulatory control, became standard rated from that date.

In effect, this means that the exemption only applies to services made under a licence duty, including those where – pursuant to a licence duty – the USP allows private postal operators access to its postal facilities. Supplies of services that a USP is not required to make under a licence duty (such as those made by Parcelforce) and services provided on terms and conditions that have been freely negotiated, are now subject to standard rate VAT.

VAT exemption for psychologists services – 1 July 2009

[21.11] With effect from 1 July 2009, practitioner psychologists became regulated by the Health Professionals Council. This means that any supplies of medical care since that date became VAT exempt rather than standard rated.

Practitioner psychologists come under seven domains: clinical, counselling, educational, forensic, health, occupational, and sport/exercise. Psychologists who work purely in academic research and experimental psychology and who do not offer services to the general public are excluded from regulation meaning that there will be no change in the VAT treatment of their services.

The phrase 'medical care' means any service relating to the protection, maintenance or restoration of the health of the person concerned, including mental health. Medical care would include services such as counselling, working with children with emotional problems, dealing with criminals' behavioural problems or running stress management courses.

However, as is the case for all health professionals, the VAT exemption excludes services that are not primarily for the benefit of the patient, for example, assessing a patient's mental condition for legal reasons at the behest of a third party. This is because the primary purpose of such services is to enable a court to take a decision on whether the patient is fit to stand trial rather than any immediate concern about the patient's mental health.

See Revenue & Customs Brief 43/09 for further details.

Independent financial advisers

[21.12] The Retail Distribution Review (RDR) came into effect on 1 January 2013, one of the aims of which is to provide greater clarity in terms of the charges consumers incur for financial advice. The RDR does not change the VAT treatment of the income generated by an independent financial adviser (IFA). Commissions and fees for arranging investments in retail financial products will continue to be exempt and fees for providing general financial advice will continue to be taxable. However, one of the effects of the RDR is that many IFAs may see the proportion of their income that relates to commissions reducing and the proportion of their income that relates to fees increasing. The challenge will be to differentiate between fees for exempt intermediary services and fees for taxable financial advisory services. As retail customers (consumers) are unable to recover VAT, IFAs will generally want to avoid voluntary VAT registration.

Example 6

Ian the IFA had total income of £100,000 for the 12 months to 31 December 2012, £90,000 of which was commission income and £10,000 of which was fee income.

For the 12 months to 31 December 2013 Ian's commission income reduced to £10,000 and his fee income increased to £90,000.

When does Ian need to start thinking about VAT?

Before 1 January 2013 Ian did not need to think much about VAT. His commission income was exempt as it clearly related to his intermediary activity arranging investments and even if all of the fees were for taxable financial advisory services this was well below the VAT registration threshold.

After 1 January 2013 Ian will need to think more about VAT. Even if all of his fee income for 2013 relates to exempt intermediary activity arranging investments he will need to retain evidence to support this. If some of the fee income relates to taxable financial advisory services he will need to monitor the level of the taxable income for VAT registration threshold purposes.

Evidence such as correspondence, meeting notes, and how the services are described on invoices should be retained to support how an IFA is treating the various elements of their income for VAT purposes. The HMRC Manual VATFIN7675 states that 'If an adviser is unable to provide evidence that an exempt supply has taken place, VAT will be due on that supply.'

General financial advice is a taxable supply (standard rated) and is not covered by the exemption for finance at *VATA 1994, Sch 9, Group 5*. What can cause confusion is that the word 'advice' is often used in the context of IFAs to include recommendation, referral and intermediary work arranging transactions in retail investment products. This intermediary work is exempt by virtue of *VATA 1994, Sch 9, Group 5, Item 5* which refers to 'The provision of intermediary services in relation to any transaction comprised in Item 1, 2, 3, 4 or 6 (whether or not any such transaction is finally concluded) by a person acting in an intermediary capacity.'

Guidance as to what constitutes a supply of intermediary services is included at HMRC Notice 701/49, para 9.1 and is included below:

'A supplier of an exempt intermediary service is a person who:

- brings together a person seeking a financial service with a person who provides a financial service
- stands between the parties to a contract and acts in an intermediary capacity, and
- undertakes work preparatory to the completion of a contract for the provision of financial services, whether or not it is completed.'

In some situations it may be clear that an IFA is providing taxable financial advice and in other situations it may be clear that the IFA is providing exempt intermediary services. However, in many situations an IFA will provide general financial advice to a client before arranging for them to invest in a particular retail investment product. In situations when an IFA is providing advisory and intermediary services it will be necessary to consider which element predominates. Guidance regarding this matter is included at HMRC Notice 701/49, para 9.9, an extract from which is included below:

'If you provide both advice and you act between your customer and the provider of a financial product it is important to establish which of the two elements of your service predominates. Where your advice directly results in your customer taking out a financial product and you meet all the criteria for intermediary services in paragraph 9.1, the whole of your service – including the advice element – will be exempt. The advice is seen as ancillary to an exempt intermediary service. If you receive commission from the finance product provider, it is consideration for a separate exempt supply by you of intermediary services.

If, on the other hand, your advice far outweighs the work done to arrange a contract (for example, because a customer has received a general financial health-check, with advice covering a range of financial issues, but then only buys a minor product requiring minimal intermediation), the intermediary service is ancillary to the advice, and VAT is due on the whole supply.'

The issue of whether services of an IFA were exempt or taxable was considered in *Bloomsbury Wealth Management LLP* (TC02063) [2012] UKFTT 379 (TC), [2012] SWTI 2738. Bloomsbury is an IFA providing services to high net worth individuals in relation to financial investments. It introduced clients to fund managers and initially accounted for VAT on its charges. It then submitted a repayment claim on the basis that it should have treated its supplies as exempt under *VATA 1994, Sch 9, Group 5, Item 5.*

HMRC decided to reject the repayment claim and Bloomsbury appealed against that decision to the First Tier Tribunal.

HMRC put forward two arguments for rejecting the repayment claim:

(1) According to HMRC, Bloomsbury was not introducing clients to fund managers so that the clients could invest in funds but was introducing clients to fund managers so that the clients could receive fund management services. This is a technical argument. The legislation specifies the type of transactions the exemption for intermediary services applies to and HMRC's argument was that the exemption did not apply to the services Bloomsbury provided.

(2) Based on time spent, the intermediary services were not the predominant services Bloomsbury provided to its clients.

Paragraphs 9.1 and 9.9 of HMRC Notice 701/49, referred to above, are both relevant in relation to the above arguments put forward by HMRC.

Rejecting HMRC's first argument the Tribunal commented that:

'In our view, Bloomsbury introduced clients to the fund managers and acted as an intermediary between the clients and the fund managers for the purpose of acquiring and maintaining the portfolio of investments on behalf of the clients. The fund managers also provided fund management services to Bloomsbury's clients but that was a necessary consequence of the fact that the clients held units in the funds. Although we did not hear any evidence from clients of Bloomsbury, we regard it as extremely unlikely that any client would have said that it engaged Bloomsbury so that it could be introduced to a fund manager.'

HMRC's second argument, that the intermediary services were ancillary to advisory and management services, was undermined by the fact that Bloomsbury did not charge for advice if an individual did not invest. The Tribunal commented that:

'We consider that the fact that there was no fee for that advice if the client decided not to invest shows that it was not the most important part of the service to Bloomsbury or its clients.'

The Tribunal decided that the fees were for an exempt supply of financial intermediary services and allowed Bloomsbury's appeal.

IFA networks

[21.13] For regulatory reasons many financial advisers are Appointed Representatives (ARs) of IFA networks. IFA networks are businesses that take responsibility for ensuring that the regulatory requirements of the Financial

Services Authority (FSA) are complied with so that its ARs do not need to be directly authorised by the FSA. When an AR deals with a client on an FSA-regulated matter they act on behalf of the network. A commission or fee paid by the client or financial product providers in relation to such work is income of the network for VAT purposes. Payments made by the network to the AR are the income of the AR for VAT purposes.

Guidance regarding the VAT implications of IFA networks is included in HMRC Notice 701/49, para 9.10, an extract of which is included below:

- all payments (whether by fee or commission) received from the product providers or clients for the supplies of financial intermediary services provided via the ARs is the network's VAT exempt income and the onward payments made to the ARs is consideration for the AR's VAT exempt intermediary services supplied to the network
- fees either paid directly to the network or via the ARs, in respect of advice only services supplied via the ARs (which fall outside the exemption for financial intermediary services) is the network's standard rated income. Any onward payments made to the ARs is consideration for the provision of those services by the ARs to the network on which VAT will be due if the AR's taxable income is above the VAT registration threshold
- any optional services supplied by the network to their ARs for additional consideration (such as specific compliance or I.T. services) will be separate supplies and the relevant VAT liability will apply, and
- any non-regulated services provided by ARs fall outside the network arrangements altogether and are made directly by the IFA to the client/product provider.

General comments about other categories

[21.14] The group headings covered at **21.4–21.11** mainly focused on areas where businesses are likely to have some VAT issues to consider, ie there are 'grey' areas as to whether income in many cases is exempt or taxable.

For many of the other categories, a relevant business is likely to have income which is wholly exempt and it is therefore unlikely to be registered for VAT, eg insurance broker, private school or children's nursery. In such cases, VAT is not a concern, unless the business diversifies its activities to include supplies that are taxable, eg vending machine sales as in Example 1 at **21.2**.

VATA 1994, Sch 9, Group 6 provides details of the VAT exemption for education. The exemption for supplies of research between eligible bodies, for example, educational establishments, has been withdrawn since 1 August 2013.

Planning points to consider

[21.15] The following planning points should be given consideration.

- It is an advantage for supplies to either the general public or other exempt businesses to be exempt from VAT because there is no tax charge to customers that they cannot recover. In most cases, this situation will outweigh the disadvantages of the input tax relevant to the supply not being reclaimable.

- There are occasions when a standard rated supply being incorrectly treated as exempt could prove costly for a business. For example, a VAT charge to another registered business would not be a problem if the business could reclaim the charge as input tax. The supplier can then recover related input tax on its own expenses because it has made a taxable supply.

- Output tax is not payable on the supply of goods where the original input tax was not reclaimed because it was either non-deductible or relevant to an exempt supply.

- For non-profit making sports clubs, it is important that HMRC rules are closely followed if a source of income is to qualify as exempt from VAT. For example, there are strict conditions concerning exemption for membership subscription income, entry fees and fundraising events.

- A business that incorrectly charges output tax on its exempt sales is still blocked from claiming input tax on the related costs. An exempt sale cannot be made taxable simply by adding 20% VAT to the income source (or treating it as VAT inclusive). Input tax cannot be claimed on expenditure relevant to exempt supplies.

- Be aware of the revised exemptions for postal services provided by Royal Mail (31 January 2011) – most supplies made since that date will be standard rated rather than exempt.

Chapter 22

Zero-rated and Reduced-rated Outputs

Key topics in this chapter:

- Goods or services that qualify for zero-rating within *VATA 1994, Sch 8*.
- Situations when zero-rating applies on supplies of food and printed matter.
- Recent changes regarding the VAT liability of hot take-away food sales and premises.
- The importance of accounting for VAT correctly if a business makes both standard and zero-rated sales.
- The impact of the flat rate scheme, cash accounting scheme and annual accounting scheme for a business that wholly, or mainly, sells zero-rated items.
- Potential benefits of a business making zero-rated supplies registering for VAT on a voluntary basis.
- Procedures to adopt if VAT is incorrectly charged on a zero-rated item (unjust enrichment).
- The aim of the 5% rate of VAT and supplies within *VATA 1994, Sch 7A*.
- The opportunity for a business that wholly or mainly makes zero-rated sales to avoid registering for VAT (exemption).

Introduction

[22.1] If a supply is zero-rated, then tax is still chargeable – but at 0%. Therefore, a zero-rated supply is still a taxable supply, and, importantly, input tax is reclaimable on costs related to the supply. This means that a business wholly making zero-rated supplies will have no output tax to pay on its VAT returns – but will be able to recover input tax on costs and overheads it incurs in the business.

If a business is in a repayment situation on a regular basis, it has the option to submit monthly rather than quarterly returns. Although this requires extra administration time (12 VAT returns to complete each year instead of four), there is a cash flow advantage in receiving money from HMRC on a monthly basis.

If a business only makes zero-rated supplies, it must still register for VAT if the value of these supplies exceeds the registration limits. In some cases, HMRC may agree that a business which only makes zero-rated supplies can be relieved from the requirement to register but, in most cases, a business making zero-rated supplies will want to register for VAT in order to benefit from input tax recovery on its costs and overheads.

Supplies that are zero-rated

[22.2] The groups of zero-rated supplies, specified in the *VATA 1994, Sch 8* are listed below. For advisers who have specific queries regarding any of the categories, the relevant HMRC public notice reference is shown in brackets against each group heading. The easiest way to view the notices is on the GO V.UK website at www.gov.uk/government/collections/vat-notices-numerical-order.

- *Group 1*: Food – see **22.3** (Notices 701/14; 701/15);
- *Group 2*: Water and sewerage services (701/16);
- *Group 3*: Books and printed matter – see **22.5** (701/10);
- *Group 4*: Talking books for the blind and handicapped and wireless sets for the blind;
- *Group 5*: Construction of buildings – see Chapters 26–28 (708);
- *Group 6*: Protected buildings – see Chapter 26 (708);
- *Group 7*: International services – see Chapter 14 (741A);
- *Group 8*: Transport (744A);
- *Group 9*: Caravans and houseboats – fewer caravans qualify from 6 April 2013 (701/20);
- *Group 10*: Gold and precious metals (701/21);
- *Group 11*: Bank notes;
- *Group 12*: Dispensing of drugs, reliefs for people with disabilities (701/7);
- *Group 13*: Imports, exports etc – see Chapters 11 and 12 (702; 704);
- *Group 14*: Withdrawn on 1 July 1999;
- *Group 15*: Charities – see Chapter 35 (701/1);
- *Group 16*: Clothing and footwear (714);
- *Group 17*: Withdrawn on 1 November 2010;
- *Group 18*: European Research Infrastructure Consortia.

Food

[22.3] The general rule is that food (for ease of reference the word 'food' in this section should be taken to include drink unless the context demands otherwise) is zero-rated if it is of a kind used for human consumption – however, there are two exceptions to the general rule:

- a supply of food made in the course of catering; and
- a supply of any food specifically excluded from zero-rating by the legislation in *VATA 1994, Sch 8, Group 1*.

The basic definition of a supply in the course of catering is any supply of food for consumption on the premises in which it is supplied and any supply of hot food for consumption off those premises.

From 1 October 2012 the definition of premises has been extended to include any area set aside for the consumption of food by the supplier's customers, whether or not the area may also be used by the customers of other suppliers.

From 1 October 2012 the definition of hot food has been revised so that hot food means food which (or any part of which) is at a temperature above the ambient air temperature at the time it is provided to the customer and:

- has been heated for the purposes of enabling it to be consumed hot; or
- has been heated to order; or
- has been kept hot after being heated because the supplier stores it in an environment which provides, applies or retains heat, or takes other steps to ensure it remains hot or to slow down the natural cooling process; or
- is provided to a customer in packaging that retains heat (whether or not the packaging was primarily designed for that purpose) or in any other packaging that is specifically designed for hot food; or
- is advertised or marketed in a way that indicates that it is supplied hot.

Examples of food or drink specifically excluded from zero-rating by the legislation at *VATA 1994, Sch 8, Group 1* are:

- ice cream and similar products;
- confectionery, eg chocolate, sweets, certain biscuits;
- alcoholic drinks, including beer, wine, cider, spirits and liqueurs;
- beverages such as fruit drinks, lemonade, cola and bottled waters;
- crisps, roasted and salted nuts.
- sports drinks that are advertised or marketed as products designed to enhance physical performance, accelerate recovery after exercise or build bulk.

However, the main everyday food items are almost invariably zero-rated, including raw meat, fish, vegetables, fruit, cereals, cakes (but not some biscuits), tea, coffee and milk.

From a practical aspect, there are two main VAT challenges facing a business that sells food:

(a) identifying the correct liability of the product being sold;
(b) where goods are sold at both standard and zero-rates of VAT, it is important that there is an accurate method of recording the split – a two button till is the most common method.

See Example 1.

Example 1

ABC Ltd trades as a bakery shop. It sells sandwiches for take-away purposes (zero-rated food) and also has a seated area in the shop which serves tea, coffee and light meals (standard-rated catering). What is the best way of recording the amount of output tax payable by the company?

Solution – one possible option could be to have separate tills for the two activities (or one till with two separate buttons) – this would also be useful from an internal management aspect because it would then be easy to identify the level of sales being achieved by each part of the business. All sales from the café area would be standard rated, and all take-away sales by the bakery would be zero-rated. However, this situation assumes that all take away sales are for cold food – any hot food supplied would be standard rated as well.

When visiting a business as in Example 1, HMRC officers will look carefully at the overall split between standard rated and zero-rated sales. Their main concern will be to ensure that a business is not trying to gain an unfair advantage by overstating its zero-rated sales. It is therefore important that taxpayers have strong accounting controls in place to minimise the risk of error.

With regard to identifying the correct liability of goods, it is important to remember that there are a number of food items that are standard rated, even though they would appear to be classed as an everyday food item. Since VAT was introduced in 1973, the interpretation of zero-rating for food has been challenged at many tribunals, and this has led to some interesting decisions. For example, a biscuit is generally zero-rated – but a biscuit wholly or partly covered with chocolate or some product similar in taste and appearance is standard rated.

(HMRC Notice 701/14).

Hot take-away food – zero-rated?

[22.4] There have been a number of VAT cases relating to whether the supply of hot food for immediate consumption, away from the premises of the seller, is a zero-rated supply of food rather than a standard-rated supply of catering.

The key case in question is *Finanzamt Burgdorf v Bog: Joined Cases C-497/09, C-499/09, C-501/09 and C-502/09* ([2011] SWTI 745, ECJ) where the Court highlighted that the preparation of the hot food in question (eg chips, nachos, popcorn) was essentially limited to basic standard actions, rather than any significant service of catering being involved. Looking at the question of 'what is the customer getting for his money?' it was considered the answer was a sale of food (goods) rather than catering (services).

HMRC issued Revenue & Customs Brief 19/11 on 1 April 2011 to give its thoughts on how the cases will apply in the UK. However, it considers that the UK has no problem because the legislation in the UK makes a specific definition of 'catering' as inclusive of hot food consumed away from the premises, ie excluded from zero-rating as food.

Even if the UK position was in doubt (and some accountants think it is) then an issue of 'unjust enrichment' (see Chapter 20) will be relevant in relation to claims for a VAT repayment. For example, how did a business deal with the two increases in VAT on 1 January 2010 (15% to 17.5%) and 4 January 2011 (17.5% to 20%). If prices were increased, this confirms that the business has added VAT to its prices (rather than absorbed them within its margin) and any past windfall of tax would belong to customers rather than the business. The prospect of a windfall may have been weakened as a result of the *Finance Act*

2012 changes to the definition of hot food and premises. For example, HMRC may take the view that the changes to the legislation effective from 1 October 2012 simply clarify how the previous legislation should have been interpreted.

Books and reading matter

[22.5] With regard to printed matter, the following main supplies are zero-rated:

- books and booklets;
- brochures and pamphlets;
- leaflets;
- newspapers;
- journals and periodicals;
- children's picture books, music and maps.

The legislation does not specifically define any of the above items – but the words are to be given their ordinary everyday meaning. For example, the supply of text by electronic means (eg via the Internet) is standard rated because the supply is for a service rather than goods. In the case of the supply of services, different rules apply.

The main situation where an adviser will need to look closely at whether a printer has applied the correct rate of VAT is if his client, the printer's customer, is either a business making exempt supplies or is not registered for VAT. In both cases, an incorrect VAT charge will cause an adverse impact on the bottom line profits of the customer – see Example 2.

(HMRC Notice 701/10).

Example 2

DEF Ltd trades as an estate agent, making 30% taxable supplies (sale of houses on a commission basis) and 70% exempt sales (fees from arranging mortgages). The company has produced a new colour brochure advertising all of its services and has paid Smith Printers an amount of £7,000 plus VAT for producing 1,000 copies of the brochure.

Solution – the brochure produced by Smith Printers is zero-rated for VAT – therefore, no VAT should have been charged on the supply to DEF Ltd. As the latter company is partly exempt, it would only be able to reclaim 30% of the VAT charged as input tax (based on the standard method of partial exemption) and therefore have lost 70% of the VAT.

Note – it is common practice for many suppliers to play safe and charge VAT where they are unsure about the correct liability. This principle does not usually produce a problem for a business that is VAT registered and able to recover input tax, but it impacts heavily on exempt, partly exempt or unregistered businesses. However, be aware that HMRC also has the power to disallow input tax claimed on a supply made to a business if the supplier has charged the wrong rate of VAT. In such cases, HMRC could assess the tax claimed and instruct the business owner to request a VAT credit from the supplier who has charged the wrong rate of VAT.

Many items produced by printers are standard rated, mainly relevant to supplies that are not classed as reading matter. For example, business cards, compliment slips, letter headings, invoices and calendars are all standard-rated items and commonly purchased by most businesses. In such cases, input tax can be claimed on these items subject to the normal rules.

One of the more difficult issues involving supplies of goods is where there are two different supplies within a package, the two items attracting VAT at different rates, eg supply of zero-rated magazine with a standard-rated CD. A full analysis of the approach to adopt with mixed supply situations is given in Chapter 23.

Zero-rated supplies – schemes for small businesses

Flat rate scheme

[22.6] The flat rate scheme is available for use by a small business with taxable turnover of £150,000 per year or less (VAT exclusive) at the time of joining the scheme. The basic aim of the scheme is that a business does not reclaim input tax on its costs, but just applies a flat-rate percentage calculation to its VAT inclusive sales, and this is the amount of VAT that will be paid each quarter. The flat rate percentage depends on the trade category of the business (see Chapter 8 for further details).

For a business that wholly makes zero-rated supplies, there will be no benefit in using the flat rate scheme. This is because there is no flat rate category that has a 0% rate – and even if there was a 0% rate, this would be a negative result anyway because the business would not benefit from input tax recovery.

However, where the flat rate scheme may prove a winner is where a business sells a mixture of standard and zero-rated items, and the trade category percentage to be applied within the flat rate scheme produces a good result. See Example 3.

Note – a business that has an unpredictable level of zero-rated sales should almost certainly avoid the flat rate scheme as well. A builder doing some work on new houses (zero-rated services) could see his profit margin heavily eroded if he has to pay flat rate scheme tax on jobs where no VAT has been charged to the customer, and he is also sacrificing input tax on the materials he has bought as well (scheme users do not claim input tax unless it relates to either qualifying pre-registration expenditure or capital goods costing more than £2,000 including VAT).

Example 3

Jenny Smith trades as a confectioner, tobacconist and newsagent. The location of her shop means that the majority of her sales are confectionery items (standard rated), closely followed by cigarettes (standard rated), and finally, newspapers (zero-rated). Her taxable turnover is £145,000 per year excluding VAT and she is considering whether it would be worthwhile using the flat rate scheme.

Solution – the flat rate percentage for a business of this nature is 4%. This may be a very favourable rate for Jenny because the mark-up on confectionery (her main selling item) is higher than cigarettes, and therefore the normal method of accounting may produce a higher tax bill than the flat rate scheme.

However, if the nature of Jenny's business meant that the majority of her sales were zero-rated newspapers, then the flat rate scheme would probably not be worthwhile for her to use.

Cash accounting scheme

[22.7] The cash accounting scheme is available to any business with taxable supplies of £1,350,000 per year or less (excluding VAT), and has the main advantage of basing VAT calculations (output tax and input tax) on cash book accounting rather than day book accounting. In effect, this means that output tax is not due on a sales invoice until payment has been received from the customer (instead of the earlier date of the invoice under normal VAT accounting). However, input tax cannot be reclaimed on a supply until payment has been made to a supplier (see Chapter 6 for a full analysis of the cash accounting scheme).

For a business that wholly or mainly makes zero-rated supplies, the cash accounting scheme is unlikely to be a winner. This is because the delay in accounting for output tax does not give the business a big cash flow advantage, but it would lose out by not being able to reclaim input tax until the date of payment.

Note – in the case of a business making mainly zero-rated sales, such as a farm, where a cash book accounting system is used, it would be sensible for the business to not use the cash accounting scheme and make an input tax claim at the end of each VAT period on unpaid purchase invoices, ie on closing creditors. The amount claimed would need to be reversed the following VAT period because the invoices will then be processed through the cash book as they are paid, but then another closing creditor claim can be made at the end of this period as well. This approach gives the double benefit of simplified accounting (cash book system linked to the business bank account) and the maximum possible input tax claim on VAT returns submitted by the business.

Annual accounting scheme

[22.8] The annual accounting scheme has a number of features, the main one being that only one VAT return per year is submitted instead of four, and that payments on account are made throughout the year to pay tax to HMRC based on the previous year's returns (see Chapter 7).

For a business that makes wholly or mainly zero-rated sales, there will be no payments on account (on the basis that the business will almost certainly be a repayment trader) but the problem will be that the business will not benefit from any VAT repayment until the annual return has been submitted. This causes a lengthy cash flow delay, so the annual accounting scheme is not worthwhile, unless the business owner is particularly keen to benefit from the advantage of only submitting one VAT return each year.

Voluntary registration

[22.9] As explained at **22.1**, a business making wholly (or mainly) zero-rated sales may benefit from registering for VAT on a voluntary basis. Voluntary registration is available to a business that makes taxable supplies below the compulsory VAT registration threshold.

The advantages of registering for VAT on a voluntary basis are as follows:

- the business will not suffer a competitive disadvantage on its sales because no output tax will be charged if supplies are zero-rated;
- the business will be able to reclaim input tax on costs and overheads, which will produce a reduction in its total expenditure and therefore an improvement in its overall net profit.

Registration for VAT on a voluntary basis will be particularly worthwhile for a business that has standard-rated purchases and zero-rated sales – see Example 4.

Example 4

Ruth makes children's clothes and sells them to members of the public on the Internet. Her annual sales are £50,000 and her biggest cost is the purchase of material – a total of £25,000 per year plus VAT, ie £30,000. She has learned that she may be able to register for VAT on a voluntary basis and that it could be in her interests to do so. What is the position?

Solution – Ruth is entitled to register on a voluntary basis because she is making taxable supplies. Her sales will be zero-rated as children's clothing (*VATA 1994, Sch 8, Group 16*) but she will be able to reclaim input tax of £5,000 on the purchase of material. Her net profit will therefore increase by £5,000 as a result of being VAT registered (and there may be other costs on which input tax could be claimed, eg accountancy fees, motor costs, machine repair costs, etc).

Avoiding VAT registration

[22.10] A business that makes zero-rated sales is normally very pleased to be registered for VAT because the returns it submits usually produce a repayment from HMRC (input tax exceeding output tax).

However, in a limited number of cases, the administrative cost of being VAT registered could outweigh the benefits of these repayments. In this situation, it may be worthwhile for the business to either deregister or seek permission from HMRC to avoid being VAT registered in the first place (eg if taxable sales have exceeded the registration limit for the first time, creating a need to register). HMRC needs to be convinced that the business will always be in a net repayment position as far as VAT returns are concerned.

See **1.10** for further details on this opportunity to obtain exemption from VAT registration, including a worked example of one particular business that could benefit from this opportunity.

Incorrectly charging VAT on a zero-rated supply

[22.11] There may be occasions when a business has charged VAT on goods or services supplied to a customer, and then belatedly discovered that the item in question should have been zero-rated. This situation can be particularly common for some of the more complex groups. For example, the liability of children's clothing (*Group 16*) is based on garment measurements and how items are held out for sale, and *Group 1* (food) can also include some interesting rulings on products that may qualify for zero-rating.

A taxpayer who discovers he has incorrectly charged VAT on a zero-rated item should bear the following points in mind.

- It needs to be considered who has paid the incorrect VAT that has been charged. In many cases, this will be the customer, namely when VAT has been added to a cost price. The rule of 'unjust enrichment' states that no taxpayer can make a financial gain from making a VAT error – the correct procedure in most cases will be to refund the incorrectly charged VAT to customers who have paid the tax. The procedures for unjust enrichment are considered in depth in Chapter 20.
- Note that any adjustment for overcharged VAT can only be made by going back four years – any tax beyond this period is out of date.

Reduced-rated supplies subject to 5% VAT

[22.12] A development in the VAT world over the last ten years has been the extended use of the reduced rate of VAT.

The attraction of the 5% VAT rate is that it ensures the Treasury collects some tax on relevant supplies (as opposed to the complete loss of tax evident with zero-rating) – but obviously produces a healthy saving for the taxpayer compared to 20%.

A list of items subject to 5% VAT is contained in *VATA 1994, Sch 7A (Groups 1–13)* – the groups are shown below, along with the relevant HMRC Notices that give more detail on each category:

Group 1	Supplies of domestic fuel or power (701/19)
Group 2	Installation of energy saving materials (708/6) – but see note below regarding changes
Group 3	Grant-funded installation of heating equipment or security goods or connection of gas supply (708/6)
Group 4	Women's sanitary products (701/18) (although note that with effect from Royal Assent of the Finance Act 2016 such products will be removed from the reduced rate schedule and will become zero-rated)
Group 5	Children's car seats (701/23)
Group 6	Residential conversions (708)
Group 7	Residential renovations and alterations (708)
Group 8	Contraceptive products (701/57)
Group 9	Welfare advice or information (701/2)
Group 10	Installation of mobility aids for the elderly

Group 11	Smoking cessation products – see **22.13**
Group 12	Applies, from 6 April 2013, to static caravans and large touring caravans (longer than 7 metres) but which do not meet British Standard BS 3632 (701/20)
Group 13	Applies to the transport of passengers by small cable-suspended systems after 31 March 2013

Note – the most common supplies that advisers will encounter on a regular basis are probably relevant to building works (construction services). See **26.14** for further detail about services that can benefit from the 5% rate of VAT.

The reduced rate for energy saving materials installed in buildings used exclusively for charitable purposes has been withdrawn with effect from 1 August 2013.

Following a decision by the CJEU released on 4 June 2015 it is likely that the reduced rate for the supply and installation of energy saving materials in residential accommodation will be withdrawn, except where the supply and installation relates to social housing.

Smoking cessation products

[22.13] The 5% rate applies to supplies of pharmaceutical products designed to help people to stop smoking tobacco. However, smoking cessation products dispensed by a pharmacist on prescription by a medical practitioner are zero-rated and unaffected by the 5% rules. The 5% rate applies to all other supplies of smoking cessation products by retailers including supplies made over the internet. Examples of products included are:

- patches (eg nicotine patches);
- inhalators;
- gums.

However, the rate applies to any product where the primary purpose is to help people in their efforts to stop smoking.

Planning points to consider

[22.14] The following planning points should be given consideration.

- A business making wholly or mainly zero-rated supplies will almost certainly benefit from registering for VAT on a voluntary basis if its taxable turnover is less than the compulsory registration limits.
- If a business makes both standard-rated and zero-rated sales, it is imperative that systems and procedures are in place to correctly record the correct amount of output tax to declare.
- VAT incorrectly charged to a customer on a zero-rated item will produce reduced profits for the customer if it makes some exempt supplies or if it is not VAT registered. A review of possible items of expenditure where a supplier has incorrectly charged VAT (eg in relation to printed matter) could be worthwhile.

- It is unlikely that a business making zero-rated sales will benefit from using the cash accounting scheme or annual accounting scheme. However, there may be occasions when the flat rate scheme could be worthwhile if the percentage of zero-rated sales for a business is quite low.

- If VAT has been incorrectly charged on a zero-rated supply, then the issue of unjust enrichment needs to be fully considered before trying to obtain a VAT windfall from HMRC. No business is able to make a financial gain from making VAT errors.

- There is scope for a business that makes wholly or mainly zero-rated sales (net repayment situation) to avoid being VAT registered or to deregister, even if it is making sales that exceed the VAT registration limits.

Chapter 23

Mixed Supplies at Different Rates of VAT

Key topics in this chapter:

- The rules to consider when determining whether a single or multiple supply situation exists for VAT – and guidelines given by the European Court on this issue.
- Examples of single and multiple supply situations.
- Examples of case law to highlight the principles of single and mixed supply situations.
- Methods of apportioning income in mixed supply situations using one of two methods approved by HMRC (cost based or revenue-based calculations).
- The HMRC approach to apportionment situations – ensuring the taxpayer's calculations give a fair and reasonable result.

Introduction

[23.1] One of the more controversial subjects involving VAT has been the interpretation of the rules when a business sells two or more different items within one supply (goods or services), and these individual items attract different rates of VAT. In such situations, the suggested approach is as follows:

- the question to resolve is whether each of the individual supplies constitutes an aim in its own right – if it does, there is more than one supply;
- if one of the supplies is regarded as being insignificant or incidental to the main supply, then it can be ignored for VAT purposes – the liability will then be determined by the rate of tax applicable to the main supply (or supplies).

I often quote, as an example of the difficulties surrounding the concept of mixed versus single supplies, the typical visit to a restaurant. On arrival one is usually shown to a table by a waiter (a service), one is then offered drinks (a service), one is then provided with those drinks (goods). The waiter then takes your food order (service), the chef prepares the food (service) and the waiter delivers it to your table (service). I could go on . . . . Nobody would suggest that what is being provided by the restaurant is anything but a single supply of catering; to split any or all of these services would clearly be artificial.

In this chapter, we will consider the best approach to adopt as far as dealing with mixed supplies is concerned, looking at some useful examples where tribunals have had the difficult job of mediating in cases which are less obvious to determine.

Key principles of mixed supply situations

[23.2] The case involving *Card Protection Plan Ltd v Customs and Excise Comrs: C-349/96* [1999] 2 AC 601, [1999] STC 270, ECJ, found its way to the European Court of Justice in 1999, and is regarded as the landmark ruling on this subject, because the court gave clear guidance on whether a transaction was a single or mixed supply. HMRC considers that the tests laid down in this case will be appropriate in the majority of situations.

The following rules emerged from the *Card Protection Plan* ECJ decision. However, the background to the case and the verdict that was reached is not really of importance, it is the guidance given by the court that is of most relevance.

- Where a transaction comprises a bundle of features, the question to ask is whether each supply constitutes an aim in itself, or whether there is one main supply, with the other supplies being incidental to that main supply.

- It needs to be considered whether the aim of the secondary supply (or supplies) is to enhance the enjoyment of the main supply. For example, a customer could pay to hire a box at a football club for a big match (standard-rated supply) and then receive a match day programme as part of the facility (zero-rated). The match day programme is not an aim in itself, but a way of helping the customer to enhance his enjoyment of the main supply, which is the game.

- If there is only one main supply, this will determine the VAT liability of the entire supply to the customer. So if the main supply is zero-rated, the entire charge to the customer will also be zero-rated – if the main supply is standard rated, then VAT will be due on the whole payment.

- The perception of the customer should also be taken into account about what he expects to receive when he makes payment for goods or services. This conclusion was very important in the case of *Revenue and Customs Comrs v Weight Watchers (UK) Ltd* [2008] EWCA Civ 715, [2008] STC 2313, heard by the Court of Appeal – see **23.11**. For example, in the previous situation, if the match day programme was not provided, then this would not have created a situation where the customer would have complained to the club about not receiving something he had paid for. In reality, he paid to watch the game, ie this is clearly the main supply.

To illustrate the points above, consider Examples 1 and 2.

Example 1

John takes a flight from London to Edinburgh (supply of zero-rated air travel). During the journey, he receives a cup of tea and a biscuit (supply of standard rated catering). Does the money paid by John for his ticket need to be apportioned so that output tax is paid on the value of the tea and biscuit – the balance being zero-rated as air travel?

Solution – in this case, the purpose of John's expenditure is to benefit from the air travel. The cup of tea and biscuit serves no other purpose than to make the flying experience more comfortable for him, ie it is incidental to the main supply. The whole of the payment made by John is zero-rated. Again, would John have cancelled his flight to Edinburgh if the tea and biscuit had not been available? Would the absence of the tea and biscuit cause him to write a strong letter of complaint to the air company and request part of his money back? The answer is almost certainly 'no'.

Example 2

John and Jean have booked a day trip on the Orient Express. As well as the comfortable rail journey, their trip also includes a sumptuous five-course meal with wine and champagne. The rail journey is zero-rated – catering supplies are standard rated. Is there a single or multiple supply in this example?

Solution – imagine the likely response of John and Jean if they boarded the train and were told that the five-course meal was not available and they were only going to benefit from the train journey. They would almost certainly complain to the rail company and demand a refund of part of their fee. In other words, they expect to receive two very distinct benefits – the rail journey and the meal.

The five-course meal is an aim in itself, and cannot be dismissed as incidental to the rail travel. The rail company must account for output tax on the value of the catering supply – the rail travel can be zero-rated. See **23.17–23.21** for methods of apportioning output tax.

The key point to remember about mixed supply situations is that they only become a problem if the goods or services within the supply attract different rates of VAT. See Example 3.

Example 3

Steve has decided to go and watch a football match at the ground of Hale Town. Hale Town is VAT registered and charges Steve £12 for admission and, as a special offer just for today's match, his admission fee includes two hamburgers and a portion of chips.

Solution – in this situation, the supplies involved (admission fee to watch a football match and supply of catering when inside the ground) are both standard rated. No VAT problem here – output tax of £2 is due on the full price (£12 × 1/6 – assuming a VAT rate of 20%).

Tribunal decisions in borderline cases

[23.3] The examples given above were clear as far as the mixed supply situation is concerned. However, there have been many tribunal cases on this subject over the years and a few have been included in this section to give readers an indication of the approach to adopt when reviewing similar situations.

Multiple supply decisions

Medical Aviation Services Ltd

[23.4] In the case of *Medical Aviation Services Ltd v Customs and Excise Comrs* (30 September 1997, unreported) (LON/97/016 15308), the question concerned the supply of an air ambulance (helicopter) and pilots to two Air Ambulance Trusts.

The supply of the helicopter would be zero-rated as the hire of goods (*Sch 8, Group 15, Item 5* via notes *3(b)* and 9), the hire of the pilots being standard rated.

The taxpayer argued that there was one overall supply of a transport service (ie zero-rated) whereas Customs argued that there were two distinct supplies, the transport and the pilots. The tribunal clearly ruled in favour of a mixed supply.

Cairngorm Mountain

[23.5] In the case of *Cairngorm Mountain v Customs and Excise Comrs* (20 May 2002, unreported) (EDN/01/208 17679), the customer's payment entitled him to ski passes and also the train journey to get from the bottom of the mountain to the top. The argument put forward by HMRC was that the train journey was incidental to the main supply of the ski passes, on the basis that it was a service that made the skiing experience more pleasant, ie enhancing the enjoyment of the main supply.

The tribunal concluded that the aim of the rail travel was to get a person from 'A' to 'B' as is the aim of any transport facility. On this basis, it must therefore form an aim in its own right, confirming that the arrangement was a multiple supply with zero-rated travel and standard-rated skiing facilities.

Note – this is an interesting case because the two supplies are both for services rather than goods. The apportionment of output tax will be quite an interesting calculation – see **23.17–23.21** for the different methods that could be adopted.

Single supply decisions

Sky Broadcasting Group plc

[23.6] In *British Sky Broadcasting Group plc v Customs and Excise Comrs* [1999] V & DR 283 (LON/98/889 16220), Sky provided broadcasting services to customers in return for a monthly subscription. However, as part of the deal, the customer also received a regular copy of a magazine (zero-rated as printed matter), giving the customer details about the television programmes and their times.

Sky argued that the magazine constituted an aim in itself, and therefore the subscription payment made by the customer should be apportioned for VAT purposes. HMRC argued (successfully) that the magazine was incidental to the main supply of the subscription payment and that the whole supply was, therefore, standard rated.

Note – following the *Card Protection Plan* ruling (see **23.2**), it will be very difficult in most cases involving printed matter to convince a tribunal that the printed matter is an aim in its own right. This is supported by the findings in the *Weight Watchers (UK) Ltd* case – see **23.11**. A similar decision was reached in the case of *Manchester United plc v Customs and Excise Comrs* (11 June 2001, unreported) (MAN/00/371 17234), where the tribunal concluded that a match day programme supplied as part of a hospitality package was not an aim in its own right but a means of better enjoying the main supply of hospitality.

Byrom (t/a Salon 24)

[23.7] In *Byrom (t/a Salon 24) v Revenue and Customs Comrs* [2006] EWHC 111 (Ch), [2006] STC 992, the High Court upheld a decision of the VAT tribunal that supplies by the taxpayers, who operated a massage parlour from which they let rooms to individual masseuses, were standard rated supplies of facilities for VAT purposes and not licenses to occupy land that would have been exempt from VAT.

The benefits enjoyed by the masseuses in return for their payment to the salon, included:

* provision of laundry services;
* use of a day room;
* provision of receptionist services;
* a telephone system and credit card payment facility.

The court concluded that the facilities offered by the taxpayer were all intended to assist the masseuse in running her business (ie an aim in their own right), not a means of better enjoying the room itself.

The next question concerned the hire of the room – could that be a supply in its own right and benefit from being exempt from VAT? If so, this would mean that the payment by the masseuses would need to be apportioned as a mixed supply.

The court ruled that the room was incidental to the main supply of the services provided by the parlour – therefore the whole payment to the taxpayer was standard rated.

Note – in a simple sentence, the court ruled that the taxpayer was making a 'supply of massage parlour services' not the 'rent of a room as a license to occupy land'. This interpretation can apply to similar arrangements in other situations and advisers need to look closely at the reality of a situation, not just how it is described by a taxpayer to avoid VAT being charged on his supplies.

Tumble Tots UK Ltd

[23.8] (Note – this is an interesting case because the original decision of the tribunal was that a mixed supply situation was evident – the High Court overturned this verdict and ruled that there was just a single supply).

In the case of *Tumble Tots UK Ltd v Revenue and Customs Comrs* [2007] EWHC 103 (Ch), [2007] STC 1171 the company is franchiser of a chain of play centres for children. In order to take part in a play session, the child must be a member of the National Tumble Tots Club. An annual fee is payable, and this was the subject of the appeal. In return for the annual fee, a member receives the following benefits:

• membership card;
• special yellow Tumble Tots T-shirt;
• DVD and CD of nursery songs;
• members' handbook and gym bag;
• various newsletters and booklets.

HMRC argued that there was one main supply of membership (standard rated), entitling the children to take part in activity sessions at Tumble Tot premises. All other supplies were considered to be incidental to this main supply.

Tumble Tots argued that the main supplies were the zero-rated supplies of printed material and children's clothing (T-shirt), so overall it was making a zero-rated supply.

The tribunal concluded that the membership was the main benefit, and all other supplies were incidental apart from the T-shirt that had some monetary benefit and importance to the child.

However, HMRC appealed to the High Court ([2007] EWHC 103 (Ch), [2007] SWTI 293, [2007] All ER (D) 274 (Jan)), which ruled that the aim of the payment made by the customer was to secure attendance at the classes. Other benefits such as the t-shirt were incidental to this main supply. The entire payment made by the customer was therefore standard rated.

Metropolitan International Schools

[23.9] In the case of *Metropolitan International Schools* (*MIS*), the First Tier Tribunal decided that, on the evidence before it, what MIS supplied was a single supply of printed matter (the printed course material). As a consequence of that finding, all of the supplies were liable to VAT at the zero rate.

HMRC contended before the tribunal that what was being supplied was a course of education and that as MIS was not an eligible body for VAT purposes, its supplies of such education ought to have been liable to VAT at the standard rate.

Ultimately, the First Tier Tribunal accepted that the essential supply was the sale of the course manuals. While the 'student' had access to some tutor support and guidance, MIS contended that these were ancillary to the main supply of manuals. In the vast majority of cases, students simply learnt from reading these manuals and did not request such support. When they did, they were referred back to the course manuals. In addition, the courses offered did not lead to any form of examination or qualification. Students could, if they wished, sit an exam set by third party bodies but this was not something that was provided by MIS. As such, the First Tier Tribunal distinguished the earlier House of Lords judgment in the case of the *College of Estate Management*. In *MIS*, the First Tier Tribunal concluded that the student's motive was different in that, when he entered into a contract with MIS, he was aware that MIS did not provide an examination or qualification. As such, the First Tier Tribunal concluded that 'the customer's desired end result was to educate himself entirely by studying the self-contained manuals'. In light of that conclusion, the First Tier Tribunal decided that there was a single supply of the manuals which was zero-rated. HMRC have appealed this decision to the Upper Tribunal.

Current approach

[23.10] As explained at the beginning of this chapter, the subject of VAT and mixed supplies has kept the courts busy in recent years.

A landmark case was *Revenue and Customs Comrs v Weight Watchers (UK) Ltd* [2008] EWCA Civ 715, [2008] STC 2313, a case that was heard by three different courts culminating in a judgment from the Court of Appeal – see **23.11**.

The main conclusion from the judgment was to emphasise the importance of looking at a supply from the point of view of the customer rather than the supplier. What does the customer expect to receive for his money? What would his reaction be if he did not receive a specific benefit? Example 2 earlier in this chapter considered this process – how would John and Jean have reacted if the sumptuous five-course meal they were expecting had been absent from their trip on the Orient Express?

Weight Watchers (UK) Ltd

[23.11] The case of *Revenue and Customs Comrs v Weight Watchers (UK) Ltd* [2008] EWCA Civ 715, [2008] STC 2313 was finally concluded in the Court of Appeal. It concerned the VAT liability of payments made by customers to attend weight loss meetings. The following questions were considered:

- did the payments made by the customers wholly relate to the standard rated attendance at weight loss programme meetings? or

- did some of the payments relate to the zero-rated supply of printed matter – booklets provided to the customers to assist with their weight-loss efforts?

The Court of Appeal effectively overturned the thinking of both the VAT tribunal and High Court by ruling that there was, in fact, a single supply of standard-rated weight loss services. The lower courts had concluded that there was some zero-rated element of printed matter supplied to the customer.

The Court of Appeal concluded that the handbook given to new members when they first enrolled on a weight loss course, plus the subsequent monthly newsletters and leaflets, were all supplies that were incidental to the main supply of the standard-rated course. In effect, this conclusion supports the findings of the other cases involving printed matter mentioned in this chapter. The aim of printed matter is usually to enhance the enjoyment of another supply, ie it rarely forms an aim in its own right.

Other cases

David Baxendale Ltd

VAT treatment of a weight loss programme

[23.12] The High Court delivered a ruling in this case that was consistent with the *Weight Watchers (UK) Ltd* case considered at 23.11: *Revenue and Customs Comrs v David Baxendale Ltd* [2009] EWHC 162 (Ch), [2009] STC 825.

The court held that the provision of a weight loss programme through replacement food packages supported by counselling and advice was a single composite supply of services which was standard-rated for VAT purposes. The zero-rated supply of food was incidental to the main supply of the weight loss programme.

The court ruled that it would be artificial to split the different elements of the supply and this meant it was therefore necessary to consider whether the consumer considered that he was paying for zero-rated food or standard-rated services. The main character of the supply was of services, ie standard-rated.

Note – this case has again emphasised the importance of looking at a supply from the point of view of the customer rather than the supplier. It is also interesting that this is another case where two courts have reached different conclusions, as the VAT tribunal had acknowledged an element of zero-rating, ie a mixed supply.

Colaingrove Limited (Verandahs) (TC02746)

VAT treatment of sale of verandas with static caravans

[23.13] Colaingrove Limited (Colaingrove) operates holiday parks and re-sorts in the UK. As part of its business it sells static caravans (sometimes known as residential caravans) as holiday homes. The static caravans are zero-rated by virtue of *VATA 1994, Sch 8, Group 9*. The issue for the First Tier Tribunal and the Upper Tribunal was whether zero-rating extended to a veranda when sold with a static caravan ((TC02746) [2013] UKFTT 343 (TC); revsd [2015] UKUT 0002 (TCC)).

The First Tier Tribunal decided that a veranda was not zero-rated when sold with a static caravan but Colaingrove appealed that decision to the Upper Tribunal.

Both HMRC and Colaingrove agreed that if the principles that had their genesis in the judgment of the ECJ in *Card Protection Plan Ltd v Customs and Excise Comrs* (C-349/96) [1999] STC 270 *(CPP)* applied the sale of a caravan with a veranda would be a single supply. The nature of such a single supply would be one comprising a principal element of a caravan and an ancillary element of a veranda. The VAT treatment of the single supply would be that of the principal element, the caravan, and so the single supply would, as a whole, (the caravan and the verandah) be zero-rated.

The principal question for the Upper Tribunal was whether, in the circumstances of the case, the *CPP* principles applied, and if so how they applied. The *CPP* principles are aimed at determining from the essential features of a transaction whether the nature of what is supplied to the typical consumer is several distinct supplies or a single supply which should not be split.

The scope of the effect of the *CPP* principles had to be addressed by the ECJ in the context of *VATA 1994, Sch 8, Group 9* in the case of *Talacre Beach Caravan Sales Ltd v Customs and Excise Comrs* (C-251/05) [2006] STC 1671 *(Talacre)*. The *Talacre* case concerned the VAT treatment of items of removable contents which are specifically excluded from the scope of zero-rating by virtue of *Note (a)* to *VATA 1994, Sch 8, Group 9*. The ECJ decided that the *CPP* principles did not prevent VAT at the standard rate applying to items which the legislation had excluded from the scope of a different VAT treatment.

The Upper Tribunal in *Colaingrove*, considered that the First Tier Tribunal had erred in relation to the effect of *Talacre*. The Upper Tribunal decided that the *CPP* principles should be applied, subject to there being no relevant exclusion or limitation in the zero-rating provisions of *VATA 1994, Sch 8, Group 9*.

Note (a) to *VATA 1994, Sch 8, Group 9* specifically refers to removable contents but does not refer to a veranda. The Upper Tribunal noted that there was nothing in *VATA 1994, Sch 8, Group 9* to exclude a veranda from the scope of zero-rating by reason of being part of a single supply of which the principal supply is a caravan. There being no relevant exclusion or limitation in the zero-rating provisions of *VATA 1994, Sch 8, Group 9*, the Upper Tribunal decided that the effect of the *CPP* principles is that zero-rating applies to the whole of a single supply of a caravan and a veranda.

The Upper Tribunal allowed the appeal. In essence, what the Upper Tribunal concluded was that the customer had still purchased a caravan albeit with the added luxury of a verandah.

Colaingrove Limited (TC02534)

VAT treatment of charges for electricity based on length of holiday

[23.14] Colaingrove Limited (Colaingrove) operates holiday parks and resorts in the UK. The case ((TC02534) [2013] UKFTT 116 (TC); revsd [2015] UKUT 0080 (TCC)) related to the VAT treatment of charges for electricity supplied to static caravans and chalets in circumstances where a compulsory charge was made based on the length of the holiday rather than the amount of electricity used. The holidays were advertised in a newspaper and the charge for the accommodation was collected by the newspaper and remitted, less a commission, to Colaingrove. The charge for the electricity was collected separately by Colaingrove from the customer at the time the customer made the reservation.

VATA 1994, Sch 7A, Group 1 provides for the reduced rate of VAT to apply to supplies of domestic fuel or power and *Note 6* to the legislation confirms that domestic use includes use in self-catering holiday accommodation and caravans.

HMRC accepted that the reduced rate of VAT applied in circumstances where separate metered charges were made but did not accept that the reduced rate applied in circumstances where a fixed compulsory charge was made based on the length of the holiday. Colaingrove appealed to the First Tier Tribunal, which decided in the company's favour. HMRC did not accept the First Tier Tribunal's decision and appealed to the Upper Tribunal, which decided in HMRC's favour.

The Upper Tribunal again applied the principles that had their genesis in the judgment of the ECJ in *Card Protection Plan Ltd v Customs and Excise Comrs* (C-349/96) [1999] STC 270 (*CPP*) and concluded that there was a single standard rated supply of serviced accommodation.

Leisure trusts providing all-inclusive membership schemes

[23.15] Following the *Weight Watchers (UK) Ltd* case, HMRC sensibly issued Revenue & Customs Brief 13/09, which finally settles the VAT liability of membership schemes supplied by leisure trusts (the latter are charitable organisations so their services qualify for a range of VAT exemptions).

HMRC's previous stance was that if one benefit of a membership scheme was standard rated (eg the right to use a sauna) then the whole of the membership payment received from the customer would be standard rated, even if the majority of facilities were exempt from VAT if supplied in their own right (participation in sport provided by an eligible body).

The Brief confirms that in cases where the customer's main motive for purchasing an all-inclusive membership package is to use the range of available sports facilities, the single supply is exempt. It is irrelevant if a small proportion of the benefits would be standard rated if sold in their own right (eg sauna use) – it is the overall package that counts. This policy will hopefully end the situation where some trusts were providing free saunas or closing saunas completely because of the VAT problem – common sense has won the day.

Strategy for advisers

[23.16] So what is the key message for practitioners?

It is very difficult in the current climate to obtain an official ruling from HMRC on a mixed supply situation. The written enquiry teams are reluctant to give a ruling on any subject unless it is felt that HMRC's own published guidance is unclear about the matter. However, there are plenty of court cases to refer to about mixed supply situations – the challenge is often to remember the conclusion reached by the final appeal court when decisions have fluctuated.

The following are four key questions to consider in each case. The answers to these questions should give a strong indication about whether a single or multiple supply is evident.

* What does the customer perceive he is paying for – one main supply or a combination of two or more supplies?
* How are supplies advertised or marketed – do adverts promote one main benefit or a range of benefits, each of which will be of interest to the customer?
* What is the contractual position between the buyer and seller – is the seller obliged to provide a range of different services to the customer, eg to supply both rail travel and catering as in Example 2 considered at 23.2?
* What are the monetary values of the supplies in question? Although not totally conclusive, if a supply only forms a small element of the overall cost of the product, then it can usually be ignored as incidental to the main supply. For example, a cheap standard-rated pen supplied with an expensive zero-rated book could be ignored on the basis of cost.

Apportionment of output tax in cases of mixed supplies

[23.17] Having decided that a supply comprises two or more elements that attract different rates of VAT, the next challenge is to apportion the customer's payment to account for output tax on the standard rated element. Obviously, if both elements of the supply attract VAT at the same rate, then there is no problem.

The HMRC rule in such cases is that the business must allocate a fair proportion of the total payment to each of the supplies. There is no prescribed method of carrying out this apportionment – but the emphasis is on fairness and achieving a reasonable result.

In practice, there are two main methods of apportioning output tax – one based on the cost of the supplies, and the other on normal selling prices.

(HMRC Notice 700, para 8.1).

Apportionment of output tax using cost based method

[23.18] The basic principle of apportioning output tax using a cost-based method is to calculate the total cost of the standard-rated supply compared to total cost, and apply this percentage to the total selling price for output tax purposes. See Example 4.

Example 4

Item A sells for a VAT-inclusive price of £200 and includes a standard-rated element and a zero-rated element. It has been confirmed that each of the supplies represents an aim in itself – rather than one of the supplies being ancillary to the main supply.

The cost to the seller of the two elements of the supply is:

Standard-rated element	£80 (excluding VAT)
Zero-rated element	£40

How much output tax is due?

Solution – the key point to remember for this example is that the proportion of standard rated costs compared to total costs needs to include VAT – this is because the £200 selling price is also VAT inclusive (the figures that follow are based on a standard rate of VAT of 20%):

VAT-inclusive cost of the standard-rated element	£96.00 (ie £80 plus VAT at 20%)
VAT-inclusive cost of zero-rated element	£40.00 (ie £40 plus VAT at 0%)
Total VAT-inclusive cost	£136.00
Proportion of selling price that relates to the standard-rated element	£141.18 (ie £200 × £96/£136)
Output tax due	£23.53 (ie £141.18 × 1/6)

Note – 1/6 is the VAT fraction that applies with a VAT rate of 20%, ie to calculate the VAT element within an inclusive price.

In effect, the total selling price of £200 can be split as follows:

Standard rated goods	£117.65
Zero-rated goods	£58.82
VAT	£23.53

In Example 4, the apportionment was easy to carry out because it was possible to calculate the costs of both elements of the supply. As long as all costs were calculated correctly (with no major exclusions from the standard-rated costs) then the method is unlikely to deviate from the fair and reasonable test.

However, problems can occur if it is only possible to calculate the cost of one element of a supply, for example, where standard-rated goods are supplied with zero-rated services (or vice versa).

In such cases, HMRC has approved a calculation method as follows:

* calculate the total costs of the supply that can be worked out;
* apply a mark-up to this cost figure to give a selling price;
* the balance of the selling price will then be for the goods/services supplied at the different rate of VAT.

Another acceptable calculation for mixed supply situations where only one element can be costed is for a mark-up to be applied that relates to the mark up achieved for the overall business.

The onus is on HMRC to disprove the method of apportionment used by a business, and by and large, it will accept calculations given to it as long as a fair and reasonable approach has been taken.

For example, if a 200% mark-up is applied to costs relevant to a zero-rated item, but the overall business is only achieving a 50% mark-up, then the business would have to justify why it felt a 200% mark-up was reasonable (obviously the high mark-up applied greatly reduces the output tax due on the item in question). The high mark-up could clearly be a deviation from the fair and reasonable approach. HMRC would be justified in challenging the accuracy of the 200% mark-up figure being adopted.

A useful indicator concerning the accuracy of the applied mark-up could be to look at the profit margins being achieved by similar products within the company. Again, the business may be trading in goods where there are generally accepted mark-ups and profit margins, although individual variations will have to be taken into account.

Apportionment based upon normal selling prices

[23.19] This method of apportionment considers the prices charged by the business for separate supplies of the item in question, and uses these amounts to make a sensible apportionment. See Example 5.

Example 5

Item B includes a standard and zero-rated item, sold jointly for £10. The standard-rated item is sold on its own for £5 including VAT, and the zero-rated item is sold for £7.

Solution – in this situation, the standard rated element would be 5/12, giving an output tax liability of: £0.69 (ie £10 × 5/12 × 1/6 based on a standard rate of VAT rate of 20%).

Retrospective apportionment

[23.20] A frequently asked question is whether it is possible to go back to earlier VAT periods, and adjust calculations that have already been made.

In reality, the answer to this question depends on the circumstances of the proposed amendment and the approach taken by HMRC once the changes are analysed. Without being too controversial, it is fair to say that most requests for retrospective adjustment are intended to reduce output tax previously paid – rather than to increase it.

One situation where a business could clearly go back four years (error adjustment period since 1 April 2010) and recalculate its output tax liability is if an error was discovered in relation to the specific method being used. For example, it might be discovered that a key cost component has been omitted from the zero-rated item, which would create an output tax overpayment on any method of calculation linked to cost.

Again, it is possible that a business has made an item wholly standard rated in the past, unaware that part of it is eligible for zero-rating under the mixed supply rules. Again, there would be no problem doing an historic adjustment. However, all adjustments must fully consider the issue of unjust enrichment and whether the taxpayer or his customer is entitled to any VAT repayment (see **20.8**).

The situation where it would be more difficult to make a retrospective adjustment would be if a business has correctly applied one of the methods in the past (and paid the correct output tax each quarter) but has now discovered that an alternative method would give a better result in terms of paying less output tax. There is no doubt that HMRC would view any request to backdate a calculation using a different method with suspicion – it would be up to the business to clearly justify why the outcome of the previous method was unfair.

HMRC approach to fairness

[23.21] There may be occasions where a business has correctly carried out an apportionment calculation for many years, but HMRC then decide on a VAT visit that it is unfair, ie the output tax paid is too low. In such circumstances, HMRC should adopt the sensible approach of seeking to change methods from a current date, rather than assessing any underpaid output tax on a retrospective basis. This conclusion assumes that the taxpayer has adopted one of the approved methods highlighted in this chapter. As with most aspects of VAT, the taxpayer would generally have a right of appeal if he disagreed with the ruling made by the officer.

The other situation that might apply on a VAT visit is where errors in the method of calculation are discovered by the officer – in such cases, an assessment would be raised to correct the errors, going back a maximum of four years (error adjustment period since 1 April 2010). Examples of errors could be where incorrect selling prices are used if the method is based on sales values; there could be errors of calculation between the VAT exclusive/inclusive figures; for cost apportionment methods, key components of the cost price could have either been omitted or incorrectly calculated.

Planning points to consider

[23.22] The following planning points should be given consideration.

- When assessing whether a single or multiple supply situation exists, it is necessary to consider whether each supply constitutes an aim in itself, or whether it is incidental to the main supply.
- Remember that an analysis of mixed supply situations is only relevant if goods or services within the supply attract VAT at different rates.
- Be aware of the two different methods of apportionment in mixed supply situations (ie cost-based and revenue-based calculations) and identify if one of the methods gives a fairer result.
- Any errors of principle in apportioning output tax on mixed supplies can be adjusted by going back four years and correcting the error. If the amount of tax involved is less than £10,000 (or 1% of the Box 6 figure on the relevant VAT return up to a maximum of £50,000), this can be done by adjusting the next VAT return, otherwise, a separate disclosure must be made to HMRC.
- It is unlikely to be acceptable for a taxpayer to readjust his method of output tax apportionment on a historic basis, unless the method adopted was totally unfair. HMRC will be rightly suspicious about recalculations that are made just to try and get a better result in terms of output tax paid in the past.
- Some of the court cases considered in this chapter have emphasised the importance of looking at mixed supply situations from the perspective of the customer rather than the supplier. In other words, whether the customer considers that he is only paying for one main benefit (single supply outcome) or a range of benefits subject to different rates of VAT (multiple supply).
- The whole topic of mixed versus single supplies is fraught with difficulty; suffice to say that, in any situation where there is doubt, a business or its advisors should attempt to obtain a clear ruling from HMRC.

Chapter 24

Partial Exemption – Introduction

Key topics in this chapter:

- The allocation of expenditure between taxable, exempt and residual input tax and the importance of adopting an assertive approach to the allocation process – recent case study examples.
- Calculating the amount of residual input tax that can be reclaimed using the standard method of calculation.
- The need to make an annual adjustment for all partial exemption calculations and declare tax on the relevant VAT return.
- The *de minimis* rules – a business that is *de minimis* for partial exemption purposes can reclaim all of its input tax in a tax year.
- Simplification measures available for standard method users.
- The standard method override provisions.
- Partial exemption issues concerning foreign income, specified and incidental supplies.
- The 'clawback' and 'payback' provisions which deal with a situation where the actual use of an item is different to the intended use when expenditure was first incurred.
- An important point for house builders who temporarily rent out properties they cannot sell.

Introduction

[24.1] Partial exemption is one of the most complicated aspects of VAT, and becomes relevant to a business that makes some supplies that are taxable and some that are exempt. It should be remembered that taxable supplies include zero-rated and reduced rated goods or services – not just those that are standard rated.

In basic terms, three common situations will be evident as far as supplies made by a business are concerned:

(a)   *Taxable supplies only* – a business that wholly makes taxable supplies is able to recover all of its input tax, subject to normal rules. If most or all of these supplies are zero-rated, then this is likely to mean that the business will be a repayment trader for VAT purposes.

(b)   *Exempt supplies only* – a business that only makes exempt supplies will not be able to register for VAT – because it is not making taxable supplies. In effect, this means that it has the advantage of not having to charge output tax on its income, but the disadvantage that it will not be able to reclaim input tax on expenditure that it incurs. The VAT element of any expense will therefore form part of the cost of the item.

(c)   *Taxable and exempt supplies* – a business that makes both taxable and exempt supplies is able to benefit from input tax recovery to the extent that the input tax relates to taxable supplies. This is where the subject of partial exemption becomes relevant. Any input tax that relates to exempt supplies is known as exempt input tax, and cannot be reclaimed for VAT purposes.

Note – the expression 'subject to normal rules' is an expression which is often used by advisors and HMRC officers alike. It basically means that, in principle, the input tax is claimable provided that the taxpayer adheres to basic rules such as: having the appropriate invoice, the expenditure being for business purposes and the input VAT not being subject to a specific legal 'block' such as VAT incurred on the purchase of a motor car where the car is made available for private use.

There are two ways of apportioning input tax for a partly exempt business:

- standard method of calculation – which is adopted by most partly exempt businesses and is considered in this chapter.
  Note – see **24.21** for details of simplification measures that may help a business that uses the standard method.
- special method of calculation – a taxpayer can make a request to HMRC to adopt a special method, usually when it feels that the standard method does not give a fair and reasonable result as far as input tax recovery is concerned. Special methods are considered in Chapter 25.

(HMRC Notice 706, para 3.9).

Input tax apportionment

[24.2] In basic terms, a business that is partly exempt needs to analyse its purchases into three categories:

(a)   invoices that relate wholly to exempt supplies made by the business;
(b)   invoices that relate wholly to taxable supplies made by the business;
(c)   invoices that cannot be attributed to either activity, for example, head office expenses, overhead items, computer expenditure etc.

There are three key phrases that emerge following the above analysis.

- *Exempt input tax* – input tax attributable to exempt supplies. In most cases, this input tax will not be claimable by a business, unless the business qualifies as being *de minimis*, in which case it can recover all of its input tax in the normal way (see **24.10**).
- *Taxable input tax* – input tax attributable to taxable supplies, and wholly reclaimable, subject to normal rules.
- *Residual input tax* (sometimes known as non-attributable input tax or the 'pot') – input tax that is not wholly relevant to taxable or exempt supplies, eg general overhead items.

(HMRC Notice 706, para 2.3).

See Example 1 for an illustration of the principles of input tax allocation.

Example 1

Verity Ltd trades as an estate agent in the local High Street. It makes some taxable supplies (sale of houses on a commission basis) and some exempt supplies (sale of financial products such as mortgages on a commission or fee basis).

For the VAT quarter to 30 June, it makes the following payments:

- an advert in the local newspaper for £1,000 plus VAT to advertise its mortgage based products;
- the vehicle exclusively used by one of the property negotiators has a major service costing £700 plus VAT;
- the pool car used by the company and available to all employees also has a service costing £800 plus VAT;
- the office telephone bill is paid for £3,000 plus VAT;
- the auditors are paid for completing the annual audit, a fee of £2,000 plus VAT.

What is the input tax position on each of these expenses?

Solution – the input tax would follow the above analysis and so the advert in the local newspaper is deemed to be exempt input tax because it relates wholly to the exempt activity of the company – an amount of £200 cannot be reclaimed (assuming a VAT rate of 20%). However, good news for the service to the first vehicle – the property negotiator's work is wholly linked to the taxable activity of the business, so this input tax can be reclaimed in full.

The final three expenses in this example cannot be directly attributed to either the taxable or exempt activities of the business, so the input tax will be only partly reclaimed as residual input tax. See **24.3** to see how this partial claim is made using the standard method.

Standard method calculations

[24.3] In reality, most of the problems caused by partial exemption concern the attribution of input tax (ie which category the VAT should be attributed to) and the proportion of 'residual input tax' that can be claimed. It is a question of fact whether an item of expenditure is exclusively attributable to activity category or whether it is not attributable at all (or is attributable to both categories) and is thus an overhead. Businesses need to take care with such attribution as miscategorised input tax can lead to either underclaims of input tax or overclaims. Neither is desirable.

A business must calculate the amount of residual input tax to be reclaimed using the standard method (no permission required by HMRC) unless it makes a request to adopt a special method of calculation – see **CHAPTER 25**.

(HMRC Notice 706, paras 3.4 and 3.5).

The standard method means that residual input tax is reclaimed using the following formula:

$$\text{Reclaimable } \% = \frac{\text{Value of taxable supplies in the period (excluding VAT)}}{\text{Value of all supplies in the period (excluding VAT)}}$$

(HMRC Notice 706, para 4.3).

Some important points to remember:

- The denominator (bottom) part of the fraction includes 'all supplies'. Don't forget that income sources where no supply has taken place will be ignored, eg donations and most grant income for a charity. However, income received from services supplied to overseas customers where no VAT is charged due to the place of supply rules is included since 1 April 2009.
- The percentage calculation is always rounded up to the next whole number, eg 43.1% calculation means that 44% residual input tax can be recovered. The exception is when the amount of residual input tax to which the calculation is applied exceeds £400,000 per month on average. In such cases, the reclaimable percentage needs to be rounded up to two decimal places, eg 43.656% means 43.66% input tax is reclaimed (HMRC Notice 706, para 4.7).
- The above calculation is carried out at the end of each VAT period, however, monthly or quarterly calculations are always made on a provisional basis, and an annual adjustment must be made at the end of each tax year – see **24.9**.
- The tax year ends on 31 March, 30 April or 31 May, depending on when the VAT periods end for the business in question; the tax year ends on 31 March for a business that submits monthly VAT returns (HMRC Notice 706, para 12.2).
- Any sum receivable for capital goods must be excluded from the calculation, eg sales of fixed assets (HMRC Notice 706, para 4.8).
- Any supplies which are 'incidental' to the business can also be ignored. The main situation when this would tend to apply is relevant to bank interest income, which is not an activity in its own right but income that is dependent on the bank balance held by the business (HMRC Notice 706, para 4.8).
- The value of any supply made by the business which is neither taxable nor exempt should also be excluded, eg proceeds from the transfer of a going concern payment which is outside the scope of VAT (HMRC Notice 706, para 4.8).
- The value of certain imported services subject to the reverse charge (under the place of supply rules) should also be excluded.
- Remember that the formula above works on VAT exclusive figures, not inclusive figures.
- If a business uses the cash accounting scheme, then the standard method calculations for taxable and total supplies will also be based on payments received during the period, ie rather than the earlier invoice date.

- The Court of Justice of the European Union ruled in 2013 that income generated by overseas branches of a company should not be included in the partial exemption calculation. Le Credit Lyonnais argued that although the income was generated by overseas branches, nevertheless, as the branch was not a separate legal entity, but was part of the single taxable person, the overseas income should be included in both the numerator and the denominator (*Le Credit Lyonnais v Ministre du Budget, des Comptes publics et de la Reforme de l'Etat: Case C-388/11* [2014] STC 245).

See Example 2 for an illustration of the principles of the standard method of calculation.

Example 2

Following on from Example 1, our estate agent company is about to complete its VAT return for the quarter to 30 June and it has summarised the key figures as follows:

Standard rated sales for quarter excluding VAT	£80,000
Exempt sales for quarter	£20,000
Taxable input tax (input tax wholly relevant to taxable supplies)	£7,000
Exempt input tax (input tax wholly relevant to exempt supplies)	£2,000
Residual input tax (non-attributable)	£3,500

How much VAT will the company pay on this particular return?

Solution – output tax is simple: £80,000 × 20% = £16,000.

With regard to input tax, the total amount reclaimed will be £9,800 as follows:

Taxable input tax – reclaim in full £7,000.

Residual input tax – claim 80% based on percentage of taxable supplies compared to total supplies, ie £2,800 (£80,000 ÷ £100,000 × £3,500).

Net VAT payment for period = £6,200, ie £16,000 less £9,800.

Note – if the company is using the cash accounting scheme then all relevant figures for sales and purchases will be based on payments made and received, not invoices raised or received.

In Example 2, the company had a high percentage of input tax recovery on its residual input tax. This was because the income for this particular business was mainly taxable rather than exempt. This is one of the key outcomes of partial exemption calculations – a business with higher taxable income as a proportion of its total income gets a better rate of residual input tax recovery than a business which has mainly exempt supplies.

Potential problems with allocation of input tax

[24.4] One of the key skills for an accountant dealing with a partly exempt business is to be very clear about the correct way of allocating purchase invoices to one of the three categories of input tax, ie taxable, exempt or residual.

In most cases, the allocation process is straightforward – but in a commercial situation, there can be certain expenses that need to be very closely analysed. For example, if a business has 80% exempt income, then the decision to post a purchase invoice to residual input tax rather than taxable input tax will cost the company £800 if the total VAT on the invoice is £1,000.

See Example 3 for some interesting allocations.

Example 3

Nortons Golf Club is a partly exempt business (non-profit making golf club with exempt income from playing subscriptions and taxable income from a bar and restaurant). It has a clubhouse where the ground floor is allocated to changing room facilities for the players, and the first floor is allocated to a purpose built bar and restaurant. The club has two sources of income – membership subscriptions paid by cheque or direct debit, and bar or restaurant sales paid by cheque, cash or credit/debit card.

It incurs the following expenses in the period to 30 June:

- the disabled lift that takes customers from the ground floor to the first floor bar area has been serviced at a cost of £2,000 plus VAT;
- the club has just bought a safe in the office to store cash at a cost of £1,000 plus VAT.

The purpose of the disabled lift is to take customers to the bar area, so the cost of servicing it is wholly related to taxable supplies. It may be tempting to code the expense as residual because it relates to a general building expense but this would not be correct. Input tax of £400 can be reclaimed in full.

In the case of the safe, this input tax is also taxable – the purpose of the safe is to store cash held on the premises, and the only source of cash income is the bar and restaurant area (because membership subscriptions are only paid by cheque or direct debit). Again, it may have been tempting to code this expense as residual because it is located in the office, and office overheads tend to be residual by nature.

As a general observation, it is important that advisers fully consider the VAT allocation of each item of expenditure, and avoid the easy option of playing safe and choosing the allocation which results in the lowest input tax claim.

Case law examples of input tax allocation

Buying a sofa or insurance?

[24.5] The key point with identifying whether an expense is relevant to taxable, exempt or both activities is to establish whether there is a 'direct and immediate' link between the cost incurred and the income relevant to the cost. The phrase 'direct and immediate link' was adopted following a very important European Court case back in 1995 (*BLP Group Plc v C&E Commrs: (Case C-4/94)* [1995] ECR I-983, [1995] All ER (EC) 401, ECJ) and continues to be the key phrase in our analysis.

Let me illustrate this point by reference to a First Tier Tribunal case involving *DFS Furniture Company Ltd v Revenue and Customs Comrs* (TC00157) [2009] UKFTT 204 (TC). The input tax under consideration in this case related to advertising costs.

DFS earns income from selling sofas (taxable) but also earns exempt commission from selling insurance linked to the furniture, eg stain and damage insurance. The key question was therefore:

- is the input tax on advertising costs classed as residual input tax because it is linked to the sale of both sofas and insurance (this was the HMRC view);
- is the input tax fully reclaimable because the advert wholly relates to the sale of the sofas (needless to say, this was the taxpayer's conclusion).

There is no doubt that the more sofas that are sold, the more insurance commission will be earned. But this is not the key question, which is:

'was there a "direct and immediate link" between the advertisements and the insurance activity?'

In other words, was there anything in the advert that directly promoted the insurance activity, eg along the lines of 'protect your new sofa and buy our excellent insurance cover'? The answer was no, and therefore the tribunal ruled that the input tax was wholly reclaimable because it only related to the sofa sales.

Selling houses or mortgages?

[24.6] The outcome of the *Skipton Building Society* case (TC00146 – 31 July 2009) reaffirmed the conclusions of the *DFS* case, although the verdict went against the taxpayer on a key point. The cost in question was again linked to adverts and whether the adverts placed by an estate agency business within Skipton were relevant to both the taxable activity of earning commission on house sales or also relevant to the exempt commission earned on selling mortgage/insurance products.

The reason this case went against the taxpayer was because although the adverts were intended to promote the house sales, they gave a very brief mention to the mortgage activity as well. This mention was enough to create a direct and immediate link between the expenditure in question and the exempt activity of the business. The input tax was partly reclaimable as residual input tax.

Televisions only used for exempt bets?

[24.7] In the case of *Town and County Factors Ltd v Revenue and Customs Comrs* (20 April 2006, unreported) (LON/04/0791 19616), the company was the representative member of a VAT group that operated about 2,000 licensed betting offices throughout the UK – each shop having a mix of exempt income (placing of bets) and taxable income through gaming machines and catering.

The expenditure item that was the subject of the appeal related to the costs paid to SIS, Sky TV and Sabrinet – relevant to the TV screens placed in each betting shop. Sky TV provided the basic broadcasting service plus sports coverage and SIS provided racing information and television broadcasts to all of the appellant's betting offices.

The question at issue was whether the television costs wholly related to the exempt part of the business (ie the placing of bets) or did they relate to all aspects of the business – on the basis that customers passing the shop may be tempted to enter the premises to watch the TV, and then as a result of this decision, spend money in all parts of the shop, ie including the gaming machines and catering outlet.

The latter argument was put forward by the taxpayer, ie that the TV costs should be classed as residual input tax. HMRC maintained that the link between the expenditure and the taxable income was tenuous and that the input tax was wholly relevant to exempt supplies.

The result? The tribunal agreed with the taxpayer. It was satisfied that the presence of the TV screens was enough to draw customers into the shop, who were then likely to spend money on both the betting activity (exempt) and the gaming machines (taxable).

Cheshire Racing Ltd v Revenue and Customs Comrs [2007] V & DR 345, [2008] SWTI 194 – HMRC did not accept defeat lightly in the *Town and County Factors Ltd* case, concluding that the significance of this case was that the televisions generated taxable advertising revenue. The HMRC policy team dismissed the argument about the TV presence attracting customers into a betting shop, and decided to challenge another case in the courts, ie where no advertising revenue was generated by the televisions.

The outcome was the same – another defeat for HMRC, based on the argument that the presence of the TV screens was enough to draw customers into the shop, who were then likely to spend money on both the betting activity (exempt) and the gaming machine (taxable). The tribunal chairman observed that the televisions provided a comprehensive coverage of many sporting and gaming activities, coverage was not just restricted to horse and dog racing alone.

HMRC accepted this argument – and confirmed its revised policy in Revenue & Customs Brief 1/08 issued on 3 January 2008.

New rugby pitch – what income did it produce?

[24.8] In the case of *Cirencester Rugby Football Club v Revenue and Customs Comrs* (TC00718) [2010] UKFTT 453 (TC), a rugby club spent a large sum of money constructing a new pitch, which was used for club matches (exempt income from players' subscriptions) and there were also advertising boards around the pitch from local companies (taxable income). Was the input tax on the pitch costs exempt or residual?

HMRC's view was that the advertising income was linked to the club, and a desire to support the club on the part of the advertisers, with no direct link to the new pitch itself, ie exempt input tax.

The club put forward the view that it was the pitch that had created the opportunities for extra income sources to be generated for advertising/ sponsorship and that created a direct and immediate link with taxable income as well as exempt income from playing fees.

The taxpayer won the case.

In a more recent case (*The Berkshire Golf Club and Ors v Revenue and Customs Comrs* (TC04774) [2015] UKFTT 627 (TC)), the First Tier Tax Tribunal found that there was a sufficient link between course maintenance costs and supplies of taxable tee advertising to categorise the expenditure as residual.

Annual adjustment

[24.9] Many businesses have seasonal variations in their trading levels – or periods when the exempt or taxable income can be artificially high.

Consider the situation of the non-profit making golf club in Example 3 above. It is likely that all of its exempt membership receipts will be received in one VAT period (date when annual fees are due for renewal) and this will create an exceptionally high percentage of exempt sales in this one period. If the club has a very high residual input tax figure in this period, then the percentage recovery will be very low because of the exempt income.

The way that the regulations ensure a fair and reasonable recovery rate is by requiring all partly exempt businesses to make an annual adjustment for input tax purposes. The result of this annual adjustment is to even out the effect of any periods where the split between taxable and exempt income creates an unfair result (either too much or too little input VAT claimed by the business).

The annual adjustment needs to be made for the 12-month period to 31 March, 30 April or 31 May, depending on when the trader's VAT periods end. For a business on monthly VAT returns, the year ends on 31 March. An exception occurs if a business uses the annual accounting scheme, ie completes one VAT return each year. In such cases, the partial exemption year can coincide with its chosen year for the scheme.

When the annual adjustment has been calculated, the business has a choice of when it includes the tax payable or repayable on its VAT return:

- it can include it on the March, April or May return (this facility has been in place since 1 April 2009);
- it can include it on the following quarter's return ie June, July or August.

Note – the sensible outcome is to include it on the earlier return if the adjustment produces a rebate and the later return if more VAT is due.

See Example 4 for a full calculation of an annual adjustment.

Example 4

The estate agency company from Example 2 has now come to the end of its tax year and it has calculated the following figures in relation to the four VAT periods:

Taxable supplies for the year excluding VAT	£330,000
Exempt supplies for the year	£90,000
Residual input tax for the year	£16,000
Residual input tax claimed to date	£12,500

Solution – the percentage of taxable income for the year (rounded up to nearest whole number) is 79%. This means that residual input tax of £12,640 can be claimed, ie £16,000 × 79%. The actual amount of residual input tax claimed on a quarterly basis is £12,500 – so the business can reclaim an additional amount of £140 in Box 4 of its VAT return for the final quarter of the year or the first quarter of the following year.

Note – the annual adjustment calculation does not represent the correction of a VAT error – it is a normal VAT adjustment appropriate to the rules of partial exemption.

(HMRC Notice 706, section 12).

De minimis limits

[24.10] The calculations made so far in this chapter have worked on the basis that all exempt input tax is not reclaimed by a business, plus a proportion of residual input tax based on the value of taxable and exempt income. In other words, a partly exempt business always suffers some loss of input tax.

One important rule of partial exemption is that a business can reclaim all of its input tax if the total value of exempt input tax (and remember, exempt input tax also includes the proportion of residual input tax that is not reclaimed) is less than the following amounts:

(a)   £625 per month on average and £7,500 per year; and
(b)   50% of the total input tax.

(HMRC Notice 706, para 11.2).

Note – on 1 April 2010, two new *de minimis* tests were introduced, and also the opportunity for a business to treat itself as *de minimis* throughout a tax year if it was *de minimis* in the previous tax year. However, in the latter case, an annual adjustment is still needed at the end of the tax year, which could make the business partly exempt and subject to an input tax payback. See below for further analysis of these regulations.

The quarterly calculations are again superseded by an annual adjustment – so it is possible to have the situation where a business is partly exempt in a VAT quarter but *de minimis* for the year as a whole.

See Example 5 which gives an example of a business that is *de minimis* in a VAT quarter.

Example 5

ABC Ltd is about to complete its VAT return – it has summarised the key figures as follows:

Standard rated sales for the quarter excluding VAT	£80,000
Exempt sales for the quarter	£20,000
Taxable input tax (input tax wholly attributable to taxable supplies)	£7,000
Exempt input tax (input tax wholly attributable to exempt supplies)	£1,000
Residual input tax (non-attributable)	£3,500

Solution – output tax is simple: £80,000 × 20% = £16,000.

With regard to input tax, the total amount reclaimed before consideration of the *de minimis* rules will be £9,800 as follows:

Taxable input tax – reclaim in full £7,000.

Residual input tax – claim 80% based on 80% of taxable supplies compared to total supplies, ie £2,800.

However, the total exempt input tax for the period is £1,700 (£1,000 directly attributable to exempt supplies plus 20% of residual input tax, ie £700). The amount of £1,700 is less than £625 per month on average, and is also less than 50% of the total input tax figure of £11,500.

The company is *de minimis* for this period and is therefore entitled to reclaim input tax of £11,500 in Box 4 of its return. However, it is possible that the company will not be *de minimis* for the overall tax year, so the recovery of exempt input tax in this period could be only temporary.

Three de minimis tests

[24.11]–[24.13] On 1 April 2010 HMRC introduced two new *de minimis* tests, with the aim of simplifying the current procedures. However, it is questionable whether the extra calculations actually simplify things, although we must not complain if the end result is that certain businesses are entitled to full input tax recovery where they were not under the previous regime. Thus:

- the changes were announced in Revenue & Customs Brief 10/10;
- the changes are explained in VAT Information Sheet 04/10;
- the old *de minimis* test (£625/50% etc) is still available;

- the intention is for two new tests to be available for a business to consider if it is *de minimis*, which will be less time consuming than the £625/50% test;
- the new tests are optional – and can be used for any VAT period beginning on or after 1 April 2010;
- in effect, we now have a total of three *de minimis* tests, the long-standing method considered in Example 5 plus the two new simplified tests introduced on 1 April 2010.

Simplified 'Test 1'

- Is total input tax less than £625 per month on average?
- Is exempt income less than 50% of total income (ie taxable plus exempt income and also outside the scope income that would be taxable if supplied in the UK, eg consultancy services to overseas business customer)?

'Yes' answer to both questions – business is *de minimis* for the VAT period in question – but must still carry out an annual adjustment.

Example 6

Luton Estate Agents have the following figures for the VAT quarter to June:

- total input tax = £1,500
- income from mortgage commission = £20,000; income from house selling commission = £25,000

Solution – the business is *de minimis* because total input tax of £500 per month on average is less than £625 per month on average, and the value of exempt supplies is less than 50% of total supplies

Note – this test avoids having to analyse input tax into the three different categories relevant to partly exempt traders.

Simplified 'Test 2'

- Is total input tax less input tax directly attributable to taxable supplies less than £625 per month on average?
- Is exempt income less than 50% of total supplies (total supplies as defined in 'test 1')?

'Yes' answer to both questions – business is *de minimis* for the VAT period in question – but must still carry out an annual adjustment.

(HMRC Notice 706, para 11.7)

Example 7

For the VAT quarter to 30 September, Luton Estate Agents has calculated its input tax as follows:

- taxable input tax – expenses wholly attributable to selling houses – £2,000

- exempt input tax – expenses wholly attributable to arranging mortgages – £1,000
- residual input tax – general overheads expenses, eg accountancy fees – £500
- mortgage commission = 48% of total income

Solution – the business is *de minimis* for the period because total input tax of £3,500 less taxable input tax of £2,000 = £1,500, ie less than £625 per month on average, and exempt sales are less than 50% of total sales.

Comment – in effect, a business will be *de minimis* if it passes one of three tests. If one of the tests is passed, there is no need to do any further partial exemption calculations, ie all input tax can be claimed on a VAT return.

Annual adjustment

[24.14] At the end of the partial exemption year, ie 31 March, 30 April or 31 May, depending on when VAT periods end, a business needs to pass one of the three tests on an annual basis. If one of the tests is passed, all input tax is then reclaimable for the whole year.

Annual test

[24.15] The final time saving measure introduced in 2010 is to allow a business that was *de minimis* in its previous partial exemption year to assume it will be *de minimis* in the next partial exemption year. A partial exemption year ends on 31 March, 30 April or 31 May, depending on when VAT periods end. It will then be able to reclaim all input tax on quarterly returns – but must do an annual adjustment calculation at the end of the tax year, ie to confirm it is actually *de minimis* for this year as well. This saves the need to do quarterly *de minimis* tests.

Note – total input tax for the current year must be less than £1m to take advantage of this opportunity.

Example 8

A business was *de minimis* for a partial exemption year. Can it claim all of its input tax in the following four VAT periods?

Solution – the business can initially treat itself as *de minimis* for each of the following four VAT quarters but then must carry out an annual adjustment calculation. If the result of the annual adjustment calculation is that too much input tax has been claimed, the excess should be repaid via the VAT return for the final quarter or via the first VAT return for the following year.

Note – this 'annual test' facility is available for partial exemption years beginning on or after 1 April 2010.

The main disadvantage of adopting the annual test is that a business could be faced with a large VAT bill at the end of the tax year if it is not *de minimis*. If there are any doubts about this outcome, it is probably best to carry out the usual *de minimis* tests on a quarterly basis.

Opportunity for tax savings with de minimis tests

[24.16] Be aware that some small partly exempt businesses could achieve a *de minimis* outcome by applying the two additional *de minimis* tests that are now available, whereas the long-standing test may have made them partly exempt. It is therefore important to consider all three tests to see if a *de minimis* outcome can be achieved. Here is an example of a business that is *de minimis* under the new tests but would be partly exempt under the old test.

Example 9

Luton Estate Agents – VAT quarter to December:

- exempt input tax £950
- taxable input tax £850
- exempt supplies – 48% of total supplies

Can the business reclaim the exempt input tax of £950?

Solution – this is an example of a business that would not be *de minimis* for the period if the two additional tests had not been introduced. Under the old test, it is partly exempt because exempt input tax of £950 exceeds 50% of the total input tax figure of £1,800. But under simplified 'test 1' it is *de minimis* because total input tax is less than £625 per month on average (£1,800 divided by three months = £600), and exempt sales are less than 50% of total sales.

Standard method override

[24.17] In most cases, the standard method gives a fair and reasonable result. However, in some very rare cases (which in general only apply to large businesses) the standard method gives an unfair input tax recovery rate.

To combat this situation, HMRC introduced override provisions with effect from 18 April 2002 to address these difficulties. Except in cases of deliberate abuse (eg through complex VAT planning schemes), the application of the override provisions is very limited. As a general principle, the override provisions could be used if the standard method gives a level of input tax recovery on an expense that is widely different to the extent to which it is used in the making of taxable supplies.

The override only applies if the adjustment required to correct the distortion exceeds:

- £50,000; or
- 50% of the residual input tax, and £25,000.

(HMRC Notice 706, para 5.2).

The limits above mean that any adjustment that is less than £25,000 can be ignored. It can also be ignored if it is between £25,000 and £50,000 and less than 50% of the residual input tax figure.

In the case of *Abbeyview Bowling Club v Revenue and Customs Comrs* [2008] SWTI 1685, input tax was claimed by the club on the construction of a new rink next to its clubhouse. HMRC felt that the input tax claimed on the rink was excessive (unfair) when a turnover based calculation was adopted and it applied a calculation based instead on use. This produced an input tax adjustment that exceeded the £50,000 limit (ie the difference between the two calculation methods).

The tribunal accepted an alternative calculation put forward by the taxpayer that produced an input tax difference of less than £50,000 and therefore the override provisions did not apply. This case shows the importance of not always accepting an HMRC basis of calculation and looking at the wider issues of a transaction.

(HMRC Notice 706, section 5).

Foreign income and specified supplies

[24.18] UK VAT registered businesses can recover input tax in relation to taxable supplies made in the UK and supplies made outside of the UK that would be taxable if made in the UK. In addition, input tax in relation to the following specified supplies can be recovered:

• financial services supplied to persons belonging outside of the EU or which are directly related to an export of goods, and the making of arrangements for such supplies;

• insurance services supplied to persons belonging outside of the EU or which are directly related to an export of goods, and the making of arrangements for such supplies; and

• certain supplies of investment gold.

Subject to transitional arrangements, from 1 August 2015 UK businesses are not able to take into account supplies made by foreign branches when carrying out their partial exemption calculations. (HMRC Notice 706, section 9).

(HMRC Tax Information and Impact Note on VAT deductions relating to foreign branches).

Incidental transactions

[24.19] When applying the standard method of calculation, it is important to be clear about the sources of income that are excluded from the figures – as well as those that are included. The aim of the calculation process is that the percentage of residual input tax that is reclaimed by the business should be 'fair and reasonable', ie an amount that reflects the level of taxable supplies made by the business.

The following sources of income should be excluded as being incidental transactions:

- sale of capital assets, eg sale of car, plant and machinery etc;
- exempt supplies of finance where these supplies are incidental to the business, eg bank interest received;
- with effect from 1 April 2007, any 'real estate transaction' (sale of a building etc) where such supplies are again incidental to the main activities of the business.

Example – a firm of accountants sells the freehold of the building from which it trades and rents a new office in the next street. The proceeds from the sale of the building (exempt if no option to tax has been made on the building and it is also more than three years old) are excluded from the partial exemption calculation:

- the value of certain imported services which are subject to the reverse charge in the UK;
- proceeds from the sale of any business (or part of a business) as a going concern.

VAT incurred for non-business purposes

[24.20] The basic principle is that VAT incurred on expenditure that is for non-business purposes is not input tax at all and should be excluded from any calculations before partial exemption issues are considered. See Example 10. (HMRC Notice 706, para 2.2).

Example 10

John trades as a sole proprietor and is VAT registered, making taxable and exempt supplies. The percentage of taxable supplies is 80% of total supplies.

He has just purchased a piece of equipment for £20,000 plus VAT of £4,000 (based on VAT rate of 20%) that will be used for non-business purposes for 20% of the time. For the remainder of the time, the equipment will be used for both parts of his business, ie taxable and exempt activities. What is the input tax position?

Solution – an initial amount of input tax will be disallowed to reflect the non-business use, an amount of £800 (ie £4,000 x 20%). The remaining input tax of £3,200 will be treated as residual input tax and included within the partial exemption calculations for the business. If 80% of income is taxable for the relevant period, then the input tax recovery will be £2,560.

Standard method simplification measures

[24.21] HMRC issued Revenue & Customs Brief 19/09 and VAT Information Sheet 04/09 in March 2009 to explain important changes in relation to businesses that use the standard method. The aim of the measures is to simplify the partial exemption calculations for a business, ie to produce administrative savings in many cases. The new procedures took effect from 1 April 2009 and included three optional measures and a fourth measure that is compulsory.

The three optional measures are as follows:

(1)   *A provisional input tax recovery percentage can be adopted throughout the tax year, based on the previous year's annual adjustment calculation.*
This recovery percentage will be relevant to input tax claims on expenses where some taxable and some exempt use is evident (ie residual input tax). The actual recovery percentage will then be established when the annual adjustment calculation is made at the end of the tax year.
Example – ABC Ltd uses the standard method and reclaimed 75% of its residual input tax in the year to 31 March 2014. It will reclaim the same percentage of residual input tax in relation to VAT returns submitted during the year to 31 March 2015. It will then calculate its annual adjustment for the year and reclaim additional input tax if the percentage of taxable income exceeded 75%, ie the provisional recovery rate was too low. It will repay tax to HMRC if the percentage of taxable income was less than 75%, ie the provisional recovery rate was too high. The percentage of taxable income for the year to 31 March 2015 will then form the basis of quarterly calculations during the year to 31 March 2016.
Advantage of the measure – the adoption of an in-year recovery percentage will avoid any significant fluctuations in the percentage of residual input tax claimed on a quarterly basis because of, for example, big fluctuations in income levels (as in the earlier example of a golf club that received all of its exempt membership subscription income in one VAT period). It will also be easier for a business to complete its quarterly VAT returns, knowing that the percentage of residual input tax it will claim will not change each period during the year.
How it will work – a business does not need HMRC permission to apply this measure. Its intention to adopt the measure will be confirmed by the first VAT return it submits in the new tax year, ie if this return is based on the previous year's recovery percentage, the business must then adopt the same method for the remainder of the tax year.

(2)   *A business has the option of including the tax that is payable or repayable as a result of the annual adjustment calculation on the VAT return at the end of the tax year rather than the first return of the new tax year.*
This measure means that the tax payable or repayable as result of the annual adjustment calculation can be included on the VAT return ending 31 March, 30 April or 31 May rather than the subsequent return.

Example – ABC Ltd has a partial exemption year that ends on 31 March. The annual adjustment for the year has produced a VAT overpayment of £13,000. It would be sensible to include this adjustment on the VAT return for the quarter to 31 March rather than the VAT return for the following quarter, as allowed by the legislation, because this brings forward the repayment by three months, ie a useful cash flow benefit.

Advantage of the measure – as well as the potential cash flow benefit, if a business has a financial year that is the same as its partial exemption year (eg 31 March is a common year end for many businesses) then the inclusion of the adjustment on the earlier VAT return will also avoid the need to include the amount of the annual adjustment as a VAT debtor or creditor figure in the accounts.

How it will work – there is no need to apply to HMRC to adopt this measure.

(3)   A *'use based'* basis of input tax recovery can be made in certain circumstances, rather than the usual standard method calculation based on income.

The rules enable a new partly exempt business to recover input tax on the basis of 'use' in the following circumstances:

- During its registration period – ie from the date when it first became VAT registered to either 31 March, 30 April or 31 May, depending on when it completes its VAT returns.
- During its first tax year – normally the first period of 12 months commencing on 1 April, 1 May or 1 June following the end of the registration period. However, this only applies if the business did not incur any exempt input tax during its registration period.
- During any tax year – provided it did not incur any exempt input tax in its previous tax year.

The principle of 'use' means that input tax recovery is based on how an expense will be used in the future rather than the percentage of taxable income generated in the period when it is incurred.

Example – a business registered for VAT on 15 July and its registration period ends on 31 March the following year. During this period, it incurred input tax of £50,000 on setting up costs. These costs relate to future income that is both taxable and exempt, ie the input tax is classed as residual input tax. The business expects that its taxable income will be 70% of total income in its first three years of trading and that this would be a fair and reasonable basis to claim input tax on the £50,000 of setting up costs. This will produce an input tax claim of £35,000, ie £50,000 x 70%.

Advantage of the new measure – the measure will produce a fairer and probably improved input tax recovery rate by considering the principle of use. It will be particularly relevant for a business with negligible income in its registration period, ie where the standard method calculation could give a distortive result.

How it will work – the calculation made on quarterly VAT returns during the relevant period must also be applied to the annual adjustment calculation at the end of the tax year, ie to ensure consistency. However, a business that did not make a use based calculation on its quarterly returns can still do so for the annual adjustment calculation. This gives a new partly exempt business the maximum flexibility to ensure it can reclaim a fair amount of input tax.

Note – it is possible that the partly exempt business in the last example could benefit from the other measures after the end of its registration period. This means it could use the 70% recovery rate on a provisional basis in its next tax year, although the annual adjustment calculation would need to be based on a standard method calculation based on income.

Compulsory measure

[24.22] The three measures considered above are all optional. A fourth measure announced in the Brief is compulsory and relates to those businesses that make:

- supplies of services to customers outside the UK; or
- certain financial supplies such as shares and bonds; or
- supplies from establishments located outside the UK.

The main situation encountered by practitioners will be in relation to those clients who do some work for overseas customers, eg a UK based consultant who does some work for a Swedish client. Example 11 gives a practical example of the rule change.

Example 11

A UK business provides consultancy services to UK and non-UK business customers. It also has some exempt income in the UK from selling insurance services. No VAT is charged on the consultancy work carried out for overseas customers (place of supply is where the customer is based).

What is the input tax position?

Solution – since 1 April 2009, the amount of residual input tax claimed is based on an income based calculation (usual standard method calculation) ie to include the consultancy income as taxable income irrespective of the location of the customer.

Note – even though consultancy work for an overseas business client is outside the scope of UK VAT (because the place of supply is where the customer is based) it is classed as taxable income for partial exemption purposes because the services would be taxable if supplied in the UK.

Input tax adjustments for change of intended use

[24.23] Consider the following two examples:

(a)   A building company builds a new house and intends to sell the freehold of the property once it has been completed. Such a sale would be zero-rated supply for VAT purposes, so input tax of £20,000 incurred on building materials and professional fees can be fully reclaimed as it relates to an intended taxable supply. However, when the building is completed six months later, the company decides to rent the house to a tenant on a 15-year lease. The rental income paid by the tenant is consideration for an exempt supply for VAT purposes (and because the property is residential there is no scope to make an option to tax election).

(b)   A building company builds a new house and intends to rent it out to a tenant once the property has been completed. This is an exempt supply for VAT purposes, so input tax of £20,000 incurred on building materials and professional fees cannot be reclaimed as it relates to an intended exempt supply. However, when the building is completed six months later, the company receives an excellent offer from an individual who wants to purchase the freehold of the property, ie creating a zero-rated (taxable) supply.

In the first example, the company is correct to reclaim input tax on the initial expenditure because at the time of incurring the expenditure, it intended to make a taxable supply. However, the change of use means it is affected by the 'clawback' provisions, which apply in the following situations.

•   Input tax was originally reclaimed because the taxpayer intended to use the goods or services for the purposes of taxable supplies. However, within a period of six years from the beginning of the period covered by the VAT return in which the original intention was formed, the use or intention to use is changed to making either exempt supplies or both taxable and exempt supplies;

•   Input tax was originally treated as residual input tax because the goods or services were intended to be used for the making of taxable and exempt supplies. However, within a period of six years from the beginning of the period covered by the VAT return in which the original intention was formed, the use or intention to use is changed to making exempt supplies.

•   In effect, the 'clawback' provisions apply because the initial input tax deduction based on intended use has proved to be excessive, and an amount is now repayable to HMRC. The payment must be made on the return for the tax period in which the use occurs or the revised intention is formed.
      (HMRC Notice 706, paras 13.7 and 13.8).

•   Since 1 January 2011, the clawback provisions must also be applied to non-business expenditure, as long as there was some intended business use (exempt or taxable) at the time it was incurred. The actual business/exempt/taxable use must then be adjusted when the item is first used (or the intention changes) and actual use is different to intended use. If no input tax was claimed initially on the basis that there was no intended business use (taxable or exempt) then a clawback cannot be made because it was a wholly non-business/private expense. See Example 12.
      (HMRC VAT Information Sheet 06/11, section 4).

Example 12

During February a charity incurs expenditure of £10,000 plus £2,000 VAT on goods that it intends to use 50% for non-business purposes and 50% for taxable purposes. It reclaimed £1,000 of input tax on its VAT return for the quarter to 31 March based on this intention.

In August, when the expenditure is first used, actual taxable use is only 25% and non-business use is 75%. A clawback of input tax will take place on the VAT return for the quarter to 30 September, ie £500 will be repayable to HMRC. This is because the actual non-business use is different to the intended non-business use and this change must be recognised by the payback and clawback provisions since 1 January 2011.

There can be situations when a change of use from an intended exempt supply to an actual taxable supply means the business will benefit from the 'payback' provisions. This situation is the opposite to the 'clawback' provisions, as it means additional input tax can be reclaimed from HMRC.

The 'payback' provisions apply in the following situations.

• A business has not reclaimed input tax on relevant expenditure items because it was intended to use them in the making of exempt supplies. However, there is now a change of use or intended use so that they are either used in making taxable supplies or taxable and exempt supplies;

• A business has treated input tax on certain expenditure as residual input tax because it intended to use them in the making of taxable and exempt supplies. However, there is now a change of use or intended use so they are to be used only in the making of taxable supplies.

• Since 1 January 2011, the payback provisions must also be applied to non-business expenditure, as long as there was some intended business use (exempt or taxable) at the time it was incurred. The actual business/exempt/taxable use must then be adjusted when the item is first used (or the intention changes) and actual use is different to intended use. If no input tax was claimed initially on the basis that there was no intended business use (taxable or exempt) then a payback cannot apply because it was a wholly non-business/private expense. See Example 13. (HMRC VAT Information Sheet 06/11, section 4).

In the case of 'payback' situations, it is not acceptable to just make an entry on the next VAT return – approval has to be firstly granted by HMRC. Once approval has been received, the amount of VAT involved can be entered as an overpayment on the next return.

Note that the clawback and payback provisions only apply where there is a change of intention before the original intention was fulfilled. There may be occasions when an item is actually used as originally intended, but then the use changes subsequently. In such cases, no adjustment to the original allocation is normally needed unless the item in question needs to be adjusted over a five or ten-year period under the capital goods scheme (see Chapter 9), or the standard method override (see **24.17**) is applicable. See also 'House builders and rental income' below.

(HMRC Notice 706, paras 13.9 and 13.10).

Example 13

During February a charity incurs expenditure of £10,000 plus £2,000 VAT on goods that it intends to use 50% for non-business purposes and 50% for exempt purposes. It reclaimed no input tax on its VAT return for the quarter to 31 March because there was no intended taxable use.

In August, when the expenditure is first used, actual taxable use is 100%, with no exempt or non-business use. A payback situation is now evident. The charity can write to HMRC applying for approval to include the under-claim on its next VAT return.

Note – the provisions do not need to be treated as error adjustments because the original input tax claims were correct based on the intended use at that time.

(HMRC Notice 706, section 13).

House builders and rental income

[24.24] What happens if a house builder is unable to sell a dwelling he has built and decides to rent it out on a temporary basis ie creating exempt rental income rather than a zero-rated sale of a new home?

If a house builder rents out a property he has constructed for even a short period of time, the costs then relate to both taxable and exempt supplies – and an input tax adjustment could be needed.

HMRC took the opportunity to clarify its policy on the input tax challenges facing house builders in the above situation and full details are explained in Revenue & Customs Brief 44/08 and VAT Information Sheet 7/08. Both documents were issued on 15 September 2008.

The process for a builder is as follows:

• For past VAT returns, he must carry out a test called 'a simple check for *de minimis*' – this test identifies the past exempt input tax for relevant properties based on the expected number of letting years (out of a ten-year total period).

• If an adjustment of past input tax is then needed because the business is not *de minimis* for partial exemption purposes (see **24.10** above on *de minimis* limits) then HMRC will allow the business to adjust its input tax by using any method that 'fairly reflects the use of costs in making taxable supplies'. This could be based on income figures (expected letting income compared to expected sale proceeds from the property) or the number of letting years compared to a ten-year economic life of the building.

• For current and future VAT returns, the business must either adjust its input tax (if appropriate) by using the standard method of calculation for partial exemption (based on income) or formally request a special method from HMRC.

Note – any adjustment of past input tax is made on the VAT return relevant to when the decision was taken to rent out the property rather than sell it – there is no error notification issue because the original input tax was correctly claimed at the time.

The Information Sheet issued by HMRC gives full details and worked examples about input tax adjustments needed by builders for past, current and future VAT returns.

See Example 14 to show how input tax can be adjusted under the new rules.

Example 14

New Homes Ltd exceeded the 'simple check for *de minimis*' for the year because it decided to rent out six properties (flats) that it does not expect to sell for four years.

The company now needs to adjust some of the £30,000 input tax originally claimed on the cost of the flats. VAT Information Sheet 7/08 explains that this can be done by any method that 'fairly reflects the use of costs in making taxable supplies.' (this assumes the taxpayer does not already have an agreed partial exemption special method in place – unlikely for smaller house builders).

The directors decide to make the input tax adjustment based on the following formula:

$$\frac{\text{Expected rental income}}{\text{Expected total income}} \times \text{input tax claimed on properties}$$

Note – expected total income = expected rental income + expected selling price of flats.

The current projections are that each of the six flats in question will sell for £200,000 in four years time, and will generate rental income of £10,000 per annum in the meantime.

Input tax to be adjusted:

$$\frac{(\pounds10,000 \times 6 \text{ flats} \times 4 \text{ years})}{(\pounds200,000 \times 6 \text{ flats}) + (\pounds10,000 \times 6 \text{ flats} \times 4 \text{ years})} \times \pounds30,000 = \pounds5,000$$

Planning points to consider

[24.25] The following planning points should be given consideration.

• An accurate partial exemption calculation can only be made if an accountant (or relevant staff) clearly identifies whether an expense should be coded as taxable, exempt or residual as far as input tax recovery is concerned. A major invoice incorrectly coded as residual instead of taxable (or exempt instead of residual or taxable) could cost a business a lot of money.

- Most businesses use the standard method of calculation. However, be aware that a special method can be applied for (as long as HMRC approval is obtained) if the standard method does not give a fair and reasonable result (see Chapter 25).

- Be aware of the need to make an annual adjustment for all partial exemption calculations – and the fact that a business has the choice of including the adjustment on the VAT return at the end of the tax year in question or the return for the following quarter.

- Always check to see if a client is *de minimis* as far as partial exemption is concerned and don't forget that two additional *de minimis* tests were introduced on 1 April 2010. In such cases, all input tax can be reclaimed if one of the three tests creates a *de minimis* outcome. However, it is the annual position that matters, any quarterly calculations being made on a provisional basis.

- An 'annual test' was introduced on 1 April 2010, which means that a business that was *de minimis* in its previous tax year can reclaim all input tax on its VAT returns for the next tax year, subject to an annual adjustment at the end of that year. This new measure could simplify accounting for a partly exempt business because it avoids having to make quarterly partial exemption calculations.

- Optional procedures give the opportunity for a partly exempt business to use an in-year recovery rate in relation to residual input tax, based on the previous year's recovery percentage. A separate measure could also improve input tax recovery in some VAT periods by allowing a use rather than income-based method of calculation.

- Special rules affect businesses supplying services to customers outside the UK, certain financial supplies and supplies from establishments located outside the UK. It is important advisers consider these rules for any clients involved in such activities.

- A change in the intended use of an item or actual use being different to intended use means that input tax originally claimed on goods or services could be affected by the 'clawback' or 'payback' provisions. In the case of a 'clawback' situation, extra VAT will be payable to HMRC – the opposite applies in a 'payback' situation, with a rebate being due.

- Since 1 January 2011, the payback and clawback provisions also take into account a change in the percentage of non-business use if an intention changes or actual use is different to intended use. This assumes there is some intended business use of the expenditure at the time it is incurred – if an expense was wholly intended to be for private or non-business purposes, then no input tax adjustment will apply if this changes in the future.

- The planning measure outlined at Chapter 27 at **27.15** could be considered in relation to the problem for house builders identified at **24.24** of this chapter.

Chapter 25

Partial Exemption – Special Methods

Key topics in this chapter:

- Reasons why a special method could be appropriate for a business.
- Different methods that could be proposed, eg based on floor area, inputs, staff numbers and transaction numbers.
- HMRC approach to approving or rejecting special method proposals.
- The requirement for applicants to make a 'fair and reasonable' declaration when applying for a special method.
- Proposed methods likely to be rejected by HMRC, eg floor area applications where a large proportion of the floor area is excluded from the calculation as a non-attributable area.
- The importance of notifying HMRC of any changes in business circumstances that might affect a special method calculation.
- The inclusion of non-business adjustments in a special method since 1 January 2011.

Introduction

[25.1] In Chapter 24, we considered the key issues for a partly exempt business as far as input tax restriction was concerned on costs attributable to exempt supplies. The main principle of input tax recovery – the 'golden rule' – is that it can only be recovered to the extent that it relates to taxable supplies.

The assumption made in Chapter 24 was that a business was using the standard method for partial exemption purposes, which basically works as follows:

- input tax attributable wholly to taxable supplies can be reclaimed in full;
- input tax attributable wholly to exempt supplies cannot be reclaimed;
- residual input tax to reclaim – apportioned according to:

$$\frac{\text{value of taxable supplies excluding VAT}}{\text{value of taxable and exempt supplies excluding VAT}}$$

(Note – residual input tax is input tax on costs that cannot be directly attributed to either taxable or exempt supplies, eg input tax incurred on general overhead items.)

The main principle of partial exemption is that the input tax reclaimed by any business with taxable and exempt supplies should reflect the taxable use of costs on a basis that is considered to be 'fair and reasonable'. Although calculation methods can never be totally exact, and are always based on an estimated situation, it is important that advisers (and HMRC) look at the overall result of a calculation to determine if it is reasonable.

For example, if a business has 90% exempt supplies and 10% taxable supplies, then it will recover 10% of its residual input tax using the standard method. But what if, for example, the business has an office where 50% of the staff in the building are working for the exempt part of the business and 50% of the staff in the building are working for the taxable part of the business? Would it then be fair for this particular business to only reclaim 10% of the input tax on its office costs?

The above situation is an example of where the standard method of calculation may not give a fair and reasonable result. In such situations, a business has the opportunity to apply to HMRC to request the use of a special method of calculation.

(HMRC Notice 706, para 6.1).

When a special method should be requested

[25.2] The reason that a partly exempt business would consider a special method of calculation is solely due to the fact that it considers the standard method does not give a fair and reasonable result in terms of input tax recovery on residual expenditure.

In cases where it considers that the standard method is unfair, the approach of the taxpayer (or his adviser) should be as follows:

- identify why the standard method is considered to be unfair;
- consider alternative methods of calculation that would give a fairer result;
- make a written application to HMRC to request formal approval to use this proposed method for future VAT periods.

The situation in Example 1 below highlights one arrangement where the standard method does not give a fair result.

(HMRC Notice 706, paras 6.2 and 6.3).

Example 1

ABC Ltd has two activities – both generating equal levels of income (ie 50% taxable and 50% exempt). The main expenditure of the business on which input tax is incurred is linked to its property. The taxable activity is the organisation of fitness classes which takes up 80% of the premises; the exempt activity is the sale of insurance which takes up 20% of the premises. Is the standard method fair and reasonable in this situation?

Solution – most of the input tax for this particular business relates to the property from which it trades – and 80% of this property is used for taxable activities. But in reality only 50% of the input tax will be recovered on property costs using the standard method of calculation based on income.

In this particular situation, the business would be best advised to write to HMRC and apply for a special method of calculation based on floor area.

Different types of special method

[25.3] There are many different special methods that could be proposed by a business – some are listed at para 6.6 of HMRC Notice 706. The following are the main alternatives to the standard method.

Alternative methods

Floor area method

[25.4] The situation in Example 1 identified a common basis of calculation, namely, an apportionment method based on floor area. This method is very simple to operate and is widely used by many businesses.

For example, a major cost of most non-profit making golf clubs is the cost of their clubhouse. In many cases, the percentage of the floor area allocated to the bar activity (taxable) will be a very high proportion of the total floor area in the building, but the percentage of bar income may be quite low compared to total income (which would include golf membership and entry fees, exempt from VAT). In such cases, it may be worthwhile to request a floor space method to apportion the input tax on clubhouse expenses.

Inputs method

[25.5] The most common methods based on inputs are:

(a)   taxable input tax divided by total input tax (ie input tax wholly attributable to the making of taxable supplies as a percentage of total input tax);

(b)   taxable input tax divided by taxable input tax plus exempt input tax; and

(c)   taxable inputs (net of VAT) divided by taxable inputs plus exempt inputs (both net of VAT).

In reality, a special method based on inputs may produce a fairer result when the use of an overhead is more closely linked to costs than revenue. The limitation of the standard method in many cases is that it assumes that overhead and cost proportions are incurred in the same ratio as income percentages.

Staff numbers

[25.6] A method based on staff numbers may be appropriate for a head office of a company in the case of expenses. Alternatively, a method based on the floor space occupied by staff involved in the taxable and exempt parts of the business may also be appropriate. See Example 2.

Example 2

DEF Ltd is a national company with 50 estate agency branches throughout the UK. It uses the standard method of calculation for partial exemption purposes, but feels this method does not give a fair input tax recovery on its head office costs. The key figures for the year to 31 March are as follows:

- the percentage of taxable income for the company is 40%;
- there are 120 staff at its head office, with 60 staff working on the taxable part of the business, 30 staff working on the exempt part of the business and 30 staff in sections that encompass both parts, eg finance.

The business wants to calculate its residual input tax based on employee numbers. What is the solution?

Solution – a special method cannot be requested on a retrospective basis. An exception is if the business did not know it was partly exempt, perhaps it came to light on a VAT inspection, and finds that the standard method produces an unfair result when it calculates its retrospective input tax claim. However in other cases HMRC will not generally allow a business to backdate a method just because an alternative calculation gives a better result in terms of input tax recovery, otherwise there could be endless claims made for past windfalls.

As far as a special method is concerned, the company has two options:

- it could request a method of calculation that gives input tax recovery based on staff directly involved in taxable supplies (60) compared to total staff (120). This would give a recovery rate of 50%, which is still better than the standard method recovery rate of 40% (based on income);
- it could request a method of calculation that gives input tax recovery based on staff directly involved in taxable supplies (60) compared to total staff involved in taxable and exempt supplies (90). This calculation would give a recovery rate of 66.7%, which is the best result of all.

Note – the approach of HMRC to dealing with special method applications is considered at **25.8**. However, one of HMRC's main concerns is where a special method proposal attempts to ignore a large non-attributable element, eg as in the case of the 30 employees above who work on both taxable and exempt activities.

Number of transactions

[25.7] A proposal could be made to base a special method calculation on the number of taxable transactions carried out by a business compared to the total number of transactions, ie including exempt sales. For example, this method could apply to a shop where the number of taxable and exempt transactions can be clearly identified and there is a sensible link between the volume of transactions and the input tax recovery overall.

The Court of Appeal recently ruled that a finance company could recover residual input VAT on a transaction count basis. In *Volkswagen Financial Services (UK) Ltd v Revenue and Customs Comrs* [2015] EWCA Civ 832, [2016] STC 417, the company sold cars to customers at cost and also supplied finance. HMRC tried to argue that, as the company made all its profit from the exempt supply of finance, it ought not to be able to reclaim any residual input VAT. The Court dismissed HMRC's position as it was clear that the overheads were a cost component of the company's taxable as well as exempt supplies. Accordingly, the Court confirmed that, as for each supply there was a taxable transaction (the car) and an exempt supply (the finance), 50% of residual input VAT could be reclaimed. However, this decision has been appealed by HMRC to the Supreme Court.

However, it would not be sensible to propose a method based on the number of transactions if each taxable transaction was small in value, eg the sale of a bar of chocolate, whereas the exempt transactions were less frequent and higher value. See Example 3 for an illustration of this point.

Example 3

DEF Ltd, from Example 2, now wishes to propose a special method of calculation to deal with the input tax it can reclaim on the cost of its branch expenditure. For the year to 31 March, it made the following transactions:

- it sold 250 houses on a commission basis (taxable);
- it arranged 200 mortgages for clients and received a fee from the mortgage lender (exempt);
- it sold 3,000 books on how to be a property millionaire at £9.99 each (taxable).

It considers that an apportionment based on the number of taxable transactions to total transactions would be appropriate.

Solution – the proposed method would give an input tax recovery rate of 94.2% based on the number of taxable transactions (3,250) compared to total transactions (3,450). In reality, the proposed method would almost certainly be challenged by HMRC as it does not produce a fair and reasonable recovery rate.

A fairer approach would be to propose a method that excludes the book sales, as these supplies are really incidental to the two core business activities of house sales and mortgage services. Even if accepted by HMRC at the application stage, the company would be wise to reconsider the proposed method. This is because of the potential comeback on the taxpayer through rules that require him to certify that the proposed method is 'fair and reasonable' in terms of input tax recovery. See 25.9.

HMRC approach to special methods

[25.8] The key aim of any officer reviewing a special method application, or subsequent review of the method on a VAT inspection, should be to ask the simple question: does this method give a fair and reasonable outcome as far as residual input tax recovery is concerned?

Rules introduced in April 2007 put the onus on the taxpayer to certify that any proposed method is 'fair and reasonable' in terms of input tax recovery. If it is subsequently found to be unfair (and HMRC considers the taxpayer knew it would be unfair at the time of the application), then HMRC has the power to raise an assessment to correct any unfair recovery of input tax. The power to issue a retrospective assessment of tax means it is essential that taxpayers critically review their proposed methods before an application is made.

An officer will look at the bigger picture of any application and ask questions such as: is it reasonable that a business with, for example, 90% exempt income puts forward a special method application that produces an 80% input tax recovery on its residual costs?

The officer will confirm the method in writing – giving clear instructions as to how it should be carried out. The following points should be noted:

- with a special method, the ratio of any calculation should be made to two decimal places – not rounded up to the nearest whole number as is the case with the standard method;
  (HMRC Notice 706, para 6.7).
- all special methods must have an annual adjustment calculation – exactly the same as with the standard method. The aim of the annual adjustment is to even out any unfair results that can often occur with quarterly calculations – see **24.9** for an explanation of how the annual adjustment process is carried out;
  (HMRC Notice 706, para 6.10).
- HMRC should be informed of any change in the business that has a substantial effect on the amount of input tax reclaimable. The special method will then be reviewed and, if no longer suitable, a direction to stop using the method will be issued.

Special methods are only effective from the date the method is approved – there is no facility in the legislation for retrospective approval. The reason for this is simple; if a business was allowed to go back and recalculate its partial exemption figures because it secured a better result in terms of input tax recovery, then advisers could exploit this loophole at every opportunity.

Special method applications post 1 April 2007

[25.9] A special method application can appear to be based on a fair and reasonable proposal but contain a clause or section that distorts the overall result. This distortion may not be identified by HMRC at the time that the proposal is made, giving the taxpayer a very good outcome in terms of input tax recovery. It is probable that an officer will identify the distorted result on the next VAT visit but until 1 April 2007, he only had the power to revise the method from a current, rather than historic, date.

An important change was introduced on 1 April 2007 – any special method application now requires the taxpayer to certify that the proposed special method is 'fair and reasonable'. This declaration must be made before the application is approved for use by HMRC.

The exact wording of the new special method declaration is as follows:

> 'As the taxable person, I hereby declare that to the best of my knowledge and belief, the proposed special method fairly and reasonably represents the extent to which goods and services are used or to be used in making taxable supplies. I also confirm that I have taken reasonable steps to ensure that I am in possession of all relevant information before making this declaration.'

A responsible person within the organisation must sign the declaration – or the sole trader or partner in the case of unincorporated businesses.

In effect, HMRC now have power to set aside a special method which the business should have known was not fair and reasonable. This enables retrospective recovery of VAT in such situations, a strong incentive for businesses (or advisers) not to make special method proposals that could be challenged in the future.

For a practical example of the impact of the rules, see Example 4.

Example 4

DEF Ltd operates a 24-hour call centre in a big office in London. Virtually all of its residual input tax relates to office costs – the landlord has opted to tax the property so the rent is a major source of input tax.

The company employs 25 full-time staff processing applications on behalf of a large insurance company (which has been ruled as an exempt activity) and 50 part-time staff dealing with tax queries on behalf of a large firm of accountants (which has been ruled as a taxable activity). It has been identified that the standard method gives unfair input tax recovery for the business – so the directors have put forward a case to HMRC that a special method should be approved, based on the number of employees involved in taxable and exempt activities, ie 66.67% input tax recovery (50 divided by 75).

Solution – HMRC would probably accept this proposed method at the application stage. However, there is a key piece of information that it might not fully appreciate. This is the fact that the tax staff are working part-time and the insurance staff are working full-time. This means that the actual staff usage of the building by the two activities is the same if the tax staff are working 50% of full-time hours – the proposed method gives the taxpayer a very good result.

Note – in this situation, HMRC would probably impose a calculation method that either provides a split based on staff hours or staff numbers on a full-time basis. It could put forward the case that the company directors should have recognised the unfairness of their proposed method when they signed the declaration at the time of their application that 'to the best of their belief, the proposed special method is fair and reasonable'.

A fair result for input tax apportionment would probably be a 50% recovery rate – not the 66.67% initially proposed.

Methods likely to be refused by HMRC

[25.10] One of the main reasons why an application for a special method based on floor area can sometimes be rejected by HMRC is if it considers that the method proposed ignores a large part of the building because it is not wholly used for either taxable or exempt activities – in other words, a majority of the building is used for general purposes and is taken out of the proposed calculation.

This can mean that a business could propose a special method where, say, only 10% of the actual floor space is used in the computation – the balance of the building being ignored because it is not specific to either taxable or exempt activities. In such cases, HMRC could rule (probably with some justification) that the proposed method does not give a fair and reasonable result. This view (which has often been proposed in the past for opticians' businesses) has been supported by tribunal decisions. See Example 5.

Note – the tribunal chairman in the case of *Optika Ltd v Customs and Excise Comrs* (12 December 2003, unreported) (LON/00/1281 18627) made the comment in his case assessment that 'partial exemption methods based on floor area are seldom fair and reasonable'. However, this view was not shared by the chairman in the case of *Auchterarder Golf Club v Revenue and Customs Comrs* (3 November 2006, unreported) (EDN/06/28 19907) who concluded that a floor based method was effective in many situations, giving a fair and reasonable result in terms of input tax recovery.

Example 5

IC Clearly Ltd trades as an optician from a shop in a small town. Its taxable activity is the sale of non-prescription glasses (taxable income) and it is calculated that about 60 square metres of the premises is allocated to glasses stock. The company also carries out sight testing (exempt income) and has a 20 square metre area for this activity. The rest of the premises (1200 square metres) consist of corridors, common areas, or areas linked to both parts of the business.

An application is made to HMRC for a special method based on the square footage ratio of the taxable activity to the taxable plus exempt activity. This effectively gives a recovery rate of 75% (60 divided by 80).

Solution – in reality, the method would probably be refused because the common areas represent too large a proportion of the overall premises, ie 93%. The use of only a small percentage of the land for specific purposes can hardly be expected to give a fair and reasonable result.

With regard to methods proposed on an inputs basis, a similar outcome could be evident, namely, that the proposed method gives an unfair result because of the high proportion of expenses that come into the residual input tax or inputs category.

Changes in circumstances

[25.11] A special method approval letter from HMRC will include a paragraph that any significant change in the nature of the business must be notified to it if it has an effect on the amount of input tax being reclaimed. The method will then be reviewed, and if the fair and reasonable argument no longer applies, then a direction will be issued to stop a business from using the special method. It is then up to the taxpayer to propose an alternative special method, or accept the standard method instead.

One important power that HMRC holds is the option to issue a special method override direction.

Basically, it is recognised that if HMRC tells a business that a special method is no longer appropriate, there could be a time delay between the withdrawal letter and the date that the new method is agreed. In this case, for all VAT periods after the date of the notice, the business has to calculate the difference between the amount of input tax deductible using its current special scheme, and the amount of VAT that would be deductible in accordance with the principle of use. The difference between the two figures must then be declared by the business on its VAT returns.

In effect, the special method override direction ensures that a business cannot continue to benefit from an advantageous special method – due to delays in negotiating a new method with HMRC.

(HMRC Notice 706, paras 6.8 and 6.9).

Special methods/non-business VAT (1 January 2011)

[25.12] When deciding how much input tax can be claimed by a business on an expense, there is a two-stage process to carry out:

- identify the proportion of the expense that relates to business use (this can be done using any method that is fair and reasonable); and
- identify (and not claim) any of the remaining VAT (after the previous stage has been carried out) that needs to be blocked to reflect exempt use, ie taking into account the principles of partial exemption.

Until 1 January 2011, any partial exemption special method proposal could only deal with the second stage above, ie there was no scope to incorporate the non-business issue within the calculations for a special method. This is no longer the case – for VAT incurred on or after 1 January 2011, HMRC can approve a method that also covers non-business calculations. This is known as the combined method.

The combined method is only relevant to 'non-business' input tax adjustments – it cannot be requested for private use adjustments. In the latter case, input tax apportionment based on use is the only option. So the combined method will mainly benefit charities and educational bodies.

The same principles will apply to a request to adopt a combined method as to a normal special method.

- The taxpayer must certify that the proposed method gives a fair and reasonable result in terms of input tax recovery.
- The combined method must cover all VAT apportionments apart from those involving private use and certain partial exemption calculations that are always determined on the basis of use (eg those falling within *reg 103A* or *reg 103B* of the *VAT Regulations 1995*).
- It is not possible to propose two special methods, ie one for partial exemption purposes and one for non-business purposes. The request must be combined in one application.
- If a taxpayer has not incurred any exempt input tax in his current tax year or preceding year (ie he is fully taxable), then he can still request a special method just to deal with the non-business issue.
- If a taxpayer uses a combined method, then the *de minimis* limits for partial exemption (where exempt input tax can be claimed if it is below certain limits – see **24.10**) are irrelevant, ie the business will be treated as partly exempt at all times. This is logical because users of a combined method will not be clear about the total value of their exempt input tax (to apply the *de minimis* tests) if it is absorbed within the figure for non-business VAT.

Note – in effect, the main advantage of the combined special method should be the opportunity to allow a business to deal with the non-business and exempt disallowances of VAT in one stage rather than two. This should save time and administration costs.

(HMRC Information Sheet 06/11).

Planning points to consider

[25.13] The following planning points should be given consideration.

- It is important to regularly review the position of all partly exempt businesses and identify whether to apply to HMRC for a special method. These applications are appropriate when it is considered that the standard method does not give a fair and reasonable recovery of residual input tax.
- In many cases, the standard method gives a perfectly fair result – and overall is easy to calculate. However, it is important to be aware of alternative methods of calculation, particularly those based on inputs, square footage or staff numbers.
- The key principle of any partial exemption calculation is to ensure methods proposed are fair and reasonable. HMRC introduced regulations on 1 April 2007 that require a taxpayer to make a 'fair and reasonable' declaration at the time he submits the application. HMRC has the power to recover tax on a historic basis if this declaration is incorrect.
- Any change in circumstance for a business that could affect the fair and reasonable result of its special method calculations should be immediately notified to HMRC. A revised special method or adoption of the standard method may then be appropriate.

- Remember that it is only appropriate to spend time and effort proposing a special method if a business has a significant amount of residual input tax. If most (or all) input tax can be directly attributed to taxable or exempt supplies, there are negligible benefits to be gained by adopting a special method of calculation.

Chapter 26

Construction Services

Key topics in this chapter:

- The type of work that qualifies for zero-rating.
- The importance of the completion date for a new dwelling or qualifying building.
- Identifying what constitutes a new dwelling or qualifying residential/charitable building.
- The VAT liability of supplies made by subcontractors.
- Situations when a VAT certificate needs to be issued to enable a main contractor to zero-rate his supplies to a developer on a relevant new residential or charitable building.
- Supplies that are subject to the reduced rate of VAT (5%).
- Supplies of building materials that are always standard rated if supplied in the course of construction of a new dwelling, eg electrical appliances such as a fridge or dishwasher.
- The opportunity to obtain some zero-rating on professional fees through a 'design and build' arrangement.
- The *Finance Act 2012* changes affecting work on protected buildings.

Introduction

[26.1] The services supplied in the construction of a new or existing building are normally standard rated. However, there are a number of exceptions to this rule:

- certain supplies may qualify for zero-rating – mainly in the case of new residential dwellings or other qualifying buildings.
- some works qualify for a reduced VAT charge of 5%. This reduced rate is mainly relevant to work carried out in the course of certain residential conversions, or in carrying out work on altering certain buildings that have been empty for at least two years.

In many cases, services are supplied by subcontractors to a main contractor – the latter then works for the client who is receiving the benefit of the work. In certain cases, the work of the main contractor can be zero-rated if he receives a certificate from his client to confirm the building qualifies for zero-rating in accordance with the legislation. (Note – the main legislation concerning the zero-rating of construction services is contained in *VATA 1994, Sch 8, Group*

5.) However, the work of the subcontractor on the same building will be standard rated. This is an important principle to remember – the work of the subcontractor is not zero-rated because he does not hold a certificate from the main client.

Another important point to remember is that some of the VAT legislation relevant to construction services is largely dependent on the interpretation and meaning of certain key words, for example, 'dwelling', 'relevant charitable purpose', 'completion'. There will inevitably be occasions when appeals are made to VAT tribunals regarding the HMRC interpretation of these terms, which could extend the range of services that qualify for zero-rating. It is therefore worthwhile to read relevant articles and VAT tribunal decisions on this subject.

Zero-rated supplies

Main categories of zero-rated work

[26.2] Zero-rating applies to the following supplies:

- building services relevant to new qualifying dwellings and communal residential buildings, and certain new buildings used by charities. In the case of work on a new dwelling, zero-rating also applies to the construction of a garage if it is built at the same time as the dwelling and it is intended to be occupied with it;
  Note – see **26.4** for an explanation about the different types of building mentioned in this paragraph.
- services supplied in the course of construction of civil engineering work for the development of a new permanent residential caravan park;
- building services supplied to housing associations when non-residential buildings are being converted into residential buildings;
  Note – for a non-residential to residential conversion, the building work will be subject to 5% VAT if the property owner is not a housing association. See **26.14** below.
- building materials and certain electrical goods incorporated into a building by a builder who is also supplying any of the above zero-rated services;
- certain goods and services supplied to disabled persons – the best reference point is HMRC Notice 701/7;
- development of residential caravan parks.

(HMRC Notice 708, para 2.1).

An important point to remember is that building materials are only zero-rated if jointly supplied to the customer with construction services from the same builder – see Example 1.

Example 1

Smith Builders Ltd is installing kitchen units into a new house being built by Mr Jones. Mr Jones suggests that he buys the units himself from Kitchen Furniture Ltd and that Smith Builders Ltd just charges him for labour. Mr Jones is not registered for VAT – but Smith Builders Ltd has been registered for many years.

Solution – if Smith Builders Ltd bought the units from Kitchen Furniture Ltd, it would be able to recover input tax on the cost of the units. The company is then making an onward supply of labour and materials for work on a new residential building, and the full charge will be zero-rated.

However, if Mr Jones buys the materials himself from Kitchen Furniture Ltd, he will be charged 20% VAT by the company, even though the units are for a new residential property. This is because Kitchen Furniture Ltd is supplying materials only, and zero-rating would only apply if the company was supplying relevant services as well. In this case, Mr Jones will have an unnecessary VAT bill (although he could possibly recover this VAT under the DIY scheme – see Chapter 29).

Type of work that qualifies for zero-rating – and relevance of completion date

[26.3] A key point about zero-rating on qualifying dwellings is that it is only supplies made directly in the course of construction that can be zero-rated, not related services such as the following:

- services of architects, surveyors, consultants or supervisory services;
- the hire of goods on their own, eg plant and machinery without an operator, scaffolding without erection/dismantling.

In effect, therefore, the legislation means that the building work carried out on the building itself will be zero-rated – and this includes all work carried out until the building is completed. Once completed, any subsequent work is standard rated. The usual time when a building is deemed to be 'complete' is when a Certificate of Completion has been issued. However, there can be other relevant issues, such as the date when the building is sold, the intentions of the developer, and when the building is first occupied.

(HMRC Notice 708, para 3.4).

See Example 2.

Example 2

John has bought a 'shell' apartment from a developer, on which he has obtained a special deal because he is responsible for fitting out the property himself. He makes contact with builders covering a wide range of trades – carpenters, plumbers, kitchen fitters, electricians – and they perform a range of services on the apartment to make it a property that John can then live in. What is the VAT position of the supplies made by the builders?

Solution – even though the builder sold the property to John, it was sold before it was completed. The work carried out is therefore zero-rated as construction services carried out on a new dwelling before it has been completed. In effect, the completion date would be when John moves in to the property.

From a tax planning point of view, it is therefore important for as much work as possible to be carried out before the building is completed so that it can qualify for zero-rating. For example, if a customer agrees to buy a new house from a developer and agrees to pay an extra £10,000 for the property to have a conservatory fitted, then this payment will form part of the consideration to buy the house and will be zero-rated. However, if he bought the property without the conservatory and then asked a builder to subsequently build him a conservatory, this work would then be standard rated because it has taken place after the relevant completion date.

Note – a tribunal case *Mr and Mrs James* (30 October 2007, unreported) (LON/07/328 20426) considered the VAT liability of plastering work carried out after the completion date of a new dwelling, but with the aim of correcting defective plastering work caused by the original builder.

HMRC claimed that the work was standard rated as the alteration of an existing house, but the tribunal supported the taxpayer and confirmed the work should be zero-rated. The tribunal's approach was that the new plastering work was supplied in the course of the construction of the building because the old plastering work was inadequate and dangerous.

Scope of new qualifying dwellings, qualifying charitable buildings and other relevant residential properties

[26.4] As explained at **26.1**, zero-rating mainly applies if work is being carried out on the following buildings:

- a new dwelling (see **26.5**);
- a new qualifying charitable building (see **26.6**); or
- new properties used for a relevant residential purpose (see **26.11**).

The zero rate for dwellings is based on the design of the buildings and the zero rate for relevant residential purpose buildings is based on use of the buildings. Some buildings can qualify for zero-rating under both of these provisions at the same time so that either provision can be relied on to achieve zero-rating.

(HMRC Notice 708, paras 3.2 and 15.1).

New dwelling

[26.5] In basic terms, a new dwelling must have the following main features if the work is to qualify for zero-rating:

- it must consist of self-contained living accommodation;
- there must be no provision for direct internal access to any other dwelling;
- the separate use, letting or disposal of the dwelling is not prohibited by any legal clause or other provision. This means, for example, that the construction of a granny annex to an existing house is not classed as a new dwelling;

- statutory planning consent has been granted in respect of that dwelling and its construction or conversion has been carried out in accordance with that consent.

In most cases, it will be fairly obvious to identify if a project is both 'new' and a 'dwelling' – a key exclusion will always be if a project is for commercial purposes, eg new office, warehouse, factory, industrial unit.

An example of when a new dwelling is created is if an additional flat (or flats) is built on top of existing flats, ie to create an additional floor(s) with new units. However, the conversion of two flats on an existing floor to create three smaller flats on the same floor would not be classed as the construction of a new dwelling but the conversion of two existing dwellings. (HMRC Notice 708, para 3.2.4).

Note – if a new dwelling or building partly qualifies for zero-rating (eg a flat above a shop), then the builder must apportion his charges so that only work carried out on the dwelling is zero-rated. (HMRC Notice 708, para 3.5.1).

Building for a relevant charitable purpose

[26.6] Building work carried out by the main contractor (not subcontractor working for the main contractor) on a new building being constructed for a charity will only qualify for zero-rating if it is being used by the charity 'otherwise than in the course or furtherance of a business'.

The phrase 'business' does not necessarily relate to 'profit' – it is possible for a charity to have a loss making business activity.

Examples of *qualifying* buildings would therefore be:

- places of worship;
- offices used by charities for administering non-business activities such as the collection of donations.

Examples of *non-qualifying* buildings would be:

- child nurseries where a fee is charged;
- school buildings where a fee is charged for the provision of education;
- offices used by charities for administering business activities such as fundraising events where an entrance fee is charged.

Minor business use

[26.7] Where a building has both business and non-business use, there used to be an HMRC concession that the business use could be ignored if it was less than 10%. The 10% figure could be calculated on a floor space, staff numbers or time basis. Since 1 July 2009 (with a transitional arrangement that allowed the old method to be adopted until 30 June 2010) the 10% concession has been withdrawn. HMRC now accept that the legislation allows a small amount of business use as a matter of course, but restricted to 5% of total use. However, the 5% basis can be calculated using any method that is fair and reasonable. Any query on the new approach can be directed to HMRC's charity helpline (tel: 0300 123 1073).

Under the 10% concession the charity had to certify that there was no intention at the time of zero-rating that the building would be used for business purposes in excess of 10% of total use within ten years. So if, for example, a building was finalised in June 2008, the charity certified that it had no intention to have a business use of the building exceeding 10% of total use before June 2018. It would not be a problem if the 10% use was exceeded between these years, as long as the intention in June 2008 was for less than 10% business use to be achieved. However, a problem occurs under the new rules if an actual change in use at any time in the ten-year period means that business use of the building exceeds 5%. This will result in an extra tax payment for the charity.

Village hall

[26.8] The other main situation where zero-rating would apply is if the new building is being constructed as a 'village hall or similarly in providing social or recreational facilities for a local community'. This particular aspect of the legislation has been the subject of various tribunal decisions in recent years – the main principles being challenged have related to the scope of the facilities being offered by a building and the extent to which it is being used by the local community.

The obvious situation where zero-rating would apply is in the case of a new village hall being built solely for the use of residents in a particular area. Such buildings must be available for use by the community at large, not just isolated sections of the community. This clause would therefore exclude the construction of a theatre, swimming pool or child nursery. See Example 3 which highlights the importance of the building being intended for local community use.

(HMRC Notice 708, para 14.7.4).

Example 3

ABC Charity Ltd is a registered charity owning a property that is used by an independent fee paying school. The charity has arranged for the construction of a new building to be used as a sports hall for the school, which will be available for general community use at specific times, ie weekends, school holidays, evenings. The company trustees consider that the building work should benefit from zero-rating.

Solution – the sports hall could be available for general use, so the nature of the building is not a problem. However, the main beneficiaries of the hall are the pupils at the school, not the local community at large. The community use is effectively a secondary purpose of the building, not its main aim. The construction services will therefore be standard rated.

Case law – building for relevant charitable purpose

[26.9] The question of whether a new building was intended for use solely for a relevant charitable purpose was considered by the VAT Tribunal in the case of *Quarriers* (EDN/07/120 20660).

The issue for the tribunal was whether a new epilepsy centre being constructed by Quarriers was eligible for zero-rating on the construction costs or whether the actual use of the building was to be for business purposes, ie the building work would be standard-rated. The tribunal ruled in favour of the building being for non-business purposes.

- Although fees were received from local authorities towards the costs of caring for patients at the centre (fee income usually indicates a business purpose), these fees were not determined by reference to going rates in the market but were based on what Health Boards were willing to pay for the unique services provided by Quarriers.
- The activities carried out by the charity were at the heart of its charitable purposes.
- The tribunal did not feel that the activities were carried out on a commercial basis which might justify them being described as a business activity.
- The appeal was therefore allowed.

Annex to a charitable building

[26.10] The construction of an additional building to an existing site (eg an extension) usually means building services are subject to standard rate VAT. However, the building work can be zero-rated in the case of charity buildings if all of the following conditions are met:

- an 'annex' is being constructed rather than an 'extension' or 'enlargement';
- the whole annex, or part of it, is intended solely for use for a relevant charitable purpose; if only part is intended for charitable use, then the building work for this part only can be zero-rated;
- the annex is capable of functioning independently from the main building;
- the annex and the existing building each has its own independent main access;
- a valid certificate is held by the builder confirming charitable use.

(HMRC Notice 708, para 3.2.5).

Examples of an annex are a day hospice added to an existing residential hospice, a self-contained suite of rooms added to an existing village hall, a church hall added to an existing church or a nursery added to a school building.

(HMRC Notice 708, para 3.2.6).

Properties used for a relevant residential purpose

[26.11] This part of the legislation (*VATA 1994, Sch 8, Group 5, Note 4*) secures zero-rating for work carried out by the main contractor (not subcontractors working for the main contractor) on the following new buildings:

- a home or other institution providing residential accommodation for children;

- a home or other institution providing residential accommodation with personal care for persons in need of such care by reason of old age, disablement, past or present dependence on alcohol, drugs or past or present mental disorder;
- a hospice;
- residential accommodation for students or school pupils;
- residential accommodation for members of any of the armed forces;
- a monastery, nunnery or similar establishment;
- an institution which is the sole or main residence for at least 90% of the residents.

Note – the legislation makes an exception where use of a building is as a hospital, prison or similar establishment or an hotel, inn or similar establishment.

The First Tier Tax Tribunal recently upheld an appeal by *Pennine Care NHS Trust* (TC04998) [2016] UKFTT 222, [2016] SWTI 1420. The Trust constructed a building and claimed zero-rating on the basis that it was intended to be used for a relevant residential purpose. HMRC considered that the building was a hospital as all of the intended residents were undergoing treatment for mental health disorders. The tribunal concluded that, on the evidence, the building was intended to be a residence for up to two years. The fact that the residents may also receive some medical care did not turn the building into a hospital or similar establishment.

(HMRC Notice 708, para 14.6).

See Example 4 for an illustration of when zero-rating applies on this part of the legislation.

Example 4

Barry is the chief surveyor for BCD Construction Services Ltd. He is currently submitting quotes for three jobs and has asked his VAT advisor to confirm the VAT liability in each case:

(a) the company has been asked to build a new bedroom block comprising ten bedrooms in the grounds of a registered care home;

(b) the company has been asked to build a new home for people with mental disorders – the home will be for the people to use on a temporary basis only, while they recover from their illnesses;

(c) the company has been asked to construct a new property which will comprise 50 apartments for nurses to live in on a permanent basis as their main residence, and two apartments that will be rented out on a short-term bed and breakfast basis.

Solution – only (c) will qualify for zero-rating. In this case, the two apartments being rented out on a short-term basis is not a problem because at least 90% of the residents will be using the building as their sole or main residence.

The mental home will almost certainly be classed as a hospital, which is excluded from zero-rating. The new bedroom block is not eligible for zero-rating because it is not classed as the construction of a new home for a relevant residential purpose in its own right – but part of a larger home or institution.

(HMRC Notice 708, para 3.2.2).

Services of subcontractors and issuing of certificates for qualifying buildings

[26.12] At **26.4–26.11**, it was identified that zero-rating could be relevant to construction services carried out on three different types of new building:

(a)   a new dwelling, eg a house, flat or bungalow;
(b)   a new building for a relevant charitable purpose, eg a church;
(c)   a new building for a relevant residential purpose, eg a home for elderly persons.

In the case of a subcontractor working for the main contractor (or for any other person apart from the person who intends to use the building), it is only construction work being carried out on a new dwelling that can qualify for zero-rating, providing the main contractor (or other person the subcontractor is working for) is not working for a relevant housing association. All construction work carried out by a subcontractor for a main contractor on a new building for a relevant charitable purpose or a new building for a relevant residential purpose is always standard rated, as are supplies of construction services to main contractors working for relevant housing associations.

(HMRC Notice 708, para 2.1.3).

As an additional clause, the work carried out by a main contractor on a new building for a relevant charitable or residential purpose (ie excluding new dwellings) cannot be zero-rated unless he receives a certificate from the user of the building (his customer) confirming that the building in question is being used for a relevant residential or relevant charitable purpose.

Regarding these certificates, the following points should be noted:

* the customer can either copy the certificate from HMRC VAT Notice 708, para 18.1 or create his own certificate provided it contains the same information;
* the certificate must be issued before the supplier makes his supply;
* the customer providing the certificate could be liable to a civil penalty if it is found by HMRC that it should not have been issued, ie work should have been standard rated rather than zero-rated or subject to VAT at the reduced rate;
* the supplier has a responsibility to take reasonable steps to ensure the certificate is valid, including correspondence with the customer to confirm the use of the building;
* as long as the supplier has taken reasonable steps to ensure the certificate is valid, then HMRC will not seek to recover any VAT from the supplier if it is found that VAT has been undercharged on the work in question.

See Example 5 for a practical example of how the above chain of events works in practice.

Example 5

ABC Ltd has secured work as a main contractor on two new projects:

- the construction of a new home for the elderly for Claywell Housing Association;
- the construction of three new four-bedroom detached houses for a national house builder.

ABC Ltd intends to use the services of DEF Ltd to carry out all roofing work on these two projects. What is the VAT position for the two companies?

Solution – ABC Ltd and DEF Ltd can both zero-rate the work carried out for the national house builder, as long as the work is relevant to the construction of the property and carried out before its completion. In this case, there is no need for any certificates to be obtained from the house builder to confirm zero-rating.

The new property for Claywell Housing Association is classed as a new building for a relevant residential purpose, which means the services of DEF Ltd as the subcontractor must always be standard rated.

However, as long as Claywell Housing Association issues a certificate to ABC Ltd as the main contractor confirming that the building will be used for a relevant residential purpose, then ABC Ltd can zero-rate its supplies to the Association.

ABC Ltd is making a zero-rated supply (ie taxable) so it can reclaim the VAT charged by DEF Ltd as input tax.

Note – there is still widespread ignorance of these rules within many construction companies. Many surveyors working for main contractors think (incorrectly) that their subcontractors should zero-rate supplies to them if they give the subcontractor a copy of their certificate from the final customer. (HMRC Notice 708, para 17.4).

Other surveyors think (incorrectly again) that the certificate from the final customer only becomes relevant if requested by HMRC. The main contractor should receive a proper certificate from his customer before work is carried out on the project.

In a Technical Note published on 31 January 2014 HMRC announced the withdrawal from 1 April 2015 of the following.

(1) The extra statutory concession that allows Higher Education Institutions (HEIs) to ignore non-term time use when determining whether new student accommodation is intended to be used solely (at least 95%) for a relevant residential purpose, and therefore eligible for a certificate to support zero-rating. This will affect HEIs that let out the accommodation to tourists during the holiday season as well as businesses in the construction and property development sectors.

(2) The extra statutory concession that allows dining rooms and kitchens to be zero-rated as residential accommodation for students and school pupils if constructed at the same time as new student accommodation and if used predominantly (at least 50%) by the residents of the new student accommodations. Once the concession is withdrawn, HEIs and

schools will only be able to issue a certificate as evidence to support zero-rating for a dining hall and kitchen if the building is constructed at the same time as student accommodation and is intended to be used solely (at least 95%) by students living in that accommodation, their guests, and anyone who looks after the building.

As a transitional arrangement, if the first supply of construction services was made before 1 April 2015 and it relates to a meaningful start to the construction of the building by that date, and the works are expected to progress to completion without interruption, certificates which rely on the extra statutory concessions will still be valid. For single developments of more than one block of student accommodation constructed in phases, HMRC have confirmed that the phrase 'meaningful start to the construction of the building' means 'meaningful start to the construction of the first building' and the phrase 'expected to progress to completion without interruption' means 'expected to progress to completion of all phases without interruption.'

The construction of new student accommodation will continue to be zero-rated where it is used solely (at least 95%) as residential accommodation for students (a relevant residential purpose) or where it is designed as a dwelling or a number of dwellings. As noted at **26.4** some buildings qualify for zero-rating under both of these provisions at the same time so that either provision can be relied on to achieve zero-rating.

(HMRC Technical Note issued on 31 January 2014 and Revenue & Customs Brief 14/14 issued on 7 April 2014).

Work that is always standard rated

[26.13] A basic rule of VAT – another 'golden' rule – is that a supply is always standard rated, unless it is specifically zero-rated, reduced-rated, exempt or outside the scope of VAT.

The approach to adopt for dealing with a liability query from a construction industry client is to identify under which section of the legislation the work could qualify for zero-rating, and then see if it qualifies within that section.

However, as a general principle, the following categories of work are always standard rated for VAT purposes:

- repair or maintenance work – but see **26.14** regarding residential conversions and the reduced rate of VAT;
- alterations to an existing building – unless the transitional provisions (see **26.19**) regarding work on protected buildings apply;
- the reconstruction of an existing building – a building only ceases to be an existing building when it is demolished completely to ground level or the part remaining above the ground level consists of no more than a single façade (double façade where a corner site), the retention of which is a condition or requirement of statutory planning consent or similar permission;
- any work on a non-residential building unless it is a new qualifying building for a relevant charitable purpose;

- work on new and uncompleted non-qualifying buildings and civil engineering works, eg commercial buildings such as offices;
- extensions to existing buildings.

Note – in *Astral Construction Ltd v Revenue and Customs Comrs* [2015] UKUT 21 (TCC), [2015] STC 1033, the Upper Tribunal confirmed that a new relevant residential building had been constructed where the building incorporated a redundant church building. HMRC contended that the works were the enlargement of the existing church and were, thus, standard rated. The tribunal disagreed. The new construction was of such a scale that it dwarfed the existing church building such that, objectively, what had been created was a new building. HMRC's appeal was, therefore, dismissed.

Reduced rate supplies (subject to VAT at 5%)

[26.14] The main categories of construction work that can qualify for a reduced rate of VAT are as follows:

- qualifying services supplied in the course of certain residential conversions, the main ones being where there is a changed number of units at the end of the project compared to the beginning, eg converting a detached house into two semi-detached houses (or vice versa);
- qualifying services supplied when converting a non-residential building into a residential building, including a dwelling, eg office converted into flats.
  Note – work carried out for a housing association converting a non-residential property into a residential property is zero-rated. In the case of a non-residential building being converted, a further condition is that the property must not have been used for residential purposes in the ten-year period before the building work starts.
  (HMRC Notice 708, para 6.3).
- qualifying services supplied in the course of renovating and altering dwellings or relevant residential buildings that have been empty for two or more years (see **26.15**);
- building materials and certain electrical goods incorporated into a building by the builder who is also supplying the above services;
- installation of energy-saving materials. Note – the reduced rate for energy-saving materials installed in buildings used for a relevant charitable purpose has been withdrawn with effect from 1 August 2013. Following a decision by the CJEU released on 4 June 2015 it is likely that the reduced rate for the supply and installation of energy-saving materials in residential accommodation will be withdrawn, except where the supply and installation relates to social housing. Legislation was expected to appear in the Finance Bill 2016, but its introduction seems to have been postponed.

With regard to residential conversions, work on the following projects would all qualify for the reduced rate of VAT:

Type of conversion	Examples
A single household dwelling into a multiple occupancy dwelling, or a building for a relevant residential purpose.	Converting a four bedroom detached house into two bedsits; converting a private house into a residential home for elderly people.
A single house dwelling into two or more single house dwellings.	Conversion of a house into two flats; converting a four bedroom detached property into two semi-detached properties.
A number of single house dwellings into a different number of single house dwellings.	Conversion of property with five large flats into seven smaller flats.
A multiple occupancy dwelling into a single household dwelling or a building for a relevant residential purpose.	Converting a property with four bedsits into a large detached home; converting a property with four bedsits into a residential home for elderly people.
A relevant residential purpose building into either a single household dwelling or a multiple occupancy dwelling.	A residential home for elderly people is converted to a four bedroom house; a residential home for elderly people is converted to six bedsits.
Any other building into a single household dwelling, multiple occupancy dwelling or building for a relevant residential purpose.	Conversion of office block into flats; conversion of a public house into a four bedroom detached house. In these cases, the number of dwellings is being changed from zero to a positive number of one or more.

The main exclusion from the reduced rate of VAT is where a property starts as a multiple occupancy dwelling, and is converted into another multiple occupancy dwelling – even where the number of units has changed. This means, for example, that work carried out on the conversion of a property comprising four bedsits into a property that comprises six smaller bedsits will be subject to VAT at the standard rate.

The reduced rate would not apply if a relevant residential building was converted into another relevant residential building, eg a conversion of a home for the elderly into a children's home.

Qualifying services mean either of the following:

- carrying out work to the fabric of the building or part of the building being converted;

- carrying out work within the immediate site of the building in connection with the means of providing water, heat, power or access to the building; the means of providing drainage or security to the building; the provision of means of waste disposal for the building.

Note – the qualifying services include all works of repair, maintenance or improvement to the fabric of the building where the work forms an intrinsic part of changing the number of dwellings.

The rules concerning conversions of single/multiple occupancy dwellings can sometimes be somewhat complicated and a useful situation to highlight this point is shown at Example 6.

Example 6

Manor House is a property that comprises 12 self-contained flats, with four flats on each floor. Work is carried out to create three large flats on the first floor (instead of four) but the ground floor is altered so that this floor accommodates five smaller size flats.

> *Solution* – although the number of units remains unchanged at 12, the reduced rate of VAT can still be applied to the work carried out in connection with the conversions because the number of flats on the ground and first floors has changed.

Empty property rules

[26.15] The reduced rate of VAT can also be applied (as explained above) to supplies of qualifying services on the renovation or alteration of single household dwellings, multiple occupancy dwellings or buildings to be used for a relevant residential purpose as long as the building in question has not been lived in for two years or more from the date when the work commences.

The reduced rate charge will also apply to any building materials installed by the builder as part of his work.

The rules concerning empty building conditions are very specific and there is some responsibility on the supplier of the services to have reasonable evidence that the property has been empty for at least two years. In assessing whether a property has been lived in, any illegal occupation by squatters and non-residential use can be ignored, for example, if the building had been used for storage by a business.

(HMRC Notice 708, section 8).

Supply of building materials and other goods

[26.16] The supply of goods by a builder also providing services will qualify for zero-rating if the work being performed is zero-rated, and the goods in question relate to the services being supplied.

For example, a builder installing kitchen units to a new dwelling would be able to zero-rate the supply of both the goods and his services. However, if he also supplied a television to his customer, then this would not be zero-rated because it is not linked to the service being performed.

In general terms, the phrase 'building materials' relates to goods that are 'ordinarily' incorporated or installed as fittings by builders in a building of that description.

For example, HMRC accepts that an item is incorporated into a building if its removal would require the use of tools but they would not accept that free-standing appliances or furniture would qualify. This would therefore exclude from zero-rating the supply of plugged-in appliances and free-standing furniture such as sofas, tables and chairs.

In terms of the phrase 'ordinarily' installed, HMRC accepts that certain properties have items which it would be expected would be included within the building, for example, air conditioning, burglar alarms, fireplaces and surrounds, electric showers.

However, there are a number of items that are excluded from the general rules and which would always be standard-rated (or subject to an input tax block) if supplied by a builder. These items are listed in VAT Notice 708, for example:

- electrical or gas appliances such as refrigerators, cookers, washing and dish-washing machines, tumble dryers;
- carpets or carpeting material such as carpet tiles or underlay. However, floor coverings such as linoleum, ceramic tiles and wooden floor systems are building materials and could therefore qualify as zero-rated.

Note – if the builder installs non-building materials into a new dwelling (such as carpet) then it is only the supply of the goods that is standard-rated. If he makes a separate charge for his installation services, the latter would still be zero-rated.

(HMRC Notice 708, sections 11 and 13).

Other matters

[26.17] The VAT issues involving construction industry supplies are very extensive, and this chapter has focused on the main practical situations which advisers could be faced with on a day to day basis. A few useful issues to consider are now given to conclude the chapter:

- *Design and build supplies* – as explained at **26.3** the supply of professional services is always standard rated. However, there may be occasions when a main contractor is engaged to carry out both the design and construction elements of a project. In such cases, the VAT liability of the overall project depends on the liability of the building work. If the building work is zero-rated, the design element will also be zero-rated, which could produce a potential tax saving for the client if he is not in a position to reclaim input tax. The main contractor will be able to reclaim input tax on any fees charged by an architect or surveyor because he is making a zero-rated supply.
  (HMRC Notice 708, para 3.4.1).
- *Authenticated receipts and self-billed invoices* – both of these documents are issued by the customer rather than the supplier and are very common in the construction industry. The main principle is that the customer issues the authenticated receipt or self-billed invoice at the time that he makes payment to a supplier — and these documents form the basis of output tax declared by the supplier and input tax reclaimed by the customer. The procedure is particularly useful in the construction industry where amounts actually paid for, eg work in progress based on a valuation figure, can be different to amounts requested by a supplier on his sales invoice. In both the case of authenticated receipts and self-billed invoices, a tax invoice should not be issued by the supplier.
- *CIS deductions* – in many cases, a main contractor is required to deduct income tax from his payments to a subcontractor under the Construction Industry Scheme (CIS) arrangements. If the subcontractor is VAT registered, then VAT charges must be based on the gross value of the work carried out, not the amount remaining after the income tax has been deducted by the main contractor.
- *Work for disabled persons* – certain work carried out for disabled persons can qualify for zero-rating. However, zero-rating will depend on two main issues, namely the status of the person receiving the work

(ie the extent to which he is disabled and whether this will be accepted by HMRC) and the nature of the work being carried out ie the goods or services being supplied. A good reference point on this subject and the procedures to adopt is VAT Notice 701/7.

- *Retentions* – it is common practice in the construction industry for a customer to hold back part of the payment for services performed, usually for six months or one year. In such cases, output tax is not payable to HMRC by the supplier until either he receives payment for the retention from his customer, or he raises an invoice to the customer (whichever happens sooner).
  (HMRC Notice 708, para 23.1.2).

- *Incorrect VAT charge* – there is a tendency for many builders to adopt a play safe approach and charge VAT at the standard rate. If you think that work should be zero-rated or subject to a reduced rate VAT charge, then it is sensible to agree this position before the work begins. There could be problems recovering VAT from a builder if he has already received his payment. In such cases, if zero-rating is subsequently agreed, the builder should refund any incorrectly charged VAT by issuing a VAT credit note. He can then reduce his output tax liability on the VAT return covered by the date of the credit note.

Update – HMRC have issued Revenue & Customs Brief 9/16 which clarifies HMRC's position on the VAT treatment of conversions of certain non-residential buildings into dwellings following the introduction of additional permitted development rights (PDRs). PDRs are a substitute for full planning permission. As a result, a developer will be unable to demonstrate that statutory planning consent (SPC) has been granted in relation to works covered by a PDR. Normally, this would then fail the test of whether the works related to a 'dwelling' and zero-rating would then not be available. The Brief confirms that HMRC will continue to require evidence to be produced that the work is lawful in order for the zero or reduced rate of VAT to apply or for a claim to be eligible under the DIY House Builder Scheme. Where the builder, developer or DIY House Builder Scheme claimant establishes that the conversion is covered by a PDR and individual SPC is not required, they must be able to evidence it by at least one of the following:

(a) written notification from the LPA advising of the grant of prior approval; or
(b) written notification from the LPA advising that prior approval is not required; or
(c) evidence of deemed consent (ie evidence that you have written to the LPA and your confirmation that you have not received a response from them within 56 days) and evidence that the development is a permitted development. This will include all of the following (where the documents have been created), plans of the development, evidence of the prior use of the property (eg evidenced by its classification for business rates purposes etc), confirmation of which part of the planning legislation is relied upon for the development and a lawful development certificate where one is already held.

Developments carried out under a PDR must still meet the appropriate building standards. Should any circumstances arise where building control is not required, evidence from the local authority confirming this should be provided.

Finance Act 2012 changes affecting protected buildings

[26.18] Subject to transitional provisions (noted at **26.19**) the *Finance Act 2012* changes affect:

• Those who reconstruct protected buildings to sell, or to grant a long leasehold interest in, eg property developers.
• Those who incur cost on approved alterations to protected buildings, eg people and charities who live in or own listed buildings.
• Construction businesses that reconstruct or alter protected buildings.

VATA 1994, Sch 8 Group 6 provides a detailed definition of the term 'protected building'. In general terms a protected building is a listed building or scheduled monument that is designed to remain as or become a dwelling or a number of dwellings or is intended to be used exclusively for a relevant residential or charitable purpose.

Finance Act 2012 does not change the definition of a protected building but it restricts the ability for property developers to zero-rate the first grant of a substantially reconstructed protected building and it results in approved alterations to a protected building being standard rated (previously they were zero-rated). The changes are effective from 1 October 2012, subject to the transitional provisions noted at **26.19**.

Previously, a person (eg a property developer) could zero-rate the first grant of a major interest in a reconstructed protected building providing one of two conditions had been met. The first condition was that at least 60% of the cost of reconstructing the building related to building materials and construction services that would have qualified for zero-rating if the work being carried out was an approved alteration. The second condition was that the reconstructed building incorporated no more of the original building than the external walls and other external features of architectural or historic interest.

As only one of the two conditions explained in the previous paragraph had to be met, a property developer was, until 1 October 2012, able to zero-rate the first grant of a major interest in a reconstructed protected building if at least 60% of the cost of reconstructing the building related to building materials and construction services that would have qualified for zero-rating if the work being carried out was an approved alteration.

From 1 October 2012 approved alteration work does not benefit from zero-rating and is standard rated in the same way that unapproved alterations and repairs are standard rated.

Also from 1 October 2012 a property developer will only be able to zero-rate the first grant of a major interest in a reconstructed protected building if the reconstructed building incorporates no more of the original building than the external walls and other external features of architectural or historic interest.

The above changes are subject to the transitional provisions noted at **26.19**.

Transitional provisions affecting protected buildings

[26.19] Transitional provisions affect supplies which up to 30 September 2012 qualified for zero-rating but which would have ceased to qualify for zero-rating after that date were it not for the transitional provisions.

Approved alteration work can continue to be zero-rated until 30 September 2015 if it is work for which the contract was entered into or planning consent applied for before 21 March 2012.

As noted at **26.18**, the general rule from 1 October 2012 is that a property developer will only be able to zero-rate the first grant of a major interest in a reconstructed protected building if the reconstructed building incorporates no more of the original building than the external walls and other external features of architectural or historic interest. This general rule is not affected by the transitional provisions. The transitional provisions affect the first grant of a major interest in a reconstructed protected building where at least 60% of the cost of reconstructing the building relates to costs that would have previously qualified for zero-rating as approved alteration work. Where this applies, zero-rating will continue to apply until 30 September 2015 if:

•   the approved alterations are within the scope of a relevant consent applied for before 21 March 2012 or of a written contract entered into before 21 March 2012; or

•   at least 10% of the substantial reconstruction (measured by cost) was completed prior to 21 March 2012.

Detailed HMRC guidance regarding the application of the new rules, including how the rules apply in particular situations, for example, where minor changes are necessary to plans for which an application for relevant consent was applied for before 21 March 2012, are included in HMRC VAT Information Sheet 10/12.

Planning points to consider

[26.20] The following planning points should be given consideration.

•   Building materials are only zero-rated if they are also supplied with a service that is also eligible for zero-rating.

•   It is advisable for people buying a new residential dwelling to fit out the property to their requirements before it has been completed. The work will then be eligible for zero-rating in most cases – once the completion date has passed, the work will be standard rated.

•   Remember that supplies made by a subcontractor to a main contractor are only zero-rated if relevant to a new dwelling. All supplies involving a relevant residential building or qualifying charitable building are standard rated when supplied by a subcontractor.

•   A main contractor is only able to zero-rate work carried out on a new relevant charitable building or new relevant residential building if he obtains a certificate from his client confirming the building is eligible for zero-rating. This certificate should be received before the building supplies are made.

- There are a wide range of services that qualify for the 5% reduced rate of VAT in relation to many residential conversions – or work on residential properties that have been empty for at least two years. The 15% difference between the reduced VAT rate and standard VAT rate means there is scope for considerable savings if reduced rate work is correctly identified in advance.

- Most goods supplied by builders as part of their work on a new dwelling will be zero-rated. However, there are certain goods where the supply is always standard rated (or subject to an input tax block if bought directly by the housebuilder), and it is important to be aware of such items, eg fridges, washing machines, dishwashers.

- There are opportunities to save VAT on professional fees if a developer enters into a 'design and build' arrangement with a main contractor. In such cases, the liability of the design services will follow the same liability as the building work, ie possibly zero-rated. Design fees and professional services supplied on their own are always standard-rated.

- Be aware of the *Finance Act 2012* changes affecting work on protected buildings.

Chapter 27

Property Transactions – Introduction

Key topics in this chapter:

- What constitutes a licence to occupy land.
- Examples of exempt and standard-rated supplies involving a licence to occupy or use land.
- The approach to adopt when identifying whether a licence to occupy land arrangement is exempt or standard rated as far as VAT is concerned.
- Assessing whether an arrangement is for an exempt licence to occupy land or a standard-rated supply of services (illustrated by example of self-employed hair stylist).
- Exceptions to the rule that the grant of an interest in or right over land is exempt from VAT, ie standard rated (eg sale of new commercial building) or zero-rated (eg sale of new dwelling).
- Apportionment of output tax where the sale of a new building includes a standard-rated and zero-rated element, eg the sale of a new first floor flat and a ground floor shop.
- Temporarily renting out new dwellings that cannot be sold by a house builder.

Introduction

[27.1] The main focus of Chapter 26 was to consider the VAT issues concerning construction industry services, ie situations where work performed by a builder would be zero-rated, standard rated or, in some cases, subject to VAT at the 5% lower rate of tax.

In this chapter, we consider actual supplies involving property, ie the sale of a freehold or leasehold property and the VAT issues therein – or the letting of property to receive rental income.

There are two main situations as far as land and property are concerned:

- the granting of an interest in or right over land, eg the sale of property on a freehold or long leasehold basis;
- the granting of a licence to occupy land, eg where a landlord sublets his interest in the property to a tenant in return for payment of rent.

Property transactions are quite unique from a VAT aspect because the landlord/user of a property has the right to waive exemption in certain cases by making an election to tax the property, ie exempt supplies will become standard rated and subject to VAT. The decision to opt to tax a property has major implications and is considered in Chapter 28.

(HMRC Notice 742, para 2.2).

Exempt supplies – licence to occupy land

[27.2] The basic legislation in *VATA 1994, Sch 9, Group 1* states that, subject to certain exceptions, the 'grant' (see **27.3**) of any 'interest in or right over' land (see **27.4** and **27.10–27.12**) or 'licence to occupy' land (see **27.5** and **27.8**) is exempt as far as VAT is concerned.

Grant

[27.3] A grant of land is a sale of the freehold or other interest, or a lease or letting of land. It includes the surrender of the land (eg where a tenant renting the land returns its use back to the landlord) and assignment of the land, ie the transfer of a lease by an existing tenant to a new tenant.

Interest in or right over land

[27.4] 'Interest in or right over land' means that the person using the land has either a legal interest in the land (ie formal ownership of the land such as a freehold or leasehold interest in it), or a beneficial interest (that is, the right to receive the benefit of supplies of the land, eg sale proceeds or rental income). Rights over land include rights of entry and easements.

(HMRC Notice 742, paras 2.3 and 2.4).

Licence to occupy land

[27.5] HMRC regards a licence to occupy land as being created when the following criteria are met:

(a)   the licence should be granted in return for a payment made by the licensee;
(b)   the licence must be to occupy a specific piece of land;
(c)   the licence is for the occupation of the land by the licensee;
(d)   another person's right to enter the specified land does not impinge upon the occupational rights of the licensee; and either:
   (i)   the licence allows the licensee to physically enjoy the land for the purpose of the grant (eg to hold a party in a hall); or
   (ii)   the licence allows the licensee to exploit economically the land for the purpose of its business (eg to run a nightclub).

(HMRC Notice 742, para 2.5).

It is important to recognise when a licence to occupy land situation applies – see Example 1 for an illustration of a practical situation.

Example 1

The committee of Smitherton Golf Club has decided to rent out the kitchen area to a self-employed caterer, who can then sell light meals and snacks for members in the bar area. The rental arrangement will include full use of all the kitchen equipment.

As a separate transaction, they allow a local company to come to the club office at any time in order to use the club's photocopying machine and fax machine. The company will pay a fixed monthly fee for this facility.

What is the VAT position of the two transactions?

Solution – going back to the four main rules as to when a licence to occupy land exists:

- *Is the licence granted in return for a payment made by the licensee?*
  The answer in both situations is 'yes' as both the caterer and the local company are paying rent to the golf club.
- *Does the licence give the licensee a specific piece of land to occupy?*
  In the case of the caterer, the answer to this question is 'yes', ie he has use of the kitchen area to develop his activities. The answer is 'no' in the case of the company using the office equipment – the main users of the office will be the golf club staff, and the supply being enjoyed by the company is the use of the office equipment, ie standard rated.
- *Is the licence for the occupation of the land by the licensee?*
  In the case of the caterer, the answer is 'yes'.
- *Does the licensee have the right to enjoy the land or to exploit it for economic gains?*
  The caterer is trading from the premises he is occupying, ie he meets the economic gains clause.

Overall, the catering arrangement has met all four of the licence to occupy land rules and therefore the rental payment to the golf club will be exempt from VAT. However, if the golf club had opted to tax the premises, then the supply would become standard rated – see Chapter 28.

Examples of exempt supplies under licence to occupy land rules

[27.6] Listed below are some examples of exempt supplies under the licence to occupy land rules.

- *The provision of office accommodation* – however, this would have to be a specified bay, room or floor, and an agreement would often include the right to use shared areas such as reception, lifts or leisure facilities. The key point is that the tenant occupying the land is obtaining his own area of land from where he can conduct his business.
- *A shop-in-shop arrangement* – this situation occurs when a business is granted a specific area in a shop or store from which to trade. This situation is particularly common in large department stores, where there are a number of different entities trading from the premises in their own names.

- *Granting space to erect advertising hoardings* – this situation applies at, for example, a sporting ground where there are advertising boards around the ground to promote various companies. The company that is advertising through the board pays a rent to the sports club for the board to be displayed. The board should be fixed in its own area, ie not a mobile board that moves around the ground to different locations.
- *Hiring out a hall or other accommodation for meetings, parties etc* – this can be a difficult area as far as VAT is concerned, because sometimes the hire of a hall includes other benefits such as catering arrangements and the supply of staff to, for example, entertain delegates. In such cases, the overall supply could be standard rated. However, the basic hire of a hall/room for an event will qualify for exemption.
- *Granting a catering concession, where the caterer is granted a licence to occupy specific kitchen and restaurant areas, even if the grant includes the use of kitchen or catering equipment* – see Example 1 above.
- *Granting traders a pitch in a market or at a car boot sale* – this example illustrates the point that a short-term let can still qualify for VAT exemption – it is the principle of a licence to occupy land that counts, not the length of time that it is used.

(HMRC Notice 742, para 2.6).

How to identify if an arrangement is exempt

[27.7] The above examples of exempt supplies in licence to occupy land situations all meet the four key rules identified at **27.5**.

A useful approach to adopt when assessing the VAT liability of an arrangement is to ask three key questions as follows.

(a) In reality, what is the main supply being enjoyed by the person paying his money to the landlord? If this is clearly the right to occupy a specific area of land for his own benefit or enjoyment, then the supply will usually be exempt from VAT.

(b) Does it appear that the main benefits being enjoyed by the person paying his money are related to specific services rather than the right to occupy land, eg the use of photocopying facilities as in Example 1 above. If so, the supply will not be exempt from VAT as land related.

(c) Is there an indication that an arrangement is not for a specific area of land, for example, the fee paid for an ice cream van to be allowed into a sports venue to sell ice creams would not be exempt because the van driver has the opportunity to move his van to different parts of the ground (eg to park it where there are most potential customers). In such cases, his payment is standard rated as the right to sell ice-creams, not a licence to occupy land.

See **27.8** for examples of arrangements that would be standard rated for VAT purposes because a licence to occupy land situation does not exist.

Standard-rated supplies – use of land

Examples of standard-rated supplies

[27.8] At 27.6, the examples highlight when a supply involving land is exempt from VAT on the basis that the owner/user of the land is providing another party with a 'licence to occupy the land'.

In commercial situations, there are many examples of a business 'using' the land of another person or party for various reasons – but the arrangement falls short of the 'licence to occupy' arrangement that qualifies for exemption. In such cases, the charge to the user of the land will be standard rated.

The following examples illustrate when an arrangement is standard rated rather than exempt:

- *sharing business premises* – where more than one business has use of the same parts of the premises without having their own specified areas – the key feature here is that the business does not have its own land to enjoy, only on a shared basis;
- *use of office facilities* – as in Example 1 above;
- *facilities to park a vehicle* – eg fee to use a car park;
- *granting an ambulatory concession* – for example, the right to sell ice creams from a van on the sea front, hamburger vans at sporting events etc. The key point here is that it would be difficult for these vehicles to have their own specified area of land. In reality, they are paying for access to a potential market in which to sell their goods;
- *public admission to premises or events* – again, there is no licence to occupy land situation. The member of the public is gaining access to premises in order to enjoy the entertainment or other facilities on offer;
- *tipping facility* – allowing the public to tip rubbish on land;
- *self storage facilities* – *Finance Act 2012* has added para (*ka*) 'the grant of facilities for the self storage of goods' to the list of standard-rated supplies included at *VATA 1994, Sch 9, Group 1, Item 1*. A point to note is that the legislation will apply to many commercial landlords and not just to businesses who know that they are providing self-storage facilities. Any commercial landlord could potentially be a storage provider. Paragraph 2.4 of HMRC VAT Information Sheet 14/12 is relevant in relation to this point and is quoted below:

> **What if the storage provider doesn't know how the space he is letting out is used?**
>
> The use of the space will normally be clear from the nature of the facilities, the way they are advertised and the agreements entered into. However, in some instances, facilities may be suitable for a variety of uses and agreements may not specify a particular use by the licensee (ie the licensee is free to use the space for any purpose). In such cases it will be necessary for the grantor to obtain confirmation from his customer of the use to be made of the space. Suppliers are advised to obtain such confirmation in writing and retain it with their VAT records.

The notes to the legislation include exceptions to the general rule so that standard rating is not to apply to a grant of self storage facilities to a charity to use otherwise in the course of a business, or in certain circumstances where the self-storage provider is connected to the customer, or where the self-storage facilities are ancillary to other exempt use of a building.

- *other services* – any grant of land where the land is incidental to use of the main facilities that can be enjoyed – see **27.9** which illustrates this situation with the example of a hairdresser.

Hairdresser arrangement

[27.9] Many practitioners have hairdresser clients, so in this section the rules on hairdresser arrangements will be considered.

A common arrangement for hairdressers is as follows:

- many stylists will trade on a self-employed basis, using the facilities within a hairdressing salon (the scope of whether a person is employed or self-employed is beyond the scope of this book);
- the stylists will make payment to the landlord/main owner of the hairdressing salon – to compensate him for the facilities they enjoy in the salon;
- on occasions in the past, the payment for these benefits has been described as for 'rent a chair', ie an attempt to make the supply exempt from VAT as a licence to occupy the land covered by the chair;
- in reality, the stylists receive many other benefits for their payments – laundry services, the use of a rest room, the services of a receptionist employed by the salon owner, towels and linen, shampoos and other materials.

Finance Act 2012 has added para (*ma*) 'the grant of facilities to a person who uses the facilities wholly or mainly to supply hairdressing servces' to the list of standard-rated supplies included at *VATA 1994, Sch 9, Group 1, Item 1*. The legislation clarifies the effect of para (*ma*) at *Notes 17* and *18* of *VATA 1994, Sch 9, Group 1, Item 1*:

> 'Note [(17) Paragraph (ma) does not apply to a grant of facilities which provides for the exclusive use, by the person to whom the grant is made, of a whole building, a whole floor, a separate room or a clearly defined area, unless the person making the grant or a person connected with that person provides or makes available (directly or indirectly) services related to hairdressing for use by the person to whom the grant is made.
>
> Note (18) For the purposes of Note (17)—
>
> (a)   "services related to hairdressing" means the services of a hairdresser's assistant or cashier, the booking of appointments, the laundering of towels, the cleaning of the facilities subject to the grant, the making of refreshments and other similar services typically used in connection with hairdressing, but does not include the provision of utilities or the cleaning of shared areas in a building, and
>
> (b)   it does not matter if the services related to hairdressing are shared with other persons.'

The legislation puts beyond doubt that a VAT-registered hairdressing salon that rents out facilities to self-employed stylists (the rent a chair arrangement) must charge VAT on the rent. However, the wording of the legislation, in particular *Notes 17* and *18*, appears to have the effect that the landlord of a building that is let to a hairdressing salon will be making a standard-rated supply if the landlord (or a person connected with the landlord) also provides services related to hairdressing to the tenant, for example, the laundering of towels.

If a landlord has opted to tax the building VAT will be charged on the rent anyway, which should not be a problem for a VAT-registered hairdressing salon tenant. However, the landlord may prefer not to opt to tax the building as an option to tax generally cannot be revoked for 20 years (see Chapter 28). In certain circumstances providing services related to hairdressing to a hairdressing salon tenant may be preferable to opting to tax the building as a way of recovering input tax on costs relating to the building.

The question may be asked, 'What if separate invoices are issued?' The answer at paragraph 6 of VAT Information Sheet 13/12 is that issuing separate invoices does not change the VAT treatment. To quote an extract from VAT Information Sheet 13/12, paragraph 6:

> 'So, for the example, if you issue separate invoices for the provision of a designated area and services related to hairdressing, the new rules confirm that both supplies are standard-rated for VAT purposes.'

Exempt, standard-rated and zero-rated supplies – grant of interest in land

What constitutes the grant of an interest in or right over land?

[27.10] As explained at **27.3**, the grant of any interest in or right over land is, subject to certain exceptions, an exempt supply. The grant of an interest in, or right over, land is different to a licence to occupy land. See Example 2.

Example 2

Bill owns the freehold of a four-story office block – he agrees to rent the third floor of the block to Ben and sell him the second floor on a 999-year lease.

Solution – in the first situation, Ben has a licence to occupy the land on the third floor. In the second situation, he has an interest in and right over the land on the second floor.

Situations when the grant of an interest in, or right over, land is standard rated

[27.11] The supply of an interest in, or right over, land is exempt from VAT in most cases – but standard rated in the following main situations.

- *New and uncompleted non-qualifying buildings and civil engineering works* – if a new or uncompleted building does not qualify as a 'dwelling' or number of dwellings and is not intended for use solely for a 'relevant residential purpose' or a 'relevant charitable purpose' then its sale will be standard rated. The sale of a new building as a 'dwelling' or a number of dwellings or for a 'relevant residential purpose' or 'relevant charitable purpose' by the person constructing it is zero-rated. This means, for example, that the freehold sale of new or uncompleted office blocks, factories, warehouses and industrial units would all be standard rated. A building/civil engineering work is to be taken as 'completed' when an architect/engineer issues a certificate of practical completion in relation to it or it is fully occupied/used, whichever happens first. It is to be treated as 'new' if it was completed less than three years before the grant.
  (HMRC Notice 742, paras 3.2 and 3.3).
  Note – the sale of a building means the freehold sale, not the assignment of a lease at a premium. Once a building is three years old, any future sales of the building will be exempt from VAT unless an option to tax election is in place.
  The issue of what is classed as a building for a 'relevant residential purpose' or a 'relevant charitable purpose' is considered in Chapter 26 – the person buying the building in these cases is obliged to provide a certificate confirming the intended use of the building. See Example 3 for an illustration of this point.
- *Gaming and fishing rights.*
  (HMRC Notice 742, section 6).
- *Hotel accommodation* – standard rated under *VATA 1994, Sch 9, Group 1, Item 1(d)* but *VATA 1994, Sch 6, para 9* reduces the value of the supply for VAT purposes if the accommodation is supplied with other facilities to an individual for a continuous period exceeding four weeks. The reduced value for VAT purposes applies to the fifth and subsequent weeks so that the value of the supply for VAT purposes in those weeks is the value of the other facilities, eg, catering and laundry services, providing the value of those facilities amounts to at least 20% of the value of the whole supply during those weeks. A guest's stay must be continuous to qualify for the reduced value rule but paragraph 3.3 of the June 2013 edition of HMRC Notice 709/3 suggests that a guest's departure is not seen to end their stay if the guest is a long-term resident and leaves for an occasional weekend or holiday or is a student who leaves during the vacation but returns to the same accommodation for the following term. This concession in paragraph 3.3 of the June 2013 edition of HMRC Notice 709/3 was withdrawn from 1 April 2015 so that from that date hotels, inns, boarding houses and similar establishments must treat all breaks in the guest's stay as starting a new period for the purpose of the reduced value rule.
- *Holiday accommodation* – the grant of any interest in or right over or licence to occupy holiday accommodation, eg a chalet, caravan or houseboat, is standard rated if the accommodation is held out as holiday accommodation or suitable for holiday or leisure use.
- *Caravan and tent pitches and camping facilities.*

- *Parking facilities* – the granting of facilities for parking a vehicle is always standard rated – this would include the letting or licensing of garages or designated parking bays or spaces. However, the letting of a garage as part of the letting of a dwelling for permanent residential use is exempt from VAT because the letting of the garage is incidental to the letting of the main property.
(HMRC Notice 742, section 4).

- *Boxes, seats etc at entertainment venues* – eg a company may rent a box for a season at a football ground. In such cases, the main benefit being enjoyed by the users is the opportunity to see the sporting or entertainment activity taking place (standard rated), rather than an exempt right over land situation.
(HMRC Notice 742, para 3.4).

- *Sports facilities* – the letting of facilities for playing sport is usually standard rated, eg hiring out a football pitch. However, there are certain situations when the letting could be exempt if it is let out for a continuous period of 24 hours or more to the same person, or for at least ten different sessions to the same hirer over a period of time.
(HMRC Notice 742, section 5 explains the conditions for the ten or more different sessions to be exempt from VAT).

Example 3

Jones Builders Ltd has purchased a plot of land and intends to build two office blocks on the land and then sell the freehold interest. The first office block is built and sold to a national stationery company to use as its head office. The second property is to be sold to a national charity for them to use for non-business purposes.

What is the VAT position in each case?

Solution – the sale of the new office block to the national stationery company is standard rated because it is a new building that is not being used as a dwelling or number of dwellings, or for a relevant residential or relevant charitable purpose.

The sale of the second property to the national charity can be zero-rated because it is being used by the charity for non-business purposes. However, the charity will need to issue a certificate to confirm the use to which the property is being put. Without the certificate, it would not be possible for Jones Builders Ltd to zero-rate the sale.

Situations when the grant of an interest in or right over land is zero-rated

[27.12] The examples above illustrated when grants in or rights over land are standard rated – zero-rating would apply in the following circumstances.

- *New dwellings* – the first grant of a major interest in a new dwelling by the person constructing it is zero-rated, ie the freehold sale of the building or a long lease exceeding 21 years (20 years in Scotland). Any second sale or subsequent long lease sale will be exempt from VAT. See Example 4.
  (HMRC Notice 742, para 3.1).

- *New residential and charitable buildings* – the first grant of a major interest in a building to be used by the buyer for a 'relevant residential purpose' or a 'relevant charitable purpose' is also zero-rated. In these situations, it is necessary for the buyer of the property to issue a certificate to the seller confirming his intended use of the building. An example of a standard certificate layout can be found in HMRC's VAT Notice 708, para 18.2. For a list of the main types of properties that would be classed as being for a relevant residential or charitable purpose, see Chapter 26 at **26.4–26.11**.

- *Conversion of non-residential buildings* – if a building has been converted from non-residential into residential use, then the first grant of a major interest in the building will be zero-rated. An example of a qualifying project, quite common in this country, is for an agricultural barn to be converted into a house or bungalow. Commercial buildings (eg office blocks) may be converted into blocks of flats or a home for elderly persons (the latter is an example of a new building for a relevant residential purpose, which are also covered by these rules). Another example of a conversion project is when a mixed use building, for example a public house with a private living area for the landlord or manager, is converted into a dwelling or a number of dwellings. This was considered by the First Tier Tribunal in the case of *Alexandra Countryside Investments Ltd* (TC02751) [2013] UKFTT 348 (TC).

In *Alexandra Countryside Investments Ltd* (TC02751) [2013] UKFTT 348 (TC) a VAT registered property developer claimed input tax in relation to the conversion of a pub into two semi-detached houses on the basis that the sale of the houses would be zero-rated. HMRC denied the claim for input tax on the basis that parts of what had been the pub manager's flat were incorporated into both of the semi-detached houses. HMRC's position was that this meant that the sale of the houses was an exempt rather than a zero-rated supply and that the VAT incurred was not recoverable. The company appealed to the First Tier Tribunal against HMRC's decision and the tribunal allowed the company's appeal. The tribunal noted that when comparing the number of dwellings in the building before conversion (one dwelling) with the number after conversion (two dwellings) it is clear that there were more dwellings after the conversion than before the conversion. An additional dwelling had been created and the tribunal allowed the company's appeal.

HMRC policy is that for a dwelling or a number of dwellings that have been created from a mixed use building to qualify for zero-rating the dwelling or dwellings must only use non-residential parts of the mixed use building. This is illustrated in paragraph 5.3.5 of HMRC Notice 708, which gives an example of converting a two-storey public house containing a bar downstairs and a private living area upstairs into a pair of semi-detached houses. In the example, each of the semi-detached houses is created partly from what was previously the bar and partly from what was previously the private living area, with HMRC explaining that the onward sale or long lease of the semi-detached houses cannot be zero-rated and is exempt.

The key legislation providing the basis for zero-rating the first grant of a dwelling that has been converted from a non-residential building or a non-residential part of a building is at *VATA 1994, Sch 8, Group 5, Item 1*. In the legislation, *Group 5, Note 9* explains that a dwelling that has been converted from the non-residential part of a building that already contains a residential part does not qualify for zero-rating unless an additional dwelling or dwellings are created as a result of the conversion.

Example 4

Smith Ltd is a property development company working on two projects:

(a)   the company purchased a plot of land for £50,000 and has spent £100,000 on labour and materials to construct a new four-bedroom detached house. It intends to sell the freehold interest in the house for £200,000;

(b)   the company also bought an existing residential property for £120,000 in the next street. It intends to spend £30,000 refurbishing and repairing the property – and will then sell the freehold interest in the property for £200,000.

What is the VAT position in each case?

Solution – The first property is a new dwelling so the first sale of the freehold by the developer will be zero-rated. This has the double advantage for the company in that no output tax is payable on the proceeds of the sale but any related input tax on the project, for example on building materials, can be reclaimed. As the property in question is a new dwelling rather than for a relevant residential or charitable purpose, then zero-rating can be applied without the need for a certificate to be issued by the person buying the property.

The second property relates to the sale of an existing dwelling – it is only new dwellings that can qualify for zero-rating so the sale of this property will be exempt from VAT. This situation has an advantage in that there is no VAT to charge on the sale of the property – but a disadvantage in that the related costs of improving the property will be classed as relevant to an exempt supply and the input tax would not be reclaimable (unless the amount of input tax is small and the *de minimis* rules could apply). See Chapter 24 for an analysis of the issues concerning what is known as partial exemption.

Note – the above situation is very common for many property development companies and it is important that advisers fully appreciate the difference between a sale being zero-rated and exempt as far as input tax recovery is concerned.

Sale of new buildings with a mixed use

[27.13] Consider the following situation: a property developer builds a new property on land that he has bought, which comprises a shop on the ground floor and a first floor flat. The shop is clearly for a commercial purpose and therefore standard rated as the sale of a new non-qualifying building. The sale of the flat is zero-rated as the first time sale of a new dwelling.

In many cases, it is possible that the two separate properties will be bought by different people, in which case the VAT treatment will be straightforward, ie zero-rating will apply for the flat and the shop sale will be standard rated.

However, it is possible that the same person might buy the combined property and, in such cases, the consideration received from the buyer needs to be apportioned on a fair and reasonable basis so that output tax is correctly paid on the part of the deal relating to the shop.

Another common situation that occurs for housing associations is where they sell a percentage of a new dwelling to an individual(s) and retain ownership of the rest of the property. This type of transaction is known as a shared ownership arrangement – the intention being that the tenant will eventually buy the entire interest in the property. The tenant will pay rent to the housing association for the percentage of the property that he does not own.

In such cases, the initial payment by the occupier for his share of the new equity in the new property can be zero-rated but the subsequent rental payments are exempt from VAT, ie not zero-rated.

Temporarily renting out new houses

[27.14] A common situation that has emerged in recent years is where new house builders (or builders of any new dwellings) have been unable to sell their properties because of the downturn in the property market. In such cases, they have often decided to temporarily rent out these properties to generate short-term rental income.

The challenge for house builders is that the sale of a new dwelling they have built is zero-rated as far as VAT is concerned (input tax can be claimed) but rental income is exempt from VAT (no input tax can be reclaimed on related costs). The decision to generate rental income therefore has implications in relation to partial exemption and means that input tax already claimed may need to be repaid.

Any adviser who has a client faced with this situation should refer to Revenue & Customs Brief 44/08 and VAT Information Sheet 07/08 issued on 15 September 2008. These notes explain the potential input tax adjustment needed for a house builder generating short-term rental income. The positive news is that the procedures recognise that although a business is making exempt supplies (rental), the overall intention is to still make an eventual zero-rated supply – so not all input tax is disallowed. In fact, many house builders could be *de minimis* after the various calculations have been made and not need to repay any input tax.

Planning measure

[27.15] A possible measure to protect the input tax claimed on the cost of constructing new dwellings is to form a connected company or business and sell the completed property to this business (zero-rated sale) – the latter then generates the exempt rental income. The zero-rated sale made by the first business protects all input tax it has claimed on the construction costs. HMRC confirmed in Revenue & Customs Brief 54/08 (subsequently reissued as Revenue & Customs Brief 101/09) that such a measure is not considered to be abusive because the legislation always intended for input tax to be claimable on the costs of building new dwellings for sale.

It is important to consider the direct tax and Stamp Duty Land Tax (SDLT) or Scottish Land and Buildings Transaction Tax (LBTT) implications of such a measure. The other key issue relates to the amount of input tax actually involved in the project. For example, many house builders use subcontractors to carry out building services and these services (and any materials provided by the subcontractor) are usually zero-rated. So the only input tax incurred by the house builder could be relevant to professional fees only, which may produce the outcome where he is *de minimis* as far as partial exemption is concerned, ie able to fully recover all of his input tax.

Note – the issues considered in this section are quite complex and professional advice may be needed to ensure all relevant matters are fully considered.

Other matters

[27.16] Other situations to be taken into account are as follows.

- *Option to purchase or lease land* – it is quite common for a property developer to make a payment to a landowner for the opportunity to purchase an interest in his land or buildings at a future date for an agreed price. The payment represents the right to an interest in land and the liability of the payment will be the same as the liability of the land or buildings when it is eventually purchased. In most cases, the purchase of the land and buildings will be exempt so the option payment will also be exempt.
  (HMRC Notice 742, para 7.4).
- *Landlord inducement payments* – there may be occasions when a landlord will make a payment to a tenant in order to encourage the tenant to take out a lease on his property. In reality, such payments are outside the scope of VAT as long as there is no obligation for the tenant to give benefits to the landlord in return for the payment. For example, if it was an obligation of the payment for the tenant to carry out some building improvement work on the property, this would constitute a standard-rated supply of services.
  (HMRC Notice 742, para 10.1).

- *Reverse surrenders* – it is possible that a tenant wishes to escape from a lease and pays a sum of money to the landlord to accept the surrender. In most cases, this payment will be exempt from VAT (following the same liability as the rental payments) unless the option to tax has been taken in which case the payment will be standard rated.
  (HMRC Notice 742, para 10.4).

- *Dilapidation payments* – many lease agreements will contain a clause that a landlord can charge a tenant at the end of an agreement for the cost of any necessary repairs to return the property to its original condition. In effect, such payments reflect a claim for damages by the landlord to the tenant and are therefore not a supply for VAT purposes. The payment is therefore outside the scope of VAT.
  (HMRC Notice 742, para 10.12).

- *Rent-free periods* – the grant by a landlord of a rent-free period is not a supply for VAT purposes except where the rent-free period is given in exchange for something which the tenant agrees to do, eg carry out works for the benefit of the landlord.
  (HMRC Notice 742, para 10.2).

- *Services charges* – a service charge generally applies to a leased property where common areas are shared between more than one tenant. For example, a block of flats will often incur a service charge arrangement, so that each leaseholder contributes to the cost of upkeep of common areas, buildings insurance, gardening services to communal land etc. The VAT liability of the service charge usually follows the liability of the main rental payment to the landlord, ie exempt in most cases but standard rated if the option to tax election has been made.
  (HMRC Notice 742, section 11).

Note – HMRC issued Revenue & Customs Brief 67/09 on 27 October 2009 to confirm its policy in relation to property service charges. This followed the ruling given in the ECJ case of *RLRE Tellmer Property sro v Financni reditelstvi v Usti nad Labem: C-572/07* [2009] STC 2006, [2009] All ER (D) 120 (Sep), ECJ, relevant to cleaning charges provided by a landlord to tenants in a residential property in the Czech Republic. In this case, the Court ruled that the cleaning service was standard rated rather than exempt because the tenants had a choice as to which cleaner they used to deliver the service. In other words, the arrangement was detached from the main lease agreement covering service charge issues.

Planning points to consider

[27.17] The following planning points should be given consideration.

- The supply of a licence to occupy land is generally exempt from VAT. However, it is important to ensure that an arrangement qualifies for exemption by meeting the four key rules explained at **27.5**.

- Some supplies can be exempt from VAT if the supply is only to occupy land, eg hire of a hall. However, the supply could become standard rated if the hirer receives significant other benefits as well, eg catering. In such cases, it is important to charge VAT if appropriate.

- Many businesses have tried to describe arrangements as being relevant to an exempt supply of land – whereas the reality of a situation is that they are providing a package of services subject to VAT at the standard rate. In such situations, it is important to remember that the commercial reality of an arrangement takes precedence over how an arrangement is described in a contract or on a sales invoice.

- Remember that the sale of the first freehold (or long leasehold) interest in a new dwelling by a developer is zero-rated but the sale of an existing dwelling is exempt from VAT. Although there is no output tax due in either case, the input tax issues between the two different transactions are very different, ie no input tax is reclaimable in relation to an exempt supply.

- Certain payments relating to a property are outside the scope of VAT or exempt from VAT so it is important to recognise these situations when they arise. For example, dilapidation payments and landlord inducement payments are outside the scope of VAT and service charges are usually exempt too because they follow the VAT liability of the main rent payment.

- House builders need to be aware of the VAT implications of temporarily renting out any new dwellings they cannot sell, ie the potential input tax restriction because exempt supplies are being made. A possible measure could be to sell the completed property to a connected company (zero-rated sale) to protect any input tax claimed on the construction of the dwellings.

- Be aware that even if an input tax restriction is evident because of partial exemption rules, it is possible that this input tax can still be reclaimed if the business is *de minimis* for the VAT period or tax year in question, ie exempt input tax is below certain limits (see Chapter 24).

Chapter 28

Property Transactions – Option to Tax

Key topics in this chapter:

- The consequences of making an option to tax election.
- How to notify HMRC of an option to tax election.
- The opportunity to revoke an option to tax election on certain properties since 1 August 2009.
- The benefits of opting to tax a property – enhanced input tax recovery because land income becomes taxable rather than exempt.
- Potential problems of opting to tax a property – creating a VAT charge to some tenants or property buyers who are not able to reclaim input tax.
- Failing to notify an option to tax election to HMRC – Business Brief 13/05.
- Situations when the option to tax is overridden, eg when the buyer of an opted property intends to convert it into a dwelling.
- Rules to follow when an opted property is sold as part of a transfer of a going concern arrangement.
- The different HMRC forms to complete involving land and property transaction and the option to tax election.
- Insurance recharges to tenants by a landlord – VAT or no VAT?
- The importance of not making an unnecessary option to tax election on a building.

Introduction

[28.1] The VAT liability of goods and services is determined by relevant legislation – and will either be standard rated, zero-rated, subject to the reduced rate of VAT, exempt or, in some cases, outside the scope of VAT.

There is an extra dimension to consider as far as land and property transactions are concerned – namely that there is an opportunity for certain exempt supplies to become standard rated through exercising what is known as the 'option to tax'.

The option to tax is a decision taken by a person owning or renting land or buildings and has the effect of making all supplies relevant to his interest in that property taxable rather than exempt. It is a very important decision to make because the taxpayer's option cannot be revoked for 20 years on a property once it has been made (apart from a limited cooling-off period).

The main reason for making an option to tax election is to facilitate input tax recovery on either capital or revenue expenditure – if a supply is exempt, then input tax cannot be reclaimed in relation to that supply.

However, the option to tax election means that all supplies relevant to the land or property (eg rental income from subletting; proceeds from selling the building) will become standard rated rather than exempt. This means that tenants or purchasers will be faced with a VAT charge – no problem if they can reclaim input tax on their own VAT returns, but definitely a problem if they are either an exempt or partly exempt business or not registered for VAT.

An important point to note is that the option to tax election can only be made on commercial properties – for example, it is not possible for the owner of a three-bedroom house to opt to tax the property and charge VAT on future rents to tenants.

Implications of opting to tax a property

[28.2] As explained above, the decision to elect to tax a property has major consequences as far as VAT is concerned, and is one that should not be taken lightly. The amounts of tax involved in land and property transactions are considerable and a hasty decision to tax a property could potentially create an extra VAT cost to tenants or prospective buyers of the property who cannot reclaim input tax.

Equally, the decision to opt to tax the property could exclude a large number of potential buyers or tenants (eg businesses with exempt income such as insurance brokers) from having any interest in the property, for instance because it will be more cost effective for them to pursue an interest in a property where the option to tax has not been exercised.

Once a business has opted to tax its interest in land or property, it must charge VAT on all future supplies it makes in relation to that property:

* if the property is let or sublet to tenants, then VAT must be added to any rent charge;
* if the property is sold, then VAT must be added to the disposal proceeds.

Note that there are some situations where the option to tax a property is overruled by other legislation – see **28.6**.

An important point to remember is that it is only the taxable person's interest in the property that is subject to the option to tax – not the interests of other people also connected with the property – see Example 1.

Example 1

ABC Properties owns the freehold of a building at 67 High Street. It lets the building to a VAT registered firm of accountants, DEF Ltd, who sublet two of the four floors in the building to a training firm called GHI Ltd. ABC Properties decides to opt to tax its interest in the property. How will this situation affect DEF Ltd?

Solution – once ABC Properties has made the decision to tax the property, all rent that it charges to DEF Ltd will include VAT at the standard rate. However, the option to tax the property only relates to the supplies made by ABC Properties – there is no compulsion for DEF Ltd to also tax its own interest in the property.

However, DEF Ltd may also decide to opt to tax its interest in the property – otherwise some of the VAT charged by ABC Properties could be disallowed because it relates to an exempt supply, ie the sublease to GHI Ltd. This decision should not be a problem if GHI Ltd is also registered for VAT and able to reclaim input tax on its expenditure.

Procedures for taxing a property

[28.3] There are two stages in opting to tax:

*   making the decision to opt to tax an interest in land or a building and recording this decision, for example, in board meeting minutes or other relevant correspondence (ie this is the internal decision confirming there are benefits in making the election);
*   making a formal notification in writing to HMRC of the decision, within 30 days of the decision being made.

(HMRC Notice 742A, para 4.1).

The notifications to HMRC are dealt with centrally from one office:

Option to Tax National Unit
HM Revenue and Customs
Cotton House
7 Cochrane Street
Glasgow
G1 1GY

The HMRC Option to Tax Unit should only be contacted by telephone on 03000 530005 to discuss correspondence received from the Unit.

The HMRC VAT Helpline can be contacted on 0300 200 3700 to discuss VAT and opting to tax land or buildings.

The notification should be made by using Form VAT 1614A if no previous exempt supplies have been made in connection with the property. The form can be obtained from the VAT Helpline or downloaded from the GOV.UK website. It is acceptable to fax a notification (03000 529807) or send it by e-mail to: optiontotaxnationalunit@hmrc.gsi.gov.uk.

The written notification to HMRC must be made within 30 days of the decision to tax the property being made and cannot be made on a retrospective basis.

Important points to bear in mind as far as the option to tax notification is concerned are as follows.

*   In most cases, it will be clear as to the extent of the land or property subject to the election. To use the situation from Example 1 above:

'We, the partners of ABC Properties, wish to apply the option to tax to our freehold interest in the property we own at 67 High Street. We wish to make the election with effect from xx/xx/xxxx.'

However, in some cases it may be necessary for a taxpayer to clarify his exact interest in a property by including a map or plan with his notification form.
(HMRC Notice 742A, para 4.2.2).

• Form VAT 1614A is used where no previous exempt supplies have been made in relation to a property. In simple terms, this means that the property has not been rented out by the owner before the election was made. If a business has generated exempt income in the past in relation to the property in question, then it may need HMRC's permission to opt to tax the property, ie permission is not automatic. In such cases, VAT 1614H needs to be completed instead of VAT 1614A. To decide whether you need HMRC's permission, it is necessary to review HMRC Notice 742A, section 5 (Permission to opt to tax).

• Once made, the option to tax cannot be revoked until at least 20 years have elapsed since the date on which it had effect. The only exception to this rule is if a business meets the conditions of the 'cooling off' regulations, which give limited opportunities to revoke an option within six months of it being made. See **28.19** for further details on the 'cooling off' rules.

• HMRC expects Form VAT 1614A to be signed by a person with the appropriate authority, eg a director in the case of a limited company; the sole proprietor or one of the partners in a non-corporate entity. If a business submits an election via a third party, eg a solicitor or accountant, then HMRC must receive confirmation that the third party has been authorised to act on behalf of the business.
(HMRC Notice 742A, para 7.1).

• In the case of jointly owned land, this is classed as a partnership situation as far as VAT is concerned.
(HMRC Notice 742A, para 7.3).

Benefits of opting to tax land or property

[28.4] As explained at **28.1**, the main benefit of opting to tax land or property is that input tax relevant to an exempt supply and not reclaimable would become relevant to a taxable supply and therefore reclaimable subject to the normal rules. This is an important point – any taxpayer making an option to tax election should have an input tax motive for doing so. If a business can claim input tax on property expenses without opting to tax (eg because it is using the building for its own taxable business activities) then it should not make an election. Don't forget that an unnecessary election would mean having to charge standard rate VAT if the building was sold within 20 years of the election being made, causing cash flow and potential input tax recovery problems for the buyer (if he is an exempt business such as an insurance broker). See Example 2.

Example 2

ABC Properties has purchased a commercial property for £500,000 plus VAT of £100,000 (based on 20% rate of VAT). They intend to rent out the property on a ten-year lease to a firm of solicitors for £25,000 per year. ABC Properties will also be responsible for any property repairs (landlord repairing lease), estimated to be £5,000 per year plus VAT. The solicitors taking on the lease are VAT registered and only making taxable supplies, ie no exempt income.

Solution – this is a clear situation of when the option to tax should be adopted by ABC Properties. Failure to opt to tax the property will mean that the £100,000 of VAT on the initial purchase of the property will be lost (as being relevant to an exempt supply) because the income generated by the property will be exempt. Equally, the annual VAT incurred on repair costs will also be not reclaimable because it relates to an exempt supply.

However, if the option to tax is made at the time the property is purchased, then all input tax will be reclaimable because all supplies relating to the property are now taxable. There is no problem with VAT being added to the rent charge to the solicitors because they can reclaim it as input tax.

The situation given at Example 2 was a 'win:win' arrangement. The landlord of the property was able to benefit from a significant input tax saving by opting to tax his interest in the property; the tenants were not inconvenienced by the subsequent VAT charge on the rent because their business allows them full input tax recovery.

However, in some business arrangements, the facts may not be as clear cut and the overall benefit of opting to tax the property will need to be assessed. Consider the following circumstances:

- it is possible that a business may want to sell the property at some time in the future. If the option to tax has been made in respect of that property, then VAT will need to be added to the sale proceeds – this may deter certain prospective purchasers not able to recover input tax – see **28.5**;
- it is possible that future tenants of a property may not be registered for VAT, eg because they only make exempt supplies. The VAT charged on the rent will then become an extra cost to the business, which reduces the competitiveness of the letting arrangement;
- it is possible that an existing lease may preclude a landlord from adding VAT to his rental charge. In such cases, the landlord would have to treat rent received as VAT inclusive if he opted to tax the property in question – directly affecting his bottom line profit.

Disadvantages of opting to tax land or property

[28.5] There are two main disadvantages of opting to tax an interest in land or property:

(a)   a tenant who is paying rent to use the property may not be able to recover any VAT charged as input tax; and

(b)   the purchaser of the land or property may also be unable to reclaim VAT charged as input tax.

See Example 3 for an illustration of this point.

Example 3

ABC Properties now decides to sell the property in Example 2 for £800,000. Unfortunately, it has forgotten that VAT is chargeable on the proceeds received from the sale because it opted to tax its interest in the property.

There are two businesses interested in buying the property – an insurance broker to use as its head office and a clothes retailer, also interested in using the property as a head office function. What is the VAT situation as far as the sale of the property is concerned?

Solution – the option to tax situation will almost certainly come to light before the deal is finalised, which means that £160,000 VAT will be added to the sale value (based on standard rate of 20%).

For the clothes retailer, this should not be a problem (apart from the increased stamp duty cost it will face – stamp duty is charged on the gross proceeds of the sale) – because the sale of clothing is a taxable activity, so input tax should be reclaimable on the acquisition of the building. However, the insurance company will have a problem – insurance services are mainly exempt from VAT, so the VAT charge will almost certainly add an extra £160,000 to the cost of the building, with no scope for input tax recovery.

Note – the insurance company may be happy to buy the property for £800,000 including VAT – in which case ABC Properties will be out of pocket, effectively only receiving sale proceeds of £666,667 (£800,000 × 5/6) instead of £800,000.

Situations when the option to tax is not applied

[28.6] There are certain situations when an option to tax arrangement is effectively overridden, ie the sale of the interest in the land or property or rental income received will be exempt rather than standard rated (even though the property owner has made an option to tax election). See **28.14** for certification procedures required in many cases. The main situations when the override would apply are as follows.

•   *Dwellings* – any supply in relation to a building (or part of a building) intended for use as a dwelling or a number of dwellings or solely for a 'relevant residential purpose'. If an opted building is being sold and converted into dwellings by the buyer, the latter must complete Form VAT 1614D and give it to the seller before the price of the deal is legally fixed (usually before exchange of contracts). This means the sale of the building will then be exempt rather than standard-rated. However, this may present some input tax problems for the seller – hence the need for VAT 1614D to be issued before exchange of contracts. If the form is issued after this time, the seller can reject the request to override the exemption if he wishes.

Example – pub being converted into flats (dwelling); pub being used as a nursing home (ie for a 'relevant residential purpose').

Comment – an option to tax election is always made on land, and then applies to any building that is on the land. So in the case of a property consisting of a ground floor shop and first floor flat, the election is made on the entire premises, but then not applied to any rental income (or selling proceeds) relevant to the first floor flat. This is a key point – the option to tax election never applies to residential property. (HMRC Notice 742A, paras 3.2–3.4).

- *Charitable use* – a supply in relation to a building (or part of a building) intended for use solely for a 'relevant charitable purpose' other than as an office. (See Chapter 26 for an explanation about what constitutes a 'relevant residential purpose' or 'relevant charitable purpose'. An example of a relevant residential property is a residential home for children; a building for a relevant charitable purpose is a church or place of worship.) Note the words 'other than as an office' in this situation where the option to tax election will still apply.

  Comment – if a charity is renting two floors of a building from a landlord, and it uses one of the floors for its charitable purposes (non-office) and one floor for non-charitable purposes (eg a charity shop) there is no problem with the landlord who has opted to tax the building only charging VAT on the floor used for non-charitable purposes. This calculation can be made using any method that is fair and reasonable – it would probably be logical to apportion the exempt and standard rated rent on a floor area basis – perhaps charging VAT on 50% of the rent in the case of a two-floor letting arrangement. (HMRC Notice 742A, para 3.5).

- *Residential caravans* – a supply of a pitch for a permanent residential caravan. In effect, this means a pitch for a residential caravan where 12-month occupation is not prevented by any covenant, planning consent or similar provision.

  Comment – this is the same principle as explained above – the election does not apply to residential property. (HMRC Notice 742A, para 3.8).

- *Residential houseboats* – a supply of facilities for the mooring (including anchoring or berthing) of a residential houseboat. As with residential caravans, there should be no restrictions on all year occupation of the houseboat. (HMRC Notice 742A, para 3.9).

- *Housing associations* – a supply to a relevant housing association which has given the supplier Form VAT 1614G stating that the land is to be used for the construction of buildings or a building for use as a dwelling or number of dwellings or solely for a 'relevant residential purpose'.

  Comment – the override explained under 'Dwellings' above in relation to a building being converted into a dwelling only applies to 'buildings' and not 'land'. So a commercial property developer buying land would be charged the standard rate of VAT if the seller of the land had an option to tax election in place. The legislation at *VATA 1994, Sch 10, para 10(1)* explains that an option to tax has no effect in relation to any grant made to a relevant housing association in relation to any land if the association certifies that the land is to be used (after any necessary demolition work) for the construction of a building or buildings intended for use as a dwelling, or number of dwellings, or solely for a relevant residential purpose.

- *DIY builders* – a supply of land to an individual where the land is to be used for the construction of a building intended for use by him as a dwelling (not as a business venture).

  Comment – it is important that any person building a dwelling through the DIY scheme only pays VAT that has been correctly charged by the supplier in the first place. Any incorrectly charged VAT by a land seller or builder (most building services on a new dwelling are zero-rated) will be rejected by HMRC when a DIY claim is received. The claimant will be instructed to go back to the builder or landowner for a VAT credit. (HMRC Notice 742A, para 3.7).

- *Certain supplies affected by anti-avoidance measures* – HMRC has detailed anti-avoidance measures in place, mainly to prevent a business that has some or mainly exempt supplies obtaining an unfair recovery of input tax in a land or property transaction. Any adviser or business that thinks it will be affected by the provisions (unlikely in most cases) can review the detailed rules in VAT Notice 742A.

  Comment – think of an insurance broker (not VAT registered – exempt supplies only) who has bought a property that he will use for his trading purposes. It would be unfair if he could purchase the property (with VAT added by the seller) and create a separate legal entity that then rents the property to his trading business with an option to tax election being made by the new entity. The intention (if this was allowed) would be for the second entity to get an input tax windfall on the VAT charged on the purchase of the building and then drip-feed the output tax on the rent to the exempt insurance business over a long period of time. The block by HMRC in this case is justified on the basis that the legislation does not intend an exempt business to get input tax recovery on its costs by creating separate structures to avoid the input tax block. See **28.22**. (HMRC Notice 742A, para 3.11 and section 13).

For an illustration of a situation when an option to tax election is overridden, see Example 4.

Example 4

JKL Properties Ltd owns the freehold of a public house that it has rented out for the last ten years to a publican. The company opted to tax the property when it first bought it ten years ago and is now selling the freehold interest in the property to MNO Ltd, which intends to convert the entire property into eight self-contained flats.

Solution – in normal circumstances, JKL Properties Ltd would need to charge output tax on the disposal of the property because it made the option to tax election within the last 20 years. However, no output tax is due on the proposed sale because the conversion by MNO Ltd means the building is intended to be used as a 'dwelling or a number of dwellings'. MNO Ltd must issue Form VAT 1614D to JKL Properties Ltd to confirm its intended use of the building and that the option to tax is therefore overridden. This certificate must be issued by MNO Ltd before the price of the sale if legally fixed, ie usually exchange of contracts.

Registering for VAT following an election

[28.7] It is possible that a previously unregistered business may need to become VAT registered as a result of opting to tax land or property. This need to register may be on a compulsory basis (ie value of taxable supplies exceeding registration limits) or on a voluntary basis because the business wishes to benefit from input tax recovery on its costs.

The business may need to support the application to register with evidence concerning the land or property in question – correspondence, plans, minutes of meetings confirming intentions etc.

Forgetting to tell HMRC about an election

[28.8] As explained earlier, there are two stages to carrying out a successful option to tax election:

*   taking the decision to opt to tax ie internal action through board meeting minute, correspondence with advisers, charging VAT on income generated by the property, claiming input tax on costs etc;
*   formally notifying HMRC of the election in writing.

A common VAT problem occurs when the business making the election forgets to tell HMRC about its option – ie the second stage above. In such cases, this is not usually a problem as long as the business can prove its original intentions ie it has taken the decision to opt to tax and acted accordingly. A belated notification can then be made in accordance with the terms of HMRC Business Brief 13/05.

However, a problem would be evident if the taxpayer is attempting to gain a VAT advantage by trying to backdate his option. Any such request for backdating would then almost certainly be refused by HMRC.

(HMRC Notice 742A, para 4.2.1).

Transfer of a going concern arrangement

Buyer must opt to tax the property as well

[28.9] The proceeds received from the transfer of a going concern (sale of a business) are normally outside the scope of VAT – as long as various conditions are met – as explained in Chapter 4. The transfer of a business will often include land and buildings, and the seller may have opted to tax these buildings.

There is potential for the part of the sale relating to the land and buildings to also be outside the scope of VAT, even where the seller has opted to tax the property. The basic rules are as follows:

- the buyer must have opted to tax the land or buildings concerned and must have given written notification of the election to HMRC. The option must be notified to HMRC in writing and no later than the time of the deal;
- the buyer must also notify the seller that his option to tax the land or buildings concerned will not be disapplied. This notification should be in writing.

Note – the seller is responsible for ensuring the correct amount of output tax is charged on a property sale, so it is prudent for him to ask the buyer for evidence that his option to tax is in place by the relevant date, eg copy of the notification letter.

If the above conditions are not met, the transfer of the land and buildings with the election in place is a supply and output tax will be due at the standard rate.

(HMRC Notice 742A, para 11.2).

Property rental business

[28.10] A situation that has become quite common in recent years is where a property has been sold to a third party, but with an existing lease in place with a tenant. In these situations, the sale can qualify as a transfer of a going concern (sale of a property rental business).

However, if the seller has opted to tax the property in question, then the buyer must also elect to tax the property himself before the deal is completed. If this election is made without any problem, the VAT charge can be avoided.

Practical challenges with option to tax procedures

20-year rule – revoking an option to tax

[28.11] The option to tax regulations were introduced on 1 August 1989, so this means that it became possible for some options to be revoked for the first time after 1 August 2009 under the 20-year rule.

(HMRC Notice 742A, para 8.3).

A taxpayer will be able to automatically revoke his option in most cases (no HMRC permission needed – completion of Form VAT 1614J).

However, in completing VAT 1614J, a taxpayer needs to pass three anti-avoidance tests shown as Conditions 3 to 5 on the form. If any of the conditions are not met, then HMRC permission is needed before the election can be revoked, ie it is not automatic. The aim of the anti-avoidance tests is to prevent a business gaining an unfair tax advantage.

An important point for advisers to appreciate is that all of the tests at Conditions 3 to 5 must be met in order to revoke an option without HMRC permission, as well as Condition 2 regarding the 20-year time limit. Example 5 illustrates a situation where all of the conditions are met. The four conditions are:

- *20-year time period* (Condition 2) – the taxpayer must have held a relevant interest in the building or land at the time when the option first took effect and more than 20 years have now passed;
  Note – if this condition is not met, then the other issues are irrelevant. The option to tax election cannot be revoked.
- *capital goods scheme* – no input tax adjustments are needed under the capital goods scheme (Condition 3) – the capital goods scheme mainly applies in relation to the purchase of certain buildings and building works exceeding £250,000 – input tax is adjusted over a ten-year period;
  A small amendment to this rule was introduced on 1 August 2009 – the capital goods scheme condition is now met if adjustments still to be made with the scheme are less than £10,000.
- *valuation condition* (Condition 4) – in the ten-year period before the option to tax is revoked, there must have been no supply of a relevant interest in the building that was made at less than open market value (eg undervalued rents);
- *prepayments condition* (Condition 5) – no payments have been made in relation to the property that relate to a period that is more than 12 months after the option is revoked – see Example 6.

Example 5

Alan owns the freehold of an office block and opted to tax the property when he first bought it 21 years ago. In the last 21 years, the property has been rented out to a firm of accountants who have been able to reclaim as input tax the VAT on the rent charged by Alan.

Alan now wishes to revoke his election because the accountants are vacating his premises and the new tenants are insurance brokers (exempt activity – input tax cannot be reclaimed).

Alan has always charged a proper market rent to the accountants in the last ten years; he has not prepaid any expenses in relation to the property; there are no capital goods scheme issues . . . and more than 20 years have passed since his election.

Solution – Alan can automatically revoke his option to tax election without prior permission from HMRC but must still notify it by completing Form VAT 1614J.

Example 6

Alan from Example 5 suddenly has a bright idea. Just before he revokes his option to tax election he decides to make a payment of £200,000 plus VAT to the maintenance company that carries out all repair work on his property. The £200,000 payment will cover all repair works for the next five years. Alan thinks this will allow him to claim the VAT on the expenditure as input tax on his VAT return for the quarter in which the expenditure was incurred, ie before the election has been revoked.

Solution – in this situation, the prepayment means that Alan cannot revoke his election without prior permission from HMRC. However, all is not lost. If he does not reclaim input tax on the maintenance payment (on the basis that it relates to a period when only exempt supplies of the property will be made), then HMRC will almost certainly grant permission to revoke the election. He will need to write a letter to HMRC, giving the full facts of the transaction, at the time he submits Form VAT 1614J.

Properties that do not sell

[28.12] Many taxpayers will want to revoke an option to tax election in order that the proceeds of a property sale can be exempt from VAT. However, if the property does not sell, then the purpose of revoking the option could have been lost. Regulations introduced on 1 August 2009 give HMRC the power to grant permission to revoke an election on the basis of an event taking place. In other words, as an example, no property sale means no event and therefore no option to tax election being revoked.

Motives for revoking an election – including SDLT/LBTT savings

[28.13] Alan in Example 5 had an excellent motive for wishing to revoke his option to tax election. The new tenants renting his building are not in a position to reclaim input tax on the rent he charges, creating an extra VAT cost to their business.

The other main situation when Alan might wish to revoke his option is if he wants to sell the property – and potential buyers might also have an exempt activity (financial services, insurance, health etc) where input tax claims are restricted. A VAT charge on a £1m property deal is a lot of tax. Keep in mind that the chargeable consideration for Stamp Duty Land Tax (SDLT) and Scottish Land and Buildings Transaction Tax (LBTT) purposes includes any VAT chargeable on the sale proceeds. See Example 7 which illustrates a useful SDLT saving if an option to tax election is revoked.

Example 7

Jones Chartered Accountants are buying a building from Smith Chartered Surveyors for £230,000 plus VAT. Smith made an option to tax election on the building over 20 years ago. Jones can fully reclaim input tax on their VAT returns (no partial exemption problems) so are there any benefits in Smith revoking the option to tax election (as 20 years have now passed)?

Solution – as well as a cash flow saving for Jones (avoiding the need to pay out VAT and then wait possibly three months to claim it back on a VAT return), there is a big saving in SDLT if the option to tax election is revoked:

- £230,000 + VAT at 20% = £276,000; SDLT = £276,000 x 3% = £8,280 (because purchase price exceeds £250,000, SDLT is charged at 3% rather than 1%)
- £230,000, no VAT; SDLT = £230,000 x 1% = £2,300

SDLT saved = £8,280 – £2,300 = £5,980.

Certificates to be issued for buildings to be converted into dwelling(s) or used for a relevant residential purpose and land supplied to housing associations

[28.14] The option to tax is disapplied if a building is sold and will be converted for use as a dwelling (or number of dwellings), or for use for a relevant residential purpose (providing the purchaser has confirmed his intention to the seller). The sale of land to a housing association is also treated as exempt from VAT, assuming the association will build new dwellings or a relevant residential building such as an elderly persons home on the land.

The buyer of an opted building (or land) in such cases will need to confirm his intentions by issuing the following certificates to the seller:

- Certificate to disapply the option to tax: Land sold to Housing Associations (VAT 1614G);
- Certificate to disapply the option to tax: Buildings to be converted into dwellings etc (VAT 1614D).

The above certificates give the seller the right to waive the option and treat the sale of the building as exempt.

Note – the option will continue to apply in relation to any parts of the building that will not be converted into dwellings or used solely for a relevant residential purpose. These parts of the building will be unaffected by the issue of the certificate. The certificate must describe the parts of the building that are affected by the override, and the percentage, on the basis of floor space, that they represent of the whole building. See Example 8.

Example 8

Property Ltd owns the freehold of an office block, which is sold to New Homes Ltd, which intends to convert 60% of the property into a block of flats with a view to selling them – the other 40% will be maintained as office accommodation. Property Ltd has opted to tax its interest in the building.

Solution – the intention of New Homes Ltd to convert the property into dwellings means the option to tax made by Property Ltd is disapplied in relation to this part of the building. New Homes Ltd must issue form VAT1614D to Property Ltd confirming its intention to build dwellings. The form must be issued before the price paid for the grant is legally fixed, ie exchange of contracts, the signing of heads of agreement etc.

Note – be aware that the regulations effectively mean the option will be maintained if New Homes Ltd does not issue form VAT1614D to Property Ltd. This might not be a problem for New Homes Ltd if it is constructing the dwellings for resale (zero-rated supply) because the input tax will be relevant to a taxable supply. However, it would be a problem if New Homes Ltd rented the flats to tenants (exempt income) because the VAT charged by Property Ltd now relates to an exempt supply.

Supplies made by a 'relevant intermediary'

[28.15] It is possible that a business will acquire a property on which an option to tax election has been made, with the sole intention of reselling the building to another person that intends to convert it into a dwelling or use it for a relevant residential purpose. In more complicated transactions, there may be more than one intermediary involved in the process.

If the above situation applies, the business reselling the property can be classed as a 'relevant intermediary' and issue VAT 1614D (Condition 3 applies) to the seller to enable the option to tax to be overridden. The relevant intermediary can only issue a certificate if one of the three conditions has been met in relation to his own resale of the property:

* he has received a certified VAT 1614D from his buyer confirming his intention to convert the building for use as a dwelling or solely for a relevant residential purpose;
* he has received a certified VAT 1614D from his buyer confirming his intention to sell the property to a person who intends to convert the building for such use;
* he has received a certified VAT 1614D from his buyer confirming his intention to sell the property to a person who will, in turn, sell the property to a person who intends to convert the building for such use.

(HMRC Notice 742A, para 3.4.5).

Example 9 to illustrates the rules.

Example 9

ABC Ltd is seeking to sell a building that it opted to tax. Its customer DEF Ltd has already found a buyer GHI Ltd (the recipient) for the property which intends to convert the building into a dwelling (or number of dwellings) or for a relevant residential purpose. What are the VAT issues?

Solution – GHI Ltd provides a certified VAT 1614D to DEF Ltd confirming the intention to convert the building. Once DEF Ltd has this certificate, it can then issue a certified VAT 1614D to ABC Ltd confirming that it intends to dispose of the building to a person GHI Ltd who will convert it into a dwelling (or number of dwellings) or for a relevant residential purpose. Once ABC Ltd has the certificate, it can exempt its supply of the building to DEF Ltd and DEF Ltd can exempt its supply of the building to GHI Ltd.

'Real estate election'

[28.16] A company has always been able to make a 'universal' or 'global' option to tax election in the past, meaning that all properties it acquires become subject to an option to tax ie avoiding the need to make a separate election for each property. This outcome can now be achieved by completing Form VAT 1614E (Opting to tax land and buildings: Notification of a real estate election).

In reality, most property owners (or other parties with an interest in property) will prefer to make an option to tax election on an individual property basis, having analysed the advantages and disadvantages of making an election. If a business that has a real estate election in place wants to avoid an option being applied on a particular property it has acquired, then it can advise HMRC of the exclusion when it acquires the property.

(HMRC Notice 742A, section 14).

Automatic revocation of an option after six years

[28.17] An option to tax election is treated as being automatically revoked where the opter has held no relevant interest in the building for six years.

Example – building sold by opter in June 2007 (and no other use or occupation of the building has been made since then) – option automatically revoked in June 2013 (there are some exceptions to this clause in relation to group companies).

(HMRC Notice 742A, para 8.2).

Elections apply to land and buildings

[28.18] The regulations make it clear that an option to tax land applies equally to a building upon the land (including a building that has yet to be built). There is also an opportunity to exclude a new building and land within its curtilage (as long as the building is separate from any existing building) from an option to tax election even though the land has been subject to a previous option. In such cases, a taxpayer will need to complete Form VAT 1614F (Opting to tax land and buildings: New buildings – exclusion from an option to tax). The earliest point that an exclusion can be notified to HMRC is when construction work begins on the new building, although it will not take effect in practical terms until the building is completed. The latest time to notify an exclusion is 30 days after either completion or first time occupation of the building.

(HMRC Notice 742A, para 2.7).

The 'cooling off' rules

[28.19] The opportunities for a taxpayer to revoke an option to tax election he has made are very limited, the main opportunity being when the election was made 20 years ago (revocation date 1 August 2009 at earliest – as considered above).

An option to tax election can also be revoked under the 'cooling off' regulations but only if:

- less than six months have passed since the option to tax election took effect;
- the property has not been sold together with a business as a transfer of a going concern;
- no tax has become chargeable as a result of the option;
- any input tax claimed as a result of the election has been repaid – see section 8.1.2 of HMRC Notice 742A (Box F).

Note – until 31 March 2010, an additional condition in force was that the 'land must not have been used' since the option to tax election was made. This condition was repealed with effect from 1 April 2010 (VAT (Buildings and Land) Order 2010 (SI 2010/485).

If the conditions above are met, then a business will need to complete Form VAT 1614C (Option to tax land and buildings: Revoking an option to tax within six months (the 'cooling off' period)). HMRC can then give permission for the option to be revoked. The certificate must be sent to HMRC within six months of the date of the original election.

Note – if the input tax condition is not met, then a letter should be sent to HMRC with the form explaining the details and, in some cases, a request to revoke the option could still be granted.

The priority of HMRC will be to ensure no net tax gain has been acquired by the incorrect election, and there are no anti-avoidance motives to worry about.

(HMRC Notice 742A, para 8.1).

Revised rules for 'relevant associates'

[28.20] A 'relevant associate' situation applies to group structures and anti-avoidance issues when a corporate body is 'connected to the opter'. The revised legislation imposes new conditions for a body corporate to cease to be treated as a relevant associate of an opter. In such cases, Form VAT 1614B (Opting to tax land and buildings: Ceasing to be a relevant associate) needs to be completed.

(HMRC Notice 742A, para 6.3).

Summary of relevant forms

[28.21] The various forms that need to be completed in relation to the option to tax regulations have been considered above. They can be summarised as follows:

- VAT 1614A – Notifying an option to tax election;
- VAT 1614B – Ceasing to be a relevant associate;
- VAT 1614C – Revoking an option to tax within six months ('cooling off' period);
- VAT 1614D – Certificate to disapply the option: Buildings to be converted into dwellings etc;
- VAT 1614E – Notification of a real estate election;
- VAT 1614F – Notification of the exclusion of a new building from the effect of an option to tax;
- VAT 1614G – Certificate to disapply the option: Land sold to housing associations;
- VAT 1614H – Application for permission to opt;
- VAT 1614J – Revoking an option after 20 years.

Note – be aware of the difference between Forms VAT 1614A and VAT 1614H. Form VAT 1614A is used when an option to tax election can be made without HMRC permission. However, there may be situations when HMRC's permission to opt to tax a property is required, usually when exempt supplies have been made in connection with the property in the previous ten years. See section 5 of HMRC's Notice 742A for further details on this issue.

As a final point, all of the forms mentioned above have the force of law and must be used where appropriate.

Renting properties to connected parties – anti-avoidance pitfall

[28.22] Regulations are in place to prevent a business that mainly makes exempt supplies from buying a property in a separate company (or other connected business), making an option to tax election on the property in order to reclaim input tax, and then charging output tax on rent over a number of years.

The anti-avoidance rules prevent this strategy if:

- the landlord and tenant are connected to each other, as defined in *ICTA 1988, s 839*, ie to include husbands, wives, associated companies, brothers, sisters etc;
- the property in question cost more than £250,000, ie the capital goods scheme limit;
- the tenant using the property has exempt supplies of more than 20% of its total supplies, ie it suffers a significant input tax restriction under partial exemption rules.

If an option to tax election is incorrectly made in the above circumstances, then HMRC has the power to disapply the option, ie all charges of rent will be treated as exempt from VAT rather than standard rated.

(HMRC Notice 742A, section 13).

Don't make an unnecessary option to tax election

[28.23] There can be situations where clients have purchased a building from which they will trade, with VAT charged on the cost of the building, and advisers have told the client to make an option to tax election with HMRC so that input tax can be reclaimed. In such situations, an option to tax election by the buyer is not compulsory in order to reclaim input tax – if the buyer is using the building for a taxable activity, then input tax is reclaimable without any election being needed, eg a firm of accountants buying the freehold of a new office.

An unnecessary option to tax election means that output tax will need to be charged on the resale of the building if made within 20 years, causing a potential problem in certain cases, eg if the buyer cannot claim input tax. If the premises are to be let or sublet by our buyer then an option to tax election should be considered at this stage.

Key point – it takes two minutes to make an option to tax election with HMRC but 20 years to escape from its consequences. The decision to make an election should only be made after a full analysis of the relevant facts.

Insurance charges to tenants (if election is in place)

[28.24] It is standard practice for the landlord of a building to insure a property, and then split this charge among the tenants, ie so that the tenants effectively pay their share of the insurance cost. However, the key issue with VAT is to look at what supply is taking place.

- The supply of insurance is between the landlord and the insurance company – any claim against the policy would be made by the landlord and not the tenants.
- There is no 'insurance transaction' taking place between the landlord and tenant. Any payment from the tenant to landlord is therefore classed as 'additional rent' and if an option to tax election has been made by the landlord, this payment will be standard rated.

The above principles were confirmed in the case of *OM Properties Investment Co Ltd v Revenue and Customs Comrs* (TC00752) [2010] UKFTT 494 (TC).

Note – any transaction involving three parties needs to be treated with great care when VAT issues are involved. It is important to look at supplies between the different parties in isolation to each other to identify the nature of the supply as far as VAT is concerned.

Buying a property before VAT registration

[28.25] There is some scope to reclaim input tax on buying a property (or on the costs of refurbishing or extending a property) when the VAT was incurred before the date of a business was VAT registered. Either the VAT must qualify as pre-registration input tax or the property costs must exceed the £250,000 limit for the capital goods scheme.

See **16.8** and **9.8** for further details.

Planning points to consider

[28.26] The following planning points should be given consideration.

- Remember that once an option to tax election on land or a building has been made, it cannot usually be revoked for 20 years. It is therefore important to take all relevant factors into account before making the election (and a long-term view as to the likely use and potential sale of the property).
- The main reason for making an option to tax election is to enhance input tax recovery by making a supply taxable rather than exempt. However, this enhanced input tax recovery needs to be balanced against the possibility that potential tenants or purchasers of the property may not be able to claim input tax, eg if they are in a business that is exempt from VAT. In such cases, the option to tax creates a VAT charge on all supplies relevant to that property.
- The option to tax election can only be made on commercial properties. If a property is residential, the option to tax cannot be applied.
- Always remember that the decision to opt to tax a property is driven by input tax motives. If there is not an input tax gain to be acquired through an election, then it does not serve any purpose, and creates potential problems in the future if VAT needs to be charged when the building is sold.
- A common mistake made by many tenants renting a property is to assume that because their landlord has opted to tax the property in question, they must also opt to tax their own interest as well, eg if they sublet the property. This is not correct – each VAT registered entity must make its own decision as to whether an election is in its own interests.
- If there are any doubts at all regarding the boundary of a property being elected, then a map or plan of the premises/land should be sent to HMRC at the time the election is made. This avoids any ambiguity in the future.
- Remember there are certain situations where the option to tax is overridden, eg if an opted property is going to be used as a dwelling. Also, the option to tax is overridden if a building is sold as part of the transfer of a going concern – but only if the transferee has also elected to tax the property before the deal is finalised.
- The option to tax rules were introduced on 1 August 1989, so the first opportunities to revoke an option became available on 1 August 2009. This is because once an option to tax election has been made, it cannot

be revoked for at least 20 years. As well as saving VAT for businesses unable to reclaim VAT, a decision to revoke the option to tax could produce significant savings of Stamp Duty Land Tax or Scottish Land and Buildings Transaction Tax. As each day passes, more elections will have met the 20-year old time limit, ie an increasing number of revocations can be made.

• A recharge of building insurance costs from a landlord to a tenant will be subject to VAT if a landlord insures the building and the landlord has an option to tax election in place. This is because the charge by the landlord to the tenant is classed as 'additional rent' to meet the insurance cost – there is no supply of insurance taking place from the landlord to the tenant.

Chapter 29

DIY Refund Scheme

Key topics in this chapter:

- Purpose and aims of the DIY scheme.
- What constitutes the construction of a new dwelling that qualifies for a refund under the scheme.
- Rules to be aware of when converting a non-residential property into a residential property, eg ten-year rule for non-residential use.
- Situations when a claim cannot be made under the scheme, eg commercial ventures, speculative development projects.
- Costs that can and cannot be reclaimed under the DIY scheme.
- Rules for claiming VAT on costs where partly residential and partly non-residential buildings are converted.
- When the 5% rate of VAT applies to building works – and the importance of only claiming correctly charged VAT under the DIY scheme.
- Procedures for making a DIY claim – Form VAT 431 to be completed within three months of completion date and forwarded to the HMRC National DIY Team in Glasgow.

Introduction

[29.1] The aim of the DIY (do-it-yourself) Refund Scheme is to give private individuals not in business or registered for VAT the chance to recover VAT on the relevant costs of certain building projects. The main works where a claim could be made are as follows:

- the construction of a building designed as a dwelling or number of dwellings – for both residential and holiday home purposes;
- the construction of a building for use solely for a relevant residential purpose or for a relevant charitable purpose; or
- a residential conversion, ie the conversion of a non-residential building or the non-residential part of a building into either a building designed as a dwelling or number of dwellings or a building intended solely for a relevant residential purpose or anything which would fall into either of those categories if different parts of a building were treated as separate buildings.

The criteria for what constitutes a relevant charitable purpose or relevant residential purpose are considered in Chapter 26. However, most DIY claims tend to be relevant to dwellings, where private individuals obtain a plot of land and build a house on the land for their own occupation.

All work carried out on the property must be lawful, ie proper planning permission must have been obtained and there are formal procedures and deadline dates that must be followed in order to obtain a refund from HMRC.

Objectives of the DIY scheme

[29.2] In basic terms, the DIY scheme is intended to ensure that people who build their own houses or convert non-residential properties into dwellings are not disadvantaged in VAT terms compared to housebuilders or other VAT registered businesses who buy and sell properties as a trading activity – see Example 1.

Example 1

Smith Housebuilders Ltd buys half an acre of land at Potters Farm and builds a new house, which is subsequently sold. The company is VAT registered.

Mr Jones is a local tax consultant, who has also bought half an acre of land at Potters Farm to build a new house to live in himself. He is VAT registered as a tax consultant.

What is the position in these two situations as far as recovering VAT is concerned?

Solution – Smith Housebuilders Ltd has made a taxable (zero-rated) supply and can therefore reclaim input tax on any related costs such as building materials, fittings etc associated with the new property.

Mr Jones is VAT registered but cannot reclaim input tax on his VAT return because the cost of the house is a private expense relevant to him, not relevant to his taxable supplies as a tax consultant. However, he is eligible to make a claim to HMRC under the DIY scheme by completing Form VAT 431.

The end result is that both Smith Housebuilders Ltd and Mr Jones recover VAT on their costs – but by different methods.

The DIY scheme has clear and simple rules – further guidance is given in VAT431NB Notes (for new build projects) or VAT431C Notes for conversions. The previous VAT 719 Notice has been withdrawn.

Definition of 'constructing a building'

[29.3] Many DIY claims will be relevant to dwellings or qualifying buildings built on empty land and it will therefore be obvious that the project relates to the construction of a new building. However, there will be other occasions when a project utilises part of an existing building and this is where great care is needed to ensure the project is still eligible for a DIY refund.

The key rules are as follows:

- a building can still be classed as new if it makes use of no more than a single façade (or a double façade on a corner site) of a pre-existing building; and
- the pre-existing building is completely demolished before work on the new building is started; and
- the façade is retained as an explicit condition or requirement of statutory planning consent.

In determining whether a building has been demolished, the party walls relevant to a neighbouring property that is not being developed can also be ignored.

In addition, the construction of a self-contained semi-detached property will be classed as a newly constructed building, and also if an existing building is enlarged or extended and the enlargement or extension creates an additional dwelling.

For example, a new qualifying flat built on the top of an existing block of flats would be eligible for a claim – but the conversion of a loft space into a flat would not qualify.

Definition of a 'non-residential conversion'

[29.4] In most cases, it will be very easy to identify when a conversion from a non-residential to residential property has taken place. For example, a very common example of a conversion is where an agricultural building such as a barn is converted into a house or bungalow. Equally, a commercial building such as an office, warehouse or shop may be turned into new flats.

Again, an important point to remember is that situations such as those above are only covered by the scheme if the project is for a non-business purpose. For example, if an individual proposes to buy an office block, turn it into six flats and sell the flats, this is a clear business venture. The correct route is to register for VAT in the normal way. In effect, therefore, the following individuals cannot use the DIY scheme:

- speculative developers looking to buy and sell property at a profit;
- landlords seeking to rent out properties for commercial gain;
- bed and breakfast operators;
- care home operators who make a charge (even if not for a profit) to their residents;
- membership clubs and associations;
- theatres; and
- child nurseries where a fee is charged.

Note – in the case of the child nursery and care home examples, it is the 'business' aspect of the arrangement that creates the exclusion from the DIY scheme.

One important rule that applies to non-residential conversions is the ten-year rule. This rule states that a building only qualifies for DIY relief if it has not been lived in for at least ten years. For example, if an office block is being converted into a freehold dwelling, this project will qualify for a refund (subject to the normal rules). However, if the building in question has only been an office block for the last five years, and was previously a dwelling, then a claim is excluded by the ten-year rule.

As a final point, a claim can also be made if a person buys a 'shell' from a developer (or had the 'shell' built himself) and then incurs costs fitting it out to create a qualifying building.

A shell is a building that is structurally, but not functionally, complete. It will possess all the basic structural features (such as the walls, roof, doors, windows and utilities connections) but will lack some or all of the facilities that will enable it to function as a modern dwelling. This will include work to install fixtures and fittings such as kitchen furniture and other essential features. If the only work required to be done is to decorate the building, the house is considered to be both structurally and functionally complete and VAT on the costs of decoration may not be recovered.

Costs that can be claimed

[29.5] The first priority is to be aware of what services provided by a builder are zero-rated or chargeable at the lower VAT rate of 5%. This is important for two reasons:

- from a cash flow angle, it is better not to pay VAT in the first place, rather than pay it to the builder and then have a time delay before it is recovered from HMRC with a DIY claim; and
- under the DIY scheme, HMRC will only refund correctly charged VAT. If a builder charges VAT at 20% instead of 0%, this is not correctly charged VAT – and the claim to HMRC under the DIY scheme will be rejected. See Example 2.

Example 2

Mr C employed a builder to do all of the bricklaying works at his new house in Wilstead. The builder is also supplying all of the materials. He does a good job on the building but is not sure of the VAT rules for the work he has carried out. He invoices Mr C for £20,000 plus VAT of £4,000 (based on VAT rate of 20%) – which Mr C agrees to pay because he can recover the VAT from HMRC under the DIY scheme.

Solution – HMRC will reject the claim for £4,000 – as this is incorrectly charged VAT. The supply should have been zero-rated. The correct course of action is for the builder to issue a VAT credit to Mr C for incorrectly charged VAT – and refund the VAT to him. The adjustment is therefore made through the builder's VAT return, rather than by making an incorrect claim under the DIY scheme.

Note – VAT can only be recovered on 'building materials' with the scheme, ie excluding items such as washing machines, carpets, doorbells, freezers, etc. A detailed list is included in section 3 of VAT431NB Notes.

As far as the definition of 'building materials' is concerned, the main guideline is that the items in question tend to be permanently fixed in the building. For example, a carpet can be lifted and moved to another room or building – wood flooring that is permanently fixed to the ground cannot. Therefore, the VAT on wood flooring costs can be claimed – but not carpets.

On a positive note, all goods or services relevant to making the building suitable for construction can also be claimed, including:

- drainage;
- main paths on the site;
- driveways;
- retaining walls and boundary walls and fences.

The cost of building a garage is also eligible under the scheme, as long as the dwelling and garage are constructed at the same time and the garage is intended for occupation with the dwelling (or one of the dwellings).

Works and materials that cannot be claimed

[29.6] One common situation is where a 'granny' annex is constructed to an existing property, for example, to give independent living to an elderly relative but close to, or attached to, the main property. In such cases, a claim cannot be made unless the annex can be disposed of separately to the main house. In most cases, this is not possible so a DIY claim cannot be made.

The other main exclusion from the DIY scheme is that VAT cannot be recovered on certain services associated with the project. These exclusions mainly relate to professional and supervisory services – architects, surveyors, design fees, solicitor costs. Also, VAT cannot be recovered on the hire of plant, tools and equipment (generators, scaffolding etc).

Other costs that are excluded relate to detached workshops, playrooms or swimming pools constructed in the grounds of a new dwelling. These exclusions would also include other leisure facilities such as tennis courts, as well as fishponds, rockeries and other ornamental works.

An important point to remember is that the best way of dealing with the exclusions is for a builder to separately invoice for works carried out, for example, on a playroom built above a detached garage. If the builder raises an invoice for his total works on an inclusive basis, this could lead to an excessive amount of VAT being disallowed by HMRC. See Example 3.

Finally, a claim cannot be made for extra work that is done to a completed building that has been purchased from a builder or developer. Examples of work that cannot be claimed (once the building has been completed) are:

- a conservatory
- a patio
- double-glazed windows
- tiling
- a garage.

Example 3

Jane Smith is having a new four-bedroom detached house built on a plot of land she has bought, and intends to live in the property herself (ie the nature of the scheme qualifies for a VAT refund under the DIY scheme). The project includes a snooker room being built above the garage – the garage being detached from the property. She buys all building materials and fittings from a local merchant at a total cost of £60,000 plus VAT. The new house is 3,000 square feet and the snooker room is 600 square feet. What is the VAT position regarding the snooker room?

Solution – HMRC could seek to disallow 1/6 of the VAT claimed on the materials relevant to the snooker room by making an apportionment calculation on a square footage basis (600 divided by 3,600). This could lead to the claim being reduced by £2,000 (£60,000 × 20% divided by 6). However, this could produce an unfair result for Jane because the building materials in the snooker room are likely to have cost considerably less on a pro-rata basis than, for example, the kitchen, bathroom or bedrooms. It would almost certainly produce a better result for Jane if she isolates the material costs for the snooker room, and reduces her initial claim by this amount, ie only making a claim for the costs that qualify under the DIY scheme.

Buildings — part commercial/part residential

[29.7] What happens if a building that was partly residential and partly non-residential is converted into a residential building.

HMRC now accepts that, for the purposes of the DIY scheme, the conversion of a building that contains both a residential part and a non-residential part comes within the scope of the scheme so long as the conversion results in an additional dwelling being created. It is no longer necessary for the additional dwelling to be created exclusively from the non-residential part. However, VAT recovery is restricted to the conversion of the non-residential part and the project would also be outside the scope of the DIY scheme if the owner had a business motive, ie to sell or rent out the property. See Example 4.

Example 4

Phil has purchased a public house that includes a three-bedroom flat on the first floor (living quarters). He has obtained planning permission to convert the property to a private residence but is unsure whether to convert the pub into one large detached house or two flats. He needs some advice about the VAT position.

Solution – if Phil converts the flat into a detached house, then he cannot recover any VAT under the DIY scheme because he has not created an additional dwelling, ie the property will comprise one dwelling before and after the conversion.

However, he will be able to obtain relief for the costs of converting the non-residential part of the building if he takes the option of converting it into two flats. This is because he has created an additional dwelling. He will not be able to recover any VAT on the costs of converting the residential part of the building. However, Phil must ensure the project is a non-business venture and live in the property to qualify for a refund of VAT under the DIY scheme.

The change in HMRC policy is explained in Business Brief 22/05.

Lower rate VAT charge (5%)

[29.8] As explained at 29.4, it is only possible to reclaim correctly charged VAT under the DIY scheme. Certain construction services supplied by a builder will be eligible for a VAT charge at 5% rather than 20%, eg when a non-residential property is converted into one or more single house dwellings.

If the builder is unaware of the reduced rate charge, and adds VAT at 20%, then HMRC will reject the DIY claim because they can only repay correctly charged VAT. See Example 5.

Example 5

John has bought the freehold of a public house and has obtained planning permission to convert it into a five-bedroom detached house to live in himself (there was no living quarters within this pub, so the accommodation was wholly non-residential). ABC Builders Ltd carry out all of the building work and charge John £100,000 plus £20,000 VAT. He submits Form VAT 431 to HMRC to recover this VAT under the DIY scheme.

Solution – John is correct to make a DIY claim on the basis that the scheme represents the conversion of a non-residential building into a dwelling. However, the correct amount of the claim is only £5,000, ie ABC Builders Ltd should have charged VAT at 5% instead of 20%. John will need to obtain a VAT credit from ABC Builders Ltd for £15,000 to ensure he is not out of pocket.

Claim procedures under the DIY scheme

[29.9] Form VAT 431 needs to be completed and sent to HMRC in order to obtain a VAT refund under the DIY scheme. It is important to give plenty of detail in the relevant parts to support the application.

Note – there is a time limit for making the claim, namely three months after the construction or conversion is completed. The completion date is usually based on a certification or letter of completion issued by a local authority. If this deadline date cannot be met, then a letter needs to be sent to HMRC, advising the reasons for the delay and when a claim form will be submitted. As long as the reason for the delay is sensible, there are unlikely to be problems gaining a time extension.

Form VAT 431 is user friendly, and can either be obtained from the VAT Helpline (Tel: 0300 200 3700) or downloaded from the GOV.UK website (www.gov.uk/government/organisations/hm-revenue-customs).

Claims need to be submitted to:

Local Compliance
HMRC National DIY Team
S0987
NEWCASTLE
NE98 1ZZ

As well as Form VAT 431 being submitted, it is also necessary to send original invoices and supporting documents with the claim. Finally, the claim also needs to include a copy of the planning permission approval for the project, as well as evidence that the project is completed. This is to meet the HMRC objective that it will only provide refunds to a project if it is carried out lawfully.

In reality, the evidence of completion will usually be a certificate or letter of completion from the local authority. However, alternative evidence could be a valuation rating or Council Tax assessment – or a certificate from the bank or building society involved with lending money against the project.

As with all claims, HMRC has the right to make any enquiries about any relevant issue, and the taxpayer has the right to appeal to a VAT tribunal if he disagrees with a decision that affects his claim.

When a claim is submitted, the DIY section in Glasgow will acknowledge receipt of the claim in writing (within five working days), and usually give a date when they expect to make a repayment. As a general guide, a refund is normally made within six weeks of receiving the claim.

Planning points to consider

[29.10] The following planning points should be given consideration.

- A building can still qualify as a new dwelling under the DIY scheme if a single façade is retained from the existing building or a double façade in the case of a corner site. Party walls can also be ignored. However, the façade can only be retained if this was a requirement of planning consent.
- The construction of a new flat on top of an existing block of flats will qualify under the DIY scheme because it creates an additional dwelling, capable of being sold as a single unit in its own right.
- Remember that the conversion of a non-residential to residential property will only qualify under the scheme if a property has not been lived in for at least ten years. It is important to check this point before making a DIY claim.
- The DIY scheme excludes any claim linked to a commercial venture. In such cases, the claimant will need to register for VAT in the normal way (assuming he makes or intends to make taxable supplies) and recover VAT costs by claiming input tax on his VAT returns.
- It is important to ensure that builders charge the correct rate of VAT on works carried out on a project. If a builder charges standard rate VAT on a zero-rated supply, then HMRC will reject the DIY claim. In such

cases, it will be necessary to get a VAT credit from the builder. Be aware that most building services on non-residential to residential conversions attract VAT at the reduced rate of 5%.

- The DIY claim can include most building material costs that are permanently fixed to the building – however, be aware of exclusions relevant to items such as washing machines, freezers and carpets. Section 3 of VAT431NB Notes gives a detailed list of items that can and cannot be claimed.

- Be aware that certain aspects of a project cannot be reclaimed under the scheme, eg the costs relevant to a detached playroom. In such cases, it may be more profitable to directly exclude the VAT costs relevant to these aspects, than to allow HMRC to make an overall deduction of a claim based on an alternative method, eg square footage basis.

- Rules concerning the conversion of a property that partly included a residential element and partly included a non-residential element changed in 2005. The rules only allow a DIY claim to be made if an additional dwelling is created through the conversion project (eg a pub with one flat being converted into two flats) and only on the costs of converting the non-residential part of the building. There may be benefits in considering these rules before a project is started.

Chapter 30

VAT Planning Tips to Improve Cash Flow

> *Key topics in this chapter:*
> * The benefits of using the cash accounting scheme.
> * Opportunities to delay raising a sales invoice – 14-day rule and applications for payment.
> * Filing VAT returns online – extended payment period.
> * Utilising HMRC's Business Payment Support Service (BPSS) if a business is unable to pay some or all of the tax due on its VAT return.
> * Input tax treatment of leased vehicles.
> * The scope to reduce interim payments for users of the annual accounting scheme.

Introduction

[30.1] As far as VAT is concerned, it is fair to say that both advisers and clients will be faced with different challenges when cash rather than profits are in short supply. For example, questions such as 'Can I claim input tax on my new personalised number plate?' may be replaced by questions like 'What happens if I can't pay my VAT bill on time?' or 'What happens if my customers haven't paid their invoices for the last three months?'

Cash accounting scheme

[30.2] If a business uses the cash accounting scheme (available to a business with annual taxable sales of £1.35m or less – see Chapter 6), then output tax is not included on a VAT return until payment has been received from a customer and bad debt relief on unpaid sales invoices is automatic. This is because the main feature of the scheme is that output tax is not due on a VAT return until payment has been received from a customer. For a business that does not use cash accounting, VAT is usually due on a return when either a sales invoice is raised or payment received, whichever happens sooner. This usually means that output tax is payable according to the invoice date. See Example 1 for an illustration of this point.

Example 1

John is VAT registered as a surveyor with annual sales of £300,000. He has very little input tax to claim and completes his VAT returns on a calendar quarter basis.

It is 30 June and John has unpaid sales invoices of £45,000 plus VAT. What are the implications for John's VAT return for this quarter?

Solution – John is eligible to use the cash accounting scheme because his annual taxable sales are less than £1.35m. He can adopt the scheme at any time without HMRC approval. This means the output tax on his June VAT return will decrease if he adopts the scheme because all of the VAT on the unpaid sales invoices as at 30 June will be excluded. This produces a worthwhile cash flow saving.

Note – the one negative aspect of the scheme is that input tax cannot be reclaimed until payment has been made to a supplier – but this is not a major issue for John because, like many service related businesses, he has very little input tax to reclaim.

As explained above, if a business is not using the cash accounting scheme, then output tax is usually payable on a VAT return according to the date of the sales invoice, ie before payment has been received from the customer. However, in the event of non-payment of the invoice, there is scope to reclaim this VAT under the bad debt relief rules as long as the following conditions are met:

- the debt must be at least six months overdue for payment;
- the debt has been written off in the company accounts, eg credit entry to customer's sales ledger account and debit entry to a 'bad debt' account;
- output tax was charged on the original invoice and accounted for by the taxpayer on a previous VAT return;
- the debt must not have been paid, sold or factored under a valid legal assignment.

An essential point to remember is that a bad debt cannot be adjusted by issuing a credit note to either reduce or cancel the unpaid invoice. A credit note can only be used to correct pricing errors or situations where a customer has returned goods and an invoice correction is needed.

Delaying issuing a tax invoice

[30.3] There is an old phrase in business that 'cash is king'.

A possible method of delaying a VAT payment to keep money in a client's bank account a bit longer is to delay issuing a tax invoice for ongoing contracts – instead issuing an alternative document such as a 'request for payment' or 'application for payment'. This is a common and perfectly legal technique, eg in the construction industry.

The reason why this approach is only appropriate for ongoing jobs is because the normal tax point rules for VAT require an invoice to be issued within 14 days of a supply being made. If no invoice is raised (referred to as an actual tax point), then VAT becomes due on the date when the supply was made (known as a basic tax point). See Example 2.

Example 2

Jack supplies goods to Jill on 30 June (basic tax point) but does not raise an invoice for the goods until 31 July. Jack completes VAT returns on a calendar quarter basis. When must he include the sale on his VAT return?

Solution – the sale must be included on the VAT return for the quarter ended 30 June because the invoice was issued more than 14 days after the supply took place. If the sales invoice had been raised on 13 July, this would have delayed the VAT payment until the September return because the invoice has now been raised within 14 days of the supply taking place.

However, if a contract or job is being carried out on an ongoing basis, and involves interim payments, then a sensible strategy could be to issue an application for payment (not a tax invoice) and then advise the client that a tax invoice will be issued once payment has been received. This approach is covered by the continuous supply of service rules in VAT, whereby output tax is due according to invoice date or receipt of payment, whichever happens sooner. In other words, an application for payment is not an invoice – so output tax is not due until payment has been received. See Example 3.

Example 3

Decorators Ltd has annual turnover of £2m and is currently working on a large contract to paint all the rooms in a big office, a job which could last for many months. The company's VAT periods end on calendar quarters and they raise tax invoices at the end of each calendar month to charge the customer for work completed during the month. The customer pays the invoice at the end of the following month. It is 31 March and the company is about to raise an invoice for £100,000 plus VAT of £20,000. Can the company improve its VAT cash flow management?

Solution – if the company raises an application for payment instead of a tax invoice, output tax will not be payable on this charge until the June VAT quarter (assuming payment is made at the end of April by the customer) rather than the March period if an invoice was raised. This is because the tax point becomes the payment date in April. A tax invoice will also be issued when payment has been received. The company gains a useful three-month cash flow benefit on £20,000.

Paying VAT by direct debit

[30.4] From 1 April 2012 virtually all VAT-registered businesses are required to submit their VAT returns online and pay any VAT due electronically. One advantage of online filing and electronic payment is the extra time to submit VAT returns and make VAT payments – normally an extra seven calendar days.

For businesses who pay by online direct debit HMRC will collect payment a further three bank working days after the extended due date. This means that online VAT direct debit offers more time to pay than any other method – a minimum of ten extra calendar days. (Bank working days are Monday to Friday excluding bank holidays.)

Business Payment Support Service (BPSS)

[30.5] When cash is in short supply many businesses will be faced with the decision as to whether they pay their suppliers on time (to keep the flow of goods coming into the business) or the quarterly VAT return on time. The BPSS could ease this dilemma by giving the opportunity for businesses to spread the liability due on their VAT return over a number of months.

The BPSS deals with payments of VAT, National Insurance and other taxes managed by HMRC and is open seven days a week (telephone number 03002 003835).

Its opening hours (excluding bank holidays) are:

- Monday to Friday: 8am–8pm
- Saturday and Sunday: 8am–4pm

The key challenge is to contact the BPSS before the liability on a VAT return is due and make a time-to-pay proposal as to how a particular VAT debt can be settled. A deal agreed before the payment becomes legally due will also avoid any potential default surcharges being levied if the business complies with the agreed payment terms.

The approach to dealing with the BPSS is as follows:

- ensure you have your VAT registration number available to quote at the beginning of the telephone call;
- clearly identify the VAT that cannot be paid – this might relate to the balance due on a VAT return if a part payment has been made;
- quantify basic income and expenditure details of the business to show to HMRC that the VAT debt can be paid within future profits.

Note – HMRC's policy in the BPSS is to 'enter into realistic time to pay arrangements as a temporary option tailored to your business needs.' The main situation when an arrangement would be appropriate is if a business has encountered cash flow problems because of a major bad debt or late payment from a major customer.

Leasing rather than buying vehicles

[30.6] One decision taken by a company with cash flow difficulties could be to lease vehicles rather than buy them as an outright purchase.

The implication of leasing an asset is that VAT is usually charged on monthly hire payments made to the leasing company rather than when the asset is initially purchased by the business. The leasing company will often issue an annual tax invoice in advance, which serves as evidence for the lessee to reclaim input tax on each monthly payment. Be sure to resist the temptation to claim all of the year's input tax when the first payment is made!

The important point with leasing cars is that a 50% input tax restriction applies, unless the car is used exclusively for business purposes and never available for private use (unlikely . . . think for example, of the emergency trip to the supermarket) or is primarily used by a business involved in car hire, taxi work or driving instruction. The 50% restriction recognises the fact that the vehicle will be partly used for private or non-business purposes.

Author note – occasionally, there are queries from practitioners asking why a 50% restriction on input tax is needed in relation to car leasing charges if a business also pays output tax each VAT period using the scale charge system. The key point is that the scale charge adjustment only relates to private fuel usage – not to the private use of the actual vehicle.

Annual accounting – review payments on account

[30.7] The annual accounting scheme involves the completion of one annual VAT return and is considered in Chapter 7. A feature of the scheme is that payments on account are made throughout the year and these payments are based on the tax paid on the previous year's annual return.

To avoid making payments on account that are too high, and could therefore create cash flow problems, don't forget that a scheme user can contact HMRC (initial contact should be the VAT Helpline on tel: 0300 200 3700) and reduce these payments on account.

Planning points to consider

[30.8] The following planning points should be given consideration.

- Consider the potential benefits to clients of adopting the cash accounting scheme to improve business cash flow. No HMRC permission is needed to use the scheme if the business is eligible.
- A tax point (time when VAT is due on a return) can be delayed in some cases by raising a document such as an application for payment, fee note or payment request, ie any document other than a sales invoice. This could produce important cash flow benefits for the business by delaying the payment of output tax until perhaps the next VAT period.

- In cases where a business is unable to pay its tax, there is scope to negotiate a time to pay arrangement with HMRC's Business Payment Support Service. However, contact should be made before a VAT debt becomes overdue for payment, ie to avoid a potential default surcharge being levied.
- A business that uses the annual accounting scheme should regularly review its payments on account during the accounting year to ensure they are not too high. If they are too high, HMRC should be contacted in order to have them reduced to a more realistic level.

Chapter 31

Supply of Goods and Services

Key topics in this chapter:

- The difference between a supply of goods and services.
- Key issues for computer software supplies, hire purchase agreements and leasing arrangements.
- Procedures relating to goods supplied on a sale or return basis.
- Tax point rules – basic and actual tax points.
- Warranties, samples, compensation payments, lost or stolen goods, discount deals, part-exchange transactions.
- Mixed supplies – basic introduction to deal with the situation where goods are supplied which attract different rates of VAT.
- VAT invoices – when they should be issued and what information they should include.
- Electronic invoicing – the need for HMRC approval.
- Credit and debit notes – when they should be issued and what information they should contain.
- Bad debt relief – conditions for reclaiming bad debt relief on supplies made.
- Business gifts – £50 limit to avoid a VAT liability and definition of a 'person' for this limit.
- Samples – recent changes to interpretation of rules.
- Recharge of zero-rated expenses to a customer – form part of main supply.
- Disbursements – when they apply.
- Continuous supplies of services.
- Sales between related parties.
- Supply chains involving goods.

Introduction

[31.1] For a transaction to be within the scope of UK VAT, there are four key conditions that need to be satisfied:

(a)   it is a supply of goods or services;
(b)   it takes place within the UK;
(c)   it is made by a taxable person; and
(d)   it is made in the course or furtherance of any business carried on by that person.

The principle of VAT being a tax on the 'supply' of goods and services is in contrast to many other taxes – where calculations are based on money in and money out.

Note – don't forget that a 'taxable person' not only includes a person or business that is VAT registered but one that should be registered. So a business that exceeded the VAT registration limit but did not register for VAT at the correct time is still a taxable person.

An outcome of this basic rule is that tax can sometimes be due, even where no money has changed hands. This can cause confusion among clients and tax advisers, who struggle to understand the concept that a transaction can have nil proceeds but still produce a VAT bill.

Another important point is that, by definition, a supply can only be of goods or services. So if there are no goods being supplied, and a supply has taken place, then it must relate to services.

This chapter considers some of the important issues as to whether goods or services are being supplied to a customer and also some of the relevant issues that determine how much VAT is then due.

Difference between goods and services

[31.2] The basic HMRC definition of a supply of services is: 'You supply services if you do something, other than supplying goods, for a consideration' (VAT Notice 700, para 4.5).

The phrase, 'for a consideration', means there is no VAT to worry about on a free supply of services, eg an accountant doing the year-end accounts for a local charity without making any charge for his time.

The difference between goods and services is clear in most cases because goods are usually tangible and can be clearly seen by the customer.

To give everyday examples, a washing machine, television and dishwasher are clearly goods. In contrast, a hairdresser, opera singer and VAT lecturer are supplying services because the customer is receiving no goods and is enjoying the skills of the individual in question.

However, there are a number of borderline situations, usually when computer related supplies are involved – see Example 1.

(HMRC Notice 700, paras 4.4 and 4.5).

Example 1

DEF Ltd produces a monthly newsletter which provides UK businesses with advice and tips on marketing for a monthly subscription of £50 plus VAT. The newsletter has always been posted to subscribers' addresses in paper format but with effect from 1 June, it will be e-mailed to each subscriber on a monthly basis. The customers are all in the UK. What is the VAT position?

Solution – the paper copy of the newsletter qualifies as a supply of goods, eligible for zero-rating as printed matter under *VATA 1994, Sch 8, Group 3*. The VAT-inclusive monthly subscription for the paper newsletter is £50. The e-mail arrangement means the customer is now receiving a supply of electronic services – and the supply is standard rated. The VAT-inclusive monthly subscription for the electronic newsletter is £60.

Computer software supplies

[31.3] The VAT situation regarding computer software supplies can sometimes be difficult.

To give a simple example, if a person buys a copy of a standard accounting software package from the shelf of his local store, this is a supply of goods. This is because the software is a mass-produced item that is freely available to all customers.

In contrast, if someone orders a 'specific' software product for his own requirements (ie to create a unique programme), this is clearly a supply of services. The expertise of the person(s) producing the package means payment has been made for a supply of services.

Note – the issue of whether a supply relates to goods or services becomes relevant in relation to pre-registration input tax where the time limit for goods is four years before VAT registration compared to six months for services.

As a tip, don't be tempted to think that a supply of computer services can become a supply of goods if the end result is given to the customer on a CD or DVD. Although a CD can be touched, and is therefore classed as 'goods', it has a minimal value – it is the information within the CD that matters (eg an accounts programme designed for the customer), and that is a supply of services.

Transfer of ownership – HP or lease?

[31.4] A supply of 'goods' applies when a transaction involves:

- any transfer of the whole property in goods;
- the transfer of possession of goods.

A common situation encountered by practitioners concerns the VAT treatment of hire purchase (HP) and leasing agreements.

The key point with an HP agreement is that the intention of the agreement is that ownership of the goods will pass to the hirer at some point in the future, usually when the final payment has been made. The transaction therefore relates to a supply of goods.

The first instalment paid to the HP company usually includes a deposit on the asset and full payment of the VAT on the value of the goods. The hirer can reclaim input tax (subject to normal rules), even though he is paying for the goods over a longer period of time.

Contrast the above situation with the common lease hire arrangement for a car:

Example – Jim pays £400 per month to lease a car for three years and then return it to the leasing company at the end of the period.

In this situation, there is neither a transfer in the property of the goods, nor in the possession of the goods. The intention was always for the goods to be returned to the owner after three years. The monthly instalments of £400 therefore relate to a supply of services and should charge VAT at the standard rate. As long as the vehicle has some business use, HMRC allows 50% input tax recovery on the leasing payments, again subject to normal rules (see **33.10**).

The above examples are very clear – but the approach to adopt in any difficult situation is to study the written agreement in detail and the intention of the scheme as far as ownership is concerned. To give a legislative reference, *Directive 2006/112/EC, art 14(2)(b)* rules there is a supply of goods where 'in the normal course of events' ownership will pass at the latest upon payment of the final instalment.

Note – the Court of Appeal has recently referred a case (*Revenue & Customs Comrs v Mercedes-Benz Financial Services (UK) Ltd* [2015] EWCA Civ 1211, [2016] STC 392) to the Court of Justice concerning the interpretation of the phrase 'in the normal course of events'. Mercedes-Benz Financial Services (UK) Ltd (MBFS) sells cars under its 'Agility' contract. The contract allows a purchaser to either hand the car back at the end of the contract or to acquire the vehicle. In most cases, the purchaser does not, in fact, acquire title but, more often, will return the car and change to another. HMRC consider that the option to acquire that is granted at the beginning of the contract makes the supply one of goods. MBFS considers that the evidence points to a different conclusion. In the 'normal course of events' very few customers take title to the car. It is likely to be late 2017 or early 2018 before the question is resolved.

(HMRC Notice 700, para 8.4).

Land

[31.5] Another situation when a supply of goods is evident relates to a supply that involves 'the grant, assignment or surrender of a "major interest" in land'. A major interest in the UK relates to either a freehold sale or a lease exceeding 21 years (20 years in Scotland).

In effect, this means that the rental of a property (landlord and tenant basis) involves a supply of services.

Sale or return

[31.6] This situation arises when a customer receives goods from a supplier – but the supplier retains ownership of the goods until the point when the customer adopts them. In effect, this means the customer has the right to return them at any time.

A common example of where this type of supply may occur is when a manufacturer provides a demonstrator product to a retail outlet – allowing the latter to display the goods in his shop and show the benefits to potential customers.

The main rules to remember with supplies on sale or return are as follows:

- as the goods remain the property of the supplier, then no tax becomes due until the customer formally adopts them;
- if no formal adoption takes place, then the adoption date will automatically become 12 months after the goods were first received – creating a tax point for VAT purposes.

What happens if a supplier receives some payment for these goods – in advance of the adoption date? Such transactions will be looked at very closely by HMRC because payment normally indicates a transfer of ownership, ie confirming a supply has taken place. However, if it can be clearly shown that the adoption of the goods has not taken place, and that the payment made is a refundable deposit, then no VAT is due.

With regard to the 12-month adoption deadline, output tax will be due at this point on the market value of the goods. In the case of an item that has been sitting on the shop floor for a year, going through various demonstration procedures, this value is likely to be considerably less than for a brand new item. It is also possible that the item could have been superseded by a more up-to-date product, again reducing its open market value.

(HMRC Notice 700, para 14.4).

Slow invoicing procedures – tax point rules

[31.7] This is very common in business – a busy client is working so hard that he forgets to raise tax invoices promptly.

In these circumstances, it is useful to return to the basic tax point rules that apply as far as VAT is concerned.

- *Basic tax point* – this occurs at the time the supply of goods actually takes place, ie the point when goods are delivered to the customer. This transfer of ownership creates a supply as far as VAT is concerned – and a liability to the tax. However, the basic tax point is overridden if an 'actual' tax point is created.
- *Actual tax point* – this is created when either a supplier raises a tax invoice or payment is received from the customer. As long as one of these situations arises within 14 days of the basic tax point, then the actual tax point becomes the date when the VAT is due.

(HMRC Notice 700, para 14.2).

See Example 2.

Example 2

> ABC Ltd prepares VAT returns on a calendar quarter basis. On 15 March it supplied goods to DEF Ltd for £15,000 plus VAT. DEF Ltd has agreed to pay for the goods on 30 April.
>
> The Finance Director of ABC Ltd thinks he can improve his company's cash flow by issuing the invoice for the goods on 1 April and accounting for the VAT of £3,000 on the VAT return for the quarter to 30 June.
>
> *Solution* – the invoice date of 1 April is more than 14 days after the basic tax point of 15 March. This means that the VAT of £3,000 should be accounted for on the VAT return for the quarter to 31 March. If HMRC identified this anomaly on a VAT visit, then interest and a potential timing penalty could apply.
>
> Note – the logical solution would have been for ABC Ltd to delay the supply of goods until 18 March, so that the invoice date would then have been within 14 days of the supply.

As a final point, an application to HMRC can be made to extend the 14-day rule – but it is necessary to show why the 14-day period is inadequate. This could be, for example, that a price negotiation period takes place with a customer that always exceeds 14 days. There are several trades that have an agreement in place with HMRC to extend the 14-day period.

Warranties

[31.8] A warranty arrangement is very common with the supply of many goods and, in the case of extended warranties, has proved particularly profitable for companies that trade in electrical goods.

The first situation that normally occurs is where the manufacturer or supplier gives a guarantee, for example, for the first 12 months that any repair or defect to the goods will be repaired without charge. In this situation, all parts and labour supplied by the manufacturer or supplier are not charged to the customer – and no VAT is therefore due.

The situation that can cause complications is where a company sells an 'extended warranty arrangement', ie the customer receives assurance that if the goods break down after the standard warranty period expires, then he will still have repairs carried out without charge – apart from the cost of the extended warranty.

As far as VAT is concerned, the key question to ask is: does the supply to the customer involve a contract of insurance (and is a contract that would be recognised as insurance by the Financial Services Authority)? If the answer is 'yes' (unlikely in most cases), then the charge to the customer will be exempt under *VATA 1994, Sch 9, Group 2*. However, the supply of a non-insurance warranty by a UK business will be standard rated.

Samples

[**31.9**] Under HMRC's previous interpretation of the rules for samples, only one sample of each product supplied to another person was disregarded for output tax purposes. However, this approach was deemed to be incorrect following the 2010 case at the European Court involving *EMI Group Ltd v Revenue and Customs Comrs: C-581/08* [2010] STC 2609, ECJ.

The case related to the VAT treatment of DVD samples given away by EMI to music retailers and confirmed that according to EU law, there is no limit on the number of samples that can be supplied for VAT purposes as long as they are given away for business purposes. In the case of *EMI*, they were giving away DVDs in order to encourage the retailers to promote the sale of the music or artist in question. So EMI can give as many samples of the same DVD as they want to lots of different staff in the same organisation without creating a VAT problem. That principle applies to any other business giving away samples as well.

See Revenue & Customs Brief 51/10 which confirms that HMRC have accepted the principles of the *EMI* case. Legislation was introduced in the 2011 Finance Bill.

(HMRC Notice 700, para 8.8).

Compensation

[**31.10**] The issue of compensation is a potential problem for any business – and almost every business will, at some time, have to deal with a situation where something has gone wrong, and a distraught customer is looking for financial recompense.

The basic principle as far as VAT is concerned is to consider whether the compensation payment relates to a specific taxable supply of goods – or whether the payments are compensatory, eg for distress caused. See Examples 3 and 4.

Example 3

Garage Doors Ltd supplied a customer with a garage door for £1,000 plus VAT that had a loose nut in it. As a consequence, the garage door collapsed on the customer's head when she was opening it – she had to have hospital treatment for cuts and bruises. Garage Doors Ltd pays her £600 compensation and reduces its output tax by £100 (ie £600 × 1/6 with a VAT rate of 20%).

Solution – Garage Doors Ltd is incorrect to adjust its output tax figure. The payment to the injured customer is compensation for her inconvenience and suffering – it is not linked to the taxable supply of goods. The payment is outside the scope of VAT.

Example 4

Garage Doors Ltd supplies another customer with a red painted door for £1,000 plus VAT. However, after two weeks the customer notices that the paint is peeling from the door and she demands compensation for the poor quality of the product. Garage Doors Ltd pays her £600 compensation and reduces its output tax by £100 (ie £600 × 1/6 with a VAT rate of 20%).

Solution – in this case, the output tax adjustment is correct because the payment directly relates to the goods supplied. In effect, the customer is receiving a reduction in the original price because the goods are sub-standard – there is no compensation for damage or injury suffered (apart from the embarrassment of the neighbours noticing that she has bought a cheap garage door).

A further situation where compensation could be evident is where a supplier actually receives compensation from, for example, a local authority for loss of trade suffered as a result of the local authority's action. However, it is again important to research the reason for the repayment being made.

In the case of the local authority carrying out path improvement works outside a supplier's premises, causing a loss of trade to the supplier, any payment made will be outside the scope of VAT as compensation. However, if, for example, the local authority pay the supplier a sum of money for allowing them to store their plant and machinery on his land overnight, then this payment is consideration for a supply of services and is therefore taxable.

Deposits

[31.11] The receipt of an advance payment from a customer, before a supply has taken place, usually creates a tax point for VAT purposes. This is because the payment relates to a supply of either goods or services and the receipt of money creates an actual tax point that is in advance of the basic tax point (see **31.7** above for the definition of 'basic' and 'actual' tax points).

A common problem relates to the sale of a property (where VAT is charged on the sale in most cases if the seller has made an option to tax election on the property) that involves a deposit payment being made when contracts are exchanged. The deposit will need to include VAT (tax point created), the balance of VAT then being due on the date when the deal is completed. It is only when the deal is completed that the ownership of the property changes, ie a supply of goods has then taken place.

Note – an awareness of the above point is also important for a person buying a property with VAT charged, and the timing of input tax claims. In the case of *GD and Mrs D Lewis* (TC00983), the taxpayers bought a property and incorrectly claimed full input tax on their June 2009 return (based on the date when contracts were exchanged) rather than just on the deposit payment they made in this period. The deal was completed in July 2009, ie the majority of the input tax (90%) should have been claimed on their September 2009 VAT return, so they claimed three months too early. HMRC issued a 15% penalty on their error, which was reduced to 7.5% by the tribunal as a 'special circumstance' in the legislation (*Finance Act 2007, Sch 24, para 11*) and would now be reduced to 1.25% as a timing penalty following Revenue & Customs Brief 15/11 issued on 6 April 2011.

(HMRC Notice 700, para 15.9.2).

Note – an interesting ECJ case ruled that deposits paid by hotel guests who booked rooms in advance did not represent a taxable source of income for the hotel if the guests failed to arrive (or cancelled their booking) and lost their deposits.

It was ruled by the ECJ that the money retained by the hotel represented compensation for the loss suffered as a result of the cancellation – the money had no direct connection with the supply of any service for a consideration. The deposits retained were therefore outside the scope of VAT (*Societe thermale d'Eugenie-les-Bains v Ministere de l'Economie, des Finances et de l'Industrie: C-277/05* [2007] ECR I-6415, [2008] STC 2470, ECJ.

Note – this case should be contrasted with the Court of Justice judgment in *Air France-KLM and another v Ministère des Finances et des Comptes publics: Joined Cases C-250/14 and C-289/14* [2016] STC 1451 which related to the 'no-show' of passengers for flights. Air France/KLM argued that, as in the *d'Eugenie-les-Baines* case, the retention of the air fare paid by the no-show passenger, should not be regarded as consideration for any supply but should be regarded as compensation. The Court disagreed. According to the Court of Justice, when the passenger paid for his flight, he acquired the right to passenger transport services. These rights were available up to the moment that the gates closed for the flight in question. Moreover, the amount paid was the full consideration for the flight and was not refundable. As such, the money paid was consideration and was not compensation.

(HMRC Notice 700, para 8.13).

Lost or stolen goods

[**31.12**] It is important that any client who suffers a loss of goods for any reason, eg theft, fire, employee error or accident, retains full records concerning the circumstances of the loss. This is to reduce the risk of a problem with HMRC on a VAT visit. Consider the situation at Example 5.

(HMRC Notice 700, para 8.10).

Example 5

An officer from HMRC is carrying out a routine VAT visit, and notices that ABC Computers Ltd purchased 50 computers on a special shipment from America. The officer identifies that 30 have been sold (and output tax correctly charged on sales invoices), nine are still in stock and one is being used by the company in its own office. What about the other ten computers?

The officer may think that the ten missing computers have been sold as an off-record sale and he will be reluctant to believe any alternative explanation such as theft, accidental loss, fire damage etc.

The officer will not only try to assess output tax on the market value of the ten missing computers – but at worst, he could try to formulate an argument that the company is suppressing 20% of all of its sales, and raise an even bigger assessment of tax due. This would be on the basis that he is using the powers of 'best judgement' given to him under *VATA 1994, s 73* (see **20.2**).

Solution – the end result is a feast of problems, which could largely be avoided if the client retains supporting evidence of, for example, insurance claims (for damage or theft situations), police crime reports (for theft), notes of dates, people involved, action taken etc.

In the worst case scenario, the case could go to a VAT tribunal – where the tribunal panel would have to decide if they consider the defendant to be a witness of truth regarding the explanations given.

Discounts

[31.13] It is common practice for many businesses to offer a bulk discount deal – where the customer pays the full price for a quantity of goods, but is then entitled to a further quantity of goods free, eg three for the price of two. See Example 6.

(HMRC Notice 700, para 7.3.2).

Example 6

JKL Ltd manufacturers wood tables, selling goods to retailers throughout the country. In order to encourage bulk purchases, they give customers the chance to purchase ten tables at a standard list price – but then supply another table free of charge. In other words, '11 for the price of 10'.

On sales invoices raised for this type of deal, the eleventh table is recorded as a free sale.

Solution – VAT officers may be tempted to go down the route of assessing output tax based on the market value of the eleventh table. However, the correct outcome is that output tax is only due on the total price paid by the customer, ie the ten tables at list price. It is the consideration from the customer that is the basis of the VAT charge in this situation.

Another common form of discount is a prompt payment discount. With a prompt payment discount a customer receives a discount if they pay within a certain time, for example, 5% within 14 days of the invoice date. Prior to 1 April 2015 the consideration for VAT purposes was usually reduced by a prompt payment discount even when the customer did not take advantage of the discount. This meant that businesses accounted for output tax according to the amount of VAT shown on the invoice, which was previously calculated on the assumption that the customer took advantage of the discount.

From 1 April 2015 output tax must be accounted for on the actual consideration received. If the supplier needs to account for the output tax before it is known whether the discount will be taken up, for example, because an invoice is issued before the customer pays, the output tax must be calculated on the basis that the discount will not be taken up. If the discount is taken up after the output tax has been calculated, an adjustment to the output tax will be required.

On issuing a VAT invoice suppliers should enter the invoice into their accounts and record the VAT on the full price. If a prompt payment discount is offered suppliers must show the rate of the discount offered on their invoice. (*VAT Regulations 1995 (SI 1995/2518), reg 14*).

The supplier will not know if the discount has been taken up until they are paid in accordance with the terms of the prompt payment discount offer or the time limit for the prompt payment discount expires.

The supplier will need to decide, before they issue an invoice, which of the two methods below they will adopt to adjust their accounts in order to record a reduction in consideration if a discount is taken up.

Method one – a supplier may issue a credit note to evidence the reduction in consideration. In which case, a copy of the credit note must be retained as proof of that reduction.

Method two – alternatively, if a supplier does not wish to issue a credit note, the invoice must contain the following information (in addition to the normal invoicing requirements):

• the terms of the prompt payment discount, which must include, but need not be limited to, the time by which the discounted price must be made; and

• a statement that the customer can only recover as input tax the VAT paid to the supplier.

Additionally, it might be helpful for invoices to show:

• the discounted price;
• the VAT on the discounted price;
• the total amount due if the prompt payment discount is taken up.

If a business uses method two above the VAT invoice, containing appropriate wording as described above, together with proof of receipt of the discounted price in accordance with the terms of the prompt payment discount, for example, a bank statement, will be required to evidence the reduction in consideration and the reduction to the supplier's output tax.

HMRC recommends that businesses use the following wording on the invoice if method two above is used: 'A discount of X% of the full price applies if payment is made within Y days of the invoice date. No credit note will be issued. Following payment you must ensure you have only recovered the VAT actually paid.'

If the discounted price is paid in accordance with the prompt payment discount terms then the supplier must adjust their records to record the output tax on the amount actually received. If the full amount is received no adjustment will be necessary.

If a supplier receives a payment that falls short of the full price but which is not made in accordance with the prompt payment discount terms it cannot be treated as a prompt payment discount. The supplier must account for VAT on the full amount as stated on the invoice. If the amount not paid remains uncollected it will become a bad debt unless a price adjustment is agreed. If a price adjustment is agreed the adjustment must be made in the normal way by issuing a credit note.

The practical implications for a VAT registered customer receiving an invoice offering a prompt payment discount are as follows:

(a)   If the customer pays the full price they record it in their records and no VAT adjustment is necessary.

(b)   If the customer pays the discounted price in accordance with the prompt payment discount terms on receipt of the invoice they may record the discounted price and VAT on this in their accounts and no subsequent VAT adjustment is necessary.

(c)   If the customer does not pay when the invoice is first issued, they must record the full price and VAT in their records as shown on the invoice. If they subsequently decide to take up the prompt payment discount then:

   •   If they have received an invoice setting out the prompt payment discount terms which states no credit note will be issued they must adjust the VAT in their records when payment is made. They should retain a document that shows the date and amount of payment, for example, a bank statement, in addition to the invoice to evidence the reduction in consideration.

   •   If the supplier's invoice does not state that a credit note will not be issued, the customer must adjust the VAT they claim as input tax when the credit note is received. They must retain the credit note as proof of the reduction in consideration.

(HMRC Brief 49/14). (*VATA 1994, Sch 6 para 4*; *Finance Act 2014, s 108*).

Mixed supplies

[31.14] In most cases, the VAT liability of goods supplied will be very straightforward. However, an area of VAT that has always caused a few complications is when a bundle of goods are sold as part of a supply – and the goods attract VAT at different rates.

Chapter 23 is devoted to this topic, but the key principle of mixed supplies is explained here as it is an important issue for traders supplying goods.

The main question to ask with mixed supply situations is: 'Am I making two or more separate supplies – or one main supply with an ancillary supply to enhance the enjoyment of the main supply?' In effect, this question looks at the importance of each of the supplies in question, to consider whether there is only really one main supply, with other incidental supplies that can be ignored. It is also important to consider this question from the viewpoint of the customer – what does he perceive that he is receiving for his money?

If there is only one main supply, then the whole of the VAT charge depends on the liability of this main supply. See Example 7.

(HMRC Notice 700, para 8.1).

Example 7

> ABC Computers Ltd supplies a new computer to DEF Ltd for £10,000 plus VAT. However, the supply also includes a detailed manual explaining how the computer works, which cost ABC Computers Ltd £30 to produce. The manual is zero-rated for VAT purposes (reading material – *VATA 1994, Sch 8, Group 3*) so they only charge VAT on £9,970.
>
> **Solution** – in this situation, the aim of the manual is to assist the use and understanding of the main supply, ie the computer. The manual is not a supply in its own right – if the customer was not purchasing the computer, he would have no reason to buy the manual. The whole supply for £10,000 is therefore standard rated.

Part exchange transactions

[31.15] The basic VAT principle of part-exchange transactions is that there are two separate supplies taking place. It is important that amounts are not netted off against each other – VAT is due on the full value of supplies made. See Example 8.

(HMRC Notice 700, paras 7.4 and 8.7).

Example 8

> High Street Motors is VAT registered and sells a van to Mr Smith for £2,400 cash plus Mr Smith's Vauxhall car worth £3,000. High Street Motors account for output tax of £400 (ie £2,400 × 1/6 with a VAT rate of 20%).
>
> **Solution** – this is incorrect – the sale of the van is effectively taking place at £5,400 (£2,400 plus £3,000) and output tax needs to be accounted for on this amount (£5,400 × 1/6 = £900). In effect, the value for VAT purposes is based on the monetary and non-monetary consideration.

Note – VAT also needs to be accounted for on barter transactions. For example, consider a VAT registered business selling lawnmowers that agrees to give the local football club (not VAT registered) a free lawnmower in return for an advert in its match day programme. In effect, there are two supplies taking place, and the value of these supplies would be the open market value of the lawnmower. The lawnmower business has an output tax liability to declare on its VAT return.

The valuation of part exchange items can cause some difficulties, and a useful tribunal case on this subject is *Customs and Excise Comrs v Ping (Europe) Ltd* [2002] EWCA Civ 1115, [2002] STC 1186, (2002) Times, 23 August.

Here, the company offered to buy back illegal golf clubs it had sold to customers in return for a new club that complied with the regulations of the golfing authorities. The new club had a retail value of £72 and a wholesale price of £50. The customer's payment was £22 in cash plus his old club. HMRC contended that output tax was payable on the wholesale price of £50, giving the old club a value of £28 in part-exchange. Ping contended that the old club had a nil value because it was illegal and could not be used, so output tax was only payable on the monetary payment of £22 received from the customer. The courts agreed with Ping, ie the old club had a nil value.

VAT invoices

[31.16] A VAT invoice is an important document because it is essential evidence to support a customer's claim for input tax. In effect, therefore, a registered business must issue a VAT invoice to all customers who are also registered for VAT. However, there is no obligation to issue an invoice in the following circumstances:

- if the supplies in question are zero-rated or exempt;
- supplies where the customer cannot reclaim input tax, eg in relation to motor cars or business entertainment;
- supplies on which VAT is charged but the goods are provided free of charge, eg as in the case of gifts and goods put to private use;
- supplies where the customer operates a self-billing arrangement. Self-billing is an established practice where the customer prepares a VAT invoice in the name of the supplier and then sends it to the supplier, usually with payment. It is very common in the construction industry (see **26.17**);
- supplies by retailers unless the customer requests a VAT invoice;
- supplies by one member to another in the same VAT group.

A VAT invoice must show certain basic details:

- a unique identifying number;
- the time of the supply (tax point), name, address and VAT registration number of the supplier;
- name and address of the person to whom the goods are being supplied;
- a description to identify the goods or services being supplied;
- the rate of VAT and amount of VAT payable;
- if a supply relates to a second-hand scheme, the sales invoice should be noted along the lines of 'this is a second-hand margin scheme supply';
- a reference is also needed on any invoices relevant to the Tour Operators Margin Scheme (TOMS) – again along the lines of 'this is a Tour Operators Margin Scheme supply';
- any intra-EU supply where the customer needs to account for the reverse charge on his own VAT return needs a reference along the lines of 'this supply is subject to the reverse charge'.

Where the registered business is a retailer, there is no requirement to issue a VAT invoice unless requested by a customer. Also, if the gross amount of the sale is less than £250, and the supply is not to a person in another EU country, the VAT invoice can be less detailed – to include just the following information:

- name, address and registration number of the retailer;
- the time of supply;
- a description sufficient to identify the goods or services supplied;
- the total amount payable including VAT; and
- for each rate of VAT chargeable, the gross amount payable including VAT, and the VAT rate applicable.

Note – in effect, the main benefits of being able to issue a less detailed tax invoice (compared to a full tax invoice) are that the customer's name and address do not need to be shown, and the gross amount paid by the customer can be recorded, rather than a separate split of net and VAT amounts. (HMRC Notice 700, section 16).

Electronic invoicing

[31.17] Electronic invoicing is the transmission and storage of invoices by electronic means – as an alternative to the delivery of paper documents.

Basically, an electronic invoice should contain the same information as a paper invoice – HMRC also specifies a number of other conditions that must be met by a business. An important condition is for HMRC officers to have full access to the system being adopted, and to be able to carry out their usual checks on VAT visits to verify the accuracy of returns submitted.

Note – a business can also send invoices by fax or e-mail as an alternative to post; invoices sent in either of these two ways are acceptable as evidence for input tax deduction.

Credit and debit notes

[31.18] A credit note is issued by the supplier of goods to make any adjustments to invoices previously raised. This can apply if the goods are returned, if a pricing error on the invoice has occurred or if discounts need to be applied to a customer's account.

Note – a credit note must not be issued in relation to bad debt situations. See **31.19** for the VAT treatment of bad debts.

A debit note fulfils the same need as a credit note – but is issued by the customer rather than the supplier. A valid debit note places the same legal obligations on both parties as a valid credit note.

To be valid for VAT purposes, a credit or debit note must reflect a genuine mistake or overcharge and must be issued within one month of this overcharge being discovered or agreed.

In cases where a credit or contingent discount is allowed to a customer who can reclaim all the VAT on the supply as input tax, there is no obligation to adjust the original VAT charge provided both parties agree not to do so. If the customer is not VAT registered, then the original VAT charge must be adjusted.

(HMRC Notice 700, para 18.2.1).

A valid credit note should include the following details:

*   identifying number and date of issue;
*   supplier's and customer's name and address;
*   supplier's VAT registration number;
*   description identifying the goods for which credit is given;
*   quantity and amount credited for each description and reason for credit, eg 'returned goods';
*   total amount credited excluding VAT;
*   rate and amount of VAT credited;
*   number and date of the original VAT invoice – in other words, this will enable HMRC to verify that VAT has been accounted for on the original supply.

As far as VAT returns are concerned, a credit note issued by a supplier (or debit note received) will result in a reduction of his Box 1 figure for output tax – the net amount will also be subtracted from the Box 6 figure for outputs.

For a customer receiving a credit note, or issuing a debit note, the boxes affected by the transaction will be Boxes 4 and 7 (ie input tax and inputs respectively).

Note – the rate of VAT to be used for a credit or debit note is the one in force at the tax point of the original supply (HMRC Notice 700, para 18.2.3).

(HMRC Notice 700, section 18).

Bad debts

[31.19] A credit note cannot be issued to a customer on the basis that the customer has refused or been unable to pay the amount charged on an invoice. This is because a supply of goods or services has still taken place.

In such cases, the correct way of recovering unpaid VAT is by reclaiming bad debt relief. The basic rules are as follows:

*   the debt in question must be at least six months overdue for payment – in the case of an invoice issued on 30-day payment terms, this would mean the debt can qualify for bad debt relief seven months after the date of the original invoice;
*   the whole or part of the debt has been written off in the accounts as a bad debt – and transferred to a specific bad debt account;
*   output tax on the original invoice must have been accounted for and paid to HMRC.

(HMRC Notice 700, para 18.5).

A claim for bad debt relief is made by increasing the Box 4 (input tax) figure on the VAT return.

If a business receives future payment in relation to a bad debt that has been written off in its accounts, then the receipt of money will be included in Box 1 for output tax purposes on the relevant VAT return (assuming it relates to a standard-rated supply).

A business also has an obligation to repay input tax to HMRC on any purchase invoices that are more than six months overdue for payment. This provision is applicable even in cases where the supplier of the goods has not made a claim for bad debt relief. The basic principle is that it is unfair for a business to reclaim input tax on invoices that have remained unpaid over a long period of time. There could be a genuine reason for non-payment (eg dispute over goods or services provided on the invoice) but it is also possible that a balance remains unpaid on the ledger because a credit note has been mislaid. This would then account for why the supplier is not chasing payment of the outstanding invoice.

As a potential planning point, it is worth considering whether clients could be eligible to use the cash accounting scheme, ie where output tax and input tax entries on the VAT return are based on payments received and made rather than the date of sales and purchase invoices. The scheme is available to a business with annual taxable turnover of £1.35 million or less (excluding VAT) and is considered fully in Chapter 6. An advantage of the scheme is that bad debt relief is automatic because output tax is never declared until payment has been received from a customer.

The First Tier Tribunal case involving *Cumbria County Council* (TC01463) [2011] UKFTT 621 (TC) illustrates the recent approach of the courts on timing issues in relation to bad debt relief and credit notes.

In 2001, the Cumbria Council charged a fee of £4,245,081 to the Department for Environment Food and Rural Affairs (DEFRA) in relation to services rendered for dealing with the foot and mouth disease. Output tax was correctly accounted for on the fee.

After a lengthy dispute, the final amount agreed as being due from DEFRA in 2007 was £200,000. The Council sought a VAT credit at this stage by claiming bad debt relief, ie so that output tax was only accounted for on £200,000 rather than £4,245,081.

HMRC disallowed the claim because the adjustment was out of time in accordance with the bad debt relief rules. However, the taxpayer sought to make an adjustment through another part of the VAT regulations, separate to the bad debt relief provisions (*VAT Regulations 1995 (SI 1995/2518), reg 38*).

'Adjustments in the course of business

38–

(1)   This regulation applies where—
       (a)   there is an increase in consideration for a supply, or
       (b)   there is a decrease in consideration for a supply,

which includes an amount of VAT and the increase or decrease occurs after the end of the prescribed accounting period in which the original supply took place.

(2) Where this regulation applies, the taxable person shall adjust his VAT account in accordance with the provisions of this regulation.

(3) The maker of the supply shall—
  (a) in the case of an increase in consideration, make a positive entry; or
  (b) in the case of a decrease in consideration, make a negative entry, for the relevant amount of VAT in the VAT payable portion of his VAT account.

(4) The recipient of the supply, if he is a taxable person, shall—
  (a) in the case of an increase in consideration, make a positive entry; or
  (b) in the case of a decrease in consideration, make a negative entry, for the relevant amount of VAT in the VAT allowable portion of his VAT account.

(5) Every entry required by this regulation shall, except where paragraph (6) below applies, be made in that part of the VAT account which relates to the prescribed accounting period in which the increase or decrease is given effect in the business accounts of the taxable person.

(6) (6) Any entry required by this regulation to be made in the VAT account of an insolvent person shall be made in that part of the VAT account which relates to the prescribed accounting period in which the supply was made or received.

(7) None of the circumstances to which this regulation applies is to be regarded as giving rise to any application of regulations 34 and 35.'

The Tribunal accepted that the Regulation applied because there was a clear decrease in the consideration from the original supply of £4.2m to £200,000 – and *reg 38* is not capped by a four-year or other time period.

Note – the legislation concerning the time cap for bad debt relief is quoted below:

Bad debt relief – time cap – VAT Regulations 1995 (SI 1995/2518), reg 165A(1):

(1) ... a claim shall be made within the period of 4 years and 6 months following the later of—
  (a) the date on which the consideration (or part) which has been written off as a bad debt becomes due and payable to or to the order of the person who made the relevant supply; and
  (b) the date of the supply.

Example 9

On 1 March 2015 a supplier that prepares VAT returns on a calendar quarterly basis delivered goods to a customer and issued an invoice for the goods on terms specifying that payment is due by 31 March 2015. The customer has not paid. The supplier is entitled to claim bad debt relief on 30 September 2015, being the later of six months after the date of the supply and the date when the payment was due. The claim for bad debt relief can be included in the VAT return for the quarter to 30 September 2015.

If the claim for bad debt relief is not included in the VAT return for the quarter to 30 September 2015 the claim can be included in a later VAT return, assuming the customer has still not paid. The claim must be made within four years and six months after the later of the date of the supply and the date when the payment was due. If the customer has still not paid and a claim has not already been made the supplier can include the claim on the VAT return for the quarter to 30 September 2019.

Entitlement to claim ceases if the claim is not made within four years and six months after the later of the date of the supply and the date when the payment was due.

Comment – in relation to an input tax claim by a customer receiving a supply, this is normally made according to the date of a purchase invoice, unless the customer uses the cash accounting scheme. In the case of a cash accounting schemer user, input tax can only be claimed when payment has been made to a supplier. However, any input claim made on an unpaid purchase invoice must be credited to the customer's VAT account (ie reverse original input tax claim) if the invoice is overdue for payment by more than six months. It can be subsequently reclaimed again if payment (or part payment) is made at a future date. This adjustment is a requirement of the bad debt regulations (*SI 1995/2518, reg 172G/H*). So in cases such as *Cumbria County Council*, HMRC will not be out of pocket by the *reg 38* adjustment because the customer's opportunity to claim input tax is limited to the extent of the payment made for the goods or services in question, ie based on £200,000 in the case of DEFRA..

More information regarding bad debt relief is included in Chapter 36.

Business gifts

[31.20] An item is a gift when the donor is not obliged to give it and the recipient has provided no goods or services in return for receiving the gift.

A gift of goods can be made without accounting for output tax (and input tax still claimed on the purchase of the goods in question) if:

- the cost to the donor of acquiring or producing the goods is less than £50; and
- the gift is made in the course of business, eg gift to recognise loyal customers or hardworking staff; and
- the total value of gifts given to the same person in the same year is less than £50.

Note – the same year means in any 12-month period that includes the day on which the gift is made.

But what is the definition of 'person' as far as the business gift limit is concerned? Does it apply to a VAT-registered business as a 'person' or is each employee within that business a 'separate person'?

A recent case involving record producer EMI found its way to the European Court (*C-581/08*) and it was confirmed that a number of different gifts or samples to different employees in the same organisation did not count as a single gift or sample, ie each recipient was a person in his own right. See Example 10.

Example 10

> John is a self-employed IT consultant who has enjoyed very good business this year with Smith, Smith and Smith Chartered Accountants. He has decided to give a £20 box of chocolates and £10 bottle of wine to all 30 staff in the firm as a Christmas gift, including Mr Smith and the two other partners, Mr Smith and Mr Smith. What is the input tax position?
>
> The VAT rules on business gifts allow input tax to be reclaimed (and no output tax liability) if the total cost of gifts given to the same person in any 12-month period is less than £50, and they do not form part of a series of gifts (*VATA 1994, Sch 4, para 5*).
>
> The good news is that following the ECJ case of *EMI Group Ltd v R & C Commrs* (Case C-581/08), it has been confirmed that the word 'person' relates to each employee in this example rather than Smith, Smith and Smith as one 'person', ie one business. So John can claim input tax on the cost of his very expensive chocolates and wine, with no output tax liability to declare.

If a business gift does not meet the above criteria, then the gift becomes a taxable supply, and the value of the supply becomes the price the recipient would have to pay (excluding VAT) to purchase identical goods. Where that value cannot be quantified, the price for the purchase of goods similar to those in question (same age and condition) becomes the relevant figure. Assuming the goods in question are standard rated, output tax is then payable by the donor on the value of the goods.

Note – where a business makes a gift of goods on which VAT is due, and the recipient uses the goods for business (taxable) purposes, that person can recover the VAT as input tax (subject to normal rules). The donor cannot issue a tax invoice (because there is no consideration) but may instead issue a 'tax certificate', which can be used as evidence to support a claim for input tax.

The tax certificate is similar to an invoice in presentation (ie showing full details of goods being supplied) and will be worded along the lines of – 'no payment is necessary for these goods. Output tax of £x has been accounted for on the supply'.

(HMRC Notice 700, para 8.9).

Recharging zero-rated expenses to a customer

[31.21] A common point of misunderstanding with clients and advisers relates to the recharging of zero-rated expenses to a client. These expenses do not form part of a separate supply to the customer but part of the main supply of services. Example 11 illustrates this principle with a simple situation.

Example 11

> Larry is a tax lecturer and has agreed to carry out a lecture on tax for an insurance company for a fee of £1,000 plus VAT. Larry is based in London and the lecture is

in Scotland so Larry will travel by first class rail and pay a return fare of £200. Rail travel is zero-rated as far as VAT is concerned. Larry itemises the £200 zero-rated rail travel on his invoice to the insurance company, and only charges output tax on the balance of his fee, ie £800 x 20% = £160. Is he correct?

Solution – in this situation, the £200 rail fare is not relevant to the insurance company because the supply of rail travel is between Larry and the rail company. Larry's supply to the insurance company is for a tax lecture (not rail travel) so output tax must be charged on his full fee of £1,000.

Continuous supplies of services

[31.22] The basic VAT principle to be aware of is that a tax point is only created in such cases when either an invoice is raised by a supplier or payment is received from a customer. This situation tends to cover, for example, most supplies of services provided by an accountant to a client where a standard letter of engagement is in place. This is because the accountant is deemed to be supplying services throughout the year as part of an ongoing relationship with the client. It is irrelevant that there might be a number of different jobs performed by the accountant with a clear start and finish date, eg submitting a tax return to HMRC.

The delay in paying output tax can be legitimately extended by raising a 'fee note' or 'request for payment' document rather than a tax invoice – and then only issuing the invoice when the customer has made payment. The customer will often need a tax invoice in order to claim input tax, so the alternative documents such as 'fee notes' are delaying his potential to claim input tax until he has paid for the service.

The challenge for advisers is to identify when a continuous supply of service arrangement has taken place.

Example of a continuous supply – Jones Solicitors provides ongoing legal services by acting as a trustee for a particular client. A tax point will occur when either an invoice is raised by Jones or payment received from the customer.

Example of a non-continuous supply – Smith Decorators are painting the rooms in a large office block – a job that started on 1 May and will finish on 31 July.

In this situation, there is a single supply of services and the normal tax point rules will apply, ie a basic tax point is created on 31 July when the work is completed. VAT will be due on this date unless a sales invoice is raised or payment received within 14 days to create an actual tax point. This scenario assumes that no advance invoices have been raised or payments on account received in relation to this job. If so, then each advance invoice or payment also creates a tax point.

(HMRC Notice 700, para 14.3).

Sales between related parties

[31.23] Imagine that Company A buys goods for £10,000 plus VAT and reclaims input tax on its VAT return. The goods are sold to Company B (a wholly owned subsidiary of Company A) for £1 plus VAT. The reason for this valuation is because Company B only makes exempt supplies and therefore cannot reclaim input tax. Is there a problem with this arrangement?

The answer is that there is indeed a big problem because HMRC has anti-avoidance rules in place which means it can direct that the value of a supply is the 'open market value'. The conditions are:

- the monetary consideration paid is less than the open market value – this is clearly the case in our example;
- the supplier and customer are connected – the 'connection' is based on the provisions of *CTA 2010, s 1122*. This includes relatives of an individual and the spouse and relatives of the individual; partners in a partnership and their relatives and spouses; companies that are controlled by the same person or controlled by persons connected with each other, ie as with Company A and Company B; and
- the customer is not entitled to fully claim input tax because he is either not VAT registered or is making some exempt supplies.

Output tax is therefore due based on the amount that would be payable if there was no relationship between the parties. If it could be argued that the goods supplied by Company A in the above example are genuinely only worth £1 (because of damage, wear and tear, obsolescence etc), then there would not be a problem – but this is very unlikely.

Disbursements

[31.24] Many clients and advisers are confused about when a charge to a customer is a recharge of expenses (as explained in **31.21** above) or a disbursement arrangement that is not subject to VAT. The key issue to consider is whether the expense belongs to the final customer or if it has been incurred by the business making the charge as part of its own work.

As a simple example, an accountant may complete the annual return for a limited company client at Companies House and pay the £15 annual return filing fee on behalf of the client. If he recharges this £15 to the client (no profit element, recharged at cost), and shows the charge as a separate entry on his sales invoice, then this fee will be a disbursement situation because the expense belongs to the final client. A correct invoice would therefore be raised as follows:

Time charge for completing annual return – £50

Disbursement – annual return filing fee paid to Companies House – £15

VAT charge on £50 @ 20% = £10

Total amount payable = £75

(HMRC Notice 700, para 25.1).

Supply chains involving goods

[31.25] As a general principal the amount of VAT accounted for on a supply of goods should be proportionate to the total consideration paid by the final person in the supply chain after adjusting for any refunds made.

When the parties to a transaction are in a direct contractual relationship, for example a manufacturer (the supplier) and a distribution company (the customer) a credit note can be issued by the supplier to the customer to deal with adjustments to invoices previously raised, for example, if the goods are returned (see **31.18**). However, supply chains can be complex and sometimes a manufacturer or importer cannot issue a credit note because they are not in a direct contractual relationship with the person who receives the refund or reimbursement that the manufacturer has paid. This could happen when, for example, a manufacturer realises that a particular product is faulty and arranges for it to be recalled.

The *VAT Regulations 1995* were amended in 2014 to allow a first supplier, eg, a manufacturer, who refunds or reimburses a final consumer or a final supplier, eg, a retailer, to adjust their output tax position to reflect the fact that the consideration they have received has reduced. If the person who receives the payment, eg a retailer, is registered for VAT they are required to adjust their input tax position accordingly. The amendments took effect on 1 April 2014 and are detailed in the new *reg 38ZA* of the *VAT Regulations 1995*. The following are examples of the type of situations when *reg 38ZA* could be relevant.

- A manufacturer makes a cash refund directly to a final consumer because the goods were faulty.
- A manufacturer makes a cash refund directly to a final consumer because the consumer has provided the manufacturer with a proof of purchase voucher that entitles the consumer to a refund in accordance with the terms of a sales promotion scheme operated by the manufacturer.
- A manufacturer reimburses a retailer an amount equivalent to a money-off coupon issued by the manufacturer to promote sales of the goods.

The measure was introduced on 1 April 2014 following a consultation process and is intended to ensure that UK VAT law on this subject accords with EU law. In a document responding to comments received during the consultation process HMRC indicated that in principle it accepts that, where the amended legislation applies and subject to the relevant conditions being met, businesses will be able to submit claims for repayment of overpaid VAT.

(*SI 1995/2518 reg 38ZA*; *SI 2014/548*).

Planning points to consider

[31.26] The following planning points should be given consideration.

- Remember that a tax point is created for VAT purposes when goods supplied on a sale or return basis have been held by a customer for 12 months.

- The basic tax point for goods (date of supply) is overridden if an invoice is raised or payment is received within 14 days of the supply – this can possibly create a cash flow benefit for a business by moving the output tax liability to the next VAT period.

- When dealing with compensation payments to customers, output tax can be reduced on a payment if it relates to a specific problem with goods supplied, eg compensation to reflect the poor quality of a product.

- Clients should be encouraged to keep full details of any goods that have been lost, stolen or destroyed. This could avoid problems on VAT visits if an officer tries to assess output tax on goods he cannot trace.

- Always ensure that clients treat part exchange transactions as two separate supplies, and do not just account for output tax on the net amount of any payment received.

- Retailers can benefit from issuing less detailed tax invoices if they supply goods where the total consideration is £250 or less.

- Be aware of the potential opportunity to reclaim bad debt relief on any sales invoices that are overdue by more than six months – as long as certain conditions are met. Equally, input tax claims need to be adjusted on any unpaid purchase invoices that are overdue by more than six months as well.

- Do not forget that bad debt relief is not an issue for any business that uses the cash accounting scheme. See Chapter 6 for details of the scheme.

- Be aware that the rules for business gifts (what is a 'person') and samples (more than one sample can now be given away to the same person without a VAT charge) changed following a court case involving the record producer EMI.

- It is important to be clear about whether a charge to a customer is a disbursement situation (no output tax due) or for a recharge of expenses such as rail travel or hotel bills. In the latter case, the VAT liability of the recharge is the same as that for the main service being provided, ie standard rated in most cases.

- Consider if clients who are manufacturers or importers could adjust their output tax position to reflect refunds or reimbursements made directly to parties at the other end of the supply chain such as consumers and retailers. Remember that the person who received the refund or reimbursement will need to adjust their input tax position if they are registered for VAT.

Chapter 32

Input Tax – Non-deductible Items and Pension Funds

Key topics in this chapter:

- Input tax can only be reclaimed on genuine business expenses linked to the making of taxable supplies.
- Examples of when HMRC considers expenses to be private and non-deductible for VAT purposes.
- Rules for claiming (and not claiming) input tax on business entertaining expenses – and a possible opportunity to claim input tax on the cost of entertaining overseas customers.
- Rules for claiming input tax on specific employee benefits, domestic accommodation costs and farmhouse repairs.
- Procedures for reclaiming input tax on costs related to sporting events or leisure interests – the 'business purpose' test considered by HMRC.
- Input tax and motor cars.
- Apportioning input tax for an expense only partly used for business – rules to deal with private use of home computers provided by employers to employees.
- The need to consider whether a supply is made to a business.
- Input tax issues for costs relevant to a funded pension scheme.
- Input tax issues where three or more parties are involved in a deal.
- The main conditions for claiming input tax.

Introduction

[32.1] The basic rule for reclaiming input tax is simple: if the VAT on an expense relates to taxable supplies, then input tax can usually be reclaimed; if it relates to non-business supplies (eg private expenditure) or exempt supplies, then no input tax can be reclaimed.

There are a couple of notable exceptions when input tax cannot be reclaimed:

- business entertaining is a non-deductible expense, unless the expenditure relates to the entertaining of staff or overseas customers;
- motor cars are also non-deductible in most cases – unless it can be shown that the car is wholly used for business purposes and not available for private use, which is difficult to prove;

- input tax cannot be reclaimed on certain goods incorporated into a new residential dwelling by a developer, eg carpets, fridges, dishwashers (the latter two items are classed as 'white goods', and all white goods are subject to the input tax block).

The business argument

[32.2] A key method to adopt when considering input tax deduction on an expense is to ask the question: why was the expenditure incurred? Is there a clear business link? Was the expenditure made specifically to benefit the business? Or was it primarily made for private purposes – but the owner is trying to justify a business argument? See Example 1.

(HMRC Notice 700, para 4.6).

Example 1

Mr Jones is a sole trader (management consultant) and has claimed input tax on three expenses.

(a) He has renewed his golf club membership for £4,000 plus VAT. He has reclaimed £800 input tax because the golf club gives him important business contacts. He can prove that his biggest job last year was obtained through a golf contact.

(b) Mr Jones employs three other management consultants, and because the business has traded so well, he has decided to take them all out for the day – to watch the British Open Golf Championship. He incurs expenditure on tickets for the event, food and drink in a restaurant, plus petrol for his car – and has claimed input tax on all costs.

(c) Mr Jones has decided to hire an executive box for another day at the British Open Golf Championship. This will be used for entertaining key business customers – the charge is £10,000 plus VAT and he has reclaimed £2,000 input tax on the payment.

Solution – the second expense is the only cost that can be reclaimed for input tax purposes.

In example (a), although Mr Jones can clearly illustrate the business benefits of his golfing activities, the key point is that in reality he has joined the club because he enjoys playing golf. Think of the arguments that would be put forward across the country if input tax could be reclaimed on costs associated with every hobby or sporting interest.

Example (b) illustrates a key principle of VAT, namely, that input tax can be reclaimed on costs associated with entertaining staff. As an alternative justification, ask the question: if the business had traded badly, and made losses, would Mr Jones have taken them out for the day to reward their efforts? Unlikely – proving a clear link between the business and the motive for the expenditure.

Finally, example (c) highlights one of the main non-deductible items as far as VAT is concerned, namely, business entertainment for any non-employee apart from overseas customers.

Business entertainment

General rules for input tax deduction

[32.3] The basic rule for VAT purposes is that input tax cannot be reclaimed on business entertaining expenses, unless it relates to employees of the taxable person and overseas customers. A separate analysis of the issues concerning overseas customers is considered below. For an event that includes both employees and non-employees, the input tax on the employee costs cannot be reclaimed if their function is to act as hosts for the non-employees. (HMRC Notice 700/65, para 2.1).

The definition of business entertainment is extensive and HMRC regards entertainment as including all of the following facilities:

*   provision of food and drink;
*   accommodation in hotels;
*   entry to clubs and nightclubs;
*   theatre, concert or sporting tickets; and
*   the benefits of using capital assets such as yachts and boats for entertaining.

(HMRC Notice 700/65, para 2.2).

There are circumstances where input tax can be reclaimed on costs relevant to non-employees:

*   self-employed persons (subsistence expenses only) who are treated in the same way for subsistence purposes as the employees of a company;
*   helpers, stewards and other people essential to the running of sporting or similar events;
*   accommodation provided by airlines to delayed passengers;
*   entertainment provided by local authorities at civic functions – this is not business entertainment because the function is a non-business activity.

(HMRC Notice 700/65, paras 2.3 and 2.7).

Entertaining of staff

[32.4] However, the opportunity to reclaim input tax on staff entertaining is considerable – expenditure of this nature is regarded as a genuine business expense to boost staff welfare or reward staff success. It needs to be remembered, however, that input tax cannot be reclaimed on staff entertaining when the role of the staff member is to act as host to non-employees. (HMRC Notice 700/65, para 3.1).

Charge to guests

[32.5] One important principle established over the years is that the rules concerning input tax and business entertainment only apply if entertainment is provided free of charge.

In many cases, it is common for a staff function to be organised whereby the staff are allowed to attend free of charge, but any guests they bring must pay a per head contribution. This contribution may not be enough to cover the full cost to the company, but still represents a deviation from the 'free lunch' concept. However, it is important to note that output tax must be accounted for on the contributions from the guests. See Example 2.

Example 2

Jones Ltd has organised a Christmas party for 30 employees and 30 guests at a cost to the company of £40 plus VAT per person, ie a total charge for the evening of £2,400 plus VAT. This charge includes all food and cabaret. The employees can attend without charge but the guests must help with the costs by paying £15 each for their tickets.

Solution – the charge to the guests means that the whole of the input tax can be reclaimed on the costs of the event. This is because the company is not providing free hospitality to non-employees, which is a condition of the business entertaining rules. Output tax must be declared on the money received from non-employees from ticket sales. The fact that the charge to the non-employees is below cost is not a problem, providing the charge is not so small as to almost amount to providing free hospitality.

To quote from a VAT case on the subject involving *Ernst & Young*:

'But on the basis that there is a supply for consideration we also ask ourselves whether the £15 is so small in relation to the value of what was provided that effectively it was provided free of charge. It was a real charge which had to be paid in respect of a guest, but sufficiently low that the member of staff who brought a guest realised that the guest was receiving good value and so the price reflected a further benefit to the member of staff. We consider that although the charge was nominal it was not so small that one can say that the meal was effectively supplied free of charge.'

Entertaining for directors and business owners

[32.6] As explained above, there is a block on input tax recovery for staff acting as hosts when non-employees are being entertained. The other exception to the rule of input tax on staff entertaining being reclaimable is where directors, partners or the sole trader of a business incur entertainment costs that do not involve other staff members. In this case, the input tax is not classed as being relevant to business purposes (eg directors' day out at the races).

However, where directors and owners attend staff parties together with other employees, HMRC accepts that all of the input tax on the event can be reclaimed, including the costs relevant to the directors.

(HMRC Notice 700/65, para 3.2).

Entertaining overseas customers – beware output tax charge

[32.7] An ECJ case verdict led to HMRC reviewing its policy on whether a UK business can claim input tax on entertaining overseas customers. The legislation to implement the change took effect on 1 May 2011 (*Value Added Tax (Input Tax) (Amendment) Order 2011 (SI 2011/1071)*) but a business can go back four years and make a backdated claim if it is eligible to do so after taking the points below into account.

A block in claiming input tax on entertaining overseas customers has applied in the UK since 1985 – but this block was incorrect, so input tax can now be claimed on such expenses. However, it is not all good news:

- Although input tax can be claimed on any entertaining of overseas customers, a 'private use' output tax charge will apply if the entertaining is not business related and is not classed as being necessary to the making of taxable supplies (defined as a 'necessity test' and a 'strict business purpose test'). It means that limited hospitality provided at a business meeting to discuss business-related matters with overseas customers is not a problem – but an output tax charge will apply if the gathering is not specifically linked to business (eg a day at the races or trip to a show). HMRC also expects a business to only recover input tax (with no output tax charge for private use) if the entertaining is clearly used for the making of taxable supplies as well as being 'on a scale which is reasonable.'
  Note – 'a scale which is reasonable' seems to indicate that even if entertainment is provided at a qualifying business meeting, it cannot be excessively lavish (eg tea and biscuits rather than champagne and caviar).
- A business that is now eligible to claim input tax on entertaining of overseas customers can make a retrospective claim for the last four years under the normal 'error correction' rules. Assuming the amount of tax underclaimed is £10,000 or less (or less than £50,000 and 1% of the Box 6 outputs figure in the period when the error is being corrected) and assuming there is no private use output tax charge that will cancel out the input tax gain, the input tax can be claimed by a business on its next VAT return.
- Be aware that the potential input tax claims only relate to overseas 'customers' – there is no scope to make a claim in relation to overseas suppliers or other business contacts based outside the UK.
- HMRC lists 'corporate hospitality events' such as golf days, trips to sporting events and night clubs, track days and evening meals as events where an output tax charge will be needed because the entertaining is not essential to the making of taxable supplies.

Overall, therefore, the opportunity to make substantial input tax claims on entertaining overseas customers (without an output tax charge) is very limited.

See HMRC Revenue & Customs Brief 44/10 for further information and ECJ case *Danfoss A/S v Skatteministeriet: C-371/07* [2008] ECR I-9549, [2009] STC 701, ECJ.

Employee benefits

[32.8] A happy employee is a productive employee – so input tax can be reclaimed on many benefits and perks provided to employees. However, in some cases, output tax must be accounted for on the onward supply of the goods to the employee. The following is a brief summary of the benefits where input tax can be reclaimed.

- *Computers supplied for home working* – see **32.16**.
- *Sporting facilities available to all staff* – corporate membership of a local gym may be taken out by a company, and this will be deductible for input tax purposes as long as the facility is available to all staff. If a facility is available to only specific employees, then input tax can still be reclaimed but output tax must be declared for the same amount, ie nil tax gain. See Example 3.
- *Canteen and recreational facilities* – input tax can be reclaimed on all costs relevant to a free staff canteen and/or recreational facilities, with no corresponding output tax charge, providing the canteen and/or recreational facilities are available to all employees without charge.
- *Relocation expenses* – employers may provide assistance to employees or future employees relocating to be nearer to their main job. In such cases, input tax can be reclaimed on costs paid by the employer – as long as it is directly associated to the house move. For example, this rule would allow input tax to be reclaimed on estate agent's fees, removal costs, short-term accommodation in a hotel – even carpets and curtains. It would not allow input tax deduction on installing new windows to the property, or a new television and or DVD player.
- *Clothing* – many clients feel input tax recovery is justified on the basis that it is important to look presentable and smart to impress clients or suppliers. Unfortunately, this is not the case. Clothing is normally a private expense – and often the only time when input tax is recovered is if the clothing relates to a uniform or protective clothing, worn by an employee in the performance of his duties. A barrister can therefore reclaim input tax on the cost of his wig and gown. In some sectors, particularly the clothing retail sector, it is not unusual for businesses to recover VAT on the cost of providing examples of the current sea-son's stock to employees. For example, a clothing retailer may give its store staff selected items of new stock on the basis that the clothes are worn at work in order to promote sales of the stock. If ownership of the clothes passes to an employee when the clothes are brand new the output tax due on the gift is based on what it would cost the retailer to purchase identical items, which means that the output tax due will usually be equivalent to the input tax recovered by the business when it bought the items. Note – no output tax is due if the £50 limit for gifts to the same person in any 12-month period is not exceeded – see **31.20**.
- *Mobile phones* – in basic terms, HMRC has agreed that input tax can be recovered by an employer on all standing charge costs or costs of purchasing the phone for an employee, even if the phone is used by an employee for private calls. However, if the employee is allowed to make private calls without charge, then the input tax on the calls must be

apportioned on a fair and reasonable basis. If the employee is required to pay for the calls the business will be making a taxable supply of services for consideration on which output tax is due but input tax recoverable.

- *Gifts* – a gift to an employee for long service can be reclaimed as far as input tax is concerned, eg a clock for 20 years' service. However, the business must then account for output tax on the supply – creating a nil tax gain.

Following the CJEU judgment in Case C-40/09 [2010] ECR I-7505, [2010] STC 2298, ECJ HMRC issued Revenue & Customs Brief 28/11 on 28 July 2011 regarding changes to the VAT treatment of certain supplies made by employers under salary sacrifice arrangements. A salary sacrifice arrangement involves a contractual change to the terms and conditions of employment so that the employee's gross salary is reduced and the employer provides a non-cash benefit in exchange for the salary sacrificed. This is different from the situation where an amount is deducted from the employee's net pay in return for a non-cash benefit. When an amount is deducted from the employee's net pay HMRC policy has always been that the deduction represents consideration for a supply of goods or services (ie the benefit) and output tax is due and input tax recoverable on the same basis as it would be were the employer making the supply to a customer.

In essence, for VAT purposes the change of policy announced by Revenue & Customs Brief 28/11 puts a sacrifice of gross salary in return for a non-cash benefit on the same footing as a deduction from net salary. In other words, the deduction in gross salary represents consideration for the supply of goods or services (ie the benefit) and output tax is due and input tax recoverable on the same basis as it would be were the employer making the supply to a customer.

Where employers provide benefits at below cost to employees under a net salary reduction or a gross salary sacrifice arrangement the output tax due is based on the cost to the employer of providing the benefit. By way of contrast, output tax is not normally due if an employer provides certain facilities to employees generally in addition to their normal salary. However, see **32.9** regarding benefits for business owners.

If the benefits provided are not subject to VAT, for example childcare vouchers, no output tax charge will arise.

HMRC have confirmed in Revenue & Customs Brief 28/11 that an output tax charge will not arise when cars are provided as an employee benefit under a salary sacrifice arrangement. This is because of the input tax block (100% on purchases and 50% on leasing) that applies to cars.

When benefits are provided which are subject to VAT which is not blocked, input tax can be recovered by employers, subject to the normal partial exemption rules.

Example 3

Sally is the tax manager at Rock Band & Co Accountants and has agreed to sacrifice gross salary of £36 per month in exchange for gym membership paid by the firm.

Several of Sally's colleagues have also chosen this benefit and Rock Band & Co have negotiated a good deal so that gym membership costs the firm £30 plus VAT per month for each employee.

Solution – for each employee who sacrifices salary for gym membership the firm can recover £6 (ie £30 x 20%) as input tax in respect of the invoice it receives from the gym but must account for £6 (ie £36 x 1/6) as output tax in respect of the salary sacrificed.

Money for sport/hobbies – private or business?

[32.9] Many business owners have a strong interest in sport or other pursuits, and there will inevitably be occasions when they will question the possibility of linking these interests to their business activity in order to gain VAT benefits.

The HMRC approach largely revolves around applying the 'business purpose' test to the expenditure. This often means trying to determine the intention of the person at the time of incurring the expenditure. Although it is often easy to justify the 'business benefit' of an expense, this does not necessarily mean that the 'purpose' of the expenditure was for the business.

Overall, the aim of HMRC, as far as input tax on sponsorship costs is concerned, is to ensure that a business gets recovery on the legitimate costs incurred promoting the business – but avoiding the situation where recovery is given to a business in respect of its own favoured sporting or recreational facility.

For example, as explained at Example 1 at **32.2**, the sole trader of a business cannot justify reclaiming input tax on his golf club membership on the basis that he obtains important business contacts at the club. His primary motive (or purpose) for the expenditure is that he enjoys playing golf.

In general terms, suggested points to consider in relation to whether an item of expenditure is business or private are:

(a)   consider the likely HMRC view on expenditure of this nature (ie how it will look in the eyes of a VAT officer carrying out a routine inspection);

(b)   clearly analyse the arguments in favour of the expenditure being business, and those that suggest it could be private;

(c)   research past tribunal cases – all 'grey' areas of VAT tend to have some useful case law to assist the process.

With regard to expenditure relating to sport, questions to consider include:

- Is the owner of the business actively participating in the sport?
- Does any of his family actively take part in the sport?
- Is there a connection between the sport and the business?
- Is there related advertising or promotional material?
- Does the business name appear on the merchandise, equipment or venue of the entity receiving the sponsorship?
- Can the business produce any evidence of research into the benefits to be obtained by the advertising?

As with other aspects of the UK taxation system (eg the definition of someone being employed or self-employed), the decision will be based on an assessment of the overall package of the arrangement. For example, it would not be sufficient for just one of the above tests to be met – it is the overall picture that counts.

A good example of a sponsorship arrangement that should have no problems is the sponsorship of the Premier League in football by, eg a top bank. The exposure of such an arrangement is worldwide and there is no personal involvement in the benefits of the deal from the business owners, ie the shareholders.

See Example 4.

Example 4

John is the sole trader of a butcher's shop and is a keen motor racing competitor. It is a very expensive hobby – but he has decided that he will advertise his business on the side of his racing car; include a reference to his business in all press articles, race programmes and other literature; he will also advertise the race wins on his business literature. The question is: can he reclaim input tax on all of the costs of the activity – or would it be classed as a non-business expense, not relevant to taxable supplies?

Solution – the whole picture needs to be taken into account when making a decision regarding input tax deduction. If the circumstances are still not conclusive, a written ruling from HMRC may be the best approach.

The points in favour of the expense being for the 'purpose of the business' are as follows:

- the business is being actively advertised on the car and in various items of literature;
- the 'winning' link would certainly be a good marketing tool for the business;
- spectators at events would read details about the business – and this could have trading benefits.

The issues against the business argument are:

- the sole trader is actively participating in the sport – indicating a motive based on personal interest rather than business promotion;
- if he cannot compete because of injury, there is no substitute driver to take his place;
- the races could take place many miles away from his business (eg would an event in the north of the country benefit a local shop in the south?);
- it would be difficult to show that the venture produced a direct boost to either business turnover or profits.

Overall, it is unlikely that HMRC would allow input tax deduction on the motor racing expenditure in this particular situation because it is too closely linked to the personal interests of the business owner.

Note – an interesting tribunal case that ruled against the taxpayer is *Independent Thinking Ltd* (25 November 2008, unreported) (LON/08/927 20884). The director put forward the argument that his company was entitled to claim input tax on the purchase and refurbishment of a yacht on the basis that it was wholly used for business purposes:

- he used it as an environment for creative thinking;
- he intended to promote round-Britain cruises at some time in the future;
- he also used it as an office.

The tribunal dismissed all three arguments and ruled that the expenditure was for non-business purposes.

Domestic accommodation

[32.10] In general terms, no input tax can be reclaimed on expenditure relevant to domestic accommodation. For example, the managing director of a London company cannot buy a luxury apartment next to his office, and claim input tax on all of the fixtures and furnishings on the basis that it is important he lives close to his main place of business.

However, there are circumstances where input tax can be recovered.

- *Sole proprietors and partners* – where the owner of a business clearly allocates one part of his house solely for his business, eg third bedroom used wholly as a business office for a self-employed IT consultant, then input tax on costs relevant to that room can be reclaimed. However, it is not acceptable to claim input tax on a room only partly used for business purposes, eg a business owner who uses the dining room table to do the books once a month cannot treat this as a room used exclusively for business purposes. There are a number of non-VAT points to bear in mind in relation to using a room exclusively for business, for example, a potential charge to capital gains tax when the home is sold.
  Employees – where a business has to provide domestic accommodation to employees in order to run the business, the expenditure is classed as being wholly for a business purpose. In such cases, input tax can be reclaimed on all relevant costs (as long as the business is involved in making taxable supplies). The most common industries where this situation occurs are in the hotel and farming trades. In these industries, it important to have staff available at all times of the day – and often there are no suitable alternatives within reasonable distance of the business premises.

(HMRC Notice 700, para 12.2).

Repairs and renovations to farmhouses

[32.11] Although this tends to be a controversial topic as far as input tax recovery is concerned, clear guidelines have been agreed between HMRC and the National Farmers Union – and often the problem occurs because farmers tend to see expenditure as being more relevant to business than is really the case. The key rules are as follows:

- for a normal working farm, 70% of VAT can be reclaimed as input tax on repair and maintenance costs to the farmhouse, eg roof repair, as long as the VAT registered person in occupation is running the farm on a full-time basis. If the farm is not a full-time occupation, then only 10% to 30% of the input tax can be reclaimed on the grounds that the dominant purpose is a personal one;

- if the work is classed as an alteration or improvement to the building, then 70% input tax can be reclaimed if the dominant purpose of the expenditure is business related – but if the main purpose is personal then a maximum of 40% of the VAT would be recovered and, in some cases, none of the VAT would be recoverable.

(Business Brief 18/96).

Input tax recovery on the purchase of motor cars

[32.12] In general terms, input tax cannot be reclaimed on the purchase of a motor car – even if it is purchased by a business that wholly makes taxable supplies and intends to use the vehicle for mainly business purposes. The key test is not whether a car is 'solely' used for business purposes but whether it is 'available for private use'. If the vehicle is available for private use, then the input tax claim is blocked. For the vehicle to be blocked from private use, there needs to be a physical restriction in place to prevent private journeys, eg an insurance policy that does not allow journeys to be made if they are for social, domestic or pleasure purposes. Purchase means not only outright purchase but also any purchase under a hire purchase agreement or any other agreement whereby ownership of the car eventually passes to the business acquiring the vehicle.

If a motor car is leased or hired (rather than purchased) usually 50% of the input tax is available for credit – see **33.10–33.12**.

There are a number of exceptions to the rule regarding input tax deduction. 100% of the input tax is available for credit (subject to any partial exemption restrictions) in the following circumstances:

- cars used exclusively for the purposes of a fully taxable business and are not available for private use – see **32.13**;
- mini-cabs, self-drive hire, driving instruction;
- stock in trade of motor dealers and manufacturers;

(HMRC Notice 700/64, para 3.1).

Note – in the case of mini-cabs, self-drive hire or for driving instruction, the vehicle needs to be primarily for business use rather than exclusively for business use. This means a taxi driver can use his car for private as well as business purposes as long as the business use is dominant overall.

(HMRC Notice 700/64, para 3.4).

In the case of *Robert & Lillian Waddell (t/a LCD Plant Hire) v Revenue and Customs Comrs* (TC00140) [2009] UKFTT 185 (TC), a farmer tried to justify input tax deduction on the purchase of a motor car on the basis of exclusive business use but, as explained above, the appeal failed because there was no restriction in place to prevent the vehicle from being used for a private journey.

In the case of *Ravenfield Ltd v Revenue and Customs Comrs* (TC00641) [2010] UKFTT 359 (TC), the taxpayer claimed input tax on the purchase of a Bentley car, claiming that it was hired out to customers on a commercial basis while their own cars were being repaired following an accident. HMRC challenged whether the car was used for such a purpose, on the basis that there was a lack of evidence concerning the hirings that had supposedly taken place, ie contracts, correspondence etc. The taxpayer's appeal was dismissed – the car had not been used for such purposes and input tax could not be claimed.

Exclusive business use of a vehicle – pool car

[32.13] As explained above, input tax can be reclaimed on the purchase of a motor car which is used exclusively for business purposes and not available for private purposes. However, tribunal cases in recent years have highlighted that it is extremely difficult for a vehicle to be not available for private use.

In reality, HMRC regards a car as being used exclusively for a business purpose if it is used only for business journeys and it is not available for private use. A car is deemed to be available for private use if there is nothing to prevent the owner or employee from using the car for private use, eg an insurance restriction.

As a general exception, HMRC normally accepts that input tax can be recovered on a pool car purchased by a business, as long as it is kept at the principal place of business, it is not allocated to an individual and it is not kept at an employee's home.

Note – one positive point about the non-deductible input tax situation is that if a business sells a motor car, the supply becomes exempt under *VATA 1994, Sch 9*, Group 14 and no output tax needs to be declared. This particular group treats the supply of goods as exempt where no input tax was recovered on the initial purchase.

(HMRC Notice 700/64, paras 3.5–3.7).

Apportionment of input tax for part business/part private expenses

[32.14] When goods are acquired by a business but only partly used for business purposes (ie meaning there is partly private or non-business use), then the input tax should be apportioned so that credit is only given for the business part of the expense. This principle does not apply to motor cars, as explained at **32.13** above.

There is an alternative approach to dealing with such expenditure, which is to fully reclaim input tax on the initial expenditure, but then account for output tax on the private element over a period of time that reflects the private or non-business use. This approach is known as the *Lennartz* mechanism, named after a famous European Court case (*Lennartz v Finanzamt München III: C-97/90* [1991] ECR I-3795, [1993] 3 CMLR 689, [1995] STC 514 – see **32.17**). However, changes in the legislation now prevent the use of *Lennartz* accounting in most cases – see **32.17**.

Apportioning expenses only partly used for business

[32.15] The legislation does not specify any particular method of input tax apportionment for expenses where there is some non-business or private use. However, any method used must be fair and reasonable, taking into account the various activities and the purposes for which the expenditure is incurred.

In reality, there are many different methods of apportioning an expense and HMRC officers are instructed to only challenge a method that is completely unfair or unreasonable in its method and outcome. If the officer considers the non-business use to be minimal, he can decide to allow a waiver of apportionment. In such cases, it would not be cost effective for him to spend time and effort trying to calculate an assessment of tax for a small amount of money.

For example, input tax apportionment could be based on a fixed percentage between business and private use; an apportionment based on income figures; a time-based method; transaction-based method; area-based method.

Home computers made available by employers to employees

[32.16] Before 13 August 2007 HMRC policy was to allow full VAT recovery on computers made available to employees without any adjustment for private use, providing there was at least some business use. This policy was withdrawn by HMRC when it issued Revenue & Customs Brief 55/07 on 13 August 2007. The revised policy from this date is as follows.

- The business must now consider why the computer is being provided to the employee to determine the level of VAT that can be claimed.
- Businesses will only be able to claim full VAT recovery without any requirement to account for VAT on any private use where the provision of a computer is necessary for the employee to carry out the duties of his employment. In such cases, HMRC has concluded that the amount of private use will not be significant, ie no adjustment is required.

- Where a business cannot demonstrate that it is necessary to provide an employee with a computer in order to carry out the duties of his employment, then HMRC will accept any method of apportionment (to reflect the private use) as long as the end result fairly reflects the extent of business use.

The Lennartz mechanism

[32.17] The key principle of the *Lennartz* mechanism is that input tax can be fully recovered on capital expenditure where there is part business and part private use, but then an output tax adjustment needs to be made at the end of each VAT period in which private use takes place over the life of the asset. Records must be kept showing how the relevant item has been used.

Since 1 January 2011, the *Lennartz* method has been withdrawn if the asset in question comes into the following categories:

- land and property;
- boats;
- aircraft.

For the above assets (eg a yacht used for business hiring and private use by staff and directors at weekends), input tax apportionment at the time of buying the asset is the only acceptable option if the asset was bought on or after 1 January 2011. Changes to the capital goods scheme were also introduced on this date, so that changes in private use over the five-year life of the asset (ten years in the case of land and buildings) are properly taken into account.

As a further point, a separate restriction to *Lennartz* accounting took effect on 22 January 2010, so that it cannot be used in many other cases:

- if an asset is used for both business and private purposes (private meaning a purpose that is fully outside of the VAT system, including a non-economic business activity – see Example 5 below), then the *Lennartz* approach cannot be used unless the private use is relevant to either the business owner or his staff or, exceptionally, for other uses which are wholly outside the purposes of the taxpayer's enterprise or undertaking;

Note – the above restriction was effective following the ECJ case involving *Vereniging Noordelijke Land- en Tuinbouw Organisatie v Staatssecretaris van Financiën: C-515/07* [2009] STC 935, ECJ. Further details are given in Revenue & Customs Brief 2/10.

Example 5

Luton Homeless Charity is VAT registered and has just bought new kitchen equipment costing £30,000 plus VAT. The equipment is partly used to provide meals to customers at commercial rates (to raise funds for the charity) and partly to provide free meals to homeless people. The latter activity is funded by donations and grants from various bodies.

Solution – The *Lennartz* approach cannot be adopted (if the equipment was purchased after 22 January 2010) because the free meals activity is classed as a non-economic business activity rather than a private activity. Input tax apportionment is the only route to claim some input tax on the kitchen equipment (ie relevant to the taxable activity of selling meals to customers at commercial rates).

Note – HMRC accepts that where a taxpayer has applied *Lennartz* accounting on the basis of HMRC's pre-*VNLTO* understanding of the law, the taxpayer may opt to continue using *Lennartz* accounting in respect of the assets concerned. This assumes they had already embarked on the *Lennartz* approach before 22 January 2010.

Supply must be to business seeking to claim input tax

[32.18] Imagine that Company A and Company B are both VAT registered and connected to each other (common ownership). Company B is partly exempt so cannot fully reclaim input tax on its VAT returns – there is no similar problem for Company A. The directors therefore decide that all expenses incurred by Company B will be invoiced to and paid for by Company A so that the latter can reclaim input tax on the expenditure. Is this allowed?

The key rule is that input tax can only be claimed if an expense (goods or services) has been supplied to the business seeking to make the claim. If this condition is not met, then it is irrelevant whether they meet the other requirements for claiming input tax, ie holding a proper tax invoice, making payment of the expense etc.

A common example and way of illustrating this principle is shown in Example 6.

Example 6

Martin is a chartered accountant and VAT registered as a sole trader. He is buying the freehold of a new office for his business and has taken out a mortgage with a bank. The bank requires a full survey to be carried out on the property as a condition of the mortgage advance. The cost of the survey is £1,000 plus VAT. What is the input tax position?

Solution – the surveyor is supplying his services and professional expertise to the bank, not to Martin. This means that he cannot reclaim input tax on the expense, despite the fact that he is fully responsible for the payment.

Other conditions for claiming input tax

[32.19] The approach of a business playing safe and charging 20% VAT on the basis that the customer is VAT registered and can reclaim input tax is one that can backfire very badly. It is important that both the 5% rate of VAT and zero-rating (or exemption) are identified and charged where appropriate. This is because a business can only claim input tax where the VAT has been correctly charged in the first place.

A case that related to input tax issues was the case of *Inayat Gulam Hussein v Revenue and Customs Comrs* (TC00286) [2009] UKFTT 348 (TC). The case related to input tax evidence but the tribunal chairman usefully summarised the four key conditions for an input tax claim to be correct in accordance with the legislation (*VATA 1994, s 25* and the *VAT Regulations 1995 (SI 1995/2518), reg 29(2)(a)*) as follows.

• A supply must have taken place.
• The input tax credit must be claimed by the taxable person to whom the supply is made.
• The supply must be chargeable to tax at the rate claimed.
• The claimant must hold satisfactory evidence of his entitlement to input tax credit.

Example 7

Mike receives a routine VAT visit from HMRC and the officer has queried an input tax claim of £10,000 made in relation to some building work. The officer rules that the charge of £50,000 plus VAT should have been zero-rated.

He disallows input tax of £10,000 – Mike must approach the builder for a VAT credit and repayment of the £10,000 VAT he has paid.

What about purchase invoices addressed to an employee?

[32.20] The fourth bullet point at **32.19** referred to satisfactory evidence of entitlement to input tax credit. Usually the evidence will be a purchase invoice addressed to the business that is receiving the supply. However, it is common for travel and subsistence costs, for example, car fuel and hotel bills, to be initially paid by the employee who is then reimbursed by the employer. When this happens, providing the costs relate to the employer's business and can be supported by the relevant purchase invoices, which will often accompany the employee's expense claim, the employer should not have a problem claiming the input tax.

A point to note is that VAT on purchase invoices addressed to employees is subject to the same recovery restrictions that apply to invoices addressed to employers. For example, the employer's business may have partial exemption issues that could affect the amount of VAT it can recover on the employee's hotel bill. Likewise, if an employee incurs business entertainment costs, for example, the cost of taking a client out to dinner, the usual input tax block on business entertainment will apply.

Input tax claims involving three or more parties

[32.21] When there are three or more parties involved in a transaction, the VAT issues can be complex and need a careful analysis of the full facts. This point is highlighted in the case of *Revenue and Customs Comrs v Airtours Holiday Transport Ltd* [2010] UKUT 404 (TCC), [2011] STC 239 where—

- the taxpayer had financial difficulties – the bank called in PwC to review finances – but fees of PwC were invoiced to the company to settle payment;

- HMRC disallowed input tax claimed by Airtours because it maintained that PwC were providing services to the bank;

- HMRC had lost its appeal at the First Tier tribunal but won this case in the Upper tribunal following an appeal. The engaging body was deemed to be the bank – it was their decision to appoint PwC even though Airtours had some input into the scope of work carried out. Input tax could not be claimed by Airtours. This has now been confirmed by the Supreme Court. PwC were engaged by the banks and, although Airtours was a party to the engagement contract, it was not in receipt of the services supplied by PwC. It was named in the contract merely to bind it to the obligation to pay for the services supplied to the banks.

The decision of the Supreme Court in *Airtours* should be contrasted with that made by the House of Lords in *Redrow plc*. In *Redrow*, the Court considered that the taxpayer obtained a benefit from the services of the estate agent but also, crucially, it was a party to the contract for the agent's services. This relationship entitled Redrow to recover input VAT it had paid in respect of the agent's services. In *Airtours* there was no such contractual relationship.

The Supreme Court considered a retail promotion scheme involving Nectar cards and up to four parties.

The four parties are:

(1)   Aimia Coalition Loyalty UK Ltd (Scheme Promoter)
(2)   The members of the scheme (Collectors)
(3)   Retailers of goods and services from whom the Collectors earn points
(4)   Retailers of goods and services from whom the Collectors redeem points (Redeemers)

Sometimes, but not always, (3) and (4) above are the same party.

The Scheme Promoter's costs include payments to the Redeemers to reflect the value of the points redeemed by the Collectors as full or part payment for goods or services supplied by the Redeemers. HMRC's view was that VAT was not recoverable on these costs as the Redeemers supply the goods and services to the Collectors but not to the Scheme Promoter. However, The Supreme Court decided that the Scheme Promoter could recover VAT on these costs on the basis that a Redeemer, when making a supply of goods or services to a Collector, makes a supply of different services to the Scheme Promoter. (*Revenue and Customs Comrs v Aimia Coalition Loyalty UK Ltd* [2013] UKSC 15, [2013] 2 All ER 719, [2013] 2 CMLR 1398.)

VAT and pension schemes

[32.22] An occupational pension scheme is often managed by trustees as a separate entity from the employer. The trustees can either be individuals or corporate members. If the scheme needs to become VAT registered it will be the trustees who register because the scheme has no separate legal status.

Example 8 provides an example of a situation where a pension scheme registers for VAT because the trustees purchase commercial property as an investment and make the decision to opt to tax the property. This means that rental income from the property will be standard rated rather than exempt and allows VAT on the relevant costs to be recovered. An analysis of the option to tax rules is provided in Chapter 28.

Example 8

The trustees of ABC pension scheme intend to purchase a new commercial property for £800,000 plus VAT. The intention is to rent out the property to a firm of solicitors to generate rental income for the fund of £40,000 per year. The scheme is not registered for VAT at the current time.

What is the best option for the trustees as far as VAT is concerned?

Solution – the only way for the scheme to be able to recover the VAT on the purchase of the property, and any maintenance and repair costs, is if it registers for VAT and elects to opt to tax the property.

Registration for VAT will be on a voluntary basis because taxable supplies will be less than the VAT registration threshold, assuming the scheme has no other sources of taxable income.

The solicitors renting the property are unlikely to be concerned about the VAT charge on their rental payments because they should be able to reclaim input tax in full. However, the trustees must remember that once they have opted to tax a property, the eventual sale of the property will also require output tax to be paid on the proceeds. Once made, the option to tax cannot be revoked for 20 years.

Often the role of managing a pension fund is outsourced to one or more third parties. Historically, HMRC policy was that pension fund management services did not qualify for VAT exemption. Revenue & Customs Brief 44/14 explains a change of policy in relation to certain pension fund management services. HMRC now accepts that the services of managing and administering pension funds that have all of the following characteristics are exempt from VAT providing the services are specific and essential to the operation of the pension funds:

- the funds are solely funded, directly or indirectly, by persons to whom the retirement benefit is to be paid (the pension customers);
- the pension customers bear the investment risk;
- the funds contain the pooled contributions of several pension customers; and
- the risk borne by the pension customers is spread over a range of securities.

The VAT exemption referred to above only applies to charges made by third parties for services provided in connection with the management or administration of the contributions held in the pension fund itself.

The VAT exemption does not apply to pension fund management services provided in connection with defined benefit pension schemes as the pension customers of such schemes do not bear the investment risks. It is therefore appropriate to consider HMRC policy regarding deducting VAT in relation to pension fund management services provided in connection with defined benefit pension schemes.

Historically, HMRC policy was to differentiate between costs incurred in relation to (1) the setting up and day-to-day administration of occupational pension schemes, and (2) the investment management relating to the assets of occupational pension schemes, and to allow employers to deduct VAT in relation to the former but not the latter. HMRC regarded the costs involved in setting up and administration of an occupational pension scheme as overheads of the employer so that the costs had a direct and immediate link to the employer's business activities. HMRC considered that the investment management costs related solely to the activities of the pension scheme and it was therefore the scheme that was entitled to any VAT deduction that may be due in relation to these costs. If a single invoice was received covering both the administration of the pension scheme and the management of the investments HMRC allowed the employer to claim 30% of the VAT as relating to the administration of the scheme and the pension scheme to claim 70% of the VAT as relating to the investment management, subject to the normal rules for VAT recovery. Revenue & Customs Brief 43/14 confirms that where the pension scheme receives the services HMRC will, as a transitional measure until 31 December 2015, allow the employer and the pension scheme to apply the treatment whereby the employer claims 30% of the VAT as relating to the administration of the scheme and the pension scheme claims 70% of the VAT as relating to the investment management.

Revenue & Customs Brief 43/14 explains that HMRC now accepts that there are no grounds to differentiate between the administration of a pension scheme and the management of its assets so the 30%/70% treatment referred to above is no longer relevant, subject to the transitional measure until 31 December 2015. This also means that some employers may be able to deduct more VAT than was allowed under the previous HMRC policy and may be entitled to claim a refund of under-declared input tax, subject to the time limit for corrections explained in Chapter 16.

When deciding whether VAT on pension fund management services is deductible by an employer it is necessary to determine whether the services are supplied to the employer. In the case of defined benefit pension schemes there are normally two potential recipients of the services, (1) the employer and (2) the pension scheme through its trustees and a useful starting point is to examine the agreements between the parties. In this context, although the fact that a party pays for the services is not decisive, payment is an important indicator, particularly in circumstances where both the employer and the pension scheme use the services.

Revenue & Customs Brief 43/14 explains that HMRC will not accept that VAT incurred in relation to a pension scheme is deductible by an employer unless there is contemporaneous evidence that the services are provided to the employer, that the employer is a party to the contract for those services, and has paid for them. For some employers, directly contracting for pension fund management services can be difficult due to the regulatory environment in which they operate. Use is therefore made of tripartite contracts between (1) the supplier of pension fund management services, (2) the pension scheme trustees, and (3) the employer.

Revenue & Customs Brief 8/15 explains that tripartite contracts, in the context of defined benefit pension schemes where the regulatory regime requires the scheme to be established under a trust and it is the employer that ultimately bears the financial risks and benefits associated with the performance of the scheme, can be used to demonstrate that the employer is the recipient of the pension fund management services. In order for an employer to be able to deduct VAT on defined benefit pension fund management services provided under a tripartite contract, the contract should evidence, as a minimum, that:

- the service provider makes its supplies to the employer (albeit that the contract may recognise that, in the particular regulatory context in which defined benefit schemes operate, the service provider may be appointed by, or on behalf of, the pension scheme trustees);
- the employer directly pays for the services that are supplied under the contract;
- the service provider will pursue the employer for payment and only in circumstances where the employer is unlikely to pay (for example, because it has gone into administration) will it recover its fees from the scheme's funds or the pension scheme trustees;
- both the employer and the pension scheme trustees are entitled to seek legal redress in the event of breach of contract, albeit that the liability of the service provider need not be any greater than if the contract were with the pension scheme trustees alone and any restitution, indemnity or settlement payments for which the service provider becomes liable may be payable in whole to the pension scheme trustees for the benefit of the pension scheme (for example in circumstances where the scheme is not fully funded);
- the service provider will provide fund performance reports to the employer on request (subject to the pension scheme trustees being able to stipulate that reports are withheld, for example where there could be a conflict of interest);
- the employer is entitled to terminate the contract, although that may be subject to a condition that they should not do so without the pension scheme trustees' prior written consent (this can be in addition to any right that the pension scheme trustees' may have to terminate the contract unilaterally).

In addition to the above, evidence that the pension scheme trustees agree that it is the employer who is entitled to deduct any VAT incurred on the services will reduce the potential for disputes.

For an employer to be able to deduct any VAT, it will be necessary for them to be issued with a valid VAT invoice for the full cost of the supply and to pay the service provider directly for the full cost of the services. HMRC does not accept that an equivalent increase in contributions to the fund or any payment that is made by, or through, the fund constitutes payment by the employer.

If an employer recharges the net cost of the pension fund management services to the pension scheme, that recharge is consideration for an onward taxable supply and VAT is due accordingly. This amount is potentially deductible by the pension scheme to the extent that the pension scheme is engaged in taxable business activities.

Any non-business activities and exempt supplies need to be taken into account when calculating how much VAT can be deducted.

Pension scheme trustees and employers will normally regularly review the level of contributions required by the employer into the scheme to ensure that the scheme is able to meet the forecast pension benefit commitments. HMRC accepts that if adjustments are made to these contributions, to take account of the fact that it is the employer rather than the scheme that is paying for certain costs, that does not constitute consideration for a supply by the employer to the pension fund, provided that there is no specific reduction equal to the actual costs that were incurred in any given period.

Planning points to consider

[**32.23**] The following planning points should be given consideration.

- Input tax can be reclaimed on the costs of entertaining non-employees to attend an event or function as long as a charge is made to the non-employees and output tax is declared on this charge. The charge can be at below cost value.
- Remember that although input tax on staff entertaining costs can be reclaimed in most cases, this does not apply when the function of the staff member in question is to act as host for non-employees.
- Be aware of the opportunity to reclaim input tax on the costs of entertaining overseas customers. However, in many cases, this claim will be cancelled out by a private use output tax charge if the entertaining relates to a social event, or if the hospitality provided at a business meeting is excessive, ie not reasonable in scale and character.
- Input tax can be reclaimed (without a corresponding output tax charge) on staff benefits such as a free staff canteen and corporate membership of a gym, as long as the facility is available to all staff, not just a select few, and is provided free of charge.
- It is possible (although difficult in practice) for a business owner to justify reclaiming input tax on costs associated with a sporting or leisure activity. However, the owner (or his adviser) will need to clearly illustrate the business and commercial benefits of an arrangement. He will need to convince HMRC that he is not just trying to reclaim input tax on costs linked to a private interest.

- Review input tax recovery on motor cars to assess whether a claim could be made, for example, for a genuine pool car arrangement. There may, however, be advantages in leasing a car – 50% of the input tax on the monthly hiring charges can be reclaimed as relevant to business use.
- If a pension scheme buys a commercial property on which VAT has been charged, there may be advantages in registering the scheme for VAT and opting to tax the property so that input tax relevant to the property (including the input tax on the initial purchase price) can be reclaimed on the basis that it relates to a taxable activity.

Chapter 33

Motor, Travel and Subsistence Expenses

Key topics in this chapter:

- Private motoring for business owners and employees.
- Scale charge procedures – CO_2 basis of calculation.
- Adjusting for private use by keeping detailed mileage records.
- The option to not claim input tax on any road fuel purchased by the business.
- Claiming input tax on the fuel element of mileage claims.
- VAT treatment of other motoring expenses – leasing/hiring a vehicle; repair and maintenance costs; personalised number plates.
- Subsistence expenses for employees and business owners.
- Other travel costs – taxi fares, air travel, rail fares.

Private motoring adjustments

Introduction

[33.1] One of the main principles of VAT is that input tax can only be reclaimed on expenses that relate to 'taxable supplies made by a business'.

In effect, this means that if a business owner or employee incurs motoring costs on a visit to a client, and the business is VAT registered and makes taxable supplies, then any VAT incurred on the journey can be recovered. If, however, the journey is to watch a football match, then this expenditure cannot be reclaimed for VAT purposes because it is now a private or non-business expense.

In reality, the reason why the VAT rules can be complicated in this area is because of the practical difficulties of making input tax claims. For example, in the situation above, if the business owner fills up his car with petrol, he does not know at this stage (unless he is a meticulous planner who knows his precise travel plans for the next seven days!) how much of this petrol will be used for business purposes (ie input tax reclaimable) and how much will be for private purposes (ie input tax not reclaimable).

Note – the rules explained and examples provided in this chapter are with reference to situations where the business is not affected by the partial exemption rules.

Motoring costs and adjusting for private use

[33.2] Any business that pays for road fuel (either for employees or owners of the business) has options available to it as far as input VAT is concerned:

- reclaim all input tax on the road fuel and then pay the scale charge for each motor car used in the business – see **33.3**;
- keep detailed mileage records to separate business mileage and private mileage for each vehicle – then calculate the amount of VAT that can be reclaimed on an apportioned basis – see **33.4**;
- it can elect to claim no VAT on the road fuel it purchases – and this will then avoid the scale charge being applied – see **33.5**.
- claim all of the VAT on fuel because 100% is used for business purposes, eg because the business only funds fuel for business motoring.

From 17 July 2013 the output tax due on supplies of private fuel to employees is based on the open market value of the fuel supplied unless output tax is accounted for on the fuel scale charge.

It is, however, possible to avoid an output tax charge on fuel completely by adopting either of the methods referred to at **33.4** (only claiming input tax on fuel that relates to business mileage) and **33.5** (not claiming any input tax on fuel).

Scale charge

[33.3] The scale charge system is based on the CO_2 emissions of a car. The emissions value can be found by checking the Vehicle Registration Certificate (VC5) for the vehicle in question.

To illustrate the workings of the scale charge system, consider the following example.

Example 1

Employee A drives a company car with a 180 CO_2 emissions band. In VAT quarter ended 30 April 2015 (standard rate of VAT is 20%), the total fuel for his vehicle (paid in full by the business) is £480. What is the VAT position?

Solution – the business can recover input tax on the fuel cost (£480 × 1/6 = £80. Note – 1/6 is the relevant VAT fraction with a 20% rate of VAT). However, because some of the fuel is used for private and non-business purposes the output tax due is calculated based on a scale charge of £408, the scale charge that applies to a car in the 180 CO_2 emissions band for the relevant VAT period.

Therefore, the business will include £68 (ie £408 × 1/6) as output tax in Box 1 of its VAT return and reclaim input tax of £80 in Box 4 of its VAT return. The net amount of the scale charge, £340 (ie £408 – £68) will be included in Box 6 of its VAT return (outputs box).

For information purposes, the fuel scale rates for three-month VAT periods are shown below.

CO_2 Band	VAT inclusive 3-month charge (£) from 1 May 2016	VAT inclusive 3-month charge (£) from 1 May 2015 to 30 April 2016
120 or less	116	133
125	175	200
130	186	213
135	197	227
140	209	240
145	221	254
150	233	267
155	245	281
160	256	294
165	268	308
170	279	320
175	291	334
180	303	347
185	314	361
190	326	374
195	338	388
200	350	401
205	362	415
210	373	428
215	384	441
220	396	455
225 or more	408	468

Note – the VAT amount will be accounted for in Box 1 of a VAT return, with the net amount included in Box 6. The figures above will obviously vary on a proportionate basis for repayment traders submitting monthly VAT returns, or taxpayers on the annual accounting scheme submitting one return each year.

As a separate tip, be aware that the new rates apply for VAT periods beginning on or after 1 May 2015. So a taxpayer who adopts calendar VAT periods will use the previous scale charges rates for his quarterly return to 30 June and the new rates for his quarterly return to 30 September.

Key questions	Answers
Does it make any difference if the vehicle in question is a company car or car owned privately by the individual?	No – the scale charge applies to any vehicle where fuel is bought for private and business purposes. In effect, the scale charge deals with the situation where fuel is initially deemed to have been bought wholly for the business, but then some of this fuel is used for private purposes ie creating an output tax liability on the onward supply to the individual in question.
Is it possible for a car to be wholly used for business purposes and therefore escape the scale charge?	Possible but very difficult. A detailed mileage record would need to be kept as evidence that the car is only used for business purposes. But even then, it would be difficult to prove that private use is never an issue – think of the detours to the supermarket or emergency situations that could arise where a private journey is needed, eg visiting a relative in hospital.

Key questions	Answers
What if our client has a petrol account with one particular garage where all fuel is paid for through this account?	The business will have given the garage a list of car registration numbers that can obtain fuel via the petrol account. All cars on this list will then be subject to the quarterly scale charge.
Is there any distinction between a company director, other employee of the business or sole trader or partner?	No – the key question is not the status of the driver or vehicle owner – but the principle that some of the fuel that has been bought for the vehicle will be used for private purposes.
What if the amount of the scale charge exceeds the amount of input tax that I have claimed on road fuel?	Consider the option available to a business to reclaim no input tax on road fuel – see **33.5**.
And does the scale charge apply to commercial vehicles such as vans and lorries?	No. If the fuel bought for a commercial vehicle is used for significant private use, then a percentage of the input tax should not be claimed to reflect this situation.

Keep detailed mileage records

[33.4] The second option for dealing with the VAT implications of private motoring is for the driver(s) of the vehicle in question to keep detailed mileage records, recording every journey for both business and private purposes.

Consider Example 2 below.

Example 2

Employee B has a company car and all of his petrol expenses are paid by his employer. He keeps a detailed mileage record of all journeys, and in the VAT period ended 30 June, he travelled 4,000 miles of which 3,000 were private miles and 1,000 were business miles. The total petrol cost for the quarter was £780 including VAT. What is the VAT position in relation to his fuel expenses?

Solution – the total VAT on the fuel purchased by the business is £130 (ie £780 × 1/6 based on a VAT rate of 20%). However, the business proportion of this input tax is only £32.50 (1,000 business miles out of a total of 4,000 miles = 25% business proportion). Input tax to reclaim is therefore £32.50.

Therefore, include £32.50 in Box 4 of the quarterly VAT return; there is no Box 1 adjustment because the input tax apportionment above has avoided the need to apply the scale charge.

Key questions	Answers
Which is the best method to use – the mileage record apportionment or the scale charge system?	This will depend on a number of issues such as the total mileage of the car, the amount of private use, the impact of the scale charge etc. In reality, however, most businesses opt for the scale charge system because the administrative burden of an employee or business owner keeping a detailed mileage log can be very onerous.

Key questions	Answers
Can the employee just record his business journeys – and then the private journeys can be assumed to be the balance?	This could be prone to challenge by a VAT officer. If a client wants to opt for the mileage route, then the records must be detailed and accurate.

Opting out of the scale charge or record-keeping system

[33.5] The options at **33.3** and **33.4** could give a business two possible problems:

- in the case of the scale charge calculation at **33.3**, it is possible that output tax declared in Box 1 may exceed the total input tax recovered on fuel costs in Box 4. This situation could arise if business drivers have very little total mileage;

- the mileage records system will deal with the potential problem created by the scale charge calculation, but it could be too onerous for vehicle drivers to remember to complete their mileage details after each journey.

A third option could be adopted – consider the following example.

Example 3

Mr C is a VAT-registered sole trader accountant with no employees and he works from home. His clients are all local and he does very little business or private mileage. He drives a car with a CO_2 emissions rate of 225. What is the best solution as far as VAT is concerned?

Solution – if Mr C opted for the scale charge route, he would be able to reclaim input tax on his petrol costs but would have an output tax liability higher than this amount. If he kept detailed mileage records he would be able to claim input tax based on his actual business mileage, which may be negligible. His best option may be to simply not claim any input tax on road fuel costs – therefore avoiding the scale charge situation and the mileage record keeping requirement.

Key questions	Answers
Should I notify HMRC if I decide not to reclaim any input tax on fuel costs?	No – Paragraph 8.6 of Notice 700/64 makes no mention of the need to notify HMRC of a decision to not reclaim input tax on fuel costs.
Can I elect to keep some of the company vehicles in the scale charge system – and some of them out of the system by making an election?	No. Any decision to not reclaim input tax relates to all road fuel purchased by the business – not just the road fuel for certain vehicles. The decision would also apply to fuel purchased for commercial vehicles as well as motor cars – there are no exceptions to the system.
What if the circumstances of the business change so that it is now better to reclaim input tax on fuel costs and apply the scale charge?	Any change to existing procedures should be made at the beginning of a VAT period.

Mileage payments

Introduction

[33.6] The VAT situation for a business that purchases road fuel was considered above – we will now look at the situation where an employee purchases the fuel himself – and then claims some recompense from his employer on a mileage basis.

Note that in reality, a business is unlikely to reimburse any mileage claims for employees making private trips – this would not be commercially realistic and would also cause problems for direct tax purposes. We will therefore assume in this section that mileage claims are for business journeys only.

We will split this topic into two parts:

- where the mileage payment is to cover the petrol cost only – see **33.7**;
- where the mileage payment is to cover all motoring costs, eg wear and tear on the vehicles, contribution towards insurance/repair costs – see **33.8**.

A key point to be aware of is that input tax claims on mileage payments must be supported by petrol receipts (tax invoices) attached to the mileage claim. (HMRC Notice 700/64, para 8.10).

Mileage payment for petrol cost only

[33.7] Consider the following example.

Example 4

Bill is employed by ABC Limited and is provided with a 1,800cc petrol company car but is responsible for paying for all of the fuel. However, ABC Limited will reimburse him for the cost of fuel used on business journeys based on the advisory fuel rates published by HMRC. During the quarter to 31 May 2015 Bill submitted mileage records and fuel receipts to ABC Limited to support his claim for 1,000 business miles at 13 pence per mile, ie a claim for £130.

Solution – a VAT-registered employer can reclaim input tax on the fuel element of any mileage costs paid to an employee, as long as the mileage in question relates to business journeys for a business making taxable supplies and tax invoices (fuel receipts) are retained as evidence to support the claim.

In this example, ABC Limited will reimburse Bill £130 for business fuel (1,000 business miles × 13p per mile) and the company will reclaim input tax of £21.67 based on a VAT rate of 20% (ie £130 × 1/6).

Key questions	Answers
Does the company need to obtain petrol receipts from the employee as evidence that he has purchased the fuel?	Yes – this is a condition of being able to reclaim input tax.

Key questions	Answers
Is the VAT officer likely to challenge the mileage records in any way?	As long as the records are accurate and reasonable, they are unlikely to be challenged. Please note that there can be direct tax, National Insurance and VAT implications if accurate mileage records are not maintained and retained.
Is there a rule about what is an acceptable fuel allowance to pay to an employee?	HMRC normally accept the advisory fuel rates which they currently review four times a year and publish on the GOV.UK website. The rates are based on the engine capacity of the car and the type of fuel used. Other rates could be used providing they accurately reflect the cost of fuel used.

HMRC currently review the advisory fuel rates four times a year and the rates for the period from 1 June 2016 are noted below:

Engine size	Petrol	LPG
Up to 1400 cc	10p	7p
1401 cc to 2000 cc	13p	9p
Over 2000 cc	20p	13p

Engine size	Diesel
Up to 1600 cc	9p
1601 cc to 2000 cc	10p
Over 2000 cc	12p

Mileage payments that also include non-fuel costs

[33.8] The situation where a business pays a mileage rate that is only intended to cover the fuel cost of a journey was considered at **33.7**. In reality, if an employee uses his own car for a business journey carried out on behalf of his employer, then he will usually be paid a higher mileage rate.

The most common mileage rates paid by a business are as follows:

• 45p per mile for first 10,000 business miles in a tax year;
• 25p per mile thereafter.

The above rates are frequently adopted because they are the rates that HMRC allows a business to adopt before any income tax implications take effect.

The basic rule for reclaiming input tax on mileage rates that cover wear and tear/other costs is that the amount reclaimed should be based on the fuel element of the mileage claim only.

Consider the following example.

Example 5

Carla, a colleague of Bill's from Example 4, is employed by ABC Limited but is not provided with a company car and instead uses her own 1,800 cc petrol car travelling on business. ABC Limited will reimburse Carla at the rate of 45 pence per business mile. During the quarter to 31 May 2015 Carla submitted mileage records and fuel receipts to ABC Limited to support her expenses claim for 1,000 business miles at 45 pence per mile, ie a claim for £450.

Solution – a VAT-registered employer can reclaim input tax on the fuel element of any mileage costs paid to an employee, as long as the mileage in question relates to business journeys for a business making taxable supplies and tax invoices (fuel receipts) are retained as evidence to support the claim.

In this example, ABC Limited will reimburse Carla £450 for business mileage, £130 of which relates to business fuel (1,000 business miles × 13p per mile). The company will reclaim input tax of £21.67 based on a VAT rate of 20% (ie £130 x 1/6).

Note – if you compare the input tax claim the company makes in this example with the input tax claim the company makes in Example 4 you will see that they are identical. Although the mileage rate paid to Carla for using her own car is higher than the rate paid to Bill, who is provided with a company car, the input tax claim by the company relates only to the fuel element of the mileage rate.

Key questions	Answers
What if my client has been adopting a mileage payment system for many years and never reclaimed any input tax on the claims paid to employees?	In effect, this situation has created a VAT overpayment on past VAT returns through under-claimed input tax. The legislation allows any past VAT errors to be adjusted for the previous four years only. If the amount of the adjustment is less than £10,000 or 1% of Box 6 turnover up to a ceiling of £50,000, this can be corrected on the next VAT return submitted by the business (increase Box 4 figure). If the amount of VAT exceeds these levels, it must be corrected by submitting an error notification form (VAT 652) to HMRC. However, don't forget that input tax claimed on mileage expenses must be supported by fuel receipts.
What if my client pays a mileage rate in excess of 45p per mile?	For VAT purposes, the principle remains unchanged – namely that input tax can only be reclaimed on the fuel element of any mileage claim (and supported by receipts). However, be aware that a mileage payment in excess of 45p per mile has benefit in kind implications for the employee and employer.
What if I consider the HMRC fuel advisory rate to be too low?	A business can still assess its own fuel rates, but these must be calculated in a fair and reasonable manner.

Other motoring expenses

[33.9] It should be noted that the guidance that follows assumes that the business in question does not trade in motor vehicles, for example as a car hire company, taxi business, car dealer etc.

Leasing or hiring a motor car

Lease

[**33.10**] As a general rule, input tax cannot be recovered on the purchase of a car. If the car is leased rather than purchased by a business the leasing company will charge VAT on the monthly rental payments.

In such cases, input tax is (assuming there are no partial exemption issues) reclaimable on 50% of the lease charge. See Example 6.

The exception to the 50% rule is if the vehicle is used for a taxi business or driving school, in which case 100% input tax can be claimed. (HMRC Notice 700/64, para 4.3).

Example 6

ABC Ltd has leased a BMW car for a 3-year period for use by its sales manager. The monthly charge is £300 plus VAT of £60 (based on 20% rate of VAT).

Solution – input tax of £30 can be reclaimed on each payment made to the leasing company (ie £60 × 50%).

HMRC agreement with the British Vehicle Rental and Leasing Association about car leasing and repairs and maintenance services

[**33.11**] Many company cars, such as the BMW in Example 6, are leased under a contract hire agreement with the customer, ABC Ltd in this example, being responsible for the cost of repairs, maintenance and servicing. As noted at **33.13**, a business can usually recover 100% of the VAT on repairs, maintenance and servicing providing the business incurs the expense and there is at least some business use of the car.

Another popular option is for the business to pay the lease company an additional monthly fee to cover repairs maintenance and servicing. Providing there is at least some business use of the car and the additional monthly fee is genuinely optional, and for services separately described in the contract hire agreement, 100% of the VAT in relation to the additional monthly fee can usually be recovered.

HMRC have agreed guidelines on what is acceptable as evidence that leasing and maintenance are supplied separately with the leasing trade organisations. The full text appears in Notice 700/57 'VAT Administrative agreements', at agreement number 13, entered into with trade bodies.

Hiring a car

[**33.12**] The 50% rule also applies to the short term hire of a vehicle – unless the hire period does not exceed ten days, and the car is being hired specifically for business purposes and does not replace the company car that is usually available to the driver. See Example 7.

(HMRC Notice 700/64, para 4.4).

Example 7

ABC Ltd has hired two vehicles for eight days each – the first to replace the company car used by the sales director, which is being repaired following an accident; the second for use by the purchasing manager on a tour to visit suppliers. The purchasing manager is not usually provided with a company car.

Solution – the 50% rule will apply to the car used by the sales director because it is provided as a replacement while his company car is repaired – but 100% input tax can be reclaimed on the car for the purchasing manager because the hire period is less than ten days and the car is being hired solely for a business purpose.

Repair and maintenance costs

[33.13] If a vehicle is used for business purposes, VAT on repair and maintenance costs can be treated as input tax if the expenses are incurred and paid for by the business.

Key questions	Answers
Can a client reclaim all of the VAT on repair and maintenance costs on a business vehicle, even though the vehicle is partly used for private purposes?	100% input tax can still be reclaimed even if the vehicle is used for some private motoring and even if no VAT is reclaimed on road fuel in order to avoid the scale charge. HMRC accepts that a vehicle needs to be in sound working order in order to carry out business journeys – and therefore allow 100% recovery of relevant costs.
What if I agree to pay the repair and maintenance costs of an employee's vehicle which he owns privately?	If a car is never used for business purposes, then no input tax can be reclaimed on repair or service costs. However, if the employee's car is sometimes used for business purposes, and the cost of the repair is incurred by the employer (ie the garage invoices the employer for the work), then input tax can be reclaimed on the cost incurred. Be aware though, that such generosity by an employer can have direct tax consequences.

Car accessories

[33.14] Input tax can only be reclaimed on car accessories if they are purchased after the car has been purchased and it can be shown that the accessory has a business use, for example, a car phone to make business calls.

As for personalised number plates – it would need to be shown that the number plate clearly advertises and promotes the business. See Example 8. (HMRC Notice 700/64, paras 5.2 and 5.3).

Example 8

Jim Smith is the managing director of ABC Ltd and the company is considering buying a personalised number plate for his Mercedes car. He is undecided whether to buy the number plate 'JIM 1' after his own name, or 'ABC 1' after the company name. He is interested in the VAT issues of both choices.

Solution – there is no business advertising benefit gained from the purchase of the plate 'JIM 1' so the cost would be non-deductible as far as input tax is concerned. However, 'ABC 1' is clearly promoting the company name, so input tax could be reclaimed on this particular choice.

An interesting VAT tribunal case allowed a Mr Hooper to recover input tax on the registration plate 'HO02 PER'. Mr Hooper said the registration plate was to give publicity to his restaurant, which was known locally as Hooper's.

Subsistence costs

[33.15] A lot of work performed by employees and business owners is done away from the main place of business, which inevitably involves meal and hotel expenses being incurred.

In most cases, there is no problems with these costs being reclaimed for input tax purposes – although remember that business entertaining expenses cannot be reclaimed, including the costs of employees acting as hosts.

Hotel expenses

[33.16] VAT incurred on accommodation in the UK for employers and employees when away from their normal place of work on a business trip can be treated as input tax – see Example 9.

Example 9

John works for a firm of accountants in Luton, and spends a week away from the office doing an audit in Birmingham. He stays at the Hillfield Hotel in Birmingham – the hotel bill is paid for by his employer.

Solution – input tax can be reclaimed by the employer on the invoice from the hotel. There is no problem under current rules if the invoice from the hotel is made out in John's name, as it is common practice for hotels to invoice the guest rather than his employer. Input tax can also be reclaimed on any meal costs incurred by John on this trip – as long as a supporting tax invoice is held.

There may be occasions where an employee is required to stay at a hotel near to his place of work for business purposes. In such cases, input tax can still be claimed on the cost of the hotel – see Example 10.

Example 10

Bill has an important job for ABC Ltd in London – he is based in Luton and commutes by train each day. There is talk of a rail strike – so ABC Ltd agree to pay for him to stay overnight at a hotel next to the office.

Solution – the decision to pay for Bill's accommodation is made for business reasons so input tax can be reclaimed on the hotel cost. It is not a problem that the hotel is located very close to Bill's main place of work. The same rule would also apply if Bill was a sole trader or partner of the business – the key point being that the reason for the expense is for genuine business reasons.

Meal expenses

[33.17] Any meal cost paid for a non-employee (eg customers or suppliers) is classed as business entertainment and input tax cannot be claimed. However, there is an opportunity to claim input tax on the cost of providing food and drink to overseas customers at a business-related meeting, but only if the hospitality provided is 'reasonable in scale and character'. If the food and drink does not meet this criteria, and is excessively lavish, then the input tax can still be claimed but a private use output tax charge will apply for the same amount of VAT, ie nil tax gain overall. Any food and drink provided to overseas customers at non-business events (eg a corporate hospitality function) will be subject to the same rules of input tax being claimed but with an output tax charge for the same amount. For non-staff and non-overseas customers, there is no scope to reclaim input tax on any entertaining cost, including the costs of the employee acting as host – see Example 11.

Example 11

The directors of ABC Ltd have booked a table for ten people at the local Chinese restaurant for eight customers, plus two employees who will look after the customers and keep them entertained.

Solution – no input tax can be claimed on the charge made by the Chinese restaurant because it relates to business entertainment. This includes the cost of the employees' meals because they are acting as host for the guests. HMRC Notice 700/65, para 3.3.

If entertainment is provided only for directors or partners of a business the VAT incurred is not input tax. This is because the goods or services are not used for a business purpose. The VAT cannot, therefore, be recovered. But where directors and partners of the business attend staff parties together with other employees, HMRC accept that the tax is input tax and is not blocked from recovery (HMRC Notice 700/65, para 3.2).

In the case of directors or partners of a business, the only other time when input tax can be reclaimed on meal costs is if they are working away from their normal location on business – these costs are then classed as subsistence expenses.

Note – how many miles would be acceptable as 'away from the normal workplace'? Five miles is a useful guide and has been accepted as reasonable by most VAT officers in the past.

In some cases, a business will pay employees a flat rate for subsistence expenses, eg £15 per day to cover meal and incidental costs if they are away from the office for more than ten hours. There is no entitlement to input tax deduction on such flat rate payments.

Travel costs

[33.18] So far in this chapter, it has been assumed that the method of transport used is by a motor vehicle – looking at the VAT implications of motoring expenses. However, now we will consider the input tax treatment of travel by other means of transport.

Air travel, rail and bus

[33.19] Any form of public transport that carries at least ten passengers is usually zero-rated for VAT purposes. Therefore, a business will never be able to reclaim any input tax on train fares, for example, as no input tax will have been incurred.

Taxi fares

[33.20] As a taxi holds less than ten passengers, a taxi journey is basically standard rated. However, be aware that many taxi drivers operate as self-employed persons trading below the VAT registration threshold.

The key point is to check if the invoice issued by the driver includes a VAT registration number.

If a taxi business is VAT registered, then input tax can be reclaimed on the cost of the journey as long as it is for business purposes.

Planning points to consider

[33.21] The following planning points should be given consideration.

- Be aware of the new scale charge rates effective for accounting periods beginning on or after 1 May 2015.
- Consider whether it would be more profitable for a business to claim no input tax on road fuel and therefore avoid the need to account for scale charges.
- Where input tax has been recovered in full but the fuel scale charge system is not used, the output tax must be calculated based on the open market value of the fuel supplied to employees for private use. It is no longer possible to account for output tax on the actual charge made to employees for private fuel, unless the charge is at least equal to the open market value of the fuel supplied.
- For a business operating the scale charge system, consider whether it would be beneficial (and realistic) to keep mileage records to adjust for private motoring costs, which may produce a VAT saving.

- Be aware of the opportunity to reclaim input tax on the fuel element of mileage payments made to employees for business journeys, however, these must be supported by accurate mileage records and tax invoices.
- If a business has not reclaimed input tax on mileage payments in the past, then there is scope (subject to supporting mileage records and fuel receipts being available) to reclaim input tax for the last four years – either by making a claim in Box 4 of the next return or by submitting an error notification claim to HMRC (depending on amounts of tax involved).
- Advise clients that generally only 50% of input tax can be deducted on car leasing/hire charges.
- The VAT treatment of repair and servicing costs on a motor car with at least some business use is very generous. A claim for 100% input tax can be made on such expenses, even if the vehicle has some private use. The business must however incur the cost.

Chapter 34

Supplies Involving Agents

Key topics in this chapter:

- Identifying an agency/principal arrangement.
- The main features of an agency relationship in a business arrangement, eg the agent never takes ownership of the goods or services being provided.
- Registering an agent for VAT and potential benefits of voluntary registration.
- VAT procedures to follow for an undisclosed agency arrangement.
- Input tax treatment of costs incurred by an agent and output tax liability of recharges made to the principal.
- Rules for dealing with VAT on disbursements.
- Example of a case concerning supplies involving three parties (*Joppa Enterprises Ltd*).

Introduction

[34.1] In many business transactions, there are three key people involved:

- the customer – the beneficiary of goods or services being provided;
- the principal – the owner of goods or provider of services;
- the agent – a third party who acts for either of the two parties (or both) above in arranging supplies of goods or services. (Normally, an agent will only act for one principal. However, as demonstrated in the *Birmingham City Football Club* [2007] V & DR 149 (TC02151) case, the First Tier Tax Tribunal found that an agent acted for both the player and the club.)

The key point with an agent is that he is arranging a transaction for someone else, rather than trading in goods or services on his own account. The agent never takes ownership of the goods or services being provided – the supply is always between the principal and the customer.

The most common method of payment is for the agent to receive a commission – usually according to the value of sales achieved or the number of transactions carried out on behalf of the principal or the customer.

An agent can work for either the customer or the principal. For example, a customer may ask the agent to find him a suitable car to buy, and then pay him a fee when this objective is achieved. A principal may instruct an agent to find customers for his products, and then pay the agent a fee when sales have been finalised.

(HMRC Notice 700, para 22.2).

Identifying an agency arrangement

[34.2] The VAT liability of the services provided by an agent do not necessarily follow the liability of the goods or services being supplied between the principal and the customer. See Examples 1 and 2.

(HMRC Notice 700, para 22.4).

Example 1

John trades as an agent, trying to find customers for books produced by ABC Publishers Ltd. The latter company sells the books directly to the customer, and arranges for their delivery and invoicing. John does not take ownership of the goods at any stage, and receives £1 commission for every book that is sold – he is VAT registered.

Solution – although the books sold by ABC Publishers Ltd are zero-rated under the *VATA 1994, Sch 8, Group 3*, the services supplied by John are standard rated. He must charge output tax on his commission, which will be fully recovered by ABC Publishers Ltd because it relates to a taxable supply.

Example 2

John trades as a bookseller, buying books from ABC Publishers Ltd and then finding customers for the books by visiting various retailers across the UK. He applies a 50% mark-up to the price he paid for the books – he is VAT registered.

Solution – John is now buying the books as a principal and taking ownership of the goods. He is earning a profit by hopefully selling the books at a higher price than what he paid for them. John is making a zero-rated supply of books to his customers and therefore no output tax is due. He will be able to reclaim input tax on any related costs, eg motoring expenses, telephone, accountancy fees, advertising costs etc.

Note – in Example 1, John will be in a payment position for VAT purposes; in Example 2, the different arrangement means that he will be a repayment trader because all of his sales are zero-rated.

In most cases, it will be clear to identify if an arrangement between two parties is on an agency basis – and the following key points will assist the analysis of a situation.

- *Title of goods* – this is the most important point and is clearly illustrated by the different arrangement between Example 1 and Example 2 above. In Example 2, the situation gives added risk in that John could end up with unsold books that he has purchased – in Example 1, this situation would not apply because he never takes ownership of the goods.
- *Buying and selling prices* – the principal will be fully aware of the buying and selling prices of the goods in which he trades. In the case of an agency relationship, it is possible that the agent may never know the final selling price of the goods or services sold to the customer. For example, the agent's role may just be to find a customer for the principal – the value of the deal between the customer and the principal may not be disclosed to the agent.
- *Written agreements* – in most cases, there will be correspondence or a contract between the principal and the agent, clarifying the basis of the trading relationship, the method of remuneration for the agent etc. In most cases, it will be very clear from the correspondence if an agency arrangement is in place. However, any written agreement between two parties must be followed in practice as well.

The level of involvement by an agent in a deal will vary according to the arrangement agreed with the principal. In some cases, the agent may take responsibility for actually delivering the goods and dealing with most or all of the paperwork. However, even in these situations, it is still the principal who will invoice the customer for the final goods or services provided, and ownership/title would have been with the principal until the sale is made.

Case law example – agent or principal?

[34.3] It can sometimes be a challenge to identify whether a customer is dealing with the principal or agent in a transaction, ie to establish the output tax position.

The case of *Joppa Enterprises Ltd* [2009] SWTI 777, [2009] STC 1279 was heard in the Scottish Court of Session and the judge upheld the decision of the VAT tribunal (case verdict delivered 6 March 2009).

The case concerned supplies involving a sauna (Joppa) and the self-employed masseuses of a venue based in Edinburgh. The customer would pay Joppa on arrival at the premises, and Joppa retained £5 of the payment for expenses, the remaining fee being split on a 50:50 basis with the masseuse. The challenge for the courts was as follows:

- Was output tax payable on the full fee paid by the customer to Joppa (the latter was obviously VAT registered)? or
- Was output tax only payable by Joppa on the £5 expense payment and its 50% share of the balance, ie the main supply was between the customer and the masseuse rather than with Joppa?

The courts considered the nature of the relationships between the three parties, and the way that the financial and administrative arrangements were managed. The court acknowledged that different structures could produce different VAT outcomes but ruled in this case that Joppa was liable to output tax on the full payment received from the customer.

- The entry fee represented a consideration to Joppa for services supplied to the customer, namely access to the premises and permission to enjoy the services therein, including the lounge, refreshments, newspapers, television, the use of a private room and services of a hostess.

- Joppa was not acting as an agent for the hostess so therefore the share of money retained by Joppa could not be classed as an agent's commission.

Registering an agent for VAT

[34.4] The value of taxable supplies for an agent will be based on the fees/commission he receives from a principal and not the value of goods sold by the principal to the final customer. If an individual partly trades as an agent and partly as a principal, then the combined turnover of his activities must be taken into account.

In many cases, it will be worthwhile for an agent to register for VAT on a voluntary basis – for example, if the following situation applies:

- he is working for a principal who is registered for VAT and able to reclaim any VAT charged as input tax. This means that the agent is not losing any competitive position by adding VAT to his commission or fee; and

- the agent will then be able to recover input tax on costs relevant to his business, thereby producing a direct improvement to his bottom line profit.

(HMRC Notice 700, para 22.7).

Undisclosed agency arrangements

[34.5] It is possible that a principal selling goods will want to keep his identity secret from the final customer and arrange for the entire deal to be handled by his agent. In such cases, it will be necessary for the agent to raise the final sales invoice to the customer in his own name, and then the principal will raise his sales invoice to the agent for the same amount. The agent will still charge his fee/commission to the principal. The HMRC approach to this situation is as follows:

- the commercial basis of the transaction remains unchanged – the main supply still being between the principal and the final customer. However, special arrangements can be applied for VAT purposes so that the agent accounts for output tax on the sales invoice raised to the customer and then reclaims the same amount of input tax on the invoice raised by the principal. The agent will then raise a separate invoice to the principal for his fees;

- the output tax and input tax in the above transactions must be accounted for and reclaimed in the same VAT period. It is not acceptable for the agent to gain a cash flow advantage by reclaiming input tax in one VAT period and delaying accounting for output tax until the next VAT period.

See Example 3.

(HMRC Notice 700, para 22.6).

Example 3

Jane is acting as an undisclosed agent and sells goods to the final customer for £1,000 plus VAT on 1 April. The principal raises an invoice to her for the same amount on 31 March. Jane's commission is for £200 plus VAT, ie 20% of the sales value. She raises an invoice to the principal for this amount when the sale has been made on 1 April. Jane's VAT periods coincide with calendar quarters.

Solution – Jane can only reclaim input tax on the invoice raised by the principal in the same VAT period that she accounts for output tax on her invoice to the final customer, ie the VAT quarter to 30 June. It is not acceptable for her to reclaim input tax in the March quarter and delay accounting for output tax until the June quarter.

Jane will also account for output tax on the commission charged to the principal.

Note – the end result of this arrangement is the same as if the principal was invoicing the customer directly, ie there is no tax lost by HMRC, just a different way of collecting it.

(HMRC Notice 700, para 23.1.2).

Electronic and telecommunication services supplied after 31 December 2014 through an agent acting in his own name are treated as a supply to the agent and a supply by the agent. (*VATA 1994, s 47; Finance Act 2014, s 106*).

See Example 4.

Example 4

Kay sells music downloads (an electronic service) to consumers via Alan. Alan is a VAT registered agent, who has a website business selling music downloads on behalf of Kay and lots of other music download providers. Kay's name and the names of the other music download providers are not mentioned on any invoices, receipts, or other communications that Alan issues or makes available to people buying the music downloads and as far as they are concerned they are buying the downloads from Alan.

For VAT purposes Kay is making a business to business supply of electronic services to Alan and Alan is making a business to consumer supply of electronic services to the people who buy the music downloads. The place of supply of broadcasting, telecommunication and electronic services after 31 December 2014 is the place where the customer belongs, regardless of the status of the customer. If any of the people buying the music downloads belong in other EU countries Alan will be responsible for accounting for the output tax due on the supplies, either by registering for VAT in each of the countries where the customers belong or by using the Mini One Stop Shop (MOSS) scheme and submitting MOSS returns to HMRC (see **14.15**).

Costs incurred by an agent

[34.6] In the course of his work, an agent will incur costs trying to arrange a deal, and it is necessary for the agent to identify the cost as relevant to one of the following three categories.

(a) *Agent's own costs* – such costs are absorbed by the agent and will reduce his profit when his accounts are produced. There is no scope to recharge these costs to a client. As long as the agent's supplies are wholly taxable, he will be able to reclaim input tax on these costs subject to the normal rules.

(b) *Agent's costs that can be recharged to the client* – there may be occasions when an agent will incur a cost in the course of his business that he can recharge to the client as an additional fee. The charge to the client will still be for a supply of agency fees, it will not be acceptable to itemise some of the costs that may be zero-rated to avoid charging VAT on them. See Example 5.

(c) *Disbursements* – it is possible that an agent will pay costs to a third party on behalf of a principal, as a practical arrangement for convenience purposes. There are special rules for disbursements – see **34.7**.

Example 5

DEF Estate Agents agree to sell a property owned by Mrs Smith on a commission basis. Mrs Smith is keen to achieve a quick sale, so agrees to pay an additional £500 fee to DEF so they can produce special colour brochures giving details of the property. The brochure will hopefully generate increased interest among potential buyers. What is the VAT position?

Solution – the production of the brochure by a printer for the estate agent will be zero-rated for VAT purposes (*VATA 1994, Sch 8, Group 3*). However, the supply of the brochure is between the printer and the estate agent, to help them achieve a sale on Mrs Smith's property. The recharge to Mrs Smith by the estate agent is standard rated, as part of the agency fee in relation to her property.

Disbursements

[34.7] The VAT rules concerning disbursements are very strict, and need to be followed in every case to avoid a potential (and often unnecessary) output tax charge.

Costs incurred by an agent, eg in relation to his telephone and motoring costs cannot be recharged to his client as a non-taxable disbursement. A disbursement situation only applies when the cost properly belongs to his client, for example, a solicitor will often pay statutory fees on behalf of a client, such as court fees, stamp duty etc. These fees properly belong to the client, and are not part of the solicitor's standard-rated services to the client.

It is important to remember that a profit cannot be made on recharging a disbursement to a client – the charge must be passed on at cost price, ie the amount paid by the agent. Other important rules for disbursements are as follows:

- the agent must have acted for his client when paying the third party;
- the client authorised the agent to make the payment on his behalf;
- the client must have received and used the goods or services provided by the third party – or it is a cost that properly belongs to him as an individual;
- the client was responsible for paying the third party;
- the agent's outlay must be separately itemised when invoicing the client;
- the agent must only recover the exact amount he paid to the third party.

(HMRC Notice 700, para 25.1).

If a payment qualifies as a disbursement, the usual method of recharging a client will be for the agent to include the amount on his invoice or statement as a VAT inclusive figure. The agent cannot reclaim input tax on the costs of the disbursement (on the basis that he is not receiving the supply) but does not need to account for output tax on the onward supply – hence the VAT inclusive figure being shown. He may need to prove to an HMRC officer that no input tax has been recovered on the disbursement and that he has correctly charged the disbursement to the client at cost price, ie without a profit element.

If the client is VAT registered and able to recover input tax, then it will be necessary for the provider of the goods or services to issue a tax invoice made out to the client, not to the agent. See Example 6.

Example 6

Jones Solicitors have acted for a client who has bought the freehold of a commercial property for £200,000. The client is VAT registered and the property will wholly be used in the making of taxable supplies. Jones have paid out two costs on behalf of the client, a land registry fee of £100 and the costs of a window company in repairing a broken window for £300 plus VAT. The buyers engaged the window company to carry out the work, but will re-invoice the sellers for this work as agreed when the deal was signed. The window company has issued a tax invoice for this work, correctly made out to the buyers of the property.

Solution – Jones Solicitors will charge disbursements of £360 (£300 plus VAT) and £100 to their client. They will have no output tax liability to declare on these amounts.

The client will be able to reclaim input tax on the cost of the window repair, but must charge output tax on the onward supply of the repair work to the seller of the property.

Planning points to consider

[34.8] The following planning points should be given consideration.

- The VAT liability of services provided by an agent can be different to the VAT liability of the goods being traded. For example, the services of an estate agent selling new residential properties (zero-rated) for a national house builder will be standard rated.
- Always review correspondence between an agent and a principal to be clear that a genuine agency arrangement is in place. The main condition is normally that the agent will never take ownership of the goods or services being provided and will receive his fee on a commission basis from the principal.
- There may be benefits in registering an agent for VAT on a voluntary basis, ie giving scope for input tax recovery on his costs.
- Be aware of the special rules that exist for transactions involving undisclosed agents – but remember that output tax and input tax on the goods or services in question must be accounted for in the same VAT period.
- Be aware that electronic and telecommunication services supplied after 31 December 2014 through an agent acting in his own name are treated as a supply to the agent and a supply by the agent.
- Remember that zero-rated costs cannot be charged as a separate supply to a principal (eg as in the case of an estate agent paying a printer to produce colour brochures to help the sale of a property). The charge to the customer is part of the fee for his services as an agent.
- It is possible that agents will pay out costs on behalf of their clients – these costs can avoid a VAT charge if they are genuine disbursements and follow strict rules laid down by HMRC. One of the important rules is that a profit must not be made on the disbursement being recharged to the client.

Chapter 35

Charities

Key topics in this chapter:

- Definition of a charity and charitable status.
- Identifying the business and non-business activities of a charity.
- Registering a charity for VAT – including voluntary registration.
- Allocation of input tax between business and non-business activities.
- Input tax issues for a charity with exempt supplies (partial exemption).
- VAT liability of most common sources of income for a charity.
- Issues to consider with grant income.
- Potential VAT savings on charity expenditure – circumstances where some supplies to a charity are zero-rated or exempt.
- Possible savings with group registration if a trading subsidiary company is owned by a charity.
- Overview of the cost-sharing exemption introduced by *Finance Act 2012*.
- Overview of VAT refunds to certain charities introduced by *Finance Act 2015*.

Introduction

[35.1] From April 2012, the definition of a charity has changed. From that date, a charity means a body of persons or Trust that is established for charitable purposes and meets all of the following conditions:

- the body falls under the jurisdiction of the High Court (or corresponding jurisdiction in other EU member states);
- it complies with the requirement to register under the *Charity Act 2011* (or equivalent legislation in other member states); and
- it is managed and administered by 'fit and proper' persons.

The reason that 'charitable status' is important is because there are provisions in the VAT legislation that relate specifically to charities:

- for the income of a charity, certain sales can qualify as being zero-rated or exempt instead of standard rated. As a large percentage of charity income is generated by the general public (not able to reclaim input tax) it is important to identify potential output tax savings; and

---

- certain supplies to charities that would normally be standard rated are zero-rated or exempt and this can produce significant financial savings.

An important point to note is that if charities make taxable supplies exceeding the VAT registration threshold, they have an obligation to register in the same way as a business. They can also register for VAT on a voluntary basis. The only difference is that they may benefit from certain VAT provisions in the legislation as mentioned above.

As a useful guideline, 'charitable status' can be assessed by considering the written objectives of the body in question. If these objectives are to assist 'the relief of poverty, advance education, religion and benefits to the community' then there is a strong indication that they could be classed as a charity by HMRC. For guidelines issued by HMRC to establish charitable status, see Internal Guidance V1–9.

Trading subsidiary company

[35.2] Charity law does not allow a charity to carry out a significant amount of 'non-primary purpose trading' as a way of raising money, eg sale of Christmas cards. In such cases, the charity usually forms a separate trading subsidiary company which, although controlled by the charity, is not an actual charity. As a result, some of the VAT reliefs available to a charity are not available to subsidiary trading companies.

Example – a subsidiary trading company can still zero-rate the sale of donated goods to the public, and income from a fundraising event is still exempt from VAT. However, the company will not benefit from zero-rating on its advertising expenditure and must pay VAT at the standard rate. Courses or training fee income will not be exempt as 'education' by an 'eligible' body unless the subsidiary company is a company limited by guarantee rather than a private limited company. The fact that the company donates all of its profits to the main charity is irrelevant in such cases.

(HMRC Notice 701/1, para 2.3).

Business and non-business activities

[35.3] Two important questions that a charity will need to consider are as follows.

(a)   Will it need to register for VAT?
(b)   If registered, how much input tax can it reclaim?

A good starting point to both of the above questions is to be clear about the type of activities being carried on by the charity in question.

The activities of most charities can be divided into two clear divisions:

- business activities; and
- non-business activities.

The phrase 'business activity' normally indicates that the charity is performing some service or providing goods in return for a consideration – a key point to note, however, is that these goods or services do not need to be performed at a profit (or surplus). It is quite common for a charity to have a business activity that produces an overall loss – and is funded by other income or reserves of the charity.

As a general guide, the following common activities of a charity would all be classed as a business activity:

- providing facilities or advantages to a member of the organisation in return for payment of a subscription;
- the sale of donated and bought in goods to members of the public;
- the admission, in return for a payment, to any premises owned or used by the organisation, or any function it has arranged;
- the services for any other body or person provided by an office holder or committee of the organisation – in return for a payment;
- any activity that would be classed as a trade, profession or vocation, eg a charity providing counselling services for a fee.

A 'non-business activity' is an activity carried out by a charity that is not based on normal business principles, ie it may not be a regular activity, may not be carried out in return for payment by any third party etc.

See Example 1 for an illustration of a business and non-business activity of a charity.

Example 1

Good Causes Ltd is a registered charity and its aims are to support families who are affected by divorce. The charity has two main activities:

- It offers a telephone helpline service so that any child affected by divorce can telephone the helpline in confidence and talk to an adviser. The costs of the helpline are mainly funded by a grant from a local authority.
- It also offers a mediation service for couples who are separating – whereby the couple can speak to a mediator in private to try and find solutions to their problems. The mediation service is provided at a very low rate of £30 per hour (payable jointly by the couple), mainly because Good Causes Ltd has other sources of income from grants, donations and fundraising activities.

What is the VAT position of the charity?

Solution – the telephone service for children is a non-business activity – there is no income generated by the facility, and it is funded by a grant that is outside the scope of VAT. It is not motivated by the normal principles of business – its aim is to assist the objectives of the charity.

However, the mediation service is a business activity because there is a service being provided (taxable), in return for a consideration that is based on the use of this service, being performed by people appointed by the charity (the mediators). The fact that the activity is charged at a rate that is less than the open market value for this particular type of service is irrelevant.

Registering for VAT and input tax recovery

Registering for VAT

[35.4] As explained at **35.1**, there is no special exemption for charities as far as VAT registration is concerned – if they have made total taxable supplies during any past 12-month period that has exceeded the compulsory registration limit or they expect to make taxable supplies exceeding the registration limit in the next 30 days then they have a requirement to register for VAT.

As with profit making entities, there is a potential opportunity for charities to save tax by registering for VAT on a voluntary basis. This could occur if, for example, the charity has mainly zero-rated sales (eg selling donated goods from a shop) and would therefore be able to benefit from input tax recovery on its expenditure.

An important point to remember is that it is only taxable supplies that count as far as the VAT registration limits are concerned. Any income that is exempt or outside the scope of UK VAT is ignored. See Example 2.

Example 2

Good Causes Ltd from Example 1 has calculated its income for the previous 12 months as follows:

Mediation services:	£50,000
Local authority grant towards costs of child helpline service:	£40,000
Donations from members:	£30,000

Does the charity need to register for VAT?

Solution – the value of taxable supplies made by the charity is £50,000 in relation to the mediation services. The income from the local authority and members' donations is outside the scope of VAT. The taxable income is therefore below the VAT registration threshold and the charity does not need to register.

The next question to consider is whether it may be worthwhile for the charity to register for VAT on a voluntary basis. The answer is probably no, because this will create an output tax liability on the mediation services, which will either create an extra VAT charge to the users of this facility – or reduce the net income of the charity if fees are kept at the same rate. The input tax benefits are unlikely to outweigh the output tax charges.

Input tax recovery

[35.5] An important principle of VAT is that input tax can normally only be recovered to the extent that it relates to taxable supplies. If a source of input tax relates to non-business or private expenditure, or it relates to exempt supplies, then no input tax can be reclaimed. An important exception in the context of charities is that certain charities can recover VAT incurred after 31 March 2015 in relation to their non-business activities – see **35.23**.

A charity will therefore need to adopt a very logical approach to reclaiming input tax to ensure the amount claimed is accurate.

Stage 1 – Ensure no VAT is claimed on non-business expenses (subject to the exception explained in 35.23 for VAT refunds to certain charities from 1 April 2015)

- Any input tax relating directly to the non-business activities of the charity cannot be reclaimed – in effect, any expenditure on non-business activities should be entered into the accounting system on a gross basis (ie including VAT) and budgets or grant requests should also be based on VAT inclusive values.

- A proportion of input tax on general overheads should not be reclaimed to reflect usage on some of the non-business activities – this could relate to input tax on telephone costs, electricity bills, rent charges for offices etc. See **35.6** for possible methods of making this apportionment.

Stage 2 – Consider partial exemption – no input tax to be claimed on exempt activities

— Having carried out the stage above, any remaining input tax will be relevant to the business activities of the charity. At this stage, a further exclusion needs to be made so that input tax is not reclaimed on any expenditure that relates to exempt activities of the charity.

— Any expenditure that relates to the taxable activities of the charity can be reclaimed in full (subject to normal rules) – remember that taxable activities include zero-rated and reduced-rate supplies as well as standard-rated sales.

— A proportion of the remaining input tax on general overheads (residual input tax) will also be disallowed as relevant to exempt supplies – either through the standard method of calculation or a special method agreed with HMRC.

Note – the principles of partial exemption are covered in depth in Chapters 24 and 25 of this book. Partial exemption is a complex aspect of VAT and issues need to be considered very carefully in order to ensure input tax claims are correct.

(HMRC Notice 701/1, para 3.7).

Input tax apportionment on non-business activities

[35.6] As explained at **35.5**, with the exception of the certain charities referred to at **35.23**, any input tax that directly relates to a non-business activity cannot be reclaimed. In addition, any input tax that is partly used for business purposes (and partly for non-business purposes) also needs to be apportioned on a fair and reasonable basis.

There is no specified method of apportionment in the legislation – the key point is that the final result should be fair – and reflect the usage of the expense item between business and non-business purposes.

A number of different methods could be considered:

- income-based method – apportioning input tax according to total value of business and non-business income – see Example 3;
- time-based method – eg time that staff spend on business and non-business matters;
- transaction-based method – eg number of telephone calls received for each activity of the charity;
- floor-area based method – eg apportion premises' overheads according to floor space allocated directly to business and non-business activities.

The income-based apportionment is very common, however, it would not give a fair result if there is no real link between the income received by an activity and the costs associated with the activity.

Example 3

Good Causes Ltd, from Example 2, has received its quarterly telephone bill which includes VAT of £500. The telephone in question is used for all aspects of the charity's activities, ie it is not a specific line for any particular activity.

The charity's income for the period is as follows – and it has been identified that an input tax apportionment for non-business use based on income would achieve a fair result.

Mediation services:	£12,000
Local authority grant towards costs of child helpline service:	£2,000
Donations from members:	£1,000

How much input tax will be disallowed as relating to non-business use?

Solution – the percentage of business income is 80% (£12,000 divided by £15,000) so 80% input tax would be deemed as relevant to business purposes and 20% disallowed as relevant to non-business activities. Therefore, the input tax disallowed would be £100.

VAT liability of a charity's income

General principles to consider

[35.7] Many charities have a wide range of income sources – and each source of income needs to be considered as far as its VAT liability is concerned. Income can be generated by a charity through the supply of goods or services – or it could be income generated without a supply being provided, for example, donations from private individuals or local companies.

As a word of caution, be aware that certain sources of income could be standard-rated if supplied by a trading subsidiary of the charity – see **35.2**.

It is important to remember the logical approach to adopt as far as assessing the VAT liability of an item is concerned.

- Is the supply specifically zero-rated under any of the groups listed in *VATA 1994, Sch 8*?
  The main group in the Schedule that is relevant to the income of a charity is *Group 15* – Charities etc (see **35.8–35.10**).
- Is the supply specifically exempt from VAT under any of the groups listed in *VATA 1994, Sch 9*?
  The main groups that could be relevant to the income of charities are as follows:
  – *Group 7* – Health and welfare (see **35.11–35.13**);
  – *Group 12* – Fundraising events organised by charities and other qualifying bodies (see **35.11–35.13**);
  – *Group 13* – Cultural services – admission to museums, exhibitions, zoos and performances of a cultural nature supplied by public bodies and eligible bodies.
- Is the income specifically outside the scope of VAT?
  The main sources of income that are outside the scope of VAT are donations received from third parties and grant income received from various bodies (as long as the grant income is not based on a supply of goods or services in which case the income is likely to be taxable – see **35.16** and **35.17**).
- Is the income subject to VAT at the reduced rate?
  The reduced VAT rate of 5% applies to certain supplies that may be relevant to a charity, eg sale of contraceptive products.
- If a supply is not zero-rated, exempt, outside the scope of VAT or subject to the reduced rate of VAT it will be standard rated in the normal manner.

Charity income that is zero-rated

[35.8] A number of sources of income for a charity could be zero-rated – but the two main sources are as discussed below.

Sale of donated goods

[35.9] The main source of income which is zero-rated for many charities relates to the situation where they sell donated goods, for instance, through a charity shop in town centres.

Bought-in goods that are resold will follow the normal VAT rules, for example, the sale of items such as books and children's clothes will be zero-rated in accordance with normal rules; items sold that are not zero-rated (or subject to reduced rate VAT) will be charged at the standard rate.

Note – see Revenue & Customs Brief 14/08 which confirms that HMRC now accepts that the sale of abandoned cats and dogs by a charity represents a zero-rated sale of donated goods.

Zero-rating also applies to the sale of donated goods by a trading subsidiary company of a charity.

(HMRC Notice 701/1, para 5.5).

Supply of magazines/newsletters as part of a membership subscription

[35.10] In normal situations, it will be necessary to consider if payment for a supply of goods and services is made in return for one main benefit or a number of different benefits subject to VAT at different rates, ie mixed supply situations. In many cases, secondary supplies will be ignored as being incidental to the main supply – the VAT liability will then be entirely based on the main supply. A detailed analysis of mixed supply situations is provided in Chapter 23.

As a special concession (ESC 3.35), HMRC has confirmed that where a non-profit making body supplies, in return for membership subscriptions, a mixture of zero-rated, exempt and/or standard-rated benefits, it may apportion such subscriptions to reflect the value and VAT liability of those individual benefits, without regard to whether there is one principal benefit. This means, for example, that any zero-rated publication supplied as part of a membership subscription (eg magazine or newsletter) can be reflected in the cost of the membership fee, ie a percentage of the membership fee can be zero-rated.

Note – HMRC confirmed in Revenue & Customs Brief 6/09 (issued 20 February 2009) that it will not allow retrospective VAT adjustments to be made in relation to the split of subscription income where ESC 3.35 is being claimed by the taxpayer. This is because the original returns submitted by the charity would have been correct in law and therefore an adjustment cannot be made to correct returns that were accurate in the first place.

(HMRC Notice 701/1, para 5.13 and HMRC Notice 48, para 3.35).

Charity income that is exempt from VAT

[35.11] A number of income sources will be exempt from VAT – the most common ones are fundraising events, certain training courses and welfare services.

Fundraising events

[35.12] An important point for charities and other qualifying bodies is that they can organise certain fundraising events, the income related to this event being exempt from VAT rather than standard rated.

It should be noted that a qualifying body is generally a non-profit making body whose main aim is to provide facilities for people to take part in sport or physical recreation, for example a members' golf club.

As far as a charity (or its trading subsidiary) is concerned, the main priority is to ensure that the purpose of the event is to raise funds towards its charitable aims – and tickets sold for the event must clearly publicise the fundraising aim with wording such as 'fundraising for . . . ', 'in aid of . . . ', 'help us to build . . . '.

The VAT exemption applies to all admission charges, sale of advertising space, items sold by the charity at the event (eg T-shirts) unless the item would normally be zero-rated in which case zero-rating can still be applied (eg children's T-shirts).

A fundraising event includes the following functions:

- dinner, disco, charity concert;
- fête, fair or festival;
- fireworks display;
- games of skill, contests and quizzes;
- an auction of bought-in goods (auction of donated goods is zero-rated).

Don't forget that any input tax directly related to the event will be attributable to an exempt supply and not reclaimable unless the charity is *de minimis* as far as partial exemption is concerned (see Chapter 24 at **24.10** for an analysis of the *de minimis* rules). See Example 4 for an illustration of the VAT treatment of a fundraising event.

Example 4

Good Causes Ltd from earlier examples wishes to raise £5,000 to purchase a new computer for its child helpline facility. The chief executive of the charity decides to organise a fundraising celebrity dinner with the following budgeted income and expenditure (all figures based on 20% rate of VAT):

Sales of tickets – 150 at £40 each = £6,000.

Sale of advertising space to local companies = £2,400.

Cost of meals – 150 meals at £10 + VAT for each meal.

Cost of celebrity speaker – £1,000 (he is not VAT registered).

Hire of venue for dinner – £300 (no VAT charge because room hire is exempt).

Is it worthwhile to treat the dinner as a fund-raising event that is exempt from VAT?

Solution – the only disadvantage of the event being exempt is that the charity will not be able to reclaim input tax on the cost of the meals supplied by the caterer. This loss of input tax is £300 (ie 150 × £2).

However, the output tax savings are considerable (£8,400 × 1/6 = £1,400) even though some of the companies paying for advertising space may be in a position to reclaim input tax.

Overall, there is a significant tax saving by ensuring the dinner is a qualifying fundraising event.

As a final point, certain fund-raising events are excluded from VAT exemption:

- exemption does not normally apply to any event where in a financial year a charity or qualifying body organises more than 15 fund-raising events of the same kind in the same location but the legislation at *VATA 1994, Sch 9, Group 12* provides that an event of that kind can be disregarded for the purpose of the 15-event limit if it is an event that took place at a location during a week in which the aggregate gross takings from fund-raising events of the same kind organised by the same charity or qualifying body at the same location did not exceed £1,000;

- events where accommodation is provided – either by the charity or qualifying body organising the event (or any charity connected with the organisers), unless the accommodation is for two nights or less (whether or not consecutive) and does not fall within the tour operators margin scheme;

- events that could distort competition, eg by placing a commercial enterprise at a disadvantage through the VAT savings being achieved;

(HMRC Notice 701/1, para 5.9).

Welfare services

[35.13] The supply by a charity of welfare services, and of goods supplied in connection with those services, is exempt from VAT.

The exemption extends to catering supplied as part of welfare services, for example, meals for residents of care homes; supplies of food and drink (but not alcohol) from trolleys, canteens and shops to patients in hospitals or inmates in prisons.

- *VATA 1994, Sch 9, Group 7, item 9* exempts the supply by a charity of welfare services – and Note 6(a) confirms that item 9 relates to 'the provision of care, treatment or instruction designed to promote the physical or mental welfare of elderly, sick, distressed or disabled persons'.

Definition of distressed

[35.14] According to HMRC Notice 701/1, para 5.18, a person is 'distressed' if they are suffering severe mental or emotional pain, anguish or financial straits. So the exemption could, for example, extend to advice given by a charity to certain local people facing extreme financial or personal difficulties. However, this is a 'grey' area of the law and it is suggested that the facts in areas of doubt are submitted in writing to HMRC's Charity section in Bootle for an official ruling.

Training courses

[35.15] A charity will sometimes organise training courses, consistent with its aims and objectives, and will charge a fee to those who attend the course. In such cases, the fees will be exempt from VAT as education (*VATA 1994, Sch 9, Group 6, Item 1(a)*) as long as any profits from the courses are reinvested into future courses. The exemption only applies to registered charities or companies limited by guarantee – it would not apply to a trading subsidiary that was a private limited company.

Charity income outside the scope of VAT

Donations

[35.16] The key point to remember is that a source of income will only qualify as a donation if the person making the donation does not receive any benefits in return for his donation. HMRC has confirmed that a public acknowledgement of the donation, for example, in an event programme, will not be classed as a benefit. It has also accepted that where the benefits received are disproportionate to the amount of the payment, then the payment can be treated as outside the scope of VAT. See Example 5.

Example 5

Good Causes Ltd has decided to sell Christmas Cards at £2 each (taxable activity). On the order form, it has a separate line inviting buyers to make an additional payment to support the charity as a donation.

Jill orders 15 Christmas cards and sends a cheque for £50 to the charity including a £20 donation.

Solution – Jill was only obliged to send £30 to the charity in order to buy her Christmas cards (ie 15 cards at £2 each). The additional payment of £20 has been made on a voluntary basis and she will receive no benefits in return for that money. The amount of £20 is clearly a donation that is outside the scope of VAT.

Note – if the literature circulated by Good Causes Ltd has specified that cards were available at £2 each plus a minimum donation of £10, then the £10 donation would not be outside the scope of VAT. This is because the payment is no longer optional for the donor.

Grant income

[35.17] Many charities benefit from the receipt of grant income, either from local or central government, national bodies such as the lottery fund, or other organisations that are keen to support worthwhile causes.

There are three key questions to consider when deciding if grant income is a taxable source of income or outside the scope of VAT as follows.

- Does the donor receive anything in return for the funding he has given (but remember that insignificant benefits are ignored as explained at **35.16**)?
- If the donor does not benefit, does a third party benefit instead? If so, is there a direct link between the money paid by the funder and the supply received by the third party? (See Example 6 to give a practical example of when grant funding would be taxable and **35.18** for a case that ruled a grant was standard-rated.)
- Are any conditions attached to the funding, which go beyond the requirement to account for the funds? (For example, some funders like to receive a report on the benefits generated by their funding – this is not classed as a benefit to the funder that would make the grant taxable.)

Note – it is possible that some grants could still avoid a VAT charge in certain cases if the goods or services being supplied qualify as being VAT exempt in the legislation rather than standard rated.

Example 6

As explained in earlier examples, Good Causes Ltd is a registered charity that provides mediation services to couples who are going through a divorce.

As well as the fees charged to couples receiving mediation, Good Causes Ltd also receives a quarterly grant from a national government body, the Mediation Services Commission. The amount of the grant depends on the number of mediation hours supplied by the company during a calendar quarter.

As a separate grant, Good Causes Ltd receives £2,000 per year from the Highgrove Bank Trust, which gives grant funding to charities whose aims include the support of children.

What is the VAT position regarding these two grants?

Solution – the grant from the Mediation Services Commission is taxable and subject to standard-rated VAT. This is because there is a direct link between the services provided by the charity (to a third party) and the amount of the grant.

However, the grant from Highgrove Bank Trust is a fixed amount of money provided to the charity, irrespective of the level of services it performs or work it carries out. The grant is therefore outside the scope of VAT.

Charity income within the scope of VAT

[35.18] The case that strengthened the argument of grants being taxable in many cases was *Bath Festivals Trust Ltd* (11 September 2008, unreported) (LON/06/511 20840). The Trust was responsible for organising the Bath International Music Festival, an event that was very important to the local councils in Bath and North Somerset as part of their overall business strategy. The VAT Tribunal confirmed that the Trust was providing a service in return for the grants it received, an important conclusion that clarifies some of the 'grey' areas on this subject.

In another case a charity, Woking Museum and Arts and Crafts Centre, provided a museum and visitor information service under the terms of a service agreement with Woking Borough Council. The charity charged VAT on the invoices it issued to the Council in relation to that supply. HMRC decided that the arrangements were such that the supply did not constitute a business supply by the charity and so fell outside of the scope of VAT. HMRC's decision, if correct, not only would have meant that the charity should not have charged VAT on the invoices but also would have meant that the charity should not have recovered VAT as input tax on the related expenses. The charity appealed and the tribunal allowed the appeal, deciding that the charity was making a taxable supply. (*Woking Museum and Arts and Crafts Centre* (TC03315) [2014] UKFTT 176 (TC).)

Charity income that is standard-rated

[35.19] As explained at **35.7**, all income is standard rated, unless it is specifically zero-rated, exempt, outside the scope of VAT or subject to VAT at the reduced rate.

Common sources of a charity's income that will usually be standard rated are as follows:

- admission to premises – unless the admission relates to a qualifying fundraising event (see **35.12**) or the income is covered by the special exemption for admission to museums, galleries, art exhibitions, zoos and theatrical, musical or choreographic performances;
- advertising in brochures, programmes or annual reports – again, there is an exception for advertising space sold at a qualifying fundraising event, in which case the income will be exempt;
- the resale of bought in goods which are standard rated.

VAT issues on charity expenses

[35.20] It is important that a charity identifies possible sources of expenditure that are either zero-rated or exempt from VAT (or subject to reduced-rate VAT) because most charities will not be in a position to reclaim all of their input tax. This is because some input tax will probably be relevant to either non-business activities or exempt supplies (or a combination of both).

In general terms, the following main categories of goods and services are specifically zero-rated if supplied to a charity – specific details (if appropriate) can be obtained by reference to relevant HMRC public notices (eg 701/7 – VAT reliefs for disabled people) or by contacting the VAT Helpline (0300 200 3700):

- talking books for the blind and disabled;
- wireless sets for the blind;
- aids for disabled persons;
- donation of goods for sale, export or letting by the charity;
- lifeboats;
- advertising;
- goods used by charities in connection with collecting monetary donations;
- medicinal products;
- substances for medical or veterinary research;
- major interests in land and buildings – see Chapter 27;
- construction services – see Chapter 26;
- some charity funded equipment for medical, veterinary uses etc;
- no VAT is payable on the importation of certain goods by or for charities and other philanthropic organisations.

Note – sometimes newspapers and other publications incorrectly charge VAT on advertisements for charities, which should be zero-rated. It is important that charities and their advisers are pro-active on this aspect of the legislation, taking steps to ensure the zero-rating is correctly applied. The zero-rating applies to all advertisements placed by a charity, including adverts in relation to staff recruitment and their business as well as non-business activities.

Revenue & Customs Brief 25/10 issued on 7 June 2010 has confirmed that zero-rating can also apply to pay-per-click (PPC) charity advertising on sponsored links and other associated services, ie including copyright and design services associated with such sponsored links. HMRC retain the view, however, that services supplied by copywriters and designers for the purpose of search engine optimisation (structuring a website so that it contains as many key words as possible) do not qualify for relief.

Note also that in addition to the above supplies, a charity will obviously be able to enjoy zero-rating on goods and services that are zero-rated for all businesses, eg the cost of using a printing firm to produce a charity's annual report will be zero-rated as printed matter under *VATA 1994, Sch 9, Group 3*.

In addition, supplies of fuel and power can be subject to the reduced rate in certain circumstances. These include use in a dwelling or a building used for a relevant residential purpose, eg a children's home. Also, the reduced rate applies to a charity otherwise than in the course or furtherance of a business.

Prior to 1 August 2013 the installation of certain energy-saving materials in a building used solely for a relevant charitable purpose was liable to VAT at the reduced rate. From 1 August 2013 the standard rate of VAT applies.

Group registration

[35.21] Example 7 illustrates a useful planning point about group registration.

Example 7

Good Causes Ltd is a registered charity and owns a trading subsidiary called Good Causes Trading Ltd. Neither company is registered for VAT because their main supplies are either outside the scope of VAT or exempt from VAT. However, Good Causes Ltd incurs costs on behalf of Good Causes Trading Ltd, and wants to make a management charge of £100,000 per annum for these services.

The problem with the above situation is that Good Causes Ltd will need to charge output tax on the management services once it has exceeded the VAT registration limit but Good Causes Trading Ltd will not be able to reclaim this VAT as input tax because it is not making any taxable supplies.

Solution – the two companies could register for VAT as a group registration, which means that supplies of goods and services between group members is ignored as far as VAT is concerned. The fact that the companies are not making any taxable supplies outside of the VAT group is not a problem – the management charges would be taxable (standard-rated) but for the group structure. The group arrangement will save the charity a lot of tax.

Note – there is no problem with forming a VAT group because the main charity controls the trading subsidiary, ie the common control test for group registration has been met.

Cost-sharing exemption

[35.22] The cost-sharing exemption, introduced by *Finance Act 2012*, should be of benefit to businesses and charities with exempt and/or non-business activities.

Organisations with exempt and/or non-business activities can form an independent group and, providing certain conditions are met, qualifying supplies of services from the group to its members benefit from the VAT cost-sharing exemption.

The five conditions relating to the cost-sharing exemption are:

(1)   There must be an independent group of persons ie a cost-sharing group supplying services to its members.

(2)   All members of the cost-sharing group must carry on an activity that is either exempt from VAT or is a non-business activity for VAT purposes.

(3)   The services supplied by the cost-sharing group must be directly necessary for the recipient members' exempt and/or non-business activity in order for the VAT exemption to apply.

(4)   For the VAT exemption to apply the services must be supplied on a cost basis ie the cost-sharing group must only recover from each member the cost it incurred in making supplies of services to that member.

(5)   The VAT exemption will only apply where its application is not likely to cause a distortion of completion.

With regard to point (5) above, the distortion of competition condition was considered by the European Court of Justice in a case (*Taksatorringen* C-8/01 [2006] STC 1842, ECJ) involving a Danish cost-sharing group formed by a number of insurance companies to provide them with claims handling services. The Court found that the VAT exemption can only be denied on the distortion of competition condition when it is the use of the exemption itself that gives rise to distortion of competition. It was held that a cost-sharing group cannot fail the distortion of competition condition simply because it is in a more advantageous competitive position because it complies with the requirement that it charges only an exact reimbursement of costs.

The background to the cost-sharing exemption is EU legislation at *Directive 2006/112/EC, art 132(1)(f)*.

HMRC issued guidance regarding the cost-sharing exemption in VAT Information Sheet 07/12.

Refunds of VAT to certain charities from 1 April 2015

[35.23] Certain charities can claim a refund of the VAT incurred on goods and services used for their non-business activities (but not for private purposes) in relation to purchases, acquisitions and importations taking place after 31 March 2015. Those charities are:

- palliative care charities;
- air ambulance charities;
- search and rescue charities; and
- medical courier charities.

A palliative care charity is a charity the main purpose of which is the provision of palliative care to persons who are in need of such care as a result of having a terminal illness, where the care is provided at the direction of, or under the supervision of, a registered medical practitioner or a registered nurse. A terminal illness is a progressive disease which will result in a person's death. Palliative care charities often operate adult and children's hospices.

An air ambulance charity is a charity the main purpose of which is to provide emergency air ambulance services in pursuance of arrangements made by, or at the request of, a National Health Service (NHS) body that delivers an NHS ambulance service. The following are NHS bodies for this purpose:

- an NHS foundation trust in England;
- an NHS trust in Wales;
- a Special Health Board constituted under s 2 of the *National Health Service (Scotland) Act 1978*;
- a Health and Social Care trust established under the *Health and Personal Social Services (Northern Ireland) Order 1991*.

A search and rescue charity is a charity that meets condition A or condition B below.

Condition A is that the main purpose of the charity is to carry out the activities of searching for and rescuing persons who are, or may be, at risk of death or serious injury in the UK or the UK marine area, where the activities are coordinated by at least one of the following relevant authorities:

- the Secretary of State;
- the Scottish Fire and Rescue Service;
- a police force within the meaning of the *Police Act 1996*;
- the Police Service of Scotland;
- the Police Service of Northern Ireland;
- the Police Service of Northern Ireland Reserve;
- the British Transport Police Force;
- the Civil Nuclear Constabulary;
- the Ministry of Defence Police;
- any other person or body specified by an order made by the Treasury for the purposes of *VATA 1994, s 33D(6)*.

Condition B is that the main purpose of the charity is to support, develop and promote the activities of a charity which meets condition A above.

A medical courier charity is a charity that meets condition A or condition B below.

Condition A is that the main purpose of the charity is to provide services for the transportation of items or substances intended for use for medical purposes, including in particular, blood, medicines and other medical supplies, and items relating to people who are undergoing medical treatment.

Condition B is that the main purpose of the charity is to support, develop and promote the activities of a charity which meets condition A above.

A charity whose main purpose is to support, develop and promote other search and rescue charities or medical courier charities will undertake at least one of the following activities:

- coordinate and provide support to such charities;
- support and help with the establishment of such charities;
- promote good practice for charitable search and rescue or medical courier activities – examples may include training, knowledge and information sharing;
- arrange supplies of goods and services to such charities which are required for charitable search and rescue or medical courier activities; and
- represent such charities regionally and/or nationally.

The main purpose of a charity is its primary function. This should be evident from documents such as the charity's memorandum and articles of association, constitution, trust deed or declaration of trust and its annual report.

If a charity makes no charge for providing a service the provision of the service is likely to be a non-business activity (see **35.3** for the distinction between business and non-business activities). A hospice charity that receives grant funding from the NHS, Clinical Commissioning Group and/or local authority to support its provision of palliative care can treat the funding as non-business income for VAT purposes. A hospice charity that receives funding under a standard NHS service level contract from the NHS, Clinical Commissioning Group and/or local authority to support its provision of palliative care can treat the funding as non-business income for VAT purposes providing there is no direct link between the palliative care provided and the funding received.

Charities that provide welfare services to individuals at significantly below cost may be able to treat the income as non-business for VAT purposes.

Charities that have a mixture of business and non-business activities need to apportion any VAT incurred on overhead costs relating to both activities.

A charity that qualifies for refunds of VAT on its non-business activities can, subject to HMRC approval, be included in a VAT group with its trading subsidiaries, but the facility to recover VAT incurred on non-business activities does not extend to the VAT group as a whole.

VAT on goods and services used by a qualifying charity for its non-business purposes can be recovered if the charity places the order, receives the supply and a VAT invoice addressed to it, and pays the invoice from its own funds, which can include funds awarded to it. VAT can only be recovered where the supply takes place after 31 March 2015. The method of claiming the VAT and the time limits for claiming it vary depending on whether the charity is registered for VAT or not.

A charity that is registered for VAT should claim the VAT refund in box 4 of its VAT return for the period the VAT was incurred, and include the net value of its claim in box 7. If a claim is not included on the VAT return for the relevant period the charity can submit a claim in writing to HMRC stating the amount it is claiming, the VAT period(s) covered and the basis of the calculation of the claim. The charity must hold evidence to support the claim. A four-year time limit applies to late claims, subject to the condition that only VAT incurred after 31 March 2015 can be recovered.

A charity that is not registered for VAT should claim the VAT refund by completing a Form VAT 126 and sending it to the following address:

HM Revenue and Customs
DMB Banking 2
7th Floor
Regian House
James Street
Liverpool
L75 1AD

Claims made using a Form VAT 126 should relate to a period of at least one calendar month, or at least 12 months if the claim is for less than £100. The period of the claim should end on the last day of a calendar month and should be made within four years of the end of the month the VAT was incurred, subject to the condition that only VAT incurred after 31 March 2015 can be recovered. Invoices and other records to support the claim should be retained for six years, unless HMRC has confirmed in writing that they can be kept for a shorter period.

Claims made using a Form VAT 126 will normally be refunded by HMRC using BACS or a payable order. After the first claim using a form VAT 126 HMRC should provide the claimant with a unique number to quote on future claims. This does not mean that HMRC has registered the claimant for VAT.

The facility to recover VAT incurred on non-business activities does not extend to non-deductible input tax, for example VAT on most motor cars (see Chapter 32).

From time to time HMRC will select claims for verification.

(*VATA 1994, ss 33C, 33D; Finance Act 2015, s 66*). (VAT Notice 1001).

Planning points to consider

[35.24] The following planning points should be given consideration.

- To take advantage of VAT reliefs applicable to charities, a body must now meet the conditions set out in *Finance Act 2010, Sch 6, Part 1*.
- In some cases, it may be worthwhile for a charity to register for VAT on a voluntary basis. This would be particularly useful if the charity has a high proportion of zero-rated sales, eg sales of donated goods.

- If a charity has to register for VAT on a compulsory basis, remember that it is only the value of taxable supplies that need to be taken into account as far as the registration limit is concerned. Exempt supplies and outside the scope income are excluded from the calculations.
- An important challenge as far as VAT is concerned is to ensure that input tax is only reclaimed by a charity that relates to its taxable supplies. Effective procedures need to be in place to ensure that input tax is not reclaimed on non-business expenditure or expenditure relating to exempt supplies. This includes an apportionment of input tax on general overheads where appropriate. From 1 April 2015 palliative care charities, air ambulance charities, search and rescue charities, and medical courier charities are excepted from the general rule that VAT cannot be reclaimed on non-business expenditure.
- A charity can use any method to apportion input tax between business and non-business activities on general overhead items as long as the method gives a fair and reasonable result. Remember that an income-based apportionment may not be the most suitable method if the expenditure in question is not directly linked to income.
- Be aware that many sources of income for a charity can be zero-rated or exempt from VAT. For example, income from a fundraising event will be exempt in most cases – although any input tax relevant to the event will not be reclaimable as it relates to an exempt supply.
- A donation can be treated as outside the scope of VAT as long as the donor does not receive any benefits for his payment. It is important to ensure that donations are freely given by the donor, for example, the request for a 'minimum donation of £x' in connection with the supply of goods or services would not be classed as a freely given donation.
- Do not assume that all grant income received by a charity is outside the scope of VAT. If grant income is linked to the performance of services by a charity, then it will be standard rated in many cases. This opinion was confirmed in the tribunal case *Bath Festivals Trust Ltd* (see **35.18**).
- There are a range of provisions in the VAT legislation that are relevant to charities as far as VAT on their expenditure is concerned. For example, a charity placing an advert in a local newspaper for a new member of staff should not pay VAT because the supply is zero-rated.
- Consider if the cost-sharing exemption introduced by *Finance Act 2012* would benefit charity clients.

Chapter 36

Bad Debt Relief

Key topics in this chapter:

- The conditions for claiming bad debt relief.
- How much bad debt relief can be claimed?
- The process for claiming bad debt relief.
- What happens if bad debt relief is claimed on a debt that is subsequently paid?
- When should bad debt relief not be claimed?
- What if you are the debtor?

Introduction

[36.1] A basic principle of VAT is that it is a tax that is borne by the ultimate consumer and should not be a cost for VAT-registered businesses in the supply chain. The reality is that complying with the VAT legislation is a cost for every VAT-registered business and some VAT-registered businesses cannot fully recover VAT (see Chapter 8 for businesses using the flat rate scheme and Chapters 24 and 25 for businesses making exempt supplies).

This chapter deals with the subject of VAT bad debt relief, a relief which is consistent with the basic principle referred to in the previous paragraph that VAT should not be a cost for VAT-registered businesses. See Example 1.

Example 1

John the accountant uses normal VAT accounting and issues invoices for tax compliance services to VAT-registered businesses and private individuals. As a general principle, the VAT on the invoices should not be a cost for the business clients (subject to any partial exemption issues) but will be a cost for the private individuals.

Example 2 illustrates why bad debt relief is necessary.

Example 2

John the accountant submits VAT returns on a calendar quarterly basis and pays the VAT due by direct debit. The VAT for the quarter to 30 June is paid by direct debit on 12 August. This should not be a cost for John if all of the invoices issued during the quarter to 30 June have been paid by 12 August. However, if an invoice has not been paid by then, the VAT due on that invoice will be a cost to John, at least until such time as the client pays the invoice in full or the conditions for claiming bad debt relief have been met.

Businesses using the cash accounting scheme obtain relief from VAT on bad debts automatically because they account for output tax on a payments received basis rather than on a tax point basis (see **6.3**). Other businesses have to claim relief from VAT on bad debts.

The conditions for claiming bad debt relief

[36.2] The seven conditions for claiming VAT bad debt relief are summarised in the table below:

Number	Condition
1	You must already have accounted for the VAT on the supplies and paid it to HMRC.
2	The debt must have remained unpaid for a period of six months after the later of the time payment was due and payable and the date of the supply.
3	You must have written off the debt in your day-to-day VAT accounts and transferred it to a separate bad debt account.
4	The debt must not have been paid, sold or factored under a valid legal assignment.
5	The value of the supply must not be more than the customary selling price.
6	The claim must be made within four years and six months of the later of the time payment was due and payable and the date of the supply. (In some circumstances, VAT bad debt relief can be claimed in relation to supplies made between 1 April 1989 and 30 April 1997.)
7	Appropriate records must be kept for a period of four years from the date of making the claim.

Each of the conditions are examined in turn.

Condition 1 – You must already have accounted for the VAT on the supplies and paid it to HMRC

A business cannot claim bad debt relief before the supply of goods or services referred to on the invoice has been made and the VAT due paid to HMRC. Not surprisingly, if a business is owed a significant amount of money from a customer, they may find it difficult to fund the VAT payments that are showing on VAT returns as due to HMRC.

Following the tribunal decision in *Times Right Marketing (In Liquidation)* LON/2006/1376, HMRC changed their policy on treatment of VAT bad debt relief claims made when the net VAT due on a VAT return has not been paid in full. The company appealed against a decision by HMRC to reject a claim for bad debt relief. HMRC's grounds for rejecting the claim were that the company had not paid the output tax due. The tribunal found that the deduction of input tax from output tax due should be seen as in effect payment of that output tax. The change in HMRC policy was announced in Revenue & Customs Brief 18/09.

Example 3

John the accountant submits his VAT return for the quarter to 31 March showing output tax of £100,000 and input tax of £30,000. Sadly, £90,000 of the output tax relates to an invoice for £450,000 issued to his main client in February who has since been declared bankrupt without paying John a penny. This has caused John severe cash-flow problems and the £70,000 (ie £100,000 – £30,000) payment showing on John's VAT return as due to HMRC remains unpaid at 30 September.

John can claim VAT bad debt relief of £20,000 on his VAT return for the quarter to 30 September because:

- The total input tax for the quarter to 31 March was £30,000. Of that amount, £10,000 is treated as payment of the £10,000 of output tax due on John's non-bad debt supplies.
- The other £20,000 is treated as part payment of the £90,000 of output tax due on John's bad debt supplies and can therefore be claimed as bad debt relief on the VAT return for the quarter to 30 September.

Condition 2 – The debt must have remained unpaid for a period of six months after the later of the time payment was due and payable and the date of the supply

It is important that invoices state when payment is due. This should help reduce the incidence of late payment and support claims for bad debt relief. The phrase 'the later of' in the above condition is important in relation to situations where invoices are issued in advance of a supply being made.

Condition 3 – You must have written off the debt in your day-to-day VAT accounts and transferred it to a separate bad debt account

Details of the information that should be included in a bad debt account are included at condition 7.

Condition 4 – The debt must not have been paid, sold or factored under a valid legal assignment

It is important to consider how much of the debt is outstanding at the time bad debt relief is claimed and only claim relief in relation to the unpaid proportion.

When using a factoring company to improve cash flow it is necessary to consider the terms of the contract. To quote from paragraph 3.12 of HMRC Notice 700/18:

'If debts are factored bad debt relief is not available where an assignment of the debt is absolute (that is where there is no provision for the reassignment of the debt in the contract).

Where there is provision for the reassignment of a debt, bad debt relief will be available once the debt is reassigned to the trader. No bad debt relief can be available during the period in which the debt remains assigned to the factor.

If you receive a payment from the factor for the unencumbered sale of a debt, this is considered to be for an exempt supply of finance and therefore will be disregarded for the purposes of bad debt relief.'

Condition 5 – The value of the supply must not be more than the customary selling price

Unless the supplier has deliberately charged an excessive amount this condition should not cause a problem except in rare cases where the customary selling price is difficult to establish. Examples of situations where the customary selling price may be difficult to establish include supplies of services that are not usually provided by the supplier or supplies of goods such as rare collector's items.

Condition 6 – The claim must be made within four years and six months of the later of the time payment was due and payable and the date of the supply

This is now the general rule and it is not usually a problem complying with it. After all, most businesses will want to claim bad debt relief as soon as possible. A caveat to the general rule is that in some situations bad debt relief can be claimed in relation to supplies made between 1 April 1989 and 30 April 1997.

Condition 7 – Appropriate records must be kept for a period of four years from the date of making the claim

The records that must be kept are detailed in the *VAT Regulations 1995, regs 167* and *168* and are summarised below:

- A copy of the relevant VAT invoice or similar document showing equivalent information.
- Evidence that the VAT due has been paid to HMRC.
- A bad debt account showing the:
    - (a) amount written off as bad debt;
    - (b) amount of VAT claimed as bad debt relief;
    - (c) VAT period in which the claim for bad debt relief is made;
    - (d) total amount of VAT charged on each supply;
    - (e) VAT period in which VAT was originally accounted for on the supply;
    - (f) details of any payments received for each supply;
    - (g) customer's name;
    - (h) date and number of the invoice to which the bad debt relates or sufficient information to allow the time and type of the supply to be readily identified.

HMRC have discretion to allow claims in circumstances where not all of the above record-keeping requirements are met.

How much VAT bad debt relief can be claimed?

[36.3] In many situations the amount of bad debt relief that can be claimed is relatively straightforward. See Example 4.

Example 4

John the accountant issued an invoice for £600 plus VAT of £120 to a personal tax client on 12 November. No payment whatsoever has been received and all of the conditions for claiming bad debt relief have been met. VAT bad debt relief of £120 can be claimed on the VAT return for the quarter to 30 June the following year in relation to this invoice.

More complex situations

[36.4] In other situations the amount of bad debt relief that can be claimed is not so straightforward. Example 3 at **36.2** above is an example of such a situation. Other examples of situations where the amount of bad debt relief that can be claimed may cause a problem are included in the following paragraphs.

Part payment of an invoice

[36.5] Sometimes a client will pay part of the amount that they are contractually obliged to pay. See Example 5.

Example 5

The personal tax client in Example 4 wrote to John enclosing a cheque for £600 as soon as they received the 12 November invoice. The letter from the client states 'I enclose my payment for the fee which we agreed but do not expect me to pay the VAT you have charged'.

Providing the terms of engagement made it clear that fees were exclusive of VAT the client does not have a valid point, although they may try to argue it anyway! In reality the client has made a part payment of the invoice. The VAT bad debt relief claim amounts to £20, which is the VAT element (20/120) of the unpaid amount of £120. The fact that the unpaid amount appears to be entirely VAT is irrelevant. The cheque for £600 is part payment of the total amount due of £720.

Mutual supplies

[36.6] Sometimes a client or customer will also be a supplier and each will owe the other money. In these situations a claim for VAT bad debt relief must assume that the amounts owing are netted off. See Example 6.

Example 6

On 4 April John the accountant issues an invoice for £1,000 plus VAT for corporation tax compliance services to an office supplies company.

On 10 May the office supplies company issues an invoice to John for £400 plus VAT for goods supplied to his firm.

Despite both of the above invoices stating that payment is due within 30 days of the invoice date, no payment has been made by either party by the time John is preparing his VAT return for the quarter to 31 December.

If John had paid the invoice from the office supplies company he could have claimed bad debt relief on the entire amount of the £200 VAT showing on the invoice he issued to that company on 4 April. However, as both invoices are outstanding John must assume that the amounts owing are netted off for the purpose of claiming bad debt relief.

The client owes John £1,200 including VAT and John owes the client £480 including VAT. The net amount owed to John is therefore £720 and John will be able to claim £120 as bad debt relief (£720 x 20/120).

In this example the office supplies company will not be able to claim bad debt relief in relation to the amount owed to it by John as it owes a greater debt to John.

Non-monetary consideration

[36.7] The legislation used to refer to goods or services supplied 'for a consideration in money'. However, following the case of *Goldsmiths (Jewellers) Limited: C-330/95* [1997] ECR I-3801, [1997] 3 CMLR 978, consideration can be non-monetary and the words 'for a consideration in money' have been repealed.

Non-monetary consideration can reduce or eliminate a debt for bad debt relief purposes.

Part payment of a number of invoices

[36.8] Sometimes a customer will have an account with a supplier and make payments to the supplier from time to time, despite the supplier making it clear when payment for each invoice is due. At any one time there may be several invoices outstanding and the supplier may wonder which invoice(s) the supplier intends to settle when he makes a payment.

For VAT bad debt relief purposes the general rule is that a payment should be allocated to older invoices first unless the customer makes it clear that the payment relates to a particular invoice and that invoice is paid in full.

Things can get complicated when the outstanding invoices relate to supplies with different rates of VAT or include invoices for exempt supplies. See Example 7.

Example 7

Harry is a tax adviser and an independent financial adviser who submits VAT returns on a calendar quarterly basis. Most of the invoices he issues to a very busy client are for taxable supplies but occasionally an invoice will relate to exempt supplies. The client is so busy that he only makes occasional payments to Harry. On 29 September the following invoices, issued to this client earlier in the year, remain outstanding:

Invoice date	Net £	VAT £	Gross £
4 January	500	100	600
4 February	1,000	exempt	1,000

4 March	750	150	900
4 April	2,000	400	2,400

The invoices clearly state that payment is due within 14 days of the invoice date.

On 30 September the client pays Harry £2,400.

Harry would like to allocate the payment to the invoice dated 4 April so that he can claim bad debt relief of £250 on his VAT return for the quarter to 30 September in relation to the VAT on the invoices dated 4 January and 4 March.

However, unless the client has made it clear to Harry that the payment of £2,400 relates to the invoice for that amount dated 4 April Harry must allocate the payment as follows:

Invoice date	Gross £	Paid £	Outstanding £
4 January	600	600	
4 February	1,000	1,000	
4 March	900	800	100
4 April	2,400		2,400

The invoice issued on 4 March was due for payment by 18 March and there is £100 outstanding over six months later on 30 September. Harry can claim bad debt relief of £16.66 when he prepares his VAT return for the quarter to 30 September in relation to the VAT element of the outstanding amount (£100 × 20/120).

The invoice issued on 4 April was due for payment by 18 April and bad debt relief cannot be claimed in relation to that invoice on the VAT return for the quarter to 30 September. As noted at 36.2, a condition for claiming bad debt relief is that the debt must have remained unpaid for a period of six months after the later of the time payment was due and payable and the date of the supply.

The outcome would have been different had the client made it clear to Harry that the payment of £2,400 relates to the invoice for that amount dated 4 April.

VAT only invoices

[36.9] A question that sometimes arises in late registration cases is whether the business should issue VAT-only invoices in an attempt to recover the VAT which they should have charged, in some cases several years previously. The alternative is for the business to treat the payments it has already received as including VAT and account for output tax accordingly.

The answer to the question will vary depending on the facts of each case but it will usually be appropriate to consider issuing VAT-only invoices in situations where the customers can recover VAT and there is a reasonable prospect that at least some of the invoices will be paid. The point to note is that the bad debt relief claim in relation to a VAT-only invoice is the VAT fraction of the invoice. See Example 8.

Example 8

HMRC visit an unregistered business and a review of the business records confirms that it needs to be registered for VAT, with an effective date of VAT registration covering supplies made during the previous two years. Its turnover for the previous two years was £1,200,000 and HMRC confirm that it can treat the £1,200,000 as including output tax of £200,000 or issue VAT-only invoices to its customers for a total amount of £240,000 (£1,200,000 x 20%).

If the business issues VAT-only invoices totalling £240,000 and all of the conditions for bad debt relief are eventually met the bad debt relief claim will amount to £40,000 (£240,000 x 20/120). The net effect, after eventually accounting for bad debt relief, is that £200,000 will have been accounted for to HMRC, the same amount that would have been due had the business treated its turnover of £1,200,000 as including output tax of £200,000.

There are other issues to consider, for example, the cash-flow implications of the initial output tax payment of £240,000 rather than £200,000 referred to in Example 8. However, providing there is a reasonable prospect that at least some VAT-only invoices will be paid, many businesses will consider issuing them.

It may seem unfair that the bad debt relief available on a VAT-only invoice is restricted to the VAT fraction of the invoice. However, a VAT-only invoice needs to be seen in the context of the total amount payable by the customer. If bad debt relief was available on the entire amount of VAT-only invoices there would be little incentive, apart from the cash-flow implications, for business to apply credit control procedures to VAT-only invoices.

Insurance claims

[36.10] When solicitors act for VAT-registered businesses in relation to insurance claims it is common practice for the insurance company to pay the net amount of the legal fees and the business to pay the VAT element of the fee, which in many cases the business will be able to recover.

Example 9

A firm of solicitors provide legal services in relation to insurance claims. When the insured person is registered for VAT the insurance company pays the net amount and the client is expected to pay the VAT. Sometimes clients do not pay the VAT. This point was considered in the case of *Simpson & Marwick* (TC00662) [2010] UKFTT 380 (TC), [2011] UKUT 498 (TCC), [2013] CSIH 29 XA45/12 and was concluded at the Court of Session in Scotland in 2013.

Simpson & Marwick are a firm of solicitors in Scotland who act in relation to insurance claims. If the insured person was registered for VAT the solicitors usually received payment of their fees, net of VAT, from the insurer and payment of the VAT element from the insured person. If the insured person did not ultimately pay, the solicitors claimed bad debt relief on the entire amount of the VAT not paid.

HMRC raised an assessment on the basis that entitlement to bad debt relief was limited to the VAT fraction of the unpaid VAT.

Simpson & Marwick appealed to the First Tier Tribunal, which agreed with HMRC that entitlement to bad debt relief was limited to the VAT fraction of the unpaid VAT.

Simpson & Marwick then appealed to the Upper Tribunal, which found in their favour ie that they were entitled to bad debt relief on the entire amount of the unpaid VAT.

HMRC then appealed to the Court of Session in Scotland, which found in their favour.

The Court of Session decision confirms that bad debt relief is restricted to the VAT fraction of an outstanding amount, even if the outstanding amount appears to be entirely VAT.

This is a similar outcome to that in Example 5 where a customer pays an invoice in part and to that in Example 8 where a VAT-only invoice is not paid.

The process for claiming bad debt relief

[36.11] The process for claiming VAT bad debt relief is to include the amount of the VAT claimed in Box 4 of the VAT return for the period in which the conditions for making the claim are first met or a later VAT return.

(HMRC Notice 700/18, para 2.4).

Most businesses will want to claim bad debt relief as soon as possible so it is important that credit control procedures include identifying debts which are at least six months overdue.

The general rule is that bad debt relief must be claimed within four years and six months of the later of the date payment was due and payable or the date of the supply. However, relief can be claimed in respect of supplies made between 1 April 1989 and 30 April 1997, subject to certain conditions being met.

(HMRC Notice 700/18, para 1.5).

What happens if bad debt relief is claimed on a debt that is subsequently paid?

[36.12] Sometimes a customer will eventually pay a debt for which VAT bad debt relief has previously paid. See Example 10.

Example 10

The client in Example 7 pays Harry £2,500 on 4 December without specifying how the payment should be allocated. Harry should allocate the payment to the amounts outstanding in relation to invoices dated 4 March and 4 April.

Invoice date	Outstanding £	Paid £
		4 December
4 March	100	100
4 April	2,400	2,400

VAT bad debt relief of £16.66 was claimed on the VAT return for the quarter to 30 September in relation to the invoice dated 4 March (£100 x 20/120). Harry will need to add £16.66 to the Box 1 figure on his VAT return for the quarter to 31 December.

(HMRC Notice 700/18, para 3.14).

If the client had paid Harry £50 instead of £2,500, Harry should only add £8.33 to the Box 1 figure on his VAT return for the quarter to 31 December (£50 x 20/120).

The outcome would be different if the client specified that the £2,500 payment was to be allocated to a later invoice issued for that amount, for example an invoice issued in August. In that case Harry would not need to add £16.66 to Box 1 of his VAT return for the quarter to 31 December and he would be able to claim bad debt relief of £400 in Box 4 of the VAT return in relation to the invoice issued on 4 April.

When should bad debt relief not be claimed?

[36.13] Bad debt relief should not be claimed in situations where there is a genuine mistake or an overcharge, or an agreed reduction in the value of the supply. In these situations the solution is to issue a credit note.

Example 11

The same scenario as Example 5 except that John's engagement letter made no reference to VAT and the client understood that the £600 fee that was agreed was the amount that he would be required to pay. The client has a valid point.

The solution for John is to issue a credit note and adjust his output tax position accordingly.

Example 12

A similar scenario to Example 5 except that it became apparent after the invoice was issued that some of the work to which it related had not been completed to the client's satisfaction. John agreed with the client that the value of the supply was £500 and not £600.

The solution for John is to issue a credit note and adjust his output tax position accordingly.

Can I issue a credit note instead of claiming VAT bad debt relief?

[36.14] The short answer is no. To quote an extract from HMRC Notice 700/18, para 5.6:

'You may not issue a credit note simply because your customer has not paid you for your supply. You may only issue a credit note where there is a genuine mistake or overcharge or an agreed reduction in the value of your supply.'

What if you are the debtor?

[36.15] At the beginning of this chapter it was noted that a basic principle of VAT is that it is a tax that is borne by the ultimate consumer and should not be a cost for VAT-registered businesses in the supply chain.

Providing every business in the supply chain is making fully taxable supplies, the output tax for a supplier will be input tax for their business customer.

A situation can arise where a business customer claims input tax on an invoice which they do not pay and for which the supplier claims VAT bad debt relief. If no further action was taken this would have the effect of transferring the VAT burden to HMRC. The customer would have claimed input tax for which there is no corresponding output tax as the output tax originally paid by the supplier would have been recovered via the claim for bad debt relief.

Not surprisingly, there are rules to prevent the kind of abuse referred to in the previous paragraph. The basic rule is that if a customer does not pay their supplier within six months of the later of the date the payment was due and the date the supply was made, they are required to repay the input tax previously claimed by making a deduction from the Box 4 figure of the VAT return for the period in which the six-month period ends.

(HMRC Notice 700/18, para 4.6).

Planning points to consider

[36.16] The following planning points should be given consideration.

- Ensure payment terms are clearly stated on invoices.
- Ensure credit control procedures include identifying debts which are at least six months overdue.
- Ensure appropriate paperwork and records are in place to support claims for bad debt relief.
- Consider the effect of bad debt relief on VAT-only invoices in late registration situations.
- If bad debts are a recurring problem the cash accounting scheme may be appropriate – see Chapter 6.
- Consider the bad debt relief rules explained in Chapter 8 for businesses using the flat rate scheme.

Chapter 37

Tour Operators' Margin Scheme (TOMS)

Key topics in this chapter:

- The mandatory nature of the TOMS and its application to all businesses that buy in and resell travel services to travellers.
- What are margin scheme supplies and margin scheme packages?
- What are in-house supplies?
- What is a traveller?
- The special place of supply and time of supply rules.
- Calculating the margin and the output tax due.

Introduction

[37.1] The Tour Operators' Margin Scheme (TOMS) has applied in the UK since 1 April 1988. The European legislative background is now at *Directive 2006/112/EC, arts 306–310*. The UK legislation is at *VATA 1994, s 53* and the *Value Added Tax (Tour Operators) Order 1987*.

The main HMRC guidance regarding the scheme is in Notice 709/5 (Tour Operators Margin Scheme), some of which has the force of law. The latest edition of Notice 709/5 is available on the GOV.UK website with a publication date of 22 February 2016.

The TOMS is a mandatory scheme and applies to businesses that act in their own name, either as a principal or as an undisclosed agent, buying in and reselling travel services to travellers.

Businesses that buy in and resell travel services to travellers

[37.2] TOMS applies when a business acts in its own name, buying in and reselling travel services to travellers. Chapter 34 deals with the general rules regarding supplies involving agents, including distinguishing between a principal and an agent and the difference between an undisclosed and a disclosed agent. In the context of the travel sector, a disclosed agent does not buy in and resell travel services, a disclosed agent simply sells travel services on behalf of third parties. As a result, a business that only acts as a disclosed agent is not within the TOMS.

It is of course possible for one business to be involved in different travel service transactions in different capacities. For example to act as:

- a principal in relation to some travel service transactions – within the TOMS;
- an undisclosed agent in relation to other travel service transactions – within the TOMS;
- a disclosed agent in relation to other transactions – outside of the TOMS.

Many businesses that are involved with the TOMS are not tour operators in the traditional sense. For example TOMS will apply to:

- a hotel operator that buys in coach transport for its customers;
- a coach operator that buys in hotel accommodation for its customers;
- a conference organiser that arranges hotel accommodation for delegates.

(HMRC Notice 709/5, para 2.2).

The European Court of Justice (ECJ) has confirmed that to make the application of the scheme depend upon whether a trader was formally classified as a travel agent or tour operator would create distortion of competition.

The following are examples of travel services:

- accommodation;
- passenger transport;
- hire of a means of transport;
- trips or excursions;
- services of tour guides;
- use of special lounges at airports.

Paragraph 2.8 of Notice 709/5, describes a traveller as a person, including a business or local authority, who receives a supply of a designated travel service, other than for the purpose of re-supply.

Margin scheme supplies and margin scheme packages

[37.3] The travel services listed at **37.2** (accommodation, passenger transport, hire of a means of transport etc) are always margin scheme supplies when bought in and resold to a traveller, either individually or as part of a package, without material alteration or further processing.

Supplies such as catering, admission tickets and sports facilities are also margin scheme supplies when bought in and resold to a traveller as part of a package with one or more of the travel services listed at **37.2** without material alteration or further processing.

A margin scheme package is a single transaction, which may include one or more margin scheme supplies, or may also include margin scheme supplies sold with in-house supplies or agency services.

For VAT purposes the sale of a margin scheme package is treated as a single supply of services. The nature of the service is that of putting together the package or organising the travel services.

(HMRC Notice 709/5, paras 2.9, 2.10, 2.11 and 4.5).

Example 1

> Fast Tours buys in hotel accommodation from an hotelier and hires a coach with a driver in order to sell a package holiday to its customers. Fast Tours is making a single supply of a package holiday rather than two separate supplies of accommodation and transport.

The agency scheme

[37.4] As noted at **37.2** it is possible for one business to be involved in different travel service transactions in different capacities. For example to act as:

- a principal in relation to some travel service transactions – within the TOMS;
- an undisclosed agent in relation to other travel service transactions – within the TOMS;
- a disclosed agent in relation to other transactions – outside of the TOMS.

A possible planning measure, referred to as 'the agency scheme' in HMRC Information Sheet 4/96, involves a tour operator acting as a disclosed agent in relation to supplies of passenger transport from third party transport providers. When the agency scheme is correctly implemented the supply of passenger transport is made to the traveller by the transport provider and is not within the TOMS. As a result, the transport element of the holiday and the tour operator's service of arranging the transport is free of UK VAT (being either zero-rated or outside the scope of UK VAT).

The following is an extract from HMRC Information Sheet 4/96:

> '**2 How does the Agency Scheme operate?**
>
> Under the agency scheme the tour operator enters into an agency arrangement acting as an agent of the transport provider.
>
> The tour operator acts as the agent of the transport provider by introducing the customer to the transport provider. As it is an agent, the tour operator is entitled to a commission from the transport provider for introducing the customer. No UK VAT will be chargeable on commission relating to the making of arrangements for the provision of passenger transport.'

A key point about the agency scheme is that the tour operator must be acting as a disclosed agent when arranging the passenger transport so that the supplies are outside of the TOMS.

In-house supplies

[37.5] Many businesses in the travel sector provide one or more of the travel services listed at **37.2** from in-house supplies. For example, a hotel business that provides accommodation in its own hotels or a coach company that provides passenger transport in its own coaches. An in-house supply can also be made from goods or services that have been bought in and materially altered or further processed so that what is supplied is different from what was bought in.

Example 2

> Fast Tours from Example 1 has expanded and decides that it makes sense to buy its own coach and employ its own driver. Transport in this coach is treated as an in-house supply.

When in-house supplies are supplied with one or more accompanying margin scheme supplies, VAT must be accounted for on the entire supply within the TOMS. However, if in-house supplies are supplied without any accompanying margin scheme supplies, the normal VAT rules apply and the supplies are not subject to the TOMS.

(HMRC Notice 709/5, para 2.13).

Example 3

> Fast Tours from Example 2 decides that it will use its own coach to provide passenger transport to customers who only want passenger transport. In this situation customers are buying a coach ticket for passenger transport rather than a package holiday and the supply is outside of the TOMS.

The Charter scheme (not available after 31 March 2015)

[37.6] As noted at **37.5** an in-house supply can be made from goods or services that have been bought in and materially altered or further processed so that what is supplied is different from what was bought in. A possible planning measure was available until 31 March 2015 and was referred to as 'the charter scheme' in HMRC Information Sheet 3/96. It involved a tour operator chartering a whole aircraft for an entire season and making separate arrangements for the in-flight catering. In a technical note published on 31 January 2014 HMRC stated that it would withdraw the concession that allowed the charter scheme on 1 April 2015.

Input tax

[37.7] Input tax cannot be reclaimed on the direct costs relating to margin scheme supplies.

Example 4

Speedy Tours owns its own coaches but buys in hotel accommodation from an hotelier so that it can sell a package holiday to customers. The package holiday consists of coach transport in Speedy Tours own coaches (an in-house supply) and hotel accommodation (a margin scheme supply). The direct cost relating to the margin scheme supplies is the cost of the hotel accommodation and no input VAT can be reclaimed on this cost.

The normal rules for claiming input VAT apply in relation to:

- indirect costs, for example, costs relating to advertising, office expenses and general overheads;
- the direct costs relating to in-house supplies.

(HMRC Notice 709/5, para 4.3).

Output tax

[37.8] Output tax is accounted for on the difference between the income from margin scheme supplies and the VAT-inclusive direct costs relating to margin scheme supplies. The margin is calculated at the end of the financial year of the business, rather than at the time each supply is made, with VAT accounted for on a provisional basis during the financial year.

According to HMRC guidance at paragraph 5.12 of Notice 709/5, the TOMS calculation should not be carried out on an individual transaction basis. Instead, HMRC require tour operators to carry out their TOMS calculation annually using global figures for the year as a whole. However, the European Court of Justice (ECJ) ruled in 2013 that the TOMS calculation should be carried out on an individual transaction basis. The ECJ decision, which is binding on the UK and all other EU member states, is referred to in Revenue & Customs Brief 5/14 published on 31 January 2014. Revenue & Customs Brief 5/14 indicates that there will be no immediate changes to the operation of TOMS in the UK but confirms that businesses can choose to operate the TOMS in accordance with the ECJ decision.

As illustrated by Examples 5, 6 and 7 below, the rate of VAT is dependent on where the margin scheme supplies are enjoyed. The UK standard rate applies when the margin scheme supplies are enjoyed within the EU and the UK zero rate applies when the margin scheme supplies are enjoyed anywhere else in the world.

Example 5

EU Hotels is based in the UK and focuses exclusively on buying in hotel accommodation throughout the EU and reselling the accommodation to UK holidaymakers. It has a 31 December year end has income for the year of £1,000,000. The VAT-inclusive cost of the hotel accommodation for the year is £400,000.

In this example the margin on which output tax is accounted for is £600,000 (£1,000,000 – £400,000) and the output tax due is £100,000 (£600,000 x 20/120). VAT is accounted for at the UK standard rate as the accommodation is enjoyed within the EU.

Example 6

UK Hotels is based in the UK and focuses exclusively on buying in hotel accommodation in the UK and reselling the accommodation to UK holidaymakers. It has a 31 December year end and has income for the year of £1,000,000. The VAT inclusive cost of the hotel accommodation for the year is £400,000.

In this example the margin on which output tax is accounted for is £600,000 (£1,000,000 – £400,000) and the output tax due is £100,000 (£600,000 x 20/120). VAT is accounted for at the UK standard rate as the accommodation is enjoyed within the EU.

Example 7

Asia Hotels is based in the UK and focuses exclusively on buying in hotel accommodation in Asia and reselling the accommodation to UK holidaymakers. It has a 31 December year end and has income for the year of £1,000,000. The VAT-inclusive cost of the hotel accommodation for the year is £400,000.

In this example the margin on which output tax is accounted for is £600,000 (£1,000,000 – £400,000) and the output tax due is £0. VAT is accounted for at the UK zero-rate as the accommodation is enjoyed outside of the EU.

The transport company scheme

[37.9] There is uncertainty regarding the effectiveness of the transport company scheme because it is dependent on wholesale supplies not being covered by the TOMS. According to HMRC guidance at paragraph 3.2 of Notice 709/5, supplies made to business customers for subsequent resale by them (wholesale supplies) are not covered by the TOMS. However, the European Court of Justice (ECJ) ruled in 2013 that wholesale supplies should be covered by the TOMS. The ECJ decision, which is binding on the UK and all other EU member states, is referred to in Revenue & Customs Brief 5/14 published on 31 January 2014. Revenue & Customs Brief 5/14 indicates that there will be no immediate changes to the operation of TOMS in the UK but confirms that businesses can choose to operate the TOMS in accordance with the ECJ decision and include wholesale supplies within the TOMS.

Notice 709/5 draws a distinction between those supplies that are treated as wholesale supplies – where supplies are made for onward supply to travellers (outside of the TOMS scheme) and supplies to businesses for their own consumption (see Notice 709/5, paras 3.2 and 3.3).

Examples 5, 6 and 7 above referred to businesses that bought in and resold hotel accommodation to travellers. Many tour operators also buy in and resell transport to travellers. A possible planning measure, referred to as 'the transport company scheme' in HMRC Information Sheet 1/97, involves the tour operator setting up a transport company. The transport company buys passenger transport from a third party transport provider and sells it to the tour operator at a profit. The profit on the passenger transport is made on the supply by the transport company to the tour operator rather than on the supply by the tour operator to travellers.

The supply from the transport company to the tour operator is not a margin scheme supply as the transport company is not selling the supply to a traveller. The margin on which the tour operator accounts for output tax is then the margin on the other supplies that make up the package, for example accommodation and catering. The following is an extract from HMRC Information Sheet 1/97:

'2 How does the transport company scheme operate?

The transport provider will sell the seats to the transport company at the price at which the seat would normally be sold to the tour operator. The transport company will then sell the seat to the tour operator at an inflated mark-up which will remove from the tour operator's TOMS calculation the margin on the transport element of the package. The tour operator will then sell the package on to the customer and account for VAT at the standard rate on the complete margin. It should be noted that the margin remaining in the tour operator's TOMS calculation is in effect the margin on accommodation, catering etc, the margin on the transport being retained by the transport company. The provision of transport by the transport company will be zero-rated, or outside the scope of UK VAT depending upon the circumstances.'

The above sentence 'The provision of transport by the transport company will be zero-rated, or outside the scope of UK VAT depending upon the circumstances' is dependent on excluding wholesale supplies from the TOMS. However, as noted above, the ECJ ruled in 2013 that wholesale supplies should be covered by the TOMS.

Business customers who are travellers

[37.10] The transport company scheme referred to at **37.9** involves passenger transport being bought and sold by a transport company. Currently because the transport company is not selling the transport to a traveller the normal VAT accounting rules apply. However, see **37.9** regarding a possibility that the TOMS, rather than the normal VAT accounting rules, may apply to such supplies in the future.

The TOMS only applies to supplies to travellers. To quote from the *Value Added Tax (Tour Operators) Order 1987, art 2*: 'This Order shall apply to any supply of goods or services by a tour operator where the supply is for the benefit of travellers.'

The term 'tour operator' can apply to businesses that may not regard themselves as tour operators and the term 'travellers' can apply to businesses and local authorities as well as private individuals. In essence a traveller is any person who receives a supply of a designated travel service, other than for the purpose of re-supply.

A feature of the TOMS is that VAT invoices cannot be issued for TOMS supplies. This is because the amount of output tax charge on a supply will not usually be known at the time the supply is made. VAT can only be determined following the end of the tour operator's financial year, when the end of year TOMS calculation has been performed (see **37.15**).

When a TOMS supply is sold to a business for use in the business (for example, travel supplies used by its employees) the invoice has to include a reference to indicate that the TOMS has been applied. HMRC have suggested that the reference refers to the relevant EC Directive or the relevant UK legislation and have confirmed that examples of acceptable indications include the following:

- This is a Tour Operators' Margin Scheme supply.
- This supply falls under the *Value Added Tax (Tour Operators) Order 1987*.

(HMRC Notice 709/5, para 4.20).

Before 1 January 2010 the UK legislation provided for businesses making supplies of travel services to opt out of TOMS where the supplies were made to business customers for their own consumption, thus allowing the business customers to recover VAT on these supplies (subject to the normal rules for recovering input tax). However, with effect from 1 January 2010, a number of changes were introduced to the TOMS to comply with EU law. The changes included the withdrawal of the business to business opt out which allowed business customers to recover VAT. On 21 May 2010 HMRC issued Revenue & Customs Brief 21/10 which is relevant in situations where business customers book hotel accommodation via a booking agent.

Revenue & Customs Brief 21/10

[37.11] On 21 May 2010 HMRC issued Revenue & Customs Brief 21/10 setting out details of an agreement with representative bodies of the business travel sector about invoicing business customers for supplies under an arrangement known as 'hotel bill-back'. Under the 'hotel bill-back' arrangement, a hotel booking agent books hotel accommodation on behalf of its business client. The arrangements detailed below apply where hotel booking agents act in a disclosed capacity so that the hotels supply accommodation direct to the business clients (the travellers).

The agreed arrangements are:

- Invoices from hotels will be addressed c/o the hotel booking agent for payment. (This is to indicate that the invoice has been issued to the hotel booking agent in its capacity as an agent.)
- The booking field on the hotel invoice will identify the hotel guest, their employer and will ideally carry a unique reference number. (Until hotels can address their invoices directly to their business customers, it may be necessary for hotel booking agents to enter an employer identification number on the invoice.)
- The hotel booking agent will arrange for payment of the invoice(s) but will not recover the input tax thereon.
- The hotel booking agent will send the customer a payment request/ statement of the expenditure incurred by the hotel booking agent on its behalf, separately identifying the value of its supplies, VAT, etc.
- The payment request/statement should say something along the lines of 'The VAT shown is your input tax which can be reclaimed subject to the normal rules'.
- The customer will use the payment request/statement as a basis for their input tax reclaim.
- The hotel booking agent will retain the original hotel invoices and these will be made available if evidence of entitlement is required by VAT staff.
- The hotel booking agent will send a VAT invoice for its own services, plus the VAT. This may be consolidated with the statement of hotel charges, or it can be a separate document.
- The hotel booking agent will charge its client the exact amount charged by the bill-back supplier, as a disbursement.

The arrangements referred to in Revenue & Customs Brief 21/10 demonstrate the importance of the distinction between a disclosed agent and an undisclosed agent in the travel sector.

Place of supply for margin scheme supplies

[37.12] Examples 5, 6 and 7 at **37.8** above illustrate that the rate of VAT on margin scheme supplies is dependent on where the margin scheme supplies are enjoyed – standard-rated when enjoyed within the EU (including the UK) and zero-rated when enjoyed anywhere else in the world. Another point to note is that the place of supply of margin scheme supplies sold to a traveller in the UK is the UK regardless of where in the world the travel services are enjoyed.

In essence, the place of supply of a margin scheme supply is dependent on where the establishment selling the supply is situated. The table below summarises the place of supply rules for margin scheme supplies.

PLACE OF SUPPLY FOR MARGIN SCHEME SUPPLIES

Business established	Place of supply
In the UK only	The UK
In the UK and other countries but supply sold from an establishment in the UK	The UK

Business established	Place of supply
In the UK and other countries but supply sold from an establishment in another EU country	Outside of the UK (outside of the scope of UK VAT but within the scope of VAT in the EU country where the supply was sold)
In the UK and other countries but supply sold from an establishment outside of the EU	Outside of the EU (TOMS does not apply)

The place of supply and a tour operator's purchases

[37.13] The table above summarises the place of supply rules in relation to a tour operator's sales to travellers. The normal place of supply rules apply to the tour operator's purchases from suppliers. In Examples 5, 6 and 7 the hoteliers' supply of hotel accommodation to the tour operators is subject to VAT based on where each of the hotels was located. This is because hotel accommodation is a service relating to land.

Example 8

> Michael, an Italian hotelier sells hotel accommodation to EU Hotels in Example 5 and charges Italian VAT. (The author understands that at the time of writing Italian VAT on hotel accommodation is applied at the reduced rate of 10%.)
>
> Under the TOMS Italy keeps the Italian VAT charged by Michael on the Italian hotel accommodation and EU Hotels pays HMRC the UK VAT accounted for on the margin.

UK Hotels in Example 6 may not regard the TOMS as a simplification measure as it focuses exclusively on buying in hotel accommodation in the UK and reselling the accommodation to UK holidaymakers. Its income for the year is £1,000,000 and the VAT-inclusive cost of the hotel accommodation for the year is £400,000. If the TOMS did not exist the VAT position in relation to these figures would be:

Output VAT on income (£1,000,000 x 20/120)	£166,667
Input VAT on direct costs (£400,000 x 20/120)	£66,667
Net VAT position	£100,000

The net VAT position of £100,000 calculated above by pretending that the TOMS does not exist is the same as the output VAT due of £100,000 calculated at Example 6 on the basis that the TOMS does exist. As TOMS is a mandatory scheme, UK Hotels in Example 6 must apply it, even if it would prefer not to.

As a final point in this section, HMRC had previously, by extra-statutory concession, allowed cruise operators to use a fixed 10% margin to determine the VAT due on sales of bought in shore excursions to cruise passengers. In a Technical Note issued on 31 January 2014 HMRC announced that from 1 April 2015 the extra-statutory concession would be withdrawn and the VAT due would need to be determined in accordance with the normal TOMS rules.

Time of supply

[37.14] The usual time of supply rules do not apply to margin scheme supplies and in-house supplies sold within a margin scheme package. Instead, each business has to choose one of two methods to determine the time of supply. When a method has been chosen it must be applied consistently, unless HMRC grant written permission to change methods.

The two methods are as follows:

Method one

The tax point is the earlier of the date of the traveller's departure or the first date they occupy accommodation.

Method two

The tax point is the earlier of the tax point using method one or the date by which more than 20% of the total cost of the package has been paid. When more than 20% of the total cost has been paid, further payments will create further tax points regardless of the amount of the individual payments.

(HMRC Notice 709/5, paras 4.14 and 4.15).

Example 9 illustrates how both methods operate. A point to note is that method two will often result in an earlier, but never a later, tax point than method one.

Example 9

On 1 February Tom and Jessie each book a similar one week foreign package holiday involving a morning departure flight from Manchester on 1 August.

Tom drives to the airport on the morning of the flight. Jessie lives further away and books overnight hotel accommodation near the airport for the night of 31 July as part of the package. Tom's holiday package costs £950 and Jessie's costs £1,100.

Tom and Jessie are each required to pay a £200 deposit on 1 February, a further £50 on 1 July, and the balance by the end of August.

Method one

If the tour operator is using method one the tax point for Tom's holiday will be the date of the departure flight and the tax point for Jessie's holiday will be the previous day, that is, the date that Jessie first occupies accommodation.

Method two

If the tour operator is using method two the tax points for the holidays are as follows:

Event	Tom's holiday	Jessie's holiday
1 February – £200 deposit	Tax point	–

Event	Tom's holiday	Jessie's holiday
1 July – further £50 paid	Tax point	Tax point
31 July – first date Jessie occupies accommodation	–	Final tax point
1 August – date of departure	Final tax point	–

End of year TOMS calculation

[37.15] An end of year TOMS calculation is carried out immediately after the end of a tour operator's financial year. VAT is accounted for on a provisional basis during the financial year based on the calculations for the previous financial year. The detailed calculations set out in HMRC Notice 709/5, sections 8–12 are included in Appendix 37A of this chapter.

The year-end calculation is designed to:

- work out the total margin achieved;
- apportion the total margin between different types of supplies (margin scheme supplies, in-house supplies, agency supplies);
- apportion the total margin between supplies with different VAT liabilities (standard-rated, zero-rated, outside the scope, exempt);
- work out the output tax due on margin scheme supplies and packages;
- work out net values for supplies with different VAT liabilities.

(HMRC Notice 709/5, para 5.1).

For businesses that have just registered for VAT, or have only just started to make margin scheme supplies, it is necessary to work out a provisional percentage to use during the first relevant financial year. This may be based on:

- previous trading figures, or
- projected costings and margins, or
- actual monthly/quarterly figures during the first year (but not for subsequent years).

Whatever method is used, the first year-end calculation and appropriate adjustment should correct any under or over payment of VAT during the first year.

(HMRC Notice 709/5, para 5.13).

If a business makes a mixture of in-house supplies and bought in margin scheme supplies they must all be accounted for using the TOMS. However, the in-house supplies need to be quantified so that they can be accounted for under the normal rules. There are two different TOMS methods, the market value calculation and the cost-based calculation.

The market value calculation works on the basis of extracting from a package a selling value for the bought in designated travel services. This is done by deducting the market value of the in-house supplies from the full package price, leaving the selling value of the bought-in designated travel services on which a margin is then calculated. The market value method should be used where a business can establish a market value for a package. However, the cost-based method can be used if the same percentage mark-up is achieved on all components of the package.

A business should not change between the market value calculation and the cost-based calculation simply because one method results in less VAT being due for a package than the other method.

The simplified end of year calculation at section 11 of HMRC Notice 709/5 (see Appendix 37A) must be used if all of the margin scheme packages are liable to VAT at the standard rate.

(HMRC Notice 709/5, paras 2.13, 5.2, 5.3, 5.4 and 5.5).

Because VAT is accounted for on a provisional basis during the financial year an annual adjustment is necessary to correct any under or over payment of VAT for the year. Example 10 illustrates this point.

Example 10

World Tours has a 30 June financial year end and has calendar quarter VAT periods. It does not make any in-house supplies so no market value calculations involved.

During the year to 30 June 2014 it has provisionally accounted for output VAT of £19,000.

The actual results for the year to 30 June 2014 are as noted below, all figures being inclusive of VAT.

	£	£
Sales of holidays		1,000,000
Cost of bought in EU holidays	500,000	
Cost of bought in non-EU holidays	300,000	(800,000)
Total margin		200,000

VAT is due on the proportion of the margin that relates to EU holidays at the standard rate and on the proportion of the margin that relates to non-EU holidays at the zero rate.

The proportion of the margin that relates to EU holidays is £125,000 (£200,000 x £500,000/£800,000).

The actual output VAT due is £20,833 (£125,000 x 20/120).

The business has provisionally accounted for output VAT of £19,000.

The annual adjustment for the year to 30 June 2014 is £1,833 (£20,833 – £19,000).

The annual adjustment of £1,833 for the year to 30 June 2014 is included on the VAT return for the quarter to 30 September 2014.

The provisional percentage for the year to 30 June 2015 is 12.5% (£125,000/ £1,000,000 x 100).

If World Tours in Example 10 owned a hotel in the UK which it used to make in-house supplies with a market value of £60,000 this would be deducted from the £1,000,000 sales figure before working through the calculation. The total margin would then be £140,000 instead of £200,000. However, output VAT of £10,000 would be due on the in-house supplies (£60,000 x 20/120).

TOMS supplies forming only an incidental part of the business

[37.16] HMRC have confirmed in Notice 709/5, para 3.6 that a business does not need to use the TOMS if it:

• does not buy in any supplies of accommodation or passenger transport for resale, and;
• buys in for resale other supplies which are normally margin scheme supplies, but;
• does not expect the total gross turnover from these other supplies to exceed 1% of total gross turnover.

The following examples are provided in Notice 709/5, para 3.6:

I am a hotelier who buys in ...	My supplies...
occasional car hire for guests, the income is less than 1% of my gross annual turnover.	can be outside the TOMS.
occasional taxi trips for my guests, the income is less than 1% of my gross annual turnover.	are within the TOMS. Although the turnover from these supplies is less than 1%, the re-supply of taxi trips is considered to be passenger transport.
the services of guides for my guests, the gross income from this is 1% of my gross turnover. I also buy-in car hire, the income from this is also 1% of my gross annual turnover.	are within the TOMS. Although both types of supply are eligible for exclusion, the total income from both is greater than 1% of the total business turnover.

The TOMS and other VAT accounting schemes

[37.17] Because of the special tax point rules that apply to the TOMS (see **37.14**) a business cannot use the cash accounting scheme for any supplies falling within the TOMS.

The TOMS can be used with the annual accounting scheme, providing the business meets the eligibility criteria for the annual accounting scheme explained in **7.2**.

If a business is using the annual accounting scheme it should include the figures from the annual TOMS calculation on the VAT return for the year in which the supplies were made – see Example 11.

Example 11

Fast Tours from Example 1 uses the annual accounting scheme. The business has an annual accounting VAT return and financial year covering the 12-month period to 30 September 2014.

Immediately after 30 September 2014 the annual TOMS calculation should be dealt with so that the figures can be included on the VAT return for the 12-month period to 30 September 2014.

TOMS supplies are specifically excluded from the flat-rate scheme.

(HMRC Notice 709/5, paras 4.16, 4.17 and 4.18).

Planning points to consider

[37.18] The following planning points should be given consideration.

- Consider the mandatory nature of the TOMS and the fact that the scheme can apply to businesses who may not regard themselves as tour operators.
- Consider the agency scheme referred to in HMRC Information Sheet 4/96.
- Be aware that, following an ECJ decision in 2013, there is a possibility that the transport company scheme referred to in HMRC Information Sheet 1/97 may be withdrawn at some point.
- Consider the impact of Revenue & Customs Brief 21/10 in situations where business customers book hotel accommodation via a booking agent.
- Consider the special tax point rules and the fact that method two will often result in an earlier, but never a later, tax point than method one.
- Consider if the annual accounting scheme (see Chapter 7) would be appropriate for businesses making TOMS supplies that meet the eligibility criteria explained at **7.2**.

Appendix 37A – HMRC Notice 709/5 (February 2016) sections 8–12

8 Market value calculation (annual adjustment)

This section has the force of law and is referred to in paras 2.6, 2.13, 2.14, 5.2, 5.5 and 7.5.

Only use this section if you have packages or parts of packages being apportioned by the market value of the in-house element of the package. On completion of all the steps M1–M5 you must then follow the steps in the cost-based calculation in section 9, taking forward the figures from this section as instructed.

Step	
	Boxes requiring 'raw data' entry are in white, boxes which 'process' that data are in grey.
	Calculate the value of sales of margin scheme packages
M1	Total the VAT-inclusive selling prices of your designated travel services and margin scheme packages supplied during the financial year including any that are not 'market value' packages.
	Working out the market value
M2	Total the VAT-inclusive purchase prices of the standard-rated designated travel services included in the total at M1: **carry forward this figure to step 21 of section 9.**
M3	Total the VAT inclusive market value of the zero-rated and outside the scope in-house travel services at M1: **carry forward this figure to step 26 of section 9.**
M4	Total the VAT-exclusive direct costs to you of the standard-rated in-house supplies at step M2 + step M3.
	Working out selling value of designated travel services and non-market value in-house supplies
M5	Deduct the total at step M4 from the total at step M1: **carry forward this figure to step 1 of section 9.**

9 Cost-based calculation (annual adjustment)

This section has the force of law and is referred to in paragraphs 2.6, 5.2, 5.10, 6.1, 6.4, 6.8, 6.9, 7.5, 7.7 and 7.8.

This section applies to packages being apportioned by reference to the costs of the in-house element of the package, and imports the figures calculated by the market value method in section 8, where that method is used for all or some of the travel packages. Do not include values already entered in section 8 unless explicitly instructed.

Step	
	Working out the total sales of margin scheme packages
1	Bring forward the total calculated at step M5 of section 8. If section 8 is not used then enter the VAT-inclusive selling prices of your designated travel services and margin scheme packages supplied during the financial year.
	Working out the purchase prices of margin scheme supplies
2	Total the VAT-inclusive purchase prices of the standard-rated designated travel services included in the total at step 1.
3	Total the VAT-inclusive purchase prices of the non standard-rated designated travel services (supplies enjoyed outside the EC) included in the total at step 1.

	Working out the direct costs of in-house supplies. Steps 4 to 7 can be ignored where a market value is applied to all in-house supplies under section 8
4	Total the VAT-exclusive direct costs to you of the standard-rated in-house supplies included in step 1. Add a percentage of that amount equivalent to the standard rate of VAT.
5	Total the VAT-exclusive direct costs to you of the zero-rated in-house supplies included in step 1.
6	Total the VAT-inclusive direct costs to you of the exempt in-house supplies included in step 1. Deduct any input tax that you are entitled to recover on these costs.
7	Total the direct costs to you of the in-house supplies included in step 1 that are supplied outside the UK, exclusive of any VAT incurred on these costs that you are entitled to recover. Add to the total an uplift equivalent to the percentage VAT rate applicable to such supplies if you have accounted for VAT on these supplies to the VAT authorities in another member state.

Working out the "costs" of agency supplies

| 8 | Total the VAT-inclusive amounts paid by you to your principals in respect of the agency supplies included in step 1 for which the consideration you receive is standard-rated. |
| 9 | Total the VAT-inclusive amounts paid by you to your principals in respect of the agency supplies included in step 1 for which the consideration you receive is not standard-rated. |

Working out the total margin

| 10 | Add the totals of costs at steps 2 to 9 inclusive. |
| 11 | Calculate the total margin for all the supplies included in step 1 by deducting the total at step 10 from the total at step 1. |

Apportioning the margin

12	Calculate the margin for the standard-rated designated travel services by applying the following formula: total at step 2 ÷ by total at step 10 × total at step 11
13	Calculate the margin for the zero-rated designated travel services by applying the following formula: total at step 3 ÷ by total at step 10 × total at step 11
	Steps 14 to 17 can be ignored where a market value is applied to all in-house supplies under section 8
14	Calculate the margin for the standard-rated in-house supplies by applying the following formula: total at step 4 ÷ by total at step 10 × total at step 11
15	Calculate the margin for the zero-rated in-house supplies by applying the following formula: total at step 5 ÷ by total at step 10 × total at step 11
16	Calculate the margin for the exempt in-house supplies by applying the following formula: total at step 6 ÷ by total at step 10 × total at step 11
17	Calculate the margin for the supplies made outside the UK by applying the following formula: total at step 7 ÷ by total at step 10 × total at step 11
18	Calculate the consideration for the standard-rated agency supplies by applying the following formula: total at step 8 ÷ by total at step 10 × total at step 11
19	Calculate the consideration for the non-standard-rated agency supplies by applying the following formula: total at step 9 ÷ by total at step 10 × total at step 11

Working out your output tax

20	Calculate the output VAT due on the designated travel services by applying the following formula:
	total at step 12 × the VAT fraction
21	Calculate the output VAT due on the standard-rated in-house supplies by applying the following formula:
	total at step 4 + total at step 14 + total calculated at step M2 of section 8 × the VAT fraction.
22	Calculate the output VAT due on the standard-rated agency supplies by applying the following formula:
	total at step 18 × the VAT fraction

Working out sales values

23	Calculate the VAT-exclusive value of the standard-rated designated travel services by deducting the total at step 20 from the total at step 12.
24	Note the value of the zero-rated designated travel services at step 13.
25	Calculate the VAT-exclusive value of your standard-rated in-house supplies by applying the following formula:
	total at step 4 + total at step 14 + total calculated at step M2 of section 8 – total at step 21
26	Calculate the value of the zero-rated supplies made within the scheme by applying the following formula:
	total at step 5 + total at step 15 + total calculated at step M3 of section 8
27	Calculate the value of your exempt in-house supplies made by applying the following formula:
	total at step 6 + total at step 16
28	Calculate the value of your in-house supplies which are supplied outside the UK by applying the following formula:
	total at step 7 + total at step 17
29	Calculate the total VAT exclusive value of the supplies:
	total of steps 23 to 28. Include this total in box 6 of your VAT return.

Working out the annual adjustment

30	Calculate the total output VAT due on your designated travel services and margin scheme packages by adding the totals at steps 20 to 22 inclusive.
31	Total the provisional output VAT which has been accounted for during the financial year on the supplies included in the total at step 1.
32	Deduct the total at step 31 from the total at step 30. Include the resulting total in box 1 of your VAT return, either as a payable amount where the amount is positive or as a deductible amount where the amount is negative.

10 Accounting for VAT on the provisional value of designated travel services and margin scheme packages

This section has the force of law and is referred to in paragraphs 1.2, 2.6, 5.10, 6.4, 6.9, 7.5 and 7.7.

Step	**Working out the provisional percentage**
1	Calculate the VAT-inclusive amount of your standard-rated supplies of designated travel services and margin scheme packages for the preceding financial year by adding the totals from steps 4, 12, 14 and 18 of section 9, together with the total M2 in the market value calculation in section 8.
2	Calculate the VAT-inclusive standard-rated percentage of the total selling price of all your designated travel services and margin scheme packages for the preceding tax year by applying the following formulae:
	If you have used a market value to value in-house supplies
	total at step 1 of section 10 ÷ total at step M1 of section 8 ×100

Step	Working out the provisional percentage
	If you have not used a market value to value in-house supplies
	total at step 1 of section 10 ÷ total at step 1 of section 9 x 100
	Working out the VAT return figures
3	Total the VAT-inclusive selling prices of the designated travel services and margin scheme packages supplied during the prescribed accounting period.
4	Calculate the provisional VAT-inclusive amount of your standard-rated supplies of designated travel services and margin scheme packages made during the prescribed accounting period by applying the following formula:
	total at step 3 × percentage at step 2
5	Calculate the provisional amount of output VAT due for the prescribed accounting period by applying the following formula:
	total at step 4 × the VAT fraction

11 Simplified end-of-year calculation (annual adjustment)

This section has the force of law and is referred to in paragraphs 1.2, 2.6, 5.4, 5.10, 6.1, 6.4, 6.8, 6.9, 7.5, 7.7 and 7.8.

Step	
1	Total the VAT-inclusive selling prices of your designated travel services and margin scheme packages supplied during the financial year.
2	Total the VAT-inclusive purchase prices of the designated travel services included in the total at step 1.
3	Calculate the VAT-inclusive amount of the supplies included in step 1 by deducting the total at step 2 from the total at step 1.
4	Calculate the total output VAT due on your designated travel services and margin scheme packages by applying the following formula:
	total at step 3 × the VAT fraction.
5	Calculate the VAT-exclusive value of your designated travel services and margin scheme packages by deducting the total at step 4 from the total at step 3.
6	Total the provisional output VAT which has been accounted for during the financial year on the supplies included in the total at step 1.
7	Deduct the total at step 6 from the total at step 4. Include the resulting total in box 1 of your VAT return, either as a payable amount where the amount is positive or as a deductible amount where the amount is negative.

12 Accounting for VAT on the provisional value of designated travel services and margin scheme packages when the simplified calculation applies (all supplies standard-rated)

This section has the force of law and is referred to in paragraphs 1.2, 2.6, 5.10, 6.4, 7.5 and 7.7.

Step	
1	Calculate the VAT-inclusive standard-rated percentage of the total selling price of all your designated travel services and margin scheme packages for the preceding tax year by applying the following formula:
	total at step 3 of section 11 × 100 total at step 1 of section 11
2	Total the VAT-inclusive selling prices of all of your designated travel services and margin scheme packages supplied during the prescribed accounting period.

Step

3 Calculate the provisional VAT-inclusive amount of your standard-rated supplies of designated travel services and margin scheme packages made during the prescribed accounting period by applying the following formula:

total at step 2 × percentage at step 1.

4 Calculate the provisional amount of output VAT due for the prescribed accounting period by applying the following formula:

total at step 3 × the VAT fraction.

5 Calculate the provisional VAT-exclusive value of all of your designated travel services and margin scheme packages made during the prescribed accounting period by deducting the total at step 4 from the total at step 3.

Chapter 38

Recent VAT Cases

Introduction

[38.1] VAT cases provide a useful insight into how the legislation should be applied in practice and are often influential in shaping HMRC policy. VAT law in all EU member states is required to reflect the objectives of EU VAT law, in particular, *Directive 2006/112/EC*, also known as the *Principal VAT Directive (PVD)*. VAT cases involving taxpayers in other member states can therefore be relevant to UK taxpayers.

The cases in this chapter include the more major decisions of the First Tier Tax Tribunal, judgments of the Upper Tribunal, the Court of Appeal, Supreme Court and Court of Justice of the European Union during the year to 31 May 2016 and are dealt with as follows:

Group and divisional registration	**38.2**
Transfer of a going concern	**38.3**
International services – place of supply	**38.4**
Penalties	**38.5**
Best judgement and unjust enrichment	**38.6**
Exempt outputs	**38.7– 38.18**
Partial exemption – special methods	**38.19**
Construction services	**38.20–38.21**
Input tax – non-deductible items and pension funds	**38.22–38.25**
Supplies involving agents	**38.26**

Group and divisional registration

Beteiligungsgesellschaft Larentia + Minerva mbH & Co KG v Finanzamt Nordenham: C-108/14 [2015] STC 2101

[38.2] This case concerned two separate issues. Firstly, the recovery of input tax by a holding company on costs associated with the acquisition of subsidiary undertakings (see **38.21** below) and secondly, whether the EU VAT rules relating to VAT groups meant that only corporate bodies could be included in a VAT group and, if so, whether they were required to be under the control of another corporate body (eg a holding company).

On the VAT group questions, the CJEU has said that there is nothing in the VAT Directive to prevent the admission of non-legal persons nor is there any requirement for the members of a VAT group to be in a subordinate relationship. What matters is whether the entities in question are closely bound to each other by financial, economic and organisational links. However, member states have discretion to lay down rules relating to the formation of VAT groups if they consider it necessary to prevent avoidance or abuse. This discretion means that the VAT Directive does not have direct effect.

Transfer of a going concern

Intelligent Managed Services Ltd [2015] UKUT 341 (TCC), [2016] STC 290

[38.3] In normal circumstances and, where certain conditions are met, the transfer of a business from one entity to another is treated for VAT purposes as if there was no supply. In other words, no VAT is either chargeable or due in relation to the transaction. One of the conditions is that the assets being transferred must be used by the purchaser entity in carrying on the same kind of business as that formerly carried on by the seller entity.

In the case of *Intelligent Managed Services Ltd*, the vendor carried on the business of operating a 'banking platform' which it sold to various third party financial institutions. The purchaser (Virgin Money Management Services Ltd) was a member of the Virgin Money Group (VMG) VAT group when it acquired that business and, following the transfer, it provided services to other VMG group members. At no time did the purchaser provide services from the acquired business to other businesses outside the VMG VAT group. On that basis, HMRC took the view that, as the VAT group rules ignore intra-group supplies, the purchaser was not 'carrying on the same kind of business'. In other words, as the purchaser did not make supplies of banking platform services to third party customers, but only supplied them to fellow members of the VAT group, there could be no TOGC.

The First Tier Tribunal agreed with HMRC but the Upper Tribunal overturned that decision. Following the CJEU's decision in the *Skandia* case (see **3.1** and **3.7**), a VAT group is a single taxable person for VAT purposes. As such, it is not appropriate to look at the acquisition of the business and assets by the single company but by the VMG VAT group. In the court's judgment, there is nothing in the VAT group rules that can prevent the transfer from being a TOGC. It was clear that the business was carried on within the group and the banking platform services were incorporated into the group's own retail banking services. The group continued to use the assets transferred in the same kind of business as that formerly carried on by the vendor.

This was a surprising judgment. It is clear that the court did not accept that, just because of the VAT group rules which ignore intra-group supplies, the business was not being continued. This is likely to also apply to cases where businesses are transferred out of VAT groups.

International services – place of supply

R (oao Telefonica Europe Plc) [2016] UKUT 173 (TCC)

[38.4] Telefonica brought judicial review proceedings against HMRC's direction that it should calculate the non-vatable proportion of its line rental charges on an actual usage basis rather than on a values basis that it had previously agreed. *Telefonica* was based on three primary grounds:

- that the imposition of a method based on actual usage was ultra vires. The EU VAT system is predicated on the basis of 'value' not on 'use' – as such, any method of determining use and enjoyment should only be based on values. The taxpayer's method of determining the non-EU proportion of its network access charges was based on values. The tribunal dismissed this ground concluding that neither the VAT Directive nor the UK VAT law implementing it precludes the use of a methodology based on actual usage;
- that it had a legitimate expectation founded on agreements reached with HMRC that it could continue to use the value methodology until either the law was changed or it changed its business. Telefonica argued that neither of these events had occurred. Again, the tribunal dismissed Telefonica's ground. There was no clear or unambiguous assurance given by HMRC that the value methodology could be retained. HMRC had decided that changes in technology meant that the taxpayer could now collect actual usage data and that a method based on such usage would be more accurate. The tribunal agreed;
- that HMRC had failed to consult properly with Telefonica. The taxpayer argued that the principle of procedural legitimate expectation should have dictated that HMRC would consult with the taxpayer properly. Telefonica claimed that, as the agreement between it and HMRC (in relation to the value methodology) had been in place since 2008, there was a duty on HMRC to consult before it required the change to a usage methodology. Again, the tribunal dismissed this ground finding that, in fact, HMRC did consult properly and provided the taxpayer with opportunities to make representations.

The case serves to illustrate that taxpayers are expected to use methods that are fair and reasonable. The situation in this case was, with the technology now available to it, Telefonica was able to determine the use of services more accurately than by simply using the value of supplies as a proxy.

Penalties

Trinity Mirror plc [2015] UKUT 421 (TCC), [2016] STC 352

[38.5] Trinity Mirror plc is a well-known publisher of national and regional newspapers. As a 'large' taxpayer, it is required to make payments of its quarterly VAT liability on account. It failed to make payment of its balancing instalment for a particular quarter by the due date but paid the full amount due the next day. The amount of VAT payable was £3.5 million and the surcharge rate imposed was 2% making the surcharge in excess of £70,000.

Trinity Mirror appealed to the First Tier Tribunal arguing that a penalty of £70,000 for being a day late with its balancing payment was wholly disproportionate. The First Tier Tribunal agreed and allowed the appeal. When compared to other cases where the courts had found a default surcharge to be disproportionate, it was clear to the First Tier Tribunal that the surcharge in this case was also disproportionate and allowed the taxpayer's appeal. HMRC appealed.

The Upper Tribunal has overturned the First Tier's decision and has allowed HMRC's appeal. The Upper Tribunal considered that the First Tier erred in law. By comparing the level of the surcharge in *Trinity Mirror* to the level of surcharges in other cases, it made the wrong comparison. It should have focused on the amount of VAT that had been paid late (ie £3.5 million) and, if it had done so, it would have seen that a penalty of 2% (a 'modest' percentage of the tax paid late) was not disproportionate and did not go beyond the objective of ensuring compliance and the timely payment of tax due. In the circumstances, there was no reasonable excuse for the delay in paying the balancing payment and the imposition of the 2% surcharge was not disproportionate. HMRC's appeal was, therefore, allowed.

Best judgement and unjust enrichment

The Berkshire Golf Club and Ors (TC04774) [2015] UKFTT 627 (TC), SWTI 220

[38.6] Having lost the substantive issue – that 'green fee' income paid by visitors is exempt from VAT – HMRC decided to run an argument that the repayment of overpaid VAT would unjustly enrich a golf club if, in reality, it had not borne the economic burden of the VAT charged but had passed that burden onto the person paying the green fee. There were also a number of other issues raised during the case.

In the end, the unjust enrichment argument boiled down to 'extent'. Both parties agreed that full repayment of the VAT overpaid would unjustly enrich the golf club. The question for the tribunal to resolve was what proportion of the VAT overpaid by golf clubs should be repaid. The tribunal heard evidence from two eminent economists and from the various golf clubs that were party to the appeal. In the end, the tribunal preferred the golf clubs' economist's analysis and confirmed that the extent to which a golf club would be unjustly enriched was only by 10% of the VAT overpaid. In other words, golf clubs can expect to receive 90% of the VAT claimed.

On the other issues, the tribunal has ruled that 'Corporate' days and supplies to tour operators are liable to VAT at the standard rate. On these points, the tribunal preferred HMRC's approach. The tribunal concluded that the corporate body and not the individual playing golf was the 'true recipient' of the golf club's supply. Similarly, unless a tour operator is acting as an agent, supplies to tour operators are also liable to VAT.

The final point to resolve was whether for partial exemption purposes, expenditure on the golf course should correctly be regarded as 'residual' such that a proportion of the VAT on that expenditure could be reclaimed under a club's partial exemption method. The tribunal found that there was a direct link between course expenditure and taxable supplies of tee advertising and buggy hire such that course expenditure should be regarded as 'overhead' expenditure and clubs were entitled to reclaim a proportion of input tax in accordance with their respective partial exemption method.

The issue of supplies made to tour operators has been appealed further by the golf clubs.

Exempt outputs

Staatssecretaris van Financiën v Fiscale Eenheid X NV cs: C-595/13 [2016] SWTI 70, [2015] All ER (D) 93 (Dec)

[38.7] This was a referral from the Dutch courts which sought guidance on a number of issues. Firstly, the Court was asked to rule on whether an investment fund, which invests solely in real estate, can be regarded for VAT purposes as a 'special investment fund'. If the answer to that question is yes, then supplies of management services provided to the fund could qualify for exemption from VAT. On the question of management, the court was also asked to give guidance on what services are covered by that term and, in particular, whether the actual management of the property assets that were the subject of the investment could be regarded as the 'management of a special investment fund'.

The CJEU has confirmed that for VAT purposes, the nature of the underlying investment assets within the fund are irrelevant. There is no restriction in the VAT Directive which limits the scope of the exemption only to funds that invest in transferrable securities. The purpose of the VAT exemption for the management of special investment funds is to ensure equal treatment between direct investment (through a broker) and indirect investment through the pooling of funds. According to established case law, a fund will, therefore, be a special investment fund for VAT purposes if (a) it pools the investments for the purpose of spreading risk, (b) that risk is borne by the investors and (c) the fund is subject to comparable state supervision. The fact that, as in this case, the underlying assets are properties makes no difference.

As far as 'management' is concerned, the Court has ruled that actual management of the properties themselves does not qualify as the management of a special investment fund. Activities relating to the selection, purchase and sale of the properties and any necessary administration and accounting tasks will qualify as 'management' but activities such as letting, management of existing tenancies and monitoring of maintenance works etc are not 'management' services that qualify for VAT exemption.

This is the latest judgment from the CJEU in connection with what does and does not constitute a 'special investment fund' for VAT purposes.

The judgment will be of interest to funds invested in property. Provided that the fund is a pooled fund where the investors bear the investment risk and, provided the fund is subject to state supervision, it will be regarded as a special investment fund.

In such circumstances, the management of the fund is exempt from VAT. The good news is that any funds that have met those conditions historically should consider seeking a refund of the VAT paid to the fund managers covering fees paid during the previous four years.

Régie communale autonome du stade Luc Varenne v État Belge: C-55/14 [2015] STC 922

[38.8] The Court of Justice of the European Union (CJEU) has issued a judgment in the above case which related to whether the letting of a stadium (with other services) to a football club and for only 18 days per year, constituted a letting of immovable property (VAT exempt) or a taxable supply of services.

The taxpayer acquired a football stadium and paid VAT of €1.3 million on the purchase price. It reclaimed the VAT paid on its VAT return but the tax authority in Belgium considered that the taxpayer's supply was, in fact, predominantly, a letting of the property which was exempt from VAT. As a consequence, the authority considered that the taxpayer was only entitled to reclaim 20% of the input VAT incurred on the purchase price and issued assessments for repayment of the VAT, penalties and interest.

The CJEU considered that, in the circumstances, the taxpayer was supplying something more than merely the passive letting of the stadium for rent. It also provided services consisting of the provision of access to the sporting facilities including the supervision, management, maintenance and cleaning of those facilities. According to its previous case law, the court stated that, in the absence of quite exceptional circumstances, services linked to the practice of sport or physical education must, as far as possible, be considered as a whole (ie a single supply). As such, where 'other' services are provided in addition to making the facilities available, they are to be regarded as the main service supplied.

The Court therefore concluded that as 80% of the value charged to the football club for the use of the stadium was associated with these 'other' services, the supply was not to be regarded as an exempt letting of the property, but as a taxable supply of services. Accordingly, the taxpayer was entitled to reclaim the VAT it had paid on the acquisition of the stadium.

The Court has made it clear on many previous occasions that strict criteria must apply for a supply to qualify as a 'leasing or letting of property' (ie the landlord of the property must have assigned to the tenant, in return for rent and for an agreed period, the right to occupy his property and to exclude other persons from it). It is for the national courts of each member state to determine the facts in each case but, in this case, the Court considered that the additional services (of supervision, management, maintenance and cleaning) predominated and were not to be regarded as letting.

Directeur général des finances publiques v Mapfre asistencia compania internacional de seguros y reaseguros SA, and Mapfre warranty SpA v Directeur général des finances publiques: C-584/13 [2015] STC 2293, ECJ

[38.9] This was a French referral to the Court of Justice and related to whether the sale of mechanical breakdown warranties constituted, for VAT purposes, an exempt supply of insurance.

In this case, third party car dealers sold mechanical breakdown warranties to customers when they purchased a second hand car. The dealer put the customer in touch with Mapfre Warranty (Mapfre) which entered into a warranty contract directly with the customer. The cost of the warranty was collected by the car dealer and passed on to Mapfre which in turn, covered its risk with Mapfre Asistencia (Asistencia).

The French tax authorities considered that what was being supplied by Mapfre was a contract of insurance in return for a premium. As such, each transaction was subject to a French insurance tax at 18%. Mapfre argued that it was simply providing aftersales services to the car dealers and covering the warranty risk through an insurance contract with Asistencia.

On the evidence presented to the CJEU, it found that, in fact, Mapfre's contract with Asistencia was, effectively, a block insurance contract and that its contract was not with the car dealers but directly with each customer. Each transaction bore the hallmarks of a contract of insurance in that, in return for a premium, Mapfre agreed to cover the risk of mechanical breakdown of the customer's car. This was sufficient for the Court to indicate that what was being supplied was insurance. As such, the premiums received by Mapfre was consideration for a supply of insurance which was exempt from VAT but was subject to French insurance tax at 18%.

Where risks are covered in return for a premium, the CJEU will take some persuading that what is being supplied is anything other than a contract of insurance. As is demonstrated in this case, the court will look at the evidence presented to it. It seems that here, the evidence did not support the taxpayer's contentions but the CJEU left it to the referring court to decide the actual facts but gave a big hint that, in the circumstances, what was being supplied was, in fact, insurance.

Metropolitan International Schools (TC04675) [2015] UKFTT 517 (TC)

[38.10] In the case of *Metropolitan International Schools* (*MIS*), the First Tier Tribunal has decided that, on the evidence before it, what MIS supplied was a single supply of printed matter (the printed course material). As a consequence of that finding, all of the supplies were liable to VAT at the zero rate.

HMRC contended before the tribunal that what was being supplied was a course of education and that as MIS was not an eligible body for VAT purposes, its supplies of such education ought to have been liable to VAT at the standard rate.

Ultimately, the First Tier Tribunal accepted that the essential supply was the sale of the course manuals. While the 'student' had access to some tutor support and guidance, MIS contended that these were ancillary to the main supply of manuals. In the vast majority of cases, students simply learnt from reading these manuals and did not request such support. When they did, they were referred back to the course manuals. In addition, the courses offered did not lead to any form of examination or qualification. Students could, if they wished, sit an exam set by third party bodies but this was not something that was provided by MIS. As such, the First Tier Tribunal distinguished the earlier House of Lords judgment in the case of the *College of Estate Management*. In *MIS*, the First Tier Tribunal concluded that the student's motive was different in that, when he entered into a contract with MIS, he was aware that MIS did not provide an examination or qualification. As such, the First Tier Tribunal concluded that 'the customer's desired end result was to educate himself entirely by studying the self-contained manuals'. In light of that conclusion, the First Tier Tribunal decided that there was a single supply of the manuals which was zero-rated.

Skatteverket v Hedqvist: C-264/14 [2016] STC 372

[38.11] The Court of Justice of the European Union (CJEU) has issued an interesting judgment in this case which relates to the buying and selling of the virtual currency 'Bitcoin'.

Given the virtual nature of the currency, the referring Swedish court was unsure about the correct VAT treatment of 'commission' earned by Mr Hedqvist in connection with his dealings in Bitcoin. For each transaction (whether buying or selling) the taxpayer made a margin and the Swedish court wanted to know whether such margin should, for VAT purposes, be regarded as consideration for a supply of services. If the answer to that question was 'yes', the Court wished to understand whether such services were covered by the VAT exemptions contained in *Article 135(1)* of the *Principal VAT Directive*.

In essence, the CJEU confirmed that Bitcoin, being a virtual currency consisting of the exchange of different means of payment, cannot be characterised for VAT purposes as 'tangible property'. As such, they do not fall within the concept of being goods and must, therefore, be regarded as services. Secondly, as the exchange of currencies (Bitcoin to real currency and vice versa) were performed for an agreed margin, the margin earned by Mr Hedqvist constituted consideration for that supply bringing the transactions squarely within the scope of VAT.

Article 135(1)(e) of the Directive exempts from VAT transactions involving currency, bank notes and legal tender. As Bitcoins are used to pay for goods and services they are equivalent to any other currency and, as a consequence, transactions involving the exchange of Bitcoins should be treated in exactly the same way as transactions in real currencies. It therefore follows from the context and the aims of *Article 135(1)(e)* that to interpret that provision as including only transactions involving traditional currencies would deprive it of part of its effect. Accordingly, the transactions undertaken by Mr Hedqvist are exempt from VAT.

DPAS Ltd [2015] UKUT 585 (TCC), [2016] STC 857

[38.12] This was an appeal by HMRC against the First Tier Tax Tribunal's decision. The case concerned the questions of whether DPAS supplied services to patients and, if they did, whether those services were taxable or VAT exempt.

In October 2010, the Court of Justice issued an unexpected judgment in the case of *Axa UK Ltd* (C-175/09) – otherwise known as the 'Denplan' case. In that judgment, the Court ruled that the services that Denplan provided to dentists were not exempt from VAT but were, in fact, debt collection services which were subject to VAT at the standard rate.

DPAS Ltd provides similar services to those provided by Axa and sought to rearrange its business model so as to ensure that it was seen to be acting for the dental patient rather than for the dentist. By changing the terms and conditions, DPAS wanted to ensure that its collection of direct debits was a service provided to the patient and not seen as a debt collection service provided to the dentist. DPAS wrote to all of the dentists' patients inviting them to accept the new arrangements. However, only 30% of the patients responded – the other 70% continued to pay by direct debit but did not expressly accept the new terms and conditions of the contract. DPAS argued that the service it provided to all of the patients was an exempt supply (as a supply relating to money transfers or payments).

The First Tier Tribunal agreed with that analysis and allowed DPAS' appeal and HMRC appealed to the Upper Tribunal arguing that firstly, the First Tier Tribunal had erred in law when it found that the 70% of customers that had not responded had accepted the new terms by their conduct (ie by continuing to pay by direct debit). The Upper Tribunal agreed with HMRC on this point. As far as VAT liability of the service to patients is concerned, this question was stayed pending the outcome of litigation in the cases of *Bookit* and *NEC* the outcome of which is set out at **38.18** below.

Brockenhurst College [2015] EWCA Civ 1196

[38.13] The issue at stake here is the question of whether certain supplies made for consideration by the college to members of the public are exempt from VAT as being 'closely related' to the supply of education it makes to students. The college contends that they are so related whereas HMRC consider that they are separate supplies and are liable to VAT at the standard rate of 20%.

In earlier hearings at the First Tier Tax Tribunal and the Upper Tribunal, the matter was decided in favour of the college. This is HMRC's appeal from the Upper Tribunal.

As is common with many colleges of further education, students enrol onto various courses. The courses in question in this case were courses related to catering and to the performing arts. As part of the curriculum, students were given practical experience of catering to members of the public in the college training restaurant. Similarly, as far as performing arts were concerned, students put on shows and entertainment to members of the public. In both scenarios, the members of the public attending either the restaurant or the entertainment paid money for the meal or entrance ticket.

The college maintains that although the supplies are made directly to members of the public, nevertheless, the supplies are closely related to the principal supply of education provided to the students. The college contends (and the lower courts have agreed) that the VAT Directive provides an exemption for such closely related services.

The Court of Appeal agreed with both parties that the VAT Directive is not clear and that, in order to obtain clarity on the meaning of the term 'closely related', it is necessary for the matter to be referred to the Court of Justice for a preliminary ruling.

Finance & Business Training Ltd [2014] EWCA Civ 1412

[38.14] The EU principle of fiscal neutrality dictates that, in a VAT context, supplies of the same or very similar goods or services should not be treated differently for VAT purposes. In other words, if a supply is treated as exempt when supplied by one person, all things being equal, it should be treated as exempt when supplied by another.

This was the issue at stake in this case. As its name suggests, Finance & Business Training Ltd (FBT) is a commercial provider of finance and business training. However, in association with the University of Wales (UoW), it also provides university level education (to Master's degree level) – which leads to a degree awarded by UoW. FBT argued that, when providing these university level courses, it should be regarded for VAT purposes as an eligible body. According to FBT, the failure of the UK to recognise it as an eligible body in this regard offends the principle of fiscal neutrality. In addition, FBT argued that the UK's failure to correctly implement the provisions of the EU VAT Directive in this regard also breached the EU principle of legal certainty. As a consequence of these purported breaches of EU law principles, FBT asserted that it was entitled to rely on the direct effect of EU law which would confer VAT exemption for its supplies of university education. The Court of Appeal dismissed FBT's assertions. Essentially, the Court held that, as far as fiscal neutrality was concerned, not only must the goods or services being supplied be the same (or similar), but the objects of the person providing the education must also be the same or similar. In the Court's judgment, this was not the case here. Accordingly, FBT could not be regarded as a college of UoW and its supplies of university education could not therefore benefit from VAT exemption. The taxpayer has petitioned the Supreme Court for leave to appeal.

The Open University [2016] EWCA Civ 114

[38.15] For many years, the BBC produced and broadcast educational programmes on behalf of the Open University and charged VAT on the provision of those services.

The Open University submitted a claim to HMRC to recover the VAT that it considered had been incorrectly charged – a sum in excess of £21 million. HMRC rejected that claim and the Open University appealed that decision to the First Tier Tax Tribunal which found in its favour. HMRC then appealed to the Upper Tribunal which also found for the Open University. HMRC appealed to the Court of Appeal.

The question to resolve was whether the BBC's services to the Open University should have been exempt from VAT.

In a unanimous judgment, the Court of Appeal dismissed HMRC's appeal.

The Open University (OU) argued that the United Kingdom had failed to correctly implement the provisions of the VAT Directive. It argued that the BBC was a body governed by public law and that its charter had clear aims of an educational nature such that its provision of production and broadcasting services were services that were closely linked to education and should have been exempt from VAT. In these particular circumstances, the OU contended that, historically, VAT should not have been charged to it by the BBC and that it was entitled to seek a refund of the VAT paid in error.

Alternatively, the OU contended that if the BBC was not a body governed by public law, it was, nevertheless a body with similar objects. Although UK VAT law does not expressly define the BBC as such a body, the OU contended that the UK had, in fact, defined it but, even if that was not the case, it argued that it could rely on the direct effect of the VAT Directive and take the benefit of the VAT exemption.

The Court of Appeal held that the BBC was not a body governed by public law. It was not an organ of the state. However, it was a body with similar educational objects as a public body and, as a result, its supplies of production and broadcasting services to the OU were services that were closely related to the OU's supply of education. While the UK had not expressly defined the BBC as a body with similar objects, through the BBC charter and licence and the funding from Parliament the UK had *de facto* recognised the BBC. On the direct effect point, the Court made it clear that the OU and the BBC could rely on direct effect as the UK had clearly failed to correctly implement the VAT Directive in UK law.

It seems clear from this judgment that the UK's law on 'eligible body' status is defective and needs to be amended to bring it in line with EU law. Contrast this judgment with that at **38.14** above (*Finance & Business Training Ltd*). The VAT Directive gives member states discretion to recognise certain bodies as having similar objects to public bodies. However, that discretion has to be exercised in a way that is compliant with EU law and in a way that is consistent with the objectives of the Directive. The Directive requires member states to recognise bodies with similar educational aims as bodies governed by public law which, according to the Court of Appeal in this case, UK law seemingly fails to achieve. HMRC may appeal this judgment to the Supreme Court which in turn may refer it (along with FBT) to the Court of Justice for a preliminary ruling. It seems clear (following the CJEU's judgment in *MDDP*) that if the matter reaches the CJEU, it is likely that the UK's VAT law concerning the classification of entities as eligible bodies under the education provisions will be ruled ultra vires.

Minister Finansów v Aspiro SA: Case C-40/15 [2016] All ER (D) 23 (May)

[38.16] This was a referral to the CJEU by the Polish courts. The issue to be resolved was whether the claims handling services provided by Aspiro to an insurance company qualified for exemption from VAT. The VAT Directive provides an exemption for 'insurance transactions' including 'related services' performed by 'insurance brokers' or 'insurance agents'.

The CJEU considered that the claims handling services could not be regarded as insurance transactions. Aspiro was not involved in the provision of insurance cover to the claimant but merely handled any claims arising out of the insurance contract concluded between the claimant and the insurer. Consequently, even though the claims settlement service is an essential part of an insurance transaction in that it includes the determination of liability and the amount of damage, and the decision to pay or refuse to pay compensation to the insured person, the service does not constitute an insurance transaction.

The Court also concluded that Aspiro was neither an insurance broker nor an insurance agent. Those terms envisage that, for VAT purposes, the services of such intermediaries consist in the finding of prospective clients and their introduction to the insurer with a view to the conclusion of insurance contracts. In *Aspiro*, they simply provided claims handling services and were not involved in any way with the introduction of the customer to the insurer. While the claims handling services may be 'related services', for the exemption to apply, they had to be provided by an insurance broker or an insurance agent. That was not the case here and Aspiro's claims handling services were, therefore, taxable.

IFX Investment Company Ltd [2016] EWCA Civ 436

[38.17] The Court of Appeal has issued a unanimous judgment in favour of the taxpayer in the long-running VAT case relating to whether 'spot the ball' competitions are exempt from VAT or are subject to VAT at the standard rate.

IFX Investment Company Ltd (IFX) (and others) operate a 'spot the ball' competition and contended that the competition was a 'game of chance'. According to IFX, this meant that income from the competitions it ran were exempt from VAT under the betting and gaming provisions of the VAT Act.

HMRC took issue with that view. It did not consider that Spot the Ball was a game nor did it consider that, if it was a game, it was a game of chance. IFX appealed to the First Tier Tax Tribunal which upheld its case. The tribunal rejected HMRC's arguments that, for there to be a 'game' there had to be either an interaction between two or more players or a single player had to respond to a change in circumstances. It also ruled that Spot the Ball was, in fact, a game of chance.

HMRC appealed to the Upper Tribunal which ruled in favour of HMRC. The Upper Tribunal considered that the First Tier's decision – that there was no requirement for player interaction – was an error of law and, as such, it reversed the decision.

IFX appealed to the Court of Appeal which has unanimously decided that the First Tier Tribunal did not make any error of law. As a consequence, the operation of the Spot the Ball competition is, for the purposes of the Gaming Act 1968, a game of chance and, in turn, this means that the income received by the promoter of the game was exempt from VAT.

This is the latest step in the litigation that has taken over seven years to get this far. The victory at the Court of Appeal is worth over £97 million to IFX alone. However, given the values involved it must be anticipated that HMRC will seek leave to appeal the issue to the UK's Supreme Court.

National Exhibition Centre Ltd: C-130/15 and Bookit Ltd: C-607/14 [2016] All ER (D) 78 (Jun)

[38.18] Although separate cases, the issue at stake in *Bookit Ltd* and *NEC* were almost identical. The question referred to the Court of Justice by the UK courts was whether the charge made by the taxpayers to customers using either debit or credit cards as the means of payment for separate services was a 'financial service' which should be treated as exempt from VAT. In a previous case (known as *SDC*), the Court of Justice had held that, where a taxpayer's actions caused money to be transferred between two bank accounts thus changing the financial and legal relationship between the payer and the payee, the service provided by the taxpayer was in the nature of a financial service which was exempt from VAT.

Relying on that earlier decision, both Bookit and NEC considered that their actions caused such a transfer of money and that, as a result, they argued that the service they provided to their customer should also be exempt from VAT.

The Court of Justice has dismissed these arguments. The actions of the taxpayers here consisted of obtaining card details from the customer, transmitting those details to the taxpayer's bank and the transmission of an 'end-of-day' settlement file which contained the necessary authorisation codes. While, on the face of it, those actions could be seen as being necessary to execute the transfer of funds, according to the Court of Justice, they cannot be considered to be an essential function of the transfer of funds. In essence, the Court considers that the actions of the taxpayer are more akin to the handling of information which enable the transactions to occur. Bookit Ltd and NEC argued that they both obtain and transmit the authorisation codes without which the transactions could not occur. However, the Court ruled that such transmission is not a specific or essential function of the transfer of money between bank accounts, they simply confirm that the transaction can proceed. The card handling services cannot, therefore, be regarded as a 'financial service' and cannot be exempt from VAT.

Partial exemption – special methods

Volkswagen Financial Services (UK) Ltd [2015] EWCA Civ 832, [2016] STC 417

[38.19] The Court of Appeal has allowed the taxpayer's appeal on both grounds.

On the first ground, the issue at stake was whether 'residual' input tax (VAT incurred on general overheads) could be reclaimed by VWFS. In cases where a customer of a VW dealership wished to purchase a vehicle on HP, the dealer would sell the car to VWFS which, in turn, would then sell the vehicle to the customer along with the appropriate exempt supply of finance. VWFS made no margin on the sale of the car; its profits were made almost entirely from the exempt supply of finance.

HMRC argued that, on that basis, none of the general overheads of the business were used in making the taxable supply of the car. Instead, according to HMRC, the overheads were more accurately to be regarded as being used to make the exempt supplies of finance. As such, none of the residual input tax could be reclaimed. The First Tier Tribunal disagreed with that view and allowed VWFS's appeal considering that VWFS clearly made both taxable and exempt supplies.

That decision was overturned by the Upper Tribunal and VWFS appealed to the Court of Appeal. In a unanimous judgment, the Court of Appeal has restored the First Tier Tribunal's decision. The Court has held that there is no principled basis for HMRC's argument that the general overheads of VWFS's business should not be treated as cost components of both the taxable supplies of cars and the exempt supplies of finance. As a consequence, input VAT incurred on overheads could be classed as residual and apportioned in accordance with the taxpayer's partial exemption formula.

On the second ground, VWFS claimed that it was entitled to recover 50% of the residual input VAT (on the basis that for each transaction there were two supplies). In the circumstances, the Court of Appeal agreed that such an apportionment disclosed no error of law on the part of the First Tier Tribunal and accordingly, the appeal was allowed. It is generally thought that this part of the ruling is only applicable to VWFS. This is simply because, in the circumstances of the litigation, HMRC offered no alternative method other than to argue that no input VAT could be reclaimed. As the Court found that such an assertion was clearly wrong, and in the absence of anything else, it agreed the 50/50 approach. In the circumstances of other similar cases, it is considered likely that HMRC would offer some alternative methods.

Construction services

Wakefield College [2016] UKUT 19 (TCC)

[38.20] The Upper Tribunal has released its second judgment in this appeal having sent the original appeal back to the First Tier Tribunal for a rehearing of the facts.

The issue – whether the construction of a building qualifies for zero-rating under UK VAT law – rested in this case on whether the college intended to use the building in question for a relevant charitable purpose. The First Tier Tribunal concluded (at the second hearing) that, as the fees paid by certain students were set according to various personal factors, the fees could not (following the CJEU's judgment in *Commission v Finland*), be regarded as 'consideration' for the supply of education. As such, the income of the college was not derived from the carrying on of an economic activity and, as a result, the use of the particular building was for a relevant charitable purpose. HMRC appealed again to the Upper Tribunal.

The dispute in this case centred around those students aged over 19 where either they, or their employer were expected to contribute to the cost of their courses. HMRC considered that the contribution made in this way was consideration for a supply of education services and should, therefore, be regarded for VAT purposes as income from the operation of a business. The Upper Tribunal confirmed, however, that where students have their fees abated to reflect their personal circumstances, those supplies of education are outside the scope of VAT. However, where the student's personal circumstances do not entitle him to an abated fee, the income should be regarded as consideration and thus business income. This is the case even though the fee charged by the college is below cost. The tribunal considers that the crucial distinction here is the fact that the student (or his employer) pays the full advertised price and is not entitled to any abatement due to personal circumstances.

Although this case was primarily about whether or not zero-rating was applicable to a construction project, it also concerned the question of whether the college was undertaking an 'economic' activity. The Court of Justice had ruled in the *Commission v Finland* case that where legal aid fees were set according to the customer's ability to pay and net worth, the payment made by the customer could not be regarded as consideration in a VAT sense. If the payments were not consideration, the supplies could not be regarded as falling within the scope of VAT.

Astral Construction Ltd [2015] UKUT 21 (TC), [2015] STC 1033

[38.21] This was an appeal by HMRC against the decision of the First Tier Tribunal. The issue to be determined was whether the construction of a nursing home on the site of and incorporating a redundant church was the construction of a building intended for use for a relevant residential purpose (and thus zero-rated) or, as contended by HMRC, the works were the enlargement of, or extension to the existing church.

The taxpayer supplied construction services to the operator of a nursing home. The development incorporated an existing but redundant church. The work involved the construction of two substantial new wings with the church being used as the main entrance and reception. The First Tier Tribunal concluded that when compared to what previously existed, the new building dwarfed the old church and that, looking objectively at the physical characteristics of the building(s) before and after the works had been completed, the only conclusion that could be drawn was that the works were correctly to be classed as the construction of a new building rather than the extension or enlargement of the old church. HMRC appealed.

The Upper Tribunal could only allow HMRC's appeal if the First Tier Tribunal had made an error of law or made a finding of fact which was not supported by the evidence. HMRC's primary argument was that the First Tier Tribunal had applied the wrong test but, the Upper Tribunal concluded that it had not. The phrase 'construction of a building' contained in the VAT law is wide enough to include the construction of a new building or buildings connected to and incorporating the old church. In addition, whether the works were an enlargement or an extension to the old church is a question of fact, degree and impression. The structure which existed after the works was a single fully functional nursing home. As a matter of impression, size, shape, function and character, it was so different from the existing church that it could not be said to constitute either the conversion, enlargement of or extension to the church. These findings of fact by the First Tier Tribunal were, therefore, wholly reasonable. Accordingly, HMRC's appeal was dismissed.

Input tax – non-deductible items and pension funds

Larentia + Minerva mbH & Co KG v Finanzamt Nordenham: C-108/14

[38.22] In addition to the VAT group issues (discussed at **38.2** above), the *Larentia & Minerva* case also considered the issue of whether a holding company could recover input tax it had incurred on the cost of acquiring a subsidiary undertaking.

The German tax authority considered that the holding company had two activities. Firstly, the holding of shares in its subsidiaries and secondly, the provision of management services. In light of that duality, the tax authority concluded that the holding company should apportion its input VAT. However, the Court of Justice disagreed. Where a holding company is actively involved in managing its subsidiaries, the VAT incurred on overheads is wholly attributable to that activity and is not attributable to the passive activity of the holding of shares. As such, provided that the management services it supplied to its subsidiaries were taxable supplies, the input VAT incurred on overheads (including VAT incurred on costs associated with the acquisition of the subsidiary undertaking) could be reclaimed in full. The Court has confirmed that overhead costs have a direct and immediate link with outputs if they form a cost component of those outputs. It seems that, in light of this judgment, HMRC will now have to reconsider its existing policy in this regard.

HMRC's policy on holding companies and the recovery of input tax is a long and drawn-out affair. It had been hoped that, by the time of publication of this edition of this book, HMRC would have published its policy. A draft of a proposed Revenue & Customs Brief has been seen but, frankly, it poses more questions than it provides answers. Hopefully soon, the definitive policy will emerge.

Sveda UAB: C-126/14 [2016] STC 447

[38.23] *Article 168* of the *VAT Directive* confers a right to reclaim VAT incurred on inputs provided that they are used for the purposes of transactions that are themselves taxable transactions.

The Lithuanian tax authority considered in this case that as no VAT was chargeable on the public's use of the trail constructed by the taxpayer (because it was to be used by the public free of charge), the condition contained in *Article 168* was not satisfied.

The CJEU however confirmed that, on the face of it, as the trail allowed the public access to Sveda's taxable outlets, the necessary link existed and the VAT incurred on the construction of the trail could be reclaimed.

The taxpayer is a commercial organisation which entered into an agreement with a public body. Under the terms of that agreement, it constructed a pathway (a heritage trail) and recovered the VAT it had incurred on the construction costs. The Lithuanian tax authority refused the repayment on the basis that the trail was open to the public free of charge. As such, the authority argued that, as the trail was not to be used for the purposes of a taxable activity, Sveda had no right to reclaim the VAT incurred.

On the other hand, Sveda argued that the trail was a means for the public to access its outlets where it was to sell food and drink, souvenirs and facilities for bathing all of which were liable to VAT.

The CJEU was asked to provide guidance on whether, in such circumstances, *Article 168* of the *VAT Directive* granted the taxpayer a right to recover the VAT incurred on the construction of the trail.

In its judgment, the CJEU has confirmed that in carrying out its activities, Sveda acted at all times as a taxable person. The case law of the Court confirms that the test for recovery of input VAT is whether there is a direct and immediate link between the expenditure (inputs) and the trader's taxable outputs or whether the expenditure is part of the taxpayer's general costs. That was clearly the case here. Even though the public was entitled to use the trail for no consideration, the trail was a means for the public to access Sveda's taxable economic activities and, as such, *Article 168* of the *VAT Directive* allowed the taxpayer to reclaim the VAT incurred on the trail's construction.

Norseman Gold plc [2016] UKUT 69 (TCC)

[38.24] It is possible to register for VAT in the UK as an 'intending trader' (that is a trader who does not yet make taxable supplies but intends to do so at some point in the future) (see **1.9**). This is usually required where the trader is in a preliminary stage of development and incurs input VAT on the purchase of goods and services. A VAT registration allows the trader to reclaim that VAT.

For input tax to be reclaimable the trader must intend to make taxable supplies. Taxable supplies are supplies of goods or services that are not exempt supplies and, crucially, in *Norseman Gold plc* are made for consideration.

There are exceptions to this rule but, generally there is no supply if there is no consideration.

Norseman Gold plc (Norseman) took the view that it was entitled to reclaim VAT it had incurred as it intended – at some future date – to make taxable supplies of management services to its subsidiaries. On the evidence HMRC took the view, and the First Tier Tribunal agreed, that there was no firm agreement between Norseman and its subsidiaries as to how much the charges would be and when exactly the management charges would be made. The subsidiaries were making losses (prospecting for gold in Australia) and Norseman did not see the point of raising management charges in a situation where the subsidiaries would have had to have been funded by it in order to pay for the services.

The First Tier Tribunal concluded that the services provided by Norseman to its subsidiaries were certainly capable of being classified as taxable supplies save for one crucial omission. For VAT purposes, there can be no supply if there is no consideration. Consideration is founded on reciprocal performance of obligations and in this case, while Norseman provided services to its subsidiaries, on the evidence before the tribunal, there were no arrangements in place for the subsidiaries to provide payment in return. The First Tier Tribunal considered this as fatal to Norseman's case and dismissed its appeal.

At the Upper Tribunal, Norseman argued that, provided that there was an intention to pay for the services at some point in the future, that was enough to make the supplies taxable supplies. The Upper Tribunal disagreed and upheld the First Tier Tribunal's decision. It was not enough for Norseman to argue that the consideration for the supply would be calculated at some future point if and when the subsidiaries were in funds and were able to pay. Consideration – that which is given in return – needs to be certain at the time of supply if what is being provided is to be regarded as a supply.

Airtours Holiday Transport Ltd [2016] UKSC 21

[38.25] The issue in this case was whether Airtours was entitled to recover VAT as input tax that it had paid on the supply of professional services. The issue seems quite a simple one but the matter has taken many years to resolve.

The Supreme Court has decided by a majority of 3 to 2 that the professional services were not supplied to Airtours but were supplied to the financial institutions that commissioned the work. The fact that Airtours paid for the services under the terms of an agreement it had signed with the institutions did not mean that it was entitled to reclaim the VAT charged as input tax.

In a majority verdict the Supreme Court has ruled that Airtours was not entitled to reclaim the VAT charged on fees for professional services because, the economic reality of the situation was that the services had not been supplied to it but to the financial institutions that commissioned the work.

Airtours was in major financial difficulty and owed money to a consortium of some 70 or so banks (the financial institutions). In an attempt to resolve the financial issues, the financial institutions commissioned PriceWaterhouseCoopers (PwC) to undertake a financial review of the Airtours business. As part of that process, PwC engaged with the financial institutions by way of an engagement letter. Under the terms of that agreement, Airtours agreed to pay PwC's fees. Airtours argued that it was a party to the agreement and that it received a benefit from the PwC services. As such, following the earlier judgment of the House of Lords in the case of *Redrow*, it argued that it was, therefore, entitled to recover the VAT charged by PwC as input tax. HMRC disagreed with that view.

The case has gone through all of the tiers of the UK court system and, ultimately, the Supreme Court has decided by a narrow margin of three to two that the supply of professional services by PwC was made to the financial institutions and not to Airtours. The fact that Airtours was a party to the engagement was purely to ensure that it was contractually obliged to pay for the services. However, this did not mean that it had a right to deduct the VAT paid as input tax. The economic reality was that the financial institutions commissioned the work because they needed it in order to make an informed decision on the future viability of the Airtours business. The judgment makes it clear that, in order to reclaim input tax, a business must be the person to whom the supplies of goods or services is made. Paying a third party's costs (third party consideration) will provide no entitlement to reclaim input VAT.

Supplies involving agents

Adecco UK Ltd (TC04743) [2015] UKFTT 600 (TC)

[38.26] The supply of staff between one legal entity and another is a taxable supply of services upon which VAT is due in the UK at the rate of 20%.

The question of what constitutes a supply of staff is a complex one to resolve. However, the First Tier Tribunal ruled in *Reed Employment Ltd* [2011] UKFTT 200 that the first employer had to 'control' the employee and that such control had to be ceded to the second employer for there to be such a supply.

In *Adecco*, the First Tier Tribunal has declined to follow that reasoning.

In the First Tier Tribunal's view, the contractual obligations are such that the worker supplies his services to Adecco, which in turn supplies the worker to his customer. This constitutes a supply of staff and VAT is due on the full consideration received.

The First Tier Tribunal has issued its decision in the litigation between Adecco UK Ltd (and other group members) and HMRC. The issue in dispute is whether Adecco's supply to its customers, of temporary workers, should be regarded for VAT purposes as a supply of staff or, merely, as a supply of introductory services. HMRC contend in this litigation that there is a supply of staff and that, as a result, VAT is due on the full consideration received by Adecco, which includes the temporary worker's wages, PAYE and NI costs along with Adecco's commission. Adecco, on the other hand, argues that, in reality, all it does is simply introduce the temporary worker to the customer and that, as a result, only its commission should be subject to VAT. Adecco considers that it simply collects the wages element as a disbursement and that VAT is not due on these payments.

Adecco relied heavily on the First Tier Tribunal's previous decision in the case of *Reed Employment Ltd* (a case based on similar issues and arguments) where the tribunal found that for there to be a supply of staff, the agency had to have control of the worker and cede that control to the customer. In the absence of such control, the First Tier Tribunal allowed Reed's appeal and ruled that there was only a supply of introductory services and, consequently, VAT was only due on the commission element of the payments received.

In the *Adecco* case, the judge considered that *Reed Employment Ltd* was decided incorrectly and has refused to follow it. The contractual obligations between Adecco and the worker and the economic reality of the supply was that the worker was obliged to work for the customer. However, that obligation was owed to Adecco under the terms of the agreement between the worker and Adecco. Similarly, the customer was obliged under contract with Adecco to pay Adecco for the worker's services. In consequence, even though the customer controlled the worker during the term of the assignment, the First Tier Tribunal considers that the arrangements amounted to a supply of staff and VAT was due on the full payment.

The decision of the tribunal in *Adecco* is diametrically opposed to the decision of the tribunal in *Reed Employment Ltd*. As a consequence there is little certainty on this point and it is very difficult to know how to advise an employment agent type business. Adecco has appealed to the Upper Tribunal so some clarity should emerge in due course.

Table of Cases

C

D

E

R

W

Table of Statutes

Paragraph references printed in **bold** type indicate where the Statute is set out in part or in full.

Table of Statutory Instruments

Paragraph references printed in **bold** type indicate where the Rule, Regulation or Order is set out in part or in full.

Table of European Legislation

Paragraph or page numbers printed in **bold** type indicate where an Article is set out in part or in full.

Index

References are to paragraph number.